Fundamentals of Research in Criminology and Criminal Justice

Fifth Edition

*In memory of my mother, Jan, who was my friend, teacher, mentor in all things that mattered,
and role model—from her, I learned the importance of kindness and grace.*

R. D. B.

To Elizabeth and Julia

R. K. S.

Sara Miller McCune founded SAGE Publishing in 1965 to support
the dissemination of usable knowledge and educate a global
community. SAGE publishes more than 1000 journals and over
600 new books each year, spanning a wide range of subject areas.
Our growing selection of library products includes archives, data,
case studies and video. SAGE remains majority owned by our
founder and after her lifetime will become owned by a charitable
trust that secures the company's continued independence.

Los Angeles | London | New Delhi | Singapore | Washington DC | Melbourne

Fundamentals of Research in Criminology and Criminal Justice

Fifth Edition

Ronet D. Bachman

University of Delaware

Russell K. Schutt

University of Massachusetts Boston

Los Angeles | London | New Delhi
Singapore | Washington DC | Melbourne

FOR INFORMATION:

SAGE Publications, Inc.
2455 Teller Road
Thousand Oaks, California 91320
E-mail: order@sagepub.com

SAGE Publications Ltd.
1 Oliver's Yard
55 City Road
London EC1Y 1SP
United Kingdom

SAGE Publications India Pvt. Ltd.
B 1/I 1 Mohan Cooperative Industrial Area
Mathura Road, New Delhi 110 044
India

SAGE Publications Asia-Pacific Pte. Ltd.
18 Cross Street #10-10/11/12
China Square Central
Singapore 048423

Acquisitions Editor: Jessica Miller
Content Development Editor: Laura Kirkhuff
Editorial Assistant: Sarah Manheim
Marketing Manager: Jillian Ragusa
Production Editor: Veronica Stapleton Hooper
Copy Editor: Jared Leighton
Typesetter: C&M Digitals (P) Ltd.
Proofreader: Susan Schon
Indexer: Beth Nauman-Montana
Cover Designer: Scott Van Atta

Printed in Canada

Library of Congress Cataloging-in-Publication Data

Names: Bachman, Ronet, author. | Schutt, Russell K., author.

Title: Fundamentals of research in criminology and criminal justice / Ronet D. Bachman, University of Delaware, Russell K. Schutt, University of Massachusetts Boston.

Description: Fifth edition. | Thousand Oaks, California : SAGE Publications, Inc., [2021] | Includes bibliographical references and index.

Identifiers: LCCN 2019035164 | ISBN 9781544374055 (paperback) | ISBN 9781544374048 (epub) | ISBN 9781544374031 (epub) | ISBN 9781544374024 (pdf)

Subjects: LCSH: Criminology—Research. | Criminal justice, Administration of—Research.

Classification: LCC HV6024.5 .B32 2021 | DDC 364.072—dc23
LC record available at https://lccn.loc.gov/2019035164

This book is printed on acid-free paper.

20 21 22 23 24 10 9 8 7 6 5 4 3 2 1

BRIEF CONTENTS

Appendix F. Quantitative Data Analysis

Appendix G. Data Sets

DETAILED CONTENTS

After years of teaching courses in research methods, we have found that the best forum for learning is to link the teaching of key topics to contemporary research in the discipline. By combining discussions of research techniques with practical research examples from the field, students learn not only how to conduct research but also why it is important to do so. In the fifth edition of *Fundamentals of Research in Criminology and Criminal Justice*, we have drawn on comments by students in the classroom, insightful reviews by those who teach research methods, and our own continuing learning experience as scholars and teachers; we think the resulting innovations will add a great deal to your learning experience. We have retained our unique method of "instruction by example" that is used in our more comprehensive text, *The Practice of Research in Criminology and Criminal Justice*. We believe this approach not only increases students' understanding of complex research methods but also conveys to students the vital role that research plays in our discipline.

The purpose of this book is to introduce students to the basics of scientific methods of research and to show how they are actually used. Each chapter in this book combines instruction in research methods with investigations of key research questions in our field: What are the factors related to school shootings? What is the best police response to intimate partner violence? How do gang members perceive their world? Does wearing body cameras affect police and citizen rates of injury? Do community police officers perceive their roles as different from regular patrol officers? These and many other research questions are explored through the text, in tandem with a discussion of research methods. These substantive examples will help you see how research methods are used in practice and, perhaps more importantly, why they were selected by researchers in the field.

By the end of the course, students will not only have the ability to conduct research but also be more adept consumers of knowledge claims about "truth" that bombard us on a daily basis. But research methods cannot be learned by rote and applied mechanically. It is our hope that you will realize that all research methods come with their own strengths and limitations. In fact, the underlying theme of our book is that employing a combination of methods together to answer the same research question is often preferable. Extensive exercises are provided at the end of each chapter that allow students to engage in different research tasks both individually and within groups.

ORGANIZATION OF THE BOOK

The way this book is organized reflects our beliefs in making research methods interesting, teaching students how to critique research, and viewing specific research techniques as parts of an integrated research strategy. Our concern with ethical issues in all types of research is underscored by the fact that we have a chapter devoted exclusively to research ethics, in addition to sections on ethics in every methodology chapter. The first two chapters introduce the why and how of research in general. Chapter 1 shows how research has helped us understand the magnitude of and the factors related to youth violence. It also introduces you to different research philosophies and how these philosophies affect both our research questions and the appropriate methods for answering them. Chapter 2 illustrates the basic stages of research with a series of experiments on the police response to intimate partner violence. Chapter 3 highlights issues of research ethics by taking you inside Philip Zimbardo's prison experiment and Stanley Milgram's research on obedience to authority. Chapters 4 and 5 discuss how to evaluate the way researchers design their measures and draw their samples. Chapter 6 explores issues related to making causal connections and provides a summary of the strengths and limitations of various research designs in making causal conclusions. It offers a detailed discussion of how true experimental designs are the gold standard when making causal inferences.

Chapters 7 and 8 present the other important methods of data collection: surveys and qualitative methods (including participant observation, systematic observation, intensive interviews, and focus groups). Chapter 9 now focuses on methodologies that are often used in intelligence-led policing, including a new section on social-network analysis, along with crime mapping, research techniques that utilize Big Data, and content analysis. Chapter 10 covers evaluation research and policy analysis and highlights the different alternatives to evaluation, along with a discussion of the most appropriate methods to use for each evaluation question (e.g., process v. impact). In this chapter, you will see how various methods have been used to investigate the effects of several programs and policies, including problem-oriented policing and the use of body cameras by law enforcement officers. You will also see why "evidence-based" policy is increasingly in demand and that applied research represents an increasing proportion of all studies conducted in the criminological sciences.

Within each of the methods chapters, there are examples of studies that have used mixed methods. However, because researchers are increasingly combining methods, Chapter 11 provides an overview of the philosophy and motivation for combining methods, the various techniques for doing so, and some exciting research examples to demonstrate the fruitfulness of such multiple-methods projects. We finish up in Chapter 12 with an overview of the process of and techniques for reporting research results, along with some ethical problems in writing.

In each chapter, we have retained the substantive case studies to show how each methodology has been used to improve our understanding of criminal justice–related issues, including the factors related to violence, how question wording affects estimates of victimization in surveys, how gang members perceive their world, how community police officers describe their role in comparison with regular patrol officers, the effects of inmates' classification on institutional misconduct in prison, to name just a few of the examples provided.

NEW TO THIS EDITION

The fifth edition of *Fundamentals of Research in Criminology and Criminal Justice* retains the strengths of our other more comprehensive methods textbook while breaking new ground with newly popular research methods, enhanced tools for learning in the text and online, and contemporary, fascinating research findings. We have reorganized the chapters to better connect related techniques, along with new pedagogical learning aids at the end of each chapter and on our Student Study Site. The other distinctive feature of this text, compared with others in the field, continues to be the integration into each chapter of in-depth substantive research examples from the real world highlighting researchers' decision-making processes in their *own* words. Examples from the literature are not simply dropped here and there to keep students' attention. Rather, each chapter presents a particular research method in the context of a substantive research story. This serves several purposes: It illustrates the process of research in the real world, it underscores why particular methods were selected over others, and it highlights the important role research plays in policy decisions in our field. As such, this book's success is due in no small measure to the availability of so many excellent research examples in our discipline. New examples of research have been added in all data collection chapters. The following points are additional strengths of this text, along with a few of the new innovations in this edition.

New chapter that incorporates methods for intelligence-led policing. Chapter 9 includes a new section on social-network analysis (SNA), which provides case studies that highlight how it was used to examine the 9/11 terrorist network and how it could be used to investigate crimes. This chapter also incorporates the sections on crime mapping with a new case study highlighting how mapping can be used to predict break and entries, as well as a section on how Big Data are being used to predict both crime and recidivism. It concludes with an expanded discussion of content analysis.

New sections on research in a diverse society. Several chapters now contain new sections on the importance of making sure our samples, measurements, and methods are inclusive and sensitive to the diverse nature of our society. These sections remind us that we must recognize that cultural norms impact the research process, whether it is the willingness to participate in research activities, the meaning ascribed to abstract terms and constructs, the way data are collected, or the interpretation of the findings. The failure by researchers to adequately address the cultural context impacts the research process in different ways and, ultimately, the validity and generalizability of research findings.

We heard you! Chapter 1 is now more streamlined! This chapter retains the important discussion of how the scientific method helps to ensure research devoid of everyday errors in reasoning. It also highlights different types of research questions and provides a preview of some of the specific methods that are examined in the text. The discussion of research philosophies has been streamlined, is more integrated in the discussion of the distinction between qualitative and quantitative methods, and illuminates why this distinction is becoming less visible with the increased use of mixed methods.

New sections throughout that reflect recent developments in research methods. We have expanded and updated sections, as needed, to reflect changes in practices, including an updated discussion of how the Federal Policy for the Protection of Human Subjects has recently been revised, in Chapter 3. This chapter also includes a new section on institutional review boards. Based on reviewer comments, we have also made other changes, such as expanding our discussion of content analysis in Chapter 9. We also have continued to update the text to reflect increased attention to the Internet as an avenue for research and include electronic surveys, a growing reliance on smartphones, the use of social media for social-network analysis and other research, and the use of the Internet in qualitative techniques.

Updated examples of criminological research as they occur in real-world settings. We have incorporated contemporary and interesting studies taken from the literature on a variety of topics, including the effects of police wearing body cameras on both police and citizen injury, predicting break and entries, and the barriers that exist for older offenders reentering society from prison. These real-world research examples illustrate the exigencies and complexities that shape the application of research methods.

Hearing from other students. Most chapters open with a new quote sharing real stories from students who have taken a research methods course that explains how the class has helped them in their careers.

Increased focus on international research. We have expanded our use of research conducted in countries around the globe, as well as continuing our focus on issues involving diversity in race, ethnicity, gender, and culture within the United States and in other countries.

New "Careers and Research" highlights. Each chapter highlights the career of a researcher who has used the methods discussed. Researchers include those with bachelor's, master's, and PhD degrees who are now working in the field. What better incentive to study hard and master these methods! New careers featured in this edition include a director of research compliance and a research analyst for the World Justice Project.

New "Research in the News" highlights. We have updated these boxes that highlight the research that has made headlines in the news to illustrate the impact of our research not just on researchers and practitioners in criminal justice but also on society as a whole. New topics highlighted in this feature include school shootings, an increase in reporting of rapes, changes to the Common Rule, the impact of video games on violence, violence against women, predictive policing, suicides by jail inmates, gun violence, and the opioid epidemic.

New learning tools. End-of-chapter exercises now include two questions that refer to a chapter-specific video posted on the Student Study Site, in which researchers discuss their experiences with a method presented in that chapter. New empirical datasets are now included in the Student Study Site, and each chapter contains new SPSS or Excel exercises that correspond to the chapter material. Subsets of data are posted in the study site, with the 2013 Youth Risk Behavior Survey, 2014 General Social Survey, 2013 Monitoring the Future data, National Crime Victimization Survey lone-offender assault data for 1992 through 2013, and a 2012 state-level dataset with social and crime indicators.

Aids to effective study. The many effective study aids included in the previous editions have been updated as needed. Lists of main points and key terms provide quick summaries at the end of each chapter. In addition, key terms are highlighted in boldface type when first introduced and defined in text. Definitions for these also can be found in the glossary at the end of the book.

It is a privilege to share with you the results of excellent research related to criminal justice and criminology. If this book communicates the excitement of research and the importance of evaluating carefully the methods we use in research, then we have succeeded in representing what social scientists interested in issues related to criminal justice and criminology do. We think it conveys the latest developments in research methodology and thereby demonstrates that researchers are committed to evaluating and improving their own methods of investigation.

We hope you enjoy learning how to investigate research questions related to criminal justice and criminology and perhaps do some research of your own along the way. We guarantee that the knowledge you develop about research methods will serve you well throughout your education, in your career, and in your community.

DIGITAL RESOURCES

Companion Student Study Site

This web-based Student Study Site (available at edge.sagepub.com/bachmanfrccj5e) provides a variety of additional resources to enhance students' understanding of the book content and take their learning one step further. The site includes quizzes, eFlashcards, a "Learning From SAGE Journal Articles" feature, exercises, podcasts, videos, real data related to criminal justice and criminology (detailed previously), and appendices on how to use IBM® SPSS® Statistics* and Microsoft Excel® and how to use a qualitative analysis package. There is also an appendix on conducting descriptive data analysis.

*SPSS is a registered trademark of International Business Machines Corporation.

Instructor Teaching Site

A password-protected instructor teaching site is available at edge.sagepub.com/bachman frccj5e. It offers a variety of resources to supplement the book material, including lecture notes, PowerPoint slides, test questions with answers, and student project ideas. The site also contains SAGE journal articles, podcasts, videos, Web resources, and articles on teaching criminal justice research methods.

A NOTE ABOUT USING IBM® SPSS® STATISTICS*

To carry out the SPSS exercises at the end of each chapter, you must have SPSS installed on your computer. The Student Study Site includes several subsets of data that are listed previously. Appendix C will get you up and running with SPSS for Windows, as will Appendix E with Excel. You then may spend as much time as you like exploring the datasets provided or you may even use your own data. You also may carry out analyses of the General Social Survey at the University of California, Berkeley, website (sda.berkely.edu/archive.htm).

*SPSS is a registered trademark of International Business Machines Corporation.

ACKNOWLEDGMENTS

We must first acknowledge our heartfelt gratitude to Jessica Miller, whose hard work and guidance on this project are unrivaled. Her supervision of the project and meticulous attention to detail and demand for perfection force us to be better teachers and writers. Importantly, her guiding hand is filled with sincere empathy and care. We also thank Veronica Stapleton Hooper for making sure the trains are running on time and shuttling the manuscript through the appropriate channels. We also want to thank Jared Leighton for his meticulous attention to detail when editing this edition.

Gratitude also goes to all the reviewers of our research methods books who have helped make this *Fundamentals* version what it is, including Brian Colwell, Stanford University; Frank Cormier, University of Manitoba; Amy Craddock, Indiana State University; Michael J. DeValve, Fayetteville State University; Gennifer Furst, The College of New Jersey; Lori Guevara, Fayetteville State University; Stephen M. Haas, Marshall University; Susan B. Haire, University of Georgia; Kristy Holtfreter, Florida State University; James R. Maupin, New Mexico State University; Ira Sommers, California State University, Los Angeles; William Wells, Southern Illinois University Carbondale; and Lisa Anne Zilney, Montclair State University. Reviewers of previous editions included Hank J. Brightman, Saint Peter's College; Cathy Couglan, Texas Christian University; Phyllis B. Gerstenfeld, California State University, Stanislaus; Stephen Haas, Marshall University; Lucy Hochstein, Radford University; Kristen Kuehnle, Salem State College; Eric Metchick, Salem State College; Wilson R. Palacios, University of South Florida; and Mark Winton, University of Central Florida.

We would also like to thank reviewers of this new version of the text, including

Emmanuel N. Amadi, Mississippi Valley State University

Kevin M. Beaver, Florida State University

Deborah Baskin, Loyola University Chicago

Ashley G. Blackburn, University of Houston-Downtown

Shannyn Botsford, Bryant and Stratton College

Dena C. Carson, Indiana University—Purdue University Indianapolis

Daniel Holstein, University of Nevada, Las Vegas

Yongsok Kim, Bemidji State University

Matthew Larson, Wayne State University

Karen McElrath, Fayetteville State University

Mark A. Perry, California State University, Stanislaus

Sarah Prior, Northern Arizona University

Melissa J. Tetzlaff-Bemiller, University of Memphis Lambuth Campus

Lisa Tichavsky, Northern Arizona University

Terri L. Watson, California State University, Sacramento

We also thank Lindsay R. Reed and Margaret Leigey for their diligence and hard work on the ancillary material for instructors, Margarita Porteyeva for the appendix on Excel, Kathryn Stoeckert, Erin Kerrison, and Heather Albertson for additional interactive exercises, and Madeline Stenger for "tidying up" as only she can. And finally, thanks to Matthew Manierre, methodologist extraordinaire, who did a heroic job matching SPSS exercises to the content of each chapter.

We continue to be indebted to the many students we have had an opportunity to teach and mentor at both the undergraduate and graduate levels. In many respects, this book could not have been written without these ongoing reciprocal teaching and learning experiences. You inspire us to become better teachers!

Ronet is indebted to her terrific colleagues in the department of sociology and criminal justice who are unwavering sources of support and inspiration. Ronet is also indebted to an amazing circle of friends who endured graduate school together and continue to hold retreats one weekend of the year (29 years and counting!) for guidance, support, therapy, chocolate, and laughter: Dianne Carmody, Gerry King, Peggy Plass, and Barbara Wauchope. You are the most amazing women in the world, and I am so blessed to have you in my life. To Alex Alvarez, Michelle Meloy, and Lori Williams, my other kindred spirits for their support and guidance; and to my father, Ron, for his steadfast critical eye in all matters of life. And heart-filling gratitude to my husband, Raymond Paternoster, whose amazing spirit and wisdom are with me always even though his body is not bound to this planet. Like always, his guidance continues to make me a better person. And to our son, John Bachman-Paternoster, and our dog, Leo, who bring me joy and laughter beyond my wildest dreams!

Russ would like to thank his wife, Elizabeth Schneider Schutt, and daughter, Julia. They have provided love, support, patience, and remarkable joy in his life.

ABOUT THE AUTHORS

Ronet D. Bachman, PhD, is a professor in the Department of Sociology and Criminal Justice at the University of Delaware. She is coauthor of *Statistical Methods for Crime and Criminal Justice* (3rd ed.) and coeditor of *Explaining Crime and Criminology: Essays in Contemporary Criminal Theory*. In addition, she is author of *Death and Violence on the Reservation* and coauthor of *Stress, Culture, and Aggression in the United States* and *Violence: The Enduring Problem*, as well as numerous articles and papers that examine the epidemiology and etiology of violence. Her most recent federally funded research was a mixed-methods study that investigated the long-term trajectories of offending behavior using official data of a prison cohort released in the early 1990s and then interviewed in 2010. Her longest ongoing research project is a longitudinal study related to delinquency and crime prevention, but it has only one subject—her son, John.

Russell K. Schutt, PhD, is a professor in the Department of Sociology at the University of Massachusetts Boston and research associate in the Department of Psychiatry (Massachusetts Mental Health Center, Beth Israel Deaconess Medical Center) at the Harvard Medical School and at the Edith Nourse Rogers Veterans Hospital. His other books include *Investigating the Social World: The Process and Practice of Research*, *Fundamentals of Social Work Research* (with Ray Engel), *Making Sense of the Social World* (with Dan Chambliss), and *Research Methods in Psychology* (with Paul G. Nestor)—all with SAGE Publications, as well as *Homelessness, Housing, and Mental Illness* (Harvard University Press) and *Social Neuroscience: Brain, Mind, and Society* (coedited with Larry J. Seidman and Matcheri S. Keshavan, Harvard University Press). His research has included a mixed-methods study of a youth violence reduction program, a mixed-methods study of a bibliotherapy program for probationers, a randomized trial of a peer support program for homeless dually diagnosed veterans, mixed-methods investigations of public health programs, and a randomized evaluation of housing alternatives for homeless persons diagnosed with severe mental illness, with funding from the National Cancer Institute, the Veterans Health Administration, the National Institute of Mental Health, the John E. Fetzer Institute, and state agencies. Details are available at blogs.umb.edu/russellkschutt.

1

SCIENCE, SOCIETY, AND RESEARCH RELATED TO CRIMINAL JUSTICE AND CRIMINOLOGY

> I took a research methods class because it was required. I saw it as a hurdle I had to jump to get my BA [bachelor of arts] in criminal justice. When I first stepped into the class, I was pretty intimidated, but I'm really glad I stuck it out. I have been a detective for several years, and I know that what I learned in research methods is going to open up some career advancements in the future.
>
> **Detective W. Wentz**

WHAT DO WE HAVE IN MIND?

It is a sad reality that there is often a school shooting in the United States after this textbook goes to press, which means it is impossible to list the most recent school tragedy here. The population of the United States all too frequently mourns the deaths of young innocent lives taken in this way. The deadliest elementary school shooting took place on December 14, 2012, when a 20-year-old man named Adam Lanza walked into Sandy Hook Elementary in Newtown, Connecticut, armed with several semiautomatic weapons and killed 20 children and six adults. On April 16, 2007, Cho Seung-Hui perpetrated the deadliest college mass shooting by killing 32 students, faculty, and staff and left over 30 others injured on the campus of Virginia Tech in Blacksburg, Virginia. Cho was armed with two semiautomatic handguns that he had legally purchased and a vest filled with ammunition. As police were closing in on the scene, he killed himself. The deadliest high school shooting occurred on February 14, 2018, when Nikolas Cruz, a 19-year-old former student, killed 17 people at the Marjory Stoneman Douglas High School in Parkland, Florida.

None of these mass murderers were typical terrorists, and each of these incidents caused a media frenzy. Headlines such as "The School Violence Crisis" and "School Crime Epidemic" were plastered across national newspapers and weekly

Learning Objectives

1. Describe the four common errors in everyday reasoning.

2. Define social science compared with pseudoscience.

3. Explain the motivations of social research.

4. Identify the four types of social research.

5. Explain the difference between the positivist and constructivist orientations to social research.

6. Understand the differences between quantitative and qualitative methods and the advantages of mixed methods.

$SAGE edge™

Master the content at edge
.sagepub.com/bachmanfrccj5e

1

news journals. Unfortunately, the media plays a large role in how we perceive both problems and solutions. In fact, 95% of Americans say that mass-media sources, such as television and newspapers, are their main source of information on crime and violence (Surrette, 1998). What are your perceptions of violence committed by youth, and how did you acquire them? What do you believe are the causes of youth violence? Many factors have been blamed for youth violence in American society, including the easy availability of guns, the lack of guns in classrooms for protection, the use of weapons in movies and television, the moral decay of our nation, poor parenting, unaware teachers, school and class size, racial prejudice, teenage alienation, the Internet and the World Wide Web, anti-Semitism, rap and rock music, and the list goes on.

You probably have your own ideas about the factors related to violence in general and youth violence in particular. However, these beliefs may not always be supported by empirical research. In fact, the factors often touted by politicians and the media to be related to violence are not always supported by empirical evidence. In the rest of this chapter, you will learn how the methods of social science research go beyond stories in the popular media to help us answer questions such as "What are the causes of youth violence?" By the chapter's end, you should understand how scientific methods used in criminal justice and criminology can help us understand and answer research questions in this discipline.

Case Study: Why Do Kids Kill?

The story of just one murderous youth raises many questions. Take a few minutes to read each of the following questions about Nikolas Cruz, the 19-year-old apprehended for killing 17 people in February 2018 at Marjory Stoneman Douglas High School in Parkland, Florida. Don't ruminate about the questions or worry about your responses. This is not a test; there are no wrong answers.

- How would you describe Nikolas Cruz?

- Why do you think Cruz wanted to kill other students?

- Was Cruz typical of other perpetrators of school shootings?

- In general, why do people become murderers?

- How have you learned about youth violence?

Now let us consider the possible answers to some of these questions. Cruz did not have an arrest record before the shooting, but he did have a troubled life. He and his brother were adopted, and when their father died in 2004, they were raised by their mother, who died in November of 2017. Many who knew Cruz said he took her death very hard. A neighbor believed that Cruz had been diagnosed with autism and had trouble controlling his temper. The neighbor said that when he was younger, Cruz had gone to a school for students with special needs, and "kids were really picking on him and would gang up on him and beat him up a little" (Fausset & Kovaleski, 2018).

Do you have enough information now to understand why he went on a shooting rampage in his school?

Cruz was expelled from the Marjory Stoneman Douglas High School the year before the shootings allegedly for fighting with his ex-girlfriend's new boyfriend and for possessing a knife in school. In September of 2017, he made a post under the name 'nikolas cruz' on a YouTube channel that stated, "I'm going to be a professional school shooter" (Fausset & Kovaleski, 2018). The post was flagged and submitted to a local FBI office in Mississippi.

After the shooting, the FBI reported that nothing could be done about the posting because "no other information was included in the comment which would indicate a particular time, location, or the true identity of the person who posted the comment" (Fausset &Kovaleski, 2018). Now can you construct an adequate description of Cruz? Can you explain the reason for his murderous rampage? Or do you feel you need to know more about him? We have attempted to understand just one person's behavior, and already, our investigation is spawning more questions than answers.

REASONING ABOUT THE SOCIAL WORLD

Questions and Answers

We cannot avoid asking questions about the actions and attitudes of others. We all try to make sense of the complexities of our social world and our position in it, in which we have quite a personal stake. In fact, the more that you begin to think like a social scientist, the more questions will come to mind.

But why does each question have so many possible answers? Surely our individual perspectives play a role. One person may see a homicide offender as a victim of circumstance, while another person may see the same individual as inherently evil. Answers to questions we ask in the criminological sciences vary because individual life experiences and circumstances vary. When questions concern not just one person but many people or general social processes, the number of possible answers quickly multiplies. In fact, people have very different beliefs about the factors responsible for mass shootings. Exhibit 1.1 displays Gallup Poll results from the following question: "Thinking about mass shootings that have occurred in the U.S. in recent years, from what you know or have read, how much do you think each of the following factors is to blame for the shootings?" As you can see, a large percentage blames the mental health system—4 out of 10 blame easy access to guns as well—but nearly 1 out of 5 blames inflammatory language from political commentators.

Avoiding Errors in Reasoning

We all have different ideas about the factors related to things, but most of the time, these ideas are not based on evidence. It is simply too easy to make errors in logic, particularly when we are analyzing the social world in which we ourselves are conscious participants. We can call some of these "everyday errors" because they occur so frequently in the nonscientific, unreflective discourse about the social world that we hear on a daily basis. In fact, in the last decade, tens of books have been written that focus on how and why our judgments are usually irrational and sometimes extremely biased. These errors in reasoning have been given many fancy names including the following: anchoring heuristic, base rate fallacy, illusory correlation, just-world phenomenon, omission bias, self-reference effect, and so on (Hertenstein, 2013). In this section, we more generally describe the four areas where we typically make errors: overgeneralization, selective or inaccurate observation, illogical reasoning, and resistance to change.

Overgeneralization

Overgeneralization, an error in reasoning, occurs when we conclude that what we have observed or what we know to be true for some cases is true for all cases. We are always drawing conclusions about people and social processes from our own interactions with them, but sometimes we forget that our experiences are limited. The social (and natural) world is, after all, a complex place. We have the ability (and inclination) to interact with just a small fraction of the individuals who live in the world, especially in a limited span of time.

> **Overgeneralization:** An error in reasoning that occurs when we conclude that what we have observed or know to be true for a subset of cases holds true for the entire set

Exhibit 1.1 Responses to the Question, "Thinking About Mass Shootings That Have Occurred in the U.S. in Recent Years, From What You Know or Have Read, How Much Do You Think Each of the Following Factors Is to Blame for the Shootings?"

	Great deal %	Fair amount %	Not much %	Not at all %
Failure of the mental health system to identify individuals who are a danger to others	48	32	11	8
Easy access to guns	40	21	16	20
Drug use	37	29	17	15
Violence in movies, video games, and music lyrics	32	24	23	20
The spread of extremist viewpoints on the Internet	29	28	22	15
Insufficient security at public buildings including businesses and schools	29	29	26	14
Inflammatory language from prominent political commentators	18	19	30	28

Source: Reprinted with permission from Gallup.

Selective or Inaccurate Observation

Selective observation: Observations chosen because they are in accord with preferences or beliefs of the observer

Selective observation is choosing to look only at things that align with our preferences or beliefs. When we are inclined to criticize individuals or institutions, it is all too easy to notice their every failing. We are also more inclined to see the failings of others who are "not like us." If we are convinced in advance that all kids who are violent are unlikely to be rehabilitated and will go on to commit violent offenses in adulthood, we will probably find many cases confirming our beliefs. But what about other youths who have become productive and stable citizens after engaging in violence as adolescents? If we acknowledge only the instances that confirm our predispositions, we are victims of our own selective observation. Exhibit 1.2 depicts the difference between overgeneralization and selective observation.

Inaccurate observation: Observations based on faulty perceptions of empirical reality

Our observations also can simply be inaccurate. If a woman says she is *hungry* and we think she said she is *hunted*, we have made an inaccurate observation. If we think five people are standing on a street corner when there are actually seven, we have also made an inaccurate observation. Such errors occur often in casual conversation and in everyday observation of the world around us. In fact, our perceptions do not provide a direct window to the world around us, for what we think we have sensed is not necessarily what we have seen (or heard, smelled, felt, or tasted). Even when our senses are functioning fully, our minds have to interpret what we have sensed (Humphrey, 1992).

Illogical reasoning: Prematurely jumping to conclusions and arguing on the basis of invalid assumptions

Illogical Reasoning

When we prematurely jump to conclusions or argue on the basis of invalid assumptions, we are using **illogical reasoning**. For example, it is not reasonable to propose that depictions of violence in media, such as television and movies, cause violence if evidence indicates that the majority of those who watch such programs do not become violent. However, it is also

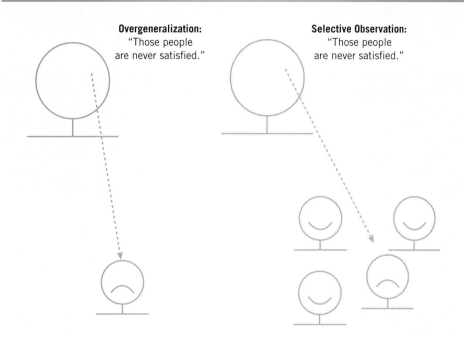

illogical to assume that media depictions of gratuitous violence have no effect on individuals. Of course, logic that seems valid to one person can seem twisted or unsound to another; the problem emerges when our reasoning stems from different assumptions rather than a failure to think straight.

Resistance to Change

Resistance to change, the reluctance to change our ideas in light of new information, may occur for several reasons:

- *Ego-based commitments.* We all learn to greet with some skepticism the claims by leaders of companies, schools, agencies, and so on that people in their organization are happy, that revenues are growing, that services are being delivered in the best possible way, and so forth. We know how tempting it is to make statements about the social world that conform to our own needs rather than to the observable facts. It also can be difficult to admit that we were wrong once we have staked out a position on an issue.

- *Excessive devotion to tradition.* Some degree of devotion to tradition is necessary for the predictable functioning of society. Social life can be richer and more meaningful if it is allowed to flow along the paths charted by those who have preceded us. But too much devotion to tradition can stifle adaptation to changing circumstances. When we distort our observations or alter our reasoning so that we can maintain beliefs that "were good enough for my grandfather, so they're good enough for me," we hinder our ability to accept new findings and develop new knowledge.

Resistance to change: Reluctance to change ideas in light of new information due to ego-based commitments, excessive devotion to tradition, or uncritical agreement with authorities

- *Uncritical agreement with authority.* If we lack the courage to critically evaluate the ideas of those in positions of authority, we will have little basis for complaint if they exercise their authority over us in ways we do not like. And if we do not allow new discoveries to call our beliefs into question, our understanding of the social world will remain limited. People often accept the beliefs of those in positions of authority without question.

Now take just a minute to reexamine the beliefs about youth violence that you recorded earlier. Did you settle on a simple explanation even though the reality was far more complex? Were your beliefs influenced by your own ego and feelings about your similarities to or differences from individuals prone to violence? Are your beliefs perhaps based on depictions of violence in the media or fiction? Did you weigh carefully the opinions of authority figures, including politicians, teachers, and even your parents, or just accept or reject those opinions? Could knowledge of research methods help to improve your own understanding of the factors related to violent behavior? By now, you can see some of the challenges faced by social scientists who study issues related to crime and the criminal justice system.

You do not have to be a scientist or use sophisticated research techniques to recognize and avoid these four errors in reasoning. If you recognize these errors for what they are and make a conscious effort to avoid them, you can improve your own reasoning. Simply stated, refrain from stereotyping people, avoid jumping to conclusions, and look at the big picture. These are the same errors that the methods of social science are designed to help us avoid.

HOW THE SCIENTIFIC APPROACH IS DIFFERENT

The **social science** approach to answering questions about the social world is designed to greatly reduce these potential sources of error in everyday reasoning. **Science** relies on systematic methods to answer questions, and it does so in a way that allows others to inspect and evaluate its methods. In the realm of social research, these methods are not so unusual. After all, they involve asking questions, observing social groups, and counting people, which we often do in our everyday lives. However, social scientists develop, refine, apply, and report their understanding of the social world more systematically, or specifically, than Joanna Q. Public.

- Social science research methods can reduce the likelihood of overgeneralization by using systematic procedures for selecting individuals or groups to study that are representative of the individuals or groups about whom we wish to generalize.

- Social science methods can reduce the risk of selective or inaccurate observation by requiring that we measure and sample phenomena systematically.

- To avoid illogical reasoning, social researchers use explicit criteria for identifying causes and for determining whether these criteria are met in a particular instance.

- Scientific methods lessen the tendency to develop answers about the social world from ego-based commitments, excessive devotion to tradition, or unquestioning respect for authority.

Science Versus Pseudoscience

In philosophical terms, the scientific method represents an **epistemology**—that is, a way of knowing that relies on objective, empirical investigation. Its techniques must be **transparent**

Social science: The use of scientific methods to investigate individuals, societies, and social processes, including questions related to criminology and criminal justice; the knowledge produced by these investigations

Science: A set of logical, systematic, documented methods for investigating nature and natural processes; the knowledge produced by these investigations

Epistemology: A branch of philosophy that studies how knowledge is gained or acquired

Transparent: An important feature of the scientific method that requires procedures, methods, and data analyses of any study to be presented clearly for the purposes of replication so that the methods, procedures, and data analyses of any study can be replicated. This transparency allows other researchers to see if the same results can be reproduced. If findings can be replicated, then we have greater confidence that the finding is real and not based on bias. Transparency also relies on **peer review**, the process by which other independent researchers evaluate the scientific merit of the study.

In contrast, if we relied on findings based on intuition, gut reactions, or our own experience, we would be open to the errors we just covered previously. If we based findings on this, it would not be science but instead fall under the classification of **pseudoscience**. Pseudoscientific beliefs are not based on the scientific method but rather on claims that may be touted as "scientifically proven" but are only bolstered by testimonials of believers who have experienced the event firsthand or who have claimed to have witnessed the phenomenon (Nestor & Schutt, 2012).

Of course, today's pseudoscience could be yesterday's science. In criminological research, **phrenology** is a good example. In the 19th century, phrenology was the belief that bumps and fissures of the skull determined the character and personality of a person. Doctors doing entry examinations at American prisons would examine a new inmate's head for bumps or cavities to develop a criminal profile. Advances in cognitive psychology and neurology have largely discredited phrenology and placed it within the domain of pseudoscience. It didn't take a genius to question phrenology, just a group of researchers adhering to the scientific method. When inmates' heads were compared with individual heads in the general population, they were essentially the same!

Criminal Justice and Criminological Research in Action

Let's get back to our topic of youth violence. This topic is not a new phenomenon of interest. It has always been a popular topic of social science research. However, the sharp increase in this violence in the United States that began in the late 1980s, along with the increased number of school shootings in recent decades, was unprecedented. Predictably, whenever a phenomenon is perceived as an epidemic, numerous explanations emerge to explain it. Unfortunately, most of these explanations are based on the media and popular culture, not on empirical research. Despite the anecdotal information floating around in the mass media about the factors that may have contributed to increases in youth violence, social scientists interested in this phenomenon have amassed a substantial body of findings that have refined knowledge about the problem and shaped social policy (Tonry & Moore, 1998). These studies fall into the four categories of purposes for social scientific research: descriptive, exploratory, explanatory, and evaluation.

Descriptive Research

Defining and describing social phenomena of interest are part of almost any research investigation, but **descriptive research** is the primary focus of many studies of youth crime and violence. Some of the central questions used in these studies were "How many people are victims of youth violence?" "How many youth are offenders?" "What are the most common crimes committed by youthful offenders?" and "How many of the different youth are arrested and incarcerated each year for crime?" Descriptive research is not interested in explaining some phenomenon, just in describing its frequency or its qualities. Measurement (see Chapter 4) and sampling (see Chapter 5) are central concerns in descriptive research.

Peer review: A process in which a journal editor sends a submitted article to two or three experts who judge whether the paper should be accepted, revised and resubmitted, or rejected; the experts also provide comments to explain their decision and guide any revisions

Pseudoscience: Dubious but fascinating claims that are touted as "scientifically proven" and bolstered by fervent, public testimonials of believers who have experienced firsthand or have claimed to have witnessed the phenomenon; however, such evidence is not based on the principles of the scientific method

Phrenology: A now-defunct field of study, once considered a science in the 19th century, which held that bumps and fissures of the skull determined the character and personality of a person

Descriptive research: Research in which phenomena are defined and described

Case Study: Description: How Prevalent Is Youth Violence?

Police Reports

One of the most enduring sources of information on lethal violence in the United States is the Federal Bureau of Investigation's (FBI) Supplementary Homicide Reports (SHR). Homicide victimization rates indicate that for those under the age of 24, vulnerability to murder increased dramatically during the mid-1980s through about 1994, when rates began a steady decline; they have remained relatively stable since (E. L. Smith & Cooper, 2013).

Data measuring the prevalence of nonlethal forms of violence, such as robbery and assaults, are a bit more complicated. How do we know how many young people assault victims each year? People who report their victimizations to police represent one avenue for these calculations. The FBI compiles these numbers in its Uniform Crime Reporting (UCR) system, which is slowly being replaced by the National Incident-Based Reporting System (NIBRS). Both of these data sources rely on state, county, and city law enforcement agencies across the United States to voluntarily participate in the reporting program. Can you imagine why relying on these data sources may be problematic for estimating prevalence rates of violent victimizations? If victimizations are never reported to police, they are not counted. This is especially problematic for victimizations between intimate partners and other offenses such as rape, in which only a fraction of incidents is ever reported to police.

Surveys

Instead of police reports, most social scientists believe the best way to determine the magnitude of violent victimization is through random-sample surveys. While we will discuss survey methodology in greater detail in Chapter 7, this basically means randomly selecting individuals in the population of interest and asking them about their victimization experiences. The only ongoing annual survey to do this is the National Crime Victimization Survey (NCVS), which is sponsored by the U.S. Department of Justice's Bureau of Justice Statistics (BJS). Among other questions, the NCVS asks questions such as "Has anyone attacked or threatened you with a weapon (for instance, a gun or knife) or by something thrown (such as a rock or bottle)? Include any grabbing, punching, or choking." Estimates indicate that youth ages 12 to 24 have the highest rates of violent victimization. Despite the recent increases observed in homicide rates for this age group in some locations, their victimization trends have generally declined since the peak of the early 1990s mentioned earlier.

The Youth Risk Behavior Survey (YRBS) is another large research survey that estimates the magnitude of youth violence (along with other risk-taking behavior, such as taking drugs and smoking) and has been conducted every two years in the United States since 1990. To measure the extent of youth violence, students are asked questions such as "During the past 12 months, how many times were you in a physical fight?" and "During the past 12 months, how many times were you in a physical fight in which you were injured and had to be seen by a doctor or nurse?"

Of course, another way to measure violence would be to ask respondents about their offending behaviors. Some surveys do this, including the Rochester Youth Development Study (RYDS). The RYDS sample consists of 1,000 students who were in the seventh and eighth grades in the Rochester, New York, public schools during the spring semester of the 1988 school year. This project has interviewed the original respondents at 12 different times, including the last interview that took place in 1997, when respondents were in their early 20s (Thornberry, Krohn, Lizotte, & Bushway, 2008). As you can imagine, respondents are typically more reluctant to reveal offending behavior compared with their victimization experiences. However, these surveys have proved to be very useful in examining the factors related to violent offending and other delinquency. We should also point out that although this discussion has been specific to violence, the measures we have discussed in this section, along with their strengths and weaknesses, apply to measuring all types of crime.

Exploratory Research

Exploratory research seeks to find out how people get along in the setting under question, what meanings they give to their actions, and what issues concern them. The goal is to answer the question "What is going on here?" and to investigate social phenomena without expectations. This purpose is associated with the use of methods that capture large amounts of relatively unstructured information. For example, researchers investigating the emergence of youth gangs in the 1980s were encountering a phenomenon of which they had no direct experience. Thus, an early goal was to find out what it was like to be a gang member and how gang members made sense of their situation.

Exploratory research: Research in which social phenomena are investigated without *a priori* expectations to develop explanations of them

Case Study: Exploration—How Did Schools Avert a Shooting Rampage?

Research that is exploratory in nature is generally concerned with uncovering detailed information about a given phenomenon, learning as much as possible about particular people and/or events. While there have been far too many school shootings in the United States during the past decade, there have also been numerous incidents in which students were plotting to kill their peers or faculty members but came to the attention of authorities before their plans could be carried out. To examine how these incidents were stopped, Eric Madfis (2014) selected 11 schools where a mass shooting had been diverted between 2000 and 2009 and conducted intensive interviews with people who were involved, including 11 principals and 21 other administrators, teachers, and police officers. He also corroborated the interview data with newspaper reports and, where possible, court transcripts and police incident reports.

Madfis's (2014) research was truly exploratory. You will learn much more about qualitative research in Chapter 8, but for now, we simply want to highlight how this study is different from the other research types listed previously. He let the people he interviewed speak for themselves; he didn't come with questions that were designed to measure concepts such as violence or delinquency before the interviews. After examining all of the interview transcripts, Madfis developed themes that emerged among them all. This is what made the research exploratory instead of explanatory.

Five out of the 11 school shootings were thwarted by other students who were not directly involved with or entrusted by the accused students but who came about the information indirectly. For example, one student reported the existence of disturbing postings and images on another student's network website. The second most common category of intervention involved people who had been told directly by students accused of plotting the attacks. For example, after one student was sent threatening messages, she told her mother, who then called the police. When the accused student was questioned, he confessed, and weapons were discovered in his bedroom.

School administrators believed that students have been more likely to come forward with information about their peers since the Columbine High School shootings than they had been before this catalyzing mass shooting. One school principal stated, "Columbine absolutely made kids much more vigilant about things going on around them. . . . I think it made kids less afraid to speak up if something wasn't sitting right with them" (Madfis, 2014,

p. 235). Another theme that was clear from the interviews was that if school environments were going to break the "student code of silence," they must be supporting, cohesive, and trusting. For example, another principal stated, "The best mechanism we have as a deterrent for these sorts of violent acts is good relationships between kids and adults, because kids will tell you" (Madfis, 2014, p. 235).

As you can see from this discussion of Madfis's results, the goal of his research was to explore the factors related to instances in which a school shooting had been successfully thwarted. He did not go into the school with a survey filled with questions because little is known about these factors in the existing literature. As such, the investigation was explorative in nature. It is different from descriptive because a prevalence estimate of some phenomenon is not the goal. Rather, a deeper understanding of the processes and perceptions of study participants is the desired outcome in exploratory research.

Explanatory Research

Explanatory research: Research that seeks to identify causes or effects of social phenomena

Many people consider explanation to be the premier goal of any science. Explanatory research seeks to identify causes and effects of social phenomena, to predict how one phenomenon will change or vary in response to variation in some other phenomenon. Researchers adopted explanation as a principal goal when they began to ask such questions as "Why do people become offenders?" and "Does the unemployment rate influence the frequency of youth crime?" Methods with which to identify causes and effects are the focus of Chapter 6.

Case Study: Explanation—What Factors Are Related to Youth Delinquency and Violence?

When we move from description to exploration and finally to explanatory research, we want to understand the direct relationship between two or more things. Does *x* explain *y*? Or if *x* happens, is *y* also likely to occur? What are some of the factors related to youth violence? Fontaine, Brendgen, Vitaro, and Tremblay (2016) were interested in how several factors, including parental supervision and attachment to school, affected the probability of adolescents engaging in violent behavior. They used a longitudinal dataset collected in Montreal, Canada, which followed boys from kindergarten until they were 17 years old. By following this sample of boys over time, the researchers could determine that parental supervision and attachments to school came before the violent offending, which is extremely important when attempting to determine factors that predict violence.

Parental supervision was assessed at ages 11, 12, 14, and 15 years and based on the following items: "Your parents know where you are when you are outside the house?" And "your parents know with whom you are when you are outside the house?" School engagement and attachments were assessed at these same ages and included six items, such as "Do you feel that you do your best at school?" Self-reported violent offending was assessed at age 17 and included fist fighting, gang fighting, carrying a deadly weapon, using a deadly weapon, threatening someone to force him/her to do something, attacking someone, and throwing an object at someone.

Several other variables were included in Fontaine et al.'s (2016) predictive models, including whether the boys had been violent as young children, family structure, and attitudes toward legal authorities, among others. Results indicated that boys who had greater parental supervision and school engagement were more likely to engage in violent delinquency compared with their less supervised and engaged counterparts. In fact, while boys who had been aggressive as children were more likely to be violent as adolescents, the relationship between childhood and adolescent violence was virtually eliminated for those boys who had high levels of parental supervision and school engagement.

Evaluation Research

Evaluation research seeks to determine the effects of a social program or other type of intervention. It is a type of explanatory research because it deals with cause and effect. However, evaluation research differs from other forms of explanatory research because it considers the implementation and outcomes of social policies and programs. These issues may not be relevant in other types of explanatory research. The increase of youth violence in the 1980s spawned many new government programs and, with them, evaluation research to assess the impact of these programs. Some of these studies are reviewed in Chapter 11, which covers evaluation research.

Evaluation research: Research about social programs or interventions

Case Study: Evaluation—Do Violence Prevention Programs in Schools Work?

As many school administrators will tell you, there are direct-mail, e-mail, and in-person direct-sales efforts to sell them programs that reduce violence, increase empathy among students, promote a positive school environment, promote other forms of mental well-being, and on and on. Unfortunately, not many of these programs have been rigorously evaluated to ensure that they actually do what they promise. One program that has been the target of rigorous evaluation is the Gang Resistance Education And Training (G.R.E.A.T.) program, which is a school-based gang and violence prevention program. This program is a cognitive-based program intended to (among other things) teach students about crime and its effects on victims, how to resolve conflicts without violence, and how to improve individual responsibility through goal setting. The G.R.E.A.T. program addresses multiple risk factors for violent offending among three domains: school, peer, and individual. Because it is curriculum-based in the school, it does not address risk factors present in the family or neighborhood. It is a 13-week program taught in sixth or seventh grade and attempts to affect several risk factors, including school commitment and performance, association with conventional or delinquent peers, empathy, and self-control, among others.

Finn-Aage Esbensen and his colleagues (Esbensen, Osgood, Peterson, Taylor, & Carson, 2013) evaluated the long-term effects of the G.R.E.A.T. program in seven cities across the United States. Schools selected for the program randomly assigned some seventh-grade classrooms to get the treatment (*experimental groups*) while the other classrooms did not (*control groups*). As you will later learn, this is called a *true experimental design*. It is an extremely strong research method for determining the effects of programs or policies because if groups are truly randomly assigned, there is a strong reason to believe that differences between the groups after program implementation, such as reduced violent offending, are because of the program and not some other factor that existed before the introduction of the treatment.

Both experimental and control group students in the Esbensen et al. (2013) study completed four follow-up surveys annually for four years. The researchers examined 33 outcome measures, including general delinquency, violent offending, gang affiliation, associations with delinquent peers, empathy, impulsivity, and problem solving. The statistical methods employed by Esbensen and his colleagues are very complicated and beyond the scope of this text, so we will simply highlight the general findings. When the data for all seven sites were combined, there were no differences in violent offending between experimental and control group students over the four-year period. Those students who participated in the G.R.E.A.T. program were, however, less likely to become members of gangs, had higher levels of altruism, showed less anger and risk taking, and had more favorable attitudes toward the police, among other things.

With these results, would you deem the G.R.E.A.T. program a success? These are the important questions evaluation research must address. Esbensen et al. (2013) agree that the program did not reduce general delinquency or violent offending but note that it was effective in reducing gang membership, which is also a risk factor for violent offending.

ALTERNATIVE RESEARCH ORIENTATIONS

Your preferences for particular research methods will be shaped, in part, by your general assumptions about how the social world can best be investigated—by your social-research philosophy. The scientific approach reflects the belief that there is an objective reality apart from the perceptions of those who observe it. This is the philosophy traditionally associated with natural science and with the belief that scientists must be objective and unbiased to see reality clearly (M. Weber, 1949, p. 72). **Positivism** asserts that a well-designed test of a specific prediction—for example, the prediction that youth who are more attached and supervised by their parents will be less likely to engage in violent behavior—can move us closer to understanding actual social processes.

Postpositivism is a philosophy that is closely related to positivism because it also assumes an external, objective reality, but postpositivists acknowledge the complexity of this reality and the limitations and biases of the scientists who study it (Guba & Lincoln, 1994, pp. 109–111). For example, postpositivists may worry that researchers who are heavy computer users themselves will be biased in favor of finding positive social effects of computer use. As a result of concerns such as this, postpositivists do not think we can ever be sure that scientific methods allow us to perceive objective reality. Instead, they believe that the goal of science is to achieve **intersubjective agreement** among scientists about the nature of reality (Wallace, 1983, p. 461). We can be more confident in the community of social researchers than in any individual social scientist (D. T. Campbell & Russo, 1999, p. 144).

In contrast to these, **interpretivism** is a research philosophy that emphasizes the importance of understanding subjective meanings people give to reality; unlike positivism and postpositivism, it does not assume that social processes can be identified objectively. Here's the basic argument: All empirical data we collect come to us through our own senses and must be interpreted with our own minds. This suggests that we can never be sure that we have understood reality properly, that we can, or that our understandings can really be judged more valid than someone else's. Concerns like this have begun to appear in many areas of social science and have begun to shape some research methods. From this standpoint, the goal of validity becomes meaningless: "Truth is a matter of the best-informed and most sophisticated construction on which there is consensus at a given time" (Schwandt, 1994, p. 128).

It is tempting to think of positivism and postpositivism as representing an opposing research philosophy to interpretivism. However, if we view them as completely distinct, we would be forced to choose the philosophy that seems closest to our own preferences and condemn the other as "unscientific," "uncaring," or perhaps just "unrealistic." Fortunately, contemporary researchers often understand the strengths of multiple philosophies and select their research methods accordingly. In fact, research can often be improved by drawing on insights from both positivist and interpretivist philosophies. In the words of Stephen P. Turner (1980), "The distinctive empirical concerns of 'interpretive' and 'statistical' research, usually thought of as antithetical or mutually irrelevant, can be made to mesh" (p. 99).

Before we move on, we also want to highlight three different orientations to research that are not so much philosophies, as they are value orientations: critical theory, feminist research, and participatory action research (PAR).

Positivism: The belief, shared by most scientists, that there is a reality that exists quite apart from our own perception of it, although our knowledge of this reality may never be complete

Postpositivism: The belief that there is an empirical reality but that our understanding of it is limited by its complexity and by the biases and other limitations of researchers

Intersubjective agreement: Agreement between scientists about the nature of reality; often upheld as a more reasonable goal for science than certainty about an objective reality

Interpretivism (interpretivist philosophy): The belief that reality is socially constructed and that the goal of social scientists is to understand what meanings people give to that reality

Like interpretivism, **critical theory** similarly focuses on examining structures, patterns of behavior, and meanings but rests on the premise that power differences, often manifested by discrimination and oppression, have shaped these structures and patterns. What is observed and described at a particular moment in time is the result of differential power relationships that have solidified over time. How people are socially located in a particular situation will construct their meanings and interests (Keenan, 2004). Researchers committed to this perspective see research as a way to challenge societal structures that reinforce oppression.

Feminist research also provides a critical lens for doing research and is a term that is often used to refer to research done by feminists (Reinharz 1992). Like critical theory, it is not a research method, as feminists utilize all types of methodologies (Reinharz 1992). However, many feminist scholars share the interpretivist concern with personal experience and subjective feelings and with the researcher's position and standpoint. Feminist researchers Sharlene Hesse-Biber and Patricia Lina Leavy (2007) emphasize the importance of viewing the social world as complex and multilayered, of sensitivity to the impact of social differences, of being an "insider" or an "outsider," and of being concerned with the researcher's position. African American feminist researcher Patricia Hill Collins (1991) suggests that researchers who are sensitive to their "outside" role within a social situation may have unique advantages: "Outsiders within occupy a special place—they become different people and their difference sensitizes them to patterns that may be more difficult for established sociological insiders to see" (p. 53).

Whyte (1991) proposed a more activist approach to research called **participatory action research (PAR)**. As the name implies, this approach encourages social researchers to get "out of the academic rut" and bring values into the research process (p. 285). In participatory action research, the researcher involves as active participants some members of the setting studied. Both the organizational members and the researcher are assumed to want to develop valid conclusions, to bring unique insights, and to desire change, but Whyte (1991) believed these objectives were more likely to be obtained if the researcher collaborated actively with the persons he studied. We will talk about PAR in Chapter 12.

Critical theory: Focuses on examining structures, patterns, and meanings but rests on the premise that power differences have shaped these structures and patterns

Feminist research: Research with a focus on women's lives that often includes an orientation to personal experience, subjective orientations, the researcher's standpoint, and emotions

Participatory action research (PAR): A type of research in which the researcher involves some organizational members as active participants throughout the process of studying an organization; the goal is making changes in the organization

Keeping Count of School Shootings

In this chapter we have talked about the different types of research, including descriptive, explanatory, exploratory, and evaluation. The *New York Times* provided a great description of the school shootings that have taken place in the United States since 1970. They examined all instances in which a gun was brandished or fired or a bullet hit school property for any reason, regardless of the number of victims. The data for the analysis came from the Center for Homeland Defense and Security.

The article highlights the fact that including those incidents where a firearm was brandished, which includes incidents in which a shooter makes threatening gestures but was stopped by a bystander or the weapon malfunctioned, are just as important as incidents where shots were actually fired. Both types of

incidents can help shed light on factors that contribute to shootings. The purpose of the article, however, was description rather than explanation. With the exception of 2018, when there was a very high number of school shootings, data show that the average number of school shootings has been around 40 for the past two decades.

For Further Thought

1. Do you think the definition of school shootings should have included both incidents in which there were shots fired and incidents where no shots were fired? Why, or why not?

2. What type of research could improve our understanding of the factors related to school shootings?

Source: Weiyi, C., & Patel, J. (2019, May 11). A half-century of school shootings like Columbine, Sandy Hook and Parkland. *New York Times*. Retrieved from https://www.nytimes.com/interactive/2019/05/11/us/school-shootings-united-states.html?searchResultPosition=15

RESEARCH IN THE NEWS

QUANTITATIVE AND QUALITATIVE METHODS

As you might expect, different research philosophies often are related to the selection of different research methods. Importantly, however, we want to make clear that the research question or purpose should always dictate the research method. This will become more obvious when you read each specific methodology chapter. However, in general, research methods can be divided into two somewhat different domains called quantitative research methods and qualitative research methods. Did you notice the difference between the types of data the case studies discussed at the beginning of the chapter used? The data collected in the YRBS were counts of the responses students gave on the survey. These data were numerical, so we say that this study used quantitative methods. In contrast, Madfis's (2014) exploratory study used in-depth interviews with school administrators who had helped prevent an attempted school shooting. This methodology was designed to capture the social reality of the participants as they experienced it, in their own words, rather than in predetermined categories. This inquiry is clearly consistent with the constructivist philosophy. Because the researchers focused on the participants' words rather than counts and numbers, we say that this study used qualitative methods.

The distinction between quantitative and qualitative methods involves more than just the type of data collected. Quantitative methods are most often used when the motives for research are explanation, description, or evaluation. Exploration is the most common motive for using qualitative methods, although researchers also use these methods for descriptive and evaluative purposes. The goals of quantitative and qualitative researchers also may differ. Whereas quantitative researchers generally accept the goal of developing an understanding that correctly reflects what is actually happening in the real world, some qualitative researchers instead emphasize the goal of developing an "authentic" understanding of a social process or social setting (Gubrium & Holstein, 1997). An authentic understanding is one that reflects *fairly* the various perspectives of participants in that setting.

As important as it is, we do not want to place too much emphasis on the distinction between qualitative and quantitative methods because social scientists often combine these methods to enrich their research. For example, "qualitative knowing" about social settings can be essential for understanding patterns in quantitative data (D. T. Campbell & Russo, 1999, p. 141). Qualitative data can be converted to quantitative data, for example, when we count the frequency of particular words or phrases in a text or measure the time elapsed between different behaviors that we have observed. Surveys that collect primarily quantitative data also may include questions asking for written responses, and these responses may be used in a qualitative, textual analysis. Researchers using quantitative methods may engage in some exploration to find unexpected patterns in their data. Qualitative researchers may test explicit explanations of social phenomena using textual or observational data.

As noted, many researchers are increasingly electing to garner the strengths of several research methods combined and, as a result, rely on mixed methods to study one research question. This is sometimes called triangulation. The latter term suggests that a researcher can get a clearer picture of the social reality being studied by viewing it from several different perspectives. Each will have some liabilities in a specific research application, and all can benefit from a combination of one or more other methods (Brewer & Hunter, 1989; Sechrest & Sidani, 1995).

As you will see in the chapters that follow, the distinction between quantitative and qualitative data is not always sharp. We'll examine such "mixed method" possibilities in each of the chapters that review specific methods of data collection.

HIGHLIGHTING A FEW SPECIFIC TYPES OF RESEARCH METHODS

As you will see in this book, the data we utilize in criminological research are derived from many different sources, and the research methods we employ in criminology and criminal justice are very diverse. In this section, we are going to highlight a few of the more traditional methods that will be covered later in the book.

An **experimental approach** is used in criminological research, particularly when the efficacy of a program or policy is being evaluated. As we will see in Chapter 6, true experiments must have three things: two groups (one receiving the treatment or intervention and the other receiving no treatment or another form thereof), random assignment to these two groups, and an assessment of change in the outcome variable after the treatment or policy has been received. Quasi-experimental designs, experiments that lack one of these three ingredients, also are used in our discipline. Chapter 10 focuses exclusively on research designs used in evaluation research.

Asking people questions in **surveys**, as we have highlighted, is another popular method used by criminological researchers and is probably the most versatile. Most concepts about individuals can be defined in such a way that measurement with one or more questions becomes an option. These surveys can be self-administered by respondents (e.g., through the mail) or can be read by an interviewer (e.g., through a telephone survey).

Although, in principle, survey questions can be a straightforward and efficient means to measure individual characteristics, facts about events, levels of knowledge, and opinions of any sort in practice survey questions can result in misleading or inappropriate answers. All questions proposed for a survey must be screened carefully for their adherence to basic guidelines and then tested and revised until the researcher feels some confidence that they will be clear to the intended respondents (Fowler, 1995). Some variables may prove to be inappropriate for measurement with any type of question. We have to recognize that memories and perceptions of the events about which we might like to ask can be limited. Specific guidelines for writing questions and developing surveys are presented in Chapter 7.

In other cases, a researcher may want to make his or her presence known and directly participate in the activity being observed. Included in this type of research design is **participant observation**, which involves developing a sustained relationship with people while they go about their normal activities. In other instances, the subject matter of interest may not be amenable to a survey, or perhaps we want more detailed and in-depth information than questions with fixed formats can answer. In these cases, we turn to research techniques such as participant observation and **intensive interviewing**. These methods are preferred when we seek in-depth information on an individual's feelings, experiences, and perceptions. Chapter 8 shows how these methods and other field research techniques can uncover aspects of the social world that we are likely to miss in experiments and surveys.

Secondary data analysis (Riedel, 2000), which is the reanalysis of already existing data, is another method used by researchers. These data usually come from one of two places: from official sources, such as local or federal agencies (e.g., rates of crime reported to police, information on incarcerated offenders from state correctional authorities, or adjudication data from the courts), or from surveys sponsored by government agencies or conducted by other researchers. Virtually all the data collected by government agencies and a great deal of survey data collected by independent researchers are made available to the public through the Inter-University Consortium for Political and Social Research (ICPSR), which is located at the University of Michigan. Another type of indirect measurement is called **content analysis**. In this type of study, a researcher studies representations of the research topic in media forms

Experimental approach: An approach in which the researcher assigns individuals to two or more groups in a way that equates the characteristics of individuals in the groups (with a certain chance of error), except for variation in the groups' exposure to the independent variable

Surveys: Popular and versatile research instruments using a question format; surveys can either be self-administered or read by an interviewer

Participant observation: Field research in which a researcher develops a sustained and intensive relationship with people while they go about their normal activities

Intensive interviewing: Open-ended, relatively unstructured questioning in which the interviewer seeks in-depth information on the interviewee's feelings, experiences, and/or perceptions

Secondary data analysis: Analysis of data collected by someone other than the researcher or the researcher's assistant

Content analysis: A research method for systematically analyzing and making inferences from text such as news articles, TV shows, and radio talk shows. An investigation of the drinking climate on campuses might examine the amount of space devoted to ads for alcoholic beverages in a sample of issues of the student newspaper. Chapter 9 covers these methods.

With the advent of computer technology, crime mapping also has become a popular method for examining the relationship between criminal behavior and other social indicators. This research technique, along with others, is increasingly being used in intelligence-based policing. Chapter 9 covers these methodologies and illustrates the importance of these unobtrusive research techniques in criminology and criminal justice. Increasingly, researchers are combining methods to more reliably answer a single research question. Although examples of mixed-methods research are highlighted in several chapters, Chapter 11 provides an overview of the philosophy and motivation for combining methods, along with the various techniques for doing so.

All research begins with a research question and then a formal process of inquiry. Chapter 2 provides an overview of the research circle from both a deductive and inductive perspective using the empirical literature on arrest and intimate partner assault as a case study. All research must also grapple with conceptualization and measuring constructs, including the extent to which these measures are valid and reliable. Chapter 4 examines these issues, followed by a discussion of sampling in Chapter 5. Of course, all research, regardless of the methodology selected, requires that it be carried out ethically, with special protections afforded the participants under study. Although every chapter that details a specific type of research method concludes with a section on ethics related to that method, Chapter 3 is devoted exclusively to the steps required to ensure research is conducted ethically.

Crime mapping: Geographical mapping strategies used to visualize a number of things, including location, distance, and patterns of crime and their correlates

STRENGTHS AND LIMITATIONS OF SOCIAL RESEARCH

These case studies are only four of the hundreds of studies investigating youth violence, but they illustrate some of the questions criminological research can address, several different methods social scientists studying these issues can use, and ways criminological research can inform public policy. Notice how each of the four studies was designed to reduce the errors common in everyday reasoning:

- The clear definition of the population of interest in each study and the selection of a broad, representative sample of that population in two studies increased the researchers' ability to draw conclusions without overgeneralizing findings to groups to which they did not apply.

- The use of surveys in which each respondent was asked the same set of questions reduced the risk of selective or inaccurate observation.

- The risk of illogical reasoning was reduced by carefully describing each stage of the research, clearly presenting the findings, and carefully testing the basis for cause-and-effect conclusions.

- Resistance to change was reduced by using an experimental design that randomly assigned classes to an experimental treatment (the G.R.E.A.T. program) and a control group to fairly evaluate the efficacy of the program.

Nevertheless, it would be misleading to suggest that simply engaging in criminological research will result in the unveiling of absolute truths! Research always has its flaws and limitations (as does any human endeavor), and findings are always subject to differing interpretations.

Social research allows us to consider and reveal more, to observe with fewer distortions, and to describe more clearly to others the basis for our opinions, but it will not settle all arguments. Other people will always have differing opinions, and some opposition will come from other social scientists who have conducted their own studies and drawn different conclusions. For example, we must ask ourselves if programs similar to G.R.E.A.T. would reduce levels of violence for younger students. Until more scientific research is conducted to evaluate these programs, it is difficult to determine whether these programs should be more widely implemented.

But even in areas of research that are fraught with controversy, where social scientists differ in their interpretations of the evidence, the quest for new and more sophisticated research has value. What is most important for improving understanding of the social world and issues in criminology is not the results of any one particular study but the accumulation of evidence from different studies of related issues. By designing new studies that focus on the weak points or controversial conclusions of prior research, social scientists contribute to a body of findings that gradually expands our knowledge about the social world and resolves some of the disagreements about it.

Grant A. Bacon, BA, Research Associate, Center for Drug and Health Studies, University of Delaware

Source: Courtesy of Grant A. Bacon

Grant Bacon graduated with degrees in history, education, and political science from the University of Delaware in 1998. He initially aspired to give back to the community, especially by helping young people as a teacher. Although he started out teaching, he found his calling by working more directly with at-risk youth as a court liaison and eventually program coordinator for a juvenile drug court/drug diversion program. It was during his time working with these drug court programs that Grant first came into contact with the University of Delaware's Center for Drug and Health Studies (CDHS), which was beginning an evaluation of the drug court programs in New Castle County, Delaware. In 2001, he accepted an offer to become a research associate with CDHS, where he has continued to work on many different research projects. Two of his most recent projects include research that investigated the factors affecting the reentry experience for inmates returning to the community and another evaluating the parole program called Decide Your Time.

Grant is happy to be working in the field on both qualitative and quantitative research. He loves working with people who share a vision of using research findings to help people in a number of ways and to give back to the world in a meaningful manner. Every day is different. Some days, Grant and other associates are on the road visiting criminal justice or health-related facilities or are trying to locate specific individual respondents or study participants. Other days, he may be gathering data, doing intensive interviewing, or administering surveys. He thinks the most rewarding part of his job is helping people who have been part of the criminal justice system and giving them a voice.

Grant's advice to students interested in research is the following:

> If doing research interests you, ask your teachers how you can gain experience through internships or volunteering. Be sure to network with as many people from as many human services organizations as possible. Being familiar with systems like GIS (geographic information systems) and data analyses is becoming important as well. If you did not receive this training during your undergraduate studies, many community colleges offer introductory and advanced classes in GIS, Microsoft Excel, Access, and SPSS. Take them!

CAREERS AND RESEARCH

Whether you plan to conduct your own research projects, read others' research reports, or even just listen to or read claims about social reality in the media, knowing about research methods has many benefits. This knowledge will give you greater confidence in your own opinions, improve your ability to evaluate others' opinions, and encourage you to refine your questions, answers, and methods of inquiry about the social world.

A COMMENT ON RESEARCH IN A DIVERSE SOCIETY

Research must always strive to reflect our increasingly diverse society, including dimensions of race/ethnicity, nationality, gender, sexual orientation, age, physical abilities, and religious or political beliefs. Although there is much that we share, there is also an increased awareness that there are distinct cultural, social, structural, and historical contexts that shape group experiences. Just as criminal justice practitioners are expected to engage in culturally competent practice, we must recognize that cultural norms impact the research process, whether it is the willingness to participate in research activities, the meaning ascribed to abstract terms and constructs, the way data are collected, or the interpretation of the findings. The failure by researchers to adequately address the cultural context impacts the research process in different ways and, ultimately, the validity and generalizability of research findings.

Historically, women and racial/ethnic minorities have been underrepresented in research studies. In addition, some groups may be reluctant to participate in research for different reasons, such as distrust of the motives of the researchers (Sobeck, Chapleski, & Fisher, 2003), historical experiences, not understanding the research process, not seeing any benefit to participation (Beals, Manson, Mitchell, Spicer, & AI-SUPERPFP Team, 2003), and misuse of findings to the detriment of their communities (Sobeck, Chapleski, & Fisher, 2003). Inadequate representation in research makes it more difficult to conclude that results of this research can be generalized to the larger, diverse population.

Measurement bias can result in misidentifying the prevalence of a condition and assuming that relationships exist for all subgroups of a population, or it can result in theories developed using homogeneous samples that do not hold up when more diverse samples are examined. For example, theories based on research using a sample of white males coming of age in the 1950s when well-paying industrial jobs were available and who, as a result, appear to have been amenable to changing their criminal behavior through "turning points" such as employment and marriage (Laub & Sampson, 2003; Sampson & Laub, 1993) have not always found support using diverse samples of individuals reentering society from prison today (Nguyen & Loughran, 2018).

The quality of information obtained from surveys is also dependent on the questions that are asked; there is an assumption that respondents share a common understanding of the meaning of the question and willingness or unwillingness to answer the question. Yet questions may have different meanings to different groups, may not be culturally appropriate, and even when translated into a different language may lack equivalent connotations (Pasick, Stewart, Bird, & D'Onofrio, 2001). For example, we know from the National Crime Victimization Survey (NCVS) that American Indian and Alaskan Native (AIAN) populations are at a greater risk of rape and sexual assault compared with other subgroups of the population. However, we also know that the NCVS may not be the best way to accurately measure the true nature of these victimizations for this population. To get a more valid estimate the magnitude of sexual assault and other victimizations against AIAN populations, the National Institute of Justice, along with the Centers for Disease Control and Prevention, in collaboration with tribal leaders, developed a new data collection instrument to ensure that the study would be "viable, culturally and community appropriate, respectful of those involved, and that the information collected would be relevant and helpful" (Crossland, Palmer, & Brooks, 2013, p. 775).

As you can see from this brief introduction, the norms that develop within population subgroups have an impact that cuts across the research process. As you read each chapter in this book, you will learn both the kinds of questions that researchers ask and the strategies they use to ensure that their research is culturally competent.

CONCLUSION

We hope this first chapter has given you an idea of what to expect in the rest of this book. Our aim is to introduce you to social-research methods by describing what social scientists have learned about issues in criminology and criminal justice as well as how they tackled systematic challenges in conducting their research. For many students, the substance of social science inevitably is more interesting than the research methods used to bring those findings to light. However, in this volume, you will see that the research methods not only demand interest and merit but also are fundamental to our understanding of criminology and criminal justice. We have focused attention on research on youth violence and delinquency in this chapter; in subsequent chapters, we will introduce research examples from other areas.

Chapter 2 continues to build the foundation for our study of social research by reviewing the types of problems that criminologists study, the role of theory, the major steps in the research process, and other sources of information that may be used in social research. We stress the importance of considering scientific standards in social research and reviewing generally accepted ethical guidelines. Throughout the chapter, we use several studies of domestic violence to illustrate the research process.

KEY TERMS

Content analysis   15
Crime mapping   16
Critical theory   13
Descriptive research   7
Epistemology   6
Evaluation research   11
Experimental approach   15
Explanatory research   10
Exploratory research   9
Feminist research   13
Illogical reasoning   4
Inaccurate observation   4

Intensive interviewing   15
Interpretivism   12
Intersubjective agreement   12
Mixed methods   14
Overgeneralization   3
Participant observation   15
Participatory action research
   (PAR)   13
Peer review   7
Phrenology   7
Positivism   12
Postpositivism   12

Pseudoscience   7
Qualitative methods   14
Quantitative methods   14
Resistance to change   5
Secondary data analysis   15
Selective observation   4
Science   6
Social science   6
Surveys   15
Transparent   6
Triangulation   14

HIGHLIGHTS

- Criminological research cannot resolve value questions or provide answers that will convince everyone and remain settled for all time.

- All empirically based methods of investigation are based on either direct experience or others' statements.

- Four common errors in reasoning are overgeneralization, selective or inaccurate observation, illogical reasoning, and resistance to change. Illogical reasoning is due to the complexity of the social world, self-interest, and human subjectivity. Resistance to change may be due to unquestioning acceptance of tradition or of those in positions of authority or to self-interested resistance to admitting the need to change one's beliefs.

- Social science is the use of logical, systematic, documented methods to investigate individuals, societies, and social processes, as well as the knowledge produced by these investigations.

- Pseudoscience involves claims based on beliefs and/or public testimonials, not on the scientific method.

- Criminological research can be motivated by policy guidance and program management needs, academic concerns, and charitable impulses.

- Criminological research can be descriptive, exploratory, explanatory, or evaluative or some combination of these.

- Positivism is the belief that there is a reality that exists quite apart from one's own perception of it that is amenable to observation.

- Intersubjective agreement is an agreement by different observers on what is happening in the natural or social world.

- Postpositivism is the belief that there is an empirical reality but that our understanding of it is limited by its complexity and by the biases and other limitations of researchers.

- Interpretivism is the belief that reality is socially constructed and the goal of social science should be to understand what meanings people give to that reality.

- Quantitative methods record variation in social life in terms of categories that vary in amount. Qualitative methods are designed to capture social life as participants experience it rather than in categories predetermined by the researcher.

- Mixed-methods research is the use of multiple methods to study a single research question.

- Cultural norms impact the research process from the willingness to participate in research, the meaning of terms, the way data are collected, or the interpretation of the findings.

EXERCISES

Discussing Research

1. What criminological topic or issue would you focus on if you could design a research project without any concern for costs? What are your motives for studying this topic? List at least four of your beliefs about this phenomenon. Try to identify the sources of each belief—for example, television, newspaper, or parental influence.

2. Develop four research questions related to a topic or issue, one for each of the four types of research (descriptive, exploratory, explanatory, and evaluative). Be specific.

3. Find a report of social science research in an article in a daily newspaper. What are the motives for the research? How much information is provided about the research design? What were the major findings? What additional evidence would you like to see in the article to increase your understanding of the findings in the research conclusions?

4. Find a CNN blog discussing some topic about crime. How do your opinions on the subject differ?

5. Outline your own research philosophy. You can base your outline primarily on your reactions to the points you have read in this chapter, but also try to think seriously about which perspective seems more reasonable to you.

Finding Research on the Web

1. You have been asked to prepare a brief presentation on a criminological topic or issue of interest to you. Go to the BJS website (www.bjs.gov). Browse the BJS publications for a topic that interests you. Write a short outline for a 5- to 10-minute presentation regarding your topic, including statistics and other relevant information.

2. Go to the FBI website (www.fbi.gov). Explore the types of programs and initiatives sponsored by the FBI. Discuss at least three of these programs or initiatives in terms of their purposes and goals. For each program or initiative examined, do you believe the program or initiative is effective? What are the major weaknesses? What changes would you propose the FBI make to more effectively meet the goals of the program or initiative?

3. Go to the website of a major newspaper, and find an article discussing the causes of violence. What conclusions does the article draw, and what research methods does the author discuss to back up his or her claims?

4. There are many interesting websites that discuss philosophy-of-science issues. Read the summaries of positivism and interpretivism at www.misq.org/misq/downloads/download/editorial/25. What do these summaries add to your understanding of these philosophical alternatives?

Critiquing Research

1. Find a story about a criminological issue in the popular press (e.g., a newspaper or periodical, such as *Time* magazine). Does the article provide a scientific basis for claims made in the story? If rates of crime are reported, does the article discuss how these rates were actually obtained?

2. Read an article in a recent issue of a major criminological journal or on the study site for this book (edge.sagepub.com/bachmanfrccj5e). Identify the type of research conducted for each study. Are the research questions clearly stated? Can you identify the purpose of the research (e.g., description, explanation, exploration, evaluation)?

3. Continue the debate between positivism and interpretivism with an in-class discussion. Be sure to review the guidelines for these research philosophies and the associated goals. You might also consider whether an integrated philosophy is preferable.

Making Research Ethical

Throughout the book, we will be discussing the ethical challenges that arise in research on crime and criminal justice. At the end of each chapter, we will ask you to consider some questions about ethical issues related to that chapter's focus. Chapter 3 is devoted to issues of ethics in research, but we will begin here with some questions for you to ponder.

1. You have now learned about the qualitative study by Madfis (2014) about schools that averted a shooting incident. We think it provided important information for policy makers about the social dynamics in these tragedies. But what would *you* do if you were conducting a similar study in a high school and you learned that another student was planning to bring a gun to school to kill some other students? What if he was only thinking about it? Or just talking with his friends about how "neat" it would be? Can you suggest some guidelines for researchers?

2. If you were part of Esbensen's research team that evaluated the G.R.E.A.T. violence reduction program in schools, would you announce your findings in a press conference and encourage schools to adopt this program? If you were a school principal who heard about this research, would you agree to let another researcher replicate (repeat) the Esbensen study in your school, with some classrooms assigned to receive the program randomly (on the basis of the toss of a coin) and others not allowed to receive the program for the duration of the study?

Developing a Research Proposal

1. What topic would you focus on if you could design a social-research project without any concern for costs? What are your motives for studying this topic?

2. Develop four questions that you might investigate about the topic you just selected. Each question should reflect a different research motive: description, exploration, explanation, or evaluation. Be specific.

3. Which question most interests you? Would you prefer to attempt to answer that question using quantitative or qualitative methods? Why?

Performing Data Analysis in SPSS or Excel

Data for Exercise	
Dataset	Description
2013 YRBS.sav	The 2013 YRBS is a national study of high school students. It focuses on gauging various behaviors and experiences of the adolescent population, including substance use and some victimization.
Monitoring the Future 2013 grade 10.sav	This dataset contains variables from the 2013 Monitoring the Future (MTF) study. These data cover a national sample of 10th graders, with a focus on monitoring substance use and abuse.

(Continued)

(Continued)

Variables for Exercise	
Variable Name	**Description**
Q44 (YRBS)	A seven-category ordinal measure that asked how many times the respondent drank five or more beverages in one sitting in the past 30 days
V7108 (MTF)	A six-category ordinal measure that asked how many times the respondent drank five or more drinks in a row in the past two weeks

First, load the "2013 YRBS.sav" file, and look at the following:

1. Create a bar chart of variable "q44" by following the menu options "graphs->legacy dialogues->bar." Select the "simple bar chart" option, and click the arrow to add "q44" to the category axis text box. At a glance, what does this bar graph tell us about binge drinking among high school students?

   a. Are the data on the YRBS qualitative or quantitative? How do you know?

2. Write at least four research questions based on the bar graph you've created. Try to make one for each type of social research (descriptive, exploratory, explanatory, and evaluative). Think about the following: What sticks out to you in this graph? Where do you need more information? On whom should the research focus?

3. Explain the possible reasons (policy, academic, or personal) for why we might want to research binge drinking or the lack thereof. What organizations might be interested in this kind of research?

4. *Triangulation* refers to using multiple methods or measures to study a single research question. Let's see if we can triangulate the results from Question 1 using a different measure in the "Monitoring the Future 2013 grade 10.sav" dataset.

5. Create a bar chart of variable "v7108." How do the estimates of binge drinking in the YRBS compare with these results? If there are any major differences, what do you think could explain them?

2

THE PROCESS AND PROBLEMS OF RESEARCH RELATED TO CRIME AND CRIMINOLOGY

> At the end of the semester, a professor asked if I would be interested in doing some research on sexual harassment in the workplace for her over the summer. For the research, I had to read research articles and summarize them for the professor. While I was reading the articles, I would come across the research methods the authors used, with data analysis tables. I thought it was incredible how I came full circle back to the research methods I learned! My research methods class set me on a course that has changed my time in college and possibly influenced my future career.
>
> **Emily G., Student**

WHAT DO WE HAVE IN MIND?

Intimate partner violence is a major problem in countries around the world. In a U.S. survey of 16,507 men and women sponsored by the Department of Justice and the Centers for Disease Control and Prevention, 35.6% of women and 28.5% of men said they had experienced rape, physical violence, or stalking by an intimate partner at some time in their lives (Black et al., 2011). An international survey by the World Health Organization (WHO) of 24,000 women in 10 countries estimated lifetime physical or sexual abuse ranging from a low of 15% in Japan to a high of 71% in rural Ethiopia (WHO, 2005) (see Exhibit 2.1).

What can be done about this problem? In 1981, the Police Foundation and the Minneapolis Police Department began an experiment to determine whether immediately arresting accused spouse abusers on the spot would deter future offending incidents. For misdemeanor cases, the experimental course of

Learning Objectives

1. Describe the importance of theory to research.

2. Understand the difference between deductive and inductive reasoning.

3. Describe the difference between a research question and a research hypothesis.

4. Explain how the research circle is really a research spiral.

5. Know the difference between an independent and dependent variable.

6. Define the different types of validity and generalizability.

$SAGE edge™

Master the content at edge .sagepub.com/bachmanfrccj5e

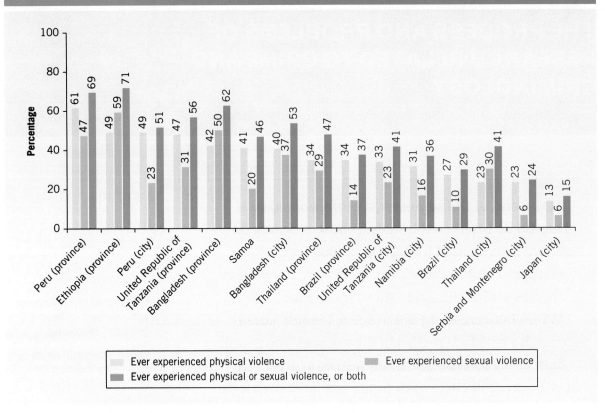

Source: **World Health Organization 2005. Multi-country Study on Women's Health and Domestic Violence: Summary Report.**

action involved the random assignment of police to respond by either arresting the suspect or giving the suspect a simple warning. The experimental treatment, then, was whether the suspect was arrested, and the researchers wanted to know whether arrest was better than not arresting the suspect in reducing recidivism. The study's results, which were widely publicized, indicated that arrest did have a deterrent effect. Partly as a result of the reported results of this experiment, the percentage of urban police departments that made arrest the preferred response to complaints of intimate partner violence (IPV) rose from 10% in 1984 to 90% in 1988 (Sherman, 1992, p. 14). Six other cities later carried out studies similar to the Minneapolis Domestic Violence Experiment (collectively, this was called the Spouse Assault Replication Program [SARP]), but from city to city, the results were mixed (Buzawa & Buzawa, 1996; Hirschel, Hutchison, & Dean, 1992; Pate & Hamilton, 1992; Sherman, 1992; Sherman & Berk, 1984). In some cities (and for some people), arrest did seem to prevent future incidents of domestic assault; in other cities, it seemed only to make matters worse, contributing to additional assault; and in still other cities, arrest seemed to have no discernible effect.

After these replications of the original Minneapolis experiment, people still wondered, "Just what is the effect of arrest in reducing IPV cases, and how should the police respond to such cases?" The answer simply was not clear. The Minneapolis experiment, the studies modeled after it, and the related controversies provide many examples for a systematic overview of the social-research process.

IDENTIFYING A RESEARCH QUESTION

The first concern in criminological research—indeed, in any research—is deciding what to study. That is, how does one go about selecting an issue, problem, or question to address? A research question is a question about some aspect of crime or deviance that the researcher seeks to answer through the collection and analysis of firsthand, verifiable, empirical data. The types of questions that can be asked are virtually limitless. For example, "Are children who are violent more likely than nonviolent children to use violence as adults?" "Does the race of a victim who is killed influence whether someone is sentenced to death rather than life imprisonment?" "Why do some kinds of neighborhoods have more crime than others? Is it due to the kinds of people who live there or characteristics of the neighborhood itself?" "Does community policing reduce the crime rate?" "Has the U.S. government's war on drugs done anything to reduce the use of illegal drugs?" So many research questions are possible in criminology that it is more of a challenge to specify what does *not* qualify as a research question than to specify what does.

That being said, specifying which research question to ask and pursuing its answer are no easy tasks. In fact, formulating a good research question can be surprisingly difficult. We can break the process into three stages: identifying one or more questions for study, refining the questions, and then evaluating the questions.

> **Research question:**
> A question that is answered through the collection and analysis of firsthand, verifiable, empirical data

Where to Start?

How does a researcher interested in criminology and criminal justice–related issues decide what to study and research?

Formulating a research question is often an intensely personal process, in addition to being a scientific or professional one. Curiosity about the social world may emerge from your "personal troubles," as Mills (1959) put it, or personal experiences. Examples of these troubles or experiences could range from how you feel about injustices raised against you in your past or present to an awareness you may have that crime is not randomly distributed within a city but that there seem to be "good" or safe parts of town and "bad" or unsafe areas. Can you think of other possible research questions that flow from your own experience in the world?

The experience of others is another fruitful source of research questions. Knowing a relative who was abused by a partner, seeing a TV special about violence, or reading a gang member's autobiography can stimulate questions about general criminological processes. Can you draft a research question based on a relative's experiences, a TV show, or a book?

The primary source of research questions for many researchers is theory. Many theoretical domains are used to inform research questions in our discipline, including sociological, psychological, and criminological theories. Some researchers spend much of their careers conducting research intended to refine an answer to one central question. For example, you may find rational choice theory to be a useful approach to understanding diverse forms of social behavior, such as crime, because you think people seem to make decisions on the basis of personal cost–benefit calculations. So you may ask whether rational choice theory can explain why some people commit crimes and others do not or why some people decide to quit committing crimes while others continue their criminal ways.

Finally, some research questions adopt a very pragmatic rationale concerning their research design. You may focus on a research question posed by someone else because doing so seems to be to your professional or financial advantage. For instance, some researchers conduct research on specific questions posed by a funding source in what is termed a *request for proposals* (RFP). (Sometimes the acronym *RFA* is used, meaning *request for applications*.) Or you may learn that the public defenders in your city are curious as to whether they are more successful in getting their clients acquitted of a criminal charge than private lawyers.

Refining Research Questions

As you have no doubt guessed, coming up with interesting criminological questions for research is less problematic than focusing on a problem of manageable size. We are often interested in much more than we can reasonably investigate with our limited time and resources (or the limited resources of a funding agency). Researchers may worry about staking a research project (and thereby a grant) on a narrowly defined problem, so they commit to addressing several research questions at once and often in a jumbled fashion. It also may seem risky to focus on a research question that may lead to results discrepant with our own cherished assumptions about the social world.

The best way to avoid these problems is to develop the research question one bit at a time with a step-by-step strategy. Do not keep hoping that the perfect research question will just spring forth from your pen. Instead, develop a list of possible research questions as you go along. Narrow your list to the most interesting, most workable candidates. Repeat this process as long as it helps to improve your research questions. Keep in mind that the research on which you are currently working will likely generate additional research questions for you to answer.

Evaluating Research Questions

In the third stage of selecting a criminological research question, you evaluate the best candidate against the criteria for good social-research questions: feasibility given the time and resources available, social importance, and scientific relevance (King, Keohane, & Verba, 1994).

The research question in the Minneapolis Domestic Violence Experiment—"Does the formal sanction of police arrest versus nonarrest inhibit IPV?"—certainly meets the criteria of social importance and scientific relevance, but it would not be a feasible question for a student project because it would require you to try to get the cooperation of a police department.

Feasibility

You must be able to conduct any study within the time frame and with the resources you have. If time is limited, questions that involve long-term change—for example, "If a state has recently changed its law so that it now permits capital punishment for those convicted of murder, does it eventually see a reduction in the homicide rate over time?"—may not be feasible. This is an interesting and important question, but it is also one that requires years of data collection and research. Another issue is the people, groups, or files that you can expect to gain access to. Although experienced researchers may be granted access to police or correctional department files to do their research, less seasoned and less well-known researchers or students may not be granted such access.

Social Importance

Criminological research is not a simple undertaking, so you must focus on a substantive area that you feel is important and that is important either to the discipline or for public policy. You also need to feel personally motivated to carry out the study; there is little point in trying to answer a question that does not interest you.

In addition, you should consider whether the research question is important to other people. Will an answer to the research question make a difference for society? Again, the Minneapolis Domestic Violence Experiment is an exemplary case. If that study showed that a certain type of police response to IPV reduced the risk of subsequent victimization, a great deal of future violence could be prevented. But clearly, criminology and criminal justice researchers are far from lacking important research questions.

Scientific Relevance

Every research question in criminology should be grounded in the existing empirical literature. By *grounded*, we mean the research we do must be informed by what others before us have done on the topic. Whether you formulate a research question because you have been stimulated by an academic article, because you want to investigate a current public policy problem, or because you are motivated by questions regarding your own personal experiences, you must turn to existing criminological literature to find out what has already been learned about this question. (Appendix A explains how to find information about previous research using both printed and computer-based resources.)

For example, the Minneapolis experiment was built on a substantial body of contradictory theories about the impact of punishment on criminality (Sherman & Berk, 1984). Deterrence theory predicted that because it was a more severe penalty, arresting people would better deter them from repeat offenses than not arresting them. Labeling theory, on the other hand, predicted that arrest would make repeat offenses more likely because it would stigmatize offenders. Studies among adults and nonexperimental research had not yielded consistent findings about the effects of arrest on recidivism in IPV cases. Clearly, the Minneapolis researchers had good reason to perform another study. Prior research and theory also helped them develop the most effective research design.

THE ROLE OF THEORY

We have already pointed out that criminological theory can be a rich source of research questions. What deserves more attention at this point is the larger role of **theory** in research. We have also noted that research investigating criminal justice and criminology-related questions relies on many theories, including criminological, sociological, and psychological theories. These theories do many things:

They help us explain or understand things, such as why some people commit crimes or commit more crimes than others, why some people quit committing crimes and others continue, and what the expected effect of good families, harsh punishment, or other factors might be on crime.

- They help us make predictions about the criminological world: "What would be the expected effect on the homicide rate if we employed capital punishment rather than life imprisonment?" "What would be the effect on the rate of property crimes if unemployment were to substantially increase?"

- They help us organize and make sense of empirical findings in a discipline.

- They help guide future research.

- They help guide public policy: "What should we do to reduce the level of IPV?"

Social scientists such as criminologists, who connect their work to theories in their discipline, can generate better ideas about what to look for in a study and develop conclusions with more implications for other research. Building and evaluating theory are therefore among the most important objectives of a social science such as criminology.

For centuries, scholars have been interested in developing theories about crime and criminals. Sometimes, these theories involve very fanciful ideas that are not well developed or

> Theory: A logically interrelated set of propositions about empirical reality; examples of criminological theories include social learning, routine activities, labeling, general strain, and social disorganization theory

organized, whereas at other times, they strike us as being very compelling and well organized. Theories usually contain what are called **theoretical constructs**. In criminology, these theoretical constructs describe what is important to look at to understand, explain, and predict crime. Some criminological theories reflect a substantial body of research and the thinking of many social scientists; others are formulated in the course of one investigation. A few have been widely accepted, at least for a time; others are the subject of vigorous controversy, with frequent changes and refinements in response to criticism and new research.

We can use the studies of the police response to domestic assault to illustrate the value of theory for social research. Even in this very concrete and practical matter, we must draw on social theories to understand how people act and what should be done about those actions. Consider three action options that police officers have when they confront a domestic assault suspect (Sherman & Berk, 1984, p. 263). Fellow officers might encourage separation to achieve short-term peace, police trainers might prefer mediation to resolve the underlying dispute, and some groups may advocate arrest to protect the victim from further harm. None of these recommendations is really a theory, but each suggests a different perspective on crime and legal sanctions. Remember that social theories do not provide the answers to research questions. Instead, social theories suggest the areas on which we should focus and the propositions that we should consider for a test. That is, theories suggest testable hypotheses about phenomena, and research verifies whether those hypotheses are true. In fact, one of the most important requirements of theory is that it be *testable*, or what philosophers of science call **falsifiable**; theoretical statements must be capable of being proven wrong. If a body of thought cannot be empirically tested, it is more likely philosophy than theory.

The original Minneapolis experiment (Sherman & Berk, 1984) was actually a test of predictions derived from two alternative theories concerning the impact of punishment on crime: deterrence theory and labeling theory.

Deterrence theory presumes that human beings are at least marginally rational beings who are responsive to the expected costs and benefits of their actions. Committing a crime nets certain benefits for offenders; therefore, if we want to inhibit crime, there must be a compensating cost that outweighs the potential benefits associated with the offense. One cost is the criminal sanction (arrest, conviction, punishment). Deterrence theory expects punishment to inhibit crime in two ways: (1) General deterrence is operating when people believe that they are likely to be caught and punished for criminal acts. Those who are punished serve as examples for those who have not yet committed an offense but who might be thinking of what awaits them should they engage in similarly punishable acts. (2) Specific deterrence occurs when persons who are punished decide not to commit another offense so they can avoid further punishment (Lempert & Sanders, 1986, pp. 86–87). Deterrence theory leads to the prediction that arresting spouse abusers will reduce the likelihood of their reoffending compared with a less serious sanction (not being arrested but being warned or counseled).

Labeling theory distinguishes between primary deviance (the acts of individuals that lead to public sanctions) and secondary deviance (the deviance that occurs in response to public sanction) (Hagan, 1994, p. 33). Arrest or some other public sanction for misdeeds labels the offender as deviant in the eyes of others. Once the offender is labeled, others will treat the offender as a deviant, and he or she is then more likely to act in a way that is consistent with the deviant label. Ironically, the act of punishment stimulates more of the very behavior that it was intended to eliminate (Tannenbaum, 1938). This theory suggests that persons arrested for IPV are more likely to reoffend than those who are caught but not punished because the formal sanction of arrest is more stigmatizing than being warned or counseled. This prediction about the effect of formal legal sanctions is the reverse of the deterrence theory prediction.

Exhibit 2.2 summarizes how these general theories relate to the question of whether or not to arrest spouse abusers.

Does either deterrence theory or labeling theory make sense to you as an explanation for the impact of punishment? Do they seem consistent with your observations of social life?

Exhibit 2.2   Two Social Theories and Their Predictions About the Effect of Arrest for Intimate Partner Violence

	Rational Choice Theory	Symbolic Interactionism
Theoretical assumption	People's behavior is shaped by calculations of the costs and benefits of their actions.	People give symbolic meanings to objects, behaviors, and other people.
Criminological component	Deterrence theory: People break the law if the benefits of doing so outweigh the costs.	Labeling theory: People label offenders as deviant, promoting further deviance.
Prediction (effect of arrest for domestic assault)	Abusing spouse, having seen the costs of abuse (namely, arrest), decides not to abuse again.	Abusing spouse, having been labeled as "an abuser," abuses more often.

More than a decade after Sherman and Berk's (1984) study, Paternoster, Brame, Bachman, and Sherman (1997) decided to study punishment of IPV from a different perspective. They turned to a social psychological theory called *procedural justice theory*, which explains law-abiding behavior as resulting from a sense of duty or morality (Tyler, 1990). People obey the law from a sense of obligation that flows from seeing legal authorities as moral and legitimate. From this perspective, individuals who are arrested seem less likely to reoffend if they are treated fairly, irrespective of the outcome of their case, because fair treatment will enhance their view of legal authorities as moral and legitimate. Procedural justice theory expands our view of the punishment process by focusing attention on how police act and how authorities treat subjects, rather than only on the legal decisions they make. Thus, it gives us a sense of the larger importance of the research question.

Are you now less certain about the likely effect of arrest for IPV? Will arrest decrease recidivism because abusers do not wish to suffer from legal sanctions again? Will it increase recidivism because abusers feel stigmatized by being arrested and thus are more likely to act as criminals? Or will arrest reduce abuse only if the abusers feel they have been treated fairly by the legal authorities? By posing such questions, social theory makes us much more sensitive to the possibilities and so helps us to design better research. Before, during, and after a research investigation, we need to keep thinking theoretically.

SOCIAL RESEARCH STRATEGIES

All social research, including criminological research, is the effort to connect theory and empirical data. As Exhibit 2.3 shows, theory and data have a two-way, mutually reinforcing relationship.

Researchers may make this connection by starting with a social theory and

Exhibit 2.3   The Links Between Theory and Data

Ideas: What we think
Theory

Inductive reasoning

Deductive reasoning

Data
Reality: What we observe

Deductive reasoning: The type of reasoning that moves from the general to the specific

Inductive reasoning: The type of reasoning that moves from the specific to the general

Serendipitous findings (anomalous findings): Unexpected patterns in data that stimulate new ideas or theoretical approaches

Research circle: A diagram of the elements of the research process, including theories, hypotheses, data collection, and data analysis

Deductive research: The type of research in which a specific expectation is deduced from a general premise and is then tested

Hypothesis: A tentative statement about empirical reality involving the relationship between two or more variables

then testing some of its implications with data. This is the process of deductive reasoning; it is most often the strategy used in quantitative methods. Alternatively, researchers may develop a connection between social theory and data by first collecting the data and then developing a theory that explains the patterns in the data. This is inductive reasoning and is more often the strategy used in qualitative methods. As you'll see, a research project can draw on both deductive and inductive strategies.

Both deductive reasoning and inductive reasoning are essential to criminologists. We cannot test an idea fairly unless we use deductive reasoning, stating our expectations in advance and then designing a way to test the validity of our claims. A theory that has not survived these kinds of tests can be regarded only as very tentative. Yet theories, no matter how cherished, cannot always make useful predictions for every social situation or research problem that we seek to investigate. We may find unexpected patterns in the data we collect, called serendipitous findings or anomalous findings. In either situation, we should reason inductively, making whatever theoretical sense we can of our unanticipated findings. Then, if the new findings seem sufficiently important, we can return to deductive reasoning and plan a new study to formally test our new ideas.

The Research Circle

This process of conducting research, moving from theory to data and back again or from data to theory and back again, can be characterized as a research circle. Exhibit 2.4 depicts this circle. Note that it mirrors the relationship between theory and data shown in Exhibit 2.3 and comprises three main research strategies: deductive research, inductive research, and descriptive research.

Deductive Research

As Exhibit 2.4 shows, deductive research proceeds from theorizing to data collection and then back to theorizing. In essence, a specific expectation is deduced from a general premise and then tested.

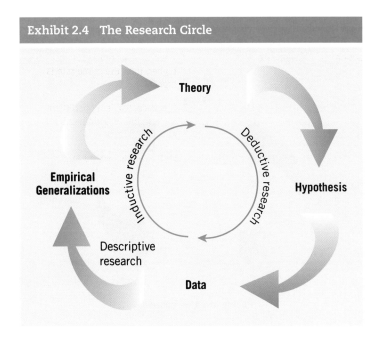

Exhibit 2.4 The Research Circle

Theory

Hypothesis

Data

Descriptive research

Empirical Generalizations

Inductive research

Deductive research

Notice that a theory leads first to a hypothesis, which is a specific implication deduced from the more general theory. Researchers actually test a hypothesis, not the complete theory itself, because theories usually contain many hypotheses. A hypothesis proposes a relationship between two or more theoretical constructs or variables. A variable is a characteristic or property that can vary. A constant is a characteristic or a property that cannot vary. For example, if we were to conduct some research in a male adult penitentiary, the theoretical construct "type of crime committed" would be a variable because persons will have been incarcerated for different offenses (one person for armed robbery, another for rape, etc.). However, the theoretical construct "gender" would be a constant because every inmate in the penitentiary would be male.

Variables are of critical importance in research because, in a hypothesis, variation in one variable is proposed to predict, influence, or cause variation in the other variable. The proposed influence is the **independent variable**; its effect or consequence is the **dependent variable**. Another way to think about this distinction is to say "the dependent variable 'depends' on the independent variable." After the researchers formulate one or more hypotheses and develop research procedures, they collect data with which to test the hypothesis.

Hypotheses can be worded in several different ways, and identifying the independent and dependent variables is sometimes difficult. When in doubt, try to rephrase the hypothesis as an if–then statement: "If the independent variable increases (or decreases), then the dependent variable increases (or decreases)." Exhibit 2.5 presents several hypotheses with their independent and dependent variables and their if–then equivalents.

Inductive Research

In contrast to deductive research, **inductive research** begins at the bottom of the research circle and then works upward (see Exhibit 2.4). The inductive researcher begins with specific data, which are then used to develop (induce) a general explanation (a theory) to account for the data. The patterns in the data are then summarized in one or more **empirical generalizations**.

The motive for inductive research is exploration. For example, in the last chapter, you read about an exploratory study of how schools averted mass shootings. In strictly inductive research, researchers already know what they have found when they start theorizing. The result can be new insights and provocative questions. But the adequacy of an explanation formulated after the fact is necessarily less certain than that of an explanation presented prior to the collection of data. Every phenomenon can always be explained in some way. Inductive explanations are thus more trustworthy if they are tested subsequently with deductive research.

> **Example of a hypothesis:** The higher the level of poverty in a community, the higher its rate of crime
>
> **Variable:** A characteristic or property that can vary (take on different values or attributes)
>
> **Constant:** A number that has a fixed value in a given situation; a characteristic or value that does not change
>
> **Independent variable:** A variable that is hypothesized to cause, or lead to, variation in another variable
>
> **Dependent variable:** A variable that is hypothesized to change or vary depending on the variation in another variable

Exhibit 2.5 Examples of Hypotheses

Original Hypothesis	Independent Variable	Dependent Variable	If–Then Hypothesis
1. The greater the social disorganization in a community, the higher the rate of crime.	Social disorganization	Crime rate	If social disorganization is higher, then the crime rate is higher.
2. As one's self-control gets stronger, the fewer delinquent acts one commits.	Self-control	Self-reported delinquency	If self-control is higher, then the number of delinquent acts is lower.
3. As the unemployment rate in a community decreases, the community rate of property crime decreases.	Unemployment rate	Rate of property crime	If the unemployment rate is lower, then the rate of property crime is lower.
4. As the level of discrepancy between one's aspirations and expectations increases, one's level of strain increases.	Discrepancy level between one's aspirations and expectations	Level of strain	If the level of discrepancy between one's aspirations and expectations is high, then the level of strain is high.
5. Crime is lower in those communities where the police patrol on foot.	Presence of foot patrols	Level of crime	If a community has police foot patrols, then the level of crime is lower.

Case Study: A History of Investigating the Effects of Arrest for Intimate Partner Violence and the Research Circle

The Sherman and Berk (1984) study of IPV is a classic example of how the research circle works. In an attempt to determine ways to prevent the recurrence of IPV, the researchers repeatedly linked theory and data, developing both hypotheses and empirical generalizations.

Phase 1: Deductive Research

The first phase of Sherman and Berk's (1984) study was designed to test a hypothesis. According to deterrence theory, punishment will reduce *recidivism*, or repeated offending. From this theory, Sherman and Berk deduced a specific hypothesis that arrest for spouse abuse would reduce the risk of repeat offenses. In this hypothesis, arrest is the independent variable, and variation in the risk of repeat offenses is the dependent variable. (It is hypothesized to depend on arrest.)

Sherman and Berk tested their hypothesis by setting up an experiment in which the police responded to the complaints of spouse abuse in one of three ways: (1) arresting the offender, (2) separating the spouses without making an arrest, or (3) simply warning the offender. When the researchers examined their data (police records for the persons in their experiment), they found that of those arrested for assaulting their spouse, only 13% repeated the offense, compared with a 26% recidivism rate for those who were separated from their spouse by the police without any arrest. This pattern in the data, or *empirical generalization*, was consistent with the hypothesis that the researchers deduced from deterrence theory. The theory thus received support from the experiment (see Exhibit 2.6).

Because of their doubts about the generalizability of their results, Sherman, Berk, and other researchers began to journey around the research circle again with funding from the National Institute of Justice for **replications** (repetitions) of the experiment in six more cities. These replications used the same basic research approach but with some improvements. The random-assignment process was tightened in most of the cities so that police officers would be less likely to replace the assigned treatment with a treatment of their own choice. In addition, data were collected about repeat violence against other victims, as well as against the original complainant. Some of the replications also examined different aspects of the arrest process to see whether professional counseling helped and whether the length of time spent in jail after the arrest mattered at all.

By the time results were reported from five of the cities in the new study, a problem was apparent. In three of the cities—Omaha, Nebraska; Charlotte, North Carolina; and Milwaukee, Wisconsin—researchers were finding long-term increases in IPV incidents among arrestees. But in two—Colorado Springs,

Exhibit 2.6 The Research Circle: Minneapolis Domestic Violence Experiment

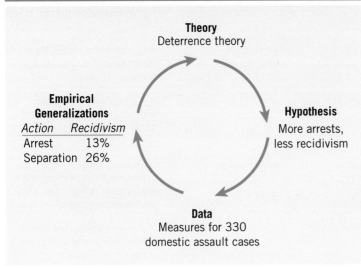

Colorado, and Dade County, Florida—the predicted deterrent effects seemed to be occurring (Sherman, Smith, Schmidt, & Rogan, 1992). Sherman and his colleagues had now traversed the research circle twice in an attempt to answer the original research question, first in Minneapolis and then in six other cities. But rather than leading to more confidence in deterrence theory, the research results were questioning it. Deterrence theory now seemed inadequate to explain empirical reality, at least as the researchers had measured this reality. So the researchers began to reanalyze the follow-up data from several cities in an attempt to explain the discrepant results, thereby starting around the research circle once again (Berk, Campbell, Klap, & Western, 1992; Pate & Hamilton, 1992; Sherman et al., 1992).

Phase 2: Adding Inductive Reasoning to Deductive Research

As we noted previously, inductive research begins with specific data, which are then used to develop (induce) a general explanation (a theory) to account for the data. Another way to think of this process is represented in Exhibit 2.7. In deductive research, reasoning from specific premises results in a conclusion that a theory is supported, but in inductive research, the identification of similar empirical patterns results in a generalization about some social process.

As we noted, inductive reasoning often enters into deductive research when we find unexpected patterns, called anomalous or serendipitous findings, in the data we have collected for testing a hypothesis.

The domestic violence research took an inductive turn when Sherman and the other researchers began trying to make sense of the differing patterns in the data collected in the different cities. Could systematic differences in the samples or in the implementation of arrest policies explain the differing outcomes? Or was the problem an inadequacy in the theoretical basis of their research? Was deterrence theory really the best way to explain the patterns in the data they were collecting?

Pate and Hamilton (1992) found that individuals who were married and employed were deterred from repeat offenses by arrest, but individuals who were unmarried and unemployed were actually more likely to commit

Exhibit 2.7 Deductive and Inductive Reasoning
Deductive
Premise 1: *All unemployed spouse abusers recidivate.*
Premise 2: *Joe is an unemployed spouse abuser.*
Conclusion: **Joe will recidivate.**
Inductive
Evidence 1: *Joe, an unemployed spouse abuser, recidivated.*
Evidence 2: *Harold, an unemployed spouse abuser, recidivated.*
Evidence 3: *George, an employed spouse abuser, didn't recidivate.*
Conclusion: **All unemployed spouse abusers recidivate.**

repeat offenses if they were arrested. What could explain this empirical pattern? The researchers turned to *control theory*, which predicts that having a "stake in conformity" (resulting from inclusion in social networks at work or in the community) decreases a person's likelihood of committing crimes (Toby, 1957). The implication is that people who are employed and married are more likely to be deterred by the threat of arrest than are those without such stakes in conformity. And this is indeed what the data revealed.

Now the researchers had traversed the research circle almost three times, a process perhaps better described as a spiral (see Exhibit 2.8). The first two times, the researchers had traversed the research circle in a deductive, hypothesis-testing way. They started with theory and then deduced and tested hypotheses. The third time, they were more inductive: They started with empirical generalizations from the data they had already obtained and then turned to a new theory to account for the unexpected patterns in the data. At this point, they believed that deterrence theory made correct predictions, given certain conditions, and that another theory, *control theory*, might specify what these conditions were.

Exhibit 2.8   The Research Spiral: Domestic Violence Experiment

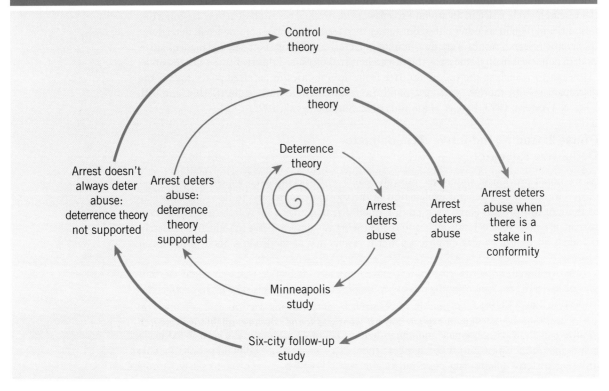

This inductive step in their research made for a more complex—but also conceptually richer—picture of the impact of arrest on IPV. The researchers seemed to have come closer to understanding how to inhibit IPV. But they cautioned us that their initial question—the research problem—was still not completely answered. Employment status and marital status do not solely measure the strength of social attachments; they are also related to how much people earn and the social standing of victims in court. So maybe social ties are not really what make arrest an effective deterrent to IPV. The real deterrent may be cost–benefit calculations ("If I have a higher income, jail is more costly for me") or perceptions about the actions of authorities ("If I am a married woman, judges will treat my complaint more seriously"). Additional research was needed (Berk et al., 1992).

Phase 3: Deductive Research

What other factors may explain the discrepancy in the findings? In 1997, Paternoster et al. reexamined data from one of the replication sites in Milwaukee to test hypotheses derived from yet another theory, procedural justice theory. As explained earlier in this chapter, procedural justice theory predicts that people will comply with the law out of a sense of duty and obligation if they are treated fairly by legal authorities. In the Milwaukee sample, arrest had a criminogenic effect: Those who were arrested were subsequently more likely to abuse their spouses than those who were simply warned. Paternoster et al. (1997) thought that this effect might have been due to the way subjects were treated when they were arrested rather than simply to the fact that they were arrested. One of their hypotheses spells out the reasoning:

Among those persons arrested for spouse assault, those who perceive themselves as being treated in a procedurally unfair manner will be more likely to commit acts of spouse assault in the future than those arrested persons who perceive themselves as being treated in a procedurally fair manner, net of other determinants of violence. (p. 173)

This reanalysis of the data qualifies as deductive research because the hypotheses were derived from theory and then tested with the data rather than being induced by the data. The procedural justice hypotheses were supported: Persons who were arrested in the Milwaukee experiment became more likely to reoffend only if they perceived that they had been treated unfairly by the police. Otherwise, their rate of rearrest was similar to that for the persons who were not arrested. Thus, another element was added to our understanding of the effects of the police response to IPV.

Clearly, our understanding of effective responses to IPV will never truly be complete, but research to date has greatly improved our knowledge of this social problem. The future should yield an even better understanding, even though at times it may be hard to make sense of conflicting findings from different studies. Science is an ongoing enterprise in which findings cumulate and eventually yield greater insight or even radical revisions in our understanding. Needless to say, researchers do not need to worry about running out of work to do.

Phase 4: Adding Exploration to the Mix

While researchers were grappling with the results of the randomized experiments, other researchers were engaged in inductive research by interviewing victims and offenders in depth and then developing an explanation for what was found. Because qualitative research is often exploratory and, hence, inductive, researchers often ask questions such as "What is going on here?" "How do people interpret these experiences?" or "Why do people do what they do?" Rather than testing a hypothesis, the researchers are trying to make sense of some social phenomenon.

Case Study: Police Decision Making

Eryn O'Neal and Cassia Spohn (2017) wanted to explore the factors that influence arrest and charging decisions in cases of intimate partner sexual assault cases. In addition to examining quantitative data on these two variables in Los Angeles, they interviewed 52 Los Angeles Police Department (LAPD) detectives and examined Los Angeles district attorney charge evaluation sheets. Results of the quantitative data indicated that the primary factor influencing whether an arrest was made was whether victims sustained injuries as the result of the attack. To explore this further, O'Neal and Spohn (2017) asked the LAPD detectives, "What are the decision rules that you follow in deciding whether to make an arrest or not?" (p. 720). To this, one detective replied, "I had a case, excuse my French, where the victim got the shit beat out of her. Her face was punched in. She was bruised all over and you could tell she fought him off her" (p. 720).

Other issues related to arrest discovered by O'Neal and Spohn were delayed reporting and victim's cooperation. Several of the detectives believed that intimate partners were less likely to cooperate with the prosecutors after reporting compared with victimizations perpetrated by strangers. This was further complicated when victims did not report the incident to police soon after the attack. For example, one LAPD detective stated:

Every victim is different. But delayed reporting results in lack of evidence. Good cases are those with a cooperative [victim], witnesses who notify the police in a timely manner so that the evidence is preserved . . . Timely reporting is a lot easier to investigate (p. 721).

These qualitative interview data allowed O'Neal and Spohn (2017) to understand the process of making an arrest from the detectives' perspective. The researchers note that the interviews allowed, "the interviewer to engage in model-building, model-testing, theory-construction, and theory verification within the same interview session" (p. 715).

Explanations developed inductively from qualitative research like these interview narratives can feel authentic because we have heard what people have to say in their own words, and we have tried to see the social world as they see it. Explanations derived from qualitative research will be richer and more finely textured than they often are in quantitative research, but they are likely to be based on fewer cases from a limited area. We cannot assume that the people studied in this setting are like others or that other researchers will develop explanations similar to ours to make sense of what was observed or heard. Because we do not initially set up a test of a hypothesis according to some specific rules, another researcher cannot come along and conduct the same test.

RESEARCH STANDARDS

Research can improve our understanding of *empirical reality*, the reality we encounter first-hand, by conducting research that leads to valid knowledge about the world. But when is knowledge valid? In general, we have reached the goal of validity when our statements or conclusions about empirical reality are correct. If you look out your window and observe that it is raining, this is probably a valid observation, if your eyes and ears are to be trusted. However, if you pick up the newspaper and read that the majority of Americans favor the death penalty, this may be of questionable validity because it is probably based on a social survey. In fact, you will see in Chapter 7 that attitudes toward the death penalty vary substantially depending on the wording of the questions asked.

Number of Reported Rapes Climbs in New York City

The New York City mayor, Bill de Blasio, held a press conference to explain his theory of why the number of reported rapes had increased by nearly 23% in 2018, while other violent crimes remained relatively stable. Recall from Chapter 1 that we measure victimization in many different ways, including official police reports and from victimization surveys. This increase was based on official reports to the police. During the preceding year, allegations of sexual misconduct by famous people sparked the #MeToo movement, which compelled many survivors to come forward. Like reports from victimization surveys, the vast majority of people who reported a rape victimization to NYC police in 2018 were attacked by intimate partners or acquaintances rather than strangers.

For Further Thought

1. What do you believe played a role in the increased number of people reporting their sexual assault victimizations to police in NYC in 2018 compared with earlier years?

2. Do you think the spike in reports represents a real spike in the number of rapes, or may it reflect an increased willingness of victims to report to law enforcement officials? Why, or why not?

Source: Southall, A. (2019, January 6). As the number of reported rapes climb, mayor points to #MeToo. *New York Times*. Retrieved from https://www.nytimes.com/2019/01/06/nyregion/rape-reports-nyc-me-too.html

To some of you, the goal of validity may sound a bit far-fetched. After all, how can we really be sure our understandings of phenomena are correct when we can perceive the world only through the filter of our own senses? Hopefully, this concern will remind you to be skeptical about new discoveries!

This book is about validity more than anything else, about how to conduct research that leads to valid interpretations of the social world. We will refer to validity repeatedly, and we ask you to register it in your brain now as the central goal of all the research conducted in our field. The goal of research conducted by social scientists investigating issues related to criminology and criminal justice is not to come up with conclusions that people will like or conclusions that suit their personal preferences. The goal is to determine the most valid answers through empirical research methods.

We must be concerned with three aspects of validity: measurement validity, generalizability, and causal validity (also known as *internal validity*). Each of these three aspects of validity is essential: Conclusions based on invalid measures, invalid generalizations, or invalid causal inferences will themselves be invalid. We will also be concerned with the goal of authenticity, a concern with reflecting fairly the perspectives of participants in a setting that we study.

Imagine that we survey a sample of 250 high school seniors and ask them two questions: "Do you have friends who have taken illegal drugs in the past six months?" (the measure of peer behavior) and "Have you taken illegal drugs in the past six months?" (respondents' behavior). We then compare the frequency of illegal drug use between students who have friends who have used illegal drugs and those whose friends have not used illegal drugs. We find that students who have friends who have used illegal drugs in the past six months are more likely to have used drugs themselves, and we conclude that drug use is, in part, due to the influence of peers.

But did our questions indeed tell us the frequency with which the students and their peers took illegal drugs? If they did, we achieved measurement validity. Do our results hold true of the larger adolescent population to which our conclusion referred? If so, our conclusion would satisfy the criterion for generalizability. Did the likelihood of students taking drugs actually increase if they had friends who also took drugs? If so, our conclusion is causally valid.

Measurement Validity

Measurement validity is our first concern in establishing the validity of research results because without having measured what we think we've measured, we really don't know what we're talking about.

The first step in achieving measurement validity is to specify clearly what it is we intend to measure. Patricia Tjaden and Nancy Thoennes (2000) identified this as one of the problems with research on IPV: "Definitions of the term vary widely from study to study, making comparisons difficult" (p. 5). To avoid this problem, Tjaden and Thoennes (2000) presented a clear definition of what they meant by *intimate partner violence*: "rape, physical assault, and stalking perpetrated by current and former dates, spouses, and cohabiting partners, with cohabiting meaning living together at least some of the time as a couple" (p. 5).

Tjaden and Thoennes also provided a measure of each type of violence. For example, "'physical assault' is defined as behaviors that threaten, attempt, or actually inflict physical harm" (Tjaden & Thoennes, 2000, p. 5). With this definition in mind, Tjaden and Thoennes (2000) then specified the set of questions they would use to measure intimate partner violence (the questions pertaining to physical assault):

Not counting any incidents you have already mentioned, after you became an adult, did any other adult, male or female, ever:

- Throw something at you that could hurt?

- Push, grab, or shove you?

> **Measurement validity:** The type of validity that is achieved when a measure measures what it is presumed to measure

- Pull your hair?

- Slap or hit you?

- Kick or bite you?

- Choke or attempt to drown you?

- Hit you with some object?

- Beat you up?

- Threaten you with a gun?

- Threaten you with a knife or other weapon?

- Use a gun on you?

- Use a knife or other weapon on you? (p. 6)

Do you believe that answers to these questions provide a valid measure of having been physically assaulted? Do you worry that some survey respondents might not report all the assaults they have experienced? Might some respondents make up some incidents? Issues like these must be considered when we evaluate measurement validity. Suffice it to say that we must be very careful in designing our measures and in subsequently evaluating how well they have performed. Chapter 4 introduces several different ways to test measurement validity. We cannot just *assume* that measures are valid.

Generalizability

The generalizability of a study is the extent to which it can be used to inform us about persons, places, or events that were not studied. You have already learned in this chapter that Sherman and Berk's findings in Minneapolis about the police response to IPV simply did not hold up in several other cities: the initial results could not be generalized. As you know, this led to additional research to figure out what accounted for the different patterns in different cities. Chapter 5 on sampling will give you the tools you need to answer questions such as these.

Generalizability has two aspects. **Sample generalizability** refers to the ability to generalize from a sample, or subset, of a larger population to that population itself. This is the most common meaning of generalizability. **Cross-population generalizability** refers to the ability to generalize from findings about one group, population, or setting to other groups, populations, or settings. Cross-population generalizability can also be referred to as **external validity**. (Some social scientists equate the term *external validity* to *generalizability*, but in this book, we restrict its use to the more limited notion of cross-population generalizability.)

Causal Validity

Causal validity, also known as **internal validity**, refers to the truthfulness of an assertion that x causes y; it is the focus of Chapter 6. A great deal of research seeks to determine what causes what, so social scientists frequently must be concerned with causal validity. Sherman and Berk (1984) were concerned with the effect of arrest on the likelihood of recidivism by people accused of IPV. To test their causal hypothesis, they designed their experiment so that some accused persons were arrested and others were not. Of course, it may seem heavy-handed for social scientists to influence police actions for the purpose of a research project, but this step reflects just how difficult it can be to establish causally valid understandings about the social world. It was only because police officials did not know whether arrest caused spouse abusers to reduce their levels of abuse that they were willing to allow an experiment to test the effect of different policies.

Sample generalizability: Exists when a conclusion based on a sample, or subset, of a larger population holds true for that population

Cross-population generalizability (external validity): Exists when findings about one group, population, or setting hold true for other groups, populations, or settings; also called *external validity*

Causal validity: Exists when a conclusion that *x* leads to or results in *y* is correct; also called *internal validity*

Chapter 6 will give you much more understanding of how some features of a research design can help us evaluate causal propositions. However, you will also learn that the solutions are neither easy nor perfect: We always have to consider critically the validity of causal statements that we hear or read.

Authenticity

The goal of **authenticity** is to fairly reflect the perspectives of the participants in a study setting and is stressed by researchers who focus attention on the subjective dimension of the social world. An authentic understanding of a social process or social setting is one that reflects fairly the various perspectives of participants in that setting (Gubrium & Holstein, 1997). Authenticity is one of several different standards proposed by some as uniquely suited to qualitative research; it reflects a belief that those who study the social world should focus first and foremost on how participants view that social world, not on developing a unique social scientists' interpretation of that world. Rather than expecting social scientists to be able to provide a valid mirror of reality, this perspective emphasizes how our recognition of participants' own reality can help us as researchers to uncover a more nuanced truth (Kvale, 2002).

For example, instead of focusing on IPV victims who sought help from police, Angela Moe (2007) interviewed victims who sought help from domestic violence shelters. She explained her basis for considering the responses of women she interviewed in the domestic violence shelter to be authentic: "Members of marginalized groups are better positioned than members of socially dominant groups to describe the ways in which the world is organized according to the oppressions they experience" (p. 682).

Moe's (2007) assumption was that "battered women serve as experts of their own lives" (p. 682). Adding to her assessment of authenticity, Moe (2007) found that the women "exhibited a great deal of comfort through their honesty and candor" as they produced "a richly detailed and descriptive set of narratives" (p. 683). You will learn more about how authenticity can be achieved in qualitative methods in Chapter 8.

> **Authenticity:** Exists when the understanding of a social process or social setting is one that reflects fairly the various perspectives of participants in the setting

Patrick J. Carr, PhD, Director, Program in Criminal Justice

Source: Patrick J. Carr

Patrick J. Carr is the program director of the Program in Criminal Justice, as well as associate professor of sociology at Rutgers University; furthermore, he is an associate member of the MacArthur Foundation's Research Network on Transitions to Adulthood. He earned his PhD in sociology from the University of Chicago in 1998 and his master's degree in sociology from University College Dublin in 1990. His research interests include communities and crime, informal social control, youth violence, and the transition to adulthood.

Carr and his wife, Maria Kefalas (Saint Joseph's University), are founders of the Philadelphia Youth Solutions Project, which "offers a safe space for Philadelphia's young people to explain their views and emotions about the danger and violence that consumes so much of their daily lives, to ask questions of themselves and the people charged with running [Philadelphia], and to have a serious conversation with teachers, parents, city officials, community leaders, state legislators, reporters, politicians, and anyone else who wants to know what is going on in the city to move forward on solutions inspired by the youth perspective." The Philadelphia Youth Solutions Project is a venue for Philadelphia's young people to offer their own expert advice on how to transform the city based on their experiences and perspectives.

Carr and Kefalas (2009) are ethnographic researchers who seek to understand people's experiences through participating in their lives and interviewing them in depth. In another project, they investigated the experiences of young adults growing up in a small Midwestern town by living in the town and sharing in community experiences. Their subsequent book was *Hollowing Out the Middle: The Rural Brain Drain and What It Means for America.*

CAREERS AND RESEARCH

CONCLUSION

Criminological researchers can find many questions to study, but not all questions are equally worthy. Those that warrant the expense and effort of social research are feasible, socially important, and scientifically relevant. The simplicity of the research circle presented in this chapter belies the complexity of the social-research process. In the following chapters, we will focus on particular aspects of that process.

Ethical issues also should be considered when evaluating research. As Chapter 3 will show, ethical issues in research are no less complex than the other issues researchers confront. It is inexcusable to jump into research involving people without paying attention to how our work can and does affect their lives.

KEY TERMS

Authenticity   39
Causal validity (internal
    validity)   38
Constant   31
Cross-population generalizability
    (external validity)   38
Deductive reasoning   30
Deductive research   30
Dependent variable   31

Empirical generalizations   32
Falsifiable   28
Hypothesis   30
Independent variable   31
Inductive reasoning   30
Inductive research   32
Measurement validity   37
Replications   32
Research circle   30

Research question   25
Sample generalizability   38
Serendipitous findings
    (anomalous findings)   30
Theoretical constructs   28
Theory   27
Variable   31

HIGHLIGHTS

- Research questions should be feasible (within the time and resources available), socially important, and scientifically relevant.

- A theory is a logically interrelated set of propositions that helps us make sense of many interrelated phenomena and predict behavior or attitudes that are likely to occur when certain conditions are met.

- Building criminological theory is a major objective of criminological research. Investigate relevant theories before starting criminological projects, and draw out the theoretical implications of research findings.

- The type of reasoning in most criminological research can be described as primarily deductive or inductive. Research based on deductive reasoning proceeds from general ideas, deduces specific expectations from these ideas, and then tests the ideas with empirical data. Research based on inductive reasoning begins with specific data and then develops general ideas or theories to explain patterns in the data.

- It may be possible to explain unanticipated research findings after the fact, but such explanations have less

credibility than those that have been tested with data collected for the purpose of the study.

- The scientific process can be represented as circular, with connections from theory to hypotheses to data to empirical generalizations. Research investigations may begin at different points along the research circle and travel along different portions of it. Deductive research begins at the point of theory; inductive research begins with data but ends with theory. Descriptive research begins with data and ends with empirical generalizations.

- Replications of a study are essential to establish its generalizability in other situations. An ongoing line of research stemming from a particular question should include a series of studies that, collectively, travel around the research circle multiple times.

- Criminologists, like all social scientists, should structure their research so that their own ideas can be proved wrong, disclose their methods for others to critique, and recognize the possibility of error. Nine specific guidelines are recommended.

- Valid knowledge is the central concern of scientific research. The three components of validity are measurement validity, generalizability (both from the sample to the population from which it was selected and from the sample to other populations), and causal (internal) validity.

EXERCISES

Discussing Research

1. State a problem for research related to a criminological topic or issue of interest to you. Write down as many questions as you can about this topic.

   a. Considering your interest, opportunities, and findings from past research, which of your research questions do not seem feasible or interesting?

   b. Pick out one question that seems feasible and that your other coursework suggests has been the focus of prior research or theorizing. Write this research question in one sentence. Elaborate on your question in a single paragraph. List at least three reasons why it is a good research question to investigate.

   c. Ultimately, how would you characterize this research effort? Does it contribute to the discipline, policy, or society at large?

2. Search the scholarly literature on your topic of interest. (You can find articles on the Student Study Site, **edge.sagepub.com/bachmanfrccj5e**.) Copy at least 10 citations to recent articles reporting research relevant to your research question.

   a. Look up at least three of these articles. Write a brief description of each article, and evaluate its relevance to your research question. What additions or changes to your thoughts about the research question are suggested by these sources?

   b. Would you characterize the findings of these articles as largely consistent or inconsistent? How would you explain discrepant findings?

   c. How well did the authors summarize their work in their abstracts for the articles you consulted? What important points would you have missed if you had relied on only the abstracts?

3. Using one of the research articles you consulted for Exercise 2, identify and look up one of the cited articles or websites. Compare the cited source with what was said about it in the original article or on the original site. Was the discussion in the cited source accurate?

Finding Research on the Web

1. Search the scholarly literature on your topic of interest. Refer to Appendix A for guidance on conducting the search, if necessary.

   a. Copy at least 10 citations to recent articles reporting research relevant to your research question.

   b. Look up at least three of these articles. Write a brief description of each article, and evaluate its relevance to your research question. What additions or changes to your thoughts about the research question are suggested by these sources?

   c. Would you characterize the findings of these articles as largely consistent or inconsistent? How would you explain discrepant findings?

   d. How well did the authors summarize their work in their abstracts for the articles you consulted? What important points would you have missed if you had relied on only the abstracts?

2. You have been assigned to write a paper on domestic violence and the law. To start, find out what the American Bar Association's stance is on the issue. Go to the American Bar Association Commission on Domestic Violence's website (www.americanbar.org/groups/domestic_violence.html). What is the American Bar Association's definition of domestic violence? How does it suggest one can identify a person as a victim of domestic violence?

3. Go to the Bureau of Justice Statistics (BJS) website (www.bjs.gov). Go to "Publications & Products." Browse the list of publications for topics related to domestic violence or intimate partner violence. List the titles of all publications focusing on violence between intimate partners. Choose the most recent publication. How does the BJS define *intimate partners*? What are some of the characteristics of IPV? What trends are identified in the report? Based on the data presented, what might you induce from the findings about police reporting of violence exhibited in particular kinds of relationships (married, divorced, by age of victim, etc.)?

Critiquing Research

1. Using one of the research articles you consulted in the last section, identify and look up one of the cited articles or websites. Compare the cited source with what was said about it in the original article or website. Was the discussion in the cited source accurate?

2. Using the same research article you focused on for the last exercise, identify the stages of the research project corresponding to the points on the research circle. Did the research cover all four stages? Identify the theories and hypotheses underlying the study. What data were collected or used for the study? What were the findings (empirical generalizations)?

Making Research Ethical

1. Review the ethical guidelines adopted by the American Sociological Association (1999, p. 63). Indicate whether you think each guideline was followed in the Sherman and Berk (1984) research on the policy response to IPV. If you find it hard to give a simple *yes* or *no* answer for each guideline, indicate the issues that make this evaluation difficult.

2. Concern with how research results are used is one of the hallmarks of ethical researchers, but deciding what form that concern should take is often difficult. You learned in this chapter about the controversy that occurred after Sherman and Berk (1984) encouraged police departments to adopt a pro-arrest policy in domestic abuse cases based on findings from their Minneapolis study. Do you agree with the researchers' decision to suggest policy changes to police departments based on their study in an effort to minimize domestic abuse? Several replication studies failed to confirm the Minneapolis findings. Does this influence your evaluation of what the researchers should have done after the Minneapolis study was completed? In one paragraph, propose a policy that researchers should follow about how much publicity is warranted and at what point in the research it should occur.

Developing a Research Proposal

The next exercises are very critical first steps in writing a research proposal.

1. State a problem for research. If you have not already identified a problem for study or if you need to evaluate whether your research problem is doable, a few suggestions should help to get the ball rolling and keep it on course:

    a. Jot down a few questions you have had about some issue. Now, take stock of your interests and your opportunities. Which of your research questions no longer seem feasible or interesting?

    b. Write out your research question in one sentence, and elaborate on it in one paragraph. List at least three reasons why it is a good research question for you to investigate.

2. Search the literature (and the Internet) for information on the research question you identified. Refer to Appendix A for guidance on conducting the search. Copy down at least 10 citations to articles and five citations to websites reporting research that seems highly relevant to your research question. Inspect the article bibliographies and the links in the websites, and identify at least one more relevant article and one more relevant website from each source. What additions or changes to your thoughts about the research question are suggested by the sources?

3. Propose at least two hypotheses that pertain to your research question. Justify these hypotheses in terms of the literature you have read.

4. Which standards for the protection of human subjects might pose the most difficulty for researchers on your proposed topic? Explain your answers, and suggest appropriate protection procedures for human subjects.

Performing Data Analysis in SPSS or Excel

Data for Exercise	
Dataset	Description
Youth.sav	These data are from a random sample of students from schools in a southern state. While not representative of the United States, this file covers a variety of important delinquent behaviors and peer influences.

Variables for Exercise	
Variable Name	**Description**
D1	A binary variable based on the number of delinquent acts a respondent reported. A 0 indicates that the respondent reported one or fewer acts, while a 1 indicates two or more.
Supervision	This is a binary variable based on a scale of parental supervision. High scores (six or greater) are coded 1; low scores (five or lower) are coded 0.
Heavytvwatcher	A binary variable based on the number of hours a respondent reported watching per week. A value of 1 indicates 15 or more hours of TV per week; a value of 0 indicates 14 or fewer.
Studyhard	A binary variable based on the number of hours a respondent reported studying per week. A value of 1 indicates nine or more hours per week; a value of 0 indicates eight or fewer.
Gender	Gender of the respondent
Drinkingnotbad	A binary variable based on a question about whether a respondent's friends view drinking as wrong

1. Consider the following pairs of variables:
   a. Delinquent behavior and parental supervision
   b. Hours watching TV per week and hours studying per week
   c. Gender and how wrong one's friends think it is to drink

2. Do the following for each pair of variables:
   a. Articulate a research question involving the two variables
   b. Hypothesize a relationship between the two variables (or lack thereof). Explain why you think the variables will be related in this fashion.
   c. Identify the independent and dependent variable.
   d. State the direction of the association that is expected.

3. With these hypotheses in hand, let's see how they hold up using real data! For these tests, you'll be constructing basic cross-tabulations, which allow you to compare two binary variables easily. Start off by clicking "analyze->descriptives->crosstabs." Then, place your independent variable in the "columns" box and your dependent variable in the "rows" box. Lastly, select the "cells" option and make sure that "column" is selected under the percentages window. The output that you get will allow you to see, for instance, if people with a high score on the independent variable also are more likely to have a high score on the dependent variable.

   a. Start off by cross-tabulating variables "d1" and "supervision."
      i. How do these results line up with your hypothesis?
      ii. What is the direction of the association found, if any?
   b. Then, compare the variables "heavytvwatcher" and "studyhard."
      i. Do these results support your hypothesis?
      ii. What is the direction of the association found, if any?
   c. Compare the variable "gender" and "drinkingnotbad."
      i. How do these results compare with your hypothesis?
      ii. What is the direction of the association found, if any?

ETHICAL GUIDELINES FOR RESEARCH

Learning Objectives

1. Describe the design of the Milgram obedience experiments and some of the controversies surrounding its methods and results.

2. Identify three other research projects that helped to motivate the establishment of human subjects' protections.

3. Define the Belmont Report's three ethical standards for the protection of human subjects.

4. Explain how an institutional review board (IRB) operates and how it classifies research.

5. List current standards for the protection of human subjects in research.

6. Describe the ethical issues related to conducting research with children and prisoners.

7. Understand the importance of institutional review boards.

⑤SAGE edge™

Master the content at edge
.sagepub.com/bachmanfrccj5e

> I wanted to let you know how useful my research methods class has already proved to be. For my internship this summer, everyone had to get the CITI [Collaborative Institutional Training Initiative] (Institutional Review Board [IRB]) training certification to conduct our research, which took a few days out of the actual projects. However, because I was already IRB certified from my class, I was able to start my project sooner. My supervisor was really appreciative that I didn't have to use my time to complete the IRB training. Additionally, I will be utilizing my knowledge about survey methods this summer for my research.
>
> **Marissa O., Student**

WHAT DO WE HAVE IN MIND?

Would You Pretend to Be a Prisoner?

Consider the following scenario: One day, as you are drinking coffee and reading the newspaper during your summer in California, you notice a small ad recruiting college students for a study at Stanford University. The ad reads as follows:

> Male college students needed for psychological study of prison life. $80 per day for 1–2 weeks beginning Aug. 14. For further information & applications, come to Room 248, Jordan Hall, Stanford U. (Zimbardo, 2008)

You go to the campus and complete an application. After you arrive at the university, you are given an information form with more details about the research (Zimbardo, 2008).

First, you are asked to complete a long questionnaire about your family background, physical and mental health history, and prior criminal involvement. Next, you are interviewed by someone, and then, you finally sign a consent form. A few days later, you are informed that you and 20 other young men have been selected to participate in the experiment. You return to the university to complete a battery of "psychological tests" and are told you will be picked up for the study the next day (Haney, Banks, & Zimbardo, 1973, p. 73).

The next morning, you hear a siren just before a squad car stops in front of your house. A police officer charges you with assault and battery, warns you of your constitutional rights, searches and handcuffs you, and drives you off to the police station. After fingerprinting and a short stay in a detention cell, you are blindfolded and driven to the "Stanford County Prison." Upon arrival, your blindfold is removed, and you are stripped naked, skin-searched, deloused, and issued a uniform (a loosely fitting smock with an ID number printed on it), bedding, soap, and a towel. You don't recognize anyone, but you notice that the other "prisoners" and the "guards" are college age, apparently almost all middle-class white men (except for one Asian) like you (Haney et al., 1973; Zimbardo, 1973).

PRISON LIFE STUDY

General Information

Purpose: A simulated prison will be established somewhere in the vicinity of Palo Alto, Stanford [sic], to study a number of problems of psychological and sociological relevance. Paid volunteers will be randomly assigned to play the roles of either prisoners and guards [sic] for the duration of the study. This time period will vary somewhat from about five days to two weeks for any one volunteer—depending upon several factors, such as the "sentence" for the prisoner or the work effectiveness of the guards. Payment will be $80 a day for performing various activities and work associated with the operation of our prison. Each volunteer must enter a contractual arrangement with the principal investigator (Dr. P. G. Zimbardo) agreeing to participate for the full duration of the study. It is obviously essential that no prisoner can leave once jailed, except through established procedures. In addition, guards must report for their 8-hour work shifts promptly and regularly since surveillance by the guards will be around-the-clock—three work shifts will be rotated or guards will be assigned a regular shift—day, evening, or early morning. Failure to fulfill this contract will result in a partial loss of salary accumulated—according to a prearranged schedule to be agreed upon. Food and accommodations for the prisoners will be provided which will meet minimal standard nutrition, health, and sanitation requirements. A warden and several prison staff will be housed in adjacent cell blocks, meals and bedding also provided for them. Medical and psychiatric facilities will be accessible should any of the participants desire or require such services. All participants will agree to having their behavior observed and to be interviewed and perhaps also taking psychological tests. Films of parts of the study will be taken, participants agreeing to allow them to be shown, assuming their content has information of scientific value.

[The information form then summarizes two of the "problems to be studied" and provides a few more details.]

Thanks for your interest in this study. We hope it will be possible for you to participate and to share your experiences with us.

Philip G. Zimbardo, PhD
Professor of Social Psychology
Stanford University

Source: Zimbardo, P. G. (2008). *The Lucifer effect: Understanding how good people turn evil* (2nd ed.). New York, NY: Random House.

The prison warden welcomes you:

As you probably know, I'm your warden. All of you have shown that you are unable to function outside in the real world for one reason or another—that somehow you lack the responsibility of good citizens of this great country. We of this prison, your correctional staff, are going to help you learn what your responsibilities as citizens of this country are. . . . If you follow all of these rules and keep your hands clean, repent for your misdeeds and show a proper attitude of penitence, you and I will get along just fine. (Zimbardo, 2008, pp. 27–28)

Among other behavioral restrictions, the rules stipulate that prisoners must remain silent during rest periods, during meals, and after lights out. They must address each other only by their assigned ID numbers, they are to address guards as "Mr. Correctional Officer," and everyone is warned that punishment will follow any rule violation (Zimbardo, 1973).

You look around and can tell that you are in the basement of a building. You are led down a corridor to a small cell (6 × 9 feet) with three cots, where you are locked behind a steel-barred black door with two other prisoners (Exhibit 3.1). Located across the hall, there is a small solitary confinement room (2 × 2 × 7 feet) for those who misbehave. There is little privacy, since you realize that the uniformed guards, behind the mirrored lenses of their sunglasses, can always observe the prisoners. After you go to sleep, you are awakened by a whistle summoning you and the others for a roll call periodically through the night.

The next morning, you and the other eight prisoners must stand in line outside your cells and recite the rules until you remember all 17 of them. Prisoners must chant, "It's a wonderful day, Mr. Correctional Officer." Two prisoners who get out of line are put in the solitary confinement unit. After a bit, the prisoners in Cell 1 decide to resist: They barricade their cell door and call on the prisoners in other cells to join in their resistance. The guards respond by pulling the beds out from the other cells and spraying several of the inmates with a fire extinguisher. The guards succeed in enforcing control and become more authoritarian, while the prisoners become increasingly docile. Punishments are regularly meted out for infractions of rules and sometimes for seemingly no reason at all; punishments include doing push-ups, being stripped naked, having legs chained, and being repeatedly wakened during the night. If this were you, would you join in the resistance? How would you react to this deprivation of your liberty by these authoritarian guards? How would you respond, given that you signed a consent form allowing you to be subjected to this kind of treatment?

By the fifth day of the actual Stanford Prison Experiment, five student prisoners had to be released due to evident extreme stress (Zimbardo, 2008). On the sixth day, Philip Zimbardo terminated the experiment. A prisoner subsequently reported, "The way we were made to degrade ourselves really brought us down and that's why we all sat docile towards the end of the experiment" (Haney et al., 1973, p. 88).

One guard later recounted his experience:

I was surprised at myself. . . . I made them call each other names and clean the toilets out with their bare hands. I practically considered the prisoners cattle, and I kept thinking: "I have to watch out for them in case they try something." (Zimbardo, 2008, p. 46)

Exhibit 3.1   Prisoner in His Cell

Source: © The Lucifer Effect by Philip G. Zimbardo, PhD, Professor Emeritus, Stanford University.

Exhibit 3.2   Chart of Guard and Prisoner Behavior

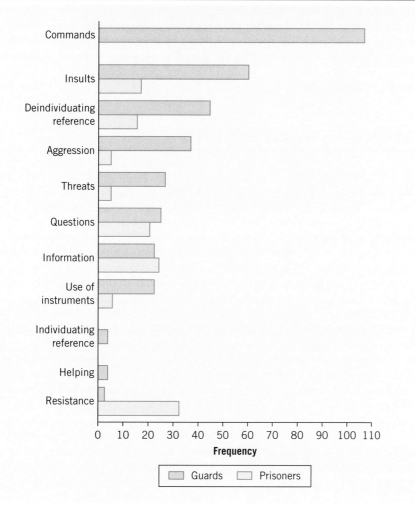

Source: Adapted from *The Lucifer Effect* by Philip G. Zimbardo.

Exhibit 3.2 gives some idea of the difference in how the prisoners and guards behaved. What is most striking about this result is that all the guards and prisoners had been screened before the study began to ensure that they were physically and mentally healthy. The roles of guard and prisoner had been assigned randomly, by the toss of a coin, so the two groups were very similar when the study began. Something about the situation appears to have led to the deterioration of the prisoners' mental states and the different behavior of the guards. Being a guard or a prisoner, with rules and physical arrangements reinforcing distinctive roles, changed their behavior.

Are you surprised by the outcome of the experiment? By the guard's report of his unexpected, abusive behavior? By the prisoners' ultimate submissiveness and the considerable psychic distress some felt? (We leave it to you to assess how you would have responded if you had been an actual research participant.)

Of course, our purpose in introducing this small "experiment" is not to focus attention on the prediction of behavior in prisons but to introduce the topic of research ethics. We will refer to **Philip Zimbardo's Stanford Prison Experiment** throughout this chapter, since it is fair to say that this research ultimately had a profound influence on the way that social scientists think about research ethics as well as on the way that criminologists understand behavior in prisons. We will also refer to **Stanley Milgram's (1963) experiments on obedience to authority**, since that research also pertains to criminal justice issues and has stimulated much debate about research ethics.

HISTORICAL BACKGROUND

Formal procedures regarding the protection of research participants emerged only after the revelation of several very questionable and damaging research practices. A defining event occurred in 1946, when the **Nuremberg war crimes trials** exposed horrific medical experiments conducted by Nazi doctors and others in the name of science. Almost 20 years later, Milgram's research on obedience also generated controversy about participant protections (Perry, 2013, p. 37). As late as 1972, Americans learned from news reports that researchers funded by the U.S. Public Health Service had followed 399 low-income African American men since the 1930s, collecting data to study the "natural" course of syphilis (Exhibit 3.3, www.tuskegee.edu/about_us/centers_of_excellence/bioethics_center/about_the_usphs_syphilis_study.aspx). At the time, there was no effective treatment for the disease, but the men were told they were being treated for "bad blood," whether they had syphilis or not. Participants received free medical exams, meals, and burial insurance but were not asked for their consent to be studied. What made this research study, known as the **Tuskegee syphilis experiment**, so shocking was that many participants were not informed of their illness, and even after penicillin was recognized as an effective treatment in 1945 and in large-scale use by 1947, the study participants were not treated. The research was ended only after the study was exposed. In 1973, congressional hearings began, and in 1974, an out-of-court settlement of $10 million was reached; it was not until 1997 that President Bill Clinton made an official apology (CDC, 2009). Of course, the United States is not the only country to have abused human subjects. For example, British military scientists exposed hundreds of Indian soldiers serving under the command of the British military to mustard gas during World War II to determine how much gas was needed to produce death (Evans, 2007).

These and other widely publicized abuses made it clear that formal review procedures were needed to protect research participants. The U.S. government created a National Commission for the Protection of Human Subjects of Biomedical and Behavioral Research and charged it with developing guidelines (Kitchener & Kitchener, 2009). The commission's 1979 **Belmont Report** (from the Department of Health, Education, and Welfare) established three basic ethical principles for the protection of human subjects (Exhibit 3.4):

Exhibit 3.3 Tuskegee Syphilis Experiment

Source: Tuskegee Syphilis Study Administrative Records. Records of the Centers for Disease Control and Prevention. National Archives—Southeast Region (Atlanta).

- **Respect for persons:** Treating persons as autonomous agents and protecting those with diminished autonomy

- **Beneficence:** Minimizing possible harms and maximizing benefits in research

- **Justice:** Distributing benefits and risks of research fairly

The Department of Health and Human Services (DHHS) and the Food and Drug Administration then translated these principles into specific regulations that were adopted in 1991 as the **Federal Policy for the Protection of Human Subjects**, also known as the **Common Rule** (Title 45 of Code of Federal Regulations [CFR], Part 46). This policy has shaped the course of social science research ever since, by requiring organizations that sponsor federally funded research—including universities—to establish committees that review all research proposed at the institution and ensure compliance with the federal human subjects requirements when the research is conducted. This policy has shaped the course of social science research ever since. This section introduces these regulations.

After 25 years, the Common Rule was revised, with modifications that were supposed to be implemented in January of 2018 but were delayed at the last minute, and the effective date was moved to July 19, 2018 (Allen, 2018). The revisions relaxed some requirements for social science research and made several other important changes that are consequential for both medical and social science researchers. These regulations, as revised, inform the discussion that follows (Chadwick, 2017).

Exhibit 3.4   Belmont Report Principles

Source: Office of Human Subjects Research, National Institutes of Health.

Some Social Scientists Are Tired of Asking for Permission

The 2017 revision of the 1991 Federal Policy for the Protection of Human Subjects (known as the Common Rule) became quite newsworthy after an opinion piece in the *Chronicle of Higher Education* noted the apparent new exemption from IRB review of research involving "benign behavioral interventions." In the opinion of coauthor Richard Nisbett, psychology professor at the University of Michigan, "There's no such thing as asking a question of a normal human being that should be reviewed by an I.R.B., because someone can just say, 'To heck with you.'" In contrast, Tom George, a lawyer and bioethicist on the institutional review board at the University of Texas at Austin worried that "there seems to be a major paradigm shift going on away from . . . protect[ing] human subjects and toward the convenience of researchers." Nathaniel Herr, psychology professor at American University observed, "It just takes one scandal to make people doubt all research and not want to participate, which would harm the whole field."

For Further Thought

1. Do you believe that social science researchers should be able to determine whether their research is subject to IRB review?

2. Professor Nisbett felt a "behavioral intervention" is benign "if it's the sort of thing that goes on in everyday life." Do you agree?

Source: Murphy, K. (2017, May 22). Some social scientists are tired of asking for permission. *New York Times.* Retrieved from https://www.nytimes.com/2017/05/22/science/social-science-research-institutional-review-boards-common-rule.html

RESEARCH IN THE NEWS

Federal regulations require that every institution, including universities that seek federal funding for biomedical or behavioral research on human subjects, have an **institutional review board (IRB)** to review research proposals. Other countries have similar entities, such as the United Kingdom's research ethics committees (RECs) (Calvey, 2014). IRBs at universities and other agencies adopt a review process that is principally guided by federally regulated ethical standards but can be expanded by the IRB itself (Sieber, 1992). To promote adequate review of ethical issues, the regulations require that IRBs include members with diverse backgrounds. The Office for Protection from Research Risks in the National Institutes of Health monitors IRBs, with the exception of research involving drugs (which is the responsibility of the federal Food and Drug Administration).

The Academy of Criminal Justice Sciences (ACJS) and the American Society of Criminology (ASC), like most professional social science organizations, have adopted ethical guidelines for practicing criminologists that are more specific than the federal regulations. The **ACJS Code of Ethics** also establishes procedures for investigating and resolving complaints concerning the ethical conduct of the organization's members.

The Code of Ethics of the ACJS (2000) is available on the ACJS website (www.acjs.org). The ASC follows the American Sociological Association's (ASA, 1999) code of ethics, which is summarized on the ASA website (www.asanet.org/membership/code-ethics).

ETHICAL PRINCIPLES

Achieving Valid Results

Achieving valid results is the necessary starting point for ethical research practice. Simply put, we have no business asking people to answer questions, submit to observations, or participate in experimental procedures if we are simply seeking to verify our preexisting prejudices or to convince others to take action on behalf of our personal interests. It is the pursuit of objective knowledge about human behavior—the goal of validity—that motivates and justifies our investigations and gives us some claim to the right to influence others to participate in our research. If we approach our research projects objectively, setting aside our personal predilections in the service of learning a bit more about human behavior, we can honestly represent our actions as potentially contributing to the advancement of knowledge.

The details in Zimbardo's articles and his recent book (2008) on the prison experiment make a compelling case for his commitment to achieving valid results—to learning how and why a prisonlike situation influences behavior. In Zimbardo's (2009) own words,

> Social-psychological studies were showing that human nature was more pliable than previously imagined and more responsive to situational pressures than we cared to acknowledge. . . . Missing from the body of social-science research at the time was the direct confrontation . . . of good people pitted against the forces inherent in bad situations. . . . I decided that what was needed was to create a situation in a controlled experimental setting in which we could array on one side a host of variables, such as . . . coercive rules, power differentials, anonymity. . . . On the other side, we lined up a collection of the "best and brightest" of young college men. . . . I wanted to know who wins—good people or an evil situation—when they were brought into direct confrontation.

Zimbardo devised his experiment so the situation would seem realistic to the participants and still allow careful measurement of important variables and observation of behavior at all times. Questionnaires and rating scales, interviews with participants as the research proceeded and after it was over, ongoing video and audio recording, and documented logs maintained by the guards all ensured that very little would escape the researcher's gaze (Haney et al., 1973).

Zimbardo's attention to validity is also apparent in his design of the physical conditions and organizational procedures for the experiment. The "prison" was constructed in a basement without any windows so that participants were denied a sense of time and place. Their isolation was reinforced by the practice of placing paper bags over their heads when they moved around "the facility," meals were bland, and conditions were generally demeaning. This was a very different "situation" from what the participants were used to—suffice it to say that it was no college dorm experience (Haney et al., 1973).

However, not all social scientists agree that Zimbardo's approach achieved valid results. British psychologists Stephen Reicher and S. Alexander Haslam (2006) argue that guard behavior was not so consistent and that it was determined by the instructions Zimbardo gave the guards at the start of the experiment rather than by becoming a guard in itself. For example, in another experiment, when guards were trained to respect prisoners, their behavior was less malicious (Lovibond, Mithiran, & Adams, 1979).

In response to such criticism, Zimbardo (2007) has pointed to several replications of his basic experiment that support his conclusions—as well as to the evidence of patterns of abuse in the real world of prisons, including the behavior of guards who tormented prisoners at Abu Ghraib during the war in Iraq.

Do you agree with Zimbardo's assumption that the effects of being a prisoner or guard could fruitfully be studied in a mock prison with pretend prisoners? Do you find merit in the criticisms? Will your evaluation of the ethics of Zimbardo's experiment be influenced by your answers to these questions? Should our ethical judgments differ when we are confident a study's results provide valid information about important social processes?

As you attempt to answer such questions, bear in mind that both Zimbardo and his critics support their conflicting ethical arguments with assertions about the validity (or invalidity) of the experimental results. It is hard to justify *any* risk for human subjects or *any* expenditure of time and resources if our findings tell us nothing about the reality of crime and punishment.

Honesty and Openness

The scientific concern with validity requires that scientists openly disclose their methods and honestly present their findings. In contrast, research distorted by political or personal pressures to find particular outcomes or to achieve the most marketable results is unlikely to be carried out in an honest and open fashion. To assess the validity of a researcher's conclusions and the ethics of his or her procedures, you need to know exactly how the research was conducted. This means that articles or other reports must include a detailed methodology section, perhaps supplemented by appendices containing the research instruments or websites or an address where more information can be obtained.

Philip Zimbardo's research reports seemed to present an honest and forthright account of the methods used in the Stanford experiment. His initial article (Haney et al., 1973) contained a detailed description of study procedures, including the physical aspects of the prison, the instructions to participants, the uniforms used, the induction procedure, and the specific data collection methods and measures. Many more details, including forms and pictures, are available on Zimbardo's website (www.prisonexperiment.org) and in his recent book (Zimbardo, 2008).

The act of publication itself is a vital element in maintaining openness and honesty. It allows others to review and question study procedures and generate an open dialogue with the researcher. Although Zimbardo disagreed sharply with his critics about many aspects of his experiment, their mutual commitment to public discourse in publications resulted in a more comprehensive presentation of study procedures and a more thoughtful discourse about research ethics (Savin, 1973; Zimbardo, 1973). Almost 40 years later, this commentary continues to inform debates about research ethics (Reicher & Haslam, 2006; Zimbardo, 2007).

Academy of Criminal Justice Sciences (ACJS) Code of Ethics: The Code of Ethics of ACJS sets forth (1) general principles and (2) ethical standards that underlie members of the academy's professional responsibilities and conduct, along with the (3) policies and procedures for enforcing those principles and standards; membership in the ACJS commits individual members to adhere to the ACJS Code of Ethics in determining ethical behavior in the context of their everyday professional activities

Openness about research procedures and results goes hand in hand with honesty in research design. Openness is also essential if researchers are to learn from the work of others. Despite this need for openness, some researchers may hesitate to disclose their procedures or results to prevent others from building on their ideas and taking some of the credit. Scientists are similar to other people in their desire to be first. Enforcing standards of honesty and encouraging openness about research are the best solutions to this problem.

Protecting Research Participants

The ACJS Code of Ethics standards concerning the treatment of human subjects include federal regulations and ethical guidelines emphasized by most professional social science organizations:

- Research should expose participants to no more than minimal risk of personal harm. (#16)

- Researchers should fully disclose the purposes of their research. (#13)

- Participation in research should be voluntary and, therefore, subjects must give their informed consent to participate in the research. (#16)

- Confidentiality must be maintained for individual research participants unless it is voluntarily and explicitly waived. (#14, #18, #19)

Philip Zimbardo (2008) himself decided that his Stanford Prison Experiment was unethical because it violated the first two of these principles: First, participants "did suffer considerable anguish . . . and [the experiment] resulted in such extreme stress and emotional turmoil that five of the sample of initially healthy young prisoners had to be released early" (pp. 233–234). Second, Zimbardo's research team did not disclose in advance the nature of the arrest or booking procedures at police headquarters, nor did they disclose to the participants' parents how bad the situation had become when they came to a visiting night. Nonetheless, Zimbardo (1973, 2008) argued that there was no long-lasting harm to participants and that there were some long-term social benefits from this research. In particular, **debriefing** participants—discussing their experiences and revealing the logic behind the experiment—and follow-up interviews enabled the participants to recover from the experience without lasting harm (Zimbardo, 2007). Also, the experience led several participants in the experiment, including Zimbardo, to dedicate their careers to investigating and improving prison conditions. As a result, publicity about the experiment has also helped focus attention on problems in prison management.

Do you agree with Zimbardo's conclusion that his experiment was not ethical? Do you think it should have been prevented from happening in the first place? Are you relieved to learn that current standards in the United States for the protection of human subjects in research would not allow his experiment to be conducted?

In contrast to Zimbardo, Stanley Milgram (1963) believed that his controversial experiments on obedience to authority were entirely ethical, so debate about this study persists today. His experiments raise most of the relevant issues we want to highlight here.

Milgram recruited community members to participate in his experiment at Yale University. His research was prompted by the ability of Germany's Nazi regime of the 1930s and 1940s to enlist the participation of ordinary citizens in unconscionable acts of terror and genocide. Milgram set out to identify through laboratory experiments the conditions under which ordinary citizens will be obedient to authority figures' instructions to inflict pain on others. He operationalized this obedience by asking subjects to deliver electric shocks (fake, of course) to a "student" supposedly learning a memory task.

Debriefing: A session after an experiment in which all instances of deception are revealed and explained and participants are allowed to ask questions

The experimental procedure had four simple steps: (1) a series of word pairs were read by the research subject, such as *blue box*, *nice day*, *wild duck*, and so on. (2) One of the first words from those pairs and a set of four words, one of which contained the original paired word, were then read. For example, "blue: sky ink box lamp" might be read. (3) The "pretend" learner stated the word that he or she thought was paired with the first word read ("blue"). If he or she gave a correct response, he or she was complimented, and the game continued. If he or she made a mistake, a switch was flipped on the console. The research subject assumed that this caused the learner to feel a shock on his or her wrist. (4) After each mistake, the next switch was flipped on the console, progressing from left to right. There was a label corresponding to every fifth mark on the dial, with the first mark labeled *slight shock*, the fifth mark labeled *moderate shock*, the 10th *strong shock*, and so on through *very strong shock*, *intense shock*, *extreme intensity shock*, and *danger: severe shock*.

Exhibit 3.5   Diagram of Milgram's Experiment

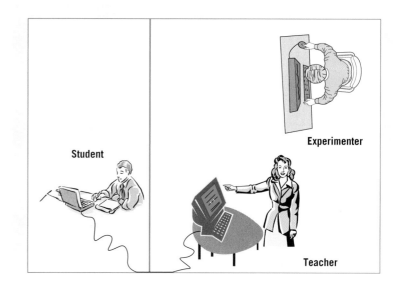

Subjects were told to increase the shocks over time, and many did so, even after the supposed "student," behind a partition, began to cry out in (simulated) pain (Exhibit 3.5). The participants became very tense, and some resisted as the shocks increased to the (supposedly) lethal range, but many still complied with the authority in that situation and increased the shocks. Like Zimbardo, Milgram debriefed participants afterward and followed up later to check on their well-being. It seemed that none had suffered long-term harm.

As we discuss how the ACJS Code of Ethics standards apply to Milgram's experiments, you will begin to realize that there is no simple answer to the question "What *is* (or *isn't*) ethical research practice?" The issues are just too complicated and the relevant principles too subject to different interpretations. But we do promise that by the end of this chapter, you will be aware of the major issues in research ethics and be able to make informed, defensible decisions about the ethical conduct of social science research.

Avoid Harming Research Participants

Although this standard may seem straightforward, it can be difficult to interpret in specific cases and harder yet to define in a way that is agreeable to all social scientists. Does it mean that subjects should not be harmed at all, psychologically or physically? That they should feel no anxiety or distress whatsoever during the study or even after their involvement ends? Should the possibility of *any* harm, no matter how remote, deter research?

Before we address these questions with respect to Milgram's experiments, a verbatim transcript of one session will give you an idea of what participants experienced (Milgram, 1965):

150 volts delivered.   You want me to keep going?

165 volts delivered.   That guy is hollering in there. There's a lot of them here. He's liable to have a heart condition. You want me to go on?

| *180 volts delivered.* | He can't stand it! I'm not going to kill that man in there! You hear him hollering? He's hollering. He can't stand it. . . . I mean who is going to take responsibility if anything happens to that gentleman? |

[The experimenter accepts responsibility.] All right.

| *195 volts delivered.* | You see he's hollering. Hear that? Gee, I don't know. *[The experimenter says: "The experiment requires that you go on."]* I know it does, sir, but I mean—Hugh—he don't know what he's in for. He's up to 195 volts. |

210 volts delivered.

225 volts delivered.

240 volts delivered. (p. 67)

This experimental manipulation generated "extraordinary tension" (Milgram, 1963):

Subjects were observed to sweat, tremble, stutter, bite their lips, groan and dig their fingernails into their flesh. . . . Full-blown, uncontrollable seizures were observed for 3 subjects. One . . . seizure [was] so violently convulsive that it was necessary to call a halt to the experiment [for that individual]. (p. 375)

An observer (behind a one-way mirror) reported, "I observed a mature and initially poised businessman enter the laboratory smiling and confident. Within 20 minutes he was reduced to a twitching, stuttering wreck, who was rapidly approaching a point of nervous collapse" (p. 377).

Psychologist Diana Baumrind (1964) disagreed sharply with Milgram's approach, concluding that the emotional disturbance subjects experienced was "potentially harmful because it could easily effect an alteration in the subject's self-image or ability to trust adult authorities in the future" (p. 422). Stanley Milgram (1964) quickly countered, "As the experiment progressed there was no indication of injurious effects in the subjects; and as the subjects themselves strongly endorsed the experiment, the judgment I made was to continue the experiment" (p. 849).

When Milgram (1964) surveyed the subjects in a follow-up, 83.7% endorsed the statement that they were "very glad" or "glad" "to have been in the experiment," 15.1% were "neither sorry nor glad," and just 1.3% were "sorry" or "very sorry" to have participated (p. 849). Interviews by a psychiatrist a year later found no evidence "of any traumatic reactions" (Milgram, 1974, p. 197). Subsequently, Milgram (1974) argued that "the central moral justification for allowing my experiment is that it was judged acceptable by those who took part in it" (p. 21).

Milgram (1974) also attempted to minimize harm to subjects with postexperimental procedures "to assure that the subject would leave the laboratory in a state of well-being" (p. 374). A friendly reconciliation was arranged between the subject and the victim, and an effort was made to reduce any tensions that arose as a result of the experiment. In some cases, the "dehoaxing" (or *debriefing*) discussion was extensive, and all subjects were promised (and later received) a comprehensive report (p. 849).

In a later article, Baumrind (1985) dismissed the value of the self-reported "lack of harm" of subjects who had been willing to participate in the experiment—and noted that 16% did *not* endorse the statement that they were "glad" they had participated in the experiment (p. 168). Baumrind also argued that research indicates most students who have participated in a deception experiment report a decreased trust in authorities as a result—a tangible harm in itself.

Many social scientists, ethicists, and others concluded that Milgram's procedures had not harmed the subjects and so were justified for the knowledge they produced, but others sided with Baumrind's criticisms (A. G. Miller, 1986). What is your opinion at this point? Does Milgram's debriefing process relieve your concerns? Are you as persuaded by the subjects' own endorsement of the procedures, as was Milgram?

Obtain Informed Consent

The requirement of informed consent is also more difficult to define than it first appears. To be informed consent, it must be given by the persons who are competent to consent, can consent voluntarily, are fully informed about the research, and comprehend what they have been told (Reynolds, 1979). Still, even well-intentioned researchers may not foresee all the potential problems and may not point them out in advance to potential participants (Baumrind, 1985). In Zimbardo's prison simulation study, all the participants signed consent forms, but they were not fully informed in advance about potential risks. The researchers themselves did not realize that the study participants would experience so much stress so quickly, that some prisoners would have to be released for severe negative reactions within the first few days, or that even those who were not severely stressed would soon be begging to be released from the mock prison. But on the other hand, are you concerned that real harm "could result from *not doing* research on destructive obedience" and other troubling human behavior (A. G. Miller, 1986, p. 138)?

> Informed consent: When a competent research participant voluntarily agrees to participate in a study

Obtaining informed consent creates additional challenges for researchers. The language of the consent form must be clear and understandable to the research participants yet sufficiently long and detailed to explain what will actually happen in the research. Exhibit 3.6 and Exhibit 3.7 illustrate two different approaches to these trade-offs.

Consent Form A was approved by the University of Delaware IRB for in-depth interviews with individuals about their experiences after release from prison. Consent Form B is the one used by Philip Zimbardo. It is brief and to the point, leaving out many of the details that current standards for the protection of human subjects require. Zimbardo's consent form also released the researchers from any liability for problems arising out of the research (such a statement is no longer allowed).

As in Milgram's (1963) study, experimental researchers whose research design requires some type of subject deception try to minimize disclosure of experimental details by withholding some information before the experiment begins but then debrief subjects at the end. In the debriefing, the researcher explains to the subjects what happened in the experiment and why and then addresses participants' concerns or questions. A carefully designed debriefing procedure can help the research participants learn from the experimental research and grapple constructively with feelings elicited by the realization that they were deceived (Sieber, 1992). However, even though debriefing can be viewed as a substitute, in some cases, for securing fully informed consent prior to the experiment, debriefed subjects who disclose the nature of the experiment to other participants can contaminate subsequent results (Adair, Dushenko, & Lindsay, 1985). Unfortunately, if the debriefing process is delayed, the ability to lessen any harm resulting from the deception may also be compromised.

If you were to serve on your university's IRB, would you allow this type of research to be conducted? Can students who are asked to participate in research by their professor be considered able to give informed consent? Do you consider informed consent to be meaningful if the true purpose or nature of an experimental manipulation is not revealed?

The process and even possibility of obtaining informed consent must take into account the capacity of prospective participants to give informed consent. For example, children cannot legally give consent to participate in research. We will talk about research with children and with prisoners, another group that requires special protections, later in this chapter. There are also special protections for other populations that are likely to be vulnerable to

Exhibit 3.6   Consent Form A

INFORMED CONSENT

ROADS DIVERGE: LONG-TERM PATTERNS OF RELAPSE, RECIDIVISM, AND DESISTANCE FOR A RE-ENTRY COHORT
(National Institute of Justice, 2008-IJ-CX-0017)

PURPOSE: You are one of approximately 300 people being asked to participate in a research project conducted by the Center for Drug and Alcohol Studies at the University of Delaware. You were part of the original study of offenders in Delaware leaving prison in the 1990s, and we want to find out how things in your life have changed since that time. The overall purpose of this research is to help us understand what factors lead to changes in criminal activity and drug use over time.

PROCEDURES: If you agree to take part in this study, you will be asked to complete a survey, which will last approximately 60 to 90 minutes. We will ask you to provide us with some contact information so that we can locate you again if we are able to do another follow-up study in the future. You will be asked about your employment, family history, criminal involvement, health history, drug use, and how these have changed over time. We will use this information, as well as information that you have previously provided or which is publicly available. We will not ask you for the names of anyone, or the specific dates or specific places of any of your activities. The interviews will be tape-recorded, but you will not be identified by name on the tape. The tapes will be stored in a locked cabinet until they can be transcribed to an electronic word processor. After the tapes have been transcribed and checked for accuracy, they will be destroyed. Anonymous transcribed data will be kept indefinitely—no audio data will be kept.

RISKS: There are some risks to participating in this study. You may experience distress or discomfort when asked questions about your drug use, criminal history, and other experiences. Should this occur, you may choose not to answer such questions. If emotional distress occurs, our staff will make referrals to services you may need, including counseling and drug abuse treatment and support services.

The risk that confidentiality could be broken is a concern, but it is very unlikely to occur. You will not be identified on the audiotape of the interview. We request that you not mention names of other people or places, but if this happens, those names will be deleted from the audiotape prior to transcription. All study materials are kept in locked file cabinets. Only three members of [the] research team will have access to study materials.

BENEFITS: You will have the opportunity to participate in an important research project, which may lead to the better understanding of what factors both help and prevent an individual's recovery from drug use and criminal activity.

COMPENSATION: You will receive $100 to compensate you for your time and travel costs for this interview.

CONFIDENTIALITY: Your records will be kept confidential. They will be kept under lock and key and will not be shared with anyone without your written permission. Your name will not appear on any data file or research report.

A Privacy Certificate has been approved by the U.S. Department of Justice. The data will be protected from being revealed to non-research interests by court subpoena in any federal, state, or local civil, criminal, administrative, legislative or other proceedings.

You should understand that a Privacy Certificate does not prevent you or a member of your family from voluntarily releasing information about yourself or your involvement in this research. If you give anyone written consent to receive research information, then we may not use the Certificate to withhold that information.

The Privacy Certificate does not prevent research staff from voluntary disclosures to authorities if we learn that you intend to harm yourself or someone else. These incidents would be reported as required by state and federal law. However, we will not ask you questions about these areas.

Because this research is paid for by the National Institute of Justice, staff of this research office may review copies of your records, but they also are required to keep that information confidential.

RIGHT TO QUIT THE STUDY: Participation in this research project is voluntary and you have the right to leave the study at any time. The researchers and their assistants have the right to remove you from this study if needed.

You may ask and will receive answers to any questions concerning this study. If you have any questions about this study, you may contact Ronet Bachman or Daniel O'Connell at (302) 831-6107. If you have any questions about your rights as a research participant, you may contact the Chairperson of the University of Delaware's Human Subjects Review Board at (302) 831-2136.

CONSENT TO BE INTERVIEWED

I have read and understand this form (or it has been read to me), and I agree to participate in the in-depth interview portion of this research project.

_____
Participant Signature   Date

_____
Signature of Witness/Interviewer   Date

CONSENT TO BE CONTACTED IN FUTURE

I have read and understand this form (or it has been read to me), and I agree to be recontacted in the future as part of this research project.

_____
Participant Signature   Date

_____
Signature of Witness/Interviewer   Date

Ronet D. Bachman, PhD

Principal Investigator

University of Delaware

Telephone: (302) 831-2181

Source: National Institute of Justice

Exhibit 3.7 Consent Form B

CONSENT

Prison Life Study
Dr. Zimbardo
August 1971

_____

(date) (name of volunteer)

I, _____, the undersigned, hereby consent to participate as a volunteer in a prison life study research project to be conducted by the Stanford University Psychology Department.

The nature of the research project has been fully explained to me, including, without limitation, the fact that paid volunteers will be randomly assigned to the roles of either "prisoners" or "guards" for the duration of the study. I understand that participation in the research project will involve a loss of privacy, that I will be expected to participate for the full duration of the study, that I will only be released from participation for reasons of health deemed adequate by the medical advisers to the research project or for other reasons deemed appropriate by Dr. Philip Zimbardo, Principal Investigator of the project, and that I will be expected to follow directions from staff members of the project or from other participants in the research project.

(Continued)

(Continued)

I am submitting myself for participation in this research project with full knowledge and understanding of the nature of the research project and of what will be expected of me. I specifically release the Principal Investigator and the staff members of the research project, Stanford University, its agents and employees, and the Federal Government, its agents and employees, from any liability to me arising in any way out of my participation in the project.

_____

(signature of volunteer)

Witness: _____

If volunteer is a minor: _____

(signature of person authorized to consent for volunteer)

Witness: _____

_____

(relationship to volunteer)

coercion—pregnant women, mentally disabled persons, and educationally or economically disadvantaged persons.

Avoid Deception in Research, Except in Limited Circumstances

Deception: Used in social experiments to create more "realistic" treatments in which the true purpose of the research is not disclosed to participants, often within the confines of a laboratory

Deception occurs when subjects are misled about research procedures in an effort to determine how they would react to the treatment if they were not research subjects. In other words, researchers deceive their subjects when they believe that knowledge of the experimental premise may actually change the subjects' behavior. Deception is a critical component of many experiments, in part because of the difficulty of simulating real-world stresses and dilemmas in a laboratory setting. The goal is to get subjects "to accept as true what is false or to give a false impression" (Korn, 1997, p. 4). In Milgram's (1963) experiment, for example, deception seemed necessary because the subjects could not be permitted to administer real electric shocks to the "student," yet it would not have made sense to order the subjects to do something that they didn't find to be so troubling. Milgram (1992) insisted that the deception was absolutely essential. The results of many other experiments would be worthless if subjects understood what was really happening to them while the experiment was in progress. The real question is this: Is that sufficient justification to allow the use of deception?

What scientific or educational or applied value would make deception justifiable, even if there is some potential for harm? Who determines whether a nondeceptive intervention is "equally effective" (A. G. Miller, 1986, p. 103)? How much risk, discomfort, or unpleasantness might be seen as affecting willingness to participate? When should a postexperimental attempt to correct any misconception due to deception be deemed sufficient?

Can you see why an IRB, representing a range of perspectives, is an important tool for making reasonable, ethical research decisions when confronted with such ambiguity?

Maintain Privacy and Confidentiality

Maintaining privacy and confidentiality is another key ethical standard for protecting research participants, and the researcher's commitment to that standard should be included in the informed consent agreement (Sieber, 1992). Procedures to protect each subject's privacy, such as locking records and creating special identifying codes, must be created to minimize the risk of access by unauthorized persons. However, statements about confidentiality should be realistic: In some cases, laws allow research records to be subpoenaed and may require reporting child abuse; a researcher may feel compelled to release information if a health- or life-threatening situation arises and participants need to be alerted. Also, the standard of confidentiality does not apply to observation in public places and information available in public records.

There are two exceptions to some of these constraints: The National Institute of Justice can issue a **privacy certificate**, and the National Institutes of Health can issue a **certificate of confidentiality**. Both of these documents protect researchers from being legally required to disclose confidential information. Researchers who are focusing on high-risk populations or behaviors, such as crime, substance abuse, sexual activity, or genetic information, can request such a certificate. Suspicions of child abuse or neglect must still be reported, as well as instances where respondents may immediately harm themselves or others. In some states, researchers also may be required to report crimes such as elder abuse (Arwood & Panicker, 2007).

The Health Insurance Portability and Accountability Act (HIPAA), passed by Congress in 1996, created much more stringent regulations for the protection of health care data. As implemented by the U.S. DHHS in 2000 (and revised in 2002), the HIPAA Final Privacy Rule applies to oral, written, and electronic information that "relates to the past, present, or future physical or mental health or condition of an individual." The HIPAA rule requires that researchers have valid authorization for any use or disclosure of protected health information (PHI) from a health care provider. Waivers of authorization can be granted in special circumstances (Cava, Cushman, & Goodman, 2007).

Privacy certificate: National Institute of Justice document that protects researchers from being legally required to disclose confidential information

Certificate of confidentiality: National Institutes of Health document that protects researchers from being legally required to disclose confidential information

Benefits of Research Should Outweigh Risks

As you can see, scientists must consider the uses to which their research is put. Although many scientists believe that personal values should be left outside the laboratory, some feel that it is proper—even necessary—for scientists to concern themselves with the way their research is used.

Milgram made it clear that he was concerned about the phenomenon of obedience precisely because of its implications for people's welfare. As you have already learned, his first article (Milgram, 1963) highlighted the atrocities committed under the Nazis by citizens and soldiers who were "just following orders." In his more comprehensive book on the obedience experiments (Milgram, 1974), he also argued that his findings shed light on the atrocities committed in the Vietnam War at My Lai, slavery, the destruction of the American Indian population, and the internment of Japanese Americans during World War II. Milgram makes no explicit attempt to "tell us what to do" about this problem. In fact, as a dispassionate social scientist, Milgram (1974) tells us, "What the present study [did was] to give the dilemma [of obedience to authority] contemporary form by treating it as subject matter for experimental inquiry, and with the aim of understanding rather than judging it from a moral standpoint" (p. xi). His research highlighted the extent of obedience to authority and identified multiple factors that could be manipulated to lessen blind obedience, and Burger's (2009) replication has unfortunately shown that people are no less willing to engage in such behavior than they were then.

The evaluation research by Lawrence Sherman and Richard Berk (1984) on the police response to domestic violence provides an interesting cautionary tale about the uses of science. As you will recall from Chapter 2, the results of this field experiment indicated that those who were arrested were less likely to subsequently commit violent acts against their partners. Sherman (1992) explicitly cautioned police departments not to adopt mandatory arrest policies based solely on the results of the Minneapolis experiment, but the results were publicized in the mass media and encouraged many jurisdictions to change their policies (Binder & Meeker, 1993; Lempert, 1989). Although we now know that the original finding of a deterrent effect of arrest did not hold up in other cities where the experiment was repeated, Sherman (1992) later suggested that implementing mandatory arrest policies might have prevented some subsequent cases of spouse abuse. JoAnn Miller's (2003) analysis of victims' experiences and perceptions concerning their safety after the mandatory arrest experiment in Dade County, Florida, found that victims reported less violence if their abuser had been arrested (or assigned to a police-based counseling program called Safe Streets; Exhibit 3.8). Should this Dade County finding be publicized in the popular press so it could be used to improve police policies? What about the results of the other replication studies where arrest led to increased domestic assault? The answers to such questions are never easy.

Social scientists who conduct research on behalf of specific organizations may face additional difficulties when the organization, instead of the researcher, controls the final report and the publicity it receives. If organizational leaders decide that particular research results are unwelcome, the researcher's desire to have findings used appropriately and reported fully can conflict with contractual obligations. Researchers can often anticipate such dilemmas in advance and resolve them when the contract for research is negotiated—or simply decline a particular research opportunity altogether. But other times, such problems come up only after a report has been drafted or the problems are ignored by a researcher who needs a job or needs to maintain particular professional relationships.

The withholding of a beneficial treatment from some subjects also is a cause for ethical concern. Recall that the Sherman and Berk (1984) experiment required the random assignment of subjects to treatment conditions and thus had the potential of causing harm to the victims of domestic violence whose batterers were not arrested. The justification for the study design, however, is quite persuasive: The researchers didn't know prior to the experiment which response to a domestic-violence complaint would be most likely to deter future incidents (Sherman, 1992). The experiment provided clear evidence about the value of arrest, so it can be argued that the benefits outweighed the risks.

In later chapters, we will continue to highlight the ethical dilemmas faced by research that uses particular types of methods. Before we begin our examination of various research methods, however, we first want to introduce you to the primary philosophies.

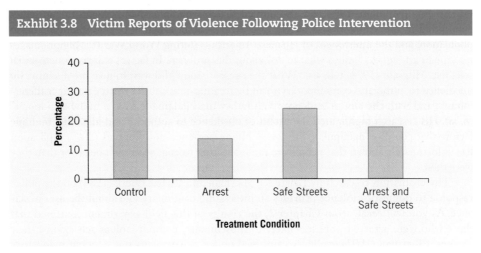

Exhibit 3.8   Victim Reports of Violence Following Police Intervention

Source: Adapted from Miller, J. (2003): 704.

MORE ON THE INSTITUTIONAL REVIEW BOARD (IRB)

How can we be certain that researchers abide by these ethical guidelines? Today, federal regulations require that every institution that seeks federal funding for biomedical or behavioral research on human subjects have an institutional review board (IRB) that reviews research proposals involving human subjects—including data about living individuals. According to federal regulations [45 CFR 46.102(d)], research is "a systematic investigation . . . designed to develop or contribute to generalizable knowledge," and according to the DHHS [45 CFR 46.102 (f)], a human subject is "a living individual about whom an investigator (whether professional or student) conducting research obtains data through intervention or interaction with the individual or just identifiable private information." The IRB determines whether a planned activity is research or involves human subjects.

IRBs at universities and other agencies apply ethical standards that are set by federal regulations but can be expanded or specified by the institution's IRB and involve all research at the institution irrespective of the funding source (Sieber, 1992, pp. 5, 10). The IRB has the authority to require changes in a research protocol or to refuse to approve a research protocol if it deems human subjects' protections inadequate. Consent forms must include contact information for the IRB, and the IRB has the authority to terminate a research project that violates the procedures the IRB approved or that otherwise creates risks for human subjects. The Office for Protection From Research Risks, National Institutes of Health, monitors IRBs, with the exception of research involving drugs (which is the responsibility of the U.S. Food and Drug Administration).

To promote adequate review of ethical issues, the regulations require that IRBs include at least five members, with at least one nonscientist and one from outside the institution (Speiglman & Spear 2009, p. 124). The new regulations for IRBs also stipulate that they "shall be sufficiently qualified through the experience and expertise of its members, including race, gender, and cultural backgrounds and sensitivity to such issues as community attitudes, to promote respect for its advice and counsel in safeguarding the rights and welfare of human subjects (*Federal Register*, 2017, p. 7263). When research is reviewed concerning populations vulnerable to coercion or undue influence, such as prisoners, the IRB must include a member knowledgeable about that population (Chadwick, 2017, p. 4). Sensitivity to community attitudes and training in human subjects protection procedures is also required (Selwitz, Epley, & Erickson, 2013).

Every member of an institution with an IRB—including faculty, students, and staff at a college or university—must submit a proposal to their IRB before conducting research with identifiable people. The IRB proposal must include research instruments and consent forms, as applicable, as well as enough detail about the research design to convince the IRB members that the potential benefits of the research outweigh any risks (Speiglman & Spear, 2009, p. 124). Most IRBs also require that researchers complete a training program about human subjects, usually the Collaborative Institutional Training Initiative (CITI) at the University of Miami (about.citiprogram.org/en/homepage). CITI training is divided into topical modules ranging from history, ethical principles, and informed consent to vulnerable populations, Internet-based research, educational research, and records-based research. Each IRB determines which CITI training modules researchers at its institution must complete.

RESEARCH INVOLVING SPECIAL POPULATIONS: CHILDREN AND PRISONERS

As you might imagine, there are special protections for certain segments of the population, including children and individuals under some form of correctional supervision. Regardless of the study being conducted, research relying on both children and prisoners usually requires a full review by an IRB.

Research With Children: By regulatory definition, any person under 18 years old is considered to be a child and, as such, has not attained the legal age for consent to treatments and procedures involved in research. Generally, IRBs analyze the same considerations as they would for other research participants, including whether the research benefits gained are worth the risks involved. The issue of informed consent, however, must be handled differently as children cannot legally provide their own consent to participate in a study. To conduct research on children, active parental consent usually is required before the child can be approached directly about the research. In active consent, parents or guardians of a child being asked to participate in a study must sign a consent form. As you might imagine, adding this requirement to a research project can dramatically reduce participation because many parents simply do not bother to respond to mailed consent forms. For example, Sloboda and colleagues (2009) used an active consent procedure for gaining parental consent along with student assent: Parents and students both had to sign forms before the student could participate. The result was that only 58% of the 34,000 eligible seventh-grade students were enrolled in the study.

When Leakey, Lunde, Koga, and Glanz (2004) were conducting research on a smoking prevention effort for middle school students, they were creative in getting parental consent forms returned. When the project began in the seventh grade, the researchers gave students project information and a consent card to take home to their parents. A pizza party was then held in every class where at least 90% of the students returned a signed consent card. In subsequent follow-ups in the eighth grade, a reminder letter was sent to parents whose children had previously participated. Classes with high participation rates also received a candy thank you. As you can see in Exhibit 3.9, the result was a very high rate of participation.

IRBs sometimes allow the use of a passive consent procedure—students can participate as long as their parents do not return a form indicating their lack of consent—which can result in much higher rates of participation. In fact, based on Article 12 of the 1989 United Nations

Exhibit 3.9 Parental Consent Response Rates and Outcomes

Survey	Population Size[a]	Consent to Parents[b]	Consent Returned[c]	Refused Consent[d]	Consent to Participate	Student Assent "Yes"[e]
7th-grade baseline[f]	4,741	4,728	89.5% (*n* = 4,231)	7.3% (*n* = 310)	92.7% (*n* = 3,921)	99.4% (*n* = 3,716)
8th-grade baseline[g]	4,222	421	58.0% (*n* = 244)	11.9% (*n* = 29)	88.1% (*n* = 215)	99.0% (*n* = 3,235)
8th-grade follow-up[g]	3,703	177	41.8% (*n* = 74)	5.4% (*n* = 4)	94.6% (*n* = 70)	98.7% (*n* = 2,999)

Source: Leakey, Tricia, Kevin B. Lunde, Karin Koga, and Karen Glanz. 2004. "Written Parental Consent and the Use of Incentives in a Youth Smoking Prevention Trial: A Case Study From Project SPLASH." *American Journal of Evaluation* 25: 509–523.

Note: Parents who had refused participation at the previous survey point were again contacted for permission at the next survey point.

a. Number of students who were enrolled in the program varies over time depending on enrollment and teacher participation rates.

b. Number of consent forms that were handed out at each time period to new students.

c. Out of the total number of consent forms distributed.

d. Out of the total number of consent forms returned.

e. Out of all students who had parental consent and were present on the day of the survey.

f. Project staff explained and distributed consent on site.

g. Teachers explained and distributed consent.

Convention on the Rights of the Child (UNCROC), which acknowledged that children are people who have a right to be heard, there has been an increased push for children to have their voices heard in research. Carroll-Lind, Chapman, and Raskauskas (2011) in New Zealand attempted just that when they surveyed children aged 9 to 13 years about their experiences with violence. They utilized a passive consent procedure that facilitated the right of children to report on their experiences of violence. To defend their use of this method, they stated,

> The Ethics Committee carefully weighed and gave credence to the issue of children's rights to protection and acknowledged and confirmed Article 12 of the UNCROC that grants children the right to speak on matters that concern them. Active consent could have compromised both of these rights. The view was held that protecting the rights of children was more important than parental rights to privacy regarding abuse in the home. (p. 7)

Research With Prisoners: Because individuals under the supervision of a correctional system are under constraints that could affect their ability to voluntarily consent to participate in research, there are also special protections for these populations. The U.S. DHHS has imposed strict limits on the involvement of prisoners as research subjects unless the research is material to their lives as prisoners. The term *prisoner*, as defined by DHHS, is as follows:

> A prisoner means any individual involuntarily confined or detained in a penal institution. The term is intended to encompass individuals sentenced to such an institution under criminal or civil statute, individuals detained in other facilities by virtue of statutes or commitment procedures which provide alternatives to criminal prosecution or incarceration in a penal institution, and individuals detained pending arraignment, trial, or sentencing. (Kiefer, 2015, p. 2)

Included are those in hospitals or alcohol and drug treatment facilities under court order. Individuals in work release programs and in at-home detention programs also qualify as prisoners. The definition applies to minors as well as to adults.

Although regulations restrict participation of prisoners to research that is material to their lives, this actually includes a great deal of research. For example, they can participate in research examining many issues including but not limited to the following: the possible causes, effects, and processes of incarceration and of criminal behavior; research on conditions particularly affecting prisoners as a class, such as research on diseases such as hepatitis and substance abuse; and all research that has the intent of improving their health and well-being.

Voluntary consent is an important issue with research involving prisoners. IRBs ensure that the decision to take part in research can have no effect on an inmate's future treatment and/or parole decision. The use of incentives for prisoners is also judged differently compared with incentives for the general population. For example, while a $10 incentive to participate may not seem like a lot to someone not in prison, the maximum wage in many state prisons is only $1 per day, so a $10 incentive is a great deal indeed! In research one of the authors just completed on examining the factors related to desistance from substance abuse and crime, former inmates who were not currently under correctional supervision were given $100 to travel to the research office for a 3-hour interview, and those who were still in prison were provided $20 in their prison spending accounts (Bachman, Kerrison, O'Connell, & Paternoster, 2013). The IRB in this case deemed that the $100 would serve to unduly influence inmates to participate in the study, since it was comparable to five months' pay in prison.

In sum, both research involving children and prisoners represent special cases for IRBs to consider when evaluating the benefits and potential harms of a study. Typically, when proposals come before IRBs that involve these special populations, there are special representatives in place who ensure their rights are protected.

Case Studies: Sexual Solicitation of Adolescents and Milgram Revisited

After reading this chapter, you may think that the ethical dilemmas from the past have been remedied by the new regulations and oversights. However, research organizations and IRBs around the world have to make decisions every day about whether the benefits of research outweigh the risks imposed to human subjects. For researchers interested in examining criminal, deviant, or otherwise hidden subcultures, obtaining informed consent is often a dubious enterprise. In addition, the growth of the Internet has provided new frontiers for observing and engaging in online communications in such forums as blogs and online chat rooms. In fact, David Calvey (2014) has described the cyber world as "a covert playground, where social researchers typically 'lurk' in order to explore this area" (p. 546). This research has generated renewed debate about informed consent and deception. Of course, some researchers contend that covert research that does not obtain voluntary consent is necessary and justified because the information would otherwise be closed to research and/or because alerting participants that they are being studied would change their behavior or put researchers at risk (Pearson, 2009). A few contemporary case studies will illuminate these ethical dilemmas well.

The first research example comes from studies examining Internet chatrooms and pedophilia. Research indicates that sexual or romantic relationships between adults and adolescents sometimes are initiated in Internet chat rooms. In fact, reality television shows like *To Catch a Predator* impersonated underage people to solicit male adults over the Internet. Of course, many police organizations (including the FBI) utilize such methods, and investigative journalists (like those who developed *To Catch a Predator*) do not have to go through an IRB for permission. But what about researchers who do? To more fully understand these chat room solicitations, Bergen, Antfolk, Jern, Alanko, and Santtila (2013) examined how adult male chat room visitors reacted to children and adolescents (they were adults posing as children) in three chat rooms. They wanted to determine whether the age of the child affected whether the adults continued to engage in sexual conversation or pursued a meeting after finding out the ages of the impersonated children. The impersonators pretended to be either 10, 12, 14, 16, or 18 years of age.

The researchers hypothesized that the older the impersonated child was, the more likely it was that adult males would express sexual interest and suggest meeting offline. All chat rooms were free and did not require registration, and one had a homosexual orientation while the other two were heterosexual in nature. Results indicated that the adult males were more likely to engage in sexual conversation and that face-to-face meetings were more likely suggested for impersonators who were 16 or older. Moreover, almost half of the adult males (46%) stopped the conversation after they learned that the impersonator was 10 or 12. However, quite disturbingly, 1 in 5 adults still expressed continuing a sexual conversation even when impersonators divulged their age to be under 13. This research confirmed previous research findings that sexual predators are more likely to solicit older adolescents; however, it revealed that there is a nontrivial percentage of predators who are not deterred from soliciting children as young as 10 years of age.

Was this knowledge worth the lack of informed consent and deception in the research? Bergen and her colleagues (2013) were aware of the ethical dilemmas but concluded that

> the value of the results from the present study would be higher than the possible harm. . . . Also, it should be noted, that we had no means (nor any interest in) gaining any information that could lead to a positive identification of those engaging in conversation, thus ensuring absolute anonymity in the study. (p. 108)

Do you agree?

You may also be surprised to learn that a few IRBs have allowed both Milgram's obedience experiment and Zimbardo's prison experiment to be replicated with the addition of more human subject protections. For example, Jerry Burger replicated Milgram's experiment with several modifications (Burger, 2009). In the experiment, the following protections were implemented: (1) No subject was allowed to go beyond the 150-volt mark; (2) a two-step screening process was used to exclude any individuals who might have a negative reaction to the experience; (3) participants were told at these two times that they could withdraw from the study at any time and still receive their $50 for participation; (4) participants were monitored by a clinical psychologist to identify excessive stress; and (5) participants were told immediately after the experiment that the "learner" had received no shocks. After all of these safeguards were implemented, the IRB at Santa Clara University, where Dr. Burger is a faculty member, approved the project. Somewhat troubling, results indicated that obedience rates in this 2006 replication were only slightly lower than those Milgram found. In fact, the majority of both men and women continued after the limit of 150 volts was reached. If you had been serving on an IRB, would you have determined that the benefits learned from this study outweighed the potential costs?

Maria Palazuelos Jorganes, PhD, Director of Research Compliance, University of Delaware

Maria Palazuelos Jorganes

The opportunity to conduct research brought Maria Palazuelos Jorganes to the U.S. from Europe. She completed her PhD in chemical engineering at the University of Florida (UF) investigating toxicity of nanomaterials at the cellular level. During her graduate studies, she developed her understanding of the scientific process, learned the importance of a methodic approach to knowledge, and honed her problem-solving abilities.

The experience provided her with a strong foundation and transferable skills that could be applied to any career path. While the classical path after her PhD may have been to pursue a job in industry, Maria accepted a management position as a research administrator of a diverse research portfolio for NSF-funded industry–university cooperative centers at UF. She enjoyed the stimulation of the academic environment so much that she changed her career trajectory.

Maria is now the director of research compliance at the University of Delaware (UD). In this role, she oversees and facilitates the ethical conduct of all research at UD. The protection of human subjects in research and the support of the Institutional Review Board (IRB) is one of her major responsibilities. Ensuring research is proposed and conducted according to the governing rules and the ethical principles upheld by the different committees charged with research review and approval is critical to the proper advancement of knowledge.

Her advice to students learning and practicing research is the following:

Keep an open mind about your own professional and personal future. A strong foundation in the scientific method and a passion for lifelong learning will enable you to make your own path. I personally never thought work on particle technology and surface science would take me to where I am today. The practical implementation of laws and ethical codes related to research are complex and technical in nature and require the input of both scientists and researchers. Being able to read and understand empirical studies from different fields has been critical to my career.

CAREERS AND RESEARCH

CONCLUSION

The extent to which ethical issues present methodological challenges for researchers varies dramatically with the type of research design. Survey research, in particular, creates few ethical problems. In fact, researchers from Michigan's Institute for Social Research Survey Center interviewed a representative national sample of adults and found that 68% of those who had participated in a survey were somewhat or very interested in participating in another; the more times respondents had been interviewed, the more willing they were to participate again. Presumably, they would have felt differently if they had been treated unethically. On the other hand, as we have also seen, some experimental studies in the social sciences that have put people in uncomfortable or embarrassing situations have generated vociferous complaints and years of debate about ethics.

The evaluation of ethical issues in a research project should be based on a realistic assessment of the overall potential for harm and benefit to research subjects rather than an apparent inconsistency between any particular aspect of a research plan and a specific ethical guideline. For example, full disclosure of what is really going on in an experimental study is unnecessary if subjects are unlikely to be harmed. Nevertheless, researchers should make every effort to foresee all possible risks and to weigh the possible benefits of the research against these risks. They should consult with individuals with different perspectives to develop a realistic risk–benefit assessment, and they should try to maximize the benefits to, as well as minimize the risks for, subjects of the research (Sieber, 1992).

Ultimately, these decisions about ethical procedures are not just up to you, as a researcher, to make. Your university's IRB sets the human subjects protection standards for your institution and will require researchers—even, in most cases, students—to submit their research proposal to the IRB for review. So we leave you with the instruction to review the human subjects guidelines of the ACJS or other professional associations in your field, consult your university's procedures for the conduct of research with human subjects, and then proceed accordingly.

KEY TERMS

Academy of Criminal Justice Sciences (ACJS) Code of Ethics   51
Belmont Report   50
Beneficence   50
Certificate of confidentiality   59
Debriefing   52
Deception   58

Federal Policy for the Protection of Human Subjects (Common Rule)   50
Informed consent   55
Institutional review board (IRB)   50
Justice (in research)   50
Nuremberg war crimes trials   48

Philip Zimbardo's Stanford Prison Experiment   48
Privacy certificate   59
Respect for persons   50
Stanley Milgram's experiments on obedience to authority   48
Tuskegee syphilis experiment   50

HIGHLIGHTS

- Philip Zimbardo's prison simulation study and Stanley Milgram's obedience experiments led to an intensive debate about the extent to which deception could be tolerated in social science research and how harm to subjects should be evaluated.

- Egregious violations of human rights by researchers, including scientists in Nazi Germany and researchers in the Tuskegee syphilis study, led to the adoption of federal ethical standards for research on human subjects.

- The 1979 Belmont Report, developed by a national commission, established three basic ethical standards for the protection of human subjects: respect for persons, beneficence, and justice.

- The DHHS adopted in 1991 a Federal Policy for the Protection of Human Subjects. This policy requires that every institution seeking federal funding for biomedical or behavioral research on human subjects have an

IRB to exercise oversight. Regulations protect special populations, including children or prisoners, whose voluntary consent is sometimes difficult to ensure.

- The ACJS standards for the protection of human subjects require avoiding harm; obtaining informed consent; avoiding deception, except in limited circumstances; and maintaining privacy and confidentiality.

- Scientific research should maintain high standards for validity and be conducted and reported in an honest and open fashion.

- Effective debriefing of subjects after an experiment can help reduce the risk of harm resulting from the use of deception in the experiment.

- Regulations protect special populations, including children and prisoners, whose voluntary consent is sometimes difficult to ensure.

Discussing Research

1. What policy would you recommend that researchers such as Sherman and Berk follow in reporting the results of their research? Should social scientists try to correct misinformation in the popular press about their research, or should they just focus on what is published in academic journals? Should researchers speak to audiences such as those at police conventions to influence policies related to their research results?

2. Now go to this book's study site (edge.sagepub.com/bachmanfrccjsr5e), and choose the "Learning from Journal Articles" option. Read one article based on research involving human subjects. What ethical issues did the research pose, and how were they resolved? Does it seem that subjects were appropriately protected?

3. Outline your own research philosophy. You can base your outline primarily on your reactions to the points you have read in this chapter, but also try to think seriously about which perspective seems the most reasonable to you.

Finding Research on the Web

1. The Collaborative Institutional Training Initiative (CITI) offers an extensive online training course in the basics of human subjects protections issues. Go to the public access CITI site (www.citiprogram.org/rcrpage.asp?affiliation=100), and complete the course in social and behavioral research. Write a short summary of what you have learned.

2. Philip Zimbardo provides extensive documentation about the Stanford Prison Experiment (www.prisonexperiment.org). Read several documents that you find on this website, and write a short report about them.

3. Read the entire ACJS Code of Ethics (www.acjs.org/?page=Code_Of_Ethics& hhSearchTerms=%22ethics%22). Discuss the meaning of each research standard.

Critiquing Research

1. Investigate the standards and operations of your university's IRB. Interview one IRB member and one researcher whose research has been reviewed by the IRB (after receiving the appropriate permissions!). How well do typical IRB meetings work to identify the ethical issues in proposed research? Do researchers feel that their proposals are treated fairly? Why, or why not?

2. How do you evaluate the current ACJS ethical code? Is it too strict, too lenient, or just about right? Are the enforcement provisions adequate? What provisions could be strengthened?

Making Research Ethical

1. Should criminologists be permitted to conduct replications of Zimbardo's prison simulation? Of Milgram's obedience experiments? Can you justify such research as permissible within the current ACJS ethical standards? If not, do you believe that these standards should be altered so as to permit this type of research?

2. Why does unethical research occur? Is it inherent in science? Does it reflect human nature? What makes ethical research more or less likely?

3. Does debriefing solve the problem of subject deception? How much must researchers reveal after the experiment is over, as well as before it begins?

Developing a Research Proposal

Now it's time to consider the potential ethical issues in your proposed study and the research philosophy that will guide your research. The following exercises involve very critical decisions in research.

1. List the elements in your research plans that an IRB might consider to be relevant to the protection of human subjects. Rate each element from "1" to "5," where "1" indicates no more than a minor ethical issue and "5" indicates a major ethical problem that probably cannot be resolved.

2. Write one page for the application to the IRB that explains how you will ensure that your research adheres to each relevant American Sociological Association standard.

3. Draft a consent form to be administered to your subjects when they enroll in your research. Use underlining and margin notes to indicate where each standard for informed consent is met.

Data for Exercise	
Dataset	**Description**
2013 YRBS.sav	The 2013 Youth Risk Behavior Survey (YRBS) is a national study of high school students. It focuses on gauging various behaviors and experiences of the adolescent population, including substance use and some victimization.

Variables for Exercise	
Variable Name	**Description**
State	The state in which the respondent lives
Schoolname	The name of the school the respondent went to
Qn23	Dichotomy based on if the respondent says they have been forced to have sex on a date in the past year, where 1 = *yes*, 0 = *no*
Qn49	Dichotomy based on if the respondent smoked marijuana in the past month, where 1 = *yes*, 0 = *no*

This time, we'll be using the YRBS 2013 subsample, which is a survey of high school students all around the United States. This survey was given to students in a classroom filled with their peers under the supervision of a trained survey administrator.

1. Let's say we'd like to see if individuals from different schools and states have higher or lower rates of sexual victimization. First, make a frequency table (analyze ->descriptives->frequencies) of the variables "state" and "schoolname."

   a. What do you see? Why do you think that the results look this way? How does this apply to what you've been reading about research ethics?

2. Calculate a frequency table for the variable "qn23," if they had been forced to have sex on a date.

a. First, what sort of ethical considerations need to be made when asking a question such as this? Bear in mind that this survey was given to students in a classroom filled with their peers under the supervision of a trained survey administrator.

   i. Consider, for instance, what the participant must be told before the survey, the setting the survey occurs in, and how datasets will be released to researchers.

b. What does this frequency table tell us about the incidence of sexual assault in the country?

c. Consider Point A again. Do you think the results in Point B might have been different if those ethical considerations hadn't been made? If yes, how so?

   i. What about in the case of "qn49"—if they'd used marijuana in the past month?

STUDENT STUDY SITE

⑤SAGE edge™

Get the tools you need to sharpen your study skills. SAGE Edge offers a robust online environment featuring an impressive array of free tools and resources. Access practice quizzes, eFlashcards, video, and multimedia at edge.sagepub.com/bachmanfrccj5e.

4

CONCEPTUALIZATION AND MEASUREMENT

> **My research methods class has already helped me. I am taking a human development class, and we are writing annotations and a synthesis for three different studies, and it's so easy to understand all the studies and data posted from SPSS! I'm even helping out a few classmates so they can include information in their annotations that they didn't understand before.**
>
> **Emma T., Student**

WHAT DO WE HAVE IN MIND?

Substance abuse is a social problem of remarkable proportions. About 18 million Americans have an alcohol use disorder (Grant et al., 2004; Hasin, Stinson, Ogburn, & Grant, 2007; National Institute on Alcohol Abuse and Alcoholism [NIAAA], 2018), and about 80,000 die every year from alcohol-related causes (NIAAA, 2018). While in college, 4 out of 10 students binge drink (Wechsler et al., 2002), and about 1 out of 3 could be diagnosed as alcohol abusers (Knight et al., 2002). Drinking is a factor in almost half of on-campus sexual assaults (Sinozich & Langton, 2014), and almost 1 in 4 victims of violence in the general population perceive their attackers to have been under the influence of drugs and/or alcohol. And finally, almost half of jail inmates report having alcohol dependence or abuse problems (Karberg & James, 2005). All told, the annual costs of prevention and treatment for alcohol and drug abuse exceed $340 billion in the United States (T. R. Miller & Hendrie, 2008). Across the globe, alcohol misuse results in about 2.5 million deaths annually (World Health Organization [WHO], 2013).

With all of these facts, we have presented several concepts including *alcohol*, *college students*, and *alcohol dependence*. While we each have our own ideas about what these concepts mean, do we all have the same idea in mind when we hear

Learning Objectives

1. Define and distinguish conceptualization, operationalization, and an indicator.

2. Identify the different forms of single questions and response choices.

3. Explain the rationale for creating multi-item indexes, and discuss the issues that should always be explored about indexes.

4. Give examples of the four levels of measurement.

5. Compare the advantages and disadvantages of the four approaches to testing the validity of measures.

6. Define four basic methods of evaluating reliability.

7. Understand the difference between measurement validity and reliability.

⬡SAGE edge™

Master the content at **edge** **.sagepub.com/bachmanfrccj5e**

these terms? For example, are community colleges classified within the term *college*? How is alcohol abuse different from dependence? The process of defining these terms in words is called **conceptualization**.

Conceptualization: The process of specifying what we mean by a term. In deductive research, conceptualization helps to translate portions of an abstract theory into testable hypotheses involving specific variables. In inductive research, conceptualization is an important part of the process used to make sense of related observations

Concept: A mental image that summarizes a set of similar observations, feelings, or ideas

CONCEPTS

Concepts such as *substance-free housing* require an explicit definition before they are used in research because we cannot be certain that all readers will share the same definition. It is even more important to define concepts that are somewhat abstract or unfamiliar. When we refer to concepts such as *poverty*, *social control*, or *strain*, we cannot be certain that others know exactly what we mean.

Clarifying the meaning of such concepts does not just benefit those unfamiliar with them; even experts often disagree about their meanings. We need not avoid using these concepts. We just have to specify clearly what we mean when we use them, and we must expect others to do the same.

Conceptualization in Practice: Defining Youth Gangs

Do you have a clear image in mind when you hear the term *youth gangs*? Although this is a very ordinary term, social scientists' attempts to define precisely the concept *youth gang* have not yet succeeded: "Neither gang researchers nor law enforcement agencies can agree on a common definition . . . and a concerted national effort . . . failed to reach a consensus" (Howell, 2003, p. 75). Exhibit 4.1 lists a few of the many alternate definitions of youth gangs.

Exhibit 4.1 Alternate Definitions of Youth Gangs

- The term gang tends to designate collectivities that are marginal members of mainstream society, loosely organized, and without a clear, social purpose. (Ball & Curry, 1995, p. 227)
- The gang is an interstitial group (between childhood and maturity) originally formed spontaneously, and then integrated through conflict. (Thrasher, 1927, p. 18)
- [A gang is] any denotable adolescent group of youngsters who (a) are generally perceived as a distinct aggregation by others in the neighborhood, (b) recognize themselves as a denotable group (almost invariably with a group name), and (c) have been involved in a sufficient number of delinquent incidents to call forth a consistently negative response from neighborhood residents and/or law enforcement agencies. (Klein, 1971, p. 13)
- A youth gang is a self-formed association of peers united by mutual interests with identifiable leadership and internal organization who act collectively or as individuals to achieve specific purposes, including the conduct of illegal activity and control of a particular territory, facility, or enterprise. (W. Miller, 1992, p. 21)
- [A gang is] an age-graded peer group that exhibits some permanence, engages in criminal activity, and has some symbolic representation of membership. (Decker &Van Winkle, 1996, p. 31)
- [A gang is] a self-identified group of kids who act corporately, at least sometimes, and violently, at least sometimes. (D. M. Kennedy, Piehl, & Braga, 1996, p. 158)
- A Criminal Street Gang is any ongoing organization, association, or group of three or more persons, whether formal or informal, having as one of its primary activities the commission of . . . criminal acts. (Street Terrorism Enforcement and Prevention Act of 1988, California Penal Code § 186.22[f])
- [A gang is] a group that has three or more members, generally aged 12–24, who share an identity, typically linked to a name and other symbols. Members view themselves as a gang and they are recognized by others as a gang. The group has some permanence and degree of organization and is involved in an elevated level of criminal activity. (National Gang Center, 2014)

As you can see, there are many different ideas about what constitutes a *gang*. What is the basis of this conceptual difficulty? Howell (2003) suggests that defining the term *youth gangs* has been difficult for four reasons:

- Youth gangs are not particularly cohesive.

- Individual gangs change their focus over time.

- Many have a "hodgepodge of features," with diverse members and unclear rules.

- There are many incorrect but popular "myths" about youth gangs. (pp. 27–28)

In addition, youth gangs are only one type of social group, and it is important to define youth gangs in a way that distinguishes them from these other types of groups—for example, childhood play groups, youth subculture groups, delinquent groups, and adult criminal organizations. Whenever you define a concept, you need to consider whether the concept is unidimensional or multidimensional. If it is multidimensional, your job of conceptualization is not complete until you have specified the related subconcepts that belong under the umbrella of the larger concept. And finally, the concept you define must capture an idea that is distinctly separate from related ideas.

FROM CONCEPTS TO VARIABLES: MEASUREMENT OPERATIONS

After defining the concepts in a theory, we can identify variables corresponding to the concepts and develop procedures to measure them. Recall that a variable is a characteristic or property that can vary (e.g., religion, socioeconomic status, self-esteem scale). This is an important step. Consider the concept of *social control*, which Donald Black (1984) defines as "all of the processes by which people define and respond to deviant behavior." What variables do you think represent this conceptualization of social control? The proportion of persons arrested in a community? The average length of sentences for crimes? Types of bystander reactions to public intoxication? Some combination of these?

Although we must proceed carefully to specify what we mean by a concept such as social control, some concepts are represented well by the specific variables in the study and therefore define themselves. We may define *binge drinking* as heavy episodic drinking and measure it, as a variable, by asking people how many drinks they consumed in succession during some period (see Wechsler, Davenport, Dowdall, Moeykens, & Castillo, 1994). That is pretty straightforward.

HOW WILL WE KNOW WHEN WE'VE FOUND IT?

After we have defined our concepts in the abstract—that is, after conceptualizing—and after we have specified the specific variables we want to measure, we must develop our measurement procedures. The goal is to devise **operations** that actually measure the concepts we intend to measure—in other words, to achieve measurement validity.

Exhibit 4.2 represents the **operationalization** process in three studies. The first researcher defines her concept (*binge drinking*) and chooses one variable (frequency of heavy episodic drinking) to represent it. This variable is then measured with responses to a single question or **indicator**: "How often within the past two weeks did you consume five or more

Operation: A procedure for identifying or indicating the value of cases on a variable

Operationalization: The process of specifying the operations that will indicate the value of a variable for each case

Indicator: The question or other operation used to indicate the value of cases on a variable

drinks containing alcohol in a row?" The second researcher defines his concept, *poverty*, as having two aspects or dimensions, subjective poverty and absolute poverty. Subjective poverty is measured with responses to a survey question: "Do you consider yourself to be poor?" Absolute poverty is measured by comparing family income with the poverty threshold. The third researcher decides that her concept, *social class*, can be indicated with three measured variables: income, education, and occupational prestige.

Good conceptualization and operationalization can prevent confusion later in the research process. For example, a researcher may find that substance abusers who join a self-help group are less likely to drink again than those who receive hospital-based substance abuse treatment. But what is it about these treatment alternatives that are associated with successful abstinence? Level of peer support? Beliefs about the causes of alcoholism? Financial investment in the treatment? If the researcher had considered such aspects of the concept of substance abuse treatment before collecting her data, she might have been able to measure different elements of treatment and then identify which, if any, were associated with differences in abstinence rates. Because she did not measure these variables, she will not contribute as much as she might have to our understanding of substance abuse treatment.

Social researchers have many options for operationalizing their concepts. Measures can be based on activities as diverse as asking people questions, reading judicial opinions, observing social interactions, coding words in books, checking census data, enumerating the contents of trash receptacles, or drawing urine and blood samples. We focus here on the operations of using published data, asking questions, observing behavior, and using unobtrusive means of measuring people's behavior and attitudes.

Using Available Data

Government reports are rich and readily accessible sources of criminal justice data, as are datasets available from nonprofit advocacy groups, university researchers, and some private businesses. For example, law enforcement and health statistics provide several community-level indicators of substance abuse (Gruenewald, Treno, Taff, & Klitzner, 1997). Statistics on arrests for the sale and possession of drugs, drunk driving arrests, and liquor law violations (such as sales to minors) can usually be obtained on an annual basis—and often quarterly—from local police departments or state crime information centers.

Still, indicators such as these cannot be compared across communities or over time without reviewing carefully how they were constructed in each community (Gruenewald et al., 1997). We also cannot assume that available data are accurate, even when they appear to measure the concept in which we are interested in a way that is consistent across communities.

Government statistics that are generated through a central agency, such as the U.S. Census Bureau, are usually of high quality, but caution is still warranted when using official

Exhibit 4.2 Concepts, Variables, and Indicators

Concept	Variable	Indicator
Binge drinking	Frequency of heavy episodic drinking	"How often within the past two weeks did you consume five or more drinks containing alcohol in a row?"
Poverty	Subjective poverty Absolute poverty	"Would you consider yourself to be poor?" Family income vs. poverty threshold
Social class	Income Education Occupational prestige	Income + education + prestige

data. Data accuracy is more of an issue for data collected by local levels of government. For example, the Uniform Crime Reports (UCR) program administered by the Federal Bureau of Investigation (FBI) imposes standard classification criteria, with explicit guidelines and regular training at the local level, but data are still inconsistent for many crimes. Different jurisdictions vary in their definition of terms such as "more than necessary force" and even in the classification of offenses as aggravated or simple assaults (Mosher, Miethe, & Phillips, 2002, p. 66). The new National Incident-Based Reporting System (NIBRS), mentioned in Chapter 1, corrects some of the problems with the UCR, but it requires much more training and documentation and has not yet been adopted by all jurisdictions (Mosher et al., 2002).

Constructing Questions

Asking people questions is the most common and probably the most versatile operation for measuring social variables. "Overall, how satisfied are you with the police in your community?" "How would you rate your current level of safety?" Most concepts about individuals are measured with these sorts of questions.

Questions can be designed with or without explicit response choices. The question that follows is considered a **closed-ended (fixed-choice) question** because respondents are offered explicit responses to choose from. It has been selected from the Core Alcohol and Drug Survey distributed by the Core Institute (Presley, Meilman, & Lyerla, 1994), Southern Illinois University.

Compared with other campuses with which you are familiar, this campus's use of alcohol is . . . (*Mark one*)

_____ Greater than for other campuses

_____ Less than for other campuses

_____ About the same as for other campuses

> **Closed-ended (fixed-choice) question:** A survey question that provides preformatted response choices for the respondent to circle or check

Response choices should be mutually exclusive and exhaustive, so that every respondent can find one—and only one—choice that applies to him or her (unless the question is of the "Check all that apply" format). To make response choices exhaustive, researchers may need to offer at least one option with room for ambiguity. For example, a questionnaire asking college students to indicate their school status should not use freshman, sophomore, junior, senior, and graduate student as the only response choices. Most campuses also have students in a "special" category, so you might add "Other (please specify)" to the five fixed responses to this question. If respondents do not find a response option that corresponds to their answer to the question, they may skip the question entirely or choose a response option that does not indicate what they are really thinking.

Most surveys of a large number of people primarily contain closed-ended questions, which are easy to process with computers and analyze with statistics. With closed-ended questions, respondents are also more likely to answer the question that the researcher really wants them to answer. Including response choices reduces ambiguity and makes it easier for respondents to answer. However, closed-ended choices may obscure what people really think if the choices do not match the range of possible responses to the question; many studies show that some respondents will choose response choices that do not apply to them simply to give some sort of answer (Peterson, 2000, p. 39). We will discuss question wording and response options in greater detail in Chapter 7.

Open-ended questions—questions without explicit response choices, to which respondents write in their answers—are preferable when the range of responses cannot adequately be anticipated. By this, we mean questions that have not previously been used in surveys and

> **Open-ended questions:** A survey question without explicit response choices

questions that are asked of new groups. Open-ended questions can also lessen confusion about the meaning of responses involving complex concepts. The question that follows is an open-ended version of the earlier closed-ended question:

How would you say alcohol use on this campus compares with that on other campuses?

Making Observations

Observations can be used to measure characteristics of individuals, events, and places. The observations may be the primary form of measurement in a study, or they may supplement measures obtained through questioning.

Robert J. Sampson and Stephen W. Raudenbush (1999) and Peter St. Jean (2007) used direct observation (and other techniques) in their studies of neighborhood disorder and crime. Teams drove in "a sport utility vehicle at a rate of five miles per hour down every street" in a sample of Chicago neighborhoods. On both sides of the vehicle, video cameras recorded activities while a trained observer completed a log for each block—a very careful method of observing phenomena termed systematic social observation (SSO) (Reiss, 1971). Sampson and Raudenbush's research resulted in 23,816 observer logs containing information about building conditions and land use, while the videotapes were coded to measure features of streets, buildings, businesses, and social interaction on 15,141 blocks. Direct observation is often the method of choice for measuring behavior in natural settings, as long as it is possible to make the requisite observations.

Systematic social observation (SSO): A strategy that increases the reliability of observational data by using explicit rules that standardize coding practices across observers

Collecting Data Through Unobtrusive Measures

Unobtrusive measures allow us to collect data about individuals or groups without their direct knowledge or participation. In their classic book (now revised), Webb et al. (Webb, Campbell, Schwartz, & Sechrest, 1966) identified four types of unobtrusive measures: physical trace evidence, archives (available data), simple observation, and contrived observation (using hidden recording hardware or manipulation to elicit a response). We will focus attention in this section on physical trace evidence and archives.

Unobtrusive measure: A measurement based on physical traces or other data that are collected without the knowledge or participation of the individuals or groups that generated the data

The physical traces of past behavior are one type of unobtrusive measure that is most useful when the behavior of interest cannot directly be observed (perhaps because it is hidden or it occurred in the past) and has not been recorded in a source of available data. To measure the prevalence of drinking in college dorms or fraternity houses, we might count the number of empty bottles of alcoholic beverages in the surrounding dumpsters. However, you can probably see that care must be taken to develop trace measures that are useful for comparative purposes. For instance, comparison of the number of empty bottles in dumpsters outside different dorms can be misleading; at the very least, you would need to take into account the number of residents in the dorms, the time since the last trash collection, and the accessibility of each dumpster to passersby.

Unobtrusive measures can also be created from such diverse forms of media as newspaper archives or magazine articles, TV or radio talk shows, legal opinions, historical documents, journals, personal letters, or e-mail messages. An investigation of the drinking climate on campuses might include a count of the amount of space devoted to ads for alcoholic beverages in a sample of issues of the student newspaper. Campus publications also might be coded to indicate the number of times that statements discouraging substance abuse appear. With this tool, you could measure the frequency of articles reporting substance abuse–related crimes, the degree of approval of drinking expressed in TV shows or songs, or the relationship between region of the country and amount of space devoted in the print media to alcohol consumption.

Combining Measurement Operations

Using available data, asking questions, making observations, and using unobtrusive indicators are interrelated measurement tools, each of which may include or be supplemented by the others. From people's answers to survey questions, the U.S. Census Bureau develops widely consulted reports containing available data on people, firms, and geographic units in the United States. Data from employee surveys may be supplemented by information available in company records. Interviewers may record observations about those whom they question. Researchers may use insights gleaned from questioning participants to make sense of the social interaction they have observed. Unobtrusive indicators can be used to evaluate the honesty of survey responses.

Questioning can be a particularly poor approach for measuring behaviors that are very socially desirable, such as voting or attending church, or that are socially stigmatized or illegal, such as abusing alcohol or drugs. **Triangulation**, the use of two or more different measures of the same variable, can strengthen measurement considerably (Brewer & Hunter, 1989). When we achieve similar results with different measures of the same variable, particularly when they are based on such different methods as survey questions and field-based observations, we can be more confident in the validity of each measure. If results diverge with different measures, it may indicate that one or more of these measures are influenced by more measurement error than we can tolerate. Divergence between measures could also indicate that they actually operationalize different concepts. An interesting example of this interpretation of divergent results comes from research on crime. Official crime statistics only indicate those crimes that are reported to and are recorded by the police; when surveys are used to measure crimes with self-reports of victims, many "personal annoyances" are included as if they were crimes (Levine, 1976). We will talk more about triangulation in Chapter 10.

> **Triangulation:** The use of multiple methods to study one research question; also used to mean the use of two or more different measures of the same variable

Case Study: Defining Inmate Misconduct

As we already highlighted in Chapter 1, it is possible to measure offending in several different ways, including with official arrest data, victimization surveys, and self-report offending data from surveys. There are different types of measurement error associated with each type of measurement tool, but generally, official data tend to indicate lower estimates compared with survey data. What if we wanted to measure offending behavior inside correctional facilities? This is an important question because one indicator of the safety of a prison or jail is often evaluated by levels of inmate offending behavior, generally termed *inmate misconduct*.

Like the victims in the general population, the detection of crime in a correctional facility is largely influenced by the willingness of victims or witnesses to report the events to authorities. Once reported, official records are also influenced by whether an incident makes it into the official record. To determine the convergence between official incident records of inmate misconduct and self-reported offending, Benjamin Steiner and John Wooldredge (2014) collected survey data from inmates, as well as official records for the same inmates, in correctional facilities in Ohio and Kentucky. They collected data for two groups of inmates: those who had previously served time and those who had not. To be eligible to participate in the survey, however, respondents had to have been in confinement for six months or longer because the survey asked about misconduct that they engaged in during the past six months. Over 5,600 inmates completed the survey.

To operationalize whether inmates had committed an assault, they were asked whether they had "physically assaulted another inmate for reasons other than because he tried to hurt you first" or "stabbed another inmate for reasons other than because he tried to hurt you first"

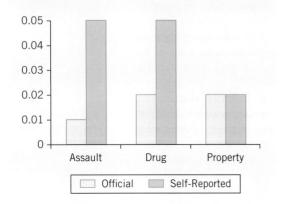

Exhibit 4.3 Comparisons of the Prevalence of Self-Reported and Official Measures of Inmate Misconduct

Source: Adapted from Steiner, B., &Wooldredge, J. (2014). Comparing self-report to official measures of inmate misconduct. *Justice Quarterly, 31*(6), 1074–1101.

(Steiner & Wooldredge, 2014, p. 1083). Official measures of assault included these behaviors, as well as attempted assaults. The authors stated, "Differences in the operational definitions of the types of offenses should be kept in mind when interpreting the findings" (p. 1084). Despite official records including attempted as well as completed assaults, results indicated that incidence of self-reported offending behavior was 80% higher than official rates of inmate-perpetrated assault. Steiner and Wooldredge also found this to be the case for drug-related offenses but not for theft-related offenses. Exhibit 4.3 summarizes their findings. As you see, how we operationalize concepts affects our findings. There are many ways we can operationalize constructs in research. We will highlight a few of them next.

HOW MUCH INFORMATION DO WE REALLY HAVE?

Whether we collect information through observations, questions, available data, or using unobtrusive measures, the data that result from our particular procedures may vary in mathematical precision. We express this level of precision as the variable's **level of measurement**. A variable's level of measurement also has important implications for the types of statistics that can be used with the variable. There are four levels of measurement: nominal, ordinal, interval, and ratio. Exhibit 4.4 depicts the differences among these four levels.

Nominal Level of Measurement

The **nominal level of measurement** (also called the *categorical* or *qualitative level*) identifies variables whose values have no mathematical interpretation; they only vary in kind or quality but not in amount. In fact, it is conventional to refer to the values of nominal variables as *attributes* instead of values. Gender is one example. The variable *gender* has two attributes (categories or qualities): male and female. We might indicate male with the value "1" and female with the value "2," but these numbers do not tell us anything about the difference between male and female, except that they are different. Female is not one unit more of gender than male nor is it twice as much gender. Ethnicity, occupation, religious affiliation, and region of the country are also measured at the nominal level. A person may be Spanish or Portuguese, but one ethnic group does not represent more ethnicity than another, just a different ethnicity. A person may be a doctor (arbitrarily valued as "4") or a truck driver (valued as "1"), but one does not represent three units more occupation than the other. The values assigned to nominal variables should be thought of as codes, not numbers.

Although the attributes of categorical variables do not have a mathematical meaning, they must be assigned to cases with great care. The attributes we use to measure, or *categorize*, cases must be mutually exclusive and exhaustive:

- A variable's attributes or values are **mutually exclusive attributes** if every case can have only one attribute.

- A variable's attributes or values are **exhaustive attributes** when every case can be classified into one of the categories.

Level of measurement: The mathematical precision with which the values of a variable can be expressed. The nominal level of measurement, which is qualitative, has no mathematical interpretation; the quantitative levels of measurement (ordinal, interval, and ratio) are progressively more precise mathematically

Nominal level of measurement: Variables whose values have no mathematical interpretation; they vary in kind or quality but not in amount

Mutually exclusive attributes: A variable's attributes or values are mutually exclusive if every case can have only one attribute

Exhaustive attributes: A variable's attributes or values in which every case can be classified as having one attribute

Exhibit 4.4   Levels of Measurement

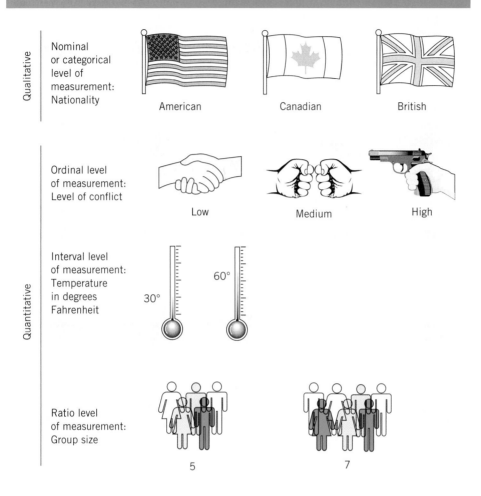

When a variable's attributes are mutually exclusive and exhaustive, every case corresponds to one and only one attribute.

Ordinal Level of Measurement

The first of the three quantitative levels is the ordinal level of measurement. At this level, the numbers assigned to cases specify only the order of the cases, permitting *greater than* and *less than* distinctions; absolute mathematical distinctions cannot be made between categories.

The properties of variables measured at the ordinal level are illustrated in Exhibit 4.4 by the contrast between the level of conflict in two groups. The first group, symbolized by two people shaking hands, has a low level of conflict. The second group, symbolized by two persons using fists against each other, has a higher level of conflict. The third group, symbolized by a hand pointing a gun has an even higher level of conflict. To measure conflict, we would put the groups "in order" by assigning the number 1 to the low-conflict group, the number 2 to the group using fists, and the number 3 to the high-conflict group using guns. The numbers thus indicate only the relative position or order of the cases. Although low level

Ordinal level of measurement: A measurement of a variable in which the numbers indicating the variable's value specify only the order of the cases, permitting *greater than* and *less than* distinctions

of conflict is represented by the number 1, it is not mathematically two fewer units of conflict than the high level of conflict, which is represented by the number 3. These numbers really have no mathematical qualities; they are just used to represent relative rank in the measurement of conflict.

As with nominal variables, the different values of a variable measured at the ordinal level must be mutually exclusive and exhaustive. They must cover the range of observed values and allow each case to be assigned no more than one value.

The Favorable Attitudes Toward Antisocial Behavior Scale measures attitudes toward antisocial behavior among high school students with a series of questions that each involves an ordinal distinction (see Exhibit 4.5). The response choices to each question range from "very wrong" to "not wrong at all"; there's no particular quantity of "wrongness" that these distinctions reflect, but the idea is that a student who responds that it is "not wrong at all" to a question about taking a handgun to school has a more favorable attitude toward antisocial behavior than does a student who says it is "a little bit wrong," which is, in turn, more favorable than those who respond "wrong" or "very wrong."

As with nominal variables, the different values of a variable measured at the ordinal level must be mutually exclusive and exhaustive. They must cover the range of observed values and allow each case to be assigned no more than one value. Often, questions that use an ordinal level of measurement simply ask respondents to rate their response to some question or statement along a continuum of, for example, strength of agreement, level of importance, or relative frequency. Like variables measured at the nominal level, variables measured at the ordinal level in this way classify cases in discrete categories and so are termed discrete measures.

A series of similar questions may be used instead of one question to measure the same concept. The set of questions in the Favorable Attitudes Toward Antisocial Behavior Scale in Exhibit 4.5 is a good example. In such a multi-item index or *scale*, numbers are assigned to reflect the order of the responses (such as 1 for "very wrong," 2 for "wrong," 3 for "a little bit wrong," and 4 for "not wrong at all"); these responses are then summed or averaged to create the index score. One person's responses to the five questions in Exhibit 4.5 could thus range from

Discrete measure: A measure that classifies cases in distinct categories

Index: A composite measure based on summing, averaging, or otherwise combining the responses to multiple questions that are intended to measure the same variable; sometimes called a *scale*

Exhibit 4.5 Example of Ordinal Measures: Favorable Attitudes Toward Antisocial Behavior Scale

1. How wrong do you think it is for someone your age to take a handgun to school?

   Very wrong   Wrong   A little bit wrong   Not wrong at all

2. How wrong do you think it is for someone your age to steal anything worth more than $5?

   Very wrong   Wrong   A little bit wrong   Not wrong at all

3. How wrong do you think it is for someone your age to pick a fight with someone?

   Very wrong   Wrong   A little bit wrong   Not wrong at all

4. How wrong do you think it is for someone your age to attack someone with the idea of seriously hurting them?

   Very wrong   Wrong   A little bit wrong   Not wrong at all

5. How wrong do you think it is for someone your age to stay away from school all day when their parents think they are at school?

   Very wrong   Wrong   A little bit wrong   Not wrong at all

Sources: **Lewis, Chandra, Gwen Hyatt, Keith Lafortune, and Jennifer Lembach. 2010.** *History of the Use of Risk and Protective Factors in Washington State's Healthy Youth Survey.* Portland, OR: RMC Research Corporation. See also Arthur, Michael W., John S. Briney, J. David Hawkins, Robert D. Abbott, Blair L. Brooke-Weiss, and Richard F. Catalano. 2007. "Measuring Risk and Protection in Communities Using the Communities That Care Youth Survey." *Evaluation and Program Planning* 30: 197–211.

5 (meaning they said each behavior is "very wrong") to 20 (meaning they said each behavior is "not wrong at all"). However, even though these are numeric scores, they still reflect an ordinal level of measurement because the responses they are based on involve only ordinal distinctions.

Interval Level of Measurement

The numbers indicating the values of a variable at the interval level of measurement represent fixed measurement units (e.g., the change in value from one unit to the next is equal and incremental) but have no absolute, or fixed, zero point. This level of measurement is represented in Exhibit 4.4 by the difference between two Fahrenheit temperatures. Although 60° is 30° hotter than 30°, 60 in this case is not twice as hot as 30. Why not? Because heat does not begin at 0 degrees on the Fahrenheit scale. The numbers can therefore be added and subtracted, but ratios between them (2 to 1, or *twice as much*) are not meaningful.

Sometimes social scientists create indexes by combining responses to a series of questions measured at the ordinal level. An index of this sort could be created with responses to the Core Institute's (2015) questions about friends' disapproval of substance use (see Exhibit 4.6). The survey has 13 questions on the topic, all of which have the same three response choices. If "Do not disapprove" is valued at 1, "Disapprove" is valued at 2, and "Strongly disapprove" is valued at 3, the summed index of disapproval would range from 13 to 39. Many social scientists would consider scores on an index like this to reflect an interval-level measure. So a score of 20 could be treated as if it were 4 more units than a score of 16.

> **Interval level of measurement:** A measurement of a variable in which the numbers indicating a variable's values represent fixed measurement units but have no absolute, or fixed, zero point

Exhibit 4.6 Ordinal-Level Variables Can Be Added to Create an Index With Interval-Level Properties: Core Alcohol and Drug Survey

How do you think your close friends feel (or would feel) about you . . . (mark one for each line)	Do Not Disapprove	Disapprove	Strongly Disapprove
a. Trying marijuana once or twice			
b. Smoking marijuana occasionally			
c. Smoking marijuana regularly			
d. Trying cocaine once or twice			
e. Taking cocaine regularly			
f. Trying LSD once or twice			
g. Taking LSD regularly			
h. Trying amphetamines once or twice			
i. Taking amphetamines regularly			
j. Taking one or two drinks of an alcoholic beverage (beer, wine, liquor) nearly every day			
k. Taking four or five drinks nearly every day			
l. Having five or more drinks in one sitting			
m. Taking steroids for bodybuilding or improved athletic performance			

Source: Core Institute. 1994. "Core Alcohol and Drug Survey: Long Form." Core Institute, Student Health Center, Southern Illinois University-Carbondale.

Ratio Level of Measurement

Ratio level of
measurement:
A measurement of a
variable in which the
numbers indicating
a variable's values
represent fixed
measuring units and an
absolute zero point

The numbers indicating the values of a variable at the ratio level of measurement represent fixed measuring units and an absolute zero point. (Zero means absolutely no amount of whatever the variable measures or represents.) For example, the following question was used on the National Minority SA/HIV Prevention Initiative Youth Questionnaire to measure number of days during the past 30 days that the respondent drank at least one alcoholic beverage. We can easily calculate the number of days that separate any response from any other response (except for the missing value of "don't know").

During the past 30 days, on how many days did you drink one or more drinks of an alcoholic beverage?

Exhibit 4.4 displays an example of a variable measured at the ratio level. The number of people in the first group is 5, and the number in the second group is 7. The ratio of the two groups' sizes is then 1.4, a number that mirrors the relationship between the sizes of the groups. Note that there does not actually have to be any group with a size of 0; what is important is that the numbering scheme begins at an absolute zero—in this case, the absence of any people. The number of days a convicted felon was sentenced to prison would represent a ratio level of measurement because sentence length begins with an absolute 0 point. The number of days an addict stays clear after treatment, too, has a ratio level of measurement.

Continuous measure:
A measure with numbers
indicating the values of
variables as points on a
continuum

For most statistical analyses in social science research, the interval and ratio levels of measurement can be treated as equivalent. In addition to having numerical values, both the interval and ratio levels also involve continuous measures: The numbers indicating the values of variables are points on a continuum, not discrete categories. But despite these similarities, there is an important difference between variables measured at the interval and ratio levels. On a ratio scale, 10 is 2 points higher than 8 and is also *2 times* greater than 5—the numbers can be compared in a ratio. Ratio numbers can be added and subtracted, and because the numbers begin at an absolute zero point, they can be multiplied and divided (so ratios can be formed between the numbers). For example, people's ages can be represented by values ranging from 0 years (or some fraction of a year) to 120 or more. A person who is 30 years old is 15 years older than someone who is 15 years old (30 − 15 = 15) and is twice as old as that person (30 ÷ 15 = 2). Of course, the numbers also are mutually exclusive and exhaustive, so that every case can be assigned one and only one value.

The Case of Dichotomies

Dichotomy: A variable
having only two values

Dichotomies, variables having only two values, are a special case from the standpoint of levels of measurement. Although variables with only two categories are generally thought of as nominally measured, we can also think of a dichotomy as indicating the presence or absence of an attribute. Suppose, for example, we were interested in differences between individuals who had never used illegal drugs in the last year and those who had used at least one illegal drug in the last year. We could create a variable that indicated this dichotomous distinction by coding those individuals who said they did not use any of the substances listed as "0" and all others as "1." Viewed in this way, there is an inherent order to the two values: In one group, the attribute of consuming illegal substances is absent (those coded "0"), and in another, it is present (those coded "1").

Comparison of Levels of Measurement

Exhibit 4.7 summarizes the types of comparisons that can be made with different levels of measurement, as well as the mathematical operations that are legitimate. All four levels of measurement allow researchers to assign different values to different cases. All three quantitative measures allow researchers to rank cases in order.

Exhibit 4.7 Properties of Measurement Levels

Relevant Level of Measurement					
Examples of Comparison Statements	Appropriate Math Operations	Nominal	Ordinal	Interval	Ratio
A is equal to (not equal to) *B*	= (≠)	✓	✓	✓	✓
A is greater than (less than) *B*	> (<)		✓	✓	✓
A is three more than (less than) *B*	+ (−)			✓	✓
A is twice (half) as large as *B*	÷ (×)				✓

An important thing to remember is that researchers *choose* levels of measurement in the process of operationalizing the variables; the level of measurement is not inherent in the variable itself. Many variables can be measured at different levels, with different procedures. For example, the Core Alcohol and Drug Survey (Core Institute, 2015) identifies binge drinking by asking students, "Think back over the last two weeks. How many times have you had five or more drinks at a sitting?" You might be ready to classify this as a ratio-level measure, but you must first examine the closed-ended options given to respondents. This is a closed-ended question, and students are asked to indicate their answer by checking *none, once, twice, 3 to 5 times, 6 to 9 times,* or *10 or more times.* Use of these categories makes the level of measurement ordinal. The distance between any two cases cannot be clearly determined. A student with a response in the *6 to 9 times* category could have binged just one more time than a student who responded with *3 to 5 times,* or he or she could have binged four more times. With these response categories, you cannot mathematically distinguish the number of times a student binged, only the relative amount of bingeing behavior.

It is usually a good idea to try to measure variables at the highest level of measurement possible. The more information available, the more ways we have to compare cases. We also have more possibilities for statistical analysis with quantitative than with qualitative variables. Thus, if doing so does not distort the meaning of the concept that is to be measured, measure at the highest level possible. For example, even if your primary concern is only to compare teenagers with young adults, measure age in years rather than in categories; you can always combine the ages later into categories corresponding to teenager and young adult.

Be aware, however, that other considerations may preclude measurement at a high level. For example, many people are very reluctant to report their exact incomes, even in anonymous questionnaires. So asking respondents to report their income in categories (such as under $10,000, $10,000–$19,999, $20,000–$29,999, etc.) will result in more responses, and thus more valid data, than asking respondents for their income in dollars.

Often, researchers treat variables measured at the interval and ratio levels as comparable. They then refer to this as the **interval-ratio level of measurement**. If you read the chapter on quantitative data analysis on the Student Study Site, you will learn that different statistical procedures are used for variables with fixed measurement units, but it usually doesn't matter whether there is an absolute zero point.

Interval-ratio level of measurement: A measurement of a variable in which the numbers indicating a variable's values represent fixed measurement units but may not have an absolute, or fixed, zero point, but it is assumed the values can be multiplied and divided

Are Teenagers Replacing Drugs With Smartphones?

As high-school-aged teens' use of smartphones and tablets has accelerated in recent years, their use of illicit drugs other than marijuana has actually been dropping. Could the first trend be responsible, to some extent, for the second? Substance abuse expert Silvia Martins of Columbia University thinks this "is quite plausible." According to Nora Volkow, the director of the National Institute on Drug Abuse, "teens can get literally high when playing these [computer] games." Teens quoted in the article agreed, but other experts proposed other explanations. Professor James Anthony of Michigan State University admitted that "there is very little hard, definitive evidence on the subject."

For Further Thought

1. Should the concept of *addiction* be applied to behavior on modern technology devices? Why, or why not? How would you define the concept of addiction?

2. Can we depend on self-report measures of drug (and technology) use? (The research described here used questions from the Monitoring the Future survey.) What measurement challenges can you think of?

Source: Richtel, M. (2017, March 13). Are teenagers replacing drugs with smartphones? *New York Times.* Retrieved from https://www.nytimes.com/2017/03/13/health/teenagers-drugs-smartphones.html

DID WE MEASURE WHAT WE WANTED TO MEASURE?

Do the operations developed to measure our concepts actually do so—are they valid? If we have weighed our measurement options, carefully constructed our questions and observational procedures, and carefully selected indicators from the available data, we should be on the right track. We cannot have much confidence in a measure until we have empirically evaluated its validity. In addition, we must also evaluate its reliability (consistency).

Measurement Validity

Measurement validity: The type of validity that is achieved when a measure measures what it is presumed to measure

As mentioned in Chapter 2, we can consider measurement validity the first concern in establishing the validity of research results because without having measured what we think we measured, we really do not know what we are talking about.

We briefly discussed the difference between official police reports and survey data in Chapter 1. We noted that official reports underestimate the actual amount of offending because a great deal of offending behavior never comes to the attention of police (Mosher et al., 2002). There is also evidence that arrest data often reflect the political climate and police policies as much as they do criminal activity. For example, let's suppose we wanted to examine whether illicit drug use was increasing or decreasing since the United States' "war on drugs," which heated up in the 1980s and is still being fought today. During this time, arrest rates for drug offenses soared, giving the illusion that drug use was increasing at an epidemic pace. However, self-report surveys that asked citizens directly about their drug use behavior during this time period found that use of most illicit drugs was actually declining or had stayed the same (Regoli & Hewitt, 1994). In your opinion, then, which measure of drug use—the UCR or self-report surveys—was more valid? The extent to which measures indicate what they are intended to measure can be assessed with one or more of four basic approaches: face validation, content validation, criterion validation, and construct validation.

Whatever the approach to validation, no one measure will be valid for all times and places. For example, the validity of self-report measures of substance abuse varies with such factors as whether the respondents are sober or intoxicated at the time of the interview, whether the measure refers to recent or lifetime abuse, and whether the respondents see their responses as affecting their chances of receiving housing, treatment, or some other desired outcome (Babor, Stephens, & Marlatt, 1987). In addition, persons with severe mental illness are, in general, less likely to respond accurately (Corse, Hirschinger, & Zanis, 1995). These types of possibilities should always be considered when evaluating measurement validity.

Face Validity

Researchers apply the term face validity to the confidence gained from careful inspection of a concept to see if it is appropriate "on its face." More precisely, we can say that a measure has face validity if it obviously pertains to the concept being measured more than to other concepts (Brewer & Hunter, 1989, p. 131). For example, if college students' alcohol consumption is what we are trying to measure, asking for students' favorite color seems unlikely on its face to tell us much about their drinking patterns. A measure with greater face validity would be a count of how many drinks they had consumed in the past week.

Although every measure should be inspected in this way, face validation on its own is not the gold standard of measurement validity. The question "How much beer or wine did you have to drink last week?" may look valid on its face as a measure of frequency of drinking, but people who drink heavily tend to underreport the amount they drink. So the question would be an invalid measure in a study that includes heavy drinkers.

Face validity: The type of validity that exists when an inspection of the items used to measure a concept suggests that they are appropriate "on their face"

Content Validity

Content validity establishes that the measure covers the full range of the concept's meaning. To determine that range of meaning, the researcher may solicit the opinions of experts and review literature that identifies the different aspects of the concept. An example of a measure that covers a wide range of meaning is the Michigan Alcoholism Screening Test (MAST). The MAST includes 24 questions representing the following subscales: recognition of alcohol problems by self and others; legal, social, and work problems; help seeking; marital and family difficulties; and liver pathology (Skinner & Sheu, 1982). Many experts familiar with the direct consequences of substance abuse agree that these dimensions capture the full range of possibilities. Thus, the MAST is believed to be valid from the standpoint of content validity.

Content validity: The type of validity that exists when the full range of a concept's meaning is covered by the measure

Criterion Validity

Consider the following scenario: When people drink an alcoholic beverage, the alcohol is absorbed into their bloodstream and then gradually metabolized (broken down into other chemicals) in their liver (NIAAA, 1997). The alcohol that remains in their blood at any point, unmetabolized, impairs both thinking and behavior (NIAAA, 1997). As more alcohol is ingested, cognitive and behavioral consequences multiply. These biological processes can be identified with direct measures of alcohol concentration in the blood, urine, or breath. Questions about alcohol consumption, on the other hand, can be viewed as attempts to measure indirectly what biochemical tests measure directly.

Criterion validity is established when the scores obtained on one measure can accurately be compared with those obtained with a more direct or already validated measure of the same phenomenon (the criterion). A measure of blood alcohol concentration or a urine test could serve as the criterion for validating a self-report measure of drinking, as long as the

Criterion validity: The type of validity that is established by comparing the scores obtained on the measure being validated with those obtained with a more direct or already validated measure of the same phenomenon (the criterion)

questions we ask about drinking refer to the same period. Observations of substance use by friends or relatives could also, in some circumstances, serve as a criterion for validating self-report substance use measures.

An attempt at criterion validation is well worth the effort because it greatly increases confidence that the measure is actually measuring the concept of interest—criterion validity basically offers evidence. However, often no other variable might reasonably be considered a criterion for individual feelings or beliefs or other subjective states. Even with variables for which a reasonable criterion exists, the researcher may not be able to gain access to the criterion, as would be the case with a tax return or employer document as criterion for self-reported income.

Construct Validity

Construct validity:
The type of validity
that is established by
showing that a measure
is related to other
measures as specified
in a theory

Measurement validity also can be established by showing that a measure is related to a variety of other measures as specified in a theory. This validation approach, known as construct validity, is commonly used in social research when no clear criterion exists for validation purposes. For example, in one study of the validity of the Addiction Severity Index (ASI), McLellan et al. (1985) compared subject scores on the ASI with a number of indicators that they felt from prior research should be related to substance abuse: medical problems, employment problems, legal problems, family problems, and psychiatric problems. They could not use a criterion validation approach because they did not have a more direct measure of abuse, such as laboratory test scores or observer reports. However, their extensive research on the subject had given them confidence that these sorts of other problems were all related to substance abuse, and thus, their measures seemed to be valid from the standpoint of construct validity. Indeed, the researchers found that individuals with higher ASI ratings tended to have more problems in each of these areas, giving us more confidence in the ASI's validity as a measure.

The distinction between criterion and construct validation is not always clear. Opinions can differ about whether a particular indicator is indeed a criterion for the concept that is to be measured. For example, if you need to validate a question-based measure of sales ability for applicants to a sales position, few would object to using actual sales performance as a criterion. But what if you want to validate a question-based measure of the amount of social support that people receive from their friends? Should you just ask people about the social support they have received? Could friends' reports of the amount of support they provided serve as a criterion? Even if you could observe people in the act of counseling or otherwise supporting their friends, can an observer be sure that the interaction is indeed supportive? There isn't really a criterion here, just a combination of related concepts that could be used in a construct validation strategy.

What construct and criterion validation have in common is the comparison of scores on one measure with scores on other measures that are predicted to be related. It is not so important that researchers agree that a particular comparison measure is a criterion rather than a related construct. But it is very important to think critically about the quality of the comparison measure and whether it actually represents a different measure of the same phenomenon. For example, it is only a weak indication of measurement validity to find that scores on a new self-report measure of alcohol use are associated with scores on a previously used self-report measure of alcohol use.

Measurement Reliability

Reliability: A measure is
reliable when it yields
consistent scores
or observations of a
given phenomenon
on different
occasions; reliability
is a prerequisite for
measurement validity

Reliability means that a measurement procedure yields consistent scores as long as the phenomenon being measured is not changing. If a measure is reliable, it is affected less by random error, or chance variation, than if it is unreliable. For example, if we gave students a survey with the same questions asking them about their alcohol consumption, the measure would be reliable if the same students gave approximately the same answers six months later (assuming their drinking patterns had not changed much). Reliability is a prerequisite for measurement validity; we cannot really measure a phenomenon if the measure we are using gives inconsistent results. Unfortunately, because it is usually easier to access reliability than validity, you are more likely to see an evaluation of measurement reliability in research compared with an evaluation of measurement validity.

Problems in reliability can occur when inconsistent measurements are obtained after the same phenomenon is measured multiple times, with multiple indicators, or by multiple observers. To assess these different inconsistencies, there are four possible methods: test–retest reliability, interitem reliability, alternate-forms reliability, and interobserver reliability.

Test–Retest Reliability

When researchers measure a phenomenon that does not change between two points separated by an interval of time, the degree to which the two measurements yield comparable, if not identical, values is the test–retest reliability of the measure. If you take a test of your math ability and then retake the test two months later, the test is performing reliably if you receive a similar score both times, presuming that nothing happened during the two months to change your math ability. Of course, if events between the test and the retest have changed the variable being measured, then the difference between the test and retest scores should reflect that change.

Interitem Reliability (Internal Consistency)

When researchers use multiple items to measure a single concept, they are concerned with interitem reliability (or *internal consistency*). For example, if we are to have confidence that a set of questions reliably measures an attitude—say, attitudes toward violence—then the answers to the questions should be highly associated with one another. The stronger the association between the individual items and the more items included, the higher the reliability of the index. Cronbach's alpha is a reliability measure commonly used to measure interitem reliability. Of course, interitem reliability cannot be computed if only one question is used to measure a concept. For this reason, it is much better to use a multi-item index to measure an important concept (Viswanathan, 2005).

Alternate-Forms Reliability

Researchers are testing alternate-forms reliability when they compare subjects' answers with slightly different versions of survey questions (Litwin, 1995). A researcher may reverse the order of the response choices in an index or modify the question wording in minor ways and then readminister that index to subjects. If the two sets of responses are not too different, alternate-forms reliability is established.

A related test of reliability is the split-halves reliability approach. A survey sample is divided in two by flipping a coin or using some other random assignment method. These two halves of the sample are then administered the two forms of the questions. If the responses of the two halves are about the same, the measure's reliability is established.

Intraobserver and Interobserver Reliability

When ratings by an observer, rather than ratings by the subjects themselves, are being assessed at two or more points in time, test–retest reliability is termed intraobserver or intrarater reliability. Let's say a researcher observes a grade school cafeteria for signs of bullying behavior on multiple days. If his observations captured the same degree of bullying on every Friday, it can be said that his observations were reliable. When researchers use

Test–retest reliability: A measurement showing that measures of a phenomenon at two points in time are highly correlated, if the phenomenon has not changed or has changed only as much as the phenomenon itself

Interitem reliability: An approach that calculates reliability based on the correlation among multiple items used to measure a single concept

Cronbach's alpha: A statistic that measures the reliability of items in an index or scale

Alternate-forms reliability: A procedure for testing the reliability of responses to survey questions in which subjects' answers are compared after the subjects have been asked slightly different versions of the questions or when randomly selected halves of the sample have been administered slightly different versions of the questions

Split-halves reliability: Reliability achieved when responses to the same questions by two randomly selected halves of a sample are about the same

Intraobserver reliability (intrarater reliability): Consistency of ratings by an observer of an unchanging phenomenon at two or more points in time

Interobserver reliability: When similar measurements are obtained by different observers rating the same persons, events, or places

more than one observer to rate the same persons, events, or places, **interobserver reliability** is their goal. If observers are using the same instrument to rate the same thing, their ratings should be very similar. In this case, the researcher interested in cafeteria bullying would use more than one observer. If the measurement of bullying is similar across the observers, we can have much more confidence that the ratings reflect the actual degree of bullying behavior.

Can We Achieve Both Reliability and Validity?

We must always assess the reliability of a measure if we hope to be able to establish its validity. Remember that a reliable measure is not necessarily a valid measure, as Exhibit 4.8 illustrates. This discrepancy is a common flaw of self-report measures of substance abuse. The multiple questions in self-report indexes of substance abuse are answered by most respondents in a consistent way, so the indexes are reliable. However, a number of respondents will not admit to drinking, even though they drink a lot. Their answers to the questions are consistent, but they are consistently misleading. So the indexes based on self-report are reliable but invalid. Such indexes are not useful and should be improved or discarded. Unfortunately, many measures are judged to be worthwhile on the basis only of a reliability test.

Exhibit 4.8 The Difference Between Reliability and Validity: Drinking Behavior

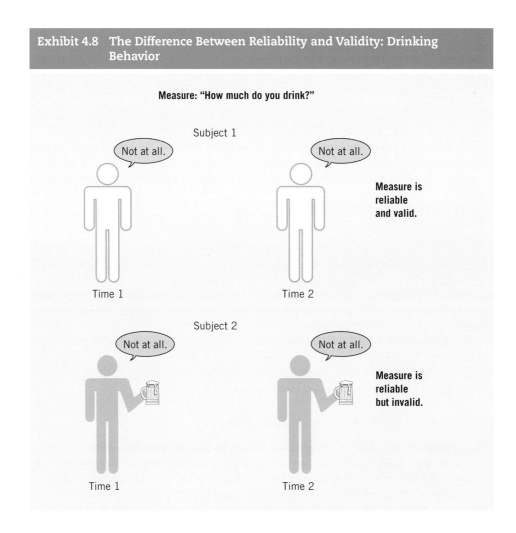

**Ryan Charles Meldrum, PhD, Assistant Professor of Criminal Justice,
Florida International University**

Source: Courtesy of Ryan Charles Meldrum

Ryan Meldrum's research focuses on the causes of juvenile delinquency. His path to becoming a delinquency researcher began when, out of sheer curiosity, he took a class on juvenile delinquency as an undergraduate student at Oregon State University. Having grown up in a small farming town in rural Oregon, Meldrum became interested in understanding why some teenagers would engage in delinquent and criminal behavior. His interest in making a career out of studying this topic was solidified during his graduate studies at Florida State University.

One of Meldrum's main areas of research concerns the measurement and operationalization of associating with delinquent peers. Traditionally, this construct is measured by having survey respondents report on the delinquent behavior of their friends. However, because of concerns over the accuracy of such reports, researchers are increasingly making use of reports of peer delinquency based on social-networking measurement strategies. With this measurement strategy, respondents are first asked to report who their friends are, and then researchers obtain self-reports of delinquency from those friends directly, bypassing concerns that someone might inaccurately recall and report on the behavior of their friends. Meldrum's research—and that of others exploring this topic—demonstrates how the empirical significance of peer delinquency for understanding individual involvement in delinquency may have been exaggerated in past studies relying solely on respondent perceptions of peer behavior.

His advice for students interested in a similar career is this:

Think like a researcher. One of the most challenging things for me early on was transitioning from a student who was responsible for consuming knowledge to a professor who was expected to produce new knowledge. What worked for me? I started to listen to news stories and read research with an eye toward thinking of new questions that needed to be answered or how a study could be conducted on the topic I was learning about. One day during my third year in graduate school the light bulb went off in my head, the floodgates of ideas opened, and I have been working ever since to answer questions related to the causes of juvenile delinquency.

The reliability and validity of measures in any study must be tested after the fact to assess the quality of the information obtained. But then, if it turns out that a measure cannot be considered reliable and valid, little can be done to save the study. Thus, it is supremely important to select, in the first place, measures that are likely to be reliable and valid. In studies that use interviewers or observers, careful training is often essential to achieving a consistent approach. In most cases, however, the best strategy is to use measures that have been used before and whose reliability and validity have been established in other contexts. However, know that the selection of "tried and true" measures still does not absolve researchers from the responsibility of testing the reliability and validity of the measure in their own studies.

It may be possible to improve the reliability and validity of measures in a study that already has been conducted if multiple measures were used. For example, in a study of housing for homeless mentally ill persons, residents' substance abuse was assessed with several different sets of direct questions, as well as with reports from subjects' case managers and others (Goldfinger et al., 1996). It was discovered that the observational reports were often inconsistent with self-reports and that different self-report measures were not always in agreement and were thus unreliable. A more reliable measure of substance abuse was initial reports of lifetime substance abuse problems. This measure was extremely accurate in identifying all those who subsequently abused substances during the project.

A COMMENT ON MEASUREMENT IN A DIVERSE SOCIETY

Throughout this chapter, we have communicated how important measurement is for research. Although it is crucial to have evidence of reliability and validity, it is important that such evidence also applies to different subgroups within the population. Often people of color, women, the poor, the LGBTQ community, and other groups have not been adequately represented in the development or testing of various measurement instruments (Witkin, 2001). Just because a measure appears valid does not mean that you can assume that it validly measures a construct for different subgroups.

Take the concept, *self-control*, which has been linked to delinquency and adult offending (for a review of this construct, see Gottfredson & Hirschi, 1990). Researchers have used several different types of variables to measure self-control, sometimes called self-regulation for young children, but the majority of research has simply assumed that these measures validly measure self-control for all individuals. Michael Sulik and his colleagues (2010) wanted to know whether the measure of self-regulation that had been used in many studies of children differentially measured the construct across different socioeconomic, gender, and racial/ethnic groups. The construct they measured was actually called effortful control (EC) and is generally conceptualized as the ability to shift and focus attention as needed and to activate and inhibit behavior (e.g. aggression) as needed, especially when one does not want to. Sulik et al. (2010) state, "Much of the work on EC has been conducted with primarily European-American sample" (p. 11).

To determine whether an EC similarly measured self-regulation across gender and racial/ethnic groups, Sulik and his colleagues (2010) tested children from 53 preschools in and around Houston, Texas, and 58 preschools in and around Tallahassee, Florida. They gave over 800 preschoolers different tasks designed to measure different factors related to self-regulation including a task called "waiting for bow," in which a wrapped gift was placed on the table within the child's reach while the researcher explained that he/she forgot the bow on the gift. Children were asked to stay in their seats and not touch or open the gift until the researcher came back from retrieving the bow in another room. Interestingly, they did not find any differences in the results of their EC measure across subgroups. They concluded, "This indicates that the construct of EC behaves in a similar way across groups, and that a wide array of tasks index a single latent EC construct" (p. 20). Still they caution, "It would be useful to examine the measurement invariance of EC across different levels of SES and in a range of cultures, including groups outside of the United States" (p. 20).

CONCLUSION

Always remember that measurement validity is a necessity for social research. Gathering data without careful conceptualization or conscientious efforts to operationalize key concepts often is a wasted effort.

The difficulties of achieving valid measurement vary with the concept being operationalized and the circumstances of the particular study. The examples in this chapter of difficulties in achieving valid measures of substance abuse should sensitize you to the need for caution, particularly when the concepts you wish to measure are socially stigmatized or illegal.

Careful planning ahead is the key to achieving valid measurement in your own research; careful evaluation is the key to sound decisions about the validity of measures in others' research. Statistical tests can help to determine whether a given measure is valid after data have been collected, but if it appears, after the fact, that a measure is invalid, little can be done to correct the situation. If you cannot tell how key concepts were operationalized when you read a research report, do not trust the findings. If a researcher does not indicate the results of tests used to establish the reliability and validity of key measures, always remain skeptical!

KEY TERMS

HIGHLIGHTS

- Conceptualization plays a critical role in research. In deductive research, conceptualization guides the operationalization of specific variables; in inductive research, it guides efforts to make sense of related observations.

- Concepts are operationalized in research by one or more indicators, or *measures*, which may derive from observation, self-report, available records or statistics, books and other written documents, clinical indicators, discarded materials, or some combination of these.

- The validity of measures should always be tested. There are four basic approaches: face validation, content validation, criterion validation, and construct validation. Criterion validation provides the strongest evidence of measurement validity, but there often is no criterion to use in validating social science measures.

- Measurement reliability is a prerequisite for measurement validity, although reliable measures are not necessarily valid. Reliability can be assessed through test–retest procedures, in terms of interitem consistency, through a comparison of responses to alternate forms of the test, or in terms of consistency among observers.

- Level of measurement indicates the type of information obtained about a variable and the type of statistics that can be used to describe its variation. The four levels of measurement can be ordered by complexity of the mathematical operations they permit: nominal (least complex), ordinal, interval, and ratio (most complex). The measurement level of a variable is determined by how the variable is operationalized.

Discussing Research

1. Pick one important, frequently used concept such as *crime, juries, community policing, racism,* or some other concept suggested by your instructor. Then, find five uses of it in newspapers, magazines, or journals. Is the concept defined clearly in each article? How similar are the definitions? Write up what you have found in a short report.

2. How would you define *rape*? Write a brief definition. Based on this conceptualization, what circumstances constitute rape? Describe a method of measurement that would be valid for a study of rape (as you define it). Now go to the Rape Victim Advocates' website (www.RapeVictimAdvocates.org). Go to "Myths & Facts." In a group, discuss some facts about rape that you were previously unaware of or some myths you believed. Rewrite your definition of rape based on your new knowledge. What additional circumstances constitute rape based on your new conceptualization?

3. Do you and your classmates share the same beliefs about the meanings of important concepts? First, divide your class into several groups, with each group having at least six students. Then assign each group a concept from the following list: promiscuity, hazing, academic success, stress, social support, mental illness, social norms, substance abuse. In each group, each student should independently write a brief definition of his or her concept and some different examples supporting it. Finally, all students who have worked on the same concept should meet together, compare their definitions and examples, and try to reach agreement on the meaning of the concept. Discuss what you learned from this effort.

4. Propose an open-ended question to measure one of the concepts you discussed in the preceding exercises. Compare your approach with those adopted by other students.

Finding Research on the Web

1. Are important concepts in criminological research always defined clearly? Are they defined consistently? Search the literature for six articles that focus on *violent crime, domestic violence,* or some other concept suggested by your instructor. Is the concept defined clearly in each article? How similar are the definitions? Write what you have found in a short report.

2. How would you define *alcoholism*? Write a brief definition. Based on this conceptualization, describe a method of measurement that would be valid for a study of alcoholism (as you define it). Now go to the National Council on Alcohol and Drug Dependence (NCADD) website (www.ncadd.org/about-addiction/alcohol/facts-about-alcohol) and read its official "Definition of Alcoholism." What is the definition of alcoholism used by NCADD? How is alcoholism conceptualized? How does this compare with your definition?

3. How would you define a *hate crime*? Write a brief definition. Now go to the Bureau of Justice Statistics (BJS) website (bjs.gov), and find a publication that presents statistics on victimizations perceived to be motivated by hate. How does BJS define a hate crime? How does it actually measure the extent to which a victimization is motivated by hate? How does this compare with your definition of a hate crime?

4. What are some of the research questions you could attempt to answer with available statistical data? Visit your library, and ask for an introduction to the government documents collection. Inspect the volumes from the FBI UCR or the *Sourcebook for Criminal Justice Statistics*, both of which report statistics on crimes by offender characteristics. List 10 questions you could explore with such data.

Critiquing Research

1. Develop a plan for evaluating the validity of a measure. Your instructor will give you a copy of a questionnaire actually used in a study. Choose one question, and define the concept that you believe it is intended to measure. Then develop a construct validation strategy involving other measures in the questionnaire that you think should be related to the question of interest—that is, does it measure what you think it does?

2. Compare two different measures of substance abuse. A site maintained by the National Institute on Alcoholism and Alcohol Abuse (www.niaaa.nih.gov/alcohol-health/overview-alcohol-consumption/moderate-binge-drinking) provides many of the most popular measures. Pick two of them. What concept of substance abuse is reflected in each measure? Is either measure multidimensional? What do you think the relative advantages of each measure might be? What evidence is provided about their reliability and validity? What other test of validity would you suggest?

Making Research Ethical

1. In order to measure disorder in Chicago neighborhoods, Sampson and Raudenbush (1999) recorded the street scene with video cameras in a van with darkened windows. Do you judge this measurement procedure to be ethical? Refer to each of the ethical guidelines in Chapter 3. How could the guidelines about anonymity/confidentiality and informed consent be interpreted to permit this type of observational procedure?

2. Both some Department of Homeland Security practices and inadvertent releases of web-searching records have raised new concerns about the use of unobtrusive measures of behavior and attitudes. If all identifying information is removed, do you think criminologists should be able to study who is stopped by police for traffic violations? Or what types of books are checked out in libraries in different communities? Or the extent of use of pornography in different cities by analyzing store purchases? Or how much alcohol different types of people use by linking credit card records to store purchases?

Developing a Research Proposal

At this point, you can begin the processes of conceptualization and operationalization. You will need to assume that your primary research method will be conducting a survey.

1. List at least 10 variables that will be measured in your research. No more than two of these should be sociodemographic indicators, such as race or age. The inclusion of each variable should be justified in terms of theory or prior research that suggests it would be an appropriate independent or dependent variable or will have some relation to either of these.

2. Write a conceptual definition for each variable. Whenever possible, this definition should come from the existing literature, either a book you have read for a course or the research literature that you have been searching. Ask two class members for feedback on your definitions.

3. Develop measurement operations for each variable. Several measures should be single questions and indexes that were used in prior research. (Search the Web and the journal literature in criminal justice abstracts, sociological abstracts, or psychology abstracts.) Make up a few questions and one index yourself. Ask classmates to answer these questions and give you feedback on their clarity.

4. Propose tests of reliability and validity for four of the measures.

Performing Data Analysis in SPSS or Excel

Data for Exercise	
Dataset	**Description**
Monitoring the future 2013 grade 10.sav	This dataset contains variables from the 2013 Monitoring the Future (MTF) study. These data cover a national sample of 10th graders, with a focus on monitoring substance use and abuse.
Variables for Exercise	
Variable Name	**Description**
V7329	Question asking how often a respondent enjoyed school in the past year. The five response categories were never (1), seldom (2), sometimes (3), often (4), and always (5).
V7333	Question asking how often the student found their school work interesting in the past year. See v7329 for response categories.
V7330_r	Question asking how often the student hated school in the past year. Response categories were never (5), seldom (4), sometimes (3), often (2), and always (1).
Gender	Gender of the respondent
Playedhooky	Dichotomous variable where "1" means a respondent has skipped school in the past month; "0" means school was never skipped

1. Take a look at the descriptions for "v7329," "v7330_r," and "v7333." Do they appear to have anything in common? What kind of concept might they be measuring?

2. Let's use those three measures together to get a more thorough measure of that concept. This process is called *scale construction*.

   a. First, tabulate all three measures. There are two ways we can compute a scale. One method is to add up all the indicators; the other is to take their average. In this case, we will take the average. This is because we can take an average score even when someone missed a question; we cannot add them up unless they answered all three items.

      i. Select "transform->compute."

      ii. Enter the following into the "numeric expression" field and then press "ok": MEAN.2(V7329, V7330_r, V7333).

3. This syntax can be read as "take the average of these three variables if at least two of the three items have been completed."

   a. Run a frequency of each of the three indicators again. Do you notice anything about v7330_r's coding compared with the others? Why was it coded that way? *Hint:* Think about the math in part 2a.

4. What do high scores on this measure reflect? Low scores?

5. Interitem reliability is often assessed to statistically make sure indicators for a scale are sufficiently correlated with one another. One measure to test this is Cronbach's α, which gives scores ranging from 0 to 1. Typically scores about 0.7 are acceptable, 0.8 are good, and 0.9 are excellent. To calculate Cronbach's α for our scale, click "analyze->scale->reliability analysis"; enter the three variables under the "items" box.

   a. What was Cronbach's alpha (α) for this scale? Does this scale have acceptable interitem reliability based on the cutoffs described previously?

6. Let's use that measure to answer a substantive research question: Is there a relationship between a person's attitudes toward school and whether they cut classes?

   a. What do you hypothesize? What is the direction of this association?

   b. To test this, we will compare average scores on your scale for people who skip class versus those who do not. To do this, select "analyze-> compare means->means" and put your scale in the "dependent list" box and the variable "playedhooky" in the independent variable list.

   c. Based on the comparison of average scores, what do you conclude about the relationship between these two items?

7. What level of measurement are the following variables? Don't trust the SPSS "measure" tab; it is often wrong because data curators often ignore it!

   a. V7329

   b. Gender

   c. Playedhooky

   d. Your scale

5

SAMPLING

WHAT DO WE HAVE IN MIND?

Whenever there is a high-profile crime or victimization, journalists typically scramble to the scene to put a "human face" on the story or turn to bystanders for their reactions. For example, after four members of a Brooklyn family, including a toddler and a teenage boy, were found shot to death on March 14, 2018, *New York Times* reporters sought insight from the neighbors about the alleged killer, Terrance Briggs, who took his own life after killing the other three. Responses to these queries are often inconsistent. For example, one neighbor stated that the family argued and that Briggs "liked to play the first-person shooter video game 'Call of Duty' on his PlayStation," while another said, "This is shocking to me. They were friendly people, nothing bad about them" (Mueller, Piccoli, & Southall, 2018). While these person-on-the-scene or on-the-street interviews are interesting and provide personal narratives to stories, they do not tell us much more than anecdotal information. In other words, we don't know how generalizable or reliable these impromptu interviews are.

In this chapter, you will learn about *sampling methods*, the procedures that primarily determine the generalizability of research findings. We first review the rationale for using sampling in research and consider two circumstances when sampling is not necessary. The chapter then turns to specific sampling methods and when they are most appropriate. By the chapter's end, you should understand which questions you need to ask to evaluate the generalizability of a study, as well as what choices you need to make when designing a sampling strategy. You should also realize that it is just as important to select the right people or objects to study as it is to ask participants the right questions.

SAMPLE PLANNING

The purpose of sampling is to generate a set of individuals or other entities that give us a valid picture of all such individuals or other entities. That is, a **sample** is a subset of the larger set of individuals or other entities in which we are interested. If we have done a good job of sampling, we will be able to generalize what we have learned from the subset to the larger set from which it was selected.

Learning Objectives

1. Identify the circumstances that make sampling unnecessary and the reason they are rare.

2. Identify the relation between the desired sample, the obtained sample, the sampling frame, and sample quality.

3. Define and distinguish probability and nonprobability sampling and both techniques' relationship to sample generalizability.

4. Define the major types of probability sampling, and indicate when each is preferred.

5. Explain when nonprobability sampling methods may be preferred.

6. Understand what units of analysis are and how errors can be made when generalizing from one unit of analysis to another.

$SAGE edge™

Master the content at edge
.sagepub.com/bachmanfrccj5e

As researchers, we call the set of individuals or other entities to which we want to be able to generalize our findings the population. For example, on April 25, 2015, over 1,000 people marched to the Baltimore City Hall to protest the death of Freddie Gray, who died of a spinal cord injury while in the custody of the Baltimore Police Department. Suppose we wanted to understand their motivations. It would be virtually impossible to interview all protesters. The entire group would be the population. Instead, we would likely interview a subset of the protesters, which is called a sample. The individual members of this sample are called elements, or elementary units.

Define Sample Components and the Population

In many studies, we sample directly from the elements in the population of interest. We may survey a sample of the entire population of students in a school based on a list obtained from the registrar's office. This list, from which the elements of the population are selected, is termed the sampling frame. The students who are selected and interviewed from that list are the elements.

In some studies, the entities that can be reached easily are not the same as the elements from which we want information, but they include those elements. For example, we may have a list of residential addresses but not a list of the entire population of a town, even though the adults are the elements that we actually want to sample. In this situation, we could draw a sample of households so that we can identify the adult individuals in these households. The households are termed enumeration units, and the adults in the households are the elements (Levy & Lemeshow, 1999).

In other instances, the individuals or other entities from which we collect information are not actually the elements in our study. For example, suppose we are interested in finding out the availability of substance abuse treatment programs in state prisons. To do this, we might first select a sample of prisons. From within those selected prisons, we might interview a sample of inmates in each prison to obtain information about substance abuse treatment program availability. In this case, both the prisons and the inmates are termed sampling units because we sample from both (Levy & Lemeshow, 1999). The prisons are selected in the first stage of the sample, so they are the *primary sampling units*. (In this case, they are also the elements in the study.) The inmates are *secondary sampling units*. (But they are not elements because they are used to provide information about the entire prison.) (See Exhibit 5.1.)

One key issue with selecting or evaluating sample components is understanding exactly what population they represent. In a survey of adult Americans, the general population may be reasonably construed as all residents of the United States who are at least 18 years old. But always be alert to ways in which the population may have been narrowed by the sample selection procedures. Perhaps only English-speaking adult residents of the continental United States were actually sampled. The population for a study is the aggregation of elements that we actually focus on and sample from, not a larger aggregation that we really wish we could have studied.

Some populations, such as the homeless, cannot easily be identified by a simple criterion, such as a geographic boundary or an organizational membership. Let us say you were interested in victimizations experienced by the homeless population. In this case, a clear definition of the homeless population is difficult but quite necessary. In research, anyone reading the study should be able to determine what population was actually examined. However, studies of homeless persons in the early 1980s "did not propose definitions, did not use screening questions to be sure that the people they interviewed were indeed homeless, and did not make major efforts to cover the universe of homeless people" (Burt, 1996, p. 15). For example, some studies relied on homeless persons in only one shelter. The result was "a collection of studies that could not be compared" (p. 15). According to Burt, several studies of homeless persons in

Sample: A subset of elements from the larger population

Population: The entire set of elements (e.g., individuals, cities, states, countries, prisons, schools) in which we are interested

Elements: The individual entities of the population whose characteristics are to be measured

Sampling frame: A list of all elements of a population from which a sample is actually selected

Enumeration units: Units that contain one or more elements and that are listed in a sampling frame

Sampling units: Units selected at each stage of a multistage sampling design

Exhibit 5.1   Sample Components in a Two-Stage Study

Sample of Prisons

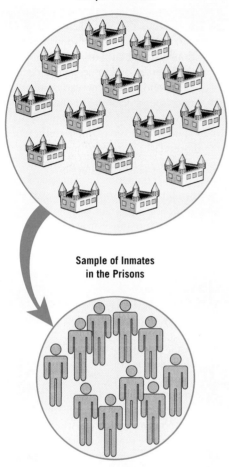

Prisons are the elements and the primary sampling unit.

Sample of Inmates in the Prisons

Inmates are the secondary sampling units; they provide information about the prisons.

urban areas addressed the problem by employing a more explicit definition of the population: People are homeless if they have no home or permanent place to stay of their own (renting or owning) and no regular arrangement to stay at someone else's place. Even this more explicit definition still leaves some questions unanswered: What is a regular arrangement? How permanent does a permanent place have to be? The more complete and explicit the definition of the population from which a sample is selected, the more precise our generalizations from a sample to that population can be.

Evaluate Generalizability

After clearly defining the population we will sample, we need to determine the scope of the generalizations we will seek to make from our sample. Let us say we are interested in the extent to which high school youth are fearful of being attacked or harmed at school or going to and from their schools. It would be easy to go down to the local high school and hand out a survey asking students to report their level of fear in these situations. But what if my local high school were located in a remote and rural area of Alaska? Would this sample reflect levels of fear perceived by suburban youth in California or urban youth in New York City? Obviously not. Often, regardless of the sample utilized, researchers will assert that "This percentage of high school students is fearful" or "First-year students are more fearful than seniors," as if their study results represented all high school students. Many researchers (and most everyone else, for that matter) are eager to draw conclusions about all individuals they are interested in, not just their samples. Generalizations make their work (and opinions) sound more important. If every high school student were like every other one, generalizations based on observations of one high school student would be valid. This, however, is not the case.

As noted in Chapter 2, generalizability has two aspects. Can the findings from a sample of the population be generalized to the population from which the sample was selected? **Sample generalizability** refers to the ability to generalize from a sample (subset) of a larger population to that population itself (e.g., using those Alaskan students' survey results to speak more generally about rural students' perceptions of fear). This is the most common meaning of generalizability. Can the findings from a study of one population be generalized to another, somewhat different population? This is **cross-population generalizability** and refers to the ability to generalize from findings about one group, population, or setting to other groups, populations, or settings (see Exhibit 5.2). In this book, we use the term *external validity* to refer only to cross-population generalizability, not to sample generalizability.

Generalizability is a key concern in research design, so this chapter focuses primarily on the problem of sample generalizability. We rarely have the resources to study the entire population that is of interest to us. For this reason, we have to select cases to study that will allow our findings to be generalized to the population of interest. We can never be sure that our propositions will hold under all conditions, so we should be cautious in generalizing to populations that we did not actually sample.

When designing our research studies, we must ask whether findings from a sample may be generalized to the population from which the sample was drawn. Social-research methods provide many tools to address this concern.

Sample generalizability depends on sample quality, which is determined by the amount of **sampling error**. Sampling error can generally be defined as the difference between the characteristics of a sample and the characteristics of the population from which it was selected. The larger the sampling error, the less representative is the sample and thus the less generalizable are the findings. To assess sample quality when you are planning or evaluating a study, ask yourself these questions:

- From what populations were the cases selected?
- What method was used to select cases from this population?
- Do the cases that are/were studied represent, in the aggregate, the population from which they were selected?

In reality, researchers often project their theories onto groups or populations much larger than—or simply different from—those they have actually studied. The **target population** consists of a set of elements larger than or different from the population that was sampled, to which the researcher would like to generalize any study findings. When we generalize findings to target populations, we must be somewhat speculative and carefully consider the claim that the findings can be applied to other groups, geographic areas, cultures, or times.

Because the validity of cross-population generalizations cannot be tested empirically, except by conducting more research in other settings, we do not focus much attention on this problem here. We will return to the problem of cross-population generalizability in Chapter 6, which addresses experimental research.

Sample generalizability: Exists when a conclusion based on a sample, or subset, of a larger population holds true for that population

Cross-population generalizability (external validity): Exists when findings about one group, population, or setting hold true for other groups, populations, or settings

Sampling error: Any difference between the characteristics of a sample and the characteristics of the population from which it was drawn; the larger the sampling error, the less representative the sample is of the population

Target population: A set of elements larger than or different from the population sampled and to which the researcher would like to generalize study findings

Exhibit 5.2   Sample and Cross-Population Generalizability

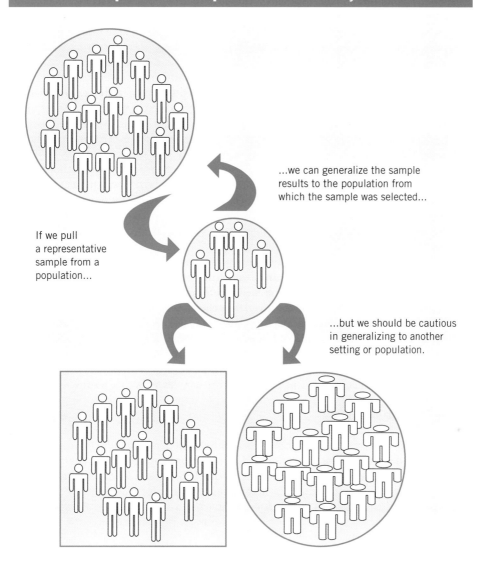

...we can generalize the sample results to the population from which the sample was selected...

If we pull a representative sample from a population...

...but we should be cautious in generalizing to another setting or population.

Assess Population Diversity

Sampling is unnecessary if all the units in the population are identical. Physicists do not need to select a **representative sample** of atomic particles to learn about basic physical processes. They can study a single atomic particle because it is identical to every other particle of its type. Similarly, biologists do not need to sample a particular type of plant to determine whether a given chemical has toxic effects on it. The idea is, "If you've seen one, you've seen 'em all."

What about people? Certainly all people are not identical—nor are animals, in many respects. Nonetheless, if we are studying physical or psychological processes that are the same among all people, sampling is not needed to achieve generalizable findings. Various types of psychologists, including social psychologists, often conduct experiments on college students to learn about processes that they think are identical for all individuals. They believe that

Representative sample: A sample that looks similar to the population from which it was selected in all respects that are potentially relevant to the study. The distribution of characteristics among the elements of a representative sample is the same as the distribution of those characteristics among the total population. In an unrepresentative sample, some characteristics are overrepresented or underrepresented.

most people will have the same reactions as the college students if they experience the same experimental conditions. Field researchers who observe group processes in a small community sometimes make the same assumption.

There is a potential problem with this assumption, however. There is no way to know whether the processes being studied are identical for all people. In fact, experiments can give different results depending on the type of people studied or the conditions for the experiment. Milgram's (1965) experiments on obedience to authority (discussed in Chapter 3) illustrate this point very well. Recall that Milgram concluded that people are very obedient to authority. But were these results generalizable to all men, to men in the United States, or to men in New Haven? We can have confidence in these findings because similar results were obtained in many replications of the Milgram experiments when the experimental conditions and subjects were similar to those studied by Milgram.

Accurately generalizing the results of experiments and of participant observation is risky because such research often studies a small number of people who do not represent a particular population. Researchers may put aside concerns about generalizability when they observe the social dynamics of specific clubs or college dorms or a controlled experiment that tests the effect of, say, a violent movie on feelings for others. Nonetheless, we should still be cautious about generalizing the results of such studies.

The important point is that social scientists rarely can skirt the problem of demonstrating the generalizability of their findings. If a small sample has been studied in an experiment or field research project, the study should be replicated in different settings or, preferably, with a representative sample of the population for which the generalizations are sought (see Exhibit 5.3).

The people in our social world are just too diverse to be considered identical units. Social psychological experiments and small field studies have produced good social science, but they need to be replicated in other settings with other subjects to claim any generalizability. Even when we believe that we have uncovered basic social processes in a laboratory experiment or field observation, we must seek confirmation in other samples and other research.

Consider a Census

Census: Research in which information is obtained through the responses that all available members of an entire population give to questions

In some circumstances, researchers can bypass the issue of generalizability by conducting a census that studies the entire population of interest rather than drawing a sample. The federal government tries to do this every 10 years with the U.S. Census. A census can also involve studies of all the employees (or students) in small organizations (or universities), studies comparing all 50 states, or studies of the entire population of a particular type of organization in a particular area. However, in all these instances—except for the U.S. Census—the population studied is relatively small.

The reason that social scientists don't often attempt to collect data from all the members of some large population is simply that doing so would be too expensive and time-consuming—and they can do almost as well with a sample. Some social scientists conduct research with data from the U.S. Census, but the government collects the data and our tax dollars pay for the effort to get one person in about 134 million households to answer 10 questions. To conduct the 2010 census, the U.S. Census Bureau spent more than $5.5 billion and hired 3.8 million people (U.S. Census Bureau, 2010a, 2010b). In most situations, then, it is much better to select a representative sample from the total population so that there are more resources for follow-up procedures that can overcome reluctance or indifference about participation.

SAMPLING METHODS

The most important distinction made about samples is whether they are based on a probability or a nonprobability sampling method. Sampling methods that allow us to know in advance

Exhibit 5.3 Representative and Unrepresentative Samples

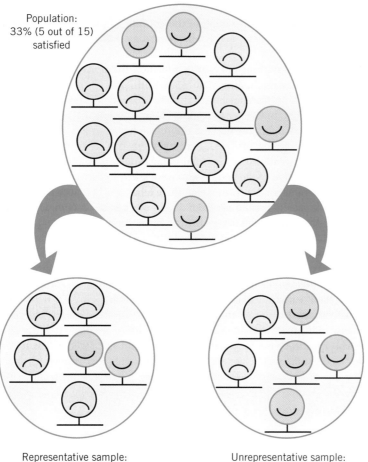

Population:
33% (5 out of 15)
satisfied

Representative sample:
33% (2 out of 6) satisfied

Unrepresentative sample:
66% (4 out of 6) satisfied

how likely it is that any element of a population will be selected for the sample are **probability sampling methods**. Sampling methods that do not reveal the likelihood of selection in advance are **nonprobability sampling methods**.

Probability sampling methods rely on a random selection procedure. In principle, this is the same as flipping a coin to decide which person wins and which one loses. Heads and tails are equally likely to turn up in a coin toss, so both persons have an equal chance to win. That chance, or the **probability of selection**, is 1 out of 2, or .5.

Flipping a coin is a fair way to select 1 of 2 people because the selection process harbors no systematic bias. You might win or lose the coin toss, but you know that the outcome was due simply to chance, not to bias (unless your opponent tossed a two-headed coin!). For the same reason, rolling a six-sided die is a fair way to choose 1 of 6 possible outcomes (the odds of selection are 1 out of 6, or .17). Similarly, state lotteries use a random process to select winning numbers. Thus, the odds of winning a lottery—the probability of selection—are known even though they are very small (perhaps 1 out of 1 million) compared with the odds

Probability sampling methods: Sampling methods that rely on a random, or chance, selection method so that the probability of selection of population elements is known

Nonprobability sampling methods: Sampling methods in which the probability of selection of population elements is unknown

Probability of selection: The likelihood that an element will be selected from the population for inclusion in the sample. In a census, of all the elements of a population, the probability that any particular element will be selected is 1.0 because everyone will be selected. If half the elements in the population are sampled on the basis of chance (say, by tossing a coin), the probability of selection for each element is one half (0.5). When the size of the sample as a proportion of the population decreases, so does the probability of selection.

of winning a coin toss. As you can see, the fundamental strategy in probability sampling is the random selection of elements into the sample. When a sample is randomly selected from the population, every element has a known and independent chance of being selected into the sample.

There is a natural tendency to confuse the concept of probability, in which cases are selected only on the basis of chance, with a haphazard method of sampling. On first impression, leaving things up to chance seems to imply the absence of control over the sampling method. But to ensure that nothing but chance influences the selection of cases, the researcher must actually proceed very methodically and leave nothing to chance except the selection of the cases themselves. The researcher must carefully follow controlled procedures if a purely random process is to occur. In fact, when reading about sampling methods, do not assume that a random sample was obtained just because the researcher used a random selection method at some point in the sampling process. Look for these two particular problems: selecting elements from an incomplete list of the total population and failing to obtain an adequate response rate (say, only 45% of the people who were asked to participate actually agreed).

If the sampling frame, or list from which the elements of the population are selected, is incomplete, a sample selected randomly from the list will not be random. How can it be when the sampling frame fails to include every element in the population? Even for a simple population, such as a university's student body, the registrar's list is likely to be at least a bit out of date at any given time. For example, some students will have dropped out, but their status will not yet be officially recorded. Although you may judge the amount of error introduced in this particular situation to be small, the problems are greatly compounded for a larger population.

A very inclusive sampling frame may still yield systematic bias if many sample members cannot be contacted or refuse to participate. Nonresponse is a major hazard in survey research because individuals who do not respond to a survey are likely to differ systematically from those who take the time to participate. You should not assume that findings from a randomly selected sample will be generalizable to the population from which the sample was selected if the rate of nonresponse is considerable (certainly if it is much above 30%).

Probability Sampling Methods

Probability sampling methods are those in which the probability of selection is known and is not zero (so there is some chance of selecting each element). These methods randomly select elements and therefore have no systematic bias; nothing but chance determines which elements are included in the sample. This feature of probability samples makes them much more desirable than nonprobability samples when the goal is to generalize to a larger population.

Even though a random sample has no systematic bias, it certainly will have some sampling error due to chance. The probability of selecting a head is .5 in a single toss of a coin—and in 20, 30, or however many tosses of a coin you like. Be aware, however, that it is perfectly possible to toss a coin twice and get a head both times. The random sample of the two sides of the coin is selected in an unbiased fashion, but it still is unrepresentative. Imagine randomly selecting a sample of 10 people from a population comprising 50 men and 50 women. Just by chance, it is possible that your sample of 10 people will include seven women and only three men. Fortunately, we can determine mathematically the likely degree of sampling error in an estimate based on a random sample (as you will see later in this chapter), assuming that the sample's randomness has not been destroyed by a high rate of nonresponse or by poor control over the selection process.

In general, both the size of the sample and the homogeneity (sameness) of the population affect the degree of error due to chance; the proportion of the population that the sample represents does not. To elaborate, consider this:

The larger the sample, the more confidence we can have in the sample's representativeness of the population from which it was drawn. If we randomly pick five people to represent the entire population of our city, our sample is unlikely to be very representative of the entire population in terms of age, gender, race, attitudes, and so on. But if we randomly pick 100 people, the odds of having a representative sample are much better; with a random sample of 1,000, the odds become very good indeed.

The more homogeneous the population, the more confidence we can have in the representativeness of a sample of any particular size. Let us say we plan to draw samples of 50 from each of two communities to estimate mean family income. One community is very diverse, with family incomes ranging from $12,000 to $85,000. In the more homogeneous community, family incomes are concentrated in a narrower range, from $41,000 to $64,000. The estimated average family income based on the sample from the homogeneous community is more likely to be representative than is the estimate based on the sample from the more heterogeneous community. With less variation, fewer cases are needed to represent the larger population.

The fraction of the total population that a sample contains does not affect the sample's representativeness, unless that fraction is large. We can regard any sampling fraction under 2% with about the same degree of confidence (Sudman, 1976). In fact, sample representativeness is not likely to increase much until the sampling fraction is quite a bit higher. Other things being equal, a sample of 1,000 from a population of 1 million (with a sampling fraction of 0.001, or 0.1%) is much better than a sample of 100 from a population of 10,000 (although the sampling fraction is 0.01, or 1%, which is 10 times higher). The size of a sample is what makes representativeness more likely, not the proportion of the whole that the sample represents.

Because they do not disproportionately select particular groups within the population, random samples that are successfully implemented avoid systematic bias. The four most common methods for drawing random samples are simple random sampling, systematic random sampling, stratified random sampling, and multistage cluster sampling.

Simple Random Sampling

Simple random sampling requires a procedure that generates numbers or identifies cases strictly on the basis of chance. As you know, flipping a coin and rolling a die can be used to identify cases strictly on the basis of chance, but these procedures are not very efficient tools for drawing a sample. A **random number table**, which can be found on many websites, simplifies the process considerably. The researcher numbers all the elements in the sampling frame and then uses a systematic procedure for picking corresponding numbers from the random number table. Alternatively, a researcher may use a lottery procedure. Each case number is written on a small card, and then the cards are mixed up and the sample selected from the cards.

When a large sample must be generated, these procedures are very cumbersome. Fortunately, a computer program can easily generate a random sample of any size. The researcher must first number all the elements to be sampled (the sampling frame) and then run the computer program to generate a random selection of the numbers within the desired range. The elements represented by these numbers are the sample.

As the percentage of the population that has only cell phones has increased (40% in 2013), it has become essential to explicitly sample cell phone numbers as well as landlines. Those who use cell phones only tend to be younger, male, and single and more likely to be black or Hispanic. As a result, failing to include cell phone numbers in a phone survey can introduce bias (Christian, Keeter, Purcell, & Smith, 2010). In the National Intimate Partner and Sexual Violence Survey (NISVS) conducted by the Centers for Disease Control and Prevention (CDC), both landline and cell phone databases of adult U.S. residents were selected through a **random digit dialing (RDD)** random sampling method (Black et al., 2011). You will learn more about this survey in Chapter 7.

Organizations that conduct phone surveys often draw random samples with RDD. A machine dials random numbers within the phone prefixes corresponding to the area in which

Simple random sampling: A method of sampling in which every sample element is selected only on the basis of chance through a random process

Random number table: A table containing lists of numbers that are ordered solely on the basis of chance; it is used for drawing a random sample

Random digit dialing (RDD): The random dialing by a machine of numbers within designated phone prefixes, which creates a random sample for phone surveys

the survey is to be conducted. RDD is particularly useful when a sampling frame is not available. The researcher simply replaces any inappropriate numbers (e.g., those no longer in service or for businesses) with the next randomly generated phone number.

The probability of selection in a true simple random sample is equal for each element. If a sample of 500 is selected from a population of 17,000 (i.e., a sampling frame of 17,000), then the probability of selection for each element is 500/17,000, or .03. Every element has an equal and independent chance of being selected, just like the odds in a toss of a coin (1/2) or a roll of a die (1/6).

Simple random sampling can be done either with or without **replacement sampling**. In replacement sampling, each element is returned to the sampling frame from which it is selected so that it may be sampled again. In sampling without replacement, each element selected for the sample is then excluded from the sampling frame. In practice, it makes no difference whether sampled elements are replaced after selection, as long as the population is large and the sample is to contain only a small fraction of the population.

In the CDC's NISVS study mentioned previously, noninstitutionalized (e.g., not in nursing homes, prisons, and so on) English- and/or Spanish-speaking residents aged 18 and older were randomly selected through an RDD sampling method. A total of 9,970 women and 8,079 men were selected, approximately 45% of the interviews were conducted by landline and 55% by cell phone. The final sample represented the U.S. population very well. For example, the proportion of the sample by gender, race/ethnicity, and age in the NISVS sample was very close to the sample proportions for the U.S. population as a whole.

Systematic Random Sampling

Systematic random sampling is a variant of simple random sampling and is a little less time-consuming. When you systematically select a random sample, the first element is selected randomly from a list or from sequential files, and then every nth element is systematically selected thereafter. This is a convenient method for drawing a random sample when the population elements are arranged sequentially. It is particularly efficient when the elements are not actually printed (i.e., there is no sampling frame) but instead are represented by folders in filing cabinets.

Systematic random sampling requires three steps:

1. The total number of cases in the population is divided by the number of cases required for the sample. This division yields the **sampling interval**, the number of cases from one sampled case to another. If 50 cases are to be selected out of 1,000, the sampling interval is 20 (1,000 ÷ 50 = 20); every 20th case is selected.

2. A number from 1 to 20 (the sampling interval) is selected randomly. This number identifies the first case to be sampled, counting from the first case on the list or in the files.

3. After the first case is selected, every nth case is selected for the sample, where n is the sampling interval. If the sampling interval is not a whole number, the size of the sampling interval is systematically varied to yield the proper number of cases for the sample. For example, if the sampling interval is 30.5, the sampling interval alternates between 30 and 31.

In almost all sampling situations, systematic random sampling yields what is essentially a simple random sample. The exception is a situation in which the sequence of elements is affected by **periodicity**—that is, the sequence varies in some regular, periodic pattern. The list

Replacement sampling: A method of sampling in which sample elements are returned to the sampling frame after being selected, so they may be sampled again; random samples may be selected with or without replacement

Systematic random sampling: A method of sampling in which sample elements are selected from a list or from sequential files, with every nth element being selected after the first element is selected randomly within the first interval

Sampling interval: The number of cases from one sampled case to another in a systematic random sample

Periodicity: A sequence of elements (in a list to be sampled) that varies in some regular, periodic pattern

or folder device from which the elements are selected must be truly random in order to avoid sampling bias. For example, we could not have a list of convicted felons sorted by offense type, age, or some other characteristic of the population. If the list is sorted in any meaningful way, this will introduce bias to the sampling process, and the resulting sample is not likely to be representative of the population.

Stratified Random Sampling

Although all probability sampling methods use random sampling, some add steps to the process to make sampling more efficient or easier. Samples are easier to collect when they require less time, money, or prior information.

Stratified random sampling uses information known about the total population prior to sampling to make the sampling process more efficient. First, all elements in the population (i.e., in the sampling frame) are differentiated on the basis of their value on some relevant characteristic. This sorting step forms the sampling strata. Next, elements are sampled randomly from within these strata. For example, race may be the basis for distinguishing individuals in some population of interest. Within each racial category selected for the strata, individuals are then sampled randomly.

Why is this method more efficient than drawing a simple random sample? Well, imagine that you plan to draw a sample of 500 from an ethnically diverse neighborhood. The neighborhood population is 15% African American, 10% Hispanic, 5% Asian, and 70% Caucasian. If you drew a simple random sample, you might end up with disproportionate numbers of each group. But if you created sampling strata based on race and ethnicity, you could randomly select cases from each stratum: 75 African Americans (15% of the sample), 50 Hispanics (10%), 25 Asians (5%), and 350 Caucasians (70%). By using **proportionate stratified sampling**, you would eliminate any possibility of error in the sample's distribution of ethnicity. Each stratum would be represented exactly in proportion to its size in the population from which the sample was drawn (see Exhibit 5.4).

In **disproportionate stratified sampling**, the proportion of each stratum that is included in the sample is intentionally varied from what it is in the population. In the case of the sample stratified by ethnicity, you might select equal numbers of cases from each racial or ethnic group: 125 African Americans (25% of the sample), 125 Hispanics (25%), 125 Asians (25%), and 125 Caucasians (25%). In this type of sample, the probability of selection of every case is known but unequal between strata. You know what the proportions are in the population, so you can easily adjust your combined sample accordingly. For instance, if you want to combine the ethnic groups and estimate the average income of the total population, you would have to weight each case in the sample. The *weight* is a number you multiply by the value of each case based on the stratum it is in. For example, you would multiply the incomes of all African Americans in the sample by 0.6 (75/125), the incomes of all Hispanics by 0.4 (50/125), and so on. Weighting in this way reduces the influence of the oversampled strata and increases the influence of the undersampled strata to what they would have been if pure probability sampling had been used.

Why would anyone select a sample that is so unrepresentative in the first place? The most common reason is to ensure that cases from smaller strata are included in the sample in sufficient numbers. For example, American Indian and Alaskan Native (AIAN) populations represent a very small percentage of the total U.S. population. To ensure that nationally representative surveys obtain enough AIAN respondents, they often oversample this population. Only then can separate statistical estimates and comparisons be made between strata (e.g., between AIAN and Caucasian respondents). Remember that one determinant of sample quality is sample size. If few members of a particular group are in the population, they need to be oversampled. Such disproportionate sampling may also result in a more efficient sampling design if the costs of data collection differ markedly between strata or if the variability (heterogeneity) of the strata differs.

Stratified random sampling: A method of sampling in which sample elements are selected separately from population strata that are identified in advance by the researcher

Proportionate stratified sampling: Sampling methods in which elements are selected from strata in exact proportion to their representation in the population

Disproportionate stratified sampling: Sampling in which elements are selected from strata in different proportions from those that appear in the population

Exhibit 5.4 **Stratified Random Sampling**

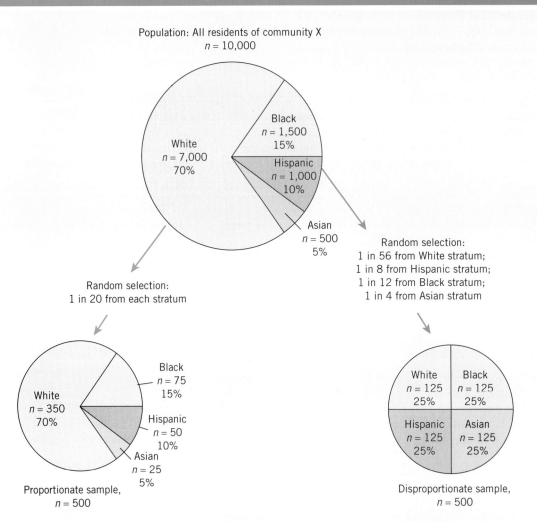

Population: All residents of community X
n = 10,000

White
n = 7,000
70%

Black
n = 1,500
15%

Hispanic
n = 1,000
10%

Asian
n = 500
5%

Random selection:
1 in 20 from each stratum

Random selection:
1 in 56 from White stratum;
1 in 8 from Hispanic stratum;
1 in 12 from Black stratum;
1 in 4 from Asian stratum

White
n = 350
70%

Black
n = 75
15%

Hispanic
n = 50
10%

Asian
n = 25
5%

Proportionate sample,
n = 500

White
n = 125
25%

Black
n = 125
25%

Hispanic
n = 125
25%

Asian
n = 125
25%

Disproportionate sample,
n = 500

Multistage cluster sampling: Sampling in which elements are selected in two or more stages, with the first stage being the random selection of naturally occurring clusters and the last stage being the random selection of multilevel elements within clusters

Cluster: A naturally occurring, mixed aggregate of elements of the population

Multistage Cluster Sampling

Although stratified sampling requires more information than usual prior to sampling (about the size of strata in the population), **multistage cluster sampling** requires less prior information. Specifically, cluster sampling can be useful when a sampling frame is not available, as is often the case for large populations spread across a wide geographic area or among many different organizations. In fact, if we wanted to obtain a sample from the entire U.S. population, there would be no list available. Yes, there are lists in telephone books of residents in various places who have telephones, lists of those who have registered to vote, lists of those who hold driver's licenses, and so on. However, all these lists are incomplete: Some people do not list their phone number or do not have a telephone, some people are not registered to vote, and so on. Using incomplete lists such as these would introduce selection bias into our sample.

In such cases, the sampling procedures become a little more complex, and we usually end up working toward the sample we want through a series of steps or stages (hence the name *multistage*!). First, researchers extract a random sample of groups or **clusters** of elements that are available and then randomly sample the individual elements of interest from within these selected clusters. So what is a cluster? A cluster is a naturally occurring, mixed aggregate of elements of the population, with each element appearing in one and only one cluster. Schools could serve as clusters for sampling students, blocks could serve as clusters for sampling city residents, counties could serve as clusters for sampling the general population, and businesses could serve as clusters for sampling employees.

Drawing a cluster sample is at least a two-stage procedure. First, the researcher draws a random sample of clusters. A list of clusters should be much easier to obtain than a list of all the individuals in each cluster in the population. Next, the researcher draws a random sample of elements within each selected cluster. Because only a fraction of the total clusters is involved, obtaining the sampling frame at this stage should be much easier.

In a cluster sample of city residents, for example, blocks could be the first-stage clusters. A research assistant could walk around each selected block and record the addresses of all occupied dwelling units. Or, in a cluster sample of students, a researcher could contact the schools selected in the first stage and make arrangements with the registrars or office staff to obtain lists of students at each school. Cluster samples often involve multiple stages (see Exhibit 5.5).

Exhibit 5.5   Cluster Sampling

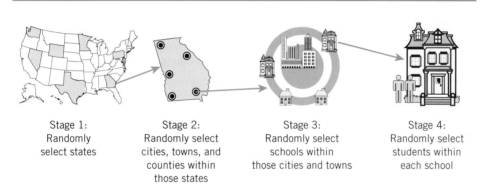

Stage 1:
Randomly
select states

Stage 2:
Randomly select
cities, towns, and
counties within
those states

Stage 3:
Randomly select
schools within
those cities and towns

Stage 4:
Randomly select
students within
each school

Many federal-government-funded surveys use multistage cluster samples or even combinations of cluster and stratified probability sampling methods. The U.S. Justice Department's National Crime Victimization Survey (NCVS) is an excellent example of a cluster sample. In the NCVS, clusters selected in the first stage are referred to as primary sampling units (PSUs) and represent a sample of rural counties and large metropolitan areas. The second stage of sampling involves the selection of geographic districts within each of the PSUs that have been listed by the U.S. Census Bureau population census. Finally, a probability sample of residential dwelling units is selected from these geographic districts. These dwelling units, or addresses, represent the last stage of the multistage sampling. Anyone who resides at a selected address who is 12 years of age or older and is a U.S. citizen is eligible for the NCVS sample. Approximately 50,500 housing units or other living quarters are designated for the NCVS each year and are selected in this manner.

How would we evaluate the NCVS sample, using the sample evaluation questions?

- *From what populations were the cases selected?* The population was clearly defined for each cluster.

- *What method was used to select cases from this population?* The random selection method was carefully described.

- *Do the cases that were studied represent, in the aggregate, the population from which they were selected?* The unbiased selection procedures make us reasonably confident in the representativeness of the sample.

Nonprobability Sampling Methods

Unlike probability samples, when collecting a sample using nonprobability sampling techniques, elements within the population do not have a known probability of being selected into the sample. Thus, because the chance of any element being selected is unknown, we cannot be certain the selected sample actually represents our population. Why, you may be asking yourself right now, would we want to use such a sample if we cannot generalize our results to a larger population? These methods are useful for several purposes, including those situations in which we do not have a population list, when we are exploring a research question that does not concern a large population or when we are doing a preliminary or exploratory study.

Nonprobability sampling methods are often used in qualitative research when the focus is on one setting or when a small sample allows a more intensive portrait of activities and actors. Suppose, for example, that we were interested in the crime of shoplifting and wanted to investigate how shoplifters rationalized their behavior. For example, do they think insurance covers the products they steal, so they are really not hurting anyone? It would be hard to define a population of shoplifters in this case because we do not have a list of shoplifters from which to randomly select. There may be lists of convicted shoplifters, but, of course, they only represent those shoplifters who were actually caught. As you can see, producing a random sample of some groups is very difficult indeed.

There are four common nonprobability sampling methods: (1) availability sampling, (2) quota sampling, (3) purposive sampling, and (4) snowball sampling. Because these methods do not use a random selection procedure, we cannot expect a sample selected with any of these methods to yield a representative sample. They should not be used in quantitative studies if a probability-based method is feasible. Nonetheless, these methods are useful when random sampling is not possible, when a research question calls for an intensive investigation of a small population, or when a researcher is performing a preliminary, exploratory study.

Availability Sampling

Availability sampling: Sampling in which elements are selected on the basis of convenience

In availability sampling, elements are selected because they are available or easy to find. Consequently, this sampling method is also known as *haphazard*, *accidental*, or *convenience* sampling. As noted earlier, news reporters often use passersby—availability samples—to inject a personal perspective into a news story and show what ordinary people may think of a given topic. Availability samples are also used by university professors and researchers all the time. Have you ever been asked to complete a questionnaire before leaving one of your classes? If so, you may have been selected for inclusion in an availability sample.

Even though they are not generalizable, availability samples are often appropriate in research—for example, when a field researcher is exploring a new setting and trying to get some sense of prevailing attitudes or when a survey researcher conducts a preliminary test of a questionnaire. There are a variety of ways to select elements for an availability sample: standing on street corners and talking to anyone walking by, asking questions of employees who come to pick up their paychecks at a personnel office, or distributing questionnaires to an available and captive audience, such as a class or a group meeting. Availability samples are also frequently used in fieldwork studies when the researchers are interested in obtaining detailed information about a particular group. When such samples are used, it is necessary to explicitly describe the sampling procedures used in the methodology section of research reports to acknowledge the nonrepresentativeness of the sample. For example, in a study investigating the prevalence of problem behavior in a sample of students pursuing policing careers, Gray (2011) stated,

> [A] convenience/purposive sample was used to survey students attending a medium-sized public, Midwestern university . . . to determine if differences existed between students majoring in criminal justice (CJ) and students with other majors in terms of deviance and delinquency, drinking and drug use, and an array of other behaviors. (p. 544)

Those of you studying for a policing career will be interested to know that over one quarter of the CJ majors had engaged in serious forms of problematic behavior, such as marijuana use. Students who engage in these forms of illegal activities, Gray (2011) points out, "should expect to have some level of difficulty with police application and hiring processes" (p. 549). But we digress.

How does the generalizability of survey responses from an availability sample compare with those obtained from probability samples? The difference is that in an availability sample, there is no clearly definable population from which the respondents were drawn, and no systematic technique was used to select the respondents. Consequently, there is not much likelihood that the sample is representative of any target population; the problem is that we can never be sure. Unfortunately, availability sampling often masquerades as a more rigorous form of research.

Quota Sampling

Quota sampling is intended to overcome availability sampling's biggest downfall: the likelihood that the sample will just consist of who or what is available, without any concern for its similarity to the population of interest. The distinguishing feature of a quota sample is that quotas are set to ensure that the sample represents certain characteristics in proportion to their prevalence in the population.

Quota samples are similar to stratified probability samples, but they are generally less rigorous and precise in their selection procedures. Quota sampling simply involves designating the population into proportions of some group that you want to be represented in your sample. Similar to stratified samples, in some cases, these proportions may actually represent the true proportions observed in the population. At other times, these quotas may represent predetermined proportions of subsets of people you deliberately want to oversample.

The problem is that even when we know that a quota sample is representative of the particular characteristics for which quotas have been set, we have no way of knowing if the sample is representative in terms of any other characteristics. In Exhibit 5.6, for example, quotas have been set for gender only. Under the circumstances, it's no surprise that the sample is representative of the population only in terms of gender, not in terms of other demographic characteristics such as age. Realistically, researchers can set quotas for only a small fraction of the characteristics relevant to a study, so a quota sample is really not much better than an availability sample (although following careful, consistent procedures for selecting cases within the quota limits always helps).

This last point leads to another limitation of quota sampling: You must know the characteristics of the entire population to set the right quotas. In most cases, researchers know what the population looks like in terms of no more than a few of the characteristics relevant to their concerns, and in some cases, they have no such information on the entire population. Does quota sampling remind you of stratified sampling? It's easy to understand why because they both select sample members partly on the basis of one or more key characteristics. The key difference is quota sampling's lack of random selection.

Quota sampling: A nonprobability sampling method in which elements are selected to ensure that the sample represents certain characteristics in proportion to their prevalence in the population

Exhibit 5.6 Quota Sampling

Population
50% male, 50% female
70% white, 30% black

Quota Sample
50% male, 50% female

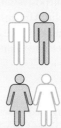

Representative of gender distribution in population, not representative of race distribution.

Purposive or Judgment Sampling

Purposive sampling:
A nonprobability sampling method in which elements are selected for a purpose, usually because of their unique position; sometimes referred to as *judgment sampling*

In **purposive sampling**, each sample element is selected for a purpose, usually because of the unique position of the sample elements. It is sometimes referred to as *judgment sampling*, because the researcher uses his or her own judgment about whom to select into the sample rather than drawing sample elements randomly. Purposive sampling may involve studying the entire population of some limited group (members of a street gang) or a subset of a population (juvenile parolees). A purposive sample may also be a key informant survey, which targets individuals who are particularly knowledgeable about the issues under investigation.

Rubin and Rubin (1995) suggest three guidelines for selecting informants when designing any purposive sampling strategy. Informants should be

- knowledgeable about the cultural arena or situation or experience being studied,
- willing to talk, and
- representative of the range of points of view. (p. 66)

In addition, Rubin and Rubin (1995) suggest continuing to select interviewees until you can pass two tests:

- *Completeness.* "What you hear provides an overall sense of the meaning of a concept, theme, or process." (p. 72)
- *Saturation.* "You gain confidence that you are learning little that is new from subsequent interview[s]." (p. 73)

Adhering to these guidelines will help ensure that a purposive sample adequately represents the setting or issues being studied. Purposive sampling does not produce a sample that represents some larger population, but it can be exactly what is needed in a case study of an organization, community, or some other clearly defined and relatively limited group. For example, in their classic book *Crimes of the Middle Class*, Weisburd, Wheeler, Waring, and Bode (1991) examined a sample of white-collar criminal offenders convicted in seven federal judicial districts. These judicial districts were not randomly selected from an exhaustive list of all federal districts but were instead deliberately selected by the researchers because they were thought to provide a suitable amount of geographical diversity. The cost of such nonprobability sampling, you should realize by now, is generalizability; we do not know if their findings hold true for white-collar crime in other areas of the country.

Snowball Sampling

Snowball sampling is useful for hard-to-reach populations for which there is no sampling frame, but in which the members are somewhat interconnected. (At least some members of the population know each other, such as drug dealers, sex workers, and so on.) In snowball sampling, you identify one member of the population and speak to him or her, then ask that person to identify others in the population and speak to them, then ask them to identify others, and so on.

St. Jean (2007) used snowball sampling for recruiting offenders in a Chicago neighborhood for interviews. After several years of participant observation (see Chapter 8) within a Chicago community, St. Jean wanted to understand the logic offenders used for setting up street drug dealing and staging robberies. He explained his sampling technique as follows:

> I was introduced to the offenders mainly through referrals from relatives, customers, friends, and acquaintances who, after several months (sometimes years), trusted me as someone whose only motive was to understand life in their neighborhood. For instance, the first three drug dealers I interviewed were introduced by their close relatives. Toward the end of each interview, I asked for leads to other subjects, with the first three interviews resulting in eleven additional leads. (p. 26)

One problem with this technique is that the initial contacts may shape the entire sample and foreclose access to some members of the population of interest. For example, in their study of gang members, Decker and Van Winkle (1996) wanted to interview members from several gangs, so they had to restart the snowball sampling procedure many times to gain access to a large number of gangs. One problem, of course, was validating whether individuals claiming to be gang members—so-called wannabes—actually were legitimate members. Over 500 contacts were made before the final sample of 99 was complete.

More systematic versions of snowball sampling can also reduce the potential for bias. The most sophisticated version, *respondent-driven sampling*, gives financial incentives, also called *gratuities*, to respondents to recruit peers (Heckathorn, 1997). Limitations on the number of incentives that any one respondent can receive increase the sample's diversity. Targeted incentives can steer the sample to include specific subgroups. When the sampling is repeated through several waves, with new respondents bringing in more peers, the composition of the sample converges on a more representative mix of characteristics. Exhibit 5.7 shows how the sample spreads out through successive recruitment waves to an increasingly diverse pool (Heckathorn, 1997). As with all nonprobability sampling techniques, however, researchers using even the most systematic versions of snowball sampling cannot be confident that their sample is representative of the population of interest.

Snowball sampling: A method of sampling in which sample elements are selected as they are identified by successive informants or interviewees

Exhibit 5.7   Respondent-Driven Sampling—A Version of Snowball Sampling

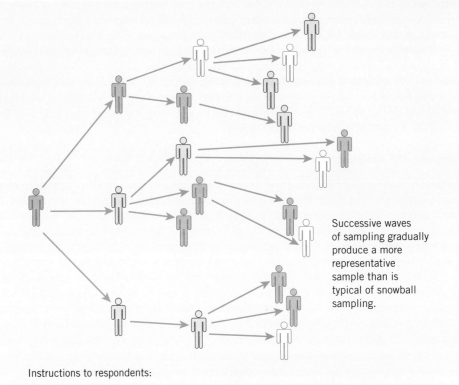

Successive waves of sampling gradually produce a more representative sample than is typical of snowball sampling.

Instructions to respondents:

"We'll pay you $5 each for up to three names, but only one of those names can be somebody from your own town. The others have to be from somewhere else."

Lessons About Sample Quality

Some lessons are implicit in our evaluations of the samples in this chapter:

- We cannot evaluate the quality of a sample if we do not know what population it is supposed to represent. If the population is unspecified because the researchers were never clear about just what population they were trying to sample, then we can safely conclude that the sample itself is no good.

- We cannot evaluate the quality of a sample if we do not know exactly how cases in the sample were selected from the population. If the method was specified, we then need to know whether cases were selected in a systematic fashion or on the basis of chance. In any case, we know that a haphazard method of sampling (as in person-on-the-street interviews) undermines generalizability.

- Sample quality is determined by the sample actually obtained, not just by the sampling method itself. That is, findings are only as generalizable as the sample from which they are drawn. If many of the people (or other elements) selected for our sample do not respond or participate in the study, even though they have been selected for the sample, generalizability is compromised.

- We need to be aware that even researchers who obtain very good samples may talk about the implications of their findings for some group that is larger than or just different from the population they actually sampled. For example, findings from a representative sample of students in one university often are discussed as if they tell us about university students in general. Maybe they do; the problem is, we just don't know.

Generalizability in Qualitative Research

Qualitative research often focuses on populations that are hard to locate or very limited in size. In consequence, nonprobability sampling methods, such as availability sampling and snowball sampling, are often used. However, this does not mean that generalizability should be ignored in qualitative research or that a sample should be studied simply because it is convenient (Gobo, 2008). Janet Ward Schofield (2002) suggests two different ways of increasing the generalizability of the samples obtained in such situations:

> *Studying the Typical.* Choosing sites on the basis of their fit with a typical situation is far preferable to choosing on the basis of convenience. (p. 181)

> *Performing Multisite Studies.* A finding emerging repeatedly in the study of numerous sites would appear to be more likely to be a good working hypothesis about some as yet unstudied site than a finding emerging from just one or two sites. . . . Generally speaking, a finding emerging from the study of several very heterogeneous sites would be more . . . likely to be useful in understanding various other sites than one emerging from the study of several very similar sites. (p. 184)

Giampietro Gobo (2008) highlights another approach to improving generalizability in qualitative research. A case may be selected for in-depth study because it is atypical or deviant. Investigating social processes in a situation that differs from the norm will improve understanding of how social processes work in typical situations: "the exception that proves the rule."

Some qualitative researchers do question the value of generalizability as most researchers understand it. The argument is that understanding the particulars of a situation in depth is an important object of inquiry in itself. In the words of sociologist Norman Denzin,

> The interpretivist rejects generalization as a goal and never aims to draw randomly selected samples of human experience. . . . Every instance of social interaction . . . represents a slice from the life world that is the proper subject matter for interpretive inquiry. (Denzin cited in Schofield, 2002, p. 173)

UNITS OF ANALYSIS AND ERRORS IN CAUSAL REASONING

In criminological research, we obtain samples from many different units, including individuals, groups, cities, prisons, countries, and so on. When we make generalizations from a sample to the population, it is very important to keep in mind the units under study, which are referred to as the **units of analysis**. These units of analysis are the level of social life on which the research question is focused, such as individuals, groups, or nations.

Units of analysis: The level of social life on which a research question is focused, such as individuals

What Are Best Practices for Sampling Vulnerable Populations?

A New York City survey estimated that there were 3,900 people living on the street, and the city's Department of Homeless Services (DHS) is opening new drop-in centers to help meet their basic needs. Finding housing prices impossibly high for meager incomes—even for some who are working—street-dwelling homeless persons have often tried and rejected the option of staying in shelters due to experiences with or fear of crime, overcrowding, or other problems. The DHS estimates that it takes an average of five months of contact to reestablish trust and convince people to return to living indoors. Although the city is also opening more shelters, some are designated as Safe Havens of limited size in order to attract more of the street homeless.

For Further Thought

1. What research question would be of most interest to you that might be the focus of a survey of a sample of homeless persons dwelling on the street?

2. How many challenges can you list that would likely be confronted by a social researcher seeking to survey a representative sample of homeless persons?

3. Can you identify strategies discussed in this chapter for overcoming some of these challenges?

Source: Stewart, N. (2017, July 19). As more opt for streets, city offers a place to go. *New York Times*, p. A20.

Individual and Group Units of Analysis

In much social science research, including criminological studies, the units of analysis are individuals. The researcher may collect survey data from individuals, analyze the data, and then report on how many individuals felt socially isolated and whether recidivism by individuals related to their feelings of social isolation. Data are collected from individuals, and the focus of analysis is on the individual.

In other instances, however, the units of analysis may be groups, such as families, schools, prisons, towns, states, or countries. In some studies, groups are the units of analysis but data are collected from individuals. For example, in their classic study of neighborhoods and crime, Sampson, Raudenbush, and Earls (1997) measured collective efficacy in Chicago neighborhoods. The construct of collective efficacy was defined as ability of neighborhood residents to trust and/or to help other neighborhood residents. To measure this, they had to survey individuals. However, to measure this construct at the neighborhood level, these individual responses were averaged to create a collective efficacy score for each neighborhood. It was this neighborhood measure of collective efficacy that was used to explain variation in the rate of violent crime between neighborhoods. The data were collected from individuals and were about individuals, but they were combined or aggregated to describe neighborhoods. The units of analysis were thus groups (neighborhoods).

In a study such as that of Sampson and colleagues, we can distinguish the concept of *units of analysis* from the **units of observation**. Data were collected from individuals (the units of observation), and then the data were aggregated and analyzed at the group level. In some studies, the units of observation and the units of analysis are the same. For example, Yili Xu, Mora Fiedler, and Karl Flaming (2005), in collaboration with the Colorado Springs Police Department, surveyed a stratified random sample of 904 residents to test whether their sense of collective efficacy and other characteristics would predict their perceptions of crime, fear of crime, and satisfaction with police. Their data were collected from individuals and analyzed

Units of observation: The cases about which measures actually are obtained in a sample

at the individual level. They concluded that collective efficacy was not as important as in Sampson et al.'s (1997) study.

The important point is to know when this is true. A conclusion that crime increases with joblessness could imply that individuals who lose their jobs are more likely to commit a crime, that a community with a high unemployment rate is likely to have a high crime rate, or both. Whether we are drawing conclusions from data or interpreting others' conclusions, we have to be clear about which relationship is referenced.

We also have to know what the units of analysis are to interpret statistics properly. Measures of association tend to be stronger for group-level than for individual-level data because measurement errors at the individual level tend to cancel out at the group level (Bridges & Weis, 1989).

The Ecological Fallacy and Reductionism

Researchers should make sure that their conclusions reflect the units of analysis in their study. For example, a conclusion that crime increases as unemployment increases could imply that individuals who lose their jobs are more likely to commit a crime, that a community with a high unemployment rate is also likely to have a high crime rate, or both. Conclusions about processes at the individual level should be based on individual-level data; conclusions about group-level processes should be based on data collected about groups. In most cases, violation of this rule creates one more reason to suspect the validity of the causal conclusions.

A researcher who draws conclusions about individual-level processes from group-level data is constructing an **ecological fallacy** (see Exhibit 5.8). The conclusions may or may not be correct, but we must recognize that group-level data do not describe individual-level processes. For example, a researcher may examine prison employee records and find that the higher the percentage of correctional workers without college education in prisons, the higher the rate of inmate complaints of brutality by officers in prisons. But the researcher would commit an ecological fallacy if he or she then concluded that individual correctional officers without a college education were more likely to engage in acts of brutality against inmates. This conclusion is about an individual-level causal process (the relationship between the education and criminal propensities of individuals), even though the data describe groups (prisons). It could actually be that college-educated officers are the ones more likely to commit acts of brutality. If more officers in prison are not college educated, perhaps the college-educated officers feel they would not be suspected.

Conversely, when data about individuals are used to make inferences about group-level processes, a problem occurs that can be thought of as the mirror image of the ecological fallacy: the **reductionist fallacy**, also known as **reductionism** or the *individualist fallacy* (see Exhibit 5.8).

The solution to these problems is to know what the units of analysis and units of observation were in a study and to take these into account when weighing the credibility of the researcher's conclusions. The goal is not to reject conclusions that refer to a level of analysis different from what was actually

Ecological fallacy: An error in reasoning in which incorrect conclusions about individual-level processes are drawn from group-level data

Reductionist fallacy (reductionism): An error in reasoning that occurs when incorrect conclusions about group-level processes are based on individual-level data

Exhibit 5.8 Errors in Causal Conclusions

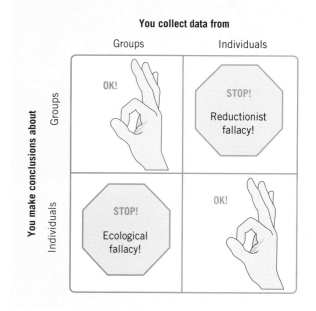

studied. Instead, the goal is to consider the likelihood that an ecological fallacy or a reduction-ist fallacy has been made when estimating the causal validity of the conclusions. The goal is not to reject conclusions that refer to a level of analysis different from what was actually stud-ied. Instead, the goal is to consider the likelihood that an ecological fallacy or a reductionist fallacy has been made when estimating the causal validity of the conclusions.

CAREERS AND RESEARCH

Captain Jennifer Griffin, PhD, Patrol Troop Commander, Delaware State Police

Source: Courtesy of Jennifer Griffin

Captain Jennifer Griffin has been a trooper with the Delaware State Police for 16 years. She has had assignments as a patrol trooper, a school resource officer, and a grant man-ager and planner in the Planning Section; she has been the director of the Internal Affairs Unit, and she is currently a patrol troop commander. But what most people don't know is that she is also a PhD from the University of Delaware. As a young woman, Captain Griffin says she always knew that her career calling was to be a police officer, and so she pursued her bachelor's degree in criminal jus-tice. However, within one year of becoming a state trooper, she realized that she wanted to earn her master's degree. During that time, she says, "I real-ized how much I enjoyed school and research, and how much more the research and the lessons meant to me because I was studying the field in which I was working." After she completed her master's, she continued on and earned her doctorate in sociology, with concentrations in gender and deviance.

Captain Griffin's doctoral studies included her writing her dissertation, which was titled "Stress in the 21st Century: Are We Protecting Those Who Protect Others?" She says she chose a research topic based on her experience as a police officer and wanted to use her research abilities and training to gain information to help police officers deal with the stress and strains of policing. Through her research, she was able to open a dialogue between police offi-cers and the Delaware State Police administration to discuss stress, burnout, work–family conflict, and the relationships among officers from different demographic groups.

Captain Griffin's research skills have provided her with opportunities that she says she never even imagined. As a result of her interest and education, she has been teaching as an adjunct instructor at the University of Delaware and other universities, and she teaches classes that range from graduate-level research methods to several undergraduate criminal justice courses. She says, "Without my PhD, teaching both undergraduate and graduate students wouldn't have been an option, and it gives me the opportunity to share not only my expertise as a researcher and scholar but also my life experiences as a state trooper. Being able to blend my academic background and life stories really helps me engage with students in ways that are both meaningful for the students and relevant to what is going on within society."

Her advice to other criminology and criminal justice students is this: "Find an area within the field that you are most interested in, and focus on how you can make it meaningful not only to you but also to the field because you really never know the doors that will open for you in the process. I could have never imagined all of the opportunities and interests that I have developed just from continuing my stud-ies within criminal justice."

CONCLUSION

Sampling is the fundamental starting point in criminological research. Probability sampling methods allow researchers to use the laws of chance, or *probability*, to draw samples from populations and maintain a standard of representativeness that can be estimated with a high degree of confidence. A sample of just 1,000 or 1,500 individuals can easily be used

114   FUNDAMENTALS OF RESEARCH IN CRIMINOLOGY AND CRIMINAL JUSTICE

to reliably estimate the characteristics of the population of a nation comprising millions of individuals.

The alternatives to random, or *probability-based*, sampling methods are almost always much less desirable, even though they typically are less expensive. Without a method of selecting cases likely to represent the population in which the researcher is interested, research findings will have to be carefully qualified. Unrepresentative samples may help researchers understand which aspects of a social phenomenon are important, but questions about the generalizability of this understanding are still left unanswered.

Social scientists often seek to generalize their conclusions from the population that they studied to some larger target population. The validity of generalizations of this type is necessarily uncertain, for having a representative sample of a particular population does not at all ensure that what we find will hold true in other populations. Nonetheless, the accumulation of findings from studies based on local or otherwise unrepresentative populations can provide important information about broader populations.

KEY TERMS

Availability sampling   106
Census   98
Cluster   104
Cross-population generalizability
    (external validity)   96
Disproportionate stratified
    sampling   103
Ecological fallacy   113
Elements   94
Enumeration units   94
Multistage cluster sampling   104
Nonprobability sampling
    method   99
Nonresponse   100

Periodicity   102
Population   94
Probability of selection   99
Probability sampling method   99
Proportionate stratified sampling   103
Purposive sampling   108
Quota sampling   107
Random digit dialing (RDD)   101
Random number table   101
Random selection   100
Reductionist fallacy
    (reductionism)   113
Replacement sampling   102
Representative sample   97

Sample   94
Sampling error   96
Sampling frame   94
Sample generalizability   96
Sampling interval   102
Sampling units   94
Simple random sampling   101
Snowball sampling   109
Stratified random sampling   103
Systematic bias   100
Systematic random sampling   102
Target population   96
Units of analysis   111
Units of observation   112

HIGHLIGHTS

- Sampling is usually necessary except in two conditions: (1) when the elements that would be sampled are identical, which is almost never the case, and (2) when you have the option of conducting a complete census of a population.

- Nonresponse undermines sample quality: It is the obtained sample, not the desired sample, which determines sample quality.

- Probability sampling methods rely on a random selection procedure to ensure there is no systematic bias in the selection of elements. In a probability sample, the odds of selecting elements are independent, equal, and known, and the method of selection is carefully controlled.

- Simple random sampling and systematic random sampling are equivalent probability sampling methods in most situations. However, systematic random sampling is inappropriate for sampling from lists of elements that have a regular, periodic structure.

- Other types of random sampling include stratified random sampling, which uses prior information about a population to make sampling more efficient, and cluster sampling.

- Nonprobability sampling methods can be useful when random sampling is not possible, when a research question does not concern a larger population, and when a preliminary exploratory study is appropriate. However, the representativeness of nonprobability samples cannot be determined.

- The likely degree of error in an estimate of a population characteristic based on a probability sample decreases as the size of the sample increases. Sampling error also decreases if the population from which the sample was selected is homogeneous.

EXERCISES

Discussing Research

1. Assess two different polls offering opinions about the same heated topic related to crime—compare CNN.com with Slate.com, for example. What information does the article provide on the sample that was selected? What additional information do you need to determine whether the sample was a representative one? What do the responses tell you about the people who participate in pools on these websites?

2. Select a random sample using the table of random numbers, which typically can be found on many websites (stattrek.com/Tables/Random.aspx). Now find information on crime rates from some source such as the government documents section of your library or online at the Bureau of Justice Statistics or the Federal Bureau of Investigation. Find a listing of crime rates (e.g., robbery, homicide) by some geographical units (e.g., states, cities) and number them. Then, apply your selected random sample to the list, and extract the sample. Compute the average crime rate from your sample. Now, compute the average for the entire population list. How does the sample average compare with the corresponding figure for the entire population?

3. Draw a snowball sample of people who have some characteristic of interest that is not common (e.g., have been skydiving). Ask friends and relatives to locate a first contact and then call or visit this person and ask for names of others. Stop when you have identified a sample of 10. Review the problems you encountered, and consider how you would proceed if you had to draw a larger sample.

4. All adult U.S. citizens are required to participate in the decennial census, but some do not. Some social scientists have argued for putting more resources into a large representative sample so that more resources are available to secure higher rates of response from hard-to-include groups. Do you think that the U.S. Census should shift to a probability-based sampling design? Why, or why not?

Finding Research on the Web

1. What can you learn about sampling on the Web? Conduct a search on "sampling" and "population" and select a few of these sites. List a few new points that you learn about sampling and how the inclusion of cell phone users will steer future research findings.

2. Go to the Bureau of Justice Statistics (bjs.gov). Search for five publications containing information on prison populations or victimization. Briefly describe the sampling procedures used to collect the information in these publications. How do these sources of information differ in their approaches to collecting information? Do they report the sampling information? What statistics do they present? What sampling methods were used? Evaluate the sampling methods in terms of representativeness and generalizability. How would you improve on the sampling methods to increase the representativeness and generalizability of the data? If no sampling methods are mentioned, propose one that would have been appropriate to obtain the statistics.

Critiquing Research

1. Select five scholarly journal articles that describe criminological research using a sample drawn from some population (you can find journal articles on the Student Study Site, edge.sagepub.com/bachmanfrccj5e). Identify the type of sample used in each study, and note any strong and weak points in how the sample was actually drawn. Did the researchers have a problem due to nonresponse? Considering the sample, how confident are you in the validity of generalizations about the population based on the sample? Do you need any additional information to evaluate the sample? Do you think a different sampling strategy would have been preferable? To what larger population were the findings generalized? Do you think these generalizations were warranted? Why, or why not?

2. What are the advantages and disadvantages of probability-based sampling designs compared

with nonprobability-based designs? Could any of the research described in this chapter with a nonprobability-based design have been conducted instead with a probability-based design? What are the difficulties that might have been encountered in an attempt to use random selection? How would you discuss the degree of confidence you can place in the results obtained from research using a nonprobability-based sampling design? Can you think of other examples where probability sampling is not an option for researchers?

Making Research Ethical

1. How much pressure is too much pressure to participate in a probability-based sample survey? Is it okay for the U.S. government to mandate that all citizens participate in the decennial census? Should companies be able to require employees to participate in survey research about work-related issues? Should students be required to participate in surveys about teacher performance? Should parents be required to consent to the participation of their high-school-aged students in a survey about substance abuse and health issues? Is it okay to give monetary incentives for participation in a survey of homeless shelter clients? Can monetary incentives be coercive? Explain your decisions.

2. The Centers for Disease Control and Prevention sampled adults using RDD in order to determine the prevalence of intimate partner violence and sexual assault. Do you believe that the researchers had any ethical obligation to take any action whatsoever when they learned that a respondent was currently being victimized? Are any of the ethical guidelines presented in Chapter 3 relevant to this situation? Teachers and medical personnel are required by law to report cases they believe represent incidents of child abuse. Should researchers have the same obligation? How would this affect large-scale surveys using RDD when you want to preserve the anonymity of respondents?

Developing a Research Proposal

Consider the possibilities for sampling:

1. Propose a sampling design that would be appropriate if you were to survey students on your campus only. Define the population, identify the sampling frame(s), and specify the elements and any other units at different stages. Indicate the exact procedure for selecting people to be included in the sample.

2. Propose a different sampling design for conducting your survey in a larger population, such as your city, state, or the entire nation.

Performing Data Analysis in SPSS or Excel

Data for Exercise	
Dataset	**Description**
2012 states data.sav	This dataset compiles official statistics from various official sources, such as the census, health department records, and police departments. It includes basic demographic data, crime rates, and incidence rates for various illnesses and infant mortality for entire states.

Variables for Exercise	
Variable Name	**Description**
State	ID for state the data are from
MurderRt	Number of murders in a state per 100,000

1. First, take a look at the 2012 state dataset. Answer these questions:

    a. How many cases are in this dataset?

    b. What does the variable "state" tell you if you look at a frequency?

    c. What are units of analysis for these data?

    d. Assume that official records are accurately collected. Are these sample data or population data?

    e. Say we took an average of the murder rates in the data. What will that average tell us?

2. Take a look at the average murder rate for the United States by looking at descriptives for the variable "murderRt" (analyze->descriptive statistics->descriptives).

   a. What do you find? Hang on to this number!

3. If you guessed that these are population-level data, you are correct! Such data are rather rare, but we can use the data to explore how close estimates from a sample from the population come to capturing the actual population mean. We'll do this taking a random sample of states using it to generalize to the population as a whole.

   a. To randomly select 25 states, select "data->select cases" and then click "sample" under the "random sample of cases" option. In the pop-up menu, tell it to select 25 of 50 states randomly.

Some rows should now be crossed off in data view.

4. Now let's look at the sample that was selected. Answer these questions:

   a. How many cases are in this dataset?

   b. What does the variable "state" tell you if you look at a frequency?

   c. What are units of analysis for these data?

   d. Assume that official records are accurately collected. Are these sample data or population data?

   e. Take a look at the average murder rate for the United States by looking at descriptives for the variable "murderRt" (analyze->descriptive statistics->descriptives). How does this mean compare with the mean from the population?

6

CAUSATION AND EXPERIMENTATION

> I am positive the skills I learned in my research methods class helped me get my position at the Office of the Child Advocate . . . I'm extremely excited and thankful! The coordinator specifically mentioned how important my research and data analysis skills will be in transitioning the data they gathered in paper copy to an electronic database.
>
> **Dillon D., Student**

WHAT DO WE MEAN BY CAUSATION?

On December 31, 2017, over 6.5 million people in the United States were under some kind of correctional supervision, including in prisons or local jails, or on probation or parole (Kaeble & Cowhig, 2018). The large prison population, coupled with lawsuits, has prompted most correctional institutions to begin classifying inmates into different security levels (e.g., minimum and maximum) based on objective criteria such as the severity of their offenses, previous records, and so forth. Obviously, the security level of an institution in which an inmate is classified will affect his or her incarceration experience. For example, someone who is assigned to a maximum-security prison instead of one with a lower level of security will also have differential access to things such as mental health services, drug treatment programs, and vocational training (Brennan & Austin, 1997). But is the classification of inmates also related to their behavior while incarcerated? Do those assigned to maximum-security prisons engage in more misconduct compared with inmates assigned to less secure facilities? How could you answer this question? If you compared rates of misconduct across prison settings, you would not have the answer because the inmates may have been very different at their time of incarceration. As such, any differences you observe in misconduct could be attributable to these "before incarceration"

Learning Objectives

1. List the three criteria for establishing a causal relationship and the two cautions that can improve understanding of a causal connection.

2. Contrast the strengths and weaknesses of dealing with nonspuriousness through statistical control and through randomization.

3. Explain the meaning of the expression "correlation does not prove causation."

4. Name two challenges to using experimental designs and two difficulties with identifying idiographic causal explanations.

5. Name and illustrate the three different quasi-experimental designs.

6. Define the individual and group units of analysis, and explain the role they play in the ecological and reductionist fallacies.

⑤SAGE edge™

Master the content at **edge**
.sagepub.com/bachmanfrccj5e

differences, not to the type of facility in which they are housed. As you can see, establishing causation is more difficult than it appears.

CAUSAL EXPLANATIONS

A *cause* is an explanation for some characteristic, attitude, or behavior of groups, individuals, or other entities (such as families, organizations, or cities) or for events. Most social scientists seek causal explanations that reflect tests of the types of hypotheses with which you are familiar (recall Chapter 2). In these tests, the independent variable is the presumed cause and the dependent variable is the potential effect. For example, does problem-oriented policing (independent variable) reduce violent crime (dependent variable)? Does experiencing abuse as a child (independent variable) increase the likelihood that the person will be a violent adult (dependent variable)? This type of causal explanation is termed *nomothetic*.

A different type of cause is the focus of some qualitative research and our everyday conversations about causes. In this type of causal explanation, termed *idiographic*, individual events or the behavior of individuals are explained with a series of related, prior events. For example, you might explain a particular crime as resulting from several incidents in the life of the perpetrator that resulted in a tendency toward violence, coupled with stress resulting from a failed marriage and a chance meeting with a suitable target.

Quantitative (Nomothetic) Causal Explanation

A nomothetic causal explanation is one involving the belief that variation in an independent variable will be followed by variation in the dependent variable, when all other things are equal (*ceteris paribus*) or when all other potentially influential conditions and factors are taken into consideration. For instance, researchers might claim that the likelihood of committing violent crimes is higher for individuals who were abused as children than it would be if these same individuals had not been abused as children. Or researchers might claim that the likelihood of committing violent crimes is higher for individuals exposed to media violence than it would be if these same individuals had not been exposed to media violence. The situation as it would have been in the absence of variation in the independent variable is termed the counterfactual (see Exhibit 6.1).

Of course, the fundamental difficulty with this perspective is that we never really know what would have happened at the same time to the same people (or groups, cities, etc.) if the independent variable had not varied because it did. We cannot rerun real-life scenarios (King, Keohane, & Verba, 1994). We could observe the aggressiveness of people's behavior before and after they were exposed to media violence. But this comparison involves an earlier time period, when, by definition, the people and their circumstances were not exactly the same.

Fortunately, we can design research to create conditions that are comparable indeed so that we can confidently assert our conclusions *ceteris paribus*. We can examine the impact on the dependent variable of variation in the independent variable alone, even though we will not be able to compare the same people at the same time in exactly the same circumstances except for the variation in the independent variable. And by knowing the ideal standard of comparability, we can improve our research designs and strengthen our causal conclusions even when we cannot come so close to living up to the meaning of *ceteris paribus*.

Quantitative researchers seek to test nomothetic causal explanations with either experimental or nonexperimental research designs. However, the way in which experimental and nonexperimental designs attempt to identify causes differs quite a bit. It is very hard to meet some of the criteria for achieving valid nomothetic causal explanations using a nonexperimental

Nomothetic causal explanation: A type of causal explanation involving the belief that variation in an independent variable will be followed by variation in the dependent variable, when all other things are equal

Causal effect (nomothetic perspective): When variation in one phenomenon, an independent variable, leads to or results, on average, in variation in another phenomenon, the dependent variable

Example of a nomothetic causal effect: Individuals arrested for domestic assault tend to commit fewer subsequent assaults than do similar individuals who are accused in the same circumstances but not arrested

Ceteris paribus: Latin term meaning "all other things being equal"

Counterfactual: The outcome that would have occurred if the subjects who were exposed to the treatment actually were not exposed but otherwise had had identical experiences to those they underwent during the experiment

Exhibit 6.1   The Counterfactual in Causal Research

Independent variable: **Dependent variable:**

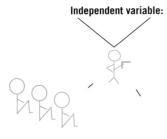   

Actual situation: People who watch violence on TV are more likely to commit violent acts.

Independent variable: **Dependent variable:**

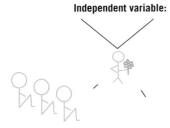   

Counterfactual situation: The same people watch nonviolent TV shows at the same time, in the same circumstances. They are not more likely to commit violent acts.

design. Most of the rest of this chapter is devoted to a review of these causal criteria and a discussion of how experimental and nonexperimental designs can help establish them.

Qualitative (Idiographic) Causal Explanation

The other meaning of the term *cause* is one that we have in mind very often in everyday speech. This is idiographic causal explanation: the concrete, individual sequence of events, thoughts, or actions that resulted in a particular outcome for a particular individual or that led to a particular event (Hage & Meeker, 1988). An idiographic explanation also may be termed an *individualist* or a *historicist explanation*.

A causal effect from an idiographic perspective includes statements of initial conditions and then relates a series of events at different times that led to the outcome, or causal effect. This narrative, or story, is the critical element in an idiographic explanation, which may therefore be classified as narrative reasoning (Richardson, 1995). Idiographic explanations focus on particular social actors, in particular social places, at particular social times (Abbott, 1992). Idiographic explanations are also typically very concerned with context, with understanding the particular outcome as part of a larger set of interrelated circumstances. Idiographic explanations thus can be termed holistic.

Elijah Anderson's (1999) field research in a poor urban community produced a narrative account of how drug addiction can result in a downward slide into residential instability and crime:

> When addicts deplete their resources, they may go to those closest to them, drawing them into their schemes. . . . The family may put up with the person for a while. They provide money if they can. . . . They come to realize that the person is on drugs. . . . Slowly the reality sets in more and more completely, and the family

Idiographic causal explanation: An explanation that identifies the concrete, individual sequence of events, thoughts, or actions that resulted in a particular outcome for a particular individual or that led to a particular event; may be termed an *individualist* or *historicist explanation*

Causal effect (idiographic perspective): When a series of concrete events, thoughts, or actions result in a particular event or individual outcome

Context: A focus of causal explanation; a particular outcome is understood as part of a larger set of interrelated circumstances

Example of an
idiographic causal
effect: An individual
is neglected by his
parents. He comes to
distrust others, has
trouble maintaining
friendships, has trouble
in school, and eventually
gets addicted to heroin.
To support his habit, he
starts selling drugs and
is ultimately arrested
and convicted for drug
trafficking.

becomes drained of both financial and emotional resources. . . . Close relatives lose faith and begin to see the person as untrustworthy and weak. Eventually the addict begins to "mess up" in a variety of ways, taking furniture from the house [and] anything of value. . . . Relatives and friends begin to see the person . . . as "out there" in the streets. . . . One deviant act leads to another. (pp. 86–87)

An idiographic explanation like Anderson's pays close attention to time order and causal mechanisms. Nonetheless, it is difficult to make a convincing case that one particular causal narrative should be chosen over an alternative narrative (Abbott, 1992). Does low self-esteem result in vulnerability to the appeals of drug dealers, or does a chance drug encounter precipitate a slide in self-esteem? The prudent causal analyst remains open to alternative explanations.

Idiographic explanation is deterministic, focusing on what caused a particular event to occur or what caused a particular case to change. As in nomothetic explanations, idiographic causal explanations can involve counterfactuals by trying to identify what would have happened if a different circumstance had occurred. But unlike nomothetic explanations, in idiographic explanations, the notion of a probabilistic relationship, an average effect, does not really apply. A deterministic cause has an effect only in the case under consideration. We focus on methods for examining idiographic causation more closely in Chapter 8.

CRITERIA FOR NOMOTHETIC CAUSAL EXPLANATIONS

Mark Twitchell wanted to be a filmmaker and become famous. One of the short movies he made was about a serial killer. Twitchell also was a big fan of the TV show *Dexter*, a drama about a serial killer. In 2008, he advanced this fiction to real life when he posed as a woman on a dating website to lure Johnny Altinger on a date. When Altinger showed up for the date on October 8, 2008, he was killed and dismembered. Fortunately, the murder was discovered before Twitchell could kill again. Not surprisingly, after his arrest, Twitchell became known as the "Dexter Killer" ("Mark Twitchell Case," n.d.). As frequently happens, some attributed Twitchell's violence to media portrayals of violence, in this case, to the series *Dexter*. How would you evaluate this claim? What evidence do we need to develop a valid conclusion about a hypothesized causal effect? As a blossoming criminological researcher, you now know that if we want to have confidence in the validity of our causal statements, we must meet a scientific standard.

How research is designed influences our ability to draw causal conclusions. In this section, we will introduce the features that need to be considered in a research design to evaluate how well it can support nomothetic causal conclusions.

Five criteria must be considered when deciding whether a causal connection exists. When a research design leaves one or more of the criteria unmet, we may have some important doubts about causal assertions the researcher may have made. The first three of the criteria are generally considered the necessary and most important basis for identifying a nomothetic causal effect: empirical association, appropriate time order, and nonspuriousness. The other two criteria, identifying a causal mechanism and specifying the context in which the effect occurs, can also considerably strengthen causal explanations, although many do not consider them requirements for establishing a causal relationship.

Conditions Necessary for Determining Causality

1. Empirical association

2. Appropriate time order

3. Nonspuriousness

1. Mechanism

2. Context

Case Study: Media Violence and Violent Behavior

We will use Brad Bushman's (see Bushman & Huesmann, 2012, for review) experiments on media violence and aggression to illustrate the five criteria for establishing causal relationships. Bushman's study focused, in part, on this specific research question: Do individuals who view a violent videotape act more aggressively than individuals who view a nonviolent videotape?

Undergraduate psychology students were recruited to watch a 15-minute videotape in a screening room, one student at a time. Half of the students watched a movie excerpt that was violent, and half watched a nonviolent movie excerpt. After viewing the videotape, the students were told that they were to compete with another student, in a different room, on a reaction time task. When the students saw a light cue, they were to react by trying to click a computer mouse faster than their opponent. On a computer screen, the students set a level of radio static that their opponents would hear when the opponents reacted more slowly. The students themselves heard this same type of noise when they reacted more slowly than their opponents at the intensity level supposedly set by their opponents.

Each student in the study participated in 25 trials, or competitions, with the unseen opponent. Their aggressiveness was operationalized as the intensity of noise that they set for their opponents over the course of the 25 trials. The louder the noise level they set, the more aggressively they were considered to be behaving toward their opponents. The question that we will focus on first is whether students who watched the violent video behaved more aggressively than those who watched the nonviolent video.

Association

Exhibit 6.2 displays the association that Brad Bushman found between watching a violent videotape and aggressive behavior (Bushman & Huesmann, 2012). Students who watched a violent videotape in his lab administered more intense noise to an opponent than those who watched a nonviolent videotape. Thus, variation in exposure to media violence is associated with a likelihood of exhibiting aggressive behavior. A change in the independent variable is associated with—correlated with—a change in the dependent variable. By contrast, if there is no association between two variables, there cannot be a causal relationship.

Association: A criterion for establishing a causal relationship between two variables; variation in one variable is related to variation in another variable as a condition to determine causality

Time Order

Association is a necessary criterion for establishing a causal effect, but it is not sufficient on its own. We must also ensure that the variation in the independent variable came *before* variation in the dependent variable—the cause must come before the presumed effect. This is the criterion of time order. Bushman's (1995) original experiment satisfied this criterion because he controlled the variation in the independent variable: All the students saw the movie excerpts (which varied in violent content) before their level of aggressiveness was measured. As you can imagine, we cannot be so sure about time order when we use a survey or

Time order: A criterion for establishing a causal relation between two variables; the variation in the independent variable must come before variation in the dependent variable

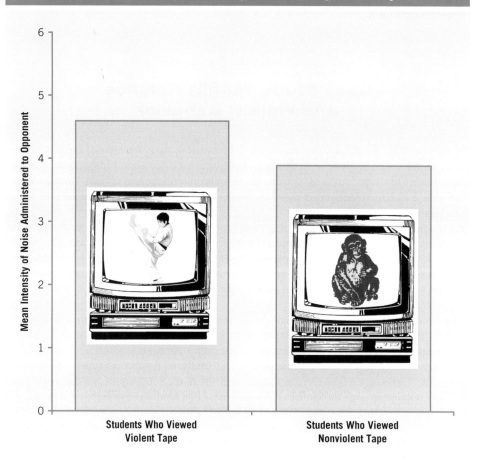

Exhibit 6.2 Association: Noise Intensity for Two Groups in an Experiment

Source: Adapted from Bushman 2012.

some other observation done at one point in time. For example, if we find that neighborhoods with higher levels of disorder have higher crime rates, we can't be sure that the level of disorder came first and that it led to more crime. Maybe higher crime rates made residents too fearful to keep things in order. Without longitudinal data or other clues to time order, we just don't know.

Nonspuriousness

Even when research establishes that two variables are associated and that variation in the independent variable precedes variation in the dependent variable, we cannot be sure we identified a causal relationship between the two variables. Have you heard the old adage among researchers, "Correlation does not prove causation"? It is meant to remind us that an association between two variables might be caused by something else. If we measure children's shoe sizes and their academic knowledge, for example, we will find a positive association. However, the association results from the fact that older children tend to have larger

Exhibit 6.3   A Spurious Relationship

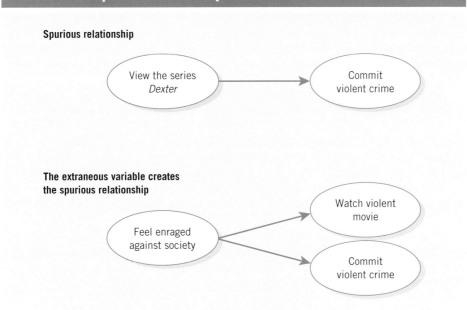

Spurious relationship

View the series *Dexter* → Commit violent crime

The extraneous variable creates the spurious relationship

Feel enraged against society → Watch violent movie

Feel enraged against society → Commit violent crime

feet, as well as more academic knowledge. As it turns out, shoe size does not cause increased knowledge or vice versa. We would say that the association between shoe size and knowledge is **spurious** (meaning apparently but not actually valid—that is, false).

Before we conclude that variation in an independent variable causes variation in a dependent variable, we must have reason to believe that the relationship is nonspurious. **Nonspuriousness** is a relationship between two variables that is not due to variation in a third variable (see Exhibit 6.3).

Does Bushman and Huesmann's (2012) claim of a causal effect rest on any stronger ground? To evaluate nonspuriousness, you need to know about one more feature of his experiment. He assigned students to watch either the violent video or the nonviolent video randomly—that is, by the toss of a coin. Because he used random assignment, the characteristics and attitudes that students already possessed when they were recruited for the experiment could not influence which video they watched. As a result, the students' characteristics and attitudes could not explain why one group reacted differently from the other after watching the videos. In fact, because Bushman used 296 students in his experiment, it is highly unlikely that the violent video group and the nonviolent video group differed in any relevant way at the outset, even on the basis of chance. This experimental research design meets the criterion of nonspuriousness. Bushman's conclusion that viewing video violence causes aggressive behavior thus rests on firm ground indeed.

Mechanism

Confidence in a conclusion that two variables have a causal connection will be strengthened if a **mechanism**—some discernible means of creating a connection—can be identified (Cook & Campbell, 1979, p. 35; Marini & Singer, 1988). Many social scientists believe that a causal explanation is not adequate until a causal mechanism is identified—what process or mechanism actually is responsible for the relationship between the independent and dependent variables.

> **Spurious relationship:** A relationship between two variables that is due to variation in a third variable
>
> **Nonspuriousness:** A relationship that exists between two variables that is not due to variation in a third variable

> **Mechanism:** A discernible process that creates a causal connection between two variables

Bushman and Huesmann (2012) did not empirically identify a causal mechanism in their experiment, though Bushman did suggest a possible causal mechanism for the effect of watching violent videos. Bushman believed that individuals who were predisposed to aggression before the study began would be more influenced by a violent film than individuals who were not aggressive at the outset. And that is what happened: Individuals who were predisposed to aggression became more aggressive after watching Bushman's violent video, but individuals who were not predisposed to aggression did not become more aggressive.

After the experiment, Bushman and Huesmann (2012) proposed a causal mechanism to explain why aggressive individuals became even more aggressive after watching the film:

> High trait aggressive individuals [people predisposed to aggression] are more susceptible to the effects of violent media than are low trait aggressive individuals because they possess a relatively large network of aggressive associations that can be activated by violent cues. Habitual exposure to television violence might be partially responsible. (p. 959)

Note that this explanation relies more on speculation than on the actual empirical evidence from this particular experiment. Nonetheless, by proposing a reasonable causal mechanism that connects the variation in the independent and dependent variables, this strengthened the argument for the causal validity of their conclusions.

Context

In the social world, it is virtually impossible to claim that one and only one independent variable is responsible for causing or affecting a dependent variable. Stated another way, no cause can be separated from the larger context in which it occurs. A cause is really only one of a set of interrelated factors required for the effect (Hage & Meeker, 1988; Papineau, 1978). When relationships among variables differ across geographic units, such as counties, or across other social settings—or even between different types of individuals—researchers say there is a contextual effect. Identification of the context in which a causal relationship occurs can help us to understand that relationship.

In a classic study of children's aggressive behavior in response to media violence, Albert Bandura, Dorothea Ross, and Sheila Ross (1963) examined several contextual factors. For example, they found that children reacted more aggressively after observing men committing violent acts than after observing women committing these same acts. Bandura and colleagues strengthened their conclusions by focusing on a few likely contextual factors. Specifying the context for a causal effect helps us understand that effect, but it is a process that can never really be complete. We can always ask what else might be important. In which country was the study conducted? What are the ages of the study participants? We need to carefully review the results of prior research and the implications of relevant theory to determine what contextual factors are likely to be important in a causal relationship.

Contextual effect: Relationships between variables that vary between geographic units or other contexts

WHY EXPERIMENT?

How research is designed influences our ability to draw causal conclusions. Obviously, if you conclude that playing violent video games causes violent behavior after watching your 8-year-old nephew playing a violent video game and then hitting his 4-year-old brother, you would be on shaky empirical ground. In this section, we will introduce features that need to be considered in a research design to evaluate how well it can support nomothetic causal conclusions.

True Experiments

Experimental research provides the most powerful design for testing causal hypotheses because it allows us to confidently establish the first three criteria for causality—association, time order, and nonspuriousness. True experiments have at least three features that help us meet these criteria:

1. Two comparison groups—one receiving the experimental condition (e.g., treatment or intervention), termed the experimental group, and the other receiving no treatment/intervention or another form thereof, termed the control group.

2. Random assignment to the two (or more) comparison groups.

3. Assessment of change in the dependent variable for both groups after the experimental condition has been applied. This is usually called a posttest. We can determine whether an association exists between the independent and dependent variables in a true experiment because two or more groups differ in terms of their value on the independent variable. One group, the experimental group, receives some "treatment" that is a manipulation of the value of the independent variable. In a simple experiment, there may be one other group that does not receive the treatment; it is termed the control or comparison group.

Let's consider the Bushman experiment in detail (see the simple diagram in Exhibit 6.4). Does watching a violent video lead to aggressive behavior? Imagine a simple experiment. Suppose you believe that watching violent movies leads people to be aggressive, commit crimes, and so on. But other people think that violent media has no effect and that it is people who are already predisposed to violence who seek out violent movies to watch. To test your research hypothesis ("Watching violent movies causes aggressive behavior"), you need to compare two randomly assigned groups of subjects, a control group and an experimental group.

First, it is crucial that the two groups be more or less equal at the beginning of the study. If you let students choose which group to be in, the more violent students may pick the violent movie, hoping, either consciously or unconsciously, to have their aggressive habits

True experiment: Experiment in which subjects are assigned randomly to an experimental group that receives a treatment or other manipulation of the independent variable and a comparison group that does not receive the treatment or receives some other manipulation; outcomes are measured in a posttest

Experimental group: In an experiment, the group of subjects that receives the treatment or experimental manipulation

Control or comparison group: The group of subjects who are either exposed to a different treatment than the experimental group or who receive no treatment at all

Exhibit 6.4 Experimental Design Used in the Bushman Research

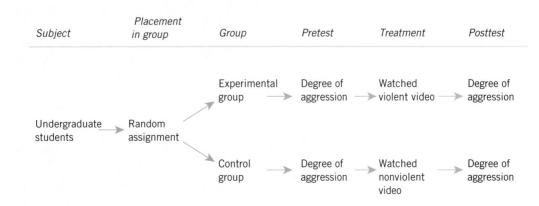

Subject	Placement in group	Group	Pretest	Treatment	Posttest
		Experimental group	Degree of aggression	Watched violent video	Degree of aggression
Undergraduate students	Random assignment				
		Control group	Degree of aggression	Watched nonviolent video	Degree of aggression

reinforced. If so, your two groups won't be equivalent at the beginning of the study. As such, any difference in their aggressiveness may be the result of that initial difference (a source of spuriousness), not whether they watched the violent video. You must randomly sort the students into the two different groups. You can do this by flipping a coin for each one of them, pulling names out of a hat, or using a random number table, as described in the previous chapter. In any case, the subjects themselves should not be free to choose nor should you (the experimenter) be free to put them into whatever group you want.

Note that the random assignment of subjects to experimental and comparison groups is not the same as random sampling of individuals from some larger population (see Exhibit 6.5). In fact, **random assignment (randomization)** does not help at all to ensure that the research subjects are representative of some larger population; instead, representativeness

> **Random assignment (randomization):** A procedure by which experimental and control group subjects are placed in groups randomly

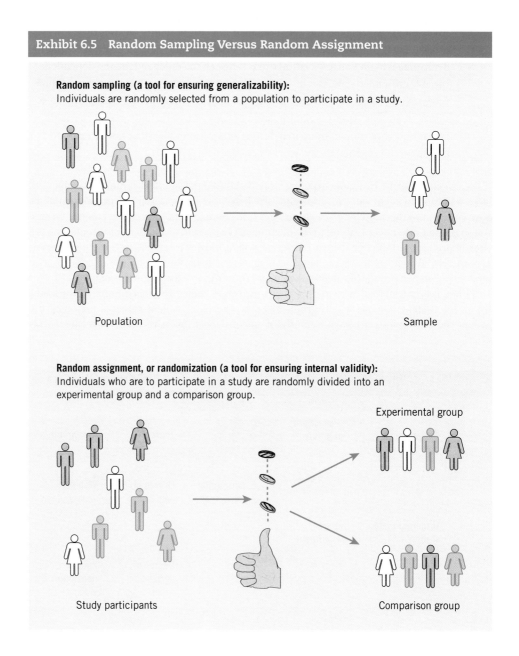

Exhibit 6.5 Random Sampling Versus Random Assignment

Random sampling (a tool for ensuring generalizability):
Individuals are randomly selected from a population to participate in a study.

Population

Sample

Random assignment, or randomization (a tool for ensuring internal validity):
Individuals who are to participate in a study are randomly divided into an experimental group and a comparison group.

Experimental group

Study participants

Comparison group

is the goal of random sampling. What random assignment does—create two (or more) equivalent groups—is useful for ensuring internal validity, not generalizability.

Next, people in the two groups will interact among themselves. Then, the control group will watch a video about gardening while the experimental group will watch a video featuring a lot of violence. Next, both groups will sit and interact again among themselves. At the end, the interactions within both groups before and after the videos will be coded, and you will see whether either group increased in aggressiveness. Thus, you may establish *association*.

Matching is another procedure sometimes used to equate experimental and comparison groups, but by itself, it is a poor substitute for randomization. Matching of individuals in a treatment group with those in a comparison group might involve pairing persons on the basis of similarity of gender, age, year in school, or some other characteristic. The basic problem is that, as a practical matter, individuals can be matched on only a few characteristics. Unmatched and unknown differences between the experimental and comparison groups may still influence outcomes.

These defining features of true experimental designs give us a great deal of confidence that we can meet the three basic criteria for identifying causes: association, time order, and nonspuriousness. However, we can strengthen our understanding of causal connections and increase the likelihood of drawing causally valid conclusions by also investigating causal mechanism and causal context.

Even after establishing the random assignment of experimental and control groups, you may find an association outside the experimental setting, but it won't establish time order. Perhaps aggressive people choose to watch violent videos, while nonaggressive people do not. So there would be an association but *not* the causal relation for which we are looking. By controlling who watches the violent video and when, we establish time order. All true experiments have a **posttest**—that is, a measurement of the outcome in both groups after the experimental group has received the treatment. Many true experiments also have **pretests** that measure the dependent variable before the experimental intervention. A pretest is exactly the same as a posttest, just administered at a different time. Strictly speaking, though, a true experiment does not require a pretest. When researchers use random assignment, the groups' initial scores on the dependent variable (or observed effect or behavior) and on all other variables are very likely to be similar. Any difference in outcome between the experimental and comparison groups is therefore likely to be due to the intervention (or to other processes occurring during the experiment), and the likelihood of a difference solely on the basis of chance can be calculated.

> Matching: A procedure for equating the characteristics of individuals in different comparison groups in an experiment; matching can be done on either an individual or an aggregate basis

> Posttest: Measurement of an outcome (dependent) variable after an experimental intervention or after a presumed independent variable has changed for some other reason

> Pretest: Measurement of an outcome (dependent) variable prior to an experimental intervention or change in a presumed independent variable

Case Study: An Experiment in Action—Prison Classification and Inmate Behavior

There is wide variability in the criteria used to classify prisoners across the United States. Regardless of how these classifications are made, once these labels are assigned, they have the effect that all labels have: They attach various stigmas and expectations to prisoners. Bench and Allen (2003) state,

> An offender classified as maximum security instantly obtains an image of one who is hard to handle, disrespectful of authority, prone to fight with other inmates, and at a high risk for escape. In contrast, an offender classified as medium security is generally regarded as more manageable, less of an escape risk, and not requiring as much supervision as a maximum-security offender. (p. 371)

To examine whether prison classification actually affects inmate behavior, Bench and Allen (2003) obtained a random sample of 200 inmates admitted to the Utah State Prison who had been classified as maximum security following their initial assessment based on the following criteria: severity of current crime, expected length of incarceration, criminal violence history, escape history, prior institutional commitment, age, history of institutional adjustment, and substance abuse history.

From this group, inmates were randomly assigned to either an experimental group, in which inmates were reclassified to medium-security status, or a control group, in which inmates retained their maximum-security status. The independent variable, then, was security classification. The dependent variable was the number of disciplinary infractions or sanctions for violation of prison rules received by each group. The severity of infractions was weighted to control for the severity of the violations (e.g., possession of unauthorized food was weighted lower than assaulting another inmate). The primary hypothesis was that the experimental group, those reclassified as medium security, would have a lower number of disciplinary infractions compared with the control group, the inmates who retained their maximum-security classification. A diagram depicting the experiment is provided in Exhibit 6.6. Results indicated that inmates reclassified to medium security did not receive a lower number of infractions; both groups received about the same number of disciplinary infractions, regardless of security classification.

Case Study: Field Experiments in Action—Determining the Effect of Incarceration on Employment

As you have seen, social experiments are not always conducted in a laboratory or controlled environment. In fact, many experiments are conducted out in the real world. Whenever studies utilize the conditions of an experimental method in a real-world setting, they are termed **field experiments**. All of the studies examining the effects of arrest on future intimate partner assaults discussed in Chapter 2 were field experiments.

One innovative field experiment was conducted by Pager (2007) to determine the effects of incarceration on the likelihood of obtaining employment. This is an extremely important research question because the prison population in the United States has vastly increased over the past 30 years. In addition to the laws barring ex-offenders in some states from obtaining employment in certain sectors, reentering offenders also face other obstacles in finding a job, particularly from the stigma attached to having a record. How could we determine the effects of a formal criminal record on the likelihood of getting a job? Well, we could examine employer attitudes about hiring ex-offenders through a survey, but as you now know, this would not help us isolate a causal relationship between having a record and getting a job. We could interview offenders reentering the community to find out their own experiences, but this would tell us only about a few individuals' experiences. The best way to determine the effects of a criminal record on employment chances would be to conduct a field experiment, which is what Pager did. Her study is diagrammed in Exhibit 6.7.

Field experiment: An experimental study conducted in a real-world setting

---

Exhibit 6.6   Experiment Examining the Effect of Prison Classification on Inmate Behavior

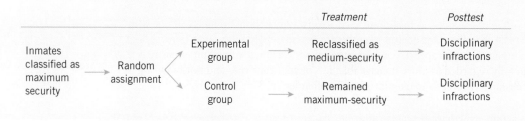

Source: Bench and Allen (2003)

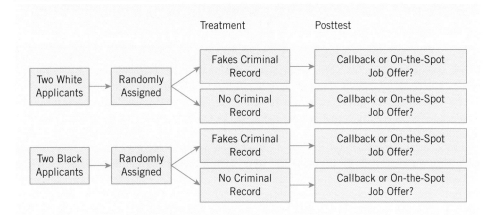

Exhibit 6.7 Experimental and Control Groups in Pager's Experiment Investigating Effect of Job Applicant's Criminal Record on Hiring Decisions

Source: Based on Pager, D. 2007. *Marked: Race, Crime and Finding Work in an Era of Mass Incarceration.* Chicago: University of Chicago Press.

Pager (2007) designed a field experiment in which pairs of applicants, one who had a criminal record and one who did not, applied for real jobs. Her study used two male teams of applicants, one composed of two African Americans and one composed of two whites. These individuals were actually college students in Milwaukee, Wisconsin, whom Pager refers to as "testers." The testers were matched on the basis of age, physical appearance, and general style of self-presentation, and all were assigned fictitious résumés that reflected equivalent levels of education (all had a high school education) and equivalent levels of steady work experience. However, one tester within each team was randomly assigned to have a criminal record and the other was not. The fictitious criminal record consisted of a felony drug conviction and 18 months of served prison time. This assignment rotated each week of the study (e.g., one individual played the job applicant with a record one week, and the other did so the next week) as a check against unobserved differences between team members. Same-race testers (one with a criminal record and one without) applied for the same job, one day apart. The African American team applied for a total of 200 jobs, and the white team applied for a total of 150 jobs.

The primary outcome of the study was the proportion of applications that elicited either callbacks from employers or on-the-spot job offers. The testers went through intensive training to become familiar with their assumed profiles and to respond similarly to potential interview questions. As such, the only difference between the two testers on each race team was that one had a criminal record and the other didn't. Because there was random assignment to these two conditions and the other characteristics of the testers were essentially the same, the differences observed in the percentage of callbacks between team members can be assumed to be related to the criminal record only and not to other factors.

The results of Pager's (2007) field experiment were stark. White testers with a criminal record were one-half to one-third less likely to receive a callback from employers, and the effect was even more pronounced for African American applicants. Pager concludes, "Mere contact with the criminal justice system in the absence of any transformative or selective effects severely limits subsequent job prospects. The mark of a criminal record indeed represents a powerful barrier to employment" (p. 145). With such a powerful randomly assigned field experiment, the internal (causal) validity of these findings is strong. The implications of these findings in light of the hundreds of thousands of offenders who attempt to reenter society from prison each year are troubling indeed.

WHAT IF A TRUE EXPERIMENT ISN'T POSSIBLE?

Often, testing a hypothesis with a true experimental design is not feasible. A true experiment may be too costly or take too long to carry out; it may not be ethical to randomly assign subjects to the different conditions, or it may be too late to do so. Researchers may instead use quasi-experimental designs that retain several components of experimental design but differ in important details.

In a quasi-experimental design, a comparison group is predetermined to be comparable with the treatment group in critical ways, such as being eligible for the same services or being in the same school cohort (Rossi & Freeman, 1989, p. 313). These research designs are only *quasi*-experimental because subjects are not randomly assigned to the comparison and experimental groups. As a result, we cannot be as confident in the comparability of the groups as in true experimental designs. Nonetheless, in order to term a research design *quasi-experimental*, we have to be sure that the comparison groups meet specific criteria.

We will discuss here the two major types of quasi-experimental designs as well as one type—ex post facto (after the fact) control group design—that is often mistakenly termed quasi-experimental. (Other types can be found in Cook & Campbell, 1979, and Mohr, 1992.)

- Nonequivalent control group designs: These designs have experimental and comparison groups that are designated before the treatment occurs but are not created by random assignment.

- Before-and-after designs: This type of design has a pretest and posttest but no comparison group. In other words, the subjects exposed to the treatment served, at an earlier time, as their own control group.

- Ex post facto control group designs: These designs use nonrandomized control groups designated after the fact.

These designs are weaker than true experiments in establishing the nonspuriousness of an observed association—that it does not result from the influence of some third, uncontrolled variable. On the other hand, because these quasi-experiments do not require the high degree of control necessary in order to achieve random assignment, they can be conducted using more natural procedures in more natural settings, so we may be able to achieve a more complete understanding of causal context. In identifying the mechanism of a causal effect, though, quasi-experiments are neither better nor worse than experiments.

Nonequivalent Control Group Designs

When random assignment is not possible, a nonequivalent control group design is often used. In this type of quasi-experimental design, a comparison group is selected to be as comparable as possible with the treatment group. Two selection methods can be used:

1. *Individual matching*: Individual cases in the treatment group are matched with similar individuals in the comparison group. This can sometimes create a comparison group that is very similar to the experimental group.

Quasi-experimental design: A research design in which there is a comparison group that is comparable with the experimental group in critical ways, but subjects are not randomly assigned to the comparison and experimental groups

Nonequivalent control group designs: A quasi-experimental design in which there are experimental and comparison groups that are designated before the treatment occurs but are not created by random assignment

Before-and-after designs: A quasi-experimental design may consist of before-and-after comparisons of the experimental group but has no control group

Ex post facto control group designs: Nonexperimental design in which comparison groups are selected after the treatment, program, or other variation in the independent variable has occurred

2. *Aggregate matching:* In most situations when random assignment is not possible, this second method of matching makes more sense: identifying a comparison group that matches the treatment group in the aggregate rather than trying to match individual cases. This means finding a comparison group that has similar distributions on key variables: the same average age, the same percentage female, and so on.

Case Study: Parole Community Resource Centers and Recidivism

While prison populations have started to decline in the United States, parole populations have continued to grow. Parole allows correctional populations to be released from prison but with continued supervision, monitoring, and treatment in the community. Parolees reentering the community from prison face many obstacles, including obtaining educational and job services, as well as finding suitable housing. One form of community supervision that has emerged is called community resource centers (CRCs). These centers allow parolees to live at their own residences, but they are mandated to attend programming at the CRC during the day, including such things as GED and/or high school classes, employment preparation services, and life skills training. Similar to other intensive-supervision parole programs, CRCs are less flexible than traditional parole programs. Typically, individuals who are at higher risk of failing in the community are sentenced to these intermediate sanctions (Hyatt & Ostermann, 2019).

To determine whether CRCs were more effective in reducing recidivism than traditional parole, Hyatt and Ostermann (2019) conducted a nonequivalent control group experiment in New Jersey. Because they were not able to randomly assign those leaving prison to the CRC, they matched individuals who had been under traditional parole to those who had been under CRC programs using such variables as age, gender, race/ethnicity, prior arrests, and so on (Exhibit 6.8). In this way, Hyatt and Ostermann made both sets of parolees as equivalent as possible despite not being able to randomly assign them to each group. They explain, "While randomization is preferable for causal estimation . . . rigorous quasi-experimental methods offer the ability to specify, with reasonable assumptions, the effects of policies" (p. 102). Unfortunately, results indicated that CRC participants had higher rates of recidivism than those under traditional supervision. The authors speculated that the increased control under the CRC may have led some parolees to abscond, which resulted in technical violations, which directly contributed to higher arrest rates.

Exhibit 6.8 Quasi-Experimental Design of Community Resource Centers

Source: Adapted from Listwan, S. J., Sundt, J. L., Halsinger, A. M., & Katessam, E. H. (2003). The effect of drug court programming on recidivism: The Cincinnati experience. *Crime and Delinquency, 49,* 389–411.

Before-and-After Designs

The common feature of before-and-after designs is the absence of a comparison group: All cases are exposed to the experimental treatment. The basis for comparison is instead provided by the pretreatment measures in the experimental group. These designs are thus useful for studies of interventions that are experienced by virtually every case in some population.

The simplest type of before-and-after design is the fixed-sample panel design (panel study). In a fixed-sample panel design, the same individuals are studied over time; the research may entail one pretest and one posttest. However, this type of before-and-after design does not qualify as a quasi-experimental design because comparing subjects with themselves at just one earlier point in time does not provide an adequate comparison group. Many influences other than the experimental treatment may affect a subject following the pretest—for instance, basic life experiences for a young subject.

A more powerful way to ensure that the independent variable actually affected the dependent variable when using a before-and-after design is by using a multiple-group before-and-after design. In this design, before-and-after comparisons are made of the same variables between different groups. Time series designs, sometimes called repeated-measures panel designs, include several pretest and posttest observations, allowing the researcher to study the process by which an intervention or treatment has an impact over time; hence, they are better than a simple before-and-after study.

These designs are particularly useful for studying the impact of new laws or social programs that affect large numbers of people and that are readily assessed by some ongoing measurement. For example, we might use a time series design to study the impact of a new seat belt law on the severity of injuries in automobile accidents using a monthly state government report on insurance claims. Specific statistical methods are required to analyze time series data, but the basic idea is simple: Identify a trend in the dependent variable up to the date of the intervention, and then control for outside influences and project the trend into the post-intervention period. This *projected* trend is then compared with the *actual* trend of the dependent variable after the intervention. A substantial disparity between the actual and projected trend is evidence that the intervention or event had an impact (Rossi & Freeman, 1989).

How well do these before-and-after designs meet the five criteria for establishing causality? The before–after comparison enables us to determine whether an *association* exists between the intervention and the dependent variable (because we can determine whether there was a change after the intervention). It also clarifies whether the change in the dependent variable occurred after the intervention, so *time order* is not a problem. However, there is no control group, so we cannot rule out the influence of extraneous factors as the actual cause of the change we observe; *spuriousness* may be a problem. Some other event may have occurred during the study that resulted in a change in posttest scores. Overall, the longitudinal nature (the measurement of a phenomenon over a long period of time) of before-and-after designs can help to identify causal mechanisms, while the loosening of randomization requirements makes it easier to conduct studies in natural settings, where we learn about the influence of contextual factors. We will discuss the element of time in research in greater detail later in the chapter.

> **Fixed-sample panel design (panel study):** A type of longitudinal study in which data are collected from the same individuals—the panel—at two or more points in time; in another type of panel design, panel members who leave are replaced with new members

> **Time series design (repeated-measures panel design):** A quasi-experimental design consisting of many pretest and posttest observations of the same group

Case Study: The Effects of the Youth Criminal Justice Act

Carrington and Schulenberg's (2008) study of the effect of the Youth Criminal Justice Act (YCJA) of 2002 in Canada on police discretion with apprehended young offenders illustrates a time series design. This design typically includes many pretest and posttest observations that allow the researcher to study the process by which an intervention or a treatment has an impact over time.

One of the major objectives of the YCJA, which came into effect in 2003 in Canada, was to reduce the number of referrals to youth court. The YCJA generally requires police officers who are thinking of charging a minor with a crime to first consider extralegal judicial measures, such as giving the youth an informal warning.

To study the effects of the YCJA, Carrington and Schulenberg (2008) examined the number of juveniles who were apprehended and charged from January 1, 1986, through December 31, 2006. The Canadian Uniform Crime Reporting Survey records the number of minors who were charged, as well as the number who were chargeable but not charged. The researchers note, "A change in the charge ratio, or proportion of chargeable youth who were charged, is an indication of a change in the use of police discretion with apprehended youth" (p. 355). To control for the actual crime rate of youth, the researchers also examined per capita ratios. Exhibit 6.9 displays the annual rates per 100,000 young persons who were (a) apprehended (i.e., chargeable), (b) charged, and (c) not charged. This clearly shows that the YCJA may have had the intended effect. Of course, the study design leaves open the possibility that something else in 2003 may have happened to effect this change in formal charges against juveniles. However, because there was no known event that could have had such a national impact, the conclusion that this effect is attributable to the YCJA is more plausible. As you can see, this time series design is particularly useful for studying the impact of new laws or social programs that affect everyone and can be readily assessed by ongoing measurement.

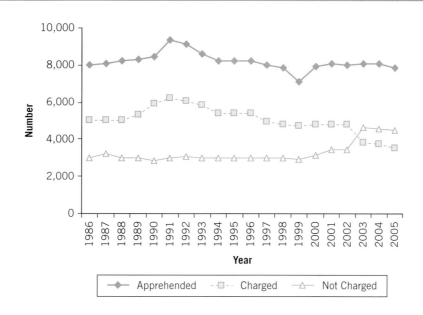

Exhibit 6.9   Results From a Repeated-Measures Panel Design Used to Examine the Efficacy of the YCJA

Source: Canadian Centre for Justice Statistics and adapted from Carrington and Schulenberg 2008.

Ex Post Facto Control Group Designs

The ex post facto control group design appears to be very similar to the nonequivalent control group design and is often confused with it, but it does not meet as well the criteria for quasi-experimental designs. Similar to nonequivalent control group designs, this design has experimental and comparison groups that are not created by random assignment. However, unlike the groups in nonequivalent control group designs, the groups in ex post facto designs are designated after the treatment has occurred. The problem with this is that if the treatment takes any time at all, people with particular characteristics may select themselves for the treatment or avoid it. Of course, this makes it difficult to determine whether an association between group membership and outcome is spurious. However, the particulars will vary from study to study; in some circumstances, we may conclude that the treatment and control groups are so similar that causal effects can be tested (Rossi & Freeman, 1989).

Case Study: Does an Arrest Increase Delinquency?

David P. Farrington's (1977) classic study of how arrest sometimes increases delinquency, called the *deviance amplification process*, is an excellent example of an ex post facto control group design (Exhibit 6.10). Farrington tested the hypothesis that juveniles who were publicly labeled as deviant through being convicted of a delinquent act would increase their deviant behavior compared with those who were not so labeled. Using secondary data from the Cambridge Study of Delinquent Development, Farrington measured outcomes of 400 London working-class youths from age 8 to 18. Results indicated that youth who were labeled as delinquent (through conviction) subsequently committed more delinquent acts than similar youth who were not labeled in this way.

Exhibit 6.10 Ex Post Facto Control Group Design: Farrington's Test of Deviance Amplification

Subject	Placement Subject in group	Group	Pretest	Treatment	Posttest
		Experimental group →	Delinquent acts at age 14 →	Convicted of offense →	Delinquent acts at age 18
Adolescents from London	No random assignment				
		Control group →	Delinquent acts at age 14 →	Not convicted of offense →	Delinquent acts at age 18

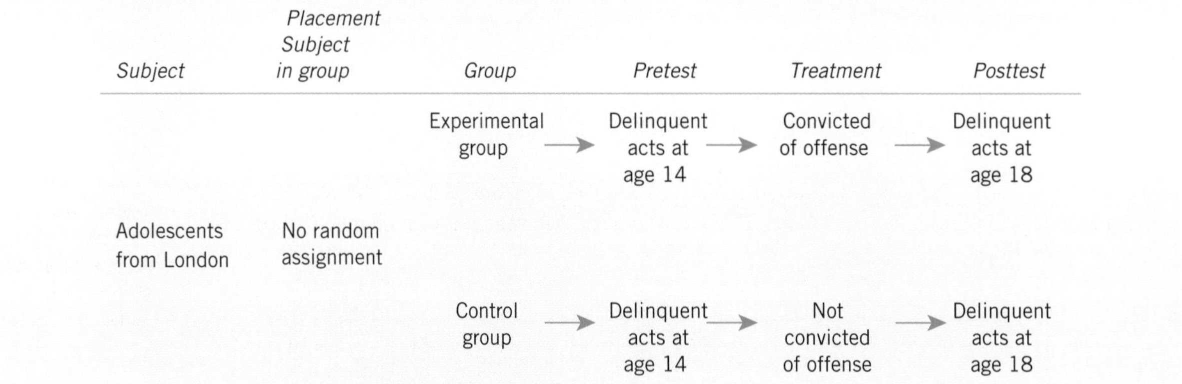

Source: Farrington (1977)

WHAT ARE THE THREATS TO INTERNAL VALIDITY AND GENERALIZABILITY IN EXPERIMENTS?

Like any research design, experimental designs must be evaluated for their ability to yield valid conclusions. True experiments are particularly well suited to producing valid conclusions about causality (internal validity), but they are less likely to fare well in achieving generalizability. Quasi-experiments may provide more generalizable results than true experiments, but they are more prone to problems of internal invalidity (although some design schemes allow the researcher to rule out almost as many potential sources of internal invalidity as does a true experiment). In general, nonexperimental designs (such as survey research and participant observation) permit less certainty about internal validity.

Causal (Internal) Validity

An experiment's ability to yield valid conclusions about causal effects is determined by the comparability of its experimental and comparison groups. First, of course, a comparison group must be created. Second, this comparison group must be so similar to the experimental group that it will show what the experimental group would be like if it did not receive the experimental treatment—that is, if the independent variable was not varied. For example, the only difference between the two groups in Bushman's (2012) study was that one group watched a violent movie and the other group did not.

There are five basic sources of internal invalidity:

1. *Selection bias*—when characteristics of the experimental and comparison group subjects differ

2. *Endogenous change*—when the subjects develop or change during the experiment as part of an ongoing process independent of the experimental treatment

3. *External events/history effects*—when something occurs during the experiment, other than the treatment, that influences outcome scores

4. *Contamination*—when either the experimental group or the comparison group is aware of the other group and is influenced in the posttest as a result (Mohr, 1992)

5. *Treatment misidentification*—when variation in the independent variable (the treatment) is associated with variation in the observed outcome, but the change occurs through a process that the researcher has not identified

Selection Bias

You may already realize that the composition of the experimental and comparison groups in a true experiment is unlikely to be affected by their difference. If it were affected, it would cause **selection bias**. Random assignment equates the groups' characteristics, though with some possibility for error due to chance. The likelihood of difference due to chance can be identified with appropriate statistics.

Even when the random assignment plan works, the groups can differ over time because of **differential attrition**, or what can be thought of as *deselection*—that is, the groups become different because, for various reasons, some subjects drop out of groups. This is not a likely problem for a laboratory experiment that occurs in one session, but for experiments in which subjects must participate over time, differential attrition may become a problem.

When subjects are not randomly assigned to treatment and comparison groups, as in nonequivalent control group designs, there is a serious threat of selection bias. Even if the researcher selects a comparison group that matches the treatment group on important variables, there is no guarantee that the groups were similar initially in terms of the dependent variable or another characteristic that ultimately influences posttest scores.

Endogenous Change

The type of problem considered an **endogenous change** occurs when natural developments in the subjects, independent of the experimental treatment, account for some or all of the

Selection bias: A source of internal (causal) invalidity that occurs when characteristics of experimental and comparison group subjects differ in any way that influences the outcome

Differential attrition: A problem that occurs in experiments when comparison groups become different because subjects are more likely to drop out of one of the groups for various reasons

Endogenous change: A source of causal invalidity that occurs when natural developments or changes in the subjects (independent of the experimental treatment itself) account for some or all of the observed change from the pretest to the posttest

observed change between pretest and posttest. Endogenous change includes three specific threats to internal validity:

1. *Testing.* Taking the pretest can in itself influence posttest scores. Subjects may learn something or be sensitized to an issue by the pretest and, as a result, respond differently when they are asked the same questions in the posttest.

2. *Maturation.* Changes in outcome scores during experiments that involve a lengthy treatment period may be due to maturation. Subjects may age or gain experience in school or grow in knowledge, all as part of a natural maturational experience, and thus respond differently on the posttest from the way they responded on the pretest.

3. *Regression.* People experience cyclical or episodic changes that result in different posttest scores, a phenomenon known as a regression effect. Subjects who are chosen for a study because they received very low scores on a test may show improvement in the posttest, on average, simply because some of the low scorers had been having a bad day. It is hard, in many cases, to know whether a phenomenon is subject to naturally occurring fluctuations, so the possibility of regression effects should be considered whenever subjects are selected because of their initial extremely high or low values on the outcome variable (Mohr, 1992).

Testing, maturation, and regression effects are generally not a problem in true experiments. Both the experimental group and the comparison group take the pretest, and they are both subject to maturation and regression effects, so even if these possibilities lead to a change in posttest scores, the comparison between the experimental and control groups will not be affected because the groups started off with similar characteristics. Of course, in experiments with no pretest, testing effects themselves are not a problem. However, in most before-and-after designs without a comparison group, endogenous-change effects could occur and lead to an invalid conclusion that there had been an effect of the independent variable.

External Events

External events (sometimes referred to as the history effect during the experiment)—things that happen outside the experiment—can also change the subjects' outcome scores. An example of this is a newsworthy event that is relevant to the focus of an experiment to which subjects are exposed. What if researchers were evaluating the effectiveness of a mandatory-arrest policy in decreasing incidents of intimate partner assault and an event such as the murder trial of O. J. Simpson occurred during the experiment? This would clearly be a historical event that might compromise the results. This trial saw a momentous amount of media coverage, and as a result, intimate partner assault and homicide were given a tremendous amount of attention. Because of this increased awareness, many victims of intimate partner violence reported their victimizations during this time—police agencies and women's shelters were flooded with calls. If a researcher had been using calls to police in a particular jurisdiction as an indicator of the incidence of intimate partner assault, this historical event would have seriously jeopardized the internal validity of his or her results. Why? Because the increase in police calls would have had more to do with the trial than with any recent change in arrest policies.

Contamination

Contamination occurs in an experiment when the comparison group is in some way affected by or affects the treatment group. This problem basically arises from failure to adequately

---

Regression effect:
A source of causal invalidity that occurs when subjects who are chosen for a study because of their extreme scores on the dependent variable become less extreme on the posttest due to natural cyclical or episodic change in the variable

External events (history effect): A source of causal invalidity that occurs when something other than the treatment influences outcome scores; also called an *effect of external events*

Contamination: A source of causal invalidity that occurs when the experimental and/or the comparison group is aware of the other group and is influenced in the posttest as a result

control the conditions of the experiment. When comparison group members become aware that they are being denied some advantage, they may increase their efforts to compensate, creating a problem called compensatory rivalry or the John Henry effect (Cook & Campbell, 1979). On the other hand, control group members may become demoralized if they feel that they have been left out of some valuable treatment and may perform worse than they would have outside the experiment. The treatment may seem, in comparison, to have a more beneficial effect than it actually did. Both compensatory rivalry and demoralization can thus distort the impact of the experimental treatment.

The danger of contamination can be minimized if the experiment is conducted in a laboratory, if members of the experimental group and the comparison group have no contact while the study is in progress, and if the treatment is relatively brief. To the degree that these conditions are not met, the likelihood of contamination will increase.

Treatment Misidentification

Treatment misidentification occurs when subjects experience a treatment that wasn't intended by the researcher. Treatment misidentification has at least three sources:

1. *Expectancies of experimental staff.* Change among experimental subjects may be due to the positive expectancies of the experimental staff who are delivering the treatment rather than due to the treatment itself. Such positive staff expectations can create a self-fulfilling prophecy and can occur even in randomized experiments when well-trained staff convey their enthusiasm for an experimental program to the subjects in subtle ways. These expectancy effects can be very difficult to control in field experiments. However, in some experiments concerning the effects of treatments such as medical drugs, double-blind procedures can be used. Staff will deliver the treatments without knowing which subjects are getting the treatment and which are receiving a placebo—something that looks similar to the treatment but has no effect. In fact, the prison experiment discussed earlier in this chapter used a double-blind procedure to randomly assign inmates to a security classification category. In the experiment, only the executive director of the corrections department and the director of classification were aware of the research. Correctional staff, other individuals who worked with the inmates, and the inmates themselves were unaware of the study. In this way, any expectancies that the staff may have had were unlikely to affect inmate behavior.

2. *Placebo effect.* Treatment misidentification may occur when subjects receive a treatment that they consider likely to be beneficial and then improve because of that expectation rather than the treatment itself. In medical research, the placebo is often a chemically inert substance that looks similar to the experimental drug but actually has no medical effect. Research indicates that the placebo effect produces positive health effects in two thirds of patients suffering from relatively mild medical problems (Goleman, 1993). Placebo effects can also occur in social science research. The only way to reduce this threat to internal validity is to treat the comparison group with something similar.

3. *Hawthorne effect.* Members of the treatment group may change in terms of the dependent variable because their participation in the study makes them feel special. This problem can occur when treatment group members compare their situation

Compensatory rivalry (John Henry effect): A type of contamination in experimental and quasi-experimental designs that occurs when control group members are aware that they are being denied some advantage and increase their efforts by way of compensation

Treatment misidentification: A problem that occurs in an experiment when the treatment itself is not what causes the outcome, but rather, the outcome is caused by some intervening process that the researcher has not identified and is not aware of

Expectancies of the experimental staff (self-fulfilling prophecy): A source of treatment misidentification in experiments and quasi-experiments that occurs when change among experimental subjects is due to the positive expectancies of the staff who are delivering the treatment rather than to the treatment itself

Double-blind procedure: An experimental method in which neither subjects nor the staff delivering experimental treatments know which subjects are getting the treatment and which are receiving a placebo

Placebo effect:
A source of treatment misidentification that can occur when subjects receive a treatment that they consider likely to be beneficial and improve because of that expectation rather than because of the treatment itself

Hawthorne effect:
A type of contamination in experimental and quasi-experimental designs that occurs when members of the treatment group change in terms of the dependent variable because their participation in the study makes them feel special

Solomon four-group design: An experimental design in which there are four groups. Two of the groups represent a classic experimental design in which there is an experimental and a control group that each receives a pretest. The final two groups represent an experimental and a control group, but neither receives a pretest. This design helps to identify the interaction of testing and treatment.

to that of the control group members who are not receiving the treatment. In this case, this is a type of contamination effect. However, experimental group members could feel special simply because they are in the experiment. The Hawthorne effect is named after a famous productivity experiment at the Hawthorne electric plant outside Chicago. Workers were moved to a special room for a study of the effects of lighting intensity and other work conditions on their productivity. After this move, the workers began to increase their output no matter what change was made in their working conditions, even when the conditions became worse. The researchers concluded that the workers felt they should work harder because they were part of a special experiment.

Interaction of Testing and Treatment

A variation of the problem of external validity occurs when the experimental treatment is effective only when particular conditions created by the experiment occur. For example, if subjects have had a pretest, it may sensitize them to a particular issue, so when they are exposed to the treatment, their reaction is different from what it would have been if they had not taken the pretest. In other words, testing and treatment interact to produce the outcome.

Suppose you were interested in the effects of a diversity training film on prejudicial attitudes. After answering questions in a pretest about their attitudes on various topics related to diversity (e.g., racial or sexual prejudice), the subjects generally became more sensitive to the issue of prejudice without seeing the training film. On the posttest, then, their attitudes may be different from pretest attitudes simply because they have become sensitized to the issue of diversity through pretesting. In this situation, the treatment may actually have an effect, but it would be difficult to determine how *much* of the effect was attributable to the sensitizing pretest and how much was due to seeing the film.

This possibility can be tested with what is called the Solomon four-group design. In this version of a true experimental design, subjects are randomly assigned to at least two experimental groups and at least two comparison groups. One experimental group and one comparison group will have a pretest, and the other two groups will not have a pretest (see Exhibit 6.11). If testing and treatment do interact, the difference in outcome scores between the experimental and comparison groups will differ between the subjects who took the pretest and those who did not.

Ultimately, the external validity of experimental results will increase with the success of replications taking place at different times and places, using different forms of the treatment. As indicated by the replications of the Sherman and Berk (1984) study of arrest for domestic violence, the result may be a more detailed, nuanced understanding of the hypothesized effect.

Exhibit 6.11	Solomon Four-Group Design Testing the Interaction of Pretesting and Treatment				
Experimental group	R	O1	X	O2
Comparison group	R	O1		O2
Experimental group	R		X	O2
Comparison group	R			O2

Note: R = random assignment; O = observation (pretest or posttest); X = experimental treatment

Generalizability

The need for generalizable findings can be thought of as the Achilles heel of the true experimental design. The design components that are essential for a true experiment and that minimize the threats to causal (internal) validity also make it more difficult to achieve sample generalizability, or the ability to apply the findings to a clearly defined, larger population.

Sample Generalizability

Subjects who can be recruited for a laboratory experiment, randomly assigned to a group, and kept under carefully controlled conditions for the study's duration are often not a representative sample of any large population of interest. In fact, most are recruited from college populations. Can they be expected to react to the experimental treatment in the same way as members of the larger population who are not students or may never have gone to college? The more artificial the experimental arrangements, the greater the problem can be (D. T. Campbell & Stanley, 1996).

Not only do the characteristics of the subjects themselves determine the generalizability of the experimental results, but the generalizability of the treatment and of the setting for the experiment also must be considered (Cook & Campbell, 1979). Field experiments are likely to yield findings that are more generalizable to broader populations than are laboratory experiments using subjects who must volunteer. When random selection is not feasible, the researchers may be able to increase generalizability by selecting several sites for conducting the experiments that offer obvious contrasts in the key variables of the population. The follow-up studies to Sherman and Berk's (1984) work, for example (see Chapter 2), were conducted in cities that differed from Minneapolis, the original site, in social class and ethnic composition. As a result, although the findings are not statistically generalizable to a larger population, they do give some indication of the study's general applicability (Cook & Campbell, 1979).

> **Sample generalizability:** Exists when a conclusion based on a sample, or subset, of a larger population holds true for that population

THE ELEMENT OF TIME IN RESEARCH

Nonexperimental research designs can be either cross-sectional or longitudinal. In a **cross-sectional research design**, all data are collected at one point in time. Identifying the time order of effects—what happened first, second, and so on—is critical for developing a causal analysis but can be an insurmountable problem with a cross-sectional design. In **longitudinal research designs**, data are collected at two or more points in time, so identification of the time order of effects can be quite straightforward. You can think of an experiment as a type of longitudinal design because subjects are often observed at two or more points in time.

Much of the research you have encountered so far in this text has been cross-sectional. Although each survey and interview takes some time to carry out, if it measures the actions, attitudes, and characteristics of respondents at only one time, it is considered cross-sectional. The name comes from the idea that a snapshot from a cross-section of the population is obtained at one point in time.

> **Cross-sectional research design:** A study in which data are collected at only one point in time
>
> **Longitudinal research design:** A study in which data are collected that can be ordered in time; also defined as research in which data are collected at two or more points in time

> ### Case Study: Cross-Sectional Research Using Life Calendars—Do Offenders Specialize in Different Crimes?

Lo, Kim, and Cheng (2008) provide an interesting example of an attempt to collect retrospective data using a cross-sectional design. The researchers wanted to determine if certain offenders were more likely to repeat the same crimes or commit different crimes. Specifically, they wanted to know if the type of crime committed early in someone's life was a reliable predictor of offenses committed later. Stated differently, do offenders specialize in different types of crime? Lo et al. obtained official arrest records from the age of 18 to the time of the study (typically around age 25) for a sample of young offenders who were incarcerated in

Do Video Games Lead to Mass Shootings?

After a mass shooting, everyone has an opinion on the factors related to these horrendous acts of violence. After the 2018 mass murder at Marjory Stoneman Douglas High School in Florida, it was reported that the shooter, Nikolas Cruz, played violent video games. The *New York Times* reported President Trump as stating, "I'm hearing more and more people say the level of violence on video games is really shaping young people's thoughts." The newspaper also reported that this claim that entertainment media violence was related to mass shootings was similarly made after the mass murders at Columbine High School, Virginia Tech, and Sandy Hook Elementary School. However, while violent video game usage has continued to increase, we have also seen violent crime actually decrease significantly since the highs in the early 1990s.

For Further Thought

1. What type of design would you use to determine not only the short-term effects of watching violent media but also the long-term effects?

2. What causal mechanisms would you investigate for such a relationship?

Source: Salam, M., & Stack, L. (2018, February 23). Do video games lead to mass shootings? Researchers say no. *New York Times.* Retrieved from https://www.nytimes.com/2018/02/23/us/politics/trump-video-games-shootings.html

---

Life calendar: An instrument that helps respondents recall events in their past by displaying each month (or some other time period) of a given year along with key dates noted within the calendar, such as birthday, arrests, holidays, anniversaries, and so on

Arrestee Drug Abuse Monitoring (ADAM): Uses standardized drug-testing methodologies and predictive models to measure the consequences of drug abuse within and across the United States boundaries

Anchors: Key dates of important events like birthdays that help trigger recall for respondents

county jails in Ohio. They then asked the inmates to reconstruct their drug and alcohol use, among other things, monthly for the same time period using a **life calendar** instrument based on the **Arrestee Drug Abuse Monitoring (ADAM)** interview schedule. This life calendar instrument helps respondents recall events in their past by displaying each month of a given year along with key dates noted within the calendar, such as birthdays, arrests, holidays, anniversaries, and so on. Respondents are given a calendar that displays these key dates, typically called **anchors**, and then are asked to recall the variables of interest (i.e., drug use, victimizations) that also occurred during the specified time frame. The use of a life calendar has been shown to improve the ability of respondents to recall events in the past compared with basic questions without a calendar (Belli, Stafford, & Alwin, 2009).

Results of Lo et al.'s (2008) research were somewhat mixed regarding offender specialization. Most offenders engaged in a variety of offenses prior to their current arrest. However, compared with drug and property offenders, violent offenders were more likely to specialize, as they were the most likely to have had violent arrest records prior to their current offenses.

It is important to note that retrospective data such as these are often inadequate for measuring variation in past psychological states or behaviors because what we recall about our feeling or actions in the past is likely to be influenced by what we feel in the present. For example, retrospective reports by both adult alcoholics and their parents appear to greatly overestimate the frequency of childhood problems (Vaillant, 1995). People cannot report reliably the frequency and timing of many past events, from hospitalization to hours worked. However, retrospective data tend to be reliable when they concern major, persistent experiences in the past, such as what type of school someone went to or how a person's family was structured (R. T. Campbell, 1992).

In contrast, longitudinal research collects data at two or more points in time and, as such, data can be ordered in time. By measuring the value of cases on an independent variable and a dependent variable at different times, the researcher can determine whether variation in the independent variable precedes variation in the dependent variable.

In some longitudinal designs, the same sample (or panel) is followed over time. In other longitudinal designs, sample members are rotated or completely replaced. The population from which the sample is selected may be defined broadly, as when a longitudinal survey of the general population is conducted, or the population may be defined narrowly, as when members of a specific age group are sampled at multiple points in time. The frequency of follow-up measurement can vary, ranging from a before-and-after design with just one follow-up to studies in which various indicators are measured every month for many years.

Collecting data at two or more points in time rather than at one time can prove difficult for a number of reasons: lack of long-term funding, participant attrition, and so on. Quite frequently, researchers cannot or are simply unwilling to delay completion of a study for even one year in order to collect follow-up data. But think of the many research questions that really should involve a much longer follow-up period: Does community-oriented policing decrease rates of violent crime? What is the impact of job training in prison on recidivism rates? How effective are batterer treatment programs for individuals convicted of intimate partner assault? Do parenting programs for young mothers and fathers reduce the likelihood of their children becoming delinquent? It is safe to say that we will never have enough longitudinal data to answer many important research questions. Nonetheless, the value of longitudinal data is so great that every effort should be made to develop longitudinal research designs when they are appropriate for the research question being asked. The following discussion of the three major types of longitudinal designs will give you a sense of the possibilities (see Exhibit 6.12).

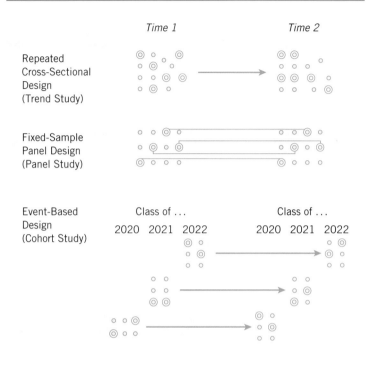

Exhibit 6.12   Three Types of Longitudinal Design

Repeated Cross-Sectional Designs

Studies that use a repeated cross-sectional design, also known as a trend study, have become fixtures of the political arena around election time. Particularly in presidential election years, we accustom ourselves to reading weekly, even daily, reports on the percentage of the population that supports each candidate. Similar polls are conducted to track sentiment on many other social issues. For example, a 1993 poll reported that 52% of adult Americans supported a ban on the possession of handguns compared with 41% in a similar poll conducted in 1991. According to pollster Louis Harris, this increase indicated a "sea change" in public attitudes (cited in Barringer, 1993, p. A14). Another researcher said, "It shows that people are responding to their experience [of an increase in handgun-related killings]" (cited in Barringer, 1993, p. A14).

Repeated cross-sectional surveys are conducted as follows:

1. A sample is drawn from a population at Time 1, and data are collected from the sample.

2. As time passes, some people leave the population, and others enter it.

3. At Time 2, a different sample is drawn from this population.

Repeated cross-sectional design (trend study): A type of longitudinal study in which data are collected at two or more points in time from different samples of the same population

Fixed-Sample Panel Designs

We talked about fixed-sample panel designs previously when we highlighted quasi-experimental designs. However, these types of designs also can be used when no experimental treatment or program is being examined. Panel designs allow us to identify changes in individuals, groups, or whatever we are studying. This is the process for conducting fixed-sample panel designs:

1. A sample (called a *panel*) is drawn from a population at Time 1, and data are collected from the sample.

2. As time passes, some panel members become unavailable for follow-up, and the population changes.

3. At Time 2, data are collected from the same people as at Time 1 (the panel), except for those people who cannot be located.

Because a panel design follows the same individuals, it is better than a repeated cross-sectional design for testing causal hypotheses. For example, Sampson and Laub (1990) used a fixed-sample panel design to investigate the effect of childhood deviance on adult crime. They studied a sample of white males in Boston when the subjects were between 10 and 17 years old and then followed up when the subjects were in their adult years. Data were collected from multiple sources, including the subjects themselves and criminal justice records. The researchers found that children who had been committed to a correctional school for persistent delinquency were much more likely than other children in the study to commit crimes as adults: 61% were arrested between the ages of 25 and 32, compared with 14% of those who had not been in correctional schools as juveniles (p. 614). In this study, juvenile delinquency unquestionably occurred before adult criminality. If the researchers had used a cross-sectional design to study the past of adults, the juvenile delinquency measure might have been biased by memory lapses, by self-serving recollections about behavior as juveniles, or by loss of agency records. The problem, of course, is that tracking people for years is extremely expensive, and many people in the original sample drop out for various reasons. Panel designs are also a challenge to implement successfully and often are not even attempted because of two major difficulties:

1. *Expense and attrition.* It can be difficult—and very expensive—to keep track of individuals over a long period, and inevitably, the proportion of panel members who can be located for follow-up will decline over time. Panel studies often lose more than one quarter of their members through attrition (D. C. Miller, 1991, p. 170), and because those who are lost are often dissimilar to those who remain in the panel, the sample's characteristics begin to change, and internal validity is compromised.

2. *Subject fatigue.* Panel members may grow weary of repeated interviews and drop out of the study, or they may become so used to answering the standard questions in the survey that they start giving stock answers rather than actually thinking about their current feelings or actions (R. T. Campbell, 1992). This is called the problem of **subject fatigue.** Fortunately, subjects do not often seem to become fatigued in this way, particularly if the research staff have maintained positive relations with them.

Subject fatigue: Problems caused by panel members growing weary of repeated interviews and dropping out of a study or becoming so used to answering the standard questions in the survey that they start giving stock or thoughtless answers

Event-Based Designs

In an **event-based design**, often called a *cohort study*, the follow-up samples (at one or more times) are selected from the same **cohort**, people who all have experienced a similar event or a common starting point. Examples include the following:

- *Birth cohorts:* those who share a common period of birth (those born in the 1940s, 1950s, 1960s, etc.)

- *Seniority cohorts:* those who have worked at the same place for about five years, about 10 years, and so on

- *School cohorts:* freshmen, sophomores, juniors, and seniors

CAUSALITY IN NONEXPERIMENTAL DESIGNS

How well do the research designs just described satisfy the criteria necessary to determine causality? Although it is relatively easy to establish that an empirical association exists between an independent and a dependent variable in these designs, the other criteria are much more difficult to assess.

Let us first illustrate the importance of time order and nonspuriousness using research that has examined the factors related to the gender and crime relationship. Suppose we want to examine whether juvenile offenders who are sentenced to boot camp facilities (a highly regimented, discipline-focused rehabilitation program) are less likely to be rearrested in the future compared with juveniles who were sentenced to traditional juvenile facilities. We are not able to randomly assign juveniles to either sanction, but in our analysis of the data, we statistically control for a number of variables that may affect recidivism, such as prior records, age, and so on.

This **statistical control**, as represented in Exhibit 6.13, is an invaluable tool used by researchers to determine which factors are most important when predicting a dependent variable (e.g. recidivism). Exhibit 6.13 presents the concept of statistical control with a hypothetical study of the relationship between attending a boot camp in prison and the likelihood of committing crimes after prison (the recidivism rate). In Exhibit 6.13, the data for all prisoners show that prisoners who attended boot camp were less likely to return to committing crimes after they left prison. However, as the more detailed data show, more female prisoners attended boot camp than male prisoners, so gender may have played a significant role in recidivism. The researchers, however, reduced the risk of spuriousness by using two statistical control methods: They examined the association between attending boot camp and postprison criminality for men and for women. After doing this, researchers determined that boot camp did not reduce recidivism. It just appeared to do so because women were more likely to attend boot camp and less likely to commit crimes after prison, regardless of whether they attended boot camp.

Nonexperimental research can be a very effective tool for exploring the context in which causal effects occur. Administering surveys in many different settings and to different types of individuals is usually much easier than administering various experiments. The difficulty of establishing nonspuriousness does not rule out using nonexperimental data to evaluate causal

Event-based design (cohort study): A type of longitudinal study in which data are collected at two or more points in time from individuals in a cohort

Cohort: Individuals or groups with a common starting point; examples of a cohort include college class of 1997, people who graduated from high school in the 1980s, General Motors employees who started work between 1990 and the year 2000, and people who were born in the late 1940s or the 1950s (the baby boom generation)

Statistical control: A technique used in nonexperimental research to reduce the risk of spuriousness. One variable is held constant so the relationship between two or more other variables can be assessed without the influence of variation in the control variable

Exhibit 6.13   The Use of Statistical Control to Reduce Spuriousness

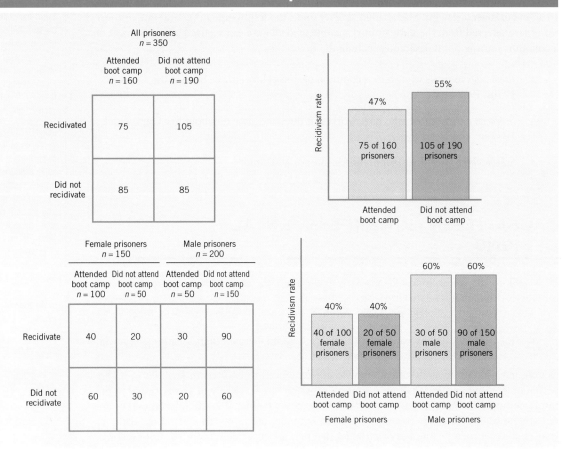

hypotheses. In fact, when enough nonexperimental data are collected to allow tests of multiple implications of the same causal hypothesis, the results can be very convincing (Rossi & Freeman, 1989).

In any case, nonexperimental tests of causal hypotheses will continue to be popular because the practical and ethical problems in randomly assigning people to different conditions preclude the test of many important hypotheses with an experimental design. Just remember to carefully consider possible sources of spuriousness and other problems when evaluating causal claims based on individual nonexperimental studies.

HOW DO EXPERIMENTERS PROTECT THEIR SUBJECTS?

Social science experiments often raise difficult ethical issues. You have already read in Chapter 3 about Philip Zimbardo's (2004) Stanford Prison Experiment. This experiment was actually ended after only six days, rather than after the planned two weeks, because of the psychological harm that seemed to result from the unexpectedly sadistic behavior of some of the "guards." Although Zimbardo's follow-up research convinced him that there had been no lasting harm to subjects, concern about the potential for harm would preclude many such experiments today.

In spite of the ethical standard of disclosure and informed consent by subjects, deception is an essential part of many experimental designs. As a result, contentious debate continues about the interpretation of this standard. Experimental evaluation of social programs also poses ethical dilemmas because they require researchers to withhold possibly beneficial treatment from some of the subjects solely on the basis of chance (Boruch, 1997). In this section, we will give special attention to the problems of deception and the distribution of benefits in experimental research.

Deception

Deception is used in social experiments to create more "realistic" treatments, often within the confines of a laboratory. You learned in Chapter 3 about Stanley Milgram's (1965) use of deception in his classic study of obedience to authority. Volunteers were recruited for what they were told was a study of the learning process, not a study of obedience to authority. The experimenter told the volunteers that they were administering electric shocks to a "student" in the next room, when there were actually neither students nor shocks. Subjects seemed to believe the deception.

Whether or not you believe that you could be deceived in this way, you are not likely to be invited to participate in an experiment such as Milgram's. Current federal regulations preclude deception in research that might trigger such upsetting feelings. However, deception is still routine in many college laboratories. The question that must always be answered is, "Is there sufficient justification to allow the use of deception?" David Willer and Henry A. Walker (2007) pay particular attention to debriefing after deception in their book about experimental research. They argue that every experiment involving deception should be followed immediately for each participant with debriefing, sometimes called dehoaxing, in which the deception is explained, and all the participants' questions are answered to their satisfaction; those participants who still feel aggrieved are directed to a university authority to file a complaint or to a counselor for help with their feelings. This is sound advice.

> **Debriefing:** A session after an experiment in which all instances of deception are revealed and explained and participants are allowed to ask questions

Selective Distribution of Benefits

Field experiments conducted to evaluate social programs also can involve issues of informed consent (Hunt, 1985). One ethical issue that is somewhat unique to field experiments is the selective distribution of benefits: How much are subjects harmed by the way treatments are distributed in the experiment? For example, Sherman and Berk's (1984) experiment—and its successors—required police to make arrests in domestic-violence cases largely on the basis of a random process. When arrests were not made, did the subjects' abused spouses suffer?

Is it ethical to give some potentially advantageous or disadvantageous treatment to people on a random basis? For example, in the drug court field experiment, is it ethical to randomly assign those who wanted extra help with their drug problem to the comparison group that did not receive extra treatment? Random distribution of benefits is justified when the researchers do not know whether some treatment actually is beneficial—and, of course, it is the goal of the experiment to find out. Chance is as reasonable a basis for distributing the treatment as any other. Also, if insufficient resources are available to fully fund a benefit for every eligible person, distribution of the benefit on the basis of chance to equally needy persons is ethically defensible (Boruch, 1997).

> **Selective distribution of benefits:** An ethical issue about how much researchers can influence the benefits subjects receive as part of the treatment being studied in a field experiment

Amanda Aykanian, Research Associate, Advocates for Human Potential

Source: Amanda Aykanian

Amanda Aykanian majored in psychology at Framingham State University and found that she enjoyed the routine and organization of research. She wrote an undergrad thesis to answer the research question, How does the way in which course content is presented affect students' feelings about the content and the rate at which they retain it?

After graduating, Aykanian didn't want to go to graduate school right away; instead, she wanted to explore her interests and get a sense of what she could do with research. Advocates for Human Potential (AHP) was the last research assistant (RA) job that Aykanian applied for. Her initial tasks as an RA at AHP ranged from taking notes, writing agendas, and assembling project materials to entering research data, cleaning data, and proofing reports. As she contributed more to project reports, she began to think about data from a more theoretical standpoint.

During seven years at AHP, Aykanian has helped lead program evaluation research, design surveys and write survey questions, conduct phone and qualitative interviews, and lead focus groups. Her program evaluation research almost always uses a mixed-methods approach, so Aykanian has learned a lot about how qualitative and quantitative methods can complement each other. She has received a lot of on-the-job training in data analysis and has learned how to think about and write a proposal in response to federal funding opportunities.

Aykanian was promoted to research associate and describes her current role as part program evaluation coordinator and part data analyst. She also has returned to graduate school, earning a master's degree in applied sociology and then starting a PhD program in social welfare.

CONCLUSION

True experiments play two critical roles in criminological research. First, they are the best research design for testing causal hypotheses. Even when conditions preclude the use of a true experimental design, many research designs can be improved by adding experimental components. Second, true experiments provide a comparison point for evaluating the ability of the other research designs to achieve causally valid results.

In spite of their obvious strengths, true experiments are used infrequently to study many research problems related to criminology and criminal justice. There are three basic reasons for this:

1. The experiments required to test many important hypotheses require more resources than most social scientists can access.

2. Most research problems of interest to social scientists simply are not amenable to experimental designs for reasons ranging from ethical considerations to the limited possibilities for randomly assigning people to different conditions in the real world.

3. The requirements of experimental design usually preclude large-scale studies and so limit generalizability to a degree that is unacceptable to many social scientists.

When a true experimental design is not feasible, researchers may instead use a quasi-experimental design, including nonequivalent control group designs, before-and-after designs, and ex post facto control group designs. As the studies highlighted in this chapter show, researchers examining issues related to criminology and criminal justice have been very creative in developing experimental research projects in the real world that can appropriately meet the demands of causal inference.

- A causal explanation relies on a comparison. The value of cases on the dependent variable is measured after they have been exposed to variation on an independent variable. This measurement is compared with what the value of cases on the dependent variable would have been if they had not been exposed to the variation in the independent variable. The validity of causal conclusions rests on how closely the comparison group comes to the ideal counterfactual.

- Three criteria are generally viewed as necessary for identifying a causal relationship: association between the variables, proper time order, and nonspuriousness of the association. In addition, the basis for concluding that a causal relationship exists is strengthened by identification of a causal mechanism and the context for the relationship.

- Association between two variables, in itself, is insufficient evidence of a causal relationship. This point is commonly made with the expression, "Correlation does not prove causation."

- Experiments use random assignment to make comparison groups as similar as possible at the outset of an experiment in order to reduce the risk of spurious effects due to extraneous variables.

- Nonexperimental designs use statistical controls to reduce the risk of spuriousness. A variable is controlled when it is held constant so that the association between the independent and dependent variables can be assessed without being influenced by the control variable.

- Longitudinal designs are usually preferable to cross-sectional designs for establishing the time order of effects. Longitudinal designs vary in terms of whether the same people are measured at different times, how the population of interest is defined, and how frequently follow-up measurements are taken. Fixed-sample panel designs provide the strongest test for the time order of effects, but they can be difficult to carry out successfully because of their expense, as well as subject attrition and fatigue.

- Ethical and practical constraints often prevent the use of experimental designs.

EXERCISES

Discussing Research

1. Review articles in several newspapers, copying down all causal assertions. These might include assertions that the presence of community policing was related positively to decreasing rates of violence, claims that the stock market declined because of uncertainty in the Middle East, or explanations about why a murder was committed. Inspect the articles carefully, noting all the evidence used to support the causal assertions. Which criteria for establishing causality are met? What other potentially important influences on the reported outcome have been overlooked?

2. Select several research articles in professional journals that assert or imply that they have identified a causal relationship between two or more variables. Is each of the criteria for establishing the existence of a causal relationship met? Find a study in which subjects were assigned randomly to experimental and comparison groups to reduce the risk of spurious influences on the supposedly causal relationship. How convinced are you by the study?

3. The web-based interactive exercises contain lessons on causation and experimental design. Try them out at this point.

Finding Research on the Web

1. Read an original article describing a true experiment. (Social psychology "readers," collections of such articles for undergraduates, are a good place to find interesting studies.) Critique the article, focusing on the extent to which experimental conditions were controlled and the causal mechanism was identified. Based on the study's control over conditions and identification of the causal mechanism, how confident were you in the causal conclusions?

2. Go to the website of the U.S. Department of Justice and examine the resources and publications available for community policing (cops.usdoj.gov). Examine a few of the publications, and note the causal assertions that are made. Pick one of these assertions, and propose a research design with which to test this assertion. Be specific.

3. Go to SocioSite (www.sociosite.net). Choose "Subject Areas." Then choose "Crime" or "Criminology." Find an example of research that has been done using experimental methods. Explain the experiment. Choose at least five of the key terms for this chapter (listed previously) that are relevant to and incorporated in the research experiment you have located on the Web. Explain how each of the five key terms you have chosen plays a role in the research example you have found.

4. Go to the FBI's Uniform Crime Reporting website (www.fbi.gov/services/cjis/ucr). Review the crime rate nationally, and then find data for state-level data. Compare the recent crime rates in at least two states and how these states may differ from national-level data. Report on the prevalence of the crimes you have examined. Propose a causal explanation for variation in crime between states, over time, or both. What research design would you propose to test this explanation? Explain.

Critiquing Research

1. Go to this book's Study Site, edge.sagepub.com/bachmanfrccj5e, and choose two research articles that include some attention to causality (as indicated by a check in that column of the article matrix). Describe the approach taken in each article to establish causality. How do the approaches differ from each other? Which approach seems stronger to you?

2. Select a true experiment, perhaps from the *Journal of Experimental Criminology* or from sources suggested in class. Diagram the experiment using the exhibits in this chapter as a model. Discuss the extent to which experimental conditions were controlled and the causal mechanism was identified. Based on a review of the threats to internal validity discussed in this chapter—selection bias, endogenous change, external events, contamination, and treatment misidentification—how confident can you be in the causal conclusions from the study? How generalizable do you think the study's results are to the population from which the cases were selected? How generalizable are they to specific subgroups in the study? How thoroughly do the researchers discuss these issues?

3. Repeat Question 2 with a quasi-experiment.

4. Go to Crime Stoppers USA's (CSUSA) website (www.crimestoppersusa.com). Check out "Profiles" and then "Programs." How is CSUSA fighting crime? What does CSUSA's approach assume about the cause of crime? Do you think CSUSA's approach to fighting crime is based on valid conclusions about causality? Explain.

Making Research Ethical

1. Under what conditions do you think that randomized assignment of subjects to a specific treatment is ethical in criminal justice research? Was it ethical for the researchers who conducted experiments on the effect of arrest in intimate partner assault (Chapter 2) to randomly assign individuals accused of domestic violence to an arrest or nonarrest treatment? What about in a laboratory study with students such as yourself? Do you think it would be ethical to assign students randomly to different groups, with some receiving stressful stimuli such as loud noises?

2. Critique the ethics of one of the experiments presented in this chapter or some other experiment about which you have read. What specific rules do you think should guide researchers' decisions about subject deception and the selective distribution of benefits?

3. Lo et al. (2008) surveyed inmates in county jails. Federal regulations require special safeguards for research on prisoners. Do you think special safeguards are necessary? Why, or why not? What type of research would you allow with prisoners: experiments, surveys, or observational studies? Do you think it is possible for prisoners to give voluntary consent to research participation? What procedures might help make prisoners' consent to research truly voluntary?

4. Bushman and Huesmann (2012) tested the impact of watching a violent video on students' level of aggressiveness. They found that watching the violent video increased aggressiveness. Do you consider it ethical to expose subjects to an intervention that might increase their aggressiveness? Are there any situations in which you would not approve of such research? Are there any types of subjects you would exclude from such research? Are there any limits you would post on the type of intervention that could be tested? Would you impose any requirements for debriefing?

Developing a Research Proposal

How will you try to establish the causal effects that you hypothesize?

1. Identify at least one hypothesis involving what you expect is a causal relationship.

2. Identify key variables that should be controlled in your survey design in order to decrease the possibility of arriving at a spurious conclusion about the hypothesized causal effect. Draw on relevant research literature and social theory to identify these variables.

3. Add a longitudinal component to your research design. Explain why you decided to use this particular longitudinal design.

4. Review the criteria for establishing a causal effect, and discuss your ability to satisfy each one.

Performing Data Analysis in SPSS or Excel

Data for Exercise	
Dataset	**Description**
Monitoring the future 2013 grade 10.sav	This dataset contains variables from the 2013 Monitoring the Future (MTF) study. These data cover a national sample of 10th graders, with a focus on monitoring substance use and abuse.

Variables for Exercise	
Variable Name	**Description**
Lowparenteduc	An ordinal variable, where "0" indicates that both parents have high school educations or greater, "1" indicates that one parent has less than high school education, and "2" indicates that both parents have less than high school education
V7234	A binary variable based on a question asking if the respondent had ever been suspended from school, where 0 = no and 1 = yes
White	Race dichotomy, where 0 = nonwhite and 1 = white

1. Take a look at some of the variables in this dataset. Is the MTF dataset suited to nomothetic or idiographic explanations? Why?

2. The link between a parent's education and a child's subsequent outcomes is well documented in many different fields, from criminology to health. Let's look at the relationship between a parent's education level and whether a respondent has ever been suspended from school.

   a. State a hypothesis about the relationship between parent education and suspension.

   b. Construct a crosstab for the variables "lowparenteduc" and "v7234" by selecting "analyze->descriptives->crosstabs." Make sure to put the independent variable in the column box and to select "column cell percentages."

   c. What does this tell us about the relationship between the two variables?

   d. Do we have sufficient evidence to say that this is a *causal* relationship? Which criteria of causality are or are not met?

   e. What else do you think we might want to account for to ensure that this is not a spurious relationship?

   f. Think of at least three intervening variables or causal mechanisms through which a parent's education might influence his or her child's risk of poor school performance.

3. Let's elaborate on this by accounting for a potential confounder. Some have argued that race is critical to understanding school discipline. They suggest that low parent education and suspension are both correlated with a parent/respondent's race. Therefore, race may be a confounder in this relationship, raising the possibility that education doesn't matter after all. We can control for the effect of race by constructing a layered crosstab, which will look at the relationship between parent education and school suspension in whites and blacks separately.

   a. Go back to the crosstab menu. This time, add the variable "white" to the "layer" field.

   b. The result here will be a bit daunting at first glance, but what you are looking for is if the pattern you found earlier is present in the nonwhite subgroup *and* the white subgroup. If the effect is not present for one group, then you have a *partial confounder*, where the relationship between the two variables is only present for certain groups. If the relationship goes away when you account for this new variable, then you have found a confounder, and the original relationship might have been spurious.

   c. In this case, is there no confounding, partial confounding, or total confounding?

   d. Does having parents with low education influence the risk of suspension for whites? For blacks? What does this tell us about our society and how punishment is distributed in schools?

4. Based on the measures in this dataset, what type of design do you think this study is using: longitudinal or cross-sectional? What are the strengths and limitations of this approach?

STUDENT STUDY SITE

$SAGE edge™

Get the tools you need to sharpen your study skills. SAGE Edge offers a robust online environment featuring an impressive array of free tools and resources. Access practice quizzes, eFlashcards, video, and multimedia at edge.sagepub.com/bachmanfrccj5e.

7

SURVEY RESEARCH

> My research methods class was a really big help for me, and I'll be honest, I did not think that I would be using this material much because I want to work as a field officer or an agent in local and federal law enforcement. But I was wrong. My internship this summer at the attorney general's office has allowed me to work alongside law enforcement, attorneys, detectives, and investigators, and I got the internship because of the knowledge I gained from my research methods class. I used these skills almost every day, and even though the internship is over, they told me I did such a good job that I could come back if I ever wanted a job working with the same supervisor I previously had.
>
> **Ricky E., Student**

SURVEY RESEARCH IN ACTION: MEASURING VICTIMIZATION

Media coverage of rape and sexual assault on college campuses has been widespread in the past few years, along with increased calls for changes in the way these crimes are handled by universities. While society appears to have given up the stereotype that people are more likely to be raped by strangers lurking in the bushes, measuring the prevalence of rape still remains a difficult task. In fact, despite over three decades of research, the magnitude of rape, stalking, and intimate partner violence (IPV) against men and women is still frequently disputed. For many reasons, including the historical stigma attached to these

Learning Objectives

1. Identify the circumstances that make survey research an appropriate methodology.

2. List the different methods for improving survey questions, along with the mistakes you do not want to make when writing questions.

3. Discuss the advantages and disadvantages of including "don't know" and neutral responses among response choices and of using open-ended questions.

4. List the strengths and weaknesses of each mode of survey design, giving particular attention to response rates.

5. Discuss the key ethical issues in survey research.

$SAGE edge™

Master the content at edge
.sagepub.com/bachmanfrccj5e

crimes, fear of retaliation from their perpetrators, and other safety concerns, estimating incidence rates of this violence has always been a difficult task. As we noted in Chapter 1, the most enduring source of statistical information about violent crime in the United States is the Uniform Crime Reporting (UCR) program compiled by the Federal Bureau of Investigation (FBI), but this data source relies on victimizations reported to the police. This is problematic, since we know that fewer than 50% of these offenses are ever reported to police. Due to weakness in estimating rates of this violence, random-sample surveys of the population are now being used as a social science tool of choice for uncovering incidents of violence. However, as can be expected, surveys employing diverse methodologies and different definitions of violence result in tremendously diverse estimates.

Importantly, gathering valid statistical data on the prevalence of these victimizations, including defining the characteristics of those most affected (e.g., subgroups by race/ethnicity and age), is the first step in preventing these victimizations. Two federal agencies have attempted to measure both rape and IPV, the Centers for Disease Control and Prevention (CDC) and the U.S. Department of Justice's Bureau of Justice Statistics (BJS). The CDC-sponsored survey is called the National Intimate Partner and Sexual Violence Survey (NISVS), and the BJS-sponsored survey, which measures most other forms of crime victimization, is called the National Crime Victimization Survey (NCVS). As we will see in this chapter, the survey questions used by both agencies are quite different, despite the fact that they are attempting to measure the same things.

WHAT IS A SURVEY?

Survey research:
Research in which
information is obtained
from a sample of
individuals through their
responses to questions
about themselves or
others

Survey research involves the collection of information from a sample of individuals through their responses to questions. Not only is survey research one of the most popular methods for science research, many newspaper editors, political pundits, and marketing gurus have also turned to survey research because it is an efficient method for systematically collecting data from a broad spectrum of individuals and social settings. In fact, surveys have become such a vital part of our nation's social fabric that we cannot assess much of what we read in the newspaper or see on TV without having some understanding of this method of data collection (Converse, 1984).

Attractive Features of Survey Research

Regardless of its scope, survey research owes its continuing popularity to three features: versatility, efficiency, and generalizability.

Versatility

The first and foremost reason for the popularity of survey methods is their versatility. Researchers can ask respondents questions about almost any topic you can imagine. Although a survey is not the ideal method for testing all hypotheses or learning about every social process, a well-designed survey can enhance our understanding of just about any social issue. In fact, there is hardly any topic of interest to social scientists that has not been studied at some time with survey methods.

Computer technology has made surveys even more versatile. Computers can be programmed so that different types of respondents are asked different questions. Short videos or pictures can be presented to respondents on a computer screen. An interviewer may give respondents a laptop on which to record their answers to sensitive personal questions, such as about illegal activities, so that not even the interviewer will know what they said (Tourangeau, 2004).

Efficiency

Surveys also are popular because data can be collected from many people at relatively low cost and, depending on the survey design, relatively quickly. Surveys are efficient research methods because many variables can be measured without substantially increasing the time or cost of data collection. Mailed questionnaires can include up to 10 pages of questions before most respondents lose interest (and before more postage must be added). The maximum time limit for phone surveys seems to be about 45 minutes. In-person interviews can last much longer, more than an hour.

Generalizability

Survey methods lend themselves to probability sampling from large populations. Thus, survey research is very appealing when sample generalizability is a central research goal. In fact, survey research is often the only means available for developing a representative picture of the attitudes and characteristics of a large population.

Surveys also are the research method of choice when cross-population generalizability is a primary concern (see Chapter 5). They allow a range of social contexts and subgroups to be sampled, and the consistency of relationships can be examined across the various subgroups.

The Omnibus Survey

Most surveys are directed at a specific research question. In contrast, an omnibus survey covers a range of topics of interest to different social scientists. It has multiple sponsors or is designed to generate data useful to a broad segment of the social science community rather than answer one particular research question.

One of the most successful omnibus surveys is the General Social Survey (GSS) of the National Opinion Research Center at the University of Chicago. Today, the GSS is administered every two years as a 90-minute interview to a probability sample of almost 3,000 Americans. It includes more than 500 questions about background characteristics and opinions, with an emphasis on social stratification, race relations, family issues, law and social control, and morale. Although the NCVS and the NISVS are not exactly omnibus surveys (they were both developed to obtain detailed information on a number of phenomena related to victimization), they do cover related information, including injuries and medical care received for victimization, the cost of victimization (including costs incurred for medical care and property lost), and whether the victimization was reported to police or other victim service agencies.

The deficiency of the omnibus approach is the limited depth that can be achieved in any one substantive area. In some years, the GSS avoids this problem by going into greater depth in one particular area. But the best way to get survey data about one particular topic is still the survey developed around the topic alone.

QUESTIONNAIRE DEVELOPMENT AND ASSESSMENT

The questionnaire (or interview schedule, as it is often called in interview-based studies) is the central feature of the survey process. Without a well-designed questionnaire tailored to the study's purposes, survey researchers have little hope of achieving their research goals.

The most effective design of a questionnaire varies with the specific survey method used and the other particulars of a survey project. There is no precise formula for a well-designed questionnaire. Nonetheless, some key principles should guide the design of any questionnaire, and some systematic procedures should be considered for refining it.

Omnibus survey: A survey that covers a range of topics of interest to different social scientists

Questionnaire: The survey instrument containing the questions for a self-administered survey

Interview schedule: The survey instrument containing the questions asked by the interviewer for an in-person interview or phone survey

Maintain Focus

A survey (with the exception of an omnibus survey) should be guided by a well-defined inquiry and a definitively targeted population. Does the study seek to describe some phenomenon in detail, explain some behavior, or explore some type of social relationship? Is your aim to explain that behavior for everyone or only as it pertains to a select group? Until the research objective is clearly formulated, survey design cannot begin. Throughout the process of questionnaire design, this objective should be the primary basis for making decisions about what to include and exclude and what to emphasize or treat with less importance. Moreover, the questionnaire should be viewed as an integrated whole in which each section and every question serve a clear purpose related to the study's objective as well as complement other sections and questions.

Build on Existing Instruments

When another researcher already has designed a set of questions to measure a key concept in your study, that existing set of questions can be called a survey instrument. If evidence from previous surveys indicates that these already formulated questions provide a good measure of the concept or behaviors you are interested in, then use them! Measurement tools have already been established for many concepts, especially those of interest to criminological research, including delinquency, self-control, depression, and so on. In the case study that follows, you will see how researchers rarely have to reinvent the wheel.

Consider Translation

Should the survey be translated into one or more languages? In the 21st century, no survey plan in the United States or many other countries can be considered complete until this issue has been considered. In 2013, 12.9% of people residing in the United States were foreign born (U.S. Census Bureau, 2015), and more than half of these adults said that they did not speak English very well. In some areas of the United States, these proportions can be much higher. Many first-generation immigrants are not fluent in English (Hakimzadeh & Cohn, 2007). As a result, they can only be included in a survey if it is translated into their native language.

This does not simply mean picking up a bilingual dictionary, clicking "translate" in a Web browser, or even hiring a translator to translate the questions. You must ensure that the concepts you are measuring have equivalence in different cultures, which is often a time-consuming task and typically involves teams of experts both in the language and in the culture for which the questionnaire is intended. Many government-sponsored surveys are currently translated into Spanish, including both the NISVS and the NCVS.

Case Study: Measuring Violent Victimizations

To assess whether respondents have experienced a victimization, the U.S. Department of Justice–sponsored NCVS asks a number of questions about experiences within the past six months. The primary screening questions of violent victimizations are displayed in Exhibit 7.1. As you can see, these questions are fairly specific and help respondents think about many different contexts, including those instances that may not be considered as victimizations, such as those committed by family and friends.

Compare the questions from the NCVS in Exhibit 7.1 with the screening questions for sexual violence from the CDC-sponsored NISVS that are displayed in Exhibit 7.2. Both

1. Has anyone attacked or threatened you in any of these ways:
   a. With any weapon, for instance, a gun or knife?
   b. With anything like a baseball bat, frying pan, scissors, or stick?
   c. By something thrown, such as a rock or bottle?
   d. Any grabbing, punching, or choking?
   e. Any rape, attempted rape, or other type of sexual assault?
   f. Any face-to-face threats?

OR

   g. Any attack or threat or use of force by anyone at all? Please mention it even if you were not certain it was a crime.

2. Incidents involving forced or unwanted sexual acts are often difficult to talk about. Have you been forced or coerced to engage in unwanted sexual activity by
   a. Someone you didn't know before?
   b. A casual acquaintance?

OR

   c. Someone you know well?

3. Were you attacked or threatened OR did you have something stolen from you
   a. At home, including the porch or yard?
   b. At or near a friend's, relative's, or neighbor's home?
   c. At work or school?
   d. In a place such as a storage shed or laundry room, a shopping mall, restaurant, bank, or airport?
   e. While riding in any vehicle?
   f. On the street or in a parking lot?
   g. At such places as a party, theater, gym, picnic area, bowling lanes, or while fishing or hunting?

OR

   h. Did anyone ATTEMPT to attack or attempt to steal anything belonging to you from any of these places?

4. People often don't think of incidents committed by someone they know. Did you have something stolen from you OR were you attacked or threatened by
   a. Someone at work or school?
   b. A neighbor or friend?
   c. A relative or family member?
   d. Any other person you've met or known?

5. Did you call the police to report something that happened to YOU which you thought was a crime?

6. Did anything happen to you which you thought was a crime but did NOT report to the police?

Source: NCVS (National Crime Victimization Survey).

surveys estimate prevalence rates of sexual violence, but as you can see, the questions on which their estimates are based are very different indeed. In the next section, we will provide you with some specific guidelines for writing questions, and you will see that the answer to this question is not so clear-cut.

How many people have ever . . . ?

   a. exposed their sexual body parts to you, flashed you, or masturbated in front of you

   b. made you show your sexual body parts to them (Remember, we are only asking about things that you didn't want to happen.)

   c. made you look at or participate in sexual photos or movies

   d. harassed you while you were in a public place in a way that made you feel unsafe

   e. kissed you in sexual way (Remember, we are only asking about things that you didn't want to happen.)

   f. fondled or grabbed your sexual body parts

When you were drunk, high, drugged, or passed out and unable to consent, how many people ever . . . ?

   a. had vaginal sex with you? By vaginal sex, we mean that (if female: a man or boy put his penis in your vagina) (if male: a women or girl made you put your penis in her vagina)

   b. (if male) made you perform anal sex, meaning that they made you put your penis into their anus

   c. made you receive anal sex, meaning they put their penis into your anus

   d. made you perform oral sex, meaning that they put their penis in your mouth or made you penetrate their vagina or anus with your mouth

   e. made you receive oral sex, meaning that they put their mouth on your (if male: penis) (if female: vagina) or anus

How many people have ever used physical force or threats to physically harm you to make you . . . ?

   a. have vaginal sex

   b. (if male) perform anal sex

   c. receive anal sex

   d. perform oral sex

   e. receive oral sex

   f. put their fingers or an object in your (if female: vagina or) anus

How many people have ever used physical force or threats of physical harm to . . . ?

   a. (if male) try to make you have vaginal sex with them, but sex did not happen

   b. try to have (if female: vaginal) oral or anal sex with you, but sex did not happen

How many people have you had vaginal, oral, or anal sex with after they pressured you by . . . ?

   a. doing things like telling you lies, making promises about the future they knew were untrue, threatening to end your relationship, or threatening to spread rumors about you

   b. wearing you down by repeatedly asking for sex or showing they were unhappy

   c. using their authority over you (for example, your boss or your teacher)

Source: From the CDC-Sponsored NISVS.

WRITING SURVEY QUESTIONS: MORE DIFFICULT THAN YOU THINK!

Questions are the centerpiece of survey research. Because the way they are worded can have a great effect on the way they are answered, selecting good questions is the single most important concern for survey researchers. All hope for achieving measurement validity is lost unless the questions in a survey are clear and convey the intended meaning to respondents. In principle, survey questions can be a straightforward and efficient means of measuring individual characteristics, facts about events, levels of knowledge, and opinions of any sort. In practice, survey questions, if misleading or unclear, can result in inappropriate and unintended answers. All questions proposed for a survey must adhere to basic guidelines and then be tested and revised until the researcher feels confident they will be clear to the intended respondents (Fowler, 1995). Structurally, questions on surveys generally fall into two categories: those with and those without explicit response choices. Recall from Chapter 4 that open-ended questions are those without explicit response choices. This type of question is usually used only for explorative purposes when there is little known about a particular topic and you want to uncover as much about it as possible without restricting responses. For example, if you are investigating the perceptions of residents regarding a new community policing program instituted in the neighborhood, open-ended questions such as the following one could be very informative:

> "In your opinion, what have been the benefits of the community policing program in your neighborhood?"

The information obtained from open-ended questions such as this could then be used as the basis for questions with fixed responses in future studies that evaluate the efficacy of community policing.

Open-ended questions are also excellent tools for obtaining respondents' interpretations in greater detail and can often illuminate flaws in other questions. A survey researcher can also try to understand what respondents mean by their responses after the fact by including additional open-ended questions in the survey. Adding such interpretive questions after key survey questions is always a good idea, but it is of utmost importance when the questions in a survey have not been pretested. An example from a study of people with driving violations illustrates the importance of interpretive questions:

> When asked whether their emotional state affected their driving at all, respondents would reply that their emotions had very little effect on their driving habits. Then, when asked to describe the circumstances surrounding their last traffic violation, respondents typically replied, "I was mad at my girlfriend," or "I had a quarrel with my wife," or "We had a family quarrel," or "I was angry with my boss." (Labaw, 1980, p. 71)

Were these respondents lying in response to the first question? Probably not. More likely, they simply did not interpret their own behavior in terms of a general concept such as *emotional state*. But their responses to the first question were likely to tell a different story without the further detail provided by answers to the second.

Open-ended questions: Survey questions to which the respondent replies in his or her own words, either by writing or by talking

Interpretive questions: Questions included in a questionnaire or interview schedule to help explain answers to other important questions

In summary, one strength of open-ended questions is the wealth of information they provide. This wealth of information, however, is exactly why many researchers do not use them. The verbatim text narratives obtained from open-ended questions take a great deal of time and energy to organize and summarize. In addition, many respondents may feel overwhelmed about writing a lengthy essay. If you want to ask a large number of open-ended questions, it is perhaps best to consider an in-person interview or phone interview instead of a questionnaire (both of which are discussed later in this chapter).

When respondents are offered explicit responses to choose from, this type of question is referred to as a **closed-ended question** or a **fixed-choice question**. For example, if we wanted to measure how safe people feel, we may ask something like the following:

Overall, would you say that personal safety in this country has improved since you were a child, gotten worse since you were a child, or stayed about the same?

____ Improved

____ Gotten worse

____ Stayed about the same

Most surveys of a large number of people primarily contain closed-ended questions, which are easy to process and analyze with the use of computers and statistical software. With closed-ended questions, respondents are also more likely to answer the question that researchers want them to answer. By including the response choices, the survey reduces ambiguity. However, closed-ended questions can also obscure what people really think unless the choices are carefully designed to match the range of all possible responses to the question.

Regardless of the format used for questions, there are several rules to follow and pitfalls to avoid that will maximize the validity of your survey instrument. We will highlight these in the next section.

Constructing Clear and Meaningful Questions

All hope for achieving measurement validity is lost unless survey questions are clear and convey the intended meaning to respondents. Even if you pose questions all the time and have no trouble understanding the responses you receive, this does not mean that clear and meaningful survey questions would not present a challenge. Consider just a few of the differences between everyday conversations and standardized surveys: Survey questions must be asked of many people, not just one person.

- The same survey questions must be used with each person, not tailored to the specifics of a given conversation.

- Survey questions must be understood in the same way by people who differ in many ways.

- You will not be able to rephrase a survey question if someone does not understand it because that would result in asking the person a different question from the one you asked the others in your sample.

- Survey respondents do not know you and so cannot be expected to share the nuances of expression that you and those close to you use to communicate.

These features make a survey very different from natural conversation and make question writing a challenging and important task for survey researchers.

Questions must be very clear and specific about what is being asked of respondents. Note the differences in specificity between the rape screening questions used by the NISVS and the NCVS displayed in Exhibits 7.1 and 7.2. It is logical that the multiple behaviorally specific questions from the NISVS will be associated with greater disclosure by survey respondents compared with the one question about sexual intercourse posed by the NCVS. Research has shown that questions that are written with more behavior-specific language, such as those used by the NISVS, result in much better recall by respondents of these types of victimizations compared with the questions used by the NCVS (Bachman, 2012; Fisher, 2009).

In addition to writing clear and meaningful questions, there are several other rules to follow and pitfalls to avoid that we will highlight next.

Avoid Confusing Phrasing and Vagueness

Good grammar is a basic requirement for clear questions. Clearly and simply phrased questions are most likely to have the same meaning for different respondents. The wordier and longer the question, the more likely you are to lose a respondent's attention and focus. Be brief, and stick to the point. Virtually all questions about behavior and feelings will be more reliable if they refer to specific times or events (Turner & Martin, 1984). Without identifying a **reference period**, or time frame around which a question is being asked, a researcher will not know how to interpret an answer. For example, the question "How often do you carry a method of self-protection, such as pepper spray?" will produce answers that have no common reference period and therefore cannot reliably be compared with answers from other respondents. A more specific way to ask the question is, "In the last month, how many days did you carry a method of self-protection, such as pepper spray?"

In general, research shows that the longer the reference period, the greater the under-reporting of a given behavior (Cantor, 1984, 1985; Kobelarcik, Alexander, Singh, & Shapiro, 1983). As a general rule, when respondents are being asked about mundane or day-to-day activities, reference periods should be no longer than "in the past month." However, when rare events are being measured, such as experiences with victimizations, "in the last six months" (as utilized by the NCVS) or "in the past 12 months" (as used by the NISVS) are both more appropriate. By using longer reference periods such as these, we will more likely capture these rarer events.

> **Reference period:** A time frame in which a survey question asks respondents to place a particular behavior (e.g., in the last six months)

Avoid Negative Words and Double Negatives

Picture yourself answering the following question: "Do you disagree that juveniles should not be tried as adults if they commit murder?" It probably took a long time for you to figure out whether you would actually agree or disagree with this statement because it is written as a **double-negative question**. For example, if you think juveniles who commit murder should be tried as adults, you would actually agree with this statement. Even questions that are written with a single negative are usually difficult to answer. For example, suppose you were asked to respond to "I can't stop thinking about a terrorist attack happening" using a 5-point response set from "very rarely" to "very often." A person who marks "very rarely" is actually saying, "I very rarely can't stop thinking about a terrorist attack happening." Confusing, isn't it? Even the most experienced survey researchers can unintentionally make this mistake.

> **Double-negative question:** A question or statement that contains two negatives, which can muddy the meaning

Avoid Double-Barreled Questions

When a question is really asking more than one thing, it is called a **double-barreled question**. For example, asking people to respond to the statement, "I believe we should stop spending so much money building prisons and put it into building more schools," is really asking them two different questions. Some respondents may believe we should stop building so many prisons but may not want the revenue to go into building more schools. Double-barreled

> **Double-barreled question:** A single survey question that actually asks two questions but allows only one answer

questions can also show up in the response categories. For example, the item below is really asking two questions:

Have you ever used cocaine, or do you know anyone who has ever used cocaine?

_____ Yes _____ No

Avoid Making Either Disagreement or Agreement Disagreeable

People often tend to agree with a statement just to avoid seeming disagreeable. You can see the impact of this human tendency in a Michigan Survey Research Center survey that asked who was to blame for crime and lawlessness in the United States (Schuman & Presser, 1981). When one item stated that individuals were more to blame than social conditions, 60% of the respondents agreed. But when the question was rephrased so respondents were asked, in a balanced fashion, whether individuals or social conditions were more to blame, only 46% chose individuals.

You can take several steps to reduce the likelihood of agreement bias. As a general rule, you should impartially present both sides of attitude scales in the question itself: "In general, do you believe that *individuals* or *social conditions* are more to blame for crime and lawlessness in the United States?" (Dillman, 2000, pp. 61–62, italics original). The response choices themselves should be phrased to make each one seem as socially approved, or as "agreeable," as the others. You should also consider replacing the word *agree* with a range of response alternatives. For example, "To what extent do you support or oppose mandatory background checks for all people who want to buy a firearm?" (response choices range from "strongly support" to "strongly oppose") is probably a better approach than the question "To what extent do you agree or disagree with the statement 'Mandatory background checks for all people who want to buy a firearm is worthy of support'?" (response choices range from "strongly agree" to "strongly disagree").

When an illegal or socially disapproved behavior or attitude is the focus, we have to be concerned that some respondents will be reluctant to agree that they have ever done or thought such a thing. In this situation, the goal is to write a question and response choices that make agreement seem more acceptable or, at the very least, not stigmatizing. For example, Dillman (2000) suggests that we ask, "Have you ever taken anything from a store without paying for it?" rather than "Have you ever shoplifted something from a store?" (p. 75). Asking about a variety of behaviors or attitudes that range from socially acceptable to socially unacceptable also will soften the impact of agreeing with those that are socially unacceptable.

Additional Guidelines for Closed-Ended Questions

Creating questions that are clear and meaningful is only half of the formula involved in creating a good survey instrument. The choices you provide respondents in closed-ended questions are also important. In this section, we provide you with several rules that will help to ensure that the response choices you provide to your questions also will be clear and concise, as well as exhaustive.

Make Response Choices Mutually Exclusive

When you want respondents to make only one choice, the fixed-response categories must not overlap. For example, if you were interested in the ways foot patrol officers spent their time while working, you might ask the following question:

On average, how much time do you spend on the job each week taking care of traffic violations?

- Less than 1 hour

- 1–3 hours

- 3–6 hours

- 6–10 hours

- 10 hours or more

The choices provided for respondents in this question are not **mutually exclusive responses** because they overlap. Which choice would an officer select if he or she spent 3 hours a week on traffic violations? Choices that are mutually exclusive would look like this:

- 1 hour or less

- 2–3 hours

- 4–6 hours

- 7–10 hours

- 11 hours or more

Make the Response Categories Exhaustive

In addition to mutual exclusivity, fixed-response categories must also allow all respondents to select an option. Consider the same research question about foot patrol officers. Suppose we asked a question such as this:

In what activity do you spend the most time in an average week on the job?

- traffic violations

- disturbance-related issues

- felony arrests

- misdemeanor arrests

Regardless of how exhaustive we think the response categories are, there must always be an option for respondents who require another choice. **Exhaustive response** categories can easily be created if respondents are provided with a choice labeled

- Other, please specify: _____

Note, however, that "Other" should be used only after you have included all options that you believe to be relevant. Otherwise, a large percentage of respondents will select the "Other" category, and you will have to spend time coding their responses.

Utilize Likert-Type Response Categories

Likert-type responses generally ask respondents to indicate the extent to which they agree or disagree with statements. This format is generally believed to have been developed by Rensis Likert in the 1930s. Likert-type response categories list choices for respondents to select their level of agreement with a statement and may look something like this:

I think "three strikes" laws that increase penalties for individuals convicted of three or more felonies will help to decrease the crime rate.

Strongly Agree	Agree	Disagree	Strongly Disagree
1	2	3	4

Minimize Fence-Sitting and Floating

Two related problems in question writing stem from the respondent's desire to choose an acceptable or socially desirable answer and the desire to get through the survey as fast as possible. There is no uniformly correct solution to these problems, so you must carefully select an alternative.

Fence-sitters are people who see themselves as neutral in their attitudes toward a particular issue. If you are truly interested in those who do not have strong feelings on an issue, one alternative is to provide a neutral or undecided response option. The disadvantage of these options is that they may encourage some respondents to take the easy way out rather than really thinking about their feelings. They also may provide an out for respondents who do not want to reveal how they truly feel about an issue. On the other hand, not providing respondents who really have no opinion on an issue with an option such as "undecided" can be very frustrating for them and may encourage them to leave the item blank. Whatever you decide, it is generally a good idea to provide respondents with instructions that ask them to "select the choice in each item that most closely reflects your opinion." This should help make all respondents feel more comfortable about their answers, particularly those who only slightly feel one way or the other.

Floaters are respondents who choose a substantive answer even when they do not know anything about a particular question. For example, research has shown that one third of the public will provide an opinion on a proposed law they know nothing about if they are not provided with a "don't know" response option (Schuman & Presser, 1981). Of course, providing a "don't know" option has the same disadvantage as providing a neutral response option: Its inclusion leads some people who have an opinion to take the easy way out. If you are really interested in informed opinions about an issue, it is best to provide detailed information about that issue when asking a question.

Utilize Filter Questions

The use of filter questions is important to ensure that questions are asked only of relevant respondents. For example, if you are interested in the utilization of police services by robbery victims, you would first need to establish victimization with a **filter question**. These filter questions create **skip patterns**. For example, respondents who answer *no* to one question are directed to skip ahead to another question, but respondents who answer *yes* are to go on to the **contingent question(s)**. (Filter questions are sometimes called *contingency questions*.) Skip patterns should be indicated clearly with arrows or other direction in the questionnaire, as demonstrated in Exhibit 7.3.

Combining Questions Into an Index

Measuring variables with single questions is very popular. Public opinion polls based on answers to single questions are reported frequently in newspaper articles and TV newscasts: "Do you favor or oppose U.S. policy for . . . ?" "If you had to vote today, for which candidate would you vote?" The primary problem with using a single question is that if respondents misunderstand the question or have some other problem with the phrasing, there is no way to tell. Single questions are prone to this **idiosyncratic variation**, which occurs when individuals' responses vary because of their reactions to particular words or ideas in the question. Differences in respondents' background, knowledge, and beliefs almost guarantee that they will

---

Fence-sitters: Survey respondents who see themselves as being neutral on an issue and choose a middle (neutral) response that is offered

Floaters: Survey respondents who provide an opinion on a topic in response to a closed-ended question that does not include a "don't know" option but will choose "don't know" if it is available

Filter question: A survey question used to identify a subset of respondents who then are asked other questions

Skip patterns: The unique combination of questions created in a survey by filter questions and contingent questions

Contingent questions: Questions that are asked of only a subset of survey respondents

Idiosyncratic variation: Variation in responses to questions that is caused by individuals' reactions to particular words or ideas in the question instead of by variation in the concept that the question is intended to measure

Exhibit 7.3   Filter Questions and Skip Patterns

14. In the past six months, has anyone taken something from you by force or the threat of force?

_____Yes (If yes, please answer questions 15 through 16)

_____No (If no, please skip to question 17)

15. What was the approximate monetary value of the items taken?

_____Under $50

_____$51 to $99

_____$100 to $299

_____$300 to $500

_____Over $500

16. Was the incident reported to the police?

_____Yes

_____No

17. How fearful are you of walking alone at night in your neighborhood?

_____Extremely afraid

_____Afraid

_____Unafraid

_____Extremely unafraid

understand the same question differently. If a number of respondents do not know some of the words in a question, we may misinterpret their answers—if they answer at all. If a question is too complex, respondents may focus on different parts of the question. If prior experiences or culturally biased orientations lead different groups in the sample to interpret questions differently, answers will not have a consistent meaning because the question meant something different to each respondent.

As noted previously, if just one question is used to measure a variable, the researcher may not realize respondents had trouble with a particular word or phrase in the question. Although writing carefully worded questions will help reduce idiosyncratic variation, when measuring concepts, the best option is to devise an index of multiple rather than single questions.

When several questions are used to measure one concept, the responses may be combined by taking the sum or average of the responses. A composite measure based on this type of sum or average is called an **index**, sometimes called a scale. The idea is that idiosyncratic variation in response to single questions will average out, so the main influence on the combined measure will be the concept focused on by the questions. In addition, the index can be considered a more complete measure of the concept than can any one of the component questions.

Creating an index, however, is not just a matter of writing a few questions that seem to focus on one concept. Questions that seem to you to measure a common concept might seem to respondents to concern several different issues. The only way to know that a given set of questions does effectively form an index is to administer the questions in a pretest to people similar to the sample you plan to study. If a common concept is being measured, people's responses to the different questions should display some consistency. Special statistics called **reliability measures** help researchers decide whether responses are consistent. Most respondent attitudes are complex and consist of many elements.

> Index: A composite measure based on summing, averaging, or otherwise combining the responses to multiple questions that are intended to measure the same variable, sometimes called a *scale*
>
> Reliability measures: Special statistics that help researchers decide whether responses are consistent

Be aware of response sets when constructing an index measuring attitudes. For example, some people tend to agree with almost everything asked of them, whereas others tend to disagree. Still others are prone to answer neutrally to everything if given the option. To decrease the likelihood of this happening, it is a good idea to make some statements both favorable and unfavorable to a particular attitude to vary the response choices and still reach an understanding of an individual's opinion. In this way, respondents are forced to be more careful in their responses to individual items. Exhibit 7.4 displays a hypothetical set of questions designed to solicit respondents' attitudes toward police in their community.

When scoring an index or scale made up of both favorable and unfavorable statements, you must remember to **reverse code** the unfavorable items. For example, marking "strongly agree" on the first item in Exhibit 7.4 should not be scored the same as a "strongly agree" response to the second item.

Demographic Questions

Almost all questionnaires include a section on demographic information, such as sex, age, race or ethnicity, income, and religion. For many research studies, these questions are important independent variables. For example, research has shown that all five of these factors are related to the probability of victimization. Many researchers, however, include demographic questions that are not necessary for purposes of their research. Try to avoid this, particularly for questions on income because it makes the questionnaire more intrusive than necessary. In fact, many respondents feel that questions about their income invade their privacy. If you believe income is an essential variable for your study, providing fixed responses that include a range of values to select from is less intrusive than asking respondents for specific annual incomes. This format is utilized by the NCVS, as shown in Exhibit 7.5.

Care should also be taken when writing questions about race and ethnicity. Many people are justifiably sensitive to these questions. Even the U.S. Census Bureau has been struggling with appropriate categories to offer respondents. In fact, the bureau still utilizes two

Reverse code: Recoding response choices that were originally coded to reflect both favorable and unfavorable attitudes toward a phenomenon as indicative of either all favorable or all unfavorable, so the index is measuring the same thing

---

Exhibit 7.4   Items in an "Attitude Toward Police" Index

1. I think police officers are generally fair to all people regardless of their race or ethnicity.

   _____ Strongly Agree   _____ Agree   _____ Disagree   _____ Strongly Disagree

2. Police officers are given too much freedom to stop and frisk community residents.

   _____ Strongly Agree   _____ Agree   _____ Disagree   _____ Strongly Disagree

3. I think if someone resisted arrest, even a little, most police officers would become assaultive if they thought they could get away with it.

   _____ Strongly Agree   _____ Agree   _____ Disagree   _____ Strongly Disagree

4. Police officers put their lives on the line every day trying to make it safe for residents of this community.

   _____ Strongly Agree   _____ Agree   _____ Disagree   _____ Strongly Disagree

5. I think the majority of police officers have lied under oath at least once.

   _____ Strongly Agree   _____ Agree   _____ Disagree   _____ Strongly Disagree

6. The majority of police officers are honest and fair.

   _____ Strongly Agree   _____ Agree   _____ Disagree   _____ Strongly Disagree

---

Exhibit 7.5   Question on Income From the NCVS

Including income from all sources, such as work, child support, and AFDC [Aid to Families with Dependent Children], how much income did you personally receive in 2015 before taxes? Stop me when I get to the category that applies. Was it:

12a.   **Household Income**

1 ☐ Less than $5,000	6 ☐ 15,000–17,499	11 ☐ 35,000–39,999
2 ☐ $5,000–7,499	7 ☐ 17,500–19,999	12 ☐ 40,000–49,999
3 ☐ 7,500–9,999	8 ☐ 20,000–24,999	13 ☐ 50,000–74,999
4 ☐ 10,000–12,499	9 ☐ 25,000–29,999	14 ☐ 75,000 and over
5 ☐ 12,500–14,999	10 ☐ 30,000–34,999	

National Crime Victimization Survey

questions, one on race and one for respondent ethnicity (Hispanic or non-Hispanic), which is obviously problematic. Most surveys now include the option of marking all categories that apply, so those with mixed racial/ethnic backgrounds can be identified. The NCVS asks a question about Hispanic origin and then asks the following question about race:

Which of the following best describes your racial background? Please mark all that apply.

1. _____ White

2. _____ Black/African American

3. _____ American Indian/Alaska Native

4. _____ Asian

5. _____ Native Hawaiian/Other Pacific Islander

6. _____ Other – Specify _____

Allowing respondents to select "all that apply" is necessary when many respondents are from a mixed-race background. Questions on marital status can also be tricky to compose. The traditional categories of married, single, divorced, and widowed, still used by novice researchers, can be interpreted very differently by respondents. Why? Well, isn't someone who is currently divorced also single? And what about someone not officially divorced but separated? To avoid confusing respondents, the U.S. Census Bureau adopted the following response categories: married, separated, widowed, divorced, and never married.

Because demographic questions are usually perceived as private by respondents, some researchers place them in a section at the end of the questionnaire with an introduction reassuring respondents that the information will remain confidential. However, when the information being gathered in the rest of the questionnaire is even more sensitive, such as violence respondents may have experienced at the hands of a family member or an intimate partner, some researchers opt to keep demographic questions near the beginning of the questionnaire.

Don't Forget to Pretest!

Adhering to the preceding question-writing guidelines will go a long way toward producing a useful questionnaire. However, simply asking what appear to be clear questions does not ensure that people will have a consistent understanding of what you are asking. You need some external feedback, and the more of it, the better.

No questionnaire should be considered ready for use until it has been **pretested**. Try answering the questionnaire yourself, and then revise it. Try it out on some colleagues or other friends, and then revise it. Then select a small sample of individuals from the population you are studying or one very similar to it, and try out the questionnaire on them. Audiotape the test interviews for later review or, for a written questionnaire, include in the pretest version some space for individuals to add comments on each key question.

It takes several drafts to create a good questionnaire. By the time you have gone through just a couple of drafts, you may not be scanning the instrument as clearly as you think. A very honest illustration of this is provided by Don Dillman, the director of the Social and Economic Sciences Research Center at Washington State University (cited in Seltzer, 1996). His research team almost mailed a questionnaire with the following response categories:

What is your opinion?

1	2	3	4	5
Strongly Oppose	Oppose	Neither Oppose nor Favor	Favor	Strongly Oppose

This Likert-type response format slipped by not only Dillman but also his typist, a research assistant, and another person working on the project. He explains,

> By the time a would-be surveyor has reached the final draft, he or she is often scanning the questionnaire for errors but not absorbing the detail. . . . All of us were looking for other things, such as spacing, punctuation, and content. The uniform appearance of the response categories looked right to all of us. (Seltzer, 1996, p. 98)

Careful scrutiny of your questionnaire using the procedures outlined in this section will help you detect these and other problems.

ORGANIZATION MATTERS

Once the basic topics and specific variables for a questionnaire have been identified, they can be sorted into categories (which may become separate sections), listed in tentative order, and later adjusted to develop the questionnaire's polish and coherence.

The first thing needed is a descriptive title for the questionnaire that indicates the overall topic. The title is essential because it sets the context for the entire survey. For example, both the NCVS and the NISVS are interested in measuring the magnitude of crime victimization in the United States. The NISVS, however, was presented as a survey interested in a number of personal-safety-related issues, including tactics used in conflict resolution. The NCVS has *crime* right in the title, and this conveys to respondents that it is a survey interested in obtaining information only about crimes respondents have experienced. Unfortunately, some survey participants still may not view assaults they have experienced by intimates and other family members as criminal acts, which may decrease the chance that they will be counted as victims.

The **cover letter** for a mailed questionnaire and the introductory statement read by interviewers in telephone or in-person interviews are also critical to the survey's success. Similar to the context set by the title of the survey, the initial statement of the cover letter sets the tone for the entire questionnaire. For example, the first thing interviewers said to respondents of the National Violence against Men and Women Survey (NVMWS), which was a precursor to the NISVS, was, "Hello, I'm _____ from SRBI, the national research organization. We are conducting a national survey on personal safety for the Center for Policy Research, under a grant from the federal government." Notice that, even though the survey's primary purpose was to uncover incidents of victimization, it was presented to respondents as a survey interested in issues of personal safety. This was done to increase the probability of respondents disclosing incidents of victimization even if they did not perceive them to be crimes. Also note that the introductory statement disclosed the researcher's affiliation and the project sponsor. In addition, the purpose of the survey should briefly be described and a contact number should be included for those who wish to ask questions or register complaints. In sum, the cover letter for a mailed questionnaire and the introductory statement for an interview should be credible, personalized, interesting, and responsible.

Question Order Matters!

In addition to these issues, question order and the use of multiple questions to uncover attitudes about emotionally charged issues are important because these factors also can influence responses. Consider the issue of capital punishment. For example, a 2013 Gallup poll revealed that 64% of those surveyed approved of the death penalty for murder. However, when respondents were given the alternative punishment of life imprisonment without the possibility of parole, the support declined to 50%. This suggests that public opinion questions that simply ask whether the person approves of capital punishment for convicted murderers are a misleading indicator of the strength of support for the death penalty. As Paternoster (1991) explains,

> What Americans may be expressing, however, is a desire for protection against
> dangerous criminals, not a desire for capital punishment. More sophisticated
> polling questions indicate that the public does not necessarily want to repay one
> life with another, but wants the murderer to be unable to offend again, and to ease
> the hardship and loss for those left behind. (p. 30)

Question order also can lead to **context effects** when one or more questions influence how subsequent questions are interpreted (Schober, 1999). For example, when a sample of the general public was asked, "Do you think it should be possible for a pregnant woman to obtain a legal abortion if she is married and does not want any more children?" 58% said yes. However, when this question was preceded by a less permissive question that asked whether the respondent would allow abortion of a defective fetus, only 40% said yes. Asking the question about a defective fetus altered respondents' frame of reference, perhaps by making abortion simply to avoid having more children seem frivolous by comparison (Turner & Martin, 1984). The point to take away from these cases is that question order is extremely important. As Schuman and Presser (1981) acknowledge,

Context effects: Occur in a survey when one or more questions influence how subsequent questions are interpreted

> Both examples illustrate the potential impact of question order on the respondents'
> answers. This potential is greatest when two or more questions concern the same
> issue or closely related issues so that asking one question affects reactions to the
> next question. The impact of question order also tends to be greatest for general
> summary-type questions. (p. 23)

There is no real cure for this potential problem. However, a **split-ballot design** may help identify problems. In a split-ballot survey, some respondents can be given a survey with a particular question order while the other respondents can be given another. This design allows researchers to determine the effect of question order on responses. What is most important is

Split-ballot design: Unique questions or other modifications in a survey administered to randomly selected subsets of the total survey sample so that more questions can be included in the entire survey or so that responses to different question versions can be compared

to be aware of the potential for problems due to question order and to carefully evaluate the likelihood of their occurrence in any particular questionnaire. Survey results should mention, at least in a footnote, the order in which key questions were asked when more than one such question was used (Labaw, 1980).

Questionnaires should conform to several other organizational guidelines as well:

- Major topic divisions within the questionnaire should be organized in separate sections, and each section should be introduced with a brief statement.

- Instructions should be used liberally to minimize respondent confusion. Instructions should explain how each type of question is to be answered (such as circling a number or writing a response) in a neutral way that is not likely to influence responses. Instructions also should guide respondents through skip patterns.

- The questionnaire should look attractive, be easy to complete, and have substantial white space. Resist the temptation to cram as many questions as possible onto one page. Response choices should be printed in a different font or format from the questions and should be set off from them.

- Response choices should be designated by numbers to facilitate coding and data entry after the questionnaire is completed.

SURVEY DESIGNS

The five basic survey designs are the mailed (self-administered) survey, group-administered survey, phone survey, in-person survey, and electronic or Web survey. Exhibit 7.6 summarizes the typical features of the five designs. Each survey design varies in its arrangement and application.

United Nations Report Highlights Violence Against Women in Families

This article provides a summary of a United Nations (UN) report titled *Families in a Changing World*. The newspaper article reported that "every single day 137 women were killed by a family member." However, it did not provide details on how those numbers were obtained. The article notes that the slowest progress in gender equality came in countries where family laws govern a woman's right to choose who and when to marry and her right to divorce and inherit money and property. The author of the article noted that some countries were making progress, including India, where the Supreme Court declared unconstitutional the practice whereby a husband can divorce his wife simply by saying "I divorce you" three times.

For Further Thought

1. What would you like to know about the data that was used for the UN report highlighted in this article?

2. Can you think of an independent variable measured at the country level that might be used to explain the dependent variable of rates of intimate partner violence in countries?

Source: Lederer, E. M. (2019, June 26). UN Report: Women too often suffer violence in families. *Washington Post*. Retrieved from https://www.washingtonpost.com/world/un-report-women-too-often-suffer-violence-in-families/2019/06/25/6839c796-97c3-11e9-9a16-dc551ea5a43b_story.html?noredirect=on&utm_term=.b6035403c2e4

Manner of Administration. Mailed, group, and electronic surveys are completed by the respondents themselves. During phone and in-person interviews, however, the researcher or a staff person asks the questions and records the respondent's answers.

Questionnaire Structure. Survey designs also differ in the extent to which the content and order of questions are structured in advance by the researcher. Most mailed, group, phone, and electronic surveys are highly structured, fixing in advance the content and order of questions and response choices. Some of these types of surveys, particularly mailed surveys, may include some open-ended questions. In-person interviews are often highly structured, but they may include many questions without fixed-response choices. Moreover, some interviews may proceed from an interview guide rather than a fixed set of questions. In these relatively unstructured interviews, the interviewer covers the same topics with respondents but varies questions according to the respondent's answers to previous questions. Extra questions are added as needed to clarify or explore answers to the most important questions.

Setting. Most mail and electronic questionnaires and phone interviews are intended for completion by only one respondent. The same is usually true of in-person interviews, although sometimes researchers interview several family members at once. On the other hand, a variant of the standard survey is a questionnaire distributed simultaneously to a group of respondents, who complete the survey while the researcher (or assistant) waits. Students in classrooms are typically the group involved, although this type of group distribution also occurs in surveys administered to employees and members of voluntary groups.

Cost. As mentioned earlier, in-person interviews are the most expensive type of survey. Phone interviews are much less expensive, but surveying by mail is cheaper still. Electronic surveys are now the least expensive method because there are no interviewer costs; no mailing costs; and, for many designs, almost no costs for data entry. Of course, extra staff time and expertise are required to prepare an electronic questionnaire.

Because of their different features, the five designs vary in the types of errors to which they are most prone and the situations in which they are most appropriate. The rest of this section focuses on the unique advantages and disadvantages of each design.

Mailed (Self-Administered) Surveys

A **mailed (self-administered) survey** is conducted by mailing a questionnaire to respondents, who then administer the survey themselves. The principal drawback in using this method of survey administration is the difficulty maximizing the response rate—we have to

> **Mailed (self-administered) survey:** A survey involving a mailed questionnaire to be completed by the respondent

Exhibit 7.6   Typical Features of the Five Survey Designs

Design	Manner of Administration	Setting	Questionnaire Structure	Cost
Mailed survey	Self	Individual	Mostly structured	Low
Group survey	Self	Group	Mostly structured	Very low
Phone survey	Professional	Individual	Structured	Moderate
In-person interview	Professional	Individual	Structured or unstructured	High
Electronic survey	Self	Individual	Mostly structured	Very low

rely on people to voluntarily return the surveys! The final response rate is unlikely to be much above 80% and almost surely will be below 70% unless procedures to maximize the response rate are precisely followed. A response rate below 60% is a disaster, and even a 70% response rate is not much more than minimally acceptable. It is hard to justify the representativeness of the sample if more than a third of those surveyed fail to respond. There are ways to increase response rates of mailed surveys, including sending a reminder postcard and sending replacement questionnaires to people who have not responded (Dillman, 2000).

Related to the threat of nonresponse in mailed surveys is the hazard of incomplete response. Some respondents may skip some questions or just stop answering questions at some point in the questionnaire. Fortunately, this problem often does not occur with well-designed questionnaires. Many researchers still rely on mailed surveys because they are relatively inexpensive and respondents are free to answer questions at their leisure, without the scrutiny of a survey administrator.

Group-Administered Surveys

A **group-administered survey** is completed by individual respondents assembled in a group. The response rate is not usually a concern in surveys that are distributed and collected in a group setting because most group members will participate. The difficulty with this method is that assembling a group is seldom feasible because it requires a captive audience. With the exception of students, employees, members of the armed forces, and some institutionalized populations, most populations cannot be sampled in such a setting.

One issue of special concern with group-administered surveys is the possibility that respondents will feel coerced to participate and, as a result, will be less likely to answer questions honestly. Also, because administering a survey to a group probably requires the approval of the group's supervisor and the survey is likely conducted on the organization's premises, respondents may infer that the researcher is not at all independent of the sponsor. Even those who volunteer may still feel uncomfortable answering all questions, which may bias their responses. No complete solution to this problem exists, but it helps to make an introductory statement that emphasizes the researcher's independence, assures respondents that their survey answers will be completely anonymous, and gives participants a chance to ask questions about the survey.

Surveys by Telephone

In a **phone survey**, interviewers question respondents over the phone and then record their answers. Phone interviewing has become a very popular method of conducting surveys in the United States because almost all families have phones. But two matters may undermine the validity of a phone survey: not reaching the proper sampling units and not getting enough complete responses to make the results generalizable.

Reaching Sampling Units

Today, drawing a random sample is easier than ever due to random digit dialing (RDD) (Lavrakas, 1987). A machine calls random phone numbers within designated exchanges, regardless of whether the numbers are published. When the machine reaches an inappropriate household (such as a business in a survey directed to the general population), the phone number is simply replaced with another.

To ensure cell phone–only households were also included in the sample, NISVS interviews were conducted both by landline and cell phone. The NISVS used RDD conducted in all 50 states and the District of Columbia so estimates of victimization could be aggregated

---

Group-administered survey: A survey that is completed by individual respondents who are assembled in a group

Phone survey: A survey in which interviewers question respondents over the phone and then record their answers

up to the state level of analysis. This allowed both individual and state-level prevalence rates to be calculated. Regardless of how individuals are contacted, the interviewers also must ask a series of questions at the start of the survey to ensure that they are speaking to the appropriate member of the household.

Maximizing Response to Phone Surveys

Three issues require special attention in phone surveys. First, because people often are not home, multiple callbacks will be necessary for many sample members. In addition, interviewers must be prepared for distractions if the respondent is interrupted by other household members. The growth of telemarketing has created another problem for telephone survey researchers: Individuals have become more accustomed to "just say no" to calls from unknown individuals and organizations or to simply use their answering machines to screen out unwanted calls (Dillman, 2000). Cell phone users are also harder (and more costly) to contact in phone surveys. Households with a cell phone but no landline tend to be younger, so the rate of phone survey participation is declining even more among those 18 to 34 years of age (Keeter, 2008).

Procedures can be standardized more effectively, quality control maintained, and processing speed maximized when phone interviewers are assisted by computers. This computer-assisted telephone interview has become known as CATI, and most large surveys are now performed in this way. There are several advantages to using CATI, but perhaps the primary one is that data collection and data entry can occur concurrently. Second, the CATI system has several machine edit features that help to minimize data entry error.

One method that dispenses with the interviewer altogether is computerized interactive voice response (IVR) survey technology. In an IVR survey, respondents receive automated calls and answer questions by pressing numbers on their touch-tone phones or speaking numbers that are interpreted by computerized voice recognition software. These surveys can also record verbal responses to open-ended questions for later transcription. Although they present some difficulties when many answer choices must be used or skip patterns must be followed, IVR surveys have been used successfully with short questionnaires and when respondents are highly motivated to participate (Dillman, 2000). When these conditions are not met, potential respondents may be put off by the impersonality of this computer-driven approach.

In summary, phone surveying is the best method to use for relatively short surveys of the general population. Response rates in phone surveys tend to be very high, often above 80%, because few individuals will hang up on a polite caller or refuse to stop answering questions (at least within the first 30 minutes or so). The NVMWS obtained a response rate of 72% in the female survey and 69% in the male survey by conducting interviews via telephone.

In-Person Interviews

What is unique to the in-person interview, compared with the other survey designs, is the face-to-face social interaction between interviewer and respondent. If financial resources are available for hiring interviewers to go out and personally conduct the surveys with respondents, in-person interviewing is often the best survey design.

Although time-consuming and costly, in-person interviewing has several advantages. Response rates are higher for this survey design than for any other when potential respondents are approached by a courteous interviewer. In addition, in-person interviews can be much longer than mailed or phone surveys; the questionnaire can be complex, with both open-ended and closed-ended questions. The order in which questions are read and answered can be controlled by the interviewer, and the physical and social circumstances of the interview

> **Computer-assisted telephone interview (CATI):** A telephone interview in which a questionnaire is programmed into a computer, along with relevant skip patterns that must be followed. It essentially combines the tasks of interviewing, data entry, and some data cleaning.

> **Computerized interactive voice response (IVR):** Software that uses a touch-tone telephone to interact with people to acquire information from or enter data into a database

> **In-person interview:** A survey in which an interviewer questions respondents and records their answers

can be monitored. Lastly, respondents' interpretations of questions can be probed and clarified, if it is done consistently with all respondents.

As with phone interviewing, computers can be used to increase control of the in-person interview. In a **computer-assisted personal interviewing (CAPI)** project, interviewers carry a laptop computer programmed to display the interview questions and process the responses that the interviewer types in as well as to check that these responses fall within the allowed ranges. Interviewers seem to like CAPI, and the quality of the data obtained is at least as good as for a noncomputerized interview (Shepherd, Hill, Bristor, & Montalvan, 1996). **Computer-assisted self-interviewing (CASI)** is also an alternative. With audio-CASI, respondents interact with a computer-administered questionnaire by using a mouse and following audio instructions delivered via headphones. Audio-CASI is considered the most reliable way to administer questionnaires that probe sensitive or potentially stigmatizing information, such as offending or victimization information (H. G. Miller, Gribble, Mazade, & Turner, 1998; Tourangeau & Smith, 1996; Turner et al., 1998). Wolf, Blitz, Shi, Bachman, and Siegel (2006) used this technology to obtain information about the physical and sexual victimization experiences of male and female state prison inmates. They explain,

> The survey was administered using audio-CASI (computer-assisted self-interviewing) and was available in English and Spanish. There were 30 computer stations set up at each facility and members of the research team were available to answer any questions and assist with the technology as needed. (p. 838)

Maximizing Response to Interviews

Even if the right balance is struck between maintaining control over interviews and achieving good rapport with respondents, in-person interviews can still have a problem. Due to the difficulty of catching all the members of a sample, response rates may suffer. As we noted in Chapter 5, many households are screening their calls and have little tolerance for unwanted solicitations.

Several factors affect the response rate in interview studies. Contact rates tend to be lower in city centers, in part because of difficulties in finding people at home and gaining access to high-rise apartments and in part because of interviewer reluctance to visit some areas at night, when people are more likely to be home (Fowler, 1988). Households with young children or elderly adults tend to be easier to contact, whereas single-person households are more difficult to reach (Groves & Couper, 1998).

Electronic Surveys

Electronic surveys have become increasingly useful for two reasons: growth in the fraction of the population using the Internet and in technological advances that make electronic survey design, often done using the Web or e-mail, relatively easy.

However, it still is not possible to obtain a true representative sample of the U.S. population on the Web, since not everyone is connected or has access to the Internet. While many specific populations have very high rates of Internet use, such as professional groups, middle-class communities, members of organizations, and, of course, college students, coverage still remains a major problem with many populations (Tourangeau, Conrad, & Couper, 2012). About one quarter of U.S. households are not connected to the Internet (Pew Research Center, 2019), so it is not yet possible to survey directly a representative sample of the U.S. population on the Web. Households without Internet access also tend to be older, poorer, and less educated than do those that are connected, so Web surveys of the general population can result in seriously biased estimates (Pew Research Center, 2019). Coverage problems can be compounded in Web surveys because of much lower rates of survey completion: It is just too

---

Computer-assisted personal interviewing (CAPI): An interview in which the interviewer carries a laptop computer programmed to display the interview questions and processes the responses that the interviewer types in, as well as checking that these responses fall within the allowed ranges

Computer-assisted self-interviewing (CASI): A system within which respondents interact with a computer-administered questionnaire by using a mouse and following audio instructions delivered via headphones

Electronic survey: A survey that is sent and answered by computer, either through e-mail or on the Web

easy to stop working on a Web survey—much easier than it is to break off interaction with an interviewer (Tourangeau et al., 2012).

The extent to which the population of interest is connected to the Web is the most important consideration when deciding whether to conduct a survey through the Web. Other considerations that may increase the attractiveness of a Web survey include the need for a large sample, the need for rapid turnaround, the need for collecting sensitive information that might be embarrassing to acknowledge in person, the availability of an e-mail list of the population, and the extent to which the interactive and multimedia features will enhance interest in the survey (Sue & Ritter, 2012).

There are many free online services to aid you in developing a Web survey, such as SurveyMonkey. However, many universities have also subscribed to more sophisticated survey engines such as Qualtrics. Using a random sample of University of Delaware students, the Center for Drug and Health Studies conducted a College Risk Behavior Survey using Qualtrics. Exhibit 7.7 displays one screen of the survey, which was devoted to ascertaining the extent to which students

Exhibit 7.7 A Page From the College Risk Behavior Survey

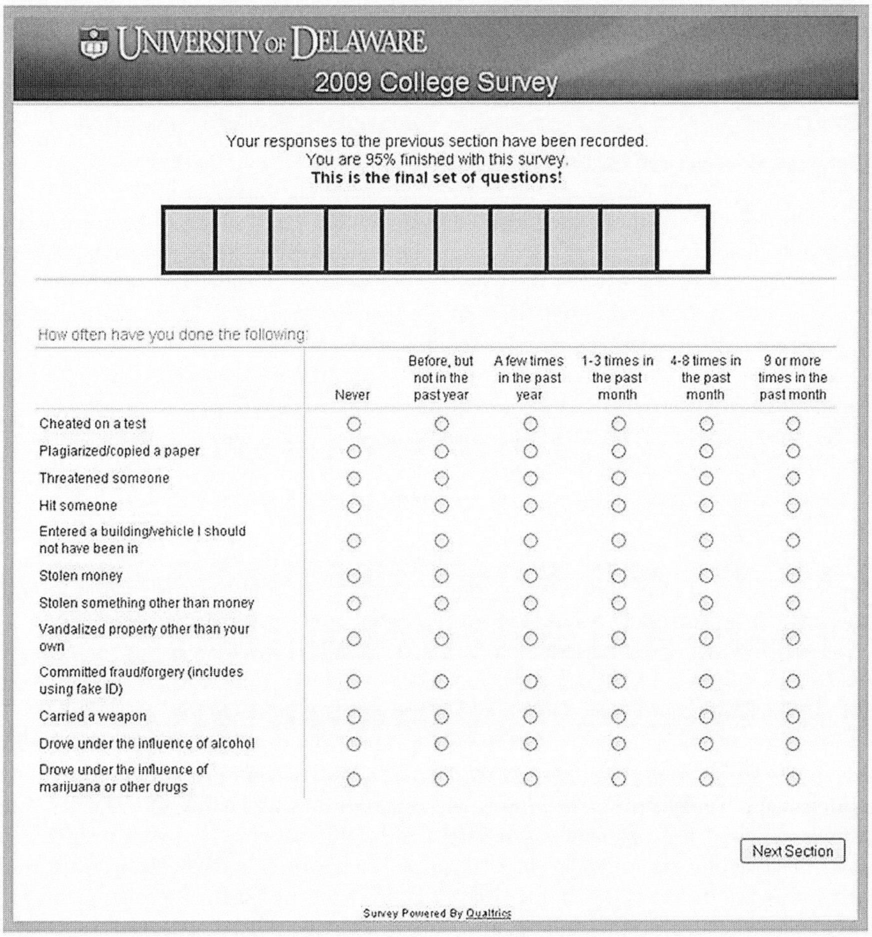

UNIVERSITY OF DELAWARE

2009 College Survey

Your responses to the previous section have been recorded.
You are 95% finished with this survey.
This is the final set of questions!

How often have you done the following:

	Never	Before, but not in the past year	A few times in the past year	1-3 times in the past month	4-8 times in the past month	9 or more times in the past month
Cheated on a test	○	○	○	○	○	○
Plagiarized/copied a paper	○	○	○	○	○	○
Threatened someone	○	○	○	○	○	○
Hit someone	○	○	○	○	○	○
Entered a building/vehicle I should not have been in	○	○	○	○	○	○
Stolen money	○	○	○	○	○	○
Stolen something other than money	○	○	○	○	○	○
Vandalized property other than your own	○	○	○	○	○	○
Committed fraud/forgery (includes using fake ID)	○	○	○	○	○	○
Carried a weapon	○	○	○	○	○	○
Drove under the influence of alcohol	○	○	○	○	○	○
Drove under the influence of marijuana or other drugs	○	○	○	○	○	○

Next Section

Survey Powered By Qualtrics

Source: University of Delaware 2009 College Survey

engaged in all types of behavior, including drinking and driving, using drugs, cheating on exams, victimizations, stealing, fighting, gambling, and illegally downloading material. Notice that the top of the screen told respondents how much of the survey they had left before they were finished. To enhance their response rate, the researchers offered students who completed the survey a $5 voucher that could be used at any university eating establishment.

Web surveys are becoming the more popular form of Internet survey because they are so flexible. The design of the questionnaire can include many types of graphic and typographic features. Respondents can view definitions of words or instructions for answering questions by clicking on linked terms. Lengthy sets of response choices can be presented with pull-down menus. Pictures and audio segments can be added when they are useful. Because answers are recorded directly in the researcher's database, data entry errors are almost eliminated, and results can be reported quickly.

Mixed-Mode Surveys

Mixed-mode surveys: Surveys that are conducted by more than one method, allowing the strengths of one survey design to compensate for the weaknesses of another and maximizing the likelihood of securing data from different types of respondents; for example, nonrespondents in a mailed survey may be interviewed in person or over the phone

Survey researchers increasingly are combining different survey designs. Mixed-mode surveys allow the strengths of one survey design to compensate for the weaknesses of another and can maximize the likelihood of securing data from different types of respondents. For example, a survey may be sent electronically to sample members who have e-mail addresses and mailed to those who do not. Alternatively, nonrespondents in a mailed survey may be interviewed in person or over the phone. As noted previously, an interviewer may use a self-administered questionnaire to present sensitive questions to a respondent.

A Comparison of Survey Designs

Which survey design should be used when? Group-administered surveys are similar in most respects to mailed surveys, except they require the unusual circumstance of having access to the sample in a group setting. We therefore do not need to consider this survey design by itself. Thus, we can focus our comparison on the four survey designs that involve the use of a questionnaire with individuals sampled from a larger population: mailed surveys, phone surveys, in-person surveys, and electronic surveys. Exhibit 7.8 summarizes their advantages and disadvantages.

The most important consideration in comparing the advantages and disadvantages of the four survey designs is the likely response rate they will generate. Because of the great weakness of mailed surveys in this respect, they must be considered the least preferred survey design from a sampling standpoint. However, researchers may still prefer a mailed survey when they have to reach a widely dispersed population and do not have enough financial resources to hire and train an interview staff or to contract with a survey organization that already has an interview staff available in many locations.

Contracting with an established survey research organization for a phone survey is often the best alternative to a mailed survey. The persistent follow-up attempts necessary to secure an adequate response rate are much easier over the phone than in person or via mail.

In-person surveys are clearly preferable in terms of the possible length and complexity of the questionnaire itself as well as the researcher's ability to monitor conditions while the questionnaire is being completed. Mailed surveys often are preferable for asking sensitive questions, although this problem can be lessened in an interview by giving respondents a separate sheet to fill out on their own. Although interviewers may themselves distort results by either changing the wording of questions or failing to record answers properly, this problem can be lessened by careful training, monitoring, and tape-recording the answers.

The advantages and disadvantages of electronic surveys must be weighed in light of the potential respondents' capabilities at the time the survey is to be conducted. At this time, over

Exhibit 7.8 Advantages and Disadvantages of Four Survey Designs

Characteristics of Design	In-Person Survey	Mail Survey	Phone Survey	Electronic Survey
Representative Sample				
Opportunity for inclusion is known				
For completely listed populations	High	High	High	Medium
For incompletely listed populations	High	Medium	Medium	Low
Selection within sampling units is controlled (e.g., specific family members must respond)	High	Medium	High	Low
Respondents are likely to be located	Medium	High	High	Low
If samples are heterogeneous	High	Medium	High	Low
If samples are homogeneous and specialized	High	High	High	High
Questionnaire Construction and Question Design				
Allowable length of questionnaire	High	Medium	Medium	Medium
Ability to include				
Complex questions	Medium	Low	High	High
Open questions	Low	High	High	Medium
Screening questions	Low	Low	High	High
Tedious, boring questions	High	High	High	High
Ability to control question sequence	Low	High	High	High
Ability to ensure questionnaire completion	Medium	High	High	High
Distortion of Answers				
Odds of avoiding social desirability bias	High	Medium	Low	High
Odds of avoiding interviewer distortion	Low	High	Medium	High
Odds of avoiding contamination by others	High	Medium	Medium	Medium
Administrative Goals				
Odds of meeting personnel requirements	High	High	Low	High
Odds of implementing quickly	Low	High	Low	High
Odds of keeping costs low	High	Medium	Low	High

Source: Adapted from Don A. Dillman, *Mail and Internet Surveys: The Tailored Design Method.* 2nd ed. Copyright © 2000 by John Wiley & Sons, Inc.

25% of households still lack Internet connections, and too many people who have computers lack adequate computer capacity for displaying complex webpages.

These various points about the different survey designs lead to two general conclusions. First, in-person interviews are the strongest design and generally preferable when sufficient resources and a trained interview staff are available, but telephone surveys still offer many of the advantages of in-person interviews at a much lower cost. Second, the best survey design for any particular study will be determined by the study's unique features and goals rather than by any absolute standard of what the best survey is.

ETHICAL ISSUES IN SURVEY RESEARCH

Survey research usually poses fewer ethical dilemmas than do experimental or field research designs. Potential respondents to a survey can easily decline to participate, and a cover letter or introductory statement that identifies the sponsors of and motivations for the survey gives them the information required to make this decision. The methods of data collection are quite obvious in a survey, so little is concealed from the respondents. The primary ethical issue in survey research involves protecting respondents.

Protection of Respondents

If the survey could possibly have any harmful effects for the respondents, these should be disclosed fully in the cover letter or introductory statement (recall the discussion of informed consent in Chapter 3). The procedures used to reduce such effects should also be delineated, including how the researcher will keep interviews confidential and anonymous. In addition, surveys such as the NISVS and NCVS that attempt to measure sensitive subject matter such as rape and intimate-perpetrated assault should also have other protections in place. When asking about victimizations, particularly those that are perpetrated by known offenders and family members, the World Health Organization (WHO) has been at the forefront of establishing policies to protect respondents. As WHO notes, "The primary ethical concern related to researching violence against women (VAW) is the potential for inflicting harm to respondents through their participation in the study" (Ellsberg & Heise, 2005, p. 38). Because many perpetrators of IPV use control as a form of abuse, a respondent may suffer physical harm if an abuser finds out that he or she disclosed information about their relationship to an interviewer. Guidelines to prevent this from happening include interviewing only one person in the household (Ellsberg & Heise, 2005). In addition, a graduated informed-consent process is also recommended. For example, when first contacting a potential respondent, the initial person who answered the telephone should be provided only general information about the survey topic (e.g., on health-related issues). Only after a respondent is selected from a household should they be told about the specific topics that would be covered (e.g., violent victimizations). Interviewers should also remind respondents that they can stop the interview at any time, and safety plans should be established between the interviewer and the respondents.

Minimizing respondents' distress from reliving victimization events and providing them with information on services and resources that can help their situation are also necessary. For example, the NISVS provided telephone numbers for the National Domestic Violence Hotline and the Rape, Abuse, and Incest National Network at the end of interviews. The College Risk Behavior Survey, discussed earlier in this chapter, also gave respondents information about a number of avenues for help seeking, including the phone numbers to the University of Delaware Center for Counseling and Student Development, the Delaware Council on Gambling Problems, and the Delaware 24-Hour Rape Crisis Hotline. As you can see in Exhibit 7.9, the last screen of the survey provided this information to respondents.

Respondent protection is even more complicated when asking about victimizations against minor children, as the NCVS does (e.g., it interviews individuals aged 12 or older). Currently, researchers do not fall under the purview of *mandatory reporters*, according to most

UNIVERSITY OF DELAWARE
2009 College Survey

Your responses to the previous section have been recorded.

Thank you for your participation. Before finishing the survey, we would like to provide you with the following information. After reading the information, please use the button at the bottom of the page to complete the survey and receive information about the $5 voucher.

ADDITIONAL INFORMATION THAT MAY BE HELPFUL TO YOU

We want to thank you for your participation in this survey. The survey touched on a number of subjects that may have raised concerns in you, either about yourself or about someone else. We want to make sure that you know of places to go to get more information or to talk to someone. All of these services are confidential and available to you free of charge.

Under any circumstances if you have a **dire emergency** involving the safety of someone, **University Police** should be contacted.

If calling from on-campus, dial: 911
If calling from off-campus, dial: 302-831-2222

For health emergencies, the **Student Health Service** in Laurel Hall is open 24 hours a day when classes are in session except during holidays, breaks and summers.

If you or a student you know is feeling extremely depressed or anxious, please call the **Center for Counseling & Student Development** (CCSD) at 831-2141. For emergencies in the evenings, or on weekends: Contact the Student Health Service (302-831-2226). You can get more information about the Counseling Center at the University at http://www.udel.edu/Counseling/

The **Center for Counseling & Student Development** is also the place to go if you or a student you know is having trouble with alcohol or other drug abuse. They have a program for students called MOSAIC that is designed to help when a student has a substance abuse problem.

For Smoking concerns, please call the **Delaware Quitline** at: 1-866-409-1858. They are available 24 hours a day to help you with programs and materials to curtail tobacco use. More information on the Quitline is available at their webpage http://www.dhss.delaware.gov/dhss/dph/dpc/quitline.html/

For Gambling concerns, please call the **Delaware Council on Gambling Problems** at 1-888-850-8888. The Council offers confidential assistance. More information is available at http://www.dcgp.org/

For concerns about sexual assault, please call the **Delaware 24-hour Rape Crisis Hotline Contact Lifeline** at 1-800-262-9800.

If you want information on a variety of issues related to your health and well-being, please contact Wellspring, the University's Student Wellness Program. You can also access their website at http://www.udel.edu/wellspring/

Finally, if you would like more information about suicide and mental health in college students, one resource is the Ulifeline web site that is funded by the Jed Foundation: http://www.ulifeline.org/

Please use the button below to complete the survey and receive information about the $5 voucher:

Next Section

Source: University of Delaware.

state statutes, and the WHO claims there is no consensus internationally about how to handle cases of child abuse (Bachman, 2012). This is true for cases of elder abuse that are reported by respondents as well. Regardless of statutes not explicitly listing researchers as mandatory reporters, however, interviewers should certainly be required to develop protocols to act in the best interests of a child or an elder when cases of these forms of abuse are revealed.

Confidentiality

Do any of the questions have the potential to embarrass respondents or otherwise subject them to adverse consequences, such as legal sanctions? If the answer to this question is no—and it often is in surveys about general social issues—other ethical problems are unlikely. But if the questionnaire includes questions about attitudes or behaviors that are socially stigmatized or generally considered to be private or questions about actions that

Ben Carleton, BA, Research Analyst

Source: Courtesy Ben Carleton

Ben Carleton graduated with degrees in political science, sociology, and Spanish from the University of Delaware in 2017. Although he was still exploring what he wanted to pursue professionally after college, Ben knew that he wanted to participate in undergraduate research while at the University of Delaware. Following his research methods and statistics course, Ben stayed in touch with Dr. Ronet Bachman, who eventually became his research advisor and mentor. Given Dr. Bachman's background in criminal justice, the two crafted two separate research projects in this area that Ben completed from start to finish during his two summers as a Summer Scholar. The two projects were cross-national studies focusing on police reporting behavior by victims of assault and trust in the police. Ben went on to complete his honors senior thesis on the topic of transnational trust in the police.

Ben's experience with undergraduate research not only taught him about the research process but also introduced him to a field of study that he was not originally pursuing. He began taking criminal justice courses after starting his research, including the Inside-Out Prison Exchange Program, and his first job after graduation was conducting research

with the Vera Institute of Justice's Policing Program in New York City. His experience reading and analyzing academic journal articles from his own research projects proved to be important for this position. After his time at Vera, Ben accepted a position at the World Justice Project in Washington, DC, where he helped with their annual Rule of Law Index. Ben's previous experiences working with different survey instruments were crucial for him landing this position and succeeding in it.

Ben's advice to students interested in research is the following:

Find a professor with whom you have taken a course and developed a relationship and see if that professor currently has any research projects that you can become involved with. Do not be turned off by the topic of a professor's research if it does not align directly with your current interests. What is most important is learning and understanding the stages of the research process. Conducting research will help you to become a better critical and analytical thinker, while potentially making you a stronger writer and introducing you to new research software. And who knows, your academic and career aspirations may shift slightly after participating in research, just as mine did.

are illegal, the researcher must proceed carefully and ensure that respondents' rights are protected.

The first step to take with potentially troublesome questions is to consider modifying them or omitting them entirely. If sensitive questions fall into this category, they probably should be omitted. There is no point in asking, "Have you ever been convicted of a felony?" if the answers are unlikely to be used in the analysis of survey results.

Many surveys—particularly surveys interested in delinquent or criminal-offending behavior—do include some essential questions that might prove damaging to the subjects if their answers were disclosed. To prevent any possibility of harm to subjects due to disclosure of such information, it is critical to preserve subject confidentiality. No one other than research personnel should have access to information that could be used to link respondents to their responses, and even that access should be limited to what is necessary for specific research purposes. Only numbers should be used to identify respondents on their questionnaires, and the researcher should keep the names that correspond to these numbers in a separate, safe, and private location, unavailable to others who might otherwise come across them. Follow-up mailings or contact attempts that require linking the ID numbers with names and addresses should be carried out by trustworthy assistants under close supervision.

Only if no identifying information about respondents is obtained can surveys provide true **anonymity** to respondents. In this way, no identifying information is ever recorded to link respondents with their responses. However, the main problem with anonymous surveys is that they preclude follow-up attempts to encourage participation by initial nonrespondents, and they prevent panel designs, which measure change through repeated surveys of the same individuals. In-person surveys rarely can be anonymous because an interviewer must, in almost all cases, know the name and address of the interviewee. However, phone surveys that are meant to sample opinion at only one point in time, as in political polls, can safely be completely anonymous. When no follow-up is desired, group-administered surveys also can be anonymous. To provide anonymity in a mail survey, the researcher should omit identifying codes from the questionnaire but could include a self-addressed, stamped postcard so the respondent can notify the researcher that the questionnaire has been returned, without being linked to the questionnaire itself (Mangione, 1995).

> **Anonymity:** Provided by research in which no identifying information is recorded that could be used to link respondents to their responses

CONCLUSION

Survey research is an exceptionally efficient and productive method for investigating a wide array of social-research questions. In addition to the potential benefits for social science, considerations of time and expense frequently make a survey the preferred data collection method. One or more of the four survey designs reviewed in this chapter can be applied to almost any research question. It is no wonder that surveys have become the most popular research method in sociology and that they frequently influence discussion and planning about important social and political questions.

The relative ease of conducting at least some types of survey research leads many people to imagine that no particular training or systematic procedures are required. Nothing could be further from the truth. As a result of this widespread misconception, you will encounter a great deal of worthless survey results. You must be prepared to carefully examine the procedures used in any survey before accepting its finding as credible. Moreover, if you decide to conduct a survey, you must be prepared to invest the time and effort required to follow proper procedures.

Anonymity   181
Closed-ended (fixed choice)
  question   160
Computer-assisted personal
  interviewing (CAPI)   174
Computer-assisted self-interviewing
  (CASI)   174
Computer-assisted telephone
  interview (CATI)   173
Computerized interactive voice
  response (IVR)   173
Context effects   169
Contingent question   164
Cover letter   168
Double-barreled question   161

Double-negative question   161
Electronic survey   174
Exhaustive responses   163
Fence-sitters   164
Filter question   164
Floaters   164
Group-administered survey   172
Index   165
Idiosyncratic variation   164
In-person interview   173
Interpretive question   159
Interview schedule   155
Likert-type responses   163
Mailed (self-administered)
  survey   171

Mixed-mode survey   176
Mutually exclusive responses   163
Omnibus survey   155
Open-ended questions   159
Phone survey   172
Pretested   168
Questionnaire   155
Reference period   161
Reliability measures   165
Reverse code   166
Skip pattern   164
Split-ballot design   169
Survey research   154

- Surveys are the most popular form of social research because of their versatility, efficiency, and generalizability. Many survey datasets, such as the GSS, are available for social scientists to use in teaching and research.

- Surveys can fail to produce useful results due to problems in sampling, measurement, and overall survey design.

- A survey questionnaire or interview schedule should be designed as an integrated whole, with each question and section serving some clear purpose and complementing the others.

- Questions must be worded carefully to avoid confusing the respondents or encouraging a less-than-honest response. Inclusion of "don't know" choices and neutral responses may help, but the presence of such options also affects the distribution of answers. Open-ended questions can be used to determine the meaning that respondents attach to their answers. The answers to any survey questions may be affected by the questions that precede them in a questionnaire or interview schedule.

- Every questionnaire and interview schedule should be pretested on a small sample that is similar to the sample to be surveyed.

- The cover letter for a mailed questionnaire and the introductory statement for an interview should be credible, personalized, interesting, and responsible.

- Phone interviews using RDD allow fast turnaround and efficient sampling.

- In-person interviews have several advantages over other types of surveys: They allow longer and more complex interview schedules, monitoring of the conditions when the questions are answered, probing for respondents' understanding of the questions, and high response rates.

- Electronic surveys may be e-mailed or posted on the Web. At this time, use of the Internet is not sufficiently widespread to allow e-mail or Web surveys of the general population, but these approaches can be fast and efficient for populations with high rates of computer use.

- Mixed-mode surveys allow the strengths of one survey design to compensate for the weaknesses of another.

- Most survey research poses few ethical problems because respondents are able to decline to participate. This option should be stated clearly in the cover letter or introductory statement. When anonymity cannot be guaranteed, confidentiality must be assured.

Discussing Research

1. Who does survey research, and how do they do it? These questions can be answered through careful inspection of ongoing surveys and the organizations that administer them at the website for the Cornell Institute for Social and Economic Research (www.ciser.cornell .edu/info/polls.shtml). Spend some time reading about the different survey research organizations, and write a brief summary of the types of research they conduct, the projects in which they are involved, and the resources they offer on their websites. What are the distinctive features of different survey research organizations?

2. Write eight to 10 questions for a one-page questionnaire on fear of crime among students. Include some questions to measure characteristics (such as income or year in school) that might help to explain the attitudes. Make all but one of your questions closed ended. What are some of the problems in trying to measure difficult concepts such as *fear*? How about attitudes such as *prejudice* and *intolerance*?

Finding Research on the Web

1. Go to the Social Science Information Gateway (SOSIG) site (www.ariadne.ac.uk/issue2/sosig). Search SOSIG for electronic journal articles that use surveys to collect information on crime, criminal behavior, or criminal victimization. Find at least five articles, and briefly describe each.

2. Go to the Research Triangle Institute website (www .rti.org). Click on "Survey Research and Services," then "Innovations." From here, you can explore many new innovations that have been applied to survey design, including cell phone surveys, computer audio-recorded interviewing, and many more. Read about their methods for computer-assisted interviewing and their cognitive laboratory methods for refining questions. What does this add to your treatment of these topics in this chapter?

3. Go to the Question Bank (surveynet.ac.uk/sqb). Go to the "UK Data Service Variable and question bank" link, and then search for a topic that interests you. Review 10 questions used in the survey, and critique them in terms of the principles for question writing that you have learned. Do you find any question features that might be attributed to the use of British English?

Critiquing Research

1. Read the original article reporting one of the surveys described in this book. (Check the text of the chapters for ideas.) Critique the article using the questions presented in Appendix B as your guide. Focus particular attention on sampling, measurement, and survey design.

2. By interviewing two students, conduct a preliminary pretest of the questionnaire you wrote for Exercise 2 under "Discussing Research." Follow up the closed-ended questions with open-ended questions that ask the students what they meant by each response or what came to mind when they were asked each question. Take account of the answers when you revise your questions. How do you draw the line between too much and too little data?

3. Make any necessary revisions to the questionnaire you wrote. Write a cover letter that presumes the survey will be administered to students in a class at your school. Submit the questionnaire and cover letter to your instructor for comment and evaluation.

Making Research Ethical

1. In this chapter, we posed the questions, "How can researchers ameliorate the negative consequences that responding to these surveys may have? What responsibility do researchers have in providing respondents with safety should they need it?" Are there any conditions in which a researcher could justify emotional harm to respondents? Write a short statement in response to each question.

2. The NISVS interviews people 18 years or older, but the NCVS selects all people in the household who are 12 years of age or older into their sample. We already asked you about the ethical dilemmas of reporting victimizations in Chapter 3. But what about respondents who are minors and are under the age of 18? What about children under the age of 12? Teachers and medical personnel are required by law to report cases they believe to represent incidents of child abuse. Should researchers have the same obligation? How would this affect large-scale surveys using RDD in which you want to preserve the anonymity of respondents?

3. Group-administered surveys are easier to conduct than other types of surveys, but they always raise an ethical dilemma. If a teacher allows a researcher to survey a class or if an employer allows employees to complete a survey on company time, are the surveys really voluntary? Is it sufficient to read a statement to the group stating that their participation is entirely up to them? What general guidelines should be followed in such situations?

Developing a Research Proposal

1. Write 10 questions for a one-page questionnaire that concerns your proposed research question. Your questions should operationalize at least three of the variables on which you have focused, including at least one independent and one dependent variable. (You may have multiple questions to measure some variables.) Make all but one of your questions closed ended. If you completed the "Developing a Research Proposal" exercises in Chapter 3, you can select your questions from the ones you developed for those exercises.

2. Conduct a preliminary pretest of the questionnaire by carrying out cognitive interviews with two students or other persons who are similar to those to whom the survey is directed. Follow up the closed-ended questions with open-ended probes that ask the students what they meant by each response or what came to mind when they were asked each question. Take account of the feedback you received when you revise your questions.

3. Polish up the organization and layout of the questionnaire, following the guidelines in this chapter. Prepare a rationale for the order of questions in your questionnaire. Write a cover letter directed to the target population that contains appropriate statements about research ethics (human subjects issues).

Performing Data Analysis in SPSS or Excel

Data for Exercise	
Dataset	**Description**
GSS 2014.sav	The GSS is a nationally representative survey that is conducted every two years. It covers a wide range of core topics, such as political and religious views, while also rotating in new topics. It is a split-ballot omnibus survey.

Variables for Exercise	
Variable Name	**Description**
Race	A three-category race measure where 1 = *white*, 2 = *black*, and 3 = *other*
Educcat	A four-category ordinal measure of respondent's education where 0 = *less than high school*, 1 = *high school*, 2 = *some college*, 3 = *college or more*
Polhitok	A yes-or-no binary question asking respondents if there is any situation in which they would feel it was okay for a police officer to hit a citizen, where 1 = *yes* and 2 = *no*
Grass	A binary asking if respondents think marijuana should be made legal or not, where 1 = *yes* and 2 = *no*
Raceint	The race of the person who administered the survey, where 1 = *white*, 2 = *black*, and 3 = *Hispanic*

1. Let's take a look at the structure of the GSS survey first.

   a. First, run frequencies for the variables "race," "educcat," and "polhitok."

   b. Look carefully at the number of cases for each of these measures. Why do you think one is so much smaller? Recall the discussion of the GSS in this chapter.

2. Look critically at how the question "grass" is written and measured. The exact question was "Do you think the use of marijuana should be made legal or not?" Look back at your frequency and notice the response categories offered.

a. Can this question's phrasing be interpreted to mean multiple things? Be specific in your answer.

b. Are response categories mutually exclusive? If not, be clear where the overlap is.

c. Does this question minimize fence-sitting?

d. How well does this question capture nuance of opinion?

e. Are there any other issues or strengths for this question?

f. Rewrite this question so it corrects for the limitations you have identified.

3. Let's answer a substantive question: Who is most likely to be pro–marijuana legalization in terms of race and education?

a. Write a hypothesis for each group.

b. Use a cross-tabulation with the variable "grass" as the dependent variable and "educcat" and "race" as independent variables.

c. What do you find? Are your hypotheses supported?

d. Consider who is most likely to be arrested and/or imprisoned for marijuana use (i.e., poor black men who do not have access to private defense attorneys). Are these results surprising or unintuitive in light of that information?

e. Do you think the question you wrote for 2f would have given comparable results? Why, or why not?

4. The GSS is administered face to face. It's important to check if the person asking questions has any influence on how people respond. For this case, let's look at whether an interviewer's race changes responses to hot-button race-related questions.

a. Let's look at how the interviewer's race (variable "raceint") affects attitudes about police violence. To do this, use crosstab "raceint" with the variable "polhitok," which asked if respondents thought it would ever be okay for police to hit a citizen.

b. Is there evidence of social-desirability bias in this variable? Can we fully trust the results for these questions? What might be causing this bias, if there is any?

c. If there is evidence of bias, what could be done about the way these questions (or the survey) are administered to reduce this desirability bias?

8

QUALITATIVE METHODS AND DATA ANALYSIS

Learning Objectives

1. Describe the features of qualitative research that most distinguish it from quantitative research.

2. Define the methods of ethnography and how they compare to netnography.

3. Compare the advantages and disadvantages of each participant observer role.

4. Discuss the major challenges at each stage of a field research project.

5. Describe the process of intensive interviewing, and compare it with the process of interviewing in survey research.

6. Discuss the advantages of focus group research, and identify particular challenges focus group researchers face.

7. Understand how grounded theory is developed.

8. Discuss the ways computer software programs can facilitate qualitative data analysis.

9. Identify the major ethical challenges faced by qualitative researchers, and discuss one qualitative research project that posed particular ethical concerns.

WHAT DO WE MEAN BY QUALITATIVE METHODS?

The five-0 [police] stopped me all the time. They checked me for drugs and guns most of the time. At first I was scared and told them I was only twelve. They didn't believe me and kept asking me where I was hiding the drugs. That made me hella mad 'cause I wasn't slanging [selling drugs] or anything.

This young man was one of the young men Victor Rios (2011) shadowed for three years in the "flatlands" of Oakland, California (p. 50). Rios wanted to understand how young men of color navigated their environment when they were under constant surveillance both at school and in their communities. As you may already surmise, an experiment or a survey was not an appropriate method to examine this research question. In this chapter, you will learn how qualitative methods are used to illuminate relationships, both individually and collectively, with this and other examples from the literature. You will see that some of our greatest insights into social processes can result from what appear to be very ordinary activities: observing, participating, listening, and talking.

You will also learn that qualitative research is much more than just doing what comes naturally in social situations. Qualitative researchers must keenly observe respondents, sensitively plan their participation, systematically take notes, and strategically question respondents. They must also prepare to spend more time and invest more of their whole selves than often occurs with experiments or surveys. Moreover, if we are to have any confidence in the validity of a qualitative study's conclusions, each element of its design must be reviewed as carefully as the elements of an experiment or survey.

FUNDAMENTALS OF QUALITATIVE METHODS

As we briefly noted in Chapter 1, qualitative methods can often be used to enrich experiments and surveys, and these methods refer to three distinctive research designs: participant observation, intensive interviewing, and focus groups. Participant observation and intensive interviewing are often used in the same project; focus groups combine some elements of these two approaches into a unique data collection strategy.

Although these three qualitative designs differ in many respects, they share several features that distinguish them from experimental and survey research designs (Denzin & Lincoln, 1994; Maxwell, 1996; Wolcott, 1995):

Collection primarily of qualitative rather than quantitative data. Any research design may collect both qualitative and quantitative data, but qualitative methods emphasize observations about natural behavior and artifacts that capture social life as it is experienced by the participants rather than in categories predetermined by the researcher.

Exploratory research questions, with a commitment to inductive reasoning. Qualitative researchers do not typically begin their projects seeking to test preformulated hypotheses but to discover what people think and how and why they act in certain social settings. Only after many observations do qualitative researchers try to develop general principles to account for their observations (recall the research circle in Chapter 2).

A focus on previously unstudied processes and unanticipated phenomena. Previously unstudied attitudes and actions cannot adequately be understood with a structured set of questions or within a highly controlled experiment. Therefore, qualitative methods have their greatest appeal when we need to explore new issues, investigate hard-to-study groups, or determine the meaning people give to their lives and actions.

An orientation to social context, to the interconnections between social phenomena rather than to their discrete features. The context of concern may be a program, an organization, a neighborhood, or a broader social context. For example, Rios's (2011) research encompassed several social and organizational entities from the social world of the 40 young men in his sample. His goal was to examine how punitive encounters with police, probation officers, teachers, and administrators shaped the meanings that young people created about themselves. To do this, he needed to observe them in their social world. He states,

> To answer my questions about criminalization, I observed and interviewed young
> males who lived in communities heavily affected by criminal justice policies and
> practices. Delinquent inner-city youths, those at the front line of the war on crime
> and mass incarceration, were the best source of data for this study. . . . I interviewed
> them . . . met with their friends and their families, advocated for them at school
> and in court, and hung out with them at parks, street corners, and community
> centers. . . . I shadowed these young men as they conducted their everyday
> routine activities such as walking the streets, "hanging out," and participating in
> community programs. (Rios, 2011, p. 8)

A focus on human subjectivity, on the meanings that participants attach to events and that people give to their lives. "Through life stories, people account for their lives. . . . The themes people create are the means by which they interpret and evaluate their life experiences and attempt to integrate these experiences to form a self-concept" (Kaufman, 1986, pp. 24–25).

A focus on the events leading up to a particular event or outcome instead of general causal explanations. With its focus on particular actors and situations and the processes that connect them, qualitative research tends to identify causes of particular events embedded within an unfolding, interconnected action sequence (Maxwell, 1996). The language of variables and hypotheses appears only rarely in the qualitative literature.

Reflexive research design and sensitivity to the subjective role of the researcher. When researchers are making observations in a social setting, there is little control over the setting or social actors within the setting. As such, the design must be open to change: "Each component of the design may need to be reconsidered or modified in response to new developments or to changes in some other component. . . . The activities of collecting and analyzing data, developing and modifying theory, elaborating or refocusing the research questions, and identifying and eliminating validity threats are usually all going on more or less simultaneously, each influencing all of the others." (Maxwell, 1996, pp. 2–3)

Moreover, little pretense is made of achieving an objective perspective on social phenomena. When conducting his study of teenage boys in Oakland, California, Victor Rios (2011) was very aware of how his past experiences shaped his research because he had also grown up in that city. He stated,

> Although I would like to pretend that this study was objective, from an outsider's perspective that could bring to light the issues that young people face in a fair and balanced way, I acknowledge that this study is affected by my own experiences. Nevertheless, as a social scientist, I committed myself to generating an empirical and systematic study. (p. 169)

We will talk more about reflexivity when we discuss qualitative data analyses later in the chapter.

Origins of Qualitative Research

Anthropologists and sociologists laid the foundation for modern qualitative methods while doing **field research** in the early decades of the 20th century. Dissatisfied with studies of native peoples that relied on secondhand accounts and inspection of artifacts, anthropologists Franz Boas and Bronislaw Malinowski went to live in or near the communities they studied. Boas visited Native American villages in the Pacific Northwest; Malinowski lived among New Guinea natives. Neither truly participated in the ongoing social life of those they studied—Boas collected artifacts and original texts, and Malinowski reputedly lived as something of a nobleman among the natives he studied—but both helped to establish the value of intimate familiarity with the community of interest and thus laid the basis for modern anthropology (Emerson, 1983).

Many of sociology's field research pioneers were former social workers and reformers. Some brought their missionary concern with the welfare of new immigrants to the Department of Sociology and Anthropology at the University of Chicago. Their successors continued to focus on sources of community cohesion and urban strain but came to view the city as a social science laboratory. They adopted the fieldwork methods of anthropology for studying the "natural areas" of the city and the social life of small towns (Vidich & Lyman, 1994). By the 1930s, 1940s, and 1950s, qualitative researchers were emphasizing the value of direct participation in community life and sharing in subjects' perceptions and interpretations of events (Emerson, 1983). An **ethnography** is the study of a culture or cultures that a group of people share (Van Maanen, 1995). As a method, it is usually meant to refer to the process by which a single investigator immerses himself or herself in a group for a long time (often one or more years), gradually establishing trust and experiencing the social world as do the participants (Madden, 2010). Ethnographic research can be called *naturalistic* because it seeks to describe and understand the natural social world as it is, in all its richness and detail.

Anthropological field research has traditionally been ethnographic, and much criminological fieldwork shares these same characteristics. But there are no particular methodological

Field research: Research in which natural social processes are studied as they happen and are left relatively undisturbed

Ethnography: The study of a culture or cultures that some group of people share and that participant observation produces over an extended period

techniques associated with ethnography, other than just "being there." The analytic process relies on the thoroughness and insight of the researcher to tell us like it is in the setting, as he or she experienced it.

Code of the Street, Elijah Anderson's (1999) award-winning study of Philadelphia's inner city, captures the flavor of this approach:

> My primary aim in this work is to render ethnographically the social and cultural dynamics of the interpersonal violence that is currently undermining the quality of life of too many urban neighborhoods. . . . How do the people of the setting perceive their situation? What assumptions do they bring to their decision making? (pp. 10–11)

Like most traditional ethnographers, Anderson (1999) describes his concern with being "as objective as possible" and using his training as other ethnographers do, "to look for and to recognize underlying assumptions, their own and those of their subjects, and to try to override the former and uncover the latter" (p. 11).

Rios's study in Oakland combined ethnography with intensive interviews and focus groups to examine the potential subtleties of expression used in a group and the multiple meanings that can be given to statements or acts (Armstrong, 2008). Good ethnographies also include some reflection by the researcher on the influence his or her own background has had on research plans, as well as on the impact of the research in the setting (Madden, 2010).

Netnography

Communities can refer not only to people in a common physical location but also to relationships that develop online. Online communities may be formed by persons with similar interests or backgrounds, perhaps to create new social relationships that location or schedules did not permit or to supplement relationships that emerge in the course of work, school, or other ongoing social activities. Like communities of people who interact face to face, online communities can develop a culture and become sources of identification and attachment (Kozinets, 2010). And like physical communities, researchers can study online communities through immersion in the group for an extended period. Netnography, also termed *cyberethnography* and *virtual ethnography* (James & Busher, 2009), is the use of ethnographic methods to study online communities.

Netnography: The use of ethnographic methods to study online communities; also termed *cyberethnography* and *virtual ethnography*

In some respects, netnography is similar to traditional ethnography. The researcher prepares to enter the field by becoming familiar with online communities and their language and customs, formulating an exploratory research question about social processes or orientations in that setting, and selecting an appropriate community to study. Unlike in-person ethnographies, netnographies can focus on communities whose members are physically distant and dispersed. The selected community should be relevant to the research question, involve frequent communication among actively engaged members, and have a number of participants who, as a result, generate a rich body of textual data (Kozinets, 2010). For example, after a residence center in Sweden that housed asylum-seeking unaccompanied minors was vandalized and its staff members threatened with violence, Katrina Hirvonen (2013) conducted a netnography to understand how the anti-immigration sentiment was rising in a country that has traditionally perceived tolerance as a national virtue. Based on the frequency of comments about the residence center, Hirvonen (2013) examined three anti-immigration websites and specifically coded data from 288 comments and 60 articles. She discovered that the "comment fields on sites serve as an echo chamber with extremists reaching out for others with the same ideas to reinforce extreme opinions already held. . . . [S]uch a forum for sharing ideas constantly encourages the development of ever more extreme thoughts and suggested action" (p. 84).

A netnographer must keep both observational and reflective field notes, but unlike a traditional ethnographer, he or she can return to review the original data—the posted text—long after it was produced. The data can then be coded, annotated with the researcher's interpretations, checked against new data to evaluate the persistence of social patterns, and used to develop a theory that is grounded in the data.

Case Study: Life in a Gang

Victor Rios's work is part of a long tradition of scholarship that has relied on the use of fieldwork techniques to study "at promise" (at-risk) youth and/or gangs in inner cities, including Thrasher's (1927) classic study of gangs in Chicago, and others, including Whyte (1943), Hagedorn (1988), Vigil (1988), Padilla (1992), Sanchez-Jankowski (1991), and Moore (1978, 1991), who spent over two decades studying the "home-boys" of Hispanic barrios all over the country. All these researchers employed a fieldwork approach to the study of gangs rather than the more structured approaches offered by quantitative methods.

Qualitative methods still must rely on operationalizing exactly what is meant by research constructs. For example, one of the first issues Decker and Van Winkle (1996) were challenged with was precisely defining a gang (recall Chapter 4). After all, the term *gang* could refer to many groups of youth, including a high school debate society or the Young Republicans. After reviewing the literature, Decker and Van Winkle developed a working definition of a gang as an "age-graded peer group that exhibits some permanence, engages in criminal activity, and has some symbolic representation of membership" (p. 31). To operationalize who was a gang member, they relied on self-identification. "Are you claiming . . . ?" was a key screening question that was also verified, as often as possible, with other gang members.

Decker and Van Winkle (1996) were interested in several questions:

> Our study revolved around a number of activities, both gang and nongang related, that our subjects were likely to engage in. First, we were interested in motivations to join gangs, the process of joining the gang, the symbols of gang membership, the strength of associational ties, the structure or hierarchy within the gang, motivations to stay (or leave) the gang. . . . The second set of issues concerned the activities gang members engaged in. These included such things as turf protection, drug sales and use, and violence, as well as conventional activities. An accurate picture of gang members must portray both the nature of their gang involvement and the legal status of their activities. (pp. 54–55)

Rios (2011) relied on several different qualitative research methods to determine how the patterns of punishment experienced by the youth in his study affected them. While his primary method was participant observation, he also used intensive interviews and focus groups. He states,

> I shadowed these young men as they conducted their everyday routine activities, such as walking the streets, "hanging out," and participating in community programs. I walked the streets and rode the bus with them from home to school and as they met with friends or went to the community center after school. There were days when I met them in front of the doorsteps at 8 a.m. and followed them throughout the day until they returned home late at night. (pp. 7–8)

Unlike the personal interviews that rely on closed-ended questions that were discussed in the last chapter, Rios relied only on an interview guide that posed several open-ended questions to the youth in his sample. He called them *life story interviews* because the goal was to place their personal testimonies about their lives at the forefront of his research.

As you can see, Rios approached his research question inductively, not deductively. First, he gathered data. Then, as data collection continued, he interpreted the data and developed analytic categories from which more questions were developed. Rios and other qualitative researchers have provided the field of criminology with in-depth descriptions and idiographic connections of sequences of events that could not have been obtained through other methodologies. They successfully used field research to explore human experiences in depth, carefully analyzing the social contexts in which the experiences occurred.

PARTICIPANT OBSERVATION

Rios's research in Oakland is a perfect example of participant observation. By watching and participating in the lives of 40 black and Latino young men for three years, he was able to obtain firsthand observations of their encounters. He states,

> Shadowing enabled me to observe regular punitive encounters and the way these became manifest in the lives of these youth in a range of different social contexts, across institutional settings. . . . I was able to conceptualize aspects of their lived experiences that would be difficult to see otherwise. (Rios, 2011, p. 8)

Participant observation is a method of studying natural social processes as they happen (in the field rather than in the laboratory), leaving them relatively undisturbed and minimizing your presence as a researcher. It is the seminal field research method, a means for seeing the social world as the research subjects see it in its totality and for understanding subjects' interpretations of that world (Wolcott, 1995). By observing people and interacting with them in the course of their normal activities, participant observers seek to avoid the artificiality of experimental designs and the unnatural structured questioning of survey research (Koegel, 1987).

The term *participant observer* actually represents a continuum of roles (see Exhibit 8.1), ranging from being a complete observer who does not participate in group activities and is publicly defined as a researcher to being a covert participant who acts just like other group members and does not disclose his or her research role. Many field researchers develop a role between these extremes, publicly acknowledging being a researcher but nonetheless participating in group activities. In some settings, it also is possible to observe covertly without acknowledging being a researcher or participating.

Participant observation: Field research in which a researcher develops a sustained and intensive relationship with people while they go about their normal activities

Choosing a Role

The first concern of all participant observers is to decide what balance to strike between observing and participating and whether to reveal their role as researchers. These decisions must take into account the specifics of the social situation being studied, the researcher's own background and personality, the larger sociopolitical context, and ethical concerns. The balance of participating and observing that is most appropriate also changes many times during the majority of projects. Ultimately, the researcher's ability to maintain either a covert or an overt role can be challenged many times throughout the research effort.

Complete Observation

In her study of community policing, Susan Miller (1999) adopted the role of a complete observer. Community policing is an approach to policing that emphasizes building closer ties

Exhibit 8.1 The Observational Continuum

To study a political activist group ...

You could take the role of complete observer:

Hello, I am a researcher. Tell me, why do you participate in these activities?

You could take the role of participant and observer:

Hello, I am a researcher and an activist. Tell me, why do you participate in these activities?

You could take the role of covert participant:

between police and members of the community. Miller was particularly interested in how gender affected the attitudes and behavior of community–police liaisons or neighborhood police officers (NPOs).

In **complete observation**, researchers try to see things as they happen, without disrupting the participants. Along with intensive interviews with police officers, Susan Miller also observed police officers on their daily shifts:

> Both neighborhood and patrol officers' shifts were observed, either on foot with neighborhood officers, or in squad cars with patrol officers. This component of the project also permitted gathering some observational information about citizens' reactions to police delivery of services. (pp. 232–233)

Of course, the researcher's presence as an observer alters the social situation being observed. It is not natural in most social situations to have an observer present who, at some point, will record his or her observations for research and publication purposes. The observer thus sees what individuals do when they are being observed, which is not necessarily what they

Complete observation: A role in participant observation in which the researcher does not participate in group activities and is publicly defined as a researcher

would do without an observer. This is called a **reactive effect**, and the extent to which it can be a problem varies with the situation. In Susan Miller's (1999) study, the extended measure of time she spent as an observer made her presence commonplace, thereby serving to decrease the problem of reactive effects. She states,

> Since I had spent so many hours over eighteen months with the Jackson City Police Department [fictional name], I had grown to be a familiar face; this, I believe, decreased respondents' tendencies toward social desirability. Officers took my presence for granted in the briefing room, the hallways, the interview rooms, and in the field, including me in jokes and informal conversation in the coffee shop. (p. 235)

Generally, in social settings involving many people, an observer may not attract attention. On the other hand, when the social setting involves few people and observing is apparent rather than camouflaged or when the observer differs in obvious respects from the participants, the complete observer is more likely to have an impact.

Reactive effect: The changes in individual or group behavior that are due to being observed or otherwise studied

Participation and Observation

Most field researchers adopt a role that involves some active participation in the setting. Usually, they inform at least some group members of their research interests, but then they participate in enough group activities to develop trust and rapport with members and to gain a direct sense of what group members experience. This is not an easy balancing act. Observational studies are generally conducted over a long period of time.

During the three years that Rios spent in Oakland conducting his research, it was inevitable that he became a participant as well as an observer. For example, one day while walking home after school with a boy Rios called Slick, they were approached by a patrol car, which followed them. Slick recognized the officer as the one who had recently beaten up another boy named Marquil in a McDonald's parking lot during lunch hour. Rios (2011) writes,

> I turned to Slick and told him, "Let's just keep walking. We'll be fine." The officer continued to follow us, driving slowly behind us. Slick became paranoid, turned around, and gave the officer a dirty look. I turned to look. The officer, a White man with a shaved head in his thirties, looked at us, grinned, and drove off. Police officers played crafty cat-and-mouse games in which the boys remained in constant fear of being humiliated, brutalized, or arrested. (p. 81)

On one occasion, Rios was even arrested. Sitting in a park with several of the youth, a police car approached. Rios and the other boys, except one, pulled their hands out of the pockets and "stood in a position of submission, with our hands to show that we didn't have a weapon," while a boy Rios called Spider kept his hands in his pockets. The officers, one white and one Latino, got out and said, "Face the wall" (Rios, 2011, p. 126). The officers searched everyone, and because Spider had a pocket knife in his pocket, he was arrested. When Rios asked the officers why they were stopped in the first place, he was handcuffed and arrested, too.

Embedded in the community as Rios was, he witnessed life as it happened, which included youth-on-youth violence, as well as harassment and abuse by the police. During his observational time, he witnessed over 40 citations imposed by the police on the boys in his study. These were usually for minor things, such as loitering, not wearing a properly fitted bicycle helmet, or disturbing the peace. Rios never participated in violence but sometimes intervened to stop it.

Disclosing your research to participants as Rios did has two clear ethical advantages. Because group members know the researcher's real role in the group, they can choose to keep some information or attitudes hidden. By the same token, the researcher can decline to participate in unethical or dangerous activities without fear of exposing his or her identity.

Even when researchers maintain a public identity as researchers, the ethical dilemmas arising from participation in group activities do not go away. In fact, researchers may have to prove themselves to group members by joining in some of their questionable activities.

Covert Participation

To lessen the potential for reactive effects and to gain entry to otherwise inaccessible settings, some field researchers have adopted the role of covert participant. By doing so, they keep their research secret and do their best to act like other participants in a social setting or group. **Covert participation** is also known as **complete participation**. Laud Humphreys (1970) served as a "watch queen" so that he could learn about men engaging in homosexual acts in a public restroom. Randall Alfred (1976) joined a group of Satanists to investigate group members and their interaction. Erving Goffman (1961) worked as a state hospital assistant while studying the treatment of psychiatric patients.

Although the role of covert participant lessens some of the reactive effects encountered by the complete observer, covert participants confront other problems. The following are a few examples:

- *Covert participants cannot openly take notes or use any obvious recording devices.* They must write up notes based solely on memory and must do so at times when it is natural for them to be away from group members.

- *Covert participants cannot ask questions that will arouse suspicion.* Thus, they often have trouble clarifying the meaning of other participants' attitudes or actions.

- *The role of covert participation is difficult to play successfully.* Covert participants will not know how regular participants act in every situation in which the researchers find themselves. Suspicion that researchers are not "one of us" may then have reactive effects, obviating the value of complete participation (Erikson, 1967).

- *Covert participants must keep up the act at all times while in the setting under study.* Researchers may experience enormous psychological strain, particularly in situations where they are expected to choose sides in intragroup conflict or to participate in criminal or other acts. Of course, some covert observers may become so wrapped up in their role that they adopt not just the mannerisms but also the perspectives and goals of the regular participants—they "go native." At this point, they abandon research goals and cease to critically evaluate their observations.

As you learned in Chapter 3, ethical issues have been at the forefront of debate over the strategy of covert participation. Covert researchers cannot anticipate the unintended consequences (e.g., gang violence) of their actions for research subjects. In addition, other social research is harmed when covert research is disclosed, either during the research or upon its publication, because distrust of social scientists increases and future access to research opportunities may decrease.

But a total ban on covert participation would "kill many a project stone dead" (Punch, 1994, p. 90). Studies of unusual religious or sexual practices and institutional malpractice would rarely be possible. According to Punch, "The crux of the matter is that some deception, passive or active, enables you to get at data not obtainable by other means" (p. 91). Therefore, some field researchers argue that covert participation is legitimate in certain circumstances. If the researcher maintains the confidentiality of others, keeps his or her commitments to them, and does not directly lie to the participants, some degree of deception may be justified in exchange for the knowledge gained.

Covert (complete) participation: A role in field research in which the researcher does not reveal his or her identity as a researcher to those who are observed; the covert participant has adopted the role of a "complete participant"

What this means for contemporary research is that it is more difficult to get covert observational studies approved by an institutional review board (IRB) than it once was. This has created what David Calvey (2014) calls a "submerged yet creative tradition" within the field of criminology (p. 541). Importantly, Calvey also cautions that there is not always a clear divide between covert and overt research. For example, while the boys Rios shadowed in Oakland were aware of this status as a researcher, not all of the people Rios encountered during his fieldwork were. In fact, it would be virtually impossible to continually make everyone aware of your role without completely changing the social world you are studying. A brief case study of research that examined football (soccer) hooligans in England is an excellent example that we will highlight next.

Case Study: The "Researcher as a Hooligan"

A riot after a sporting event is not a new phenomenon. In fact, at this writing, the most recent sporting event riot to result in injuries and arrests to occur in the United States just happened near the University of Kentucky campus after the University of Kentucky Wildcats lost to the University of Wisconsin in the NCAA basketball semifinals. Long-term trends show violent riots, however, are equally likely to occur after wins (Bialik, 2015). How do these riots happen, and what kinds of people get involved? To find out, Geoff Pearson (2009) engaged in covert participation in the illegal behavior of English football (soccer) supporters, commonly referred to as *hooligans* (see Exhibit 8.2). He was not just interested in individual and group behavior but in police responses to this behavior as well. He first attempted to interview self-professed hooligans about their behavior, but he found that their reports were unreliable, with nonviolent fans often exaggerating their violent behavior and violent fans often downplaying theirs because they feared being reported. To obtain more valid information about the culture of hooliganism, Pearson began to study this social world as a covert participant. He stated, "The only way I could gain an understanding of the 'lifeworld' of the subjects was to fully immerse myself in the group's activities through participant observation" (p. 246). He spent three years as part of a fan club for an English football club, who regularly engaged in a wide range of low-level criminal offenses, including drinking and drug offenses, disorderly and threatening behavior, damage to property, and sometimes assaults. In his research, Pearson committed minor offenses, which "the majority of the research subjects were committing and that I considered necessary to carry out the research" (p. 247). He justified his covert participation because he believed soccer hooligans have been misunderstood and subject to "serious injustices and maltreatment by those in authority" (p. 249). Among other findings, this research concluded that when the police adopt a more targeted and less confrontational approach, the risk of rioting decreased (Stott & Pearson, 2007).

Exhibit 8.2 Soccer Hooligans Assaulting a Rival Fan After a Match

Michael Campanella/Getty Images Sport/Getty Images

Entering the Field

Entering the field or the setting under investigation is a critical stage in a participant observation project, as the introduction can shape many subsequent experiences. Some background work is necessary before entering the field, at least enough to develop a clear understanding of what the research questions are likely to be and to review one's personal stance toward the people and problems likely to be encountered. With participant observation, researchers must also learn in advance about the participants' dress and their typical activities to avoid being caught completely unprepared.

Rios (2011) had lived in the flatlands of Oakland, California, where he conducted his study, but he still spent a great deal of time learning about the community context into which he was about to enter. In fact, his book, *Punished*, provides a detailed discussion of the political and structural conditions of the community under study. Among many other statistics that described policies relevant to his study, he noted,

> From 2002 to 2005 Oakland continued to focus on punitive social control in attempts to reduce the crime rate. The city prioritized funding for law enforcement, resulting in declines in spending for educational and social programs. In 2002, Oakland spent $128,331 per law-enforcement employee; by 2005, this rate had increased to $190,140. This approach was further evidence in the demands made by the Oakland City Council to the city's new chief of police: "You said you can't arrest our way out of this problem. Well you sure better try. We all have our jobs to do and your job is to arrest people." (p. 34)

Examining the larger community context as Rios did was an important component to understanding how the factors related to the individual lives of his study participants. Developing trust with at least one member of the research setting is another necessity in qualitative research. Such a person can become a valuable informant throughout the project, and most participant observers make a point of developing trust with at least one informant in a group under study.

In short, field researchers must be very sensitive to the impression they make and the ties they establish when entering the field. This stage of research lays the groundwork for collecting data from people who have different perspectives and for developing relationships that the researcher can use to overcome the problems that inevitably arise in the field.

Developing and Maintaining Relationships

Researchers must be careful to manage their relationships in the research setting so they can continue to observe and interview diverse members of the social setting throughout the long period typical of participant observation (Maxwell, 1996). Making valid observations, of course, will be impossible if researchers do not have the trust of the people whom they are studying.

Rios originally recruited participants in his study from a youth leadership organization and community center in Oakland. The boys were "'at promise' [at-risk] young men, ages fourteen to seventeen, who had previously been arrested" (p. 10). Because he had formally lived in the area and was only 25 years old when he began his research, Rios (2011) probably had a relatively easy time developing trust and rapport with his participants. In fact, he stated,

> Many of the boys acknowledged me as someone they could trust and look up to. The majority referred to me as "O.G. Vic." "O.G." stands for "original gangster." This label is often ascribed to older members of the neighborhood who have proven themselves and gained respect on the street and, as a result, are respected by younger residents. I told the young men not to consider me an O.G. since I believed, and still do, that I did not deserve the label. My belief was that any researcher who considered himself an O.G. was being deceptive. . . . At the time of the study, I was a graduate student with many privileges that many of these young people did not have. I was an "outsider" as much as an "insider." (p. 13)

While having personal knowledge or experience with a social setting certainly helps researchers gain entry into that world, many researchers who have not had backgrounds with their areas of study have also been successful. For example, Jody Miller (2000) describes her efforts to develop trust with the female gang members she interviewed for her book, *One of the Guys*:

> First, my research approach proved useful for establishing rapport. The survey began with relatively innocuous questions (demographics, living arrangements, attitudes toward school) and slowly made the transition from these to more sensitive questions about gang involvement, delinquency, and victimization. In addition, completing the survey interview first allowed me to establish a relationship with each young woman, so that when we completed the in-depth interview, there was a preexisting level of familiarity between us. . . . In addition, I worked to develop trust in the young women I interviewed through my efforts to protect their confidentiality. (pp. 29–30)

Sampling People and Events

Decisions to study one setting or several settings and to pay attention to specific people and events will shape field researchers' ability to generalize about what they have found, as well as the confidence that others can place in the results of their study. Limiting a particular study to a single setting allows a more intensive portrait of actors and activities in that setting but also makes generalization of the findings questionable.

It is easy to be reassured by information indicating that a typical case was selected for study or that the case selected was appropriate in some way for the research question. We also must keep in mind that many of the most insightful participant observation studies were conducted in only one setting and draw their credibility precisely from the researcher's thorough understanding of that setting. Nonetheless, studying more than one case or setting almost always strengthens the causal conclusions and makes the findings more generalizable (King, Keohane, & Verba, 1994).

Most qualitative researchers utilize a purposive sampling technique (Chapter 5), often adding a snowball aspect by asking respondents to recommend others. Rios (2011) added a snowball sample component to the original participants he obtained from the community center. He stated, "With snowball sampling, I was able to uncover a population of young men who were surrounded by or involved in crime and who had consistent interaction with police" (p. 11).

Theoretical sampling is a systematic approach to sampling in participant observational research (Glaser & Strauss, 1967). Decker and Van Winkle (1996) used this technique to ensure that various subgroups, such as race, sex, and type of gang, were represented within their sample. When field researchers discover in an investigation that particular processes seem to be important, implying that certain comparisons should be made or that similar instances should be checked, the researchers then modify their settings and choose new individuals, as diagrammed in Exhibit 8.3 (Ragin, 1994). Based on the existing literature and anecdotal knowledge, Decker and Van Winkle (1996) knew that not all gang members were young minority group males. They describe their strategy to obtain a full range of gang members as follows:

> We aggressively pursued leads for female gangs and gang members as well as opportunities to locate older and nonblack gang members. These leads were more difficult to find and often caused us to miss chances to interview other gang members. Despite these "missed opportunities," our sample is strengthened in that it more accurately represents the diverse nature of gangs and gang members in St. Louis. (p. 43)

Theoretical sampling:
A sampling method recommended for field researchers by Glaser and Strauss (1967); a theoretical sample is drawn in a sequential fashion, with settings or individuals selected for study as earlier observations or interviews indicate that these settings or individuals are influential

Exhibit 8.3 Theoretical Sampling

Original cases interviewed in a study of cocaine users:

Realization: Some cocaine users are businesspeople.
Add businesspeople to sample:

Realization: Sample is low on women.
Add women to sample:

Realization: Some female cocaine users are mothers of young children.
Add mothers to sample:

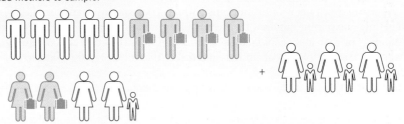

The resulting sample of gang members in Decker and Van Winkle's (1996) study represents 29 different gangs. Thus, Decker and Van Winkle's ability to draw from different gangs in developing conclusions gives us greater confidence in their study's generalizability. Using some type of intentional sampling strategy within a particular setting can allow tests of some hypotheses that would otherwise have to wait until comparative data could be collected from several settings (King et al., 1994). However, because it is rarely possible to obtain a probability sample when engaging in participant observation, researchers rarely make claims that their findings are generalizable to other settings. For example, Rios (2011) stated, "This study, while grounded in Oakland, California, may provide a deeper understand of the punishment that other youth experience in other marginalized communities" (p. 19).

Taking Notes

Written **field notes** are the primary means of recording participant observation data (Emerson, Fretz, & Shaw, 1995). It is almost always a mistake to try to take comprehensive notes while engaged in the field; the process of writing extensively is just too disruptive. The usual

Field notes: Notes that describe what has been observed, heard, or otherwise experienced in a participant observation study; these notes usually are written after the observational session

procedure is to jot down brief notes about the highlights of the observation period. These brief notes, called jottings, then serve as memory joggers when writing the actual field notes at a later time. With the aid of the brief notes and some practice, researchers usually remember a great deal of what happened, as long as the comprehensive field notes are written within the next 24 hours, usually that night or upon arising the next day. Many field researchers jot down partial notes while observing and then retreat to their computers to write up more complete notes on a daily basis. The computerized text can then be inspected and organized after it is printed out, or it can be marked up and organized for analysis using one of several computer programs designed especially for the task.

Usually, writing up notes takes as long as making the observations. Field notes must be as complete, detailed, and true to what was observed and heard as possible. Quotes should clearly be distinguished from the researcher's observations and phrased in the local vernacular; pauses and interruptions should be indicated. The surrounding context should receive as much attention as possible, and a map of the setting should always be included, with indications of where individuals were at different times.

Complete field notes must provide more than just a record of what was observed or heard. Notes also should include descriptions of the methodology: where researchers were standing while observing, how they chose people for conversation or observation, and what numerical counts of people or events they made and why. Sprinkled throughout the notes should be a record of the researchers' feelings and thoughts while observing, such as when they were disgusted by some statement or act, when they felt threatened or intimidated, or why their attention shifted from one group to another. Notes such as these provide a foundation for later review of the likelihood of bias or inattention to some salient features of the situation.

Managing the Personal Dimensions

Our overview of participant observation is not complete without considering its personal dimensions. Because field researchers become a part of the social situation they are studying, they cannot help but be affected on a personal, emotional level. At the same time, those being studied react to researchers not just as researchers but as personal acquaintances—often as friends, sometimes as personal rivals. Managing and learning from this personal side of field research is an important part of any qualitative project.

The impact of personal issues varies with the depth of researchers' involvement in the setting. The more involved researchers are in multiple aspects of the ongoing social situation, the more important personal issues become and the greater the risk of "going native." Even when researchers acknowledge their role, "increased contact brings sympathy, and sympathy in its turn dulls the edge of criticism" (Fenno, 1978, p. 277).

There is no formula for successfully managing the personal dimension of field research. It is much more art than science and flows more from the researcher's own personality and natural approach to other people than from formal training. Novice field researchers often neglect to consider how they will manage personal relationships when they plan and carry out their projects. Then, suddenly, they find themselves doing something they do not believe they should, just to stay in the good graces of research subjects, or juggling the emotions resulting from conflict within the group. These issues are even more salient when researchers place themselves in potentially dangerous situations.

SYSTEMATIC OBSERVATION

Observations can be made in a more systematic, standardized design that allows systematic comparisons and more confident generalizations. A researcher using systematic observation develops a standard form on which to record variation within the observed setting in terms of his or her variables of interest. Such variables might include the frequency of some behavior(s), the particular people observed, the weather or other environmental conditions, and the number and state of repair of physical structures. In some systematic-observation studies, records are obtained from a random sample of places or times.

Case Study: Systematic Observation in Chicago Neighborhoods

You first learned about Robert Sampson and Stephen Raudenbush's classic study of disorder and crime in urban neighborhoods in Chapter 4. In this section, we will elaborate on their use of the method of systematic social observation of public spaces to learn more about Chicago neighborhoods. A systematic observational strategy increases the reliability of observational data by using explicit rules that standardize coding practices across observers (Reiss, 1971).

Sampson and Raudenbush's study was a multiple-methods investigation that combined observational research, survey research, and archival research. The observational component involved a stratified probability (random) sample of 196 Chicago census tracts. A specially equipped sport utility vehicle was driven down each street in these tracts at the rate of 5 miles per hour. Two video recorders taped the blocks on both sides of the street, while two observers peered out the vehicle's windows and recorded their observations in logs. The result was an observational record of 23,816 face blocks (the block on one side of the street is a face block). The observers recorded codes that indicated land use, traffic, physical conditions, and evidence of physical disorder (see Exhibit 8.4). Physical disorder was measured by counting such features as cigarettes or cigars in the street, garbage, empty beer bottles, graffiti, condoms, and syringes. Indicators of social disorder included adults loitering, drinking alcohol in public, fighting, and selling drugs.

Peter St. Jean (2007) advanced the research of Sampson and Raudenbush by examining the variation in collective efficacy, community disorder, and crime within specific blocks in one high-crime police district in Chicago. After examining official data and combining them with interviews asking residents where crime typically took place in the neighborhood, St. Jean found that pockets of crime emerged in which most crimes occurred on particular blocks within a neighborhood while other blocks remained relatively untouched. The goal of St. Jean's work was to determine why. He used multiple methods for this project, including resident surveys, participant observation, in-depth interviews with residents and offenders, and systematic social observation. For this last method, video cameras were mounted on each side of a vehicle while it was slowly driven through neighborhood streets so that physical and social appearances could be captured. An example of the video St. Jean captured is available on the Student Study Site for this text. Using the tapes, neighborhood characteristics were then coded for social disorder by using the conditions of the buildings, properties, and vacant lots and the prevalence of behaviors such as loitering, public drinking, and panhandling. A snapshot from one of St. Jean's videos is displayed in Exhibit 8.5.

Innovatively, St. Jean (2007) not only coded the videos, he also used the footage as a visual cue when interviewing offenders about their reasons for selecting particular locations and victims. He explains,

> For instance, drug dealers and robbers were able to use the [systematic social observation] movie to explain in detail how and why certain locations are more attractive than others. It also allowed offenders to identify the specific features of neighborhoods that they considered distasteful, and to explain associated meanings, especially as such meanings pertain to the crimes they commit . . . it refreshed the subjects' memories of relevant events that they often claimed they would have forgotten to mention [without the video]. (p. 27)

Exhibit 8.4 Neighborhood Disorder Indicators Used in Systematic Observation Log

Variable	Category	Frequency
Physical Disorder		
Cigarettes or cigars on street or gutter	No	6,815
	Yes	16,758
Garbage or litter on street or sidewalk	No	11,680
	Yes	11,925
Empty beer bottles visible in street	No	17,653
	Yes	5,870
Tagging graffiti	No	12,859
	Yes	2,252
Graffiti painted over	No	13,390
	Yes	1,721
Gang graffiti	No	14,138
	Yes	973
Abandoned cars	No	22,782
	Yes	806
Condoms on sidewalk	No	23,331
	Yes	231
Needles or syringes on sidewalk	No	23,392
	Yes	173
Political message graffiti	No	15,097
	Yes	14
Social Disorder		
Adults loitering or congregating	No	14,250
	Yes	861
People drinking alcohol	No	15,075
	Yes	36
Peer group or gang indicators present	No	15,091
	Yes	20
People intoxicated	No	15,093
	Yes	18
Adults fighting or hostilely arguing	No	15,099
	Yes	12
Prostitutes on street	No	15,100
	Yes	11
People selling drugs	No	15,099
	Yes	12

Source: Raudenbush, Stephen W. and Robert J. Sampson. 1999. "Ecometrics: Toward a Science of Assessing Ecological Settings, With Application to the Systematic Social Observation of Neighborhoods." *Sociological Methodology* 29:1–41.

Exhibit 8.5   One Building in St. Jean's (2007) Study

Source: Courtesy of Peter K. B. St. Jean, Quality of Life Solutions.

Among other things, St. Jean discovered that even when offenders faced opposition from neighborhood reformers, they were not deterred from engaging in crime in an area when it offered "ecological advantages" such as retail establishments and bus stops.

These studies illustrate both the value of multiple methods and the technique of recording observations in a systematic form. The systematic observations, when combined with residents' own perceptions, provide us with much greater confidence in the measurement of relative neighborhood disorder. When these are combined with rich narrative accounts from neighborhood residents and active offenders, both the measurement validity of the constructs and the overall validity of the findings are significantly enhanced.

INTENSIVE INTERVIEWING

Intensive interviewing:
Open-ended, relatively
unstructured
questioning in which
the interviewer seeks
in-depth information
on the interviewee's
feelings, experiences,
and/or perceptions

Asking questions is part of almost all qualitative research designs (Wolcott, 1995). Many qualitative researchers employ intensive interviewing exclusively, without systematic observation of respondents in their natural setting. Unlike the more structured interviewing that may be used in survey research (discussed in Chapter 7), intensive interviewing relies on open-ended questions. Qualitative researchers do not presume to know the range of answers that respondents might give, and they seek to hear these answers in the respondents' own words. Rather than asking standard questions in a fixed order, intensive interviewers allow the specific content and order of questions to vary from one interviewee to another.

What distinguishes intensive interviewing from more structured forms of questioning is consistency and thoroughness. The goal is to develop a comprehensive picture of the interviewees' background, attitudes, and actions, in their own terms—to "listen to people as they describe how they understand the worlds in which they live and work" (Rubin & Rubin, 1995, p. 3). For example, even though Decker and Van Winkle (1996) had an interview guide, they encouraged elaboration on the part of their respondents and "went to great lengths to insure that each person we interviewed felt they had received the opportunity to tell their story in their own words" (p. 45).

Random selection is rarely used to select respondents for intensive interviews, but the selection method still must be considered carefully. Researchers should try to select interviewees who are knowledgeable about the subject of the interview, who are open to talking, and who represent the range of perspectives (Rubin & Rubin, 1995). Selection of new interviewees should continue, if possible, at least until the **saturation point** is reached, the point when new interviews seem to yield little additional information (see Exhibit 8.6). As new issues are uncovered, additional interviewees may be selected to represent different opinions about these issues.

Saturation point: The point at which subject selection is ended in intensive interviewing, when new interviews seem to yield little additional information

Establishing and Maintaining a Partnership

Because intensive interviewing does not engage researchers as participants in subjects' daily affairs, the problems associated with entering the field are greatly reduced. However, the logistics of arranging long periods for personal interviews can still be fairly complicated. It is important to establish rapport with subjects by considering in advance how they will react to the interview arrangement and by developing an approach that does not violate their standards for social behavior. Interviewees should be treated with respect, as knowledgeable partners whose time is valued. (In other words, avoid being late for appointments.) Once again, a commitment to confidentiality should be stated and honored (Rubin & Rubin, 1995).

It is important to highlight, however, that the intensive interviewer's relationship with the interviewee is not an equal partnership, for the researcher seeks to gain certain types of information and strategizes throughout to maintain an appropriate relationship. In the first

Exhibit 8.6 The Saturation Point in Intensive Interviewing

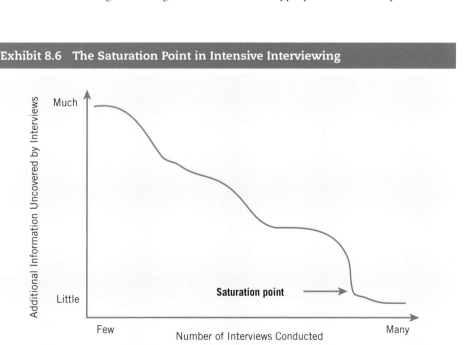

few minutes of the interview, the goal is to show interest in the interviewee and to clearly explain the purpose of the interview (Kvale, 1996). During the interview, the interviewer should maintain an appropriate distance from the interviewee, one that does not violate cultural norms; the interviewer should maintain eye contact and not engage in distracting behavior. An appropriate pace is also important; pause to allow the interviewee to reflect, elaborate, and generally not feel rushed (Gordon, 1992). When an interview covers emotional or otherwise stressful topics, at the end, the interviewer should give the interviewee an opportunity to unwind (Rubin & Rubin, 1995).

Asking Questions and Recording Answers

Intensive interviewers must plan their main questions around an outline of the interview topic. The questions should generally be short and to the point. More details can then be elicited through nondirective probes (such as "Can you tell me more about that?"), and follow-up questions can be tailored to answers to the main questions. Interviewers should strategize throughout an interview about how best to achieve their objectives while taking into account interviewees' answers.

Decker and Van Winkle's (1996) interview narrative illustrates this well:

Nearly half of the gang members identified leaders as persons who could provide material advantage, thus ascribing a functional character to leadership within the gang. Since half of our sample were in their early teens, someone with the ability to procure cars, drugs, guns, or alcohol could play a valuable role in the gang. Consequently, it was no surprise to find that over half of gang members identified leaders as persons who could "deliver." Because of the situational nature of leadership, persons moved in and out of this role. This was especially true in the case of being able to provide drugs in large quantities for street sales:

Q: Does someone have more juice in the gang?

A: Yeah, you always got someone that got more juice.

Q: What is the type of person who usually has more juice?

A: The one who got the connection with the drugs.

Q: Who has the most juice?

A: Dude named T-Loc.

Q: Why does he have more juice than everybody else?

A: 'Cause he travels a lot. Gets the good stuff.

Q: What's the good stuff?

A: Like guns, cocaine, weed.

Q: What gives him the juice? (pp. 97–98)

Do you see how the interviewer actively encouraged the subject to elaborate on answers? More important, intensive interviews can also uncover true meanings that questions utilizing fixed formats would surely miss.

Tape or digital voice recorders commonly are used to record intensive interviews. Most researchers who have recorded interviews feel that they do not inhibit most interviewees and, in fact, are routinely ignored. The occasional respondent who is very concerned with his or her public image may speak "for the recorder," but such individuals are unlikely to speak frankly in any research interview. In any case, constant note taking during an interview prevents adequate displays of interest and appreciation by the interviewer and hinders the degree of concentration that results in the best interviews.

Case Study: Barriers to Reentry for Older Offenders

While the age–crime curve reveals that criminal offending is most likely for young people, many prison inmates are older; in fact, over 1 in 10 state and federal prisoners are 50 years of age or older. While 50 is not the boundary for "old age" in the general population, among incarcerated populations, individuals of this age often experience the illnesses and disease that do not typically onset in nonincarcerated populations until the 60s or 70s. Reintegrating into society from a correctional setting is difficult for all, but it is particularly difficult for older individuals who have spent their lives in and out of prison. To understand the issues facing this population, Jessica Wyse (2018) interviewed 20 men aged 50 and older who had been released from prison for one year or less. Wyse recruited her sample "through flyers hung at halfway houses, non-profit and governmental offices serving disadvantaged and ex-offending populations" (p. 2157). The interview guide contained open-ended questions designed to solicit information about social integration and well-being. For example, questions such as, "What family members and friends have you spent most of your time with since you were released? Can you tell me a little about those people? Can you describe any health problems that you have? . . . How likely do you think it is that you will return to prison and/or commit another crime? Why do you think that is?" (p. 2157). Wyse also conducted follow-up interviews two to three months after the initial interview to assess any changes in levels of integration.

While virtually all of the respondents had a desire to become part of conventional society, they all faced substantial barriers, including disconnections from family and friends and an inability to secure employment. One 52-year-old explained the importance of finding employment,

> I don't feel productive. I don't feel like I'm a part of society yet . . . But maybe by finding a good job or, naw, it don't have to be a good job. Any job. And I'll be able to do something where I can wake up in the morning, go to work, . . . plan my day where I get like it was when I was in prison . . . every day I knew exactly what I had to do. . . . out here I need to do the same thing" (p. 2165).

Wyse would not have been able to uncover these perceptions without open-ended questions. As she stated, "Interviews allow for investigation of subjects' expectations, experiences, and beliefs, for instance, in allowing subjects to self-define success, rather than imposing an external definition upon them" (p. 2157).

Combining Participant Observation and Intensive Interviewing

Many large research projects aimed at uncovering detailed information about a particular phenomenon often combine the qualitative research techniques of participant observation and intensive interviewing. As we have already seen, Victor Rios (2011) combined these methods, as did Susan Miller (1999) in her study of community policing. In fact, Miller contends that the information obtained from both methodologies was vital to her conclusions. For example, the observational component of Miller's research shows how traditional patrol officers' perceptions and experiences differ from those of neighborhood patrol officers. Her observations also uncovered how rarely the paths of patrol officers crossed with their community-policing counterparts. These limited interactions contributed, Miller believed, to patrol officers' misconceptions about community policing. Patrol officers believed that neighborhood police officers did not do real police work and spent too much time responding to residents and political needs, not to crime-fighting goals.

Whereas both male and female patrol officers would engage in masculine teasing while in the field, such as talking about their physical fitness and shooting ability, during the one-on-one interviews, she discovered a more gendered nature of the patrol officers' perceptions and experiences:

> Even though the patrolwomen joined in the banter and told their share of crime-fighting war stories [in the field], it became clear during one-on-one conversations with them they dropped their aggressive facade when their actions were less visible to other patrol officers. The women were more than superficially involved in some of the local people's lives, particularly with the children. (p. 176)

FOCUS GROUPS

Focus group:
A qualitative method that involves unstructured group interviews in which the focus group leader actively encourages discussion among participants on the topics of interest

Focus groups are groups of individuals that are formed by a researcher and then led in group discussion of a topic. The researcher asks specific questions and guides the discussion to ensure that group members address these questions, but the resulting information is qualitative and relatively unstructured. Unlike most other survey designs, focus groups do not involve representative samples; instead, a few individuals are recruited for the group who have the time to participate and who share key characteristics with the target population.

Most focus groups involve seven to 10 people, a size that facilitates discussion by all in attendance. Although participants usually do not know one another, they are chosen so that they are relatively homogeneous, which tends to reduce their inhibitions in discussion. Of course, the characteristics of individuals that determine their inclusion are based on the researcher's conception of the target population for the study. Focus group leaders must begin the discussion by creating the expectation that all will participate and that the researcher will not favor any particular perspective or participant.

Focus groups are interviewed to collect qualitative data using open-ended questions posed by the researcher (or group leader). Thus, a focused discussion mimics the natural process of forming and expressing opinions and may give some sense of validity. The researcher also may want to conduct a more traditional survey, asking a representative sample of the target population to answer closed-ended questions, to weigh the validity of data obtained from the focus group. No formal procedure exists for determining the generalizability of focus group answers, but the careful researcher should conduct at least several focus groups on the same topic and check for consistency in the findings as a partial test of generalizability.

As with other field research techniques, focus group methods emphasize discovering unanticipated findings and exploring hidden meanings. Although they do not provide a means for developing reliable, generalizable results (the traditional strong suits of survey research), focus groups can be an indispensable aid for developing hypotheses and survey questions, for investigating the meaning of survey results, and for quickly identifying the range of opinion about an issue.

Case Study: An Analysis of Police Searches

Racial profiling has generally been defined as the use of race by police as a key factor in deciding whether to make a traffic stop—that is, to pull over a driver for an infraction (B. N. Williams & Stahl, 2008). As a response to lawsuits alleging racial profiling, many state and local law enforcement agencies have been mandated or have volunteered to collect traffic stop data to monitor the behavior of officers to determine the extent of such profiling. However, to actually determine if racial minorities were being stopped for an infraction like speeding more than whites, researchers would first have to determine the percentage of minority drivers relative to whites who were actually driving along a given highway and then the percentage of these motorists who were actually speeding to get a true base rate of speeding per population group. This would entail many hours of monitoring a given highway during various times of day.

While some researchers have actually collected these data, Williams and Stahl decided to examine whether race was a determining factor in whether a driver was searched after a stop. The questions they asked were, "Who is being searched, and what are the results of these searches?" Using data collected in 24 local Kentucky law enforcement agencies, along with two state agencies, they concluded that of the motorists pulled over on the interstate for compliance and courtesy stops, African American and Hispanic motorists were significantly more likely to be searched compared with white motorists. To test the second question, they examined whether there were differences in positive search results (e.g., finding contraband) across racial or ethnic groups. Consistent with other research, there was no statistical difference in the likelihood that white, African American, or Hispanic motorists who were searched actually had illegal material.

To better understand these quantitative findings, B. N. Williams and Stahl (2008) conducted focus groups with police officers to determine their perceptions about a number of issues, including whether traffic stops and searches were effective in preventing some of the problems in their communities. A purposive sample of 24 officers participated in five focus groups. After comparing the perceptions, attitudes, and experiences across groups and individual officers, several themes emerged. The first was that drug use and sales, as well as drunk driving, were major community problems. The second was that the police perception was that if you wanted to target a particular problem, you had to target a particular group: African Americans were perceived to be associated with crack cocaine, driving under the influence was perceived to be associated with Hispanic motorists, and methamphetamine was perceived to be associated with whites. Moreover, officers were confident that traffic stops helped deter the drug trade and improve the quality of life of their local communities. Williams and Stahl concluded that the officers shared a perception that they were community problem solvers who profile the problems and not a particular group. Recall, however, that the quantitative data showed no difference in contraband found across racial groups. The researchers concluded, "If police want to be efficient and effective in their efforts to stop drugs, it seems that they need to disregard the 'profile,' as our analysis has found that it is an ineffective tool for turning up illegal substances" (p. 238). This triangulation of methods was extremely helpful in placing the quantitative data within the perceptions shared by police officers.

ANALYZING QUALITATIVE DATA

The distinctive features of qualitative data collection methods are also reflected in the methods used to analyze the data collected. The focus on text, on qualitative data rather than on

Qualitative data analysis:Techniques used to search and code textual, visual, or other content and to explore relationships among the resulting categories

numbers, is the most important feature of qualitative data analysis. The "text" that qualitative researchers analyze is most often transcripts of interviews or notes from participant observation sessions, but text can also refer to pictures or other images that the researcher examines.

Good qualitative data analyses are distinguished by their focus on the interrelated aspects of the setting, group, or person under investigation—the entire case—rather than breaking the whole into separate parts. The whole is always understood to be greater than the sum of its parts, and so the social context of events, thoughts, and actions becomes essential for interpretation. Within this framework, it would not make sense to focus on two variables out of an interacting set of influences and test the relationship between just those two.

Qualitative data analysis is a reflexive process that begins as data are being collected rather than after data collection has ceased (Stake, 1995). Next to his or her field notes or interview transcripts, the qualitative analyst jots down ideas about the meaning of the text and how it might relate to other issues. This process of reading through the data and interpreting them continues throughout the project. The analyst adjusts the data collection process itself when it begins to appear that additional concepts need to be investigated or new relationships explored. This process is termed progressive focusing (Parlett & Hamilton, 1976).

Progressive focusing: The process by which a qualitative analyst interacts with the data and gradually refines his or her focus

Qualitative Data Analysis as an Art

The process of qualitative data analysis is described by some as involving as much art as science, or as a "dance," in the words of W. L. Miller and Crabtree (1999). In this artful way, analyzing text involves both inductive and deductive processes. The researcher generates concepts and linkages between them based on reading the text and also checks the text to see whether those concepts and interpretations are reflected.

Qualitative Compared With Quantitative Data Analysis

With these points in mind, let us review the ways in which qualitative data analysis differs from quantitative analysis (Denzin & Lincoln, 2000; Patton 2002). Qualitative analysis features the following:

- A focus on meanings rather than on quantifiable phenomena

- Collection of many data on a few cases rather than few data on many cases

- In-depth study and attention to detail, without predetermined categories or directions, rather than emphasis on analyses and categories determined in advance

- A conception of the researcher as an instrument rather than as the designer of objective instruments to measure particular variables

- Sensitivity to context rather than a seeking of universal generalizations

- Attention to the impact of the researcher's and others' values on the course of the analysis rather than presuming the possibility of value-free inquiry

- A goal of rich descriptions of the world rather than measurement of specific variables

You will also want to keep in mind features of qualitative data analysis that are shared with those of quantitative data analysis. Both qualitative and quantitative data analysis can involve making distinctions about textual data. You also know that textual data can be transposed to quantitative data through a process of categorization and counting. Some qualitative analysts also share with quantitative researchers a positivist goal of describing the world as it really is, but others have adopted a postmodern goal of trying to understand how different people see and make sense of the world without believing that there is any correct description.

TECHNIQUES OF QUALITATIVE DATA ANALYSIS

The most typical steps that are shared by most approaches to qualitative data analysis include

- documentation of the data and the process of data collection;

- organization or categorization of the data into concepts;

- connection of the data to show how one concept may influence another;

- corroboration or legitimization by evaluating alternative explanations, challenging validity, and searching for negative cases; and

- representing the account (reporting the findings).

The analysis of qualitative research notes begins while interviewing or as early as the researcher enters the field; researchers identify problems and concepts that appear likely to help in understanding the situation. Simply reading the notes or transcripts is an important step in the analytic process. Researchers should make frequent notes in the margins to identify important statements and to propose ways of coding the data.

An interim stage may consist of listing the concepts reflected in the notes and diagramming the relationships among concepts (Maxwell, 1996). In a large project, weekly team meetings are an important part of this process. Susan Miller (1999) described this process in her study of NPOs. Miller's research team members met both to go over their field notes and to resolve points of confusion, as well as to dialogue with other skilled researchers who helped to identify emerging concepts.

This process continues throughout the project and should assist in refining concepts during the report-writing phase, long after data collection has ceased. Let us examine each of the stages of qualitative research in more detail.

Documentation

The first formal analytical step is documentation. The various contacts, interviews, written documents, and whatever it is that preserves a record of what happened must all be saved and listed. Documentation is critical to qualitative research for several reasons: It is essential for keeping track of what will become a rapidly growing volume of notes, tapes, and documents; it provides a way of developing an outline for the analytic process; and it encourages ongoing conceptualizing and strategizing about the text.

What to do with all this material? Many field research projects have slowed to a halt because a novice researcher becomes overwhelmed by the quantity of information that has been collected. A 1-hour interview can generate 20 to 25 pages of single-spaced text (Kvale, 1996). Analysis is less daunting, however, if the researcher maintains a disciplined transcription schedule.

Making Sense of It: Conceptualization, Coding, and Categorizing

Identifying and refining important concepts is a key part of the iterative process of qualitative research. Sometimes conceptualizing begins with a simple observation that is interpreted directly, pulled apart, and then put back together more meaningfully. Stake (1995) provides an example: "More often, analytic insights tested against new observations, the initial statement of problems and concepts is refined, the researcher then collects more data, interacts with the data again, and the process continues" (p. 75).

Jody Miller (2000) provides an excellent illustration of the developmental process of conceptualization in her study of girls in gangs:

> I paid close attention to and took seriously respondents' reactions to themes raised in interviews, particularly instances in which they "talked back" by labeling a topic irrelevant, pointing out what they saw as misinterpretations on my part, or offering corrections. In my research, the women talked back the most in response to my efforts to get them to articulate how gender inequality shaped their experiences in the gang. Despite stories they told to the contrary, many maintained a strong belief in their equality within the gang. . . . As the research progressed, I also took emerging themes back to respondents in subsequent interviews to see if they felt I had gotten it right. In addition to conveying that I was interested in their perspectives and experiences, this process also proved useful for further refining my analyses. (p. 30)

The process described in this quote illustrates the reflexive nature of qualitative data collection and analysis. In qualitative research, the collection of data and their analysis are not typically separate activities. This excerpt shows how the researcher first was alerted to a concept by observations in the field, then refined her understanding of this concept by investigating its meaning. By observing the concept's frequency of use, she came to realize its importance.

Examining Relationships and Displaying Data

Examining relationships is the centerpiece of the analytic process because it allows the researcher to move from simple description of the people and settings to explanations of why things happened as they did with those people in that setting. The process of examining relationships can be captured in a matrix that shows how different concepts are connected or perhaps what causes are linked with what effects.

Exhibit 8.7 provides an excellent example of a causal model developed by Baskin and Sommers (1998) to explain the desistance process for the sample of violent female offenders they interviewed in the state of New York. They described the process for the women who made it out of their lives of crime as follows:

> Desistance is a process as complex and lengthy as the process of initial involvement. It was interesting to find that some of the key concepts in initiation of deviance—social bonding, differential association, deterrence, age—were equally important in the process of desistance. We see the aging offender take the threat of punishment seriously, reestablish links with conventional society and sever associations with subcultural street elements. We found, too, that the decision to give up crime was triggered by a shock of some sort that was followed by a period of crisis. They arrived at a point at which the deviant way of life seemed senseless. (p. 139)

Exhibit 8.7   The Desistance Process for Violent Female Offenders

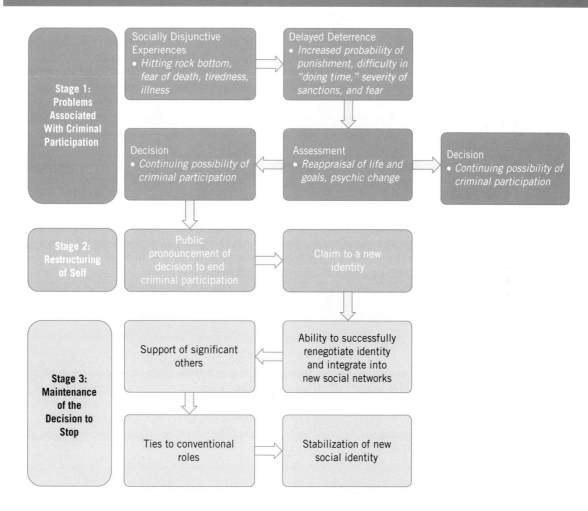

Source: Adapted from *Casualties of Community Disorder: Women's Careers in Violent Crime* by Deborah R. Baskin and Ira B. Sommers.

Corroboration and Authenticating Conclusions

No set standards exist for evaluating the validity or authenticity of conclusions in a qualitative study, but the need to consider carefully the evidence and methods on which conclusions are based is just as great as with other types of research. Data can be assessed in terms of at least three criteria (Becker, 1958):

- *How credible was the informant?* Were statements made by someone with whom the researcher had a relationship of trust or by someone the researcher had just met? Did the informant have reason to lie? If the statements do not seem to be trustworthy as indicators of actual events, can they at least be used to help understand the informant's perspective?

- *Were statements made in response to the researcher's questions, or were they spontaneous?* Spontaneous statements are more likely to indicate what would have been said had the researcher not been present.

- *How does the presence or absence of the researcher or the researcher's informant influence the actions and statements of other group members?* Reactivity to being observed can never be ruled out as a possible explanation for some directly observed social phenomena. However, if the researcher carefully compares what the informant says goes on when the researcher is not present, what the researcher observes directly, and what other group members say about their normal practices, the extent of reactivity can be assessed to some extent.

A qualitative researcher's conclusions should be assessed by their ability to provide a credible explanation for some aspect of social life. That explanation should capture group members' **tacit knowledge** of the social processes that were observed, not just their verbal statements about these processes. Tacit knowledge, "the largely unarticulated, contextual understanding that is often manifested in nods, silences, humor, and naughty nuances," is reflected in participants' actions, as well as their words, and in what they fail to state but nonetheless feel deeply and even take for granted (Altheide & Johnson, 1994, pp. 492–493). These features are evident in Whyte's (1955) analysis of Cornerville social patterns.

Comparing conclusions from a qualitative research project with those obtained by other researchers conducting similar projects can also increase confidence in their authenticity.

Reflexivity

Confidence in the conclusions from a field research study is also strengthened by an honest and informative account about how the researcher interacted with subjects in the field, what problems he or she encountered, and how these problems were or were not resolved. Such a natural history of the development of the evidence, sometimes termed **reflexivity**, enables others to evaluate the findings. Such an account is important primarily because of the evolving nature of field research.

Qualitative data analysts, more often than quantitative researchers, display real sensitivity to how a social situation or process is interpreted from a particular background and set of values and not simply based on the situation itself (Altheide & Johnson, 1994). Researchers are only human, after all, and must rely on their own senses to process information through their own minds. By reporting how and why they think they did what they did, they can help others determine whether or how the researchers' perspectives influenced their conclusions. "There should be clear 'tracks' indicating the attempt [to show the hand of the ethnographer] has been made" (Altheide & Johnson, 1994, p. 493).

Victor Rios (2011) was very aware of the effects of his subjective experiences and how they may have affected what he heard and witnessed in the field. He reflected on his goal of producing findings that could be reproduced by others:

> I reflected on my own experience so that I could distinguish between my person "truths" and the "truths" of others. My goal has been to utilize my experience in the production of knowledge but also to generate a study that could be replicated by anyone who is interested in doing so. . . . I constantly reflected on how I collected data and what consequences, positive or negative, this may have had on my subjects." (pp. 169–170)

Tacit knowledge: In field research, a credible sense of understanding of social processes that reflect the researcher's awareness of participants' actions, as well as their words, and of what they fail to state, feel deeply, and take for granted

Reflexivity: An accounting by a qualitative researcher that describes the natural history of the development of evidence; this enables others to more adequately evaluate the findings

Reflexive thinking like this is extremely important in qualitative analyses and increases the likelihood that findings are both valid and reliable. As we have already learned, replication is a key ingredient of the scientific process.

ALTERNATIVES IN QUALITATIVE DATA ANALYSIS

The qualitative data analyst can choose from many interesting alternative approaches. Of course, the research question under investigation should shape the selection of an analytic approach, but the researcher's preferences and experiences will inevitably steer the research method selection. The approach we present here, **grounded theory**, is one of the approaches most frequently used (Patton, 2002).

Grounded theory: Systematic theory developed inductively, based on observations that are summarized into conceptual categories, reevaluated in the research setting, and gradually refined and linked to other conceptual categories

Grounded Theory

Theory development occurs continually in qualitative data analysis (Coffey & Atkinson, 1996). The goal of many qualitative researchers is to create grounded theory—that is, to inductively build up a systematic theory that is grounded in or based on the observations. The observations are summarized into conceptual categories, which are tested directly in the research setting with more observations. Over time, as the conceptual categories are refined and linked, a theory evolves (Glaser & Strauss, 1967; Huberman & Miles, 1994). Exhibit 8.8 illustrates this process.

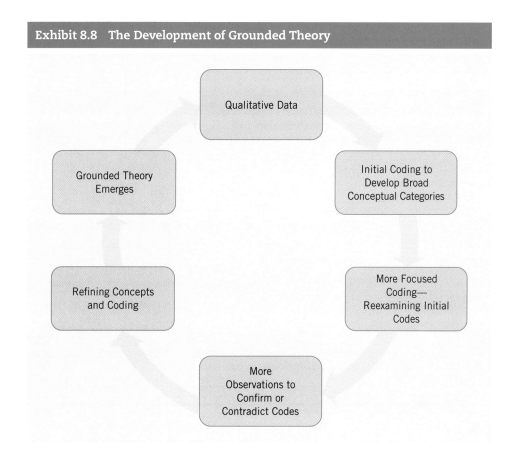

Exhibit 8.8 The Development of Grounded Theory

- Qualitative Data
- Initial Coding to Develop Broad Conceptual Categories
- More Focused Coding—Reexamining Initial Codes
- More Observations to Confirm or Contradict Codes
- Refining Concepts and Coding
- Grounded Theory Emerges

As observation, interviewing, and reflection continue, researchers refine their definitions of problems and concepts and select indicators. They can then check the frequency and distribution of phenomena: How many people made a particular type of comment? Which people assigned similar meaning to the same patterns, behavior, or comparable social events? How often did social interaction lead to arguments? Social system models may then be developed, which specify the relationships among different phenomena. These models are modified as researchers gain experience in the setting. For the final analysis, the researchers check their models carefully against their notes and make a concerted attempt to discover negative evidence that might suggest the model is incorrect.

Heidi Levitt, Rebecca Todd Swanger, and Jenny Butler (2008) used a systematic grounded method of analysis to understand the perspective of male perpetrators of violence on female victims. Research participants were recruited from programs the courts used in Memphis to assess and treat perpetrators who admitted to having physically abused a female intimate partner. The researchers began the analysis of their interview transcripts by dividing them into "meaning units"—"segments of texts that each contain one main idea"—and labeling these units with terms like those used by participants (pp. 437–438). They then compared these labels and combined them into larger descriptive categories. This process continued until they had combined all the meaning units into seven different clusters. Exhibit 8.9 gives an example of two of their clusters and the four categories of meaning units combined within each (Levitt et al., 2008, p. 439).

Here is how Levitt and her colleagues (2008) discuss the comments that were classified in Cluster 2, Category 3:

> Accordingly, when conflicts accumulated that could not be easily resolved, many of the men (5 of 12) thought that ending the relationship was the only way to stop violence from recurring. (p. 440)

Exhibit 8.9 Clusters and Categories in a Grounded Theory Analysis

Clusters (endorsement)	Categories (endorsement)
1. The arrest incident is a hurdle or a test from god that I alone have to deal with, although the responsibility for the abuse was not all my own. (10)	1. If alcohol or drugs had not been in the picture, we wouldn't have come to blows: Substance use is thought to increase the rate of IPV (2)
	2. I don't want to get involved in conflict because I don't want to deal with its consequences (9)
	3. Joint responsibility in conflict depends on who did more fighting (8)
	4. How women cause IPV: Being treated as a child through nagging and being disrespected (5)
2. Passive avoidance and withdrawal from conflict is the best way to prevent aggression and to please god. (10)	1. DV thought to be "cured" by passively attending classes and learning anger management (6)
	2. Religious interventions have been vague or guilt producing, we need explicit advice and aren't getting it (9)
	3. Intimate partner violence can be stopped by cutting off relationships, but this can be a painful experience (5)
	4. Should resolve conflict to create harmony and avoid depression—but conflict may increase as a result (10)

Source: Levitt, H. M., Todd-Swanger, R., & Butler, J. B. (2008). Male perpetrators' perspectives on intimate partner violence, religion, and masculinity. *Sex Roles: A Journal of Research, 58*, 435–448. Reprinted with permission from Springer Science + Business Media, LLC.

"I don't deal with anybody so I don't have any conflicts. . . . It makes me feel bad because I be lonely sometime, but at the same time, it's the best thing going for me right now. I'm trying to rebuild me. I'm trying to put me on a foundation to where I can be a total leader. Like I teach my sons, 'Be leaders instead of followers.'" (p. 440)

Although this interviewee's choice to isolate himself was a strategy to avoid relational dependency and conflict, it left him without interpersonal support and it could be difficult for him to model healthy relationships for his children. (p. 440)

With procedures such as these, the grounded-theory approach develops general concepts from careful review of text or other qualitative materials and can then suggest plausible relationships between these concepts.

Computer-Assisted Qualitative Data Analysis

The analysis process can be enhanced in various ways by using a computer. Programs designed for qualitative data can speed up the analysis process, make it easier for researchers to experiment with different codes, test different hypotheses about relationships, and facilitate diagrams of emerging theories and preparation of research reports (Coffey & Atkinson, 1996; Richards & Richards, 1994). The steps involved in computer-assisted qualitative data analysis parallel those used traditionally to analyze such text as notes, documents, or interview transcripts: preparation, coding, analysis, and reporting. There are several of these programs available that analyze qualitative data, including HyperRESEARCH, ATLAS.ti, and QSR NVivo. In this section, we will focus on QSR NVivo to illustrate the basic steps of qualitative data analysis.

> **Computer-assisted qualitative data analysis:** Uses special computer software to assist qualitative analyses through creating, applying, and refining categories; tracing linkages between concepts; and making comparisons between cases and events

This section is not meant to be a "primer" on learning NVivo. We simply want to show you the things that are possible when examining qualitative data with the aid of a computer program. Importantly, a computer software program such as this does *not* think for you but simply helps you work through narrative or pictorial data. Text preparation using this software program begins with typing or scanning text in a word processor or directly into NVivo's text editor. NVivo will create or import a rich-text file, a Word file, or even videos or other narrative material. The collective term for research material in NVivo is *sources*, and data that are imported directly into NVivo are called *internals*. Data that cannot be imported but can still be used by creating summaries of their content are called *externals*.

Case Study: Narratives of Desistance From Crime and Substance Abuse

One of the textbook authors is currently involved in a research project examining the factors related to desistance for a sample of drug-involved offenders (Bachman, Kerrison, O'Connell, & Paternoster, 2013). One phase of the project involved intensive interviews with over 300 individuals originally released from prison in the early 1990s. Interviews lasted between 1.5 and 2 hours and were primarily open-ended and resembled conversations rather than formal questions and answers. The goal of the interviews was to uncover what Agnew (2006) refers to as *storylines* in understanding criminal offending. A storyline is a "temporally limited, interrelated set of events and conditions that increase the likelihood that individuals will engage in crime" (p. 121). As you can imagine, there were many hundreds of pages of transcripts!

Exhibit 8.10 displays the basic NVivo program with the internals in this screen shot listing the interview ID numbers from respondents.

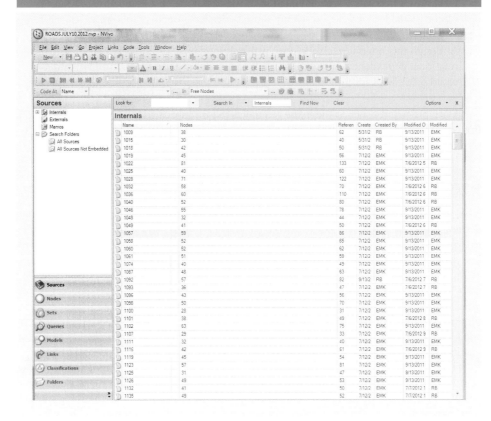

Source: **NVivo**

The first step for our coding team was to categorize particular text segments within these interviews. This is the foundation of much qualitative analysis. You can assign a code to any segment of text. You can make up codes as you go through a document and also assign codes that you have already developed to text segments. You can also have the program autocode text by identifying a word or phrase that should always receive the same code. NVivo also lets you examine the coded text *in context*, embedded in its place in the original document.

How did we begin? The coding process began with a list of initial categories developed from the existing literature on desistance, including such key indicators as turning points, indicators of agency and readiness for change, and the psychological indicators of discontent and fear. Before coding began, training sessions ensured that definitions of each category were understood, along with the coding guidelines. Next, all researchers coded the same transcripts and discussed their coding strategies in group meetings. In these team meetings, the decision to add new categories was adjudicated, and coding discrepancies were illuminated. The coding process continued with weekly marathon reliability meetings in which the same interview was coded by all four researchers. Not only did this increase intercoder reliability, but these meetings also were forums for the discussion of emerging categories and opportunities to clarify coding strategies for ambiguous narratives.

Codes in our scheme ranged from purely descriptive (e.g., narrative describing first arrest or first incarceration) to more interpretive concepts, such as reflections of whether respondents ever perceived themselves as addicts, when they wanted to get clean, and so on. All themes that emerged from the interview transcripts were coded; this resulted in over 20 main categories (e.g., discontent, turning points, incarceration) with over 100 subcategories used in the coding scheme.

After all interviews were coded, NVivo allowed us to perform analyses by viewing all interview narratives that had been coded within a particular domain. For example, some respondents who had gotten clean and stayed out of prison were motivated by fear; they often feared who they would become if they continued to use drugs or engage in crime. Indicators of this phenomenon included statements such as "I was afraid of dying alone in prison without my family" or "I knew that if I didn't get clean, I would never be able to get my family back and I would end up on the street alone." We coded all narratives reflecting these sentiments under the larger domain of *desistance* within a subdomain of *fear*. One example of such a narrative was from a 54-year-old white male:

> **Interviewer**: So I know people say all the time "I just got tired." You used the word *crushed*. What does that mean?
>
> **Respondent:** I'll be honest with you, more than tired, I got scared. The last time I went back I said I can't do this anymore. I told myself over and over again I can't do this anymore. I'm hurting myself, my loved ones, I was afraid that I'd be alone in life. And I didn't know whether I liked myself so I had to work hard to make myself better. . . . It scared the hell out of me. I finally realized I was my own worst enemy.

Another respondent, an African American woman, talked about almost dying from a heroin overdose:

> I overdosed and I was in a coma for 9 days. They told my mom that if I was gonna live, I was going to be a complete vegetable; there was a time to start making funeral arrangements. I had no brain waves or anything. It was a complete miracle. They had no explanation why I lived or why I woke up. . . . When I woke up, I had to gain back all my muscle strength; I couldn't even walk. . . . My mom had to take care of me. That's how I got clean. It scared the shit out of me.

The actual term for a code in NVivo is a *node*, and you can have large domain *nodes* (e.g., drugs) with small subgroup nodes that fall within the larger domain. For example, we had a large domain node labelled *drugs*, and within this domain, there were several subgroup nodes, including age at first use, *drug of choice*, *relapse*, and so on.

Once your data are coded, you can begin your analysis. In NVivo, you can examine all interview transcripts that were coded within particular nodes (coding categories). These analyses are called *queries*. For example, Exhibit 8.11 displays narratives that were coded under the node called *relapse*. When a query is performed on a single node, it will display the source number (in this case, internals/1009 stands for interview number 1009), along with the text that was coded within that particular category (node). As can be seen, respondent 1009 talked about getting out of prison the first time and ending up with the same "people, places, and things" that led to his drug use, which eventually led to relapse.

NVivo will also allow you to examine a domain separately based on other variables. For example, we could examine how fear was expressed differently for males and females in the sample—or by race or age. When a multiple query such as this is performed, called a *matrix coding query*, NVivo will first present a table displaying how many times each interview was coded within the grouping variable (usually a demographic indicator) and the category

Exhibit 8.11 Results of a Query in NVivo for "Relapse"

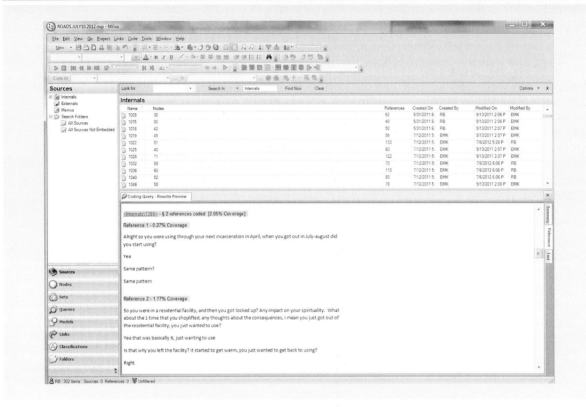

Source: NVivo

(nodes). Exhibit 8.12 displays one of these tables for a matrix coding query grouped by gender (1 = male, 2 = female) and by the nodes called *periods of abstinence* and *relapse.* You can see that within the interviews, 78 of the male interviews had narratives coded for *periods of abstinence,* along with 54 females, and so on. When you click directly on a cell within this table, the text narratives that were coded will appear so that narratives can be compared and contrasted.

As you can see, computer software programs such as NVivo are an extremely useful way to organize and analyze qualitative data. In fact, when there is a great deal of data to be analyzed, a computer software program is not only a luxury but a necessity!

ETHICAL ISSUES IN QUALITATIVE RESEARCH

Qualitative research can raise some complex ethical issues. No matter how hard the field researcher strives to study the social world naturally, leaving no traces, the very act of research itself imposes something unnatural on the situation. It is up to the researchers to identify and take responsibility for the consequences of their involvement. Several ethical issues arise: voluntary participation, subject well-being, identity disclosure, confidentiality, establishing boundaries, and maintaining the safety of researchers in the field.

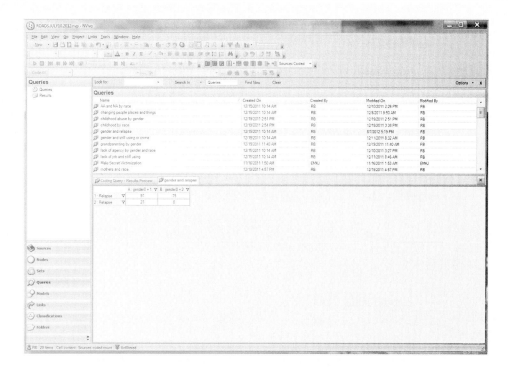

Source: NVivo

Voluntary Participation

Ensuring that subjects are participating in a study voluntarily is not often a problem with intensive interviewing and focus group research, but it is often a point of contention in participant observation studies. Few researchers or IRBs are willing to condone covert participation because it does not offer a way to ensure that participation by the subjects is voluntary. Even when the researcher's role is more open, interpreting the standard of voluntary participation still can be difficult. Most field research would be impossible if the participant observer were required to request permission of everyone having some contact, no matter how minimal, with a group or setting being observed. For instance, should the requirement of voluntary participation apply equally to every member of an organization being observed? What if the manager consents, the workers are ambivalent, and the union says no? Requiring everyone's consent would limit participant observation research only to settings without serious conflicts of interest.

As we noted in Chapter 3, the issue of voluntary participation is particularly important when interviewing/observing institutionalized populations, such as prisoners and children. For example, at what age can individuals validly give their voluntary consent to participate in a project? This requirement poses a problem for research that may be investigating issues that parents or guardians may not want uncovered, such as abuse or neglect. In other instances, alerting parents or guardians about the nature of the study may compromise the confidentiality of the participants.

Subject Well-Being

Before beginning a project, every field researcher should carefully consider how to avoid harm to subjects. It is not possible to avoid every theoretical possibility of harm or to be sure that any project will not cause adverse consequences to any individual. Direct harm to the reputations or feelings of particular individuals is what researchers must carefully avoid. They can do so, in part, by maintaining the confidentiality of research subjects. They must also avoid adversely affecting the course of events while engaged in a setting.

Jody Miller (2000) encountered a unique ethical dilemma while she was recruiting young women from a residential facility by paying them to refer other girls who were gang members to her research. These referral gratuities are common in snowball samples such as this. Unfortunately, in this case, one young woman decided to cash in on the deal by initiating new young women into her gang. Here, the ethical dilemma regarding "subject well-being" was that the initiation ceremony for this particular gang involved recruits to the gang being "beaten into the gang." Miller decided to stop conducting research at this location and ultimately lost several interviews. She states,

> It was a difficult decision to make because I had struggled for so long to locate gang girls in Columbus [Ohio]. Ultimately, I believe it was the right thing to do. My presence had stirred up trouble for the agency, and I had an ethical obligation to back away, regardless of the cost to me. (p. 26)

Identity Disclosure

How much disclosure about the study is necessary, and how hard should researchers try to make sure that their research purposes are understood? Less educated subjects may not readily comprehend what a researcher does or be able to weigh the possible consequences of the research for themselves. Should researchers inform subjects if the study's interests and foci change while it is in progress? Current ethical standards require informed consent of research subjects. Can this standard be met in any meaningful way if researchers do not fully disclose their identity in the first place? But isn't some degree of deception a natural part of social life (Punch, 1994)? Can a balance be struck between the disclosure of critical facts and a coherent research strategy?

Confidentiality

Field researchers normally use fictitious names for the people in their reports, but doing so does not always guarantee confidentiality for their research subjects. Individuals in the setting studied may be able to identify those whose actions are described and may thus become privy to some knowledge about their colleagues or neighbors that would otherwise have been kept from them. Researchers should therefore make every effort to expunge possible identifying material from published information and to alter unimportant aspects of a description when necessary to prevent identity disclosure. In any case, no field research project should begin if it is clear that some participants will suffer serious harm by being identified in project publications.

Confidentiality is particularly important if the research is uncovering deviant or illegal behavior. In Rios's (2011) research in Oakland, it was almost inevitable that he would witness illegal activity and/or be told about past criminal behavior. However, he told the boys he was not there to study their criminality. He stated,

> This could put them in danger if the records would ever end up with the police. Inevitably I would witness and hear a plethora of stories about crime. Later I would find myself reminding the young men not to provide me with details about the crimes that they had committed. (p. 170)

As we discussed in Chapter 3, researchers generally are not compelled to report past offending behavior to authorities unless information is reported that indicates a research subject intends to harm himself, herself, or others in the future.

Appropriate Boundaries

This is an ethical issue that cuts across several of the others, including identity disclosure, subject well-being, and voluntary participation. You probably are familiar with this issue in the context of guidelines for professional practice: Therapists are cautioned to maintain appropriate boundaries with patients; teachers must maintain appropriate boundaries with students. This is a special issue in qualitative research because it often involves loosening the boundary between the researcher and the research subject. Qualitative researchers may seek to build rapport with those they plan to interview by expressing an interest in their concerns and conveying empathy for their situation. Is this just faking friendship for the purpose of the research? Jean Duncombe and Julie Jessop (2002) posed the dilemma clearly in a book chapter titled "'Doing Rapport' and the Ethics of 'Faking Friendship.'"

> With deeper rapport, interviewees become more likely to explore their more intimate experiences and emotions. Yet they also become more likely to discover and disclose experiences and feelings which, upon reflection, they would have preferred to keep private from others . . . or not to acknowledge even to themselves. (p. 112)

Researcher Safety

Research in the field, whether researchers are studying gang life or anything else, should not begin until any potential risks to researcher safety have been evaluated. Qualitative methods may provide the only opportunity to learn about organized crime in Russian ports (Belousov et al., 2007), street crime in the Dominican Republic (Gill, 2004), or the other topics examined by studies in this chapter, but they should not be used if the risks to the researchers are unacceptably high. Safety needs to be considered at the time of designing the research, not as an afterthought upon arriving at the research site. As Hannah Gill learned in the Dominican Republic, such advance planning can require more investigation than just reading the local newspapers: "Due to the community's marginality, most crimes, including murders, were never reported in newspapers, making it impossible to have known the insecurity of the field site ahead of time" (p. 2).

Being realistic about evaluating risk does not mean simply accepting misleading assumptions about unfamiliar situations or communities. For example, reports of a widespread breakdown in law and order in New Orleans were broadcast repeatedly after Hurricane Katrina, but researchers found that most nontraditional behavior in that period was actually prosocial rather than antisocial (Rodríguez, Trainor, & Quarantelli, 2006):

> One group named itself the "Robin Hood Looters." The core of this group consisted of eleven friends who, after getting their own families out of the area, decided to remain at some high ground and, after the floodwaters rose, commandeered boats and started to rescue their neighbors. . . . For about two weeks they kept searching in the area. . . . They foraged for food and water from abandoned homes, and hence [acquired] their group name. Among the important norms that developed were that they were going to retrieve only survivors and not bodies and that group members would not carry weapons. The group also developed informal understandings with the police and the National Guard. (p. 91)

Reporters Engage in Observation in Honduran Gang Territory

This story highlights the research of *New York Times* journalists who spent a year roaming the streets of San Pedro Sula observing and documenting the ravages that gang violence had wrought in the city. Because of this gang violence, Honduras has one of the highest homicide rates in the world. Unlike many news articles, this exposé gives readers a very graphical account of what life is like in a city where gangs rule, and corrupt government and police officials do nothing to stop them.

Similar to the qualitative research methods explored in this chapter, the goal of this investigative journalism was to provide an intimate look into this world. For example, the article describes one shooting reporters witnessed like this: "Three sharp cracks rang out, followed by three more in quick succession. The thoroughfare emptied. Two old men ducked behind a corrugated fence. A taxi jerked onto a side street. A mother shoved her barefoot toddler indoors. The shooter, an MS-13 gunman in a tank top and black baseball cap, stood calmly on the corner in broad daylight, the only person left on the commercial strip. He stuck the gun in his waistband and watched the neighborhood shake in terror."

For Further Thought

1. How is this research different from research conducted by social scientists?

2. Imagine you are a researcher at your university. If you were going to embark on a research project of this nature, what steps must you take before entering the field?

Source: Ahmen, A. (2019, May 13). Inside gang territory in Honduras: Either they kill us or we kill them. *New York Times*. Retrieved from https://www.nytimes.com/interactive/2019/05/04/world/americas/honduras-gang-violence.html?action=click&module= RelatedLinks&pgtype=Article

WHO OWNS THE QUALITATIVE DATA?

Who owns my field notes and analyses: me, my organization, or my funders? And once my reports are written, who controls their diffusion? Of course, these concerns arise in any social-research project, but the intimate involvement of the qualitative researcher with participants in the setting studied makes conflicts of interest between different stakeholders much more difficult to resolve. Working through the issues as they arise is essential. Such approaches that allow participants access to conclusions in advance and the privilege to comment on them should be considered in relation to qualitative projects. The public availability of visual images on websites does not eliminate concerns about ownership. Copyright law in the United States, as well as in the United Kingdom and Australia, provides copyright to content on the Internet as soon as it is uploaded, but there are disagreements about the requirement of informed consent before reproducing images from publicly accessible sites (Tinkler, 2013).

It is prudent to develop understandings early in the project with all major participants and stakeholders that specify what actions will be taken to encourage appropriate use of project results and to respond to what is considered misuse of these results. Do I have an obligation to help my findings to be used appropriately? What if they are used harmfully or wrongly?

These ethical issues cannot be evaluated independently. The final decision to proceed must be made after weighing the relative benefits and risks to participants. Few qualitative research projects will be barred by consideration of these ethical issues, except for those involving covert participation. The more important concern for researchers is to identify the ethically troublesome aspects of their proposed research, resolve them before the project begins, and act on new ethical issues as they come up during the project.

Victor Rios, PhD, Associate Professor in the Department of Sociology, University of California, Santa Barbara

Source: Courtesy of Victor Rios

Dr. Rios grew up in Oakland, California, and, as a young man, joined a street gang because he thought it would provide him the protection that the police and other authority figures failed to provide. During an encounter with a rival gang when he was 15, his best friend was shot and killed. When he asked a police officer if the police were going to catch the kid who killed his friend, Rios was told, "What for? We want you to kill each other." It was perhaps this traumatic moment when he realized that the treatment he was enduring was directed not just at him but also at his entire community, and he wanted to know why. After a high school teacher reached out as a mentor and a police officer gave him another chance while he was on parole, he committed himself to pursuing an education.

After completing his BA while working full time, Rios was accepted into graduate school and completed his PhD at the University of San Francisco. The research from his award-winning book, *Punished*, is highlighted in this chapter. Dr. Rios's research addresses many questions, but it focuses primarily on how juvenile crime policies and criminalization affect the everyday lives of urban youth. In addition to conducting research, he has committed himself to making a difference in the world by participating in motivational programming for educational equity and resilience and by speaking about transforming the juvenile justice system. You can see him on TED Talks.

He wants both students and teachers to stop labeling others as "at risk" and begin seeing them "at promise"! He encourages students to never give up despite the roadblocks in their way.

CONCLUSION

Qualitative research allows the careful investigator to obtain a richer and more intimate view of the social world than can be achieved with more quantitative methods. It is not hard to understand why so many qualitative studies have become classics in the literature. The emphases in qualitative research on inductive reasoning and incremental understanding help to stimulate and inform other research approaches. Research charting the dimensions of previously unstudied social settings and intensive investigations of the subjective meanings that motivate individual action are particularly well served by the techniques of participant observation, intensive interviewing, and focus groups.

The very characteristics that make qualitative research techniques so appealing restrict their use to a limited set of research problems. It is not possible to draw representative samples for study using participant observation, and for this reason, the generalizability of any particular field study's results cannot really be known. Only the accumulation of findings from numerous qualitative studies permits confident generalization, but here again, the time and effort required to collect and analyze the data make it unlikely that many particular field research studies will be replicated.

Even if qualitative researchers made an effort to replicate key studies, attempting to compare findings would be hampered by their notion of developing and grounding explanations inductively in the observations made in a particular setting. Measurement reliability is thereby hindered, as are systematic tests for the validity of key indicators and formal tests for causal connections. Qualitative researchers do not necessarily seek to achieve the same generalizability standards as quantitative researchers; the agenda here is usually to tell *one* truth in the words of study participants.

In the final analysis, qualitative research involves a mode of thinking and investigating that is different from that used in experimental and survey research. Qualitative research is inductive; experiments and surveys tend to be conducted in a deductive, quantitative framework. Both approaches can help social scientists learn about the social world; the proficient researcher must be ready to use either. Qualitative data are often supplemented with many quantitative characteristics or activities, and quantitative data are often enriched with written comments and observations. The distinction between qualitative and quantitative research techniques is not always clear-cut, and increasingly, researchers are combining methods to advance knowledge.

KEY TERMS

Complete observation   192
Computer-assisted qualitative data analysis   215
Covert (complete) participation   194
Ethnography   188
Field notes   198
Field research   188
Focus group   206
Grounded theory   213
Intensive interviewing   202
Jottings   199
Netnography   189
Participant observation   191
Progressive focusing   208
Qualitative data analysis   208
Reactive effect   193
Reflexivity   212
Saturation point   203
Systematic observation   199
Tacit knowledge   212
Theoretical sampling   197

HIGHLIGHTS

- Qualitative researchers tend to develop ideas inductively, try to understand the social context and sequential nature of attitudes and actions, and explore the subjective meanings that participants attach to events. They rely primarily on participant observation, intensive interviewing, and, in recent years, focus groups.

- Participant observers may adopt one of several roles for a particular research project. Each role represents a different balance between observing and participating, which may or may not include public acknowledgment of the researcher's real identity. Many field researchers prefer a moderate role, participating as well as observing in a group but publicly acknowledging the researcher role.

- Field researchers must develop strategies for entering the field, developing and maintaining relations in the field, sampling, and recording and analyzing data.

- Recording and analyzing notes is a crucial step in field research. Detailed notes should be recorded and analyzed daily to refine methods and to develop concepts, indicators, and models of the social system observed.

- Intensive interviews involve open-ended questions and follow-up probes, with the content and order of specific questions varying from one interview to the next.

- Focus groups combine elements of participant observation and intensive interviewing. They can increase the validity of attitude measurement by revealing what people say when presenting their opinions in a group context.

- Case studies use qualitative techniques to provide a holistic picture of a setting or group.

- Grounded theory connotes a general explanation that develops in interaction with the data and is continually tested and refined as data collection continues.

- The main ethical issues in field research concern voluntary participation, subject well-being, identity disclosure, confidentiality, appropriate boundaries, and researcher safety.

EXERCISES

Discussing Research

1. Review the experiments and surveys described in previous chapters. Choose one, and propose a field research design that would focus on the same research question but with participant observation techniques in a local setting. Propose the role that you would

play in the setting, along the participant observation continuum, and explain why you would favor this role. Describe the stages of your field research study, including your plans for entering the field, developing and maintaining relationships, sampling, and recording and analyzing data. Then, discuss what you would expect your study to add to the findings resulting from the study described in the book.

2. Develop an interview guide that focuses on a research question addressed in one of the studies in this book. Using this guide, conduct an intensive interview with one person who is involved with the topic in some way. Take only brief notes during the interview, and then write as complete a record of the interviews as you can immediately afterward. Turn in an evaluation of your performance as an interviewer and note taker, together with your notes.

3. Find the qualitative research lesson in the interactive exercises on the Student Study Site. Answer the questions in this lesson in order to review the types of ethical issues that can arise in the course of participant observation research.

4. Read about focus groups in one of the references cited in this chapter, and then devise a plan for using a focus group to explore and explain student perspectives about crime on campus. How would you recruit students for the group? What types of students would you try to include? How would you introduce the topic and the method to the group? What questions would you ask? What problems would you anticipate (e.g., discord between focus group members or digressions from the chosen topic)? How would you respond to these problems?

Finding Research on the Web

1. Go to the Annual Review of Sociology's website (www .annualreviews.org/journal/soc). Search for articles that use field research as the primary method of gathering data on gangs or delinquency. Find at least three articles, and report on the specific method of field research used in each.

2. Search the Web for information on focus groups (previous, upcoming, or ongoing) involving victims, offenders, fear of crime, crime prevention, or another criminological topic. List the websites you find, and write a paragraph about the purpose of each focus group and the sample involved. How might these focus groups be used to influence public policy?

3. Go to the Social Science Information Gateway (SOSIG) (www.ariadne.ac.uk/issue2/sosig). Conduct a search for "qualitative methods," and then choose three or four interesting sites to find out more about field research—either professional organizations of field researchers or journals that publish their work. Explore the sites to find out what information they provide regarding field research, what kinds of projects are being done that involve field research, and the purposes that specific field research methods are being used for.

4. The *Qualitative Report* is an online journal about qualitative research. Inspect the table of contents (www.nova.edu/ssss/QR/index.html) for a recent issue. Read one of the articles, and write a brief article review.

Critiquing Research

1. Read and summarize one of the qualitative studies discussed in this chapter or another classic study recommended by your instructor. Review and critique the study using the article review questions presented in Chapter 1. What questions are answered by the study? What questions are raised for further investigation?

2. Read the complete text of one of the qualitative studies presented in this chapter, and evaluate its conclusions for authenticity using the criteria in this chapter. If validity and authenticity are in any way debatable, what suggestions would you offer to improve the researcher's methodology?

3. Review one of the articles on the book's Student Study Site that used qualitative methods. Describe the data that were collected and identify the steps used in the analysis. What type of qualitative data analysis was this? If it is not one of the methods presented in this chapter, describe its similarities to and differences from one of these methods. How confident are you in the conclusions, given the methods of analysis used?

Making Research Ethical

1. Alice Goffman's book, *On the Run: Fugitive Life in an American City*, sparked a great deal of controversy regarding her ethnographic methods. A Slate article (slate.com/news-and-politics/2015/06/alice-goffmans-on-the-run-is-the-sociologist-to-blame-for-the-inconsistencies-in-her-book.html) discusses the controversies in detail and also provides links to other articles about the issue. What are the ethical issues that have emerged regarding Goffman's research? Is it possible to do ethnographic research that avoids these ethical issues? Why, or why not?

2. Covert participation may be the only way for researchers to observe the inner workings of some criminal or other deviant groups, but this strategy is likely to result in the researcher witnessing and perhaps being asked to participate in illegal acts. Do you think that covert participation is ever ethical? If so, under what conditions? Can the standards of *no harm to subjects*, *identity disclosure*, and *voluntary participation* be maintained in covert research? In what circumstances would researcher safety advance to a priority status?

3. A *New York Times* reporter (Wines, 2006) talked about the dilemma many reporters have: whether or not to provide monetary or other compensation, such as food or medical supplies, to people they interview for a story. In journalism, paying for information is a "cardinal sin" because journalists are indoctrinated with the notion that they are observers. They are trained to report on situations but not to influence a situation. This is what many scholars believe a researcher's role should be. Nevertheless, as we learned in this chapter, it is common in research to offer small gratuities for information and interviews. However, does paying for information unduly influence the truthfulness of the information being sought? What are your thoughts on paying for information? What if you were investigating the problems faced by families living below the poverty level, and during an interview, you noticed that the family refrigerator and cupboards were empty and the baby was crying from hunger? What is the ethical reaction? If you believe the most ethical response would be to provide food or money for food, is it fair that there is another family next door in the same condition who did not happen to be on your interview list? How should gratuities be handled?

4. Recall our discussion of social norms and interpersonal comfort levels. Should any requirements be imposed on researchers who seek to study other cultures to ensure that procedures are appropriate and interpretations are culturally sensitive? What practices would you suggest for cross-cultural researchers to ensure that ethical guidelines are followed? (Consider the wording of consent forms and the procedures for gaining voluntary cooperation.)

Developing a Research Proposal

Add a qualitative component to your proposed study. You can choose to do this with a participant observation project or intensive interviewing. Choose the method that seems most likely to help answer the research question for the overall survey project.

1. For a participant observation component, propose an observational plan that would complement the overall survey project. Present in your proposal the following information about your plan:

   a. Choose a site, and justify its selection in terms of its likely value for the research.

   b. Choose a role along the participation–observation continuum, and justify your choice.

   c. Describe access procedures, and note any likely problems.

   d. Discuss how you will develop and maintain relations in the site.

   e. Review any sampling issues.

   f. Present an overview of the way in which you will analyze the data you collect.

2. For an intensive interview component, propose a focus for the intensive interviews that you believe will add the most to findings from the survey project. Present in your proposal the following information about your plan:

   a. Present and justify a method for selecting individuals to interview.

   b. Write out three introductory biographical questions and five general overview questions for your interview schedule.

   c. List at least six different probes you may use.

   d. Present and justify at least two follow-up questions for one of your grand-tour questions.

   e. Explain what you expect this intensive-interview component to add to your overall survey project.

3. Which qualitative data analysis alternative is most appropriate for the qualitative data you proposed to collect for your project? Using the approach, develop a strategy for using the techniques of qualitative data analysis to analyze your textual data.

Performing Data Analysis in SPSS or Excel

Data for Exercise	
Dataset	**Description**
Youth.sav	These data are from a random sample of students from schools in a southern state. While not representative of the United States, these data cover a variety of important delinquent behaviors and peer influences.

Variables for Exercise	
Variable Name	Description
V77	A five-category ordinal measure asking a respondent how wrong they think their friends think it is to steal. Responses range from 1 (always wrong) to 5 (never wrong)
V79	A five-category ordinal measure asking a respondent how wrong they think their friends think it is to drink. Responses are the same as "v77"
V109	A five-category ordinal measure asking the respondent how much of a problem they thought it would be if they were taken to court for underage drinking
D1	A binary variable based on the number of delinquent acts a respondent reported. A "0" indicates that the respondent reported one or fewer acts, while "1" indicates two or more

1. Thinking inductively, write several research questions and hypotheses about how you think these variables will be related to one another.

   a. Friends' attitudes about drinking and stealing

   b. Respondent views on the consequences of delinquency

   c. If the individual has engaged in delinquency

   Consider drawing a diagram to help to visualize the relationships you expect to find, paying close attention to the causal ordering you might expect. Recall that it is conceptually very possible for causes and effects to reinforce one another over time, such as the case of a vicious circle!

   d. Is this set of research questions and hypotheses better answered by quantitative or qualitative methods? Why?

2. Now, look at cross-tabulations between the variables "v77," "v79," "v109," and "d1." That's a lot of crosstabs, but that is partly the point! What sort of relationships do you find? What hypotheses are and are not supported?

   a. Is this analysis able to establish causal ordering?

   b. Is there the possibility of spuriousness?

   c. Is it reasonable to generalize from this analysis to other schools?

   d. What remains unanswered or assumed?

   e. What strengths and disadvantages might this study have compared with a qualitative study?

3. Consider your results and research question in Question 2 and ask yourself the next logical question—why are we getting these results? We can guess, but we need a study to answer that question. Take a few minutes to write about how you would approach your research questions using the following:

   a. interviews

   b. participant observation

   c. focus groups

Also consider the strengths and limitations of each approach—think about complications concerning sampling, ethics, data reliability, and time commitment.

STUDENT STUDY SITE

$SAGE edge™

9

ANALYZING CONTENT AND POLICE DATA

Social-Network Analysis, Crime Mapping, Big Data, and Content Analysis

Learning Objectives

1. Explain how secondary data analysis is different from the methods we have already examined in this book.

2. Understand how social-network analysis and crime mapping can be used for intelligence-led policing as well as basic research.

3. Understand how computer technology has ushered in our ability to analyze Big Data and the effects this has had on criminal justice–related research.

4. Describe the steps necessary when performing a content analysis.

> There are few classes that will provide you with skills that will open doors in your career the way a research methods class will. I currently work for the Department of Services for Children, Youth, and their Families (DSCYF), and my current role includes managing projects and organizing data for state services programs. I would not have been able to move into this position without the skills I learned in my research methods class.
>
> **Danielle G., Student**

WHAT DO WE HAVE IN MIND?

When researchers and policy makers want to understand how crime rates have fluctuated across time or how they compare across different locations (e.g., cities, states, countries), they generally rely on existing data sources. It would be virtually impossible for anyone to collect these types of data on their own. The research methods we have examined so far in this text have relied on researchers collecting the data or information themselves. Increasingly, however, those interested in many criminological research questions, not just those related to patterns and trends in crime, are relying on data previously collected by other investigators (Riedel, 2000). As we noted in Chapter 1, this is referred to as secondary data analysis. Secondary data analysis is simply the act of compiling or analyzing data that were originally collected by someone else at another time (Riedel, 2000). Thus, if a researcher goes to a police department and personally compiles information from police reports to examine a research question, she is still engaging in secondary data analysis because the police records were originally collected prior to her own research.

In this chapter, we will first introduce you to the concept of secondary data analysis. We next discuss social-network analysis and examine how this technique has also been applied to police practice. This is followed by other investigative research techniques, including crime mapping and analyzing Big Data. The chapter ends with a discussion of content analysis, a technique used to analyze all types of content, including newspapers and other media.

> **Secondary data analysis:** Analysis of data collected by someone other than the researcher or the researcher's assistant

ANALYZING SECONDARY DATA

In general, there are four major types of secondary data: surveys, official statistics, official records, and other historical documents. Although a dataset can be obtained by an agreement between two or more researchers, many researchers obtain data through the University of Michigan's Inter-university Consortium for Political and Social Research (ICPSR) (www .icpsr.umich.edu). Data stored at ICPSR primarily include surveys, official records, and official statistics. ICPSR stores data and information for nearly 5,000 sources and studies, including those conducted independently and those conducted by the U.S. government. Riedel (2000) has documented the majority of datasets that are available from ICPSR and that are appropriate for crime research, including the following:

Census Enumerations: Historical and Contemporary Population Characteristics. The most well-known datasets within this category are the surveys conducted every decade by the U.S. Census Bureau. Linking information from this dataset (e.g., neighborhood characteristics, including such things as poverty and residential mobility) to crime data at the same level (e.g., census block, county) has provided researchers with a rich source of data to test theories of crime.

The National Archive of Criminal Justice Data (NACJD). The Bureau of Justice Statistics and National Institute of Justice cosponsored NACJD, which provides more than 600 criminal justice data collections to the public. A sample of these datasets includes the following:

- Capital Punishment in the United States
- Expenditure and Employment Data for the Criminal Justice System
- Gang Involvement in Rock Cocaine Trafficking in Los Angeles, 1984–1985
- Criminal Careers and Crime Control in Massachusetts
- Longitudinal Research Design, Phase I, 1940–1965
- Changing Patterns of Drug Use and Criminality Among Crack Cocaine Users in New York City: Criminal Histories and CJ Processing, 1983–1984, 1986
- The National Crime Victimization Survey, ongoing
- National Jail Census
- National Judicial Reporting Program
- National Survey of Jails
- Survey of Adults on Probation
- Survey of Inmates of Federal Correctional Facilities

- Survey of Inmates of Local Jails

- Survey of Inmates of State Correctional Facilities

- Federal Bureau of Investigation (FBI) Uniform Crime Reporting (UCR) Program data, including the Supplementary Homicide Reports (SHR)

Social Indicators and Behavior. There is a series of annual surveys under this heading, including the General Social Survey, which has been conducted annually by the National Opinion Research Center since 1972. In addition, Monitoring the Future: A Continuing Study of the Lifestyles and Values of Youth is a survey of a nationally representative sample of high school seniors that asks them for many things, including self-reports of drug and alcohol use and their attitudes toward a number of issues.

Qualitative Data Sources. Far fewer qualitative datasets are available for secondary analysis, but the number is growing. European countries, particularly England, have been in the forefront of efforts to promote archiving of qualitative data. The United Kingdom's Economic and Social Research Council established the Qualitative Data Archiving Resource Center at the University of Essex in 1994 (Heaton, 2008). Now part of the Economic and Social Data Service, UK Data Service QualiBank (2014) provides access to data from over 8,000 datasets. After registering at the UK Data Service site, interview transcripts and other materials from many qualitative studies can be browsed or searched directly online, but access to many studies is restricted to users in the United Kingdom or according to other criteria.

In the United States, the ICPSR collection includes an expanding number of studies containing at least some qualitative data or measures coded from qualitative data. Studies range from transcriptions of original handwritten and published materials relating to infant care and child care from the beginning of the 20th century to World War II (LaRossa, 1995) to transcripts of open-ended interviews with high school students involved in violent incidents (Lockwood, 1996). Harvard University's Institute for Quantitative Social Science has archived more than 400 studies that contain at least some qualitative data.

SOCIAL-NETWORK ANALYSIS

Social-network analysis (SNA): An approach to analysis and a set of methodological techniques that help researchers describe and explore relationships that both individuals and groups have with each other

Social networks: Types of relationships that can include many different forms, such as face to face, online and digital, economic transactions, interaction with a criminal justice agency, etc.

It is virtually impossible today not to be part of social networks. Everyone you interact with, including those in the virtual as well as in the real world, are part of your social network. We inherently think about the world in terms of these networks, including such networks as familial and friendship networks, other students in your major in college, people who work out at the same time as you at the gym, and the many "friends" you may not actually know in real life on platforms such as Facebook or those who similarly liked something on Twitter. The method of **social-network analysis (SNA)** has increasingly been used since the Internet and these social-media platforms emerged. There are entire textbooks devoted to SNA, so the goal here is simply to introduce you to the basics, along with a few case studies that highlight their applicability in the field. SNA is not one type of method but is an approach to analysis and a set of methodological techniques that help researchers describe and explore relationships that both individuals and groups have with each other (Scott, 2017).

Social networks are types of relationships that can include many different forms, such as face-to-face and online interactions, digital economic transactions, interaction with a criminal justice agency, geopolitical relations among nation states, and so on. As you can see, there are numerous types of networks available for analysis. The most important component of any network is that it is relational. That is an important assumption. So far in this book, we have talked about variables that measure attributes of the units of analysis, such as the behavior of people, the crime rates of cities, and so on. Relational data measure the contacts, connections, attachments, and ties that relate one unit to the next (Scott, 2017). As a result, these relational data are not properties of any particular unit (e.g., individual, group, city) but are "relational systems" of units that are created by connecting pairs of interacting units. Importantly, then, it is the technique used to describe and examine relational data that is the key to SNA. Many of the traditional methods that we have already discussed in this book can also be used to collect relational data. For example, surveys, interviews, participant observation, and secondary data can all be used to generate relational data for SNA, as we will see in the case studies that follow.

Although literally thousands of articles examined aspects of social structure in the early 20th century, one of the first graphical applications of social networks was created by Jacob Moreno to examine friendship choices. In his classic book, *Who Shall Survive?* Moreno (1953) describes his definition of sociometry as being in accordance with its etymology from Latin and Greek, "but with the emphasis . . . on the second half of the term, 'metrum,' meaning measure, but also on the first half, 'socius' meaning companion" (p. 51). Instead of focusing exclusively on the individual or exclusively on an aggregate entity, Moreno believed that the relationship between individuals within a group also must be examined. Using a sociometric test, which required individuals to choose their associates from a group in which they were a member, *attractions* and *repulsions* were determined. For example, if your instructor wanted to understand the social structure of the class you are in right now, she or he might ask each student to hypothetically choose among the students whom they wanted to have sit next to them (attraction) and whom they would like to have moved to another class (repulsion). Responses received from each individual in the group could then be graphed in a sociogram, which is a way of representing the social configurations, with individuals (or some other unit) represented by points and their social relationships to one another depicted by lines (Moreno, 1953). The formal terminology that describes these graphs, as well as the units and relationships therein, are called several things depending on the discipline. The social sciences generally call the basic units in a graph nodes (sometimes called *actors* or *vertices*), and nodes are connected by relations (sometimes called *ties*, *links*, *arcs*, or *edges*). As noted above, relationship data like these can be collected from many places, like official records, Facebook friends, and so on (Yang, Keller, & Zheng 2017).

SNA usually consists of at least two datasets. The first is called the nodelist, where all of the units of observation are stored. The second defines the relations between these units. One of the most common types of relations data is called an adjacency matrix (sometimes called *network matrix*), in which the nodes constitute both the rows and the columns, and the cells specify if and what kind of relationship exists between the nodes at the intersection of each row and column. We are going to stick with the simplest case of a binary network, which only distinguishes whether a relation does or does not exist between a pair of nodes (Yang et al., 2017). An example of a network graph and the nodelist and adjacency matrix upon which it is based is presented in Exhibit 9.1. As you can imagine, nodes and relations can be much more complicated than this simple example, and special software is required to mathematically describe the numerous networks that emerge from such data. A discussion of these issues is beyond the scope of this text, but we want to provide you with some exciting case studies of how SNA is being used in research related to criminology and criminal justice.

Case Study: Networks of Terrorist Cells

On September 11, 2001, nineteen members of the Islamic extremist group al-Qaeda hijacked four airplanes and carried out suicide crashes into four places in the United States The targets included the north and south towers of the World Trade Center, the Pentagon, and

Relational data: Measures the contacts, connections, attachments, and ties that relate one unit to the next

Sociogram: A graph representing the social configurations, with individuals (or some other unit) represented by points and their social relationships to one another depicted by lines

Nodes: The basic units (e.g., people) in a network graph, sometimes called *actors* or *vertices*

Relations: The connections in a network graph, sometimes called *ties*, *links*, *arcs*, or *edges*

Nodelist: The dataset containing the nodes (units of observation) for a social-network analysis

Adjacency matrix: A dataset containing information about the relations between the units of observation, sometimes called a *network matrix*

Binary network: Distinguishes whether a relationship does or does not exist between nodes

Exhibit 9.1 Example of a Network Graph With Its Nodelist and Adjacency Matrix

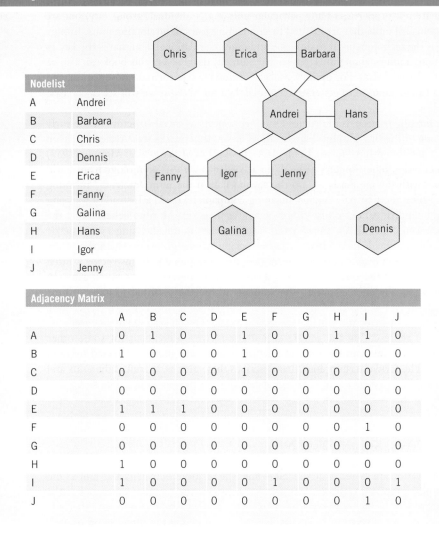

Nodelist

A	Andrei
B	Barbara
C	Chris
D	Dennis
E	Erica
F	Fanny
G	Galina
H	Hans
I	Igor
J	Jenny

Adjacency Matrix

	A	B	C	D	E	F	G	H	I	J
A	0	1	0	0	1	0	0	1	1	0
B	1	0	0	0	1	0	0	0	0	0
C	0	0	0	0	1	0	0	0	0	0
D	0	0	0	0	0	0	0	0	0	0
E	1	1	1	0	0	0	0	0	0	0
F	0	0	0	0	0	0	0	0	1	0
G	0	0	0	0	0	0	0	0	0	0
H	1	0	0	0	0	0	0	0	0	0
I	1	0	0	0	0	1	0	0	0	1
J	0	0	0	0	0	0	0	0	1	0

Source: Adapted from Yang, Keller, and Zheng, 2017, Figure 1.4, p. 9.

Washington, DC. (In the last instance, the passengers fought the hijackers, preventing the plane from hitting its target and causing it to crash into an empty field in Pennsylvania instead.) Almost 3,000 people were killed, including all of the passengers on the planes, along with the 19 hijackers, and many hundreds of people in the targeted buildings, which included rescuers. About a month before the 9/11 attack, Zacarias Moussaoui, a French citizen of Moroccan descent, sometimes referred to as the 20th hijacker, was arrested after he raised suspicion at a flight school in Oklahoma by requesting information on flying a 747. Moussaoui was eventually indicted and found guilty in 2006 of six charges, including conspiracy to commit acts of terrorism. Information from his indictment (*United States of America v. Zacarias Moussaoui*, 2001), along with other information uncovered by the *New York Times* and the *Washington Post*, has been used to conduct social-network analyses of the terrorist cell that carried out 9/11. One of the first attempts was made by Valdis Krebs (2002), who created one of the first network graphs of the terrorist network. An adapted snippet of his graph is displayed in Exhibit 9.2.

Exhibit 9.2   Partial Network Graph of the 9/11 Terrorist Attackers

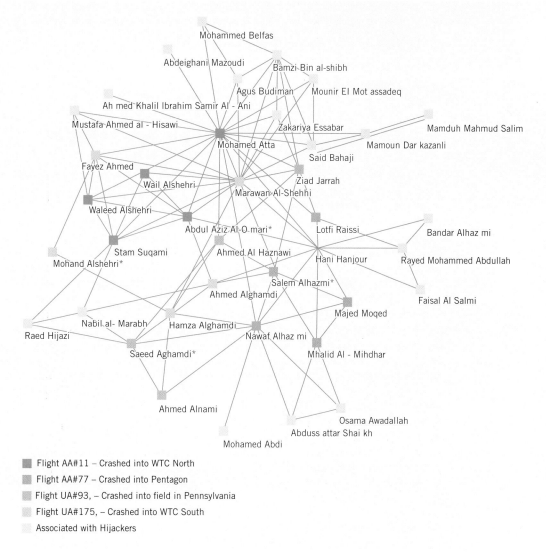

Flight AA#11 – Crashed into WTC North
Flight AA#77 – Crashed into Pentagon
Flight UA#93, – Crashed into field in Pennsylvania
Flight UA#175, – Crashed into WTC South
Associated with Hijackers

Source: Adapted from Krebs, 2002, Figure 4, p. 50.

Without going into the advanced statistical analysis performed by Krebs to describe the strength of the relations for the terrorists, many conclusions can be drawn from this graph, including the meticulousness with which the hijackers kept their identities unknown even from each other. Krebs (2002) explains, "Many pairs of team members were beyond the horizon of observability. . . . Keeping cell members distant from each other, and from other cells, minimizes damage to the network if a cell member is captured or otherwise compromised" (p. 46). Krebs's graph also confirms the fact that Mohamed Atta was the likely leader of the cell as he has the most relations with other nodes.

Krebs's analysis shows the benefits of SNA when putting together a case for prosecution. It also highlights the inherent difficulty of using SNA for preventing or uncovering secret illegal networks. Krebs concludes,

The best solution for network disruption may be to discover possible suspects and then, via snowball sampling, map their ego networks—see whom else they lead to, and where they overlap. To find these suspects it appears that the best method is for diverse intelligence agencies to aggregate their information—their individual pieces to the puzzle—into a larger emergent map. (p. 51)

While using SNA for investigative purposes has its challenges, our next case study demonstrates the merits of doing so.

Case Study: Finding a Serial Killer

The Green River serial killer (GRK) killed his first victim, 16-year-old Wendy Coffield, in Kings County, Washington. Her body was found in July of 1982 in the Green River, which became the name given to the then-unidentified killer. After 48 other murders, Gary Leon Ridgway was finally charged as the serial killer in September 2001, despite the fact that he was on the list of suspects much earlier. Media interest of the cases generated thousands of leads, and these leads compounded with every new victim, which resulted in a huge amount of data to examine. However, large amounts of data are not the only hindrance to solving a case. Like all of us, police detectives can have cognitive biases (see Chapter 1 for a list of common biases), and when combined with an overabundance of information coming from the public, both reliable and unreliable, investigations can go awry.

In a recent paper, Bichler, Lim, and Larin (2017) have demonstrated how SNA can be used to aid in connecting the pieces of a growing body of evidence. Bichler and her colleagues collected data about the Green River murders from multiple sources, including newspaper reports, books, and court transcripts of Ridgway's trial. They then performed a SNA analysis of the evidence over time to determine if SNA could have prevented investigators from keeping another man on top of their suspect list instead of Gary Ridgway. They state, "We argue that by identifying which actors shift in structural position during the investigation, it may be possible to reduce the damaging effects of tunnel vision, emphasis on specific evidence, and intuition" (p. 141). The goal of their analysis was to find the connections between the victims and the suspects, along with the places they frequented. Because these murders likely involved strangers, Bichler et al. (2017) explain that other sources of information must be added to find clusters. They state,

> People sharing social space will emerge when we link witnesses, friends, and associates to the places they frequent, but finding individuals positioned *between* different clusters will be even more informative. . . . Who else but the suspect in a crime series would link the victims from different social spaces. (p. 141)

The categories of the data Bichler and her colleagues examined included victims, suspects, investigatory involvement (e.g., witnesses, body finders), family and associates, body disposal sites, last-seen locations, and other investigative material. Because there were different levels of geographical aggregation (e.g., a red-light district, a specific hotel), all data points were placed within a census track. Without going into the statistical details of the study, they were particularly interested in a "middleman" who connected others not directly linked to each other. This is statistically measured with a **betweenness centrality score**. The researchers also created multiple graphs using data over time, beginning with graphs using data that were available from the beginning of the investigation and creating more graphs until the data were exhausted (about 30 months into the investigation). Exhibit 9.3 A displays a graph using data from the first six months of the investigation while Exhibit 9.3 B depicts the investigation at 18 months,

Betweenness centrality score: A statistic that measures the extent to which nodes connect to other nodes that are not directly linked to each other in SNA

(A)

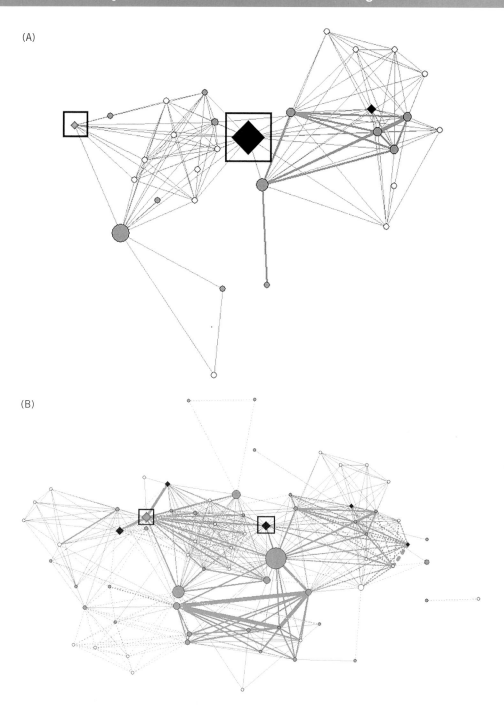

(B)

Source: Adapted from Bichler, Lim, and Larin (2017), Table 3, p. 146.

after which there was not much new data to incorporate. Line thickness indicates the number of shared places between pairs, diamonds depict suspects, gray circles indicate victims, and other circles represent other case nodes (e.g., witnesses, body disposal sites).

The size of the shapes in the graphs (e.g., circles, diamonds) indicate the degree of betweenness centrality. The highest scoring individual at the beginning of the investigation was Melvyn Foster, who is represented by the square containing the large diamond in Exhibit 9.3A. By 18 months, however, Gary Leon Ridgway, becomes more noticeable (depicted by the shaded triangle in the second box). Unfortunately, the task force did not focus on Ridgway but continued to focus exclusively on Foster. Bichler and her colleagues concluded,

> It is hard to know in hindsight if these results would sway the organization momentum that led investigators to focus on Foster to the exclusion of Ridgway. . . . it might have prevented the working hypothesis from solidifying so early on in the investigation by encouraging members of the Green River Killer Task Force to pay greater attention to Gary Leon Ridgway.

While this research cannot predict what would have happened had SNA been available then, it certainly highlights the utility of SNA for investigative purposes today. We move on next to a research technique that is frequently being used for predictive purposes in law enforcement.

CRIME MAPPING

Many of us have adopted the image of crime mapping that involves a police precinct wall with pushpins stuck all over it identifying the location of crime incidents. Shows like *The Wire*, *The District*, and episodes of *CSI* have also presented the drama behind the use of crime mapping in generating crime counts within various police beats. Crime mapping for intelligence-led policing has been increasing in the past few decades, but **crime mapping** for research purposes has a very long history; it is generally used to identify the spatial distribution of crime along with the social indicators such as poverty and social disorganization that are similarly distributed across areas (e.g., neighborhood, census tract). Rachel Boba (2009) defines crime mapping as "the process of using a geographic information system to conduct special analysis of crime problems and other police-related issues" (p. 7). She also describes the three main functions of crime mapping:

1. It provides visual and statistical analyses of the spatial nature of crime and other events.

2. It allows the linkage of crime data to other data sources, such as census information on poverty or school information, which allows relationships among variables to be established.

3. It provides maps to visually communicate analysis results.

Although applied crime mapping like this has been used for over 100 years to assist the police in criminal apprehension and crime prevention, the advent of computing technology has enabled crime mapping to become an advanced form of statistical data analysis. The **geographic information system (GIS)** is the software tool that has made crime mapping increasingly available to researchers since the 1990s.

Today, crime mapping is being used by the majority of urban law enforcement agencies to identify crime hot spots (Caplan & Kennedy, 2015). Hot spots are geospatial locations

Crime mapping: Geographical mapping strategies used to visualize a number of things, including location, distance, and patterns of crime and their correlates.

Geographic information system (GIS): The software tool that has made crime mapping increasingly available to researchers since the 1990s.

within jurisdictions where crimes are more likely to occur compared with other areas. Being able to understand where crime is more likely to occur helps agencies deploy resources more effectively, especially for crime prevention purposes. These hot spots can be specific addresses, blocks, or even clusters of blocks (Eck, Chainey, Cameron, Leitner, & Wilson, 2005). Of course, crime-mapping data with insight from criminological theory is the ideal. As Eck and his colleagues explain, "Crime theories are critical for useful crime mapping because they aid interpretation of data and provide guidance as to what actions are most appropriate" (Eck et al., 2005, p. 3). This is important because the ability to understand why crimes are occurring has a great deal to do with underlying factors related to the environment in which they occur. Kennedy, Caplan, and Piza (2012) provide a very illuminating example:

> A sole analytical focus on crime hotspots is like observing that children frequently play at the same place every day and then calling that place a hotspot for children playing, but without acknowledging the presence of swings, slides, and open fields—features of the place (i.e., suggestive of a playground) that attract children there instead of other locations absent such entertaining features. (Kennedy et al., 2012, pp. 245–246)

Through various symbols, maps can communicate a great deal of information. Exhibit 9.4, which was published by the National Institute of Justice, displays some common symbols used

Exhibit 9.4   Symbols Used in Crime Maps

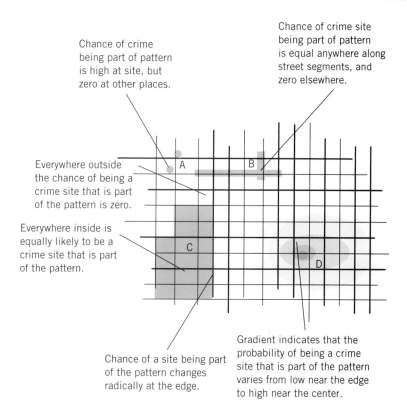

Source: Eck et al. 2005, Exhibit 3.

by crime analysts (Eck et al. 2005). As the map shows, dots (A) point to specific places where crime is likely to occur, a crime site (B and C) indicates where crime is equally likely to occur within a particular site, and a crime gradient (D) indicates that the probability of crime is most likely inside the site and decreases as you move toward the edge of the site.

Case Study: Predicting Break and Entries (BNEs)

Intelligence-led policing: Using data, analysis, and criminal theory to guide police allocation and decision making

Contemporary researchers and law enforcement officials interested in issues related to crime and criminology have access to more sophisticated computer technology that allows for the creation of more enhanced crime maps. In fact, the easy availability of mapping tools, including mobile GIS technology, is providing many more opportunities for intelligence-led policing, which includes using "data, analysis, and criminal theory . . . to guide police allocation and decision making" (Fitterer, Nelson, & Nathoo, 2015, p. 121). The purpose of crime maps, however, remains the same: to illuminate the relationship between categories of crime and corresponding characteristics such as poverty and disorganization across given locations.

Break and entries (BNEs) are one type of crime that are patterned; in fact, one of the things we know about them is that the probability of a repeat BNE increases for either the original BNE site and/or for homes near it for several weeks after the original BNE. To determine the effectiveness of mapping in predicting residential and commercial BNEs, Jessica Fitterer and her colleagues (Fitterer et al., 2015) used data from the Vancouver police districts (VPD), along with data on other characteristics of the districts, including variables such as population density, property values, dominant housing types, and street light density. Using BNE data by location, hour, day, month, and year from 2001 to 2012, the researchers then created a map of the Vancouver area composed of 200 m by 200 m grids, placing the data within each grid. For example, Exhibit 9.5 displays the map depicting residential BNE hot spots for the time period. The goal of their research, however, was not just to describe the BNE data but to use data from the early time period to predict later occurrences of BNEs. For example, Fitterer and her colleagues (2015) found that the probability of a repeat BNE occurring up to 850 m from the originating BNE increased 53% for the next 24 hours after the first event. While there was still an increase in the likelihood of near BNEs over time, this increased risk decreased to 24% after a week of the original BNE. Importantly, the proportion of historical crime did significantly predict future crime. The authors concluded,

> We found [that] both residential and commercial crimes had a strong spatial clustering over short time periods suggesting a near-repeat offense dynamic . . . [indicating] that perpetrators prefer to reoffend where they have local knowledge about residents' routine activities, possessions, and can confirm successful property entry. (p. 130)

Big Data: A very large dataset (e.g., contains thousands of cases), accessible in computer-readable form, that is used to reveal patterns, trends, and associations between variables with new computer technology.

BIG DATA

When do secondary data become what is now referred to as *Big Data*? Big Data is a somewhat vague term that has been used to describe large and rapidly changing datasets and the analytic techniques used to extract information from them. It generally refers to data involving an entirely different order of magnitude than what we are used to thinking about as large datasets. For our purposes, Big Data is simply defined as a very large dataset (e.g., contains thousands of cases), accessible in a computer-readable form, that is used to reveal patterns, trends,

Exhibit 9.5   Vancouver's 2001–2011 Break-and-Enter Hot-Spot Map for Residential Break-Ins

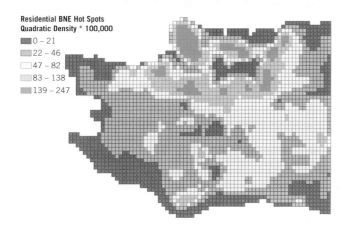

Residential BNE Hot Spots
Quadratic Density * 100,000
- 0 – 21
- 22 – 46
- 47 – 82
- 83 – 138
- 139 – 247

Source: Adapted from Fitterer et al. (2015), Figure 9, page 129.

RESEARCH IN THE NEWS

Predictive Policing in Los Angeles

This article highlights the use of predictive-policing techniques used by the Los Angeles Police Department, including such tools as LASER, which is a data analysis tool that identifies crime hot spots. While the article highlights that using such data can help protect the public when used appropriately, it also reports on an investigation by California's inspector general. While computer algorithms are supposed to eliminate biases by individual police offers, the inspector general's report found that in some cases, these programs actually enhanced bias. The newspaper article notes, "We have data that show police arrest African Americans and Latinos more often than whites who have committed the same crimes, in part because their neighborhoods are more heavily patrolled. . . . The cycle of inequity will be repeated, this time enhanced by the data 'science' that is supposed to erase it."

For Further Thought

1. What type of research should be done to examine the issues presented in this article?

2. In your opinion, how would you assess, in a research study, the effectiveness of a computer program identifying such things as crime hot spots?

Source: The Times Editorial Board. (2019, March 16). The problem with LAPD's predictive policing. *Los Angeles Times.* Retrieved from https://www.latimes.com/opinion/editorials/la-ed-lapd-predictive-policing-20190316-story.html

and associations among variables. The technological advancements in computing power over the past decade have made analyses of these huge datasets more available to everyone, including government, corporate, and research entities alike. Importantly, many researchers now contend that, "Big Data holds great promise for improving the efficiency and effectiveness of law enforcement and security intelligence agencies" (Chan & Moses, 2017, p. 299).

Here are some examples of what now qualifies as Big Data (Mayer-Schönberger & Cukier, 2013): Facebook users upload more than 10 million photos every hour and leave a comment or click on a "like" button almost three billion times per day; YouTube users upload more than an hour of video every second; Twitter users were already sending more than 400 million tweets per day. If all this and other forms of stored information in the world were printed in books, one estimate in 2013 was that these books would cover the face of the earth 52 layers thick. That's "big."

All this information would be of no more importance than the number of grains of sand on the beach except that these numbers describe information produced by people, available to social scientists, and manageable with today's computers. Already, Big Data analyses are being used to predict the spread of flu, the behavior of consumers, and the prevalence of crime.

Here's a quick demonstration: We talked about school shootings in Chapter 1, which are a form of mass murder. We think of mass murder as a relatively recent phenomenon, but you may be surprised to learn that it has been written about for decades. One way to examine inquiries into mass murder is to see how frequently the term *mass murder* has appeared in all the books ever written in the world. It is now possible with the click of a mouse to answer that question, although with two key limitations: We can only examine books written in English and in several other languages, and as of 2014, we are limited to "only" one quarter of all books ever published—a mere 30 million books (Aiden & Michel, 2013).

Ngrams: Frequency graphs, produced by Google's database, of all words printed in more than one third of the world's books over time (with coverage still expanding).

To check this out, go to the Google **Ngrams** site (books.google.com/ngrams), type in *mass murder* and *serial murder*, and check the *case-insensitive* box (and change the ending year to 2015). Exhibit 9.6 shows the resulting screen. (If you don't obtain a graph, try using a different browser.) Note that the height of a graph line represents the percentage that the term represents of all words in books published in each year, so a rising line means greater relative interest in the term, not simply more books being published. You can see that *mass murder* emerges in the early 20th century, while *serial murder* did not begin to appear until much later, in the 1980s. It's hard to stop checking other ideas by adding in other terms, searching in other languages, or shifting to another topic entirely. Our next case study illuminates how law enforcement agencies are also harnessing Big Data to make predictions.

Exhibit 9.6 Ngram of *Mass Murder* and *Serial Murder*

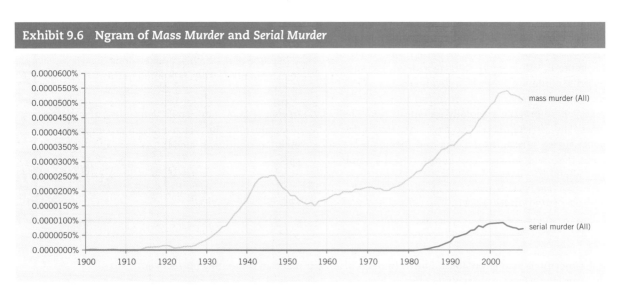

Source: Google Books Ngram Viewer, http://books.google.com/ngrams.

Case Study: Predicting Where Crime Will Occur

If you have seen the film *Minority Report*, you have gotten a far-fetched glimpse of a world where people are arrested for criminal acts that they are *predicted* they will commit, not that they have actually committed. FOX also had a television series called *Minority Report* that was based on the same premise. While crime predictions in these shows are based on clairvoyants (people who can see into the future) and not real data, law enforcement agencies are beginning to use Big Data to predict both future behavior in individuals and, as we just saw with crime mapping, areas where crime is likely to occur in the future.

As we just highlighted, crime mapping allows law enforcement agencies to estimate where hot spots of crime are occurring, that is, where they have been most likely to occur in the past. Joel Caplan and Leslie Kennedy from the Rutgers School of Criminal Justice have pioneered a new way to forecast crime using Big Data called **risk terrain modeling (RTM)** (Caplan & Kennedy, 2015). Using data from several sources, this modeling predicts the probability of crime occurring in the future using the underlying factors of the environment that are associated with illegal behavior. The important difference between this and regular crime mapping is that it takes into account features of the area that enable criminal behavior.

The process weights these factors, which are the independent variables, and places them into a final model that produces a map of places where criminal behavior is most likely to occur. In this way, the predicted probability of future crime is the dependent variable. This modeling is essentially special risk analysis in a more sophisticated form than the early maps of the Chicago school presented previously. Kennedy and his colleagues (2012) explain,

> Operationalizing the spatial influence of a crime factor tells a story, so to speak, about how that feature of the landscape affects behaviors and attracts or enables crime occurrence at places nearby to and far away from the feature itself. When certain motivated offenders interact with suitable targets, the risk of crime and victimization conceivably increases. But, when motivated offenders interact with suitable targets at certain places, the risk of criminal victimization is even higher. Similarly, when certain motivated offenders interact with suitable targets at places that are not conducive to crime, the risk of victimization is lowered.
> (p. 24)

Using data from many sources, RTM statistically computes the probability of particular kinds of criminal behavior occurring in a place. For example, Exhibit 9.7 displays a risk terrain map that was produced for Irvington, New Jersey. From the map, you can see that several

Risk terrain modeling (RTM): Modeling that uses data from several sources to predict the probability of crime occurring in the future, using the underlying factors of the environment that are associated with illegal behavior.

Exhibit 9.7 Risk Terrain Map

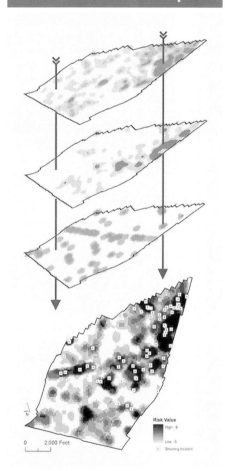

Source: Obtained from personal correspondence with Leslie Kennedy and Joel Caplan.

variables were included in the model predicting the potential for shootings to occur, including the presence of gangs and drugs, along with other infrastructure information, such as the location of bars and liquor stores. Why were these some of the factors used? Because previous research and police data indicated that shootings were more likely to occur where gangs, drugs, and these businesses were present. This does not mean that a shooting will occur in the high-risk areas, it only means that it is more likely to occur in these areas compared with other areas. RTM is considered a use of Big Data because it examines multiple datasets that share geographic location as a common denominator.

Case Study: Predicting Recidivism With Big Data

As you learned in Chapter 2, the Minneapolis Domestic Violence Experiment and the National Institute of Justice's Spousal Abuse Replication Project, which were experiments to determine the efficacy of different approaches to reducing recidivism for intimate partner violence (IPV), changed the way IPV was handled by law enforcement agencies across the United States and across the globe. No longer were parties simply separated at the scene, but mandatory-arrest policies were implemented in many jurisdictions across the country, which "swamped the system with domestic violence cases" (K. R. Williams & Houghton, 2004, p. 438). In fact, some states now see thousands of perpetrators arrested annually for assaults against their intimate partners. Many jurisdictions are attempting to more objectively determine whether these perpetrators present a risk of future violence should they be released on parole or probation.

Kirk Williams developed one instrument to determine this risk, which is called the Revised Domestic Violence Screening Instrument (DVSI-R) (K. R. Williams, 2012). To determine the effectiveness of the DVSI-R in predicting recidivism, Stansfield and Williams (2014) used a huge dataset that would be deemed *Big Data*, since it contains information on 29,317 perpetrators arrested on family violence charges in 2010 in Connecticut and is continuously updated for recent arrests and convictions. To measure the risk of recidivism for new family violence offenses (NFVO), the DVSI-R includes 11 items: Seven measure the behavioral history of the perpetrator, including such things as prior nonfamily assaults, arrests, or criminal convictions; prior family violence assaults, threats, or arrests; prior violations of protection orders; the frequency of family violence in the previous six months; and the escalation of family violence in the past six months. The other four items include substance abuse, weapons or objects used as weapons, children present during violent incidents, and employment status. The range of the DVSI-R is from 0 to 28, with 28 representing the highest risk score.

To examine how the DVSI-R predicted future arrests, Stansfield and Williams (2014) used two measures of recidivism during an 18-month follow-up: rearrests for NFVOs and rearrests for violations of protective or restraining orders only. Results indicated that of the over 29,000 cases, nearly 1 in 4 (23%) perpetrators were rearrested, with 14% of those rearrested for a violation of a protective order. Perpetrators who had higher DVSI-R risk scores were more likely to be rearrested compared with those with lower risk scores. As you can see, using Big Data to improve decision making by criminal justice professionals is not a thing of the future, it is happening now. The availability of Big Data and advanced computer technologies for its analysis mean that researchers can apply standard research methods in exciting new ways, and this trend will only continue to grow.

ETHICAL ISSUES IN USING BIG DATA

Subject confidentiality is a key concern when original records are analyzed with either secondary data or Big Data. Whenever possible, all information that could identify individuals should be removed from the records to be analyzed so that no link is possible to the identities of living subjects or the living descendants of subjects (Huston & Naylor, 1996, p. 1698). When you use data that have already been archived, you need to find out what procedures were used to preserve subject confidentiality. The work required to ensure subject confidentiality probably will have been done for you by the data archivist. For example, the Inter-university Consortium for Political and Social Research (ICPSR) examines carefully all data deposited in the archive for the possibility of disclosure risk. All data that might be used to identify respondents are altered to ensure confidentiality, including removal of information such as birth dates or service dates, specific incomes, or place of residence that could be used to identify subjects indirectly (see www.icpsr .umich.edu/icpsrweb/content/ICPSR/access/restricted/index.html). If all information that could be used in any way to identify respondents cannot be removed from a dataset without diminishing dataset quality (e.g., by preventing links to other essential data records), ICPSR restricts access to the data and requires that investigators agree to conditions of use that preserve subject confidentiality. Those who violate confidentiality may be subject to a scientific misconduct investigation by their home institution at the request of ICPSR (Johnson & Bullock, 2009, p. 218).

It is not up to you to decide whether there are any issues of concern regarding human subjects when you acquire a dataset for secondary analysis from a responsible source. The institutional review board (IRB) for the protection of human subjects at your college or university or other institution has the responsibility to decide whether they need to review and approve proposals for secondary data analysis. Data quality is always a concern with secondary data, even when the data are collected by an official government agency and even when the data are "Big." Researchers who rely on secondary data inevitably make trade-offs between their ability to use a particular dataset and the specific hypotheses they can test. If a concept that is critical to a hypothesis was not measured adequately in a secondary data source, the study might have to be abandoned until a more adequate source of data can be found.

Political concerns intersect with ethical practice in secondary data analyses. How are *race* and *ethnicity* coded in the U.S. Census? You learned in Chapter 4 that changing conceptualizations of race have affected what questions are asked in the census to measure race. This data collection process reflects, in part, the influence of political interest groups, and it means that analysts using the census data must understand why the proportion of individuals choosing "other" as their race and the proportion in a "multiracial" category has changed.

Big Data also creates some new concerns about research ethics. When enormous amounts of data are available for analysis, the procedures for making data anonymous no longer ensure that it stays that way. For example, in 2006, AOL released 20 million search queries from 657,000 users, after all personal information had been erased and only a unique numeric identifier remained to link searches. However, staff of the *New York Times* conducted analyses of sets of search queries and were able to quickly identify a specific individual user by name and location, based on their searches. The collection of Big Data also makes possible surveillance and prediction of behavior on a large scale. Crime control efforts and screening for terrorists now often involve developing predictions from patterns identified in Big Data. Without strict rules and close monitoring, potential invasions of privacy and unwarranted suspicions are enormous (Mayer-Schönberger & Cukier, 2013).

CONTENT ANALYSIS

Do media accounts of crime, such as newspaper and television news coverage, accurately portray the true nature of crime? Has the media covered the recent opioid epidemic differently than earlier substance abuse problems, such as the earlier methamphetamine epidemic? How was the drug oxycodone marketed to physicians in a way that increased the likelihood that it would be overprescribed? You now know that you probably could find data about each of these issues for a secondary data analysis, but in this section, we will introduce you to a specific technique that is well suited to answering these types of questions. Content analysis is "the systematic, objective, quantitative analysis of message characteristics" (Neuendorf, 2002, p. 1) and would be an appropriate tool. Using this method, we can learn a great deal about popular culture and many other issues through studying the characteristics of messages delivered through the mass media and other sources. Content analysis methods usually begin with text, speech broadcasts, or visual images. The content analyst develops procedures for coding various aspects of the textual, aural (spoken), or visual material and then analyzes this coded content.

The goal of a content analysis is to develop inferences from communication in any of its forms, including books, articles, songs, films, speeches, and so on (Weber, 1990). You can think of a content analysis as a "survey" of some documents or other records of prior communication. In fact, a content analysis is a survey designed with fixed-choice responses so that it produces quantitative data that can be analyzed statistically.

Content analysis bears some similarities to qualitative data analysis because it involves coding and categorizing text, discovering relationships among constructs identified in the text, and a statistical analysis of those findings. Content analysis also bears some similarities to secondary data analysis because it involves taking data (texts) that already exist and subjecting them to a new form of "analysis," but unlike secondary analysis of previously collected quantitative data, content analysis also involves sampling and measurement of primary data. The first step is to identify your content.

Identifying a Population of Documents or Other Textual Sources

The population of documents that is selected for analysis should be appropriate to the research question of interest. The units that can be surveyed in a content analysis are numerous and can range from newspapers, books, films, nomination speeches, or TV shows to persons referred to in other communications, themes expressed in documents, or propositions made in different statements. Often, a comprehensive archive can provide the primary data for the analysis (Neuendorf, 2002). Words or other features of these units are then coded in order to measure the variables involved in the research question. The content analysis proceeds through several stages (R. P. Weber, 1985). In the case study that follows, Taylor, Boisvert, Sims, and Garver (2013) used LexisNexis to select a sample of newspaper articles to examine the coverage of missing children.

Determine the Units of Analysis

The units of analysis could be items such as newspaper articles, whole newspapers, speeches, or political conventions, or they could be more microscopic units, such as words, interactions, time periods, or other bits of communication (Neuendorf, 2002, p. 71). The content analyst has to decide what units are most appropriate to the research question and how the communication content can be broken into those units. If the units are individual issues of a newspaper, in a study of changes in news emphases, this step may be relatively easy. However, if the units are most appropriately the instances of interaction between characters in a novel or a movie, in a study of conflict patterns between different types of characters, it will require a careful process of testing to determine how to define operationally the specific units of interaction (Weber, 1990, pp. 39–40).

Select a sample of units from the population. The simplest strategy might be a simple random sample of documents. However, a stratified sample might be needed to ensure adequate representation of community newspapers in large and small cities, of weekday and Sunday papers, or of political speeches during election years and in off years (see Chapter 4). Nonrandom sampling methods have also been used in content analyses when the entire population of interest could not be determined (Neuendorf, 2002, pp. 87–88).

Design coding procedures for the variables to be measured. Designing coding procedures requires deciding what variables to measure, using the unit of text to be coded, such as words, sentences, themes, or paragraphs. Then, the categories into which the text units are to be coded must be defined. These categories may be broad, such as a *child abducted by known offender*, or narrow, such as *a child abducted by a parent*. Reading or otherwise reviewing some of the documents or other units to be coded is an essential step in thinking about variables that should be coded and in developing coding procedures. Development of clear instructions and careful training of coders are essential.

Developing Reliable and Valid Coding Procedures Is Not an Easy Task

The meaning of words and phrases is often ambiguous. Homographs (words such as *mine* that have different meanings in different contexts) create special problems, as do many phrases that have special meanings (such as *point of no return*) (R. P. Weber, 1985). As a result, coding procedures cannot simply categorize and count words; text segments in which the words are embedded must also be inspected before codes are finalized. Because different coders may perceive different meanings in the same text segments, explicit coding rules are required to ensure coding consistency. Special dictionaries can be developed to keep track of how the categories of interest are defined in the study (R. P. Weber, 1985).

After coding procedures are developed, their reliability should be assessed by comparing different coders' codes for the same variables. Computer program content analysis can be used to enhance reliability (R. P. Weber, 1985). Whatever rules the computer is programmed to use to code text will be applied consistently. The criteria for judging quantitative content analyses of text reflect the same standards of validity applied to data collected with other quantitative methods. We must review the sampling approach, the reliability and validity of the measures, and the controls used to strengthen any causal conclusions.

Base Statistical Analyses on Counting Occurrences of Particular Items

The content analyst creates variables for analysis by counting occurrences of particular words, themes, or phrases and then tests relations between the resulting variables. These analyses could use some of the statistics introduced in Appendix F on the Student Study Site, including frequency distributions, measures of central tendency and variation, cross-tabulations, and correlation analysis. Computer-aided qualitative analysis programs, like those you learned about in Chapter 8, can also be used to develop coding procedures and then carry out the content coding.

In sum, the criteria for judging quantitative content analyses of text are the same standards of validity applied to data collected with other quantitative methods. We must review the sampling approach, the reliability and validity of the measures, and the controls used to strengthen any causal conclusions.

Case Study: Media Portrayals of Abducted Children

Researchers interested in the media and crime have used content analysis in a number of ways. For example, scholars analyzing crime depictions presented in the media often conclude that newspaper and television coverage of crime is frequently inaccurate and misleading; stories disproportionately report violent crimes, and reporters tend to focus attention on sensational matters, such as the capture of criminal or high-status offenders.

Over the past few decades, policy makers and the media alike have been paying increasing attention to child abductions. Unfortunately, similar to media coverage for other crimes, the media tends to focus on sensational abductions, such as those perpetrated by strangers, compared with the more common family abduction incidents. Justine Taylor and her colleagues (2013) wanted to determine whether media representations of abductions actually represented the most common characteristics of abductions. To do this, they relied on data from the United States Justice Department–sponsored National Incidence Studies of Missing, Abducted, Runaway, and Throwaway Children 2 (NISMART-2), the federal government's most accurate accounting of children abductions in the United States. NISMART-2 not only collects information on abductions from law enforcement agencies but also employs a random sample survey of youth households about their experiences with missing children. NISMART classifies several different types of abductions, including family, nonfamily, and stereotypical abductions, which is a nonfamily abduction in which a child is detained overnight, transported at least 50 miles, held for ransom, or abducted with intent to keep the child permanently or to kill the child. These NISMART data were used to describe the actual incidences and characteristics of child abductions in the U.S., which were compared with how newspapers reported on abductions across the United States.

To obtain a sample of newspaper articles, Taylor et al. (2013) searched LexisNexis Academic, which provides articles from most major newspapers in the United States, using the terms *kidnap* or *abduct*. Only articles related to abductions of children were retained and coded for information related to the victim, including such things as their age and gender and their relationship to the offender. A comparison of the empirical data from NISMART-2 indicated that male and female children were equally likely to have been abducted by family members, but the print media was more likely to report on female family abductions compared with males (Taylor et al., 2013). However, newspaper articles presented females as more likely to be abducted by strangers and for stereotypical kidnappings compared with males, which was also true for the NISMART-2 data. Still, compared with males, articles of female children abductions were significantly longer for all types of abductions. This was also generally true for younger victims (age 11 and younger) compared with older children victims. The authors concluded, "When [the media sensationalizes inaccurate portrayals of abductions], the media fails to meet moral and ethical reporting standards that society expects, but also causes a disservice to certain victims (i.e., males and nonfamily abduction victims aged 12 and over)" (Taylor at al., 2013, p. 162).

METHODOLOGICAL ISSUES WHEN USING SECONDARY DATA

Analysis of secondary data presents several challenges, ranging from uncertainty about the methods of data collection to the lack of maximal fit between the concepts that the primary study measured and each of the concepts that are the focus of the current investigation. Responsible use of secondary data requires a good understanding of the primary data source. The researcher should be able to answer the following questions (most of which were adopted from Riedel, 2000, and Stewart, 1984):

1. What were the agency's goals in collecting the data? If the primary data were obtained in a research project, what were the project's purposes?

2. Who was responsible for data collection, and what were their qualifications? Are they available to answer questions about the data? Each step in the data collection process should be charted and the personnel involved identified.

3. What data were collected, and what were they intended to measure?

4. When was the information collected?

5. What methods were used for data collection? Copies of the forms used for data collection should be obtained, and the way in which these data are processed by the agency or agencies should be reviewed.

6. How is the information organized (by date, event, etc.)? Are there identifiers that are used to identify the different types of data available on the same case? In what form are the data available (computer tapes, disks, paper files)? Answers to these questions can have a major bearing on the work that will be needed to carry out the study.

7. How consistent are the data with data available from other sources?

8. What is known about the success of the data collection effort? How are missing data indicated? What kind of documentation is available?

Answering these questions helps ensure that the researcher is familiar with the data he or she will analyze and can help identify any problems with it.

Researchers who rely on secondary data inevitably make trade-offs between their ability to use a particular dataset and the specific hypotheses they can test. If a concept that is critical to a hypothesis was not measured adequately in a secondary data source, the study might have to be abandoned until a more adequate source of data can be found. Alternatively, hypotheses or even the research question itself may be modified in order to match the analytic possibilities presented by the available data (Riedel, 2000).

ETHICAL ISSUES WHEN ANALYZING AVAILABLE DATA AND CONTENT

When analyzing data collected by others, the potential for harm to human subjects that can be a concern when collecting primary data is greatly reduced. It is still, however, important to be honest and responsible in working out arrangements for data access and protection.

Researchers who conclude that they are being denied access to public records of the federal government may be able to obtain the data by filing a Freedom of Information Act (FOIA) request. The FOIA stipulates that all persons have a right to access all federal agency records unless the records are specifically exempted (Riedel, 2000). Researchers who review historical or government documents must also try to avoid embarrassing or otherwise harming named individuals or their descendants by disclosing sensitive information.

Subject confidentiality is a key concern when original records are analyzed. Whenever possible, all information that could identify individuals should be removed from the records to be analyzed so that no link is possible to the identities of living subjects or the living descendants of subjects (Huston & Naylor, 1996). When you use data that have already been archived, you need to find out what procedures were used to preserve subject confidentiality. The work required to ensure subject confidentiality probably will have been done for you by the data archivist. For example, the ICPSR examines carefully all data deposited in the archive for the possibility of disclosure risk. All data that might be used to identify respondents is altered to ensure confidentiality, including removal of information such as birth dates or service dates, specific incomes, or place of residence that could be used to identify subjects indirectly (see www.icpsr.umich.edu/icpsrweb/content/datamanagement/confidentiality). If all information that could be used in any way to identify respondents cannot be removed from a dataset without diminishing its quality (such as by preventing links to other essential data records), ICPSR restricts access to the data and requires that investigators agree to conditions of use that preserve subject confidentiality.

CAREERS AND RESEARCH

Jennifer A. Herbert, MA, Crime Intelligence Analyst, Crime Analysis and Strategic Evaluation Unit

Source: Courtesy of Jennifer A. Herbert

Jennifer Herbert graduated with a double major in political science and justice studies from James Madison University in 2007. She had aspirations of becoming a police officer and eventually a detective. She was hired as a police officer after graduation, but she realized while at the police academy that she wanted to pursue the crime analysis career path in law enforcement. She became a crime analyst at Chesterfield County Police Department in Virginia. While working full time as an analyst, Jennifer pursued an MA degree in intelligence at the American Military University. She then accepted a promotion to crime intelligence analyst at Henrico County Police Division. After working as a crime analyst for six years, Jennifer cannot imagine doing anything else.

Every day is different working as a crime intelligence analyst. Some days, Jennifer analyzes phone records and maps the location of and time of crime incidents. Other days, she maps the latest residential burglary trend and predicts where the next burglary will occur. She also completes research projects that examine quality-of-life issues for the community, including estimating crimes per 1,000 residents by neighborhood. Jennifer's role as a crime analyst is equally important in preventing crime and in apprehension of offenders by patrol officers. She thinks the most rewarding part of her job is helping people who have been victimized by apprehending offenders and improving the quality of life for county residents. Jennifer has some good advice for students interested in careers involving analysis:

If crime analysis interests you, ask your local police department if you can do an internship (paid or unpaid) to gain experience. Be sure to network with other crime analysts and let them know you are interested in pursuing a career in crime analysis. Courses in all forms of data analysis and GIS (geographic information systems) are almost essential to a career in crime analysis. Even if you did not take GIS classes during your undergraduate studies, many community colleges offer introductory and advanced classes in GIS. Other qualifications that will help you stand out as an applicant include competency in basic statistics and proficiency in data analysis programs, including Microsoft Excel, Access, and SPSS.

It is not up to you to decide whether there are any issues of concern regarding human subjects when you acquire a dataset for secondary analysis from a responsible source. The institutional review board (IRB) for the protection of human subjects at your college, university, or other institution has the responsibility to decide whether it needs to review and approve proposals for secondary data analysis. The federal regulations are not entirely clear on this point, so the acceptable procedures will vary among institutions based on what their IRBs have decided.

CONCLUSION

In our data-driven world, data generally—and the methods examined in this chapter specifically—increasingly are being used in research and in intelligence-led policing. For example, using social-network analysis and crime mapping are also now common techniques used in large police agencies not only to respond to crime but also to reduce, disrupt, and prevent it. As one police investigator explained,

> Any data that we can collate online, whether it be that online evidence that may indicate the commission of offense or assist in making a nexus, a link to that offense, such as photographs, emails, text messages. . . .

we use any data that we can get our hands on lawfully, certainly, to assist in our investigations. (Chan & Bennett Moses, 2017, p. 305)

The use of such methodological techniques is requiring police academies to incorporate data analysis components into their training. So even if you do not plan to become a researcher yourself, you will likely be required to make sense of data in virtually any career you pursue. Hopefully, you should now have the knowledge and skills required to find and use secondary data and to review analyses of big data to answer applied criminal justice and criminological research questions.

KEY TERMS

Adjacency matrix   231
Betweenness centrality score   234
Big Data   238
Binary network   231
Content analysis   244
Crime mapping   236
Freedom of Information Act
   (FOIA)   248

Geographic information system
   (GIS)   236
Intelligence-led policing   238
Ngrams   240
Nodes   231
Nodelist   231
Relational data   231

Relations   231
Risk terrain modeling (RTM)   241
Secondary data analysis   229
Social networks   230
Social-network analysis
   (SNA)   230
Sociogram   231

HIGHLIGHTS

- Secondary data analysis is the act of collecting or analyzing data that were originally collected for another purpose.

- Social-network analysis uses relational data to examine the patterns in social relationships that individuals and groups have with each other.

- Crime mapping for research purposes is generally used to identify the spatial distribution of crime, along with the social indicators, such as poverty and social disorganization, that are similarly distributed across areas (e.g., neighborhoods, census tracts).

- Using huge datasets, often termed *Big Data*, to determine trends and patterns of social phenomena is becoming increasingly possible because of advanced computer technology. Big Data and advanced computer technology have helped to advance crime-mapping techniques in creative ways, including new predictive modeling techniques like risk terrain modeling (RTM).

- Content analysis is a tool for systematic analysis of documents and other textual data. It requires careful testing and control of coding procedures to achieve reliable measures.

EXERCISES

1. Write down at least five different research questions that crime mapping can answer. Then, find an article that used crime mapping. Describe how GIS offered new and different information compared with the other criminological research articles reviewed from previous chapter exercises.

2. In this chapter, you learned that social-network analysis is a fairly new methodological technique than can account for relationships that both individuals and groups have with each other. Think about different friends you have now who have different attitudes toward alcohol use. One person may not use alcohol while another may drink alcohol frequently. Construct a graph depicting the past four weekends and the friends you hung out with for each weekend. Does your alcohol consumption change depending on the friends with whom you are socializing? What are some ways in which the social-network analysis could help explain the individual and group behavior differences and similarities when it comes to alcohol consumption?

3. Imagine you are responsible for training police officers regarding the use of data for intelligence-led policing. In this training, you need to communicate at least five ways using data for intelligence-led policing could potentially lead to better or improved policing. Write down these five things and at least three challenges you believe you may encounter during this training on data-informed policing.

Discussing Research

1. Recall some of the other studies mentioned in this text. Think of how historical events may change our conceptualization of social behavior (e.g., recent mass shootings). Pick one phenomenon, and assess how you would perform a media content analysis concerning this particular theme. Focus particular attention on procedures for measurement, sampling, and establishing causal relations.

2. What are the similarities and differences between secondary data analysis and Big Data analysis? Do you feel one of these approaches is more likely to yield valid conclusions? Explain your answer.

3. As it was described in this chapter, social-network analysis was used in assessing the investigation of the Green River Killer. Can you think of other situations in which this type of analysis could help researchers or practitioners learn about or address a problem in society? Write these thoughts down in a one-page report.

4. Read the original article reporting one of the studies described in this chapter. Critique the article, using the article review questions presented in Appendix B as your guide. Focus particular attention on procedures for measurement, sampling, and establishing causal relations.

Finding Research on the Web

The National Institute of Justice has a wealth of information on crime mapping located at nij.gov. Search the site for information on crime mapping, and you will find that it contains a multitude of information, including the latest technological advances in crime-mapping strategies for police departments as well as full-text articles discussing recent research that uses crime-mapping techniques. Select a report available online, and summarize its findings.

1. Go to the Rutgers Center on Public Security (rutgerscps.weebly.com), and then go the RTM menu. There, you will find several places to browse, including a publications page. Find a recent publication that has used RTM, and describe the methodology. What were the independent variables, and what was used as the dependent variable? Are there any other variables that could have been added to predict the dependent variable?

2. Select a current topic, and write a research question about this topic that could be answered with counts of words in books. Use the Google Ngrams program described in this chapter to answer your question. Discuss the limitations of your approach, including the words you searched and the way in which you identified relationships.

Critiquing Research

1. Review the survey datasets available through the ICPSR, using either its published directory or its Internet site (www.icpsr.umich.edu). Select two datasets that might be used to study a research question in which you are interested. Use the information ICPSR reports about them to determine whether the datasets contain the relevant variables you will need to answer your research question. Are the issues of confidentiality and anonymity appropriately addressed? Is enough information provided to ensure that all ethical guidelines were followed? What are the advantages and disadvantages of using one of these datasets to answer your research question compared with designing a new study?

2. Read the original article reporting one of the studies described in this chapter. Critique the article using the article review questions presented in Chapter 1 as your guide. Focus particular attention on procedures for measurement, sampling, and establishing causal relations.

Making Research Ethical

1. In your opinion, does a researcher have an ethical obligation to urge government officials or others to take action in response to social problems that they have identified? Why, or why not?

2. Big Data begin as little data—that is, as the records of phone calls, Twitter posts, or pictures taken by individuals in their daily lives. What limitations on access should be imposed on access to and use of such data once they have become aggregated into massive datasets? Is removing explicit identifiers sufficient protection? When does access to Big Data violate rights to privacy?

3. In January 2012, Facebook conducted an experiment in which emotional cues were manipulated for 689,003 users. Some saw news stories and photos on Facebook's homepage containing many positive words, while others saw negative, unpleasant words. The messages sent subsequently by these users were a little more likely to reflect the emotional tone of the words they had been chosen randomly to see. When this experiment was reported in the *Proceedings of the National Academy of Sciences* (Kramer, Guillory, & Hancock, 2014), some people were outraged. What do you think of the ethics of this type of Big Data experiment?

Developing a Research Proposal

Add a mapping dimension to your proposed study.

1. For your research question, there is likely an opportunity to describe some phenomenon (e.g., crime rates) either globally, nationally, or locally. Select the units of analysis you wish to describe (e.g., census areas, cities, states, nations).

2. Review the possible sources of data for your project. Search the Web and relevant government, historical, and international-organization sites or publications. Search the social science literature for similar studies, and read about the data sources that they used.

3. Your university or library may have some mapping software that is user friendly. For example, many libraries have a program called "PolicyMap" that already contains data in many domains, including crime. Users can request variables to be mapped using various units of analysis, including states, counties, and so forth. Using software like this, attempt to create several maps using variables related to your research project.

Performing Data Analysis in SPSS or Excel

Data for Exercise	
Dataset	Description
2012 states data.sav	This state-level dataset compiles official statistics from various official sources, such as the census, health department records, and police departments. It includes basic demographic data, crime rates, and incidence rates for various illnesses and infant mortality for entire states.

Variables for Exercise	
Variable Name	**Description**
Tobaccodeathrt	The tobacco-related death rate per 100,000 for a state
Perindpoverty	The proportion of individuals below the poverty line in a state
BurglarytRt	The burglary rate reported per 100,000 for a state

1. Dr. Smartypants says, "Let's see how state characteristics end up predicting the robbery rate. Consider the following question: Is there a link between the unhealthy behaviors people engage in and the crime rate? I'm just fishing for results here, but let's see what we find!" He tells you to look into the relationship between the variables "tobaccodeathrt" and "burglaryRt" to see if there is a relationship. He wants a graph of the relationship, a regression model, and an estimate of the strength of the relationship.

   a. Before running the regression model, we should look at the relationship of the two variables using a scatterplot. This is done by selecting "graphs-> legacy dialogues->scatter/dot->simple scatter." Then, put your independent variable on the *y* axis and the dependent variable on the *x* axis. Hang on to this graph.

   b. Second, we'll estimate the strength of the relationship using a Pearson's correlation coefficient. This is a value ranging from –1 to 0 to 1, with negative values indicative a negative (inverse) association and positive values indicating a positive association. Values of ±.1 to .3 are considered a weak correlation, .4 to .6 are moderate, and ±.7 or higher are considered strong. To estimate Pearson's correlation coefficient, select "analyze->correlate->bivariate." Hang on to your correlation coefficient.

   c. Third, estimate a regression model by selecting "analyze->regression->linear" and putting the independent and dependent variables in the correct spots. The regression coefficient you want is in the row named after your independent variable in the "unstandardized coefficients: B" column. This value reflects the expected change in the robbery rate in light of a 1-unit increase in the tobacco death rate per 100,000.

   d. Now, put together a few sentences summarizing your results to Dr. Smartypants. Don't worry about the *why* part; focus on incorporating Questions 1a, 1b, and 1c.

   e. How comfortable are you with these accuracy results? Can you detect any caveats or concerns that must be considered?

2. You turn in your report to Dr. Smartypants, who is clearly very excited. He says, "Holy macaroni! This proves it! The smokers are also robbing everyone; smoking causes criminal impulses! I've got to publish this right away!"

   a. What do you think of his conclusion? Do you think it is an accurate interpretation of the data? Write a statement of support of his interpretation, or, if you disagree, write a rebuttal and alternative interpretation.

3. You decide that you want to be sure about these results before publishing them by checking for another plausible relationship—perhaps poverty is linked to a high robbery rate.

   a. Run all the analyses that you did for Question 1 again, this time using the variable "perindpoverty" as your independent variable.

   b. Write a summary of your results for Dr. Smartypants that incorporates the results from your scatterplot, correlation, and regression analysis.

4. Based on the analyses you have conducted thus far, what seems to be the most plausible explanation for robbery? If both variables are associated, why might that be the case, and which one do you think is the root cause? Which explanation seems to be more theoretically sound? Are you in a position to make claims of causality?

5. Dr. Smartypants asks you one more favor before you publish your paper together. He wants you to see if the dependent variable, "burglaryRt," has any problems that might weaken your certainty of your conclusions.

   a. What level of measurement is this variable?

   b. Use SPSS's graphing functions to construct a histogram. How would you describe this distribution: skewed left, skewed right, or normally distributed?

   i. Optional: If you are familiar with the assumptions of regression models, how do you think this might impact your results?

c. Is there any evidence of extreme outliers?

d. Think carefully about the data you are looking at. They come from official police records. Can you think of anything that might threaten the data's accuracy?

STUDENT STUDY SITE

§SAGE edge™

Get the tools you need to sharpen your study skills. SAGE Edge offers a robust online environment featuring an impressive array of free tools and resources. Access practice quizzes, eFlashcards, video, and multimedia at **edge.sagepub.com/bachmanfrccj5e**.

10

EVALUATION AND POLICY ANALYSIS

⑤SAGE edge™

WHAT DO WE HAVE IN MIND?

Every year, the federal government, combined with state and local governments, spends several billion dollars to help state law enforcement and communities prevent crime, along with programs designed to help victims themselves. Several of the studies we have already highlighted in this text were conducted to evaluate the effectiveness of some program or policy (e.g., violence prevention programs in schools, mandatory-arrest policies, the effects of a lawyer at bail hearings, the effects of drug courts). Results from studies such as these generally have an impact on policy choices in the immediate future, and as such, this research is often referred to as **applied research**.

In this chapter, you will read about a variety of social-program evaluations as we introduce the evaluation research process, illustrate the different types of evaluation research, highlight alternative approaches, and review ethical concerns. You will learn in this chapter about attempts to determine the effectiveness of several programs and policies, including whether law enforcement agencies (LEAs) that utilize conducted energy devices (such as Tasers®) decrease the risk of injuries to both officers and suspects. We will first provide you with a brief history of evaluation research. Then, after describing the different types of evaluation research, we will provide you with case studies that illustrate the various methodologies used to assess these different evaluation questions. We will conclude with a discussion of the differences between basic science and applied research and highlight the emerging demand for evidence-based policy.

A BRIEF HISTORY OF EVALUATION RESEARCH

Evaluation research is not a method of data collection, as are survey research or experiments, nor is it a unique component of research designs, as are sampling or measurement. Instead, evaluation research is social research that is conducted for a distinctive purpose: to investigate social programs (such as substance abuse treatment programs, welfare programs, criminal justice programs, or employment and training programs). Rossi and Freeman (1989) define evaluation research as "the systematic application of social-research procedures for assessing the conceptualization, design, implementation, and utility of social intervention programs" (p. 18). What exactly does *systematic* mean? Well, regardless of the treatment or program being examined, evaluations are systematic because they employ social-research approaches to gathering valid and reliable data. Note the plural *approaches* instead of the singular *approach*. Evaluation research covers the spectrum of research methods that we have discussed in this text.

For each project, an evaluation researcher must select a research design and a method of data collection that are useful for answering the particular research questions posed and appropriate for the particular program investigated.

You can see why we placed this chapter after most of the others in the text: When you review or plan evaluation research, you have to think about the research process as a whole and how different parts of that process can best be combined.

Although scientific research methods had been used prior to the 1950s (in fact, as early as the 1700s) to evaluate **outcomes** of particular social experiments and programs, it was not until the end of the 1950s that social research became immersed in the workings of government with the common goal of improving society. During the 1960s, the practice of evaluation research increased dramatically, not only in the United States but also around the world. By the mid-1970s, evaluators were called on not only to assess the overall effectiveness of programs but also to determine whether programs were being implemented as intended and to provide feedback to help solve programming problems as well.

By the 1990s, the public wanted even more accountability. Unfortunately, clear answers were not readily available. Few social programs could provide hard data on results achieved and outcomes obtained. Of course, government bureaucrats had produced a wealth of data on other things, including exactly how funds in particular programs were spent, for whom this money was spent, and for how many. However, these data primarily measured whether government staff were following the rules and regulations, not whether the desired results were being achieved.

Today, professional evaluation researchers have realized that it is not enough simply to perform rigorous experiments to determine program efficacy; they must also be responsible for making sure their results can be understood and utilized by the practitioners (e.g., government officials, corporations, and nonprofit agencies) to make decisions about scrapping or modifying existing programs. In addition, there has been increased concern in the field regarding fiscal accountability, documenting the worth of social-program expenditures in relation to their costs. Let's get started with some evaluation basics.

> **Applied research:** Research that has an impact on policy and can be immediately utilized and applied

> **Outcomes:** The impact of the program process on the cases processed

> **Inputs:** Resources, raw materials, clients, and staff that go into a program

EVALUATION BASICS

Exhibit 10.1 illustrates the process of evaluation research as a simple systems model. First, clients, customers, students, or some other persons or units—cases—enter the program as **inputs**. Students may begin a new Drug Abuse Resistance Education (DARE) program, sex offenders may enter a new intense-probation program, or crime victims may be sent to a victim advocate. Resources and staff required by a program are also program inputs.

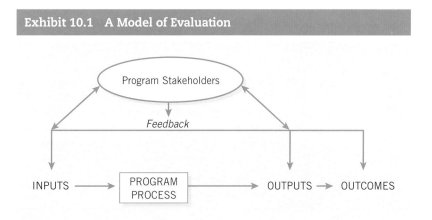

Exhibit 10.1   A Model of Evaluation

Source: Adapted from Martin and Kettner 1996.

Next, some service or treatment is provided to the cases. This may be attendance in a class, assistance with a health problem, residence in new housing, or receipt of special cash benefits. The process of service delivery (program process) may be simple or complicated, short or long, but it is designed to have some impact on the cases, as inputs are consumed and outputs are produced.

The direct products of the program's service delivery process are its outputs. Program outputs may include clients served, case managers trained, food parcels delivered, or arrests made. The program outputs may be desirable in themselves, but they primarily serve to indicate that the program is operating.

Program outcomes indicate the impact of the program on the cases that have been processed. Outcomes can range from improved test scores or higher rates of job retention to fewer criminal offenses and lower rates of poverty. There are likely to be multiple outcomes of any social program, some intended and some unintended, some positive and others that are viewed as negative.

Variation in both outputs and outcomes, in turn, influences the inputs to the program through a feedback process. If not enough clients are being served, recruitment of new clients may increase. If too many negative side effects result from a trial medication, the trials may be limited or terminated. If a program does not appear to lead to improved outcomes, clients may go elsewhere.

Evaluation research enters into this picture as a more systematic approach to feedback that strengthens the feedback loop through credible analyses of program operations and outcomes. Evaluation research also broadens this loop to include connections to parties outside of the program itself. A funding agency or political authority may mandate the research, outside experts may be brought in to conduct the research, and the evaluation research findings may be released to the public—or at least funders—in a formal report.

The evaluation process as a whole—and the feedback process in particular—can only be understood in relation to the interests and perspectives of program stakeholders. Stakeholders are those individuals and groups who have some basis of concern with the program. They might be clients, staff, managers, funders, or the public. The board of a program or agency, the parents or spouses of clients, the foundations that award program grants, the auditors who monitor program spending, and members of Congress are all potential program stakeholders, and each has an interest in the outcome of any program evaluation. Some may fund the evaluation, some may provide research data, and some may review—and even approve—the research report (Martin & Kettner, 1996). Who the program stakeholders are and what role they play in the program evaluation will have tremendous consequences for the research.

Can you see the difference between evaluation research and traditional social science research? Unlike explanatory social science research, evaluation research is not designed to test the implications of a social theory; the basic issue is often just "What is the program's impact?" Process evaluation often uses qualitative methods, but unlike traditional exploratory research, the goal is not to create a broad theoretical explanation for what is discovered; instead, the question is "How does the program do what it does?" Unlike social science research, the researchers cannot design evaluation studies simply in accord with the highest scientific standards and the most important research questions; instead, it is program stakeholders who set the agenda, but there is no sharp boundary between the two: In their attempt to explain how and why the program has an impact and whether the program is needed, evaluation researchers often bring social theories into their projects.

QUESTIONS FOR EVALUATION RESEARCH

Evaluation projects can focus on several questions related to the operation of social programs and the impact they have:

Program process: The complete treatment or service delivered by the program

Outputs: The services delivered or new products produced by the program process

Feedback: Information about service delivery system outputs, outcomes, or operations that is available to any program inputs

Stakeholders: Individuals and groups who have some basis of concern with the program

- Is the program needed? (evaluation of need)

- Can the program be evaluated? (evaluability assessment)

- How does the program operate? (evaluation of process)

- What is the program's impact? (evaluation of impact)

- How efficient is the program? (evaluation of efficiency)

The specific methods used in an evaluation research project depend, in part, on which of these questions is being addressed.

Do We Need the Program?

Is a new program needed, or is an old one still required? Is there a need at all? A needs assessment attempts to answer these questions with systematic, credible evidence. The initial impetus for implementing programs to alleviate social problems and other societal ailments typically comes from a variety of sources, including advocacy groups, moral leaders, community advocates, and political figures. Before a program is designed and implemented, however, it is essential to obtain reliable information on the nature and the scope of the problem, as well as the target population in need of the intervention. Evaluation researchers often contribute to these efforts by applying research tools to answer such questions as "What is the magnitude of this problem in this community?" "How many people in this community are in need of this program?" "What are the demographic characteristics of these people (e.g., age, gender, and race or ethnicity)?" and "Is the proposed program or intervention appropriate for this population?"

Needs assessment is not as easy as it sounds (Posavac & Carey, 1997). Whose definitions or perceptions should be used to shape our description of the level of need? How will we deal with ignorance of need? How can we understand the level of need without understanding the social context from which that level of need emerges? (Short answer to that one: We can't!) What, after all, does *need* mean in the abstract? We won't really understand what the level of need is until we develop plans for implementing a program in response to the identified needs.

> Needs assessment: A type of evaluation research that attempts to determine the needs of some population that might be met with a social program

Can the Program Be Evaluated?

Evaluation research will be pointless if the program itself cannot be evaluated. Yes, some type of study is always possible, but a study conducted specifically to identify the effects of a particular program may not be possible within the available time and resources. So researchers may carry out an evaluability assessment to learn this in advance rather than expend time and effort on a fruitless project.

Knowledge about the program gleaned through the evaluability assessment can be used to refine evaluation plans. Because they are preliminary studies to check things out, evaluability assessments often rely on qualitative methods. Program managers and key staff may be interviewed in depth, or program sponsors may be asked about the importance they attach to different goals. These assessments also may have an "action research" aspect because the researcher presents the findings to program managers and encourages changes in program operations.

> Evaluability assessment: A type of evaluation research conducted to determine whether it is feasible to evaluate a program's effects within the available time and resources

Is the Program Working as Planned?

What actually happens in a program? Once a program has been started, evaluators are often called on to document the extent to which implementation has taken place, whether the program is reaching the target individuals or groups, whether the program is actually operating as expected, and what resources are being expended in the conduct of the program. This is often called **process evaluation** or **program monitoring**. Rossi and Freeman (1989) define program monitoring as the systematic attempt by evaluation researchers to examine program coverage and delivery. Assessing program coverage consists of estimating the extent to which a program is reaching its intended target population; evaluating program delivery consists of measuring the degree of congruence between the plan for providing services and treatments and the ways they are actually provided.

Process evaluations are extremely important, primarily because there is no way to reliably determine whether the intended outcomes have occurred without being certain the program is working according to plan. For example, imagine you are responsible for determining whether an antibullying curriculum implemented in a school has been successful in decreasing the amount of bullying behavior by the students. You conduct a survey of the students both before and after the curriculum began and determine that rates of bullying have not significantly changed in the school since the curriculum started. After you write your report, however, you find out that, instead of being given in a five-day series of 1-hour sessions as intended, the curriculum was actually crammed into a 2-hour format delivered on a Friday afternoon. A process evaluation would have revealed this implementation problem. If a program has not been implemented as intended, there is obviously no need to ask whether it had the intended outcomes.

A process evaluation can take many forms. Because most government and private organizations inherently monitor their activities through such things as application forms, receipts, and stock inventories, it should be relatively easy to obtain quantitative data for monitoring the delivery of services. This information can be summarized to describe things such as the clients served and the services provided. In addition to this quantitative information, a process evaluation will also likely benefit from qualitative methodologies, such as unstructured interviews with people using the service or program. Interviews can also be conducted with staff to illuminate what they perceive to be obstacles to their delivery of services.

Process evaluation can employ a wide range of indicators. Program coverage can be monitored through program records, participant surveys, community surveys, or number of utilizers versus dropouts and ineligibles. Service delivery can be monitored through service records completed by program staff, a management information system maintained by program administrators, or reports by program recipients (Rossi & Freeman, 1989).

Qualitative methods are often a key component of process evaluation studies because they can be used to understand internal program dynamics, even those that were not anticipated (Patton, 2002; Posavac & Carey, 1997). Qualitative researchers may develop detailed descriptions of how program participants engage with each other, how the program experience varies for different people, and how the program changes and evolves over time.

Case Study: Process Evaluation of an Antigang Initiative

As part of its Project Safe Neighborhoods, the U.S. Department of Justice (DOJ) provided funding to 12 relatively large cities to develop and implement a comprehensive antigang initiative (CAGI) intended to prevent and reduce gang violence. The CAGI comprised several strategies to achieve these goals through suppression (i.e., arrests and surveillance), social intervention (i.e., emergency responses to acts of violence), organizational change (i.e., creating broad consensus about gang problems), community mobilization (i.e., mobilizing community resources to address factors related to gangs), and social-opportunities provision (i.e., expansion of job-end educational opportunities). Edmund McGarrell and his colleagues

(2013) conducted both a process and impact evaluation of the CAGI initiative. To evaluate whether the initiative was implemented as planned, the process evaluation component of the project surveyed CAGI project coordinators in all sites along with site visits and interviews with federal partners coordinating with the CAGI.

To measure the degree to which various components of CAGI were implemented, the survey asked site coordinators if their program incorporated various dimensions of the program, including the rigor of *research* (i.e., if there was a research partner gathering data for the project), the commitment of *law enforcement* strategies (i.e., the different policing strategies that were employed), and the diversity and range of *prevention* strategies that were adopted by the site. In addition to subscales that measured each of these domains of research, law enforcement, and prevention, McGarrell et al. (2013) created a standardized scale that measured the degree of implementation across sites that ranged from a low of 3 to a high of 13. Control cities in the analysis that did not have CAGI implemented in their city were given a value of 0 for the index. Exhibit 10.2 provides a list of the survey questions that asked about the possible prevention strategies that were implemented by sites.

The average implementation scale score for all cities was 1.22. This is relatively low, considering the possible high score was equal to 9, indicating that many of the strategies that could have been implemented across the CAGI sites were not. Still, when this implementation scale was used to predict gun homicide rates across cities, it was found to reduce gun homicides by about 12%. When McGarrell and his colleagues (2013) examined the type of programs that had the most effect on gun homicides, law enforcement strategies appeared to have the largest effect. These law enforcement strategies included comprehensive police partnerships and proactive enforcement strategies, such as directed patrols, antigang ordinances, and comprehensive gun tracing. Unfortunately, these strategies only affected the gun homicide rate in the short term and did not have a sustained impact.

Did the Program Work?

If a process study shows that the implementation of the program has been delivered to the target population as planned, the next role for an evaluator is to assess the extent to which the program achieved its goals. "Did the program work?" and "Did the program have the intended consequences?" are questions that should be familiar to you by now; stated more like a research question we are used to, "Did the treatment or program (independent variable) effect change in the dependent variable?" It all comes back to the issue of causality. This part of the research is variously called **impact evaluation** or impact analysis.

Impact evaluation:
Analysis of the extent to which a treatment or other service has the intended effect

The bulk of the published evaluation studies in our field are devoted to some type of impact assessment. Have new seat belt laws (independent variable) increased rates of seat belt usage (dependent variable)? Have rape reform statutes increased the willingness of rape victims to report their victimizations to police? Are boot camps more likely to reduce recidivism among juveniles compared with more traditional juvenile detention settings? Have mandatory minimum sentencing guidelines decreased the probability that extralegal factors, such as sex and race, will affect an individual's sentence? The list could go on and on.

As in other areas of research, an experimental design is the preferred method for maximizing internal validity—that is, for making sure your causal claims about program impact are justified. Cases are assigned randomly to one or more experimental treatment groups and to a control group so that there is no systematic difference between the groups at the outset (see Chapter 6). The goal is to achieve a fair, unbiased test of the program itself so that the judgment about the program's impact is not influenced by differences between the types of people who are in the different groups. It can be a difficult goal to achieve because the usual practice in social programs is to let people decide for themselves whether they want to enter a program or not and also to establish eligibility criteria that ensure that people who enter

Exhibit 10.2   Survey Questions That Asked CAGI Site Coordinators About the Prevention Strategies That Were Implemented

Measure	Indicator	Coding
Prevention Programs		
Please identify the prevention and intervention programs that have been employed as part of CAGI:		
Outreach and education to juvenile groups	no/yes	0–1
Truancy strategies	no/yes	0–1
Clergy outreach	no/yes	0–1
Ex-offender outreach	no/yes	0–1
Employment programs	no/yes	0–1
Substance abuse programs	no/yes	0–1
Vocational training programs	no/yes	0–1
Education programs	no/yes	0–1
School-based programs	no/yes	0–1
Neighborhood development programs	no/yes	0–1
Youth street worker programs	no/yes	0–1
Hospital trauma center outreach	no/yes	0–1
Other (described)	no/yes	0–1
	Potential item range	**0–13**

Source: McGarrell, et al. 2013. Adapted from Table 2.

the program are different from those who do not (Boruch, 1997). In either case, a selection bias is introduced.

Of course, program impact may also be evaluated with quasi-experimental designs or survey or field research methods without a randomized experimental design. But if current participants who are already in a program are compared with nonparticipants, it is unlikely that the treatment group will be comparable to the control group. Participants will probably be a selected group, different at the outset from nonparticipants. As a result, causal conclusions about program impact will be on much shakier ground. For instance, when a study at New York's maximum-security prison for women found that "Inmate Education [i.e., classes] Is Found to Lower Risk of New Arrest," the conclusions were immediately suspect: The research design did not ensure that the women who enrolled in the prison classes were similar to (e.g., in offense type) those who had not enrolled in the classes, "leaving open the possibility that the results were due, at least in part, to self-selection, with the women most motivated to avoid reincarceration being the ones who took the college classes" (Lewin, 2001).

Case Study: The Risk Skills Training Program (RSTP) Compared With Drug Abuse Resistance Education-Abbreviated (DARE-A)

The Risk Skills Training Program (RSTP) was designed to target multiple risk behaviors such as drinking and drug use, along with changing adolescents' personal beliefs about such behavior. Elizabeth D'Amico and Kim Fromme (2002) studied the impact of the RSTP and how it compared with the Drug Abuse Resistance Education–Abbreviated (DARE-A) program, as well as how both of these programs affected outcomes compared with students who received no programming (a control group).

To evaluate the efficacy of these programs in reducing drinking and drug use, they randomly selected 150 students to participate in their study. Then, students were randomly assigned to one of the three conditions: 75 students received RSTP programming, 75 students received the DARE-A programming, and another 150 students were randomly selected to participate but received no programming. The students received a pretest assessment and then posttest assessments, which took place at both two and six months after the programs.

The impacts (dependent variables) D'Amico and Fromme (2002) examined included positive and negative "alcohol expectancies" (the anticipated effects of drinking), as well as perceptions of peer risk taking and actual alcohol consumption. D'Amico and Fromme found that negative alcohol expectancies increased for the RSTP group in the posttest but not for the DARE-A group or the control group, while weekly drinking and "positive expectancies" for drinking outcomes actually *increased* for the DARE-A group and/or the control group by the six-month follow-up but not for the RSTP group (see Exhibit 10.3).

You should recognize the design used by D'Amico and Fromme as a true experimental design (see Chapter 6). This is the preferred method for maximizing internal validity—that is, for making sure your causal claims about program impact are justified. Cases are assigned randomly to one or more experimental treatment groups and to a control group so that there is no systematic difference between the groups at the outset. The goal is to achieve a fair, unbiased test of the program itself so that the judgment about the program's impact is not influenced by differences between the types of people who are in the different groups. It can be a difficult goal to achieve because the usual practice in social programs is to let people decide for themselves whether they want to enter a program and also to establish eligibility criteria that ensure that people who enter the program are different from those who do not (Boruch, 1997). In either case, a selection bias is introduced.

An impact evaluation is an important undertaking that fully deserves the attention it has been given in government program funding requirements. However, you should realize that more rigorous evaluation designs are less likely to conclude that a program has the desired effect; as the standard of proof goes up, success is harder to demonstrate. We will provide other case studies of impact evaluations at the end of the chapter.

Is the Program Worth It?

Whatever the program's benefits, are they sufficient to offset the program's costs? Are taxpayers getting their money's worth? What resources are required by the program? These efficiency questions can be the primary reason that funders require evaluation of the programs they fund. As a result, an **efficiency analysis**, which compares program effects with costs, is often a necessary component of an evaluation research project.

A **cost–benefit analysis** must identify the specific program costs and the procedures for estimating the economic value of specific program benefits. This type of analysis also requires

Efficiency analysis: A type of evaluation research that compares program costs with program effects; it can be either a cost–benefit analysis or a cost-effectiveness analysis

Cost-benefit analysis: A type of evaluation research that compares program costs with the economic value of program benefits

Exhibit 10.3   Impact of RSTP and DARE-A

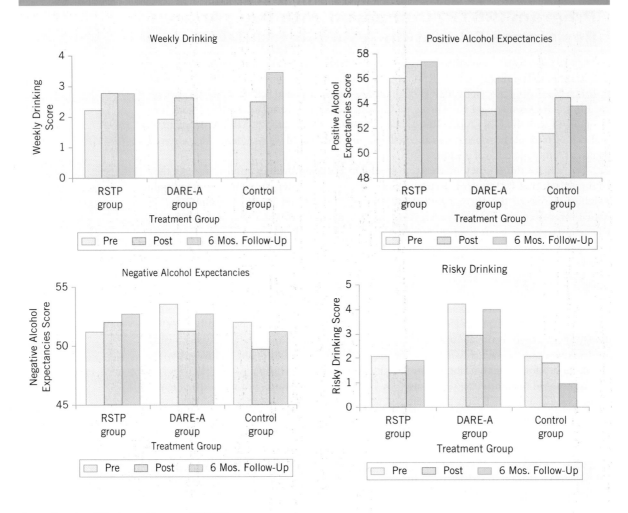

Source: Based on D'Amico and Fromme 2002, 569.

that the analyst identify whose perspective will be used to determine what can be considered a benefit rather than a cost.

A **cost-effectiveness analysis** focuses attention directly on the program's outcomes rather than on the economic value of those outcomes. In a cost-effectiveness analysis, the specific costs of the program are compared with the program's outcomes, such as the number of jobs obtained, the extent of improvement in reading scores, or the degree of decline in crimes committed. For example, one result might be an estimate of how much it cost the program for each job obtained by a program participant.

Social science training often does not give much attention to cost–benefit analysis, so it can be helpful to review possible costs and benefits with an economist or business school professor or student. Once potential costs and benefits have been identified, they must be measured. It is a need highlighted in recent government programs.

Cost-effectiveness analysis: A type of evaluation research that compares program costs to actual program outcomes

In addition to measuring services and their associated costs, a cost–benefit analysis must be able to make some type of estimation of how clients benefited from the program. Normally, this will involve a comparison of some indicators of client status before and after clients received program services or between clients who received program services and a comparable group who did not.

Case Study: Cost–Benefit Analysis of CCTV Monitoring and Direct Police Patrol

Communities across the globe have increasingly begun using closed-circuit television (CCTV) cameras for crime prevention. In general, results of impact evaluations for CCTV in preventing crimes show that they deter property crime more than violent crime and are most effective in small areas, such as parking lots. Unfortunately, CCTV cameras are extremely expensive, costing millions of dollars to install and even more to maintain and staff. Are the costs of CCTV systems worth this investment? To find out, Piza, Gilchrist, Caplan, Kennedy, and O'Hara (2016) conducted a cost–benefit analysis of a program in Newark, New Jersey, which paired proactive CCTV monitoring with directed police patrol, which was called the CCTV Directed Patrol Strategy. The directed-patrol component of the program increased CCTV monitoring staff and placed unmarked patrol units in areas to respond to incidents detected by CCTV operators.

Without going into the advanced statistical analysis used to calculate the benefits of this program net of the costs, Piza et al. (2016) created a total net effect (TNE) estimate of the crimes prevented or generated by the CCTV Directed Patrol Strategy. Their estimates included several different costs, including victim costs, criminal justice system costs, policing costs, court costs, and corrections costs. Because Newark already had a CCTV system in place, the costs associated with the new program were related to personnel costs, vehicle costs, and camera maintenance and wireless network costs. For example, during each 4-hour "tour-of-duty," five additional officers, three patrol officers, one patrol supervisor, and one video surveillance operator were worked, which resulted in a cost of nearly $74,000 over the 11-week period of the study. So did the crime prevention efforts exceed the costs? Results generally suggest that the directed-patrol strategy increased the cost-effectiveness of the CCTV system. However, investing in a new CCTV system would lead to a cost deficit. In short, the crime prevention effects of a CCTV system are not worth the bucks.

DESIGN DECISIONS

Once we have decided on or identified the goal or focus for a program evaluation, there are still important decisions to be made about how to design the specific evaluation project. The most important decisions are the following:

- Black-box or program theory: Do we care how the program gets results?
- Researcher or stakeholder orientation: Whose goals matter most?
- Quantitative or qualitative methods: Which methods provide the best answers?

Black-Box Evaluation or Program Theory

The "meat and potatoes" of most evaluation research involves determining whether a program has the intended effect. If the effect occurred, the program worked; if the effect didn't occur, then some would say the program should be abandoned or redesigned. In this approach, the process by which a program has an effect on outcomes is often treated as a **black-box evaluation** —that is, the focus of the evaluation researcher is on whether cases seem to have changed as a result of their exposure to the program between the time they entered the program as inputs and when they exited the program as outputs (H. Chen, 1990). The assumption is that program evaluation requires only the test of a simple input–output model. There may be no attempt to open the black box of the program process.

If an investigation of program process is conducted, a **program theory** may be developed. A program theory describes what has been learned about how the program has its effect. When a researcher has sufficient knowledge before the investigation begins, outlining a program theory can help to guide the investigation of program process in the most productive directions. This is termed a **theory-driven evaluation**.

A program theory specifies how the program is expected to operate and identifies which program elements are operational (H. Chen, 1990). In addition, a program theory specifies how a program is to produce its effects and so improves understanding of the relationship between the independent variable (the program) and the dependent variable (the outcome or outcomes).

Researcher or Stakeholder Orientation

Whose prescriptions specify how the program should operate, what outcomes it should try to achieve, or whom it should serve? Most social science research assumes that the researcher specifies the research questions, the applicable theory or theories, and the outcomes to be investigated. Social science research results are most often reported in a professional journal or at professional conferences, where scientific standards determine how the research is received. In program evaluation, however, the research question is often set by the program sponsors or the government agency that is responsible for reviewing the program. It is to these authorities that research findings are reported. Most often, this authority also specifies the outcomes to be investigated. The first evaluator of the evaluation research is therefore the funding agency, not the professional social science community. Evaluation research is research for a client, and its results may directly affect the services, treatments, or even punishments (e.g., in the case of prison studies) that program users receive. In this case, the person who pays the piper gets to call the tune.

Should an evaluation researcher insist on designing the evaluation project and specifying its goals, or should he or she accept the suggestions and adopt the goals of the funding agency? What role should the preferences of program staff or clients play? What responsibility does the evaluation researcher have to politicians and taxpayers when evaluating government-funded programs? The different answers that various evaluation researchers have given to these questions are reflected in different approaches to evaluation (H. Chen, 1990).

Stakeholder approaches encourage researchers to be responsive to program stakeholders. Issues for study are to be based on the views of people involved with the program, and reports are to be made to program participants. The program theory is developed by the researcher to clarify and develop the key stakeholders' theory of the program (Shadish, Cook, & Leviton, 1991). In one stakeholder approach, termed *utilization-focused evaluation*, the evaluator forms a task force of program stakeholders who help to shape the evaluation project so that they are more likely to use its results (Patton, 2002). In evaluation research termed *action research* or *participatory research*, program participants are engaged with the researchers as coresearchers and help to design, conduct, and report the research. One research approach that has been termed *appreciative inquiry* eliminates the professional researcher altogether in favor of a structured dialogue about needed changes among program participants themselves (Patton, 2002).

Black box evaluation: This type of evaluation occurs when an evaluation of program outcomes ignores and does not identify the process by which the program produced the effect

Program theory: A descriptive or prescriptive model of how a program operates and produces its effects

Theory-driven evaluation: A program evaluation that is guided by a theory that specifies the process by which the program has an effect

Stakeholder approaches: An orientation to evaluation research that expects researchers to be responsive primarily to the people involved with the program

Social science approaches emphasize the importance of researcher expertise and maintenance of some autonomy to develop the most trustworthy, unbiased program evaluation. It is assumed that "evaluators cannot passively accept the values and views of the other stakeholders" (H. Chen, 1990, p. 78). Evaluators who adopt this approach derive a program theory from information they obtain on how the program operates and extant social science theory and knowledge, not from the views of stakeholders.

Integrated approaches attempt to cover issues of concern to both stakeholders and evaluators, as well as include stakeholders in the group from which guidance is routinely sought (H.-T. Chen & Rossi, 1987). The emphasis given to either stakeholder or social concern is expected to vary with the specific project circumstances. Integrated approaches seek to balance the goal of carrying out a project that is responsive to stakeholder concerns with the goal of objective, scientifically trustworthy, and generalizable results. When the research is planned, evaluators are expected to communicate and negotiate regularly with key stakeholders and to take stakeholder concerns into account. Findings from preliminary inquiries are reported back to program decision makers so that they can make improvements in the program before it is formally evaluated. When the actual evaluation is conducted, the evaluation research team is expected to operate more autonomously, minimizing intrusions from program stakeholders.

Ultimately, evaluation research takes place in a political context, in which program stakeholders may be competing or collaborating to increase program funding or to emphasize particular program goals. It is a political process that creates social programs, and it is a political process that determines whether these programs are evaluated and what is done with evaluation findings (Weiss, 1993). Developing supportive relations with stakeholder groups will increase the odds that political processes will not undermine evaluation practice.

> Social science approaches: An orientation to evaluation research that expects researchers to emphasize the importance of researcher expertise and maintenance of autonomy from program stakeholders
>
> Integrated approaches: An orientation to evaluation research that expects researchers to respond to concerns of people involved with stakeholders, as well as to the standards and goals of the social scientific community

EVALUATION IN ACTION

Case Study: Problem-Oriented Policing in Violent Crime Areas—A Randomized Controlled Experiment

Several studies have found that over half of all crimes in a city are committed at a few criminogenic places within communities. Even within the most crime-ridden neighborhoods, it has been found that crime clusters at a few discrete locations while other areas remain relatively crime free. The clustering of violent crime at particular locations suggests that there are important features or dynamics at these locations that give rise to violent situations. As such, focused crime prevention efforts should be able to modify these criminogenic conditions and reduce violence.

Problem-oriented policing strategies, sometimes called focused deterrence strategies, are increasingly used by urban jurisdictions to reduce crime in these high-activity crime places. Problem-oriented policing challenges officers to identify and analyze the causes of problems behind a string of criminal incidents. Once the underlying conditions that give rise to crime problems are known, police officers can then develop and implement appropriate responses. One of the only true experiments to examine the efficacy of problem-oriented policing was conducted by Anthony Braga and his colleagues in 1999, and it remains a model evaluation study today. Importantly, research has continued to support the effectiveness of these strategies (Braga, Weisburd, & Turchan, 2018). The original field experiment to determine the effectiveness of problem-oriented policing in decreasing the rate of violent street crime was conducted in Jersey City, New Jersey. Recall from Chapter 6 that a true experiment allows researchers to assume that the only systematic difference between a control and an experimental group is the presence of the intervention, in this case, the presence or absence of problem-oriented policing strategies.

To determine which places would receive the problem-oriented strategies and which places would not, 56 neighborhoods were matched into 28 pairs with equal levels of crime, which were then randomly assigned to receive the problem-oriented policing treatment (experimental places). Remember that a key feature of true experimental designs is this

random assignment. The places that were not selected from the flip in each pair did not receive the new policing strategies (control places). The design of this experimental evaluation is illustrated in Exhibit 10.4.

In each of the experimental places, police officers from the Violent Crime Unit (VCU) of the Jersey City Police Department established networks consistent with problem-oriented policing. For example, community members were used as information sources to discuss the nature of the problems the community faced, the possible effectiveness of proposed responses, and the assessment of implemented responses. In most places, the VCU officers believed that the violence that distinguished these places from other areas of the city was closely related to the disorder of the place. Although specific tactics varied from place to place, most attempts to control violence in these places were actually targeted at the social-disorder problems. For example, some tactics included cleaning up the environment of the place through aggressive order maintenance and making physical improvements, such as securing vacant lots or removing trash from the street. The independent variable or treatment, then, was the use of problem-oriented policing, which comprised a number of specific tactics implemented by police officers to control the physical and social disorder at experimental violent places. In contrast, control places did not receive these problem-solving efforts; they received traditional policing strategies, such as arbitrary patrol interventions and routine follow-up investigations by detectives. No problem-oriented strategies were employed.

The effectiveness of these problem-oriented policing strategies was determined with three separate dependent variables: incident report data, citizen emergency calls for service within each place, and physical observation of each place during the pretest and posttest periods. This variable was used to indicate changes in both physical incivilities at places, such as vacant lots, trash, graffiti, or broken windows, and social incivilities, such as drinking in public and loitering. These variables were measured for six-month preintervention and postintervention periods. If the problem-oriented policing approach was effective, then Braga and colleagues should have seen a decrease in incidents and emergency calls for service in the experimental

Exhibit 10.4 Randomized Experimental Design Used to Evaluate Problem-Oriented Policing Strategies

Places	Placement	Group	Pretest	Treatment/Condition	Posttest
56 high violent crime places	Random assignment	Experimental group	Citizen calls for police service	Problem-oriented policing	Citizen calls for police service
		Control group	Citizen calls for police service	Traditional policing	Citizen calls for police service

Source: Braga, et al. 1999.

areas in the posttest compared with the control areas. They also should have seen decreased signs of physical and social incivilities in the experimental areas compared with the control areas. Results indicated that the problem-oriented policing strategies examined in this evaluation research appear to have had a great deal of success in controlling and preventing crime.

STRENGTHS OF RANDOMIZED EXPERIMENTAL DESIGNS IN IMPACT EVALUATIONS

The research design used by Braga et al. (1999) meets all three criteria for a true experimental design. First, they used at least two comparison groups. In the Braga et al. research, some communities received the problem-oriented patrol strategies (experimental groups), while the other comparison communities received traditional police patrol (control groups).

Recall the three criteria necessary for establishing a causal relationship between independent and dependent variables (see Chapter 6):

1. Association between the independent and dependent variables

2. Correct time order (the independent variable precedes the dependent)

3. Nonspuriousness (rule out influence of other variables)

Data obtained from a true experimental design provide the best way to determine that all three of these criteria have been met. Because the assessment of change in the dependent variables used in Braga et al.'s study was performed after the experimental condition (problem-oriented strategies) had been delivered, they could also ensure that the time order was correct and that the only factors that affected the reduction in violent crime was likely the new patrol strategies and not some other factor.

Many U.S. Jails Fail to Stop Inmate Suicides

This article highlights an Associated Press investigation of local news reports, lawsuits against local jails, and investigations within several local jails to understand the increasing rate of suicides in jails. They found that more than half of suicides and attempts occurred during the first seven days of custody, and many of these were in the first 48 hours. About a third of inmates who committed or attempted suicide did so after correctional staff allegedly failed to provide them with prescription medicines to manage mental illness. Other cases involved inmates who were withdrawing from drugs after incarceration. Many sheriff's offices responded that they do not have the resources to serve as mental health or drug treatment facilities.

For Further Thought

1. Describe a policy that you would implement to reduce suicides in jails. Now, what research method(s) would you use to determine whether the policy was actually implemented as planned?

2. Now describe the research method(s) you would use to determine whether the policy actually reduced suicides and attempts in jails.

Source: Cohen, S., & Eckert, N. (2019, June 18). AP investigation: Many US jails fail to stop inmate suicides. *New York Times*. Retrieved from https://www.apnews.com/5a61d556a0a14251bafbeff1c26d5f15

RESEARCH IN THE NEWS

Because the communities in Braga et al.'s (1999) study were randomly assigned to receive either problem-oriented or traditional patrol strategies, the relationship found between these strategies (independent variable) and the dependent variables (e.g., incidents of crime) is unambiguous. Braga and colleagues monitored their dependent variables both before and after the different policing strategies were implemented, so there is also no question that the strategies came before the change in the dependent variable. Finally, the random assignment of the communities to either the problem-oriented or traditional police conditions controlled for a host of possible extraneous influences that may have created spurious relationships.

The extent to which the findings of these studies can be generalized to the larger population, however, is another issue. Can their findings be generalized to the larger population in New Jersey (sample generalizability) or to other states and communities (external validity)? Issues of sample generalizability, you will recall, are related to selecting a random sample from the population in the first place (random selection), not random assignment. However, because Braga and colleagues' study used several experimental and control communities, this increases the likelihood that their findings are generalizable to their respective populations. In addition, because the study was performed in the field (i.e., the real world) and not in a laboratory, their findings are more likely to be generalizable to the larger population.

WHEN EXPERIMENTS ARE NOT FEASIBLE

We have already learned that many research questions or situations are not amenable to a true experimental design. The same is true in evaluation research. There are many reasons why it may be impossible to use randomized experiments to evaluate the impacts of programs and policies. For this reason, quasi-experimental designs are frequently used (Chapter 6).

Quasi-experimental design: A research design in which there is a comparison group that is comparable with the experimental group in critical ways, but subjects are not randomly assigned to the comparison and experimental groups

Recall that a **quasi-experimental design** is one in which at least one or more elements of a true experimental design is absent. In evaluation research, the element that is often missing is random assignment to experimental and control conditions. The primary reason why randomization is likely not possible in evaluation research is that the program is usually outside the control of the evaluator. As Rossi and Freeman (1989) state, "For political, human subject or other considerations, program staff, sponsors, or other powerful stakeholders resist randomization" (p. 313). Obtaining the cooperation of the program staff and sponsors is often an obstacle in evaluation research. In fact, when there are several locations implementing similar programs, the sites included in an evaluation study may be selected based primarily on the cooperation of the staff and sponsors.

In general, quasi-experimental designs are the most powerful alternatives to true randomized experimental designs. The more alike the experimental and control groups are to each other, particularly on characteristics thought to be related to the intervention or treatment, the more confident we can be in a study's findings. In this section, we will highlight the most frequently used quasi-experimental design, a *nonequivalent control group design* (for review of this design, see Chapter 6).

Case Study: Nonequivalent Control Group Design: Decreasing Injuries From Police Use of Force

As noted in the introduction of this chapter, although there has been a great deal of media attention on police use of force, there is a dearth of research investigating ways to curtail both injuries and death as a result of police–citizen encounters. One weapon, the CED (or Tasers®), holds promise to reduce injuries to both officers and suspects. Although there is some controversy about CEDs, including Amnesty International's call for a moratorium on their use until standards can be reached on their safe use, very few research attempts have been undertaken to determine whether the use of CEDs reduces injuries. Bruce Taylor and Daniel Woods (2010) were some of the first to compare injury rates of both officers and suspects in LEAs that used CEDs with a matched sample of LEAs that did not use them. Because they could not randomly assign LEAs to experimental and control conditions, they used a **nonequivalent control group design**. They selected 13 LEAs that could provide data for four years (two years pre– and two years post–CED deployment and a comparable time period for non-CED sites). To ensure the LEAs were comparable in other ways, they were matched on several criteria, including violent crime levels, violent crime arrests, agency size, and population size of jurisdiction. All LEAs also provided detailed training for their officers on use-of-force issues regardless of whether they employed CEDs. LEAs that did not use CEDs did use other nonlethal weapons, such as pepper spray and batons.

Taylor and Woods (2010) defined use of force by an officer as any

> physical strike or instrumental contact with a person by an officer or any significant physical contact that restricted the movement of a person by an officer, including the discharge of firearms, use of a CED, use of chemical spray, use of any other weapon, choke holds, or hard hands, taking the suspect to the ground, and deployment of a canine. (p. 268)

The measurement of injuries included a simple injury variable coded *yes* or *no*, a measure indicating the severity of the injury, whether the injury required medical attention, and whether it required hospitalization. The researchers also controlled for other characteristics of the incident, including suspect's race, gender, and age. After these factors were controlled, results indicated that LEAs that used CEDs had improved safety outcomes compared with the matched non-CED sites on three injury measures: reductions in (a) officer injuries overall, (b) suspect severe injuries, and (c) both officers and suspects receiving an injury requiring medical attention. Appropriately, Taylor and Woods (2010) caution that because they did not use a true experimental design, they could not control for all possible unmeasured variables related to injury. However, they conclude, "We have considered various alternative explanations for our results and believe the most plausible explanation is that the availability of CEDs to officers is a key factor in reducing injuries to officers and suspects" (p. 281).

> **Nonequivalent control group design:** A quasi-experimental design in which there are experimental and comparison groups that are designated before the treatment occurs but are not created by random assignment

QUALITATIVE AND QUANTITATIVE METHODS

Evaluation research that attempts to identify the effects of a treatment, law, or program typically is quantitative. It is fair to say that when there is an interest in comparing outcomes between an experimental and a control group or tracking change over time in a systematic manner, quantitative methods are favored.

But qualitative methods can add much to quantitative evaluation research studies, including more depth, detail, nuance, and exemplary case studies (Patton, 1997). Perhaps the greatest contribution qualitative methods can make in many evaluation studies is in investigating the program process—finding out what is inside the black box. Although it is possible—and even recommended—to track the process of service delivery with quantitative measures, such as staff contact hours, frequency of complaints, and the like, the goal of finding out what is happening to program clients and how clients experience the program can often best be achieved by observing program activities and interviewing staff and clients intensively.

Another good reason for using qualitative methods in evaluation research is the importance of learning how different individuals react to the treatment. Qualitative methods can also help in understanding how social programs actually operate. Complex social programs have many different features, and it is not always clear whether it is the combination of those features or some particular features that are responsible for the program's effect or for the absence of an effect.

The more complex the social program, the more value qualitative methods can add to the evaluation process. For the most part, the strengths and weaknesses of methodologies used in evaluation research are those of the methods we have already discussed throughout this text. As Patton (1997) contends, "There are no perfect [evaluation] studies. And there cannot be, for there is no agreement on what constitutes perfection" (p. 23). There are, however, methods that are better able to infer cause and effect. Because the basic question of most impact evaluations is "Does the program (cause) have its intended consequences (effect)?" there are basic methodological criteria we can use to judge the methods discussed in this chapter.

Despite the fact that a randomized experiment is the best way to determine the impact of a program, it is also important to remember that the methodology selected for an evaluation project should be relevant to the policy makers and planners who intend to use the results. Although some researchers vehemently contend that only a randomized experimental design can provide reliable information on the impacts of a program, others just as vehemently disagree.

INCREASING DEMAND FOR EVIDENCE-BASED POLICY

Policy research:
A process in which research results are used to provide policy actors with recommendations for action that are based on empirical evidence and careful reasoning

Evidence-based policy:
A policy that has been evaluated with a methodologically rigorous design and has been proven to be effective

Systematic review:
Summary review about the impact of a program in which the analyst attempts to account for differences across research designs and samples, often using statistical techniques such as a meta-analysis

Policy research is a process rather than a method: "a process that attempts to support and persuade actors by providing them with well-reasoned, evidence-based, and responsible recommendations for decision making and action" (Majchrzak & Markus, 2014, p. 3). Because policy research often draws on the findings of evaluation research projects and involves working for a client, as is the case in evaluation research, policy researchers confront many of the same challenges as do evaluation researchers. Because policy researchers must summarize and weigh evidence from a wide range of sources, they need to be familiar with each of the methods presented in this book.

The goal of policy research is to inform those who make policy about the possible alternative courses of action in response to some identified problem, their strengths and weaknesses, and their likely positive and negative effects. Reviewing the available evidence may lead the policy researcher to conclude that enough is known about the issues to develop recommendations without further research, but it is more likely that additional research will be needed using primary or secondary sources. Policies that have been evaluated with a methodologically rigorous design and have been proven effective are sometimes called **evidence-based policies**.

As you have seen, evaluation studies come in many forms. A single study, such as the Minneapolis Domestic Violence Experiment (recall Chapter 2), can be very influential and have an enormous effect on police policies. But we have seen that replications of studies answering the same question often result in very different conclusions. Obviously, learning what works should rely on more than one study. Evaluation specialists are increasingly encouraging policy makers to enact evidence-based policies, which are based on a **systematic review** of all available evidence that assesses what works and what doesn't. Petrosino and Lavenberg (2007) define systematic reviews as follows:

In systematic reviews, researchers attempt to gather relevant evaluative studies, critically appraise them, and come to judgments about what works using explicit, transparent, state-of-the-art methods. In contrast to traditional syntheses, a systematic review will include detail about each stage of the decision process, including the question that guided the review, the criteria for studies to be included, and the methods used to search for and screen evaluation reports. It will also detail how analyses were done and how conclusions were reached. (p. 1)

The reviews often try to quantify the successfulness of particular programs and interventions, sometimes using a technique called *meta-analysis*, which we describe in the next chapter. Although these reviews are designed to be objective, there are still controversies surrounding any particular review, including conflict about the inclusion or exclusion of studies and what qualifies as a rigorous study design (e.g., is a true experimental design the only way to determine causality?).

Systematic reviews are increasingly sponsored by both private and government entities. One private organization that has become a leader in publicizing reviews related to criminal justice policy research is the Campbell Collaboration. The Campbell Collaboration is an international research network that prepares and disseminates systematic reviews of social science evidence in three fields: crime and justice, education, and social welfare. The collaboration's mission "is to promote positive social change by contributing to better-informed decisions and better-quality public and private services around the world" (www.campbell collaboration.org). All reports are peer reviewed and are available on the collaboration's website.

> Campbell Collaboration: Group producing systematic reviews of programs and policies in many areas, including criminal justice, social work, and education

ETHICS IN EVALUATION

Evaluation research can make a difference in people's lives while it is in progress, as well as after the results are reported. Educational and vocational training opportunities in prison, the availability of legal counsel, and treatment for substance abuse are all potentially important benefits, and an evaluation research project can change both their type and their availability. This direct impact on research participants—and potentially their families—heightens the attention that evaluation researchers have to give to human subjects concerns. Although the particular criteria that are at issue and the decisions that are most ethical vary with the type of evaluation research conducted and the specifics of a particular project, there are always serious ethical as well as political concerns for the evaluation researcher (Boruch, 1997; Dentler, 2002).

Assessing needs, determining evaluability, and examining the process of treatment delivery have few special ethical dimensions. Cost–benefit analyses in themselves also raise few ethical concerns. It is when the focus is program impact that human subjects considerations multiply. What about assigning persons randomly to receive some social program or benefit? One justification given by evaluation researchers has to do with the scarcity of these resources. If not everyone in the population who is eligible for a program can receive it (due to resource limitations), what could be a fairer way to distribute the program benefits than through a lottery? Random assignment also seems like a reasonable way to allocate potential program benefits when a new program is being tested with only some members of the target recipient population. However, when an ongoing entitlement program is being evaluated and experimental subjects would normally be eligible for program participation, it may not be ethical simply to bar some potential participants from the programs. Instead, evaluation researchers may test alternative treatments or provide some alternative benefit while the treatment is being denied.

It is important to realize that it is costly to society and potentially harmful to participants to maintain ineffective programs. In the long run, at least, it may be more ethical to conduct an evaluation study than to let the status quo remain in place.

Kristin M. Curtis, MA, Senior Research Program Coordinator, The Senator Walter Rand Institute for Public Affairs at Rutgers University–Camden

Source: Courtesy of Kristin M. Curtis

Kristin Curtis graduated with a master's degree in criminal justice from Rutgers University–Camden in 2010. While a graduate student, she worked on a nationwide research project examining policymaker and practitioner perspectives on sex offender laws, and this experience convinced her that pursuing a career in research was the best fit for her interests and talents. She secured a position at the Walter Rand Institute (WRI) as a graduate project assistant and worked on statewide prisoner reentry studies. Kristin has quickly moved up the ranks at the WRI and, in the process, has worked on myriad criminal justice projects. Her research assignments require varied methodological approaches, including interviews, focus groups, surveys, network analysis, regression models, and geographic information systems (GIS).

One feature of working at WRI that Kristin truly values is the fact that she can participate in other areas of study outside the criminal justice realm. For instance, she has worked on projects that examine the impact of social service organization collaboration on child well-being, financial stability of families, and relationships between children and their caregivers. These projects involve the evaluation of collaborations among social service organizations in multiple New Jersey counties and employ both qualitative and quantitative research methods. Kristin has been at WRI for eight years and still enjoys her position as each day presents new challenges and different tasks, including data collection and analysis, finalizing reports, writing grant proposals for potential new projects, and supervising graduate students.

Kristin has advice for students interested in careers conducting research or using research results:

Locate faculty who engage in research in your areas of interest. Even if you are unsure what your primary research areas are, working on a research project allows you to gain exposure to different research methodologies and techniques (i.e., quantitative and qualitative). You might find you enjoy research and pick up conference presentations and academic publications along the way. Remember, college is an opportunity to explore the different career choices in the world, so take advantage of this.

CONCLUSION

In recent years, the field of evaluation research has become an increasingly popular and active research specialty within the fields of criminology and criminal justice. Many social scientists find special appeal in evaluation research because of its utility.

The research methods applied to evaluation research are no different from those covered elsewhere in this text; they can range from qualitative intensive interviews to rigorous randomized experimental designs.

In process evaluations, qualitative methodologies can be particularly advantageous. However, the best method for determining cause and effect—or for determining whether a program had its intended consequences (impacts)—is the randomized experimental design. Although this may not always be possible in the field, it is the gold standard with which to compare methodologies used to assess the impacts of all programs or policies.

KEY TERMS

Applied research   255
Black-box evaluation   264
Campbell Collaboration   271
Cost–benefit analysis   261
Cost-effectiveness analysis   262
Efficiency analysis   261
Evaluability assessment   257
Evidence-based policy   270
Feedback   256
Impact evaluation   259

Inputs   255
Integrated approaches   265
Needs assessment   257
Nonequivalent control group design   269
Outcomes   255
Outputs   256
Policy research   270
Process evaluation (program monitoring)   258

Program process   256
Program theory   264
Quasi-experimental design   268
Random assignment   266
Social science approaches   265
Stakeholder approaches   264
Stakeholders   256
Systematic review   270
Theory-driven evaluation   264

HIGHLIGHTS

- The evaluation process in general—and the feedback process in particular—can be understood only in relation to the interests and perspectives of program stakeholders.

- The process by which a program has an effect on outcomes is often treated as a black box, but there is good reason to open the black box and investigate the process by which the program operates and produces or fails to produce an effect.

- A program theory may be developed before or after an investigation of program process is completed. It may be either descriptive or prescriptive.

- There are five primary types of program evaluation: needs assessment, evaluability assessment,

process evaluation (including formative evaluation), impact evaluation, and efficiency (cost–benefit) analysis.

- True randomized experiments are the most appropriate method for determining cause and effect and, as such, for determining the impact of programs and policies.

- Evidence-based policy is increasingly demanded by government agencies, which require systematic reviews that synthesize the results of the best available research on a given topic using transparent procedures.

- Evaluation research raises complex ethical issues because it may involve withholding desired social benefits.

EXERCISES

Discussing Research

1. Read one of the articles reviewed in this chapter. Fill in the answers to the article review questions (Chapter 1) not covered in the chapter. Do you agree with the answers to the other questions discussed in the chapter? Could you add some points to the critique provided by the author of the text or to the lessons on research design drawn from these critiques?

2. Propose a randomized experimental evaluation of a social program with which you are familiar. Include in your proposal a description of the program and

its intended outcomes. Discuss the strengths and weaknesses of your proposed design.

Finding Research on the Web

1. Go to the American Evaluation Association website (www.eval.org). Choose "Publications" and then "Guiding Principles for Evaluators." What are the five guiding principles discussed in this document? Provide a summary of each principle.

2. Go to the National Criminal Justice Reference Service (NCJRS) at www.ncjrs.gov, and search for a publication

that reports on an evaluation of a program of your choice. Read the report, and write a brief summary, making sure to include a summary of the methodology used in the report.

3. Describe the resources available for evaluation researchers at the following websites: ieg.worldbankgroup.org, www.wmich.edu/evalctr, and www.apcrc.nhs.uk/evaluation/methodology.htm.

4. Go to the Campbell Collaboration website (www.campbellcollaboration.org), and access the library. Find a study that evaluates a topic of interest to you. What were the selection criteria used for the review? How did the researchers operationalize the constructs they were measuring (e.g., mentoring, delinquency, recidivism)? What do they conclude?

5. Evaluation research is a big industry. There are several large research firms that contract with the federal government to evaluate programs and/or policies. Two examples are the Rand Corporation (www.rand.org) and Abt Associates (www.abtassociates.com). Check out their websites, and summarize at least one evaluation study related to criminal justice or criminology. What type of evaluation study was it? What methods were used? Were these methods appropriate for the evaluation question? If an outcome evaluation study was conducted, was a true experiment used, or was it a quasi-experimental design?

Critiquing Research

1. Evaluate the ethics of one of the studies reviewed in which human subjects were used. Sherman and Berk's (1984) study of domestic violence raises some interesting ethical issues, but there are also points to consider in most of the other studies. To which ethical guidelines (see Chapter 2) does it seem most difficult to adhere? Where do you think the line should be drawn between not taking any risks at all with research participants and developing valid scientific knowledge? Be sure to consider various costs and benefits of the research.

2. Find a recent article that evaluates a policy or program from a criminal justice policy journal such as *Crime and Public Policy*. Describe its strengths and weaknesses. Do the author(s) make claims about causality that are supported by their methodology?

3. Go to the Campbell Collaboration website (www.campbellcollaboration.org), and find a systematic review that interests you. Read the report, and write

a brief summary, making sure to include a summary of the methodology used in the report. If the review examined the outcome effects of some program or policy, did the author(s) include only studies that used a true experimental design? If not, how did the author(s) select the articles for inclusion in the review? What were the follow-up times used in the selected studies (i.e., 30 days, six months, or longer)?

Making Research Ethical

1. The Manhattan Bail Project randomly assigned some defendants with strong community ties to be recommended for release without bail and some not to be recommended. The project found a very high (99%) rate of appearance at trial for those released without bail, but of course, the researchers did not know that this would be the case before they conducted the study. Would you consider this study design ethical? What if one of the persons in the 1% who did not come to trial murdered someone when they should have been at court? Are there any conditions when randomization should not be permitted when evaluating criminal justice programs?

2. A large body of evaluation research suggested that the DARE program was not effective in reducing drug use in schools, but many school and police officials, parents, and students insisted on maintaining the program without change for many years. Do you think that government agencies should be allowed to defund programs that numerous evaluation research studies have shown to be ineffective? Should government agencies be required to justify funding for social programs on the basis of evaluation research results?

Developing a Research Proposal

Imagine that you are submitting a proposal to the U.S. Justice Department to evaluate the efficacy of a new treatment program for substance abusers within federal correctional institutions.

1. What would your research question be if you proposed a process evaluation component to your research?

2. For the outcome evaluation, what is your independent variable, and what would your dependent variable be? How would you operationalize both?

3. What type of research design would you propose to answer both the process evaluation and outcome evaluation components in your proposal?

Performing Data Analysis in SPSS or Excel

Data for Exercise	
Dataset	**Description**
NCVS lone offender assaults 1992 to 2013. sav	This is data from the National Crime Victimization Survey (NCVS), a nationally representative study of individuals' experience of criminal victimization. This particular dataset contains responses from 1992 to 2013, allowing for larger numbers of uncommon offenses to be used in analyses. It also only includes data from respondents who reported either violent or nonviolent assault by a single offender.

Variables for Exercise	
Variable Name	**Description**
Year	The year in which the data were collected, ranges from 1992 to 2013
Maleoff	The sex of the offender, where 1 = *male* and 0 = *female*
Injury	A binary variable indicating if the respondent was physically injured during the assault, where 1 = *injured* and 0 = *uninjured*
Age_r	The age (in years) at which victimization occurred. This variable is cut off at 75.
Victimreported	A binary variable indicating whether the respondent reported their victimization to the police, where 1= *reported* and 0 = *not reported*
Vic18andover	An age binary, where 0 = *victimization occurred below 18 years old* and 1 = *victimization occurred after 18*
Relationship	Nominal level variable where 0 = *stranger*, 1 = *slightly known*, 2 = *casual acquaintance*, 3 = *well known*

1. The NCVS has been conducted for many years using roughly the same measures. As such, it is an excellent tool for tracking trends over time. To begin with, let's look at this theory: Some criminologists have suggested that as women enter the workforce and adopt more traditionally masculine roles, they will also engage in other more masculine behaviors. In particular, they will be more likely to commit crimes!

   a. To test this assertion, we'll look at if assault victims report a male or a female offender at different rates over time. To do this select "graphs->legacy dialogues->line->simple." Then, put the variable year in the "category axis" box. In the "line represents" area, select "other statistic," and insert the variable "maleoff" into the box that lights up. Then select "ok."

      i. What is the general trend over time? The *y*-axis can be multiplied by 100 to get the percentage of offenders who are male.

      ii. Do these results support the theory presented previously?

   iii. Look carefully at the scale of your graph. How large are these changes that have occurred over time?

   b. Let's elaborate on these results by looking at whether the trend you saw in Question 1a appears if we distinguish between violent and nonviolent assaults (e.g., verbal assault, threat with a weapon). To do this, go back to the line dialogue, and repeat Question 1a. This time, put the variable "injury" in the "panel by: rows" box.

      iv. What do you conclude? Does it appear that women are becoming more violent, or are they just more prone to nonviolent assaults?

2. Another application for line graphs is to look at trends across age rather than time. Often, we tell our kids that if they are in trouble, they should report it to the police. In the case of assault, are younger individuals reporting their victimization at the same rate as adults?

   a. First, run a frequency of the variable "victimreported." Overall, what proportion of assaults were reported to the police?

b. Take a second to think about the implications of this result. What does it suggest about conclusions based solely on police data?

c. Create a line graph using the instructions in Question 1a. This time, put "age_r" in the "category axis," and for "line represents," select "other statistic," and use the variable "victimreported."

    i. The *x*-axis of this graph is the age at which the assault occurred. The *y*-axis reflects the percentage of victims that reported the assault to the police.

    ii. What do you conclude about the relationship between assault reporting and age?

    iii. Why do you think these patterns exist? Are these the same kinds of assaults we see among adults?

3. Let's try to explain those results from Question 2a a bit further by looking at the relationship between victim and offender.

a. Cross-tabulate the variable "vic18andover" with the variable "relationship." Be sure to put "vic18andover" in the column box and to ask for column percentages under the "cell" menu.

b. Describe your results. Who appears to be assaulting these youth at a disproportionately high rate?

c. Consider these two explanations, and explain which one (or both) is appropriate, given these results:

    i. Assaults against children are underreported because family members abuse kids at a higher rate than adults. Kids do not want to have their parents arrested, so they do not report.

    ii. Assaults against children are underreported because violence within schools is rarely reported to the police. This is because schools deal with issues in-house and students fear retribution from their assailants if they report the problem.

STUDENT STUDY SITE

$SAGE edge™

Get the tools you need to sharpen your study skills. SAGE Edge offers a robust online environment featuring an impressive array of free tools and resources. Access practice quizzes, eFlashcards, video, and multimedia at edge.sagepub.com/bachmanfrccj5e.

11

MIXING AND COMPARING METHODS

WHAT DO WE HAVE IN MIND?

Over 2.2 million people in the United States were incarcerated in prisons or local jails at the end of 2017. Except for those under sentences of death or life without the possibility of parole (LWOP), these individuals will be returning to their communities. A large percentage of individuals under correctional supervision have been convicted of drug law violations, primarily possession (Dorsey & Zawitz, 2005), and once released, a majority of these offenders will return to prison for new offenses or for parole violations (Alper, Durose, & Markman, 2018.). Research indicates that the drug-addicted offender appears to be particularly vulnerable to long-term patterns of relapse and reoffending. Except for intensive experiences with long-term aftercare programming (Inciardi & Harrison, 2000), there appear to be very few programs that significantly increase the probability of success for ex-offenders attempting to become conforming members of society, particularly for those with substance abuse issues. The high number of offenders reentering society annually, coupled with the less-than-ideal projection for their future success, gives urgency to research investigating how to increase their chances for success.

Sampson and Laub contended that martial attachment and job stability were key factors associated with desistance from crime (Sampson & Laub, 1993; Laub & Sampson, 2003). The sample studied by Sampson and Laub, however, was exclusively white and came of age in the 1950s, when the American economy was expanding. Recent research has questioned the ability of their theory to explain desistance for contemporary samples of offenders (Giordano, Cernkovich, & Rudolph, 2002). A recent project by one of the authors (Bachman, Kerrison, O'Connell, & Paternoster, 2013) sought to increase our understanding about the process of desistance from crime and drug use among current urban, drug-involved, largely minority, and increasingly female criminal offenders. We consciously developed our project using a mixed-methods design to "combine the inherent strengths of both qualitative and quantitative methodologies to maximize our understanding of the life-course trajectories of substance abuse and crime for a contemporary cohort of drug using offenders" (Bachman et al., 2013, p. 32). This decision is not unique, as scholars are increasingly using mixed-methods research (Snelson, 2016).

In earlier chapters, we gave you examples of research that combined research methods, but in this chapter, we will explain in more detail the logic of mixed methods and different ways of combining methods. We then review the

Learning Objectives

1. Understand the history of mixed methods, and explain the appeal of this approach.

2. Explain the philosophy of pragmatism and its relevance for mixed methods.

3. Identify in a table or diagram the major features that distinguish the four major types of mixed methods.

4. State at least one reason for the use of each major type of mixed method.

5. Define *triangulation*, and explain its value.

⑤SAGE edge™

Master the content at edge
.sagepub.com/bachmanfrccj5e

strengths and limitations of the methods we have discussed; this review will help you choose the most appropriate research design for a particular investigation and decide when a combination of methods—"mixed methods"—is most useful. Finally, we introduce the methods of meta-analysis and meta-synthesis, which allow systematic evaluation of findings from numerous published studies that have all used similar quantitative and qualitative methods.

WHAT ARE MIXED METHODS?

Social scientists have long used multiple methods in their research, but only in recent decades have some focused attention on how best to combine qualitative and quantitative methods to better achieve research goals. We have seen several examples in this book already of research that has employed more than one method to investigate the same research question. For example, in his ethnography in Oakland, California, Victor Rios (2011) conducted participant observation, focus groups, and intensive interviews. But what exactly does mixed-methods research mean? While there are many definitions of mixed-methods research, the operationalization provided by the National Institute of Health's Office of Behavioral and Social Sciences Research is useful. It defines *mixed methods* as

> focusing on "research questions that call for real-life contextual understandings . . . employing rigorous quantitative research assessing the magnitude and frequency of constructs and rigorous qualitative research exploring the meaning and understanding of constructs . . . intentionally integrating or combining these methods to draw on the strengths of each." (Creswell, Klassen, Plano Clark, & Smith, 2011, p. 4)

As you can see, the use of mixed methods should be an intentional design decision, not the addition of another aspect of research that is an afterthought or fishing expedition.

You learned in Chapter 2 that research involves both deductive processes (testing ideas against observations) and inductive processes (developing ideas from observations). You have also learned that quantitative methods are used most often in deductively oriented research and that qualitative methods often are used in inductively oriented research. A common reason for mixing both quantitative and qualitative methods in one research project is to take advantage of the unique strengths of each methodological approach when engaged in different stages of the research process (Teddlie & Tashakkori, 2010).

Another reason for mixing methods is to add unique insights about the intervention process that cannot easily be obtained from the primary method used in an investigation. This function is underscored in the name often given to mixed-methods research: triangulation. The term **triangulation** is actually derived from land surveying, where knowing a single landmark allows you to locate yourself only somewhere along a line in a single direction from the landmark. However, with two landmarks, you can take bearings on both and locate yourself at their intersection. Extrapolated to research, triangulation suggests that a researcher can get a clearer picture of the social reality being studied by viewing it from two different perspectives or two different methods. The term **mixed methods** more specifically indicates that research has combined qualitative and quantitative methods in an investigation of the same or related research question(s).

Should Methods Be Mixed?

To reiterate the general argument, a researcher who accepts a positivist philosophy believes that there is a reality that exists apart from our perceptions or interpretations of it. As

Triangulation: The use of multiple methods to study one research question; also used to mean the use of two or more different measures of the same variable

Mixed methods: Combining both qualitative and quantitative methods to study one research question

researchers, we test ideas that we have about the real world to see if the evidence we obtain with our research methods indicates that the real world is consistent with our ideas about it. We need to be objective so that our view of the real world is not distorted by what we want to see. If the evidence we obtain with our research methods indicates that our ideas were wrong, we have to revise our ideas accordingly (D. L. Morgan, 2014).

By contrast, a researcher who accepts an interpretivist philosophy believes that the reality experienced by individuals differs because reality exists only in relation to each individual's unique perspective. As researchers, we can learn about others' experiences and beliefs and interpret what we learn with our theories, but there is no single reality that we can test our ideas against. The evidence we obtain with our research methods enables us to understand others' perspectives and to develop an understanding of larger social contexts, but it does not allow us to conclude one perspective is correct (D. L. Morgan, 2014).

As you can see, these different research philosophies can lay the groundwork for conflict in a discipline! Those who insist that there is an objective reality can find little basis for collaborating with those who believe that reality exists only in the eyes of the beholder. Therefore, if the logic of quantitative methods necessarily reflects a positivist philosophy and the logic of qualitative methods necessarily reflects a constructivist philosophy, there is little basis for combining these methods in one project. However, beginning in the 1970s, researchers began to question the utility of such a dichotomy, and this resulted in a decline in disagreements between researchers who endorsed a particular research philosophy (Creswell & Plano Clark, 2011).

Increasingly, researchers are sidestepping the conflicting philosophies altogether in favor of using what seems to work best for answering a given research question. Does a mandatory-arrest policy reduce recidivism in domestic-violence cases? Let's count the number of times those arrested for domestic violence repeat the offense, compared with the number of times those who are not arrested repeat the offense. Do those accused of domestic violence feel the police treat them fairly? The bottom line is that no one method can be graded as superior to the others, and each varies in its suitability to different research questions and goals.

In addition to these philosophical questions, you should also consider some practical questions before you decide to mix methods in an investigation or review other investigations using mixed methods. Is a mixed-methods approach consistent with your own goals and prior experiences? Are you well trained to mix methods, or will you need to include collaborators? Do your research questions allow for unanticipated results? Are your different research questions congruent, and do they convey a need for integration? Is it feasible to carry out a mixed-methods design, or do you lack sufficient time or resources to carry it out? Are participants accessible to you (Plano Clark & Badiee, 2010)? Of course, we have to answer these questions before we embark on any research project.

TYPES OF MIXED-METHODS DESIGNS

If you do conclude that a mixed-methods design fits the purpose of the study and provides the best strategy to answer your research question, then you have different options for your design. Creswell and Plano Clark (2011) identify six major mixed-methods designs (see Exhibit 11.1):

Convergent parallel design: The quantitative and qualitative methods are implemented at the same time. The findings are integrated and interpreted together.

Exploratory sequential design: The qualitative method is implemented first, followed by the quantitative method.

Convergent parallel design: In mixed-methods research, when quantitative and qualitative methods are implemented at the same time; the findings are integrated and interpreted together

Exploratory sequential design: The qualitative method is implemented first, followed by the quantitative method

Exhibit 11.1   Six Major Mixed-Methods Research Designs

1. The convergent parallel design

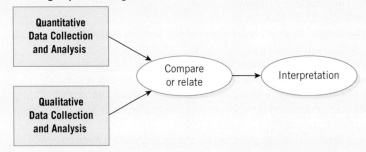

2. The explanatory sequential design

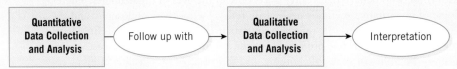

3. The exploratory sequential design

4. The embedded design

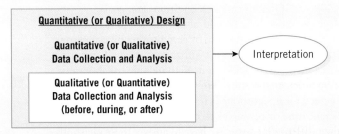

5. The transformative design

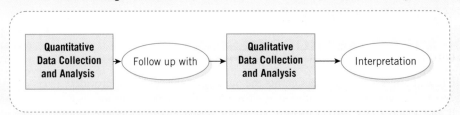

6. The multiphase design

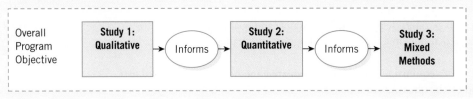

Source: Creswell and Plano Clark (2011, pp. 69–70).

Embedded design: This occurs when the primary method is qualitative or quantitative, but the researcher adds the other component to gain additional insight. For example, a quantitative design might be supplemented by a case study. These designs may be either concurrent or sequential.

Transformative design: Cresswell and Plano Clark (2011) suggest that the unique feature of a transformative design is that it uses a theoretical perspective with a social-justice focus, such as feminist research or participatory action research. Such research is done to improve the well-being of vulnerable populations.

Multiphase design: This design involves a series of quantitative and qualitative designs. Each design and its findings inform the next phase.

Creswell and Plano Clark (2011) have also helped popularize a simple notational system for distinguishing different ways of mixing quantitative and qualitative methods. This system distinguishes the priority given to one method over the other and the sequence in which they are used in a research project. For example,

- QUAL + QUAN: equal importance of the two approaches and their concurrent use

- QUAL → quan: sequenced use, with qualitative methods given priority

- QUAN(qual): qualitative methods embedded within a primarily quantitative project

Sometimes researchers will develop a study flowchart to describe the mixed-methods process and sequence of events. Of course, rather than being planned in advance, steps to combine research designs may emerge naturally as a project is developed. For example, an experiment conducted in the field can be supplemented with qualitative observations about delivery of the experimental treatment; some intensive open-ended questions can follow closed-ended survey questions; field research may use quantitative counts of phenomena or random samples of events; and comparative historical studies may add survey research results to an inspection of historical documents or the compilation of national statistics. As you will see in the case studies that follow, researchers typically describe their decision making when embarking on a mixed-methods project.

> **Embedded design:** In mixed-methods research, when the primary method is qualitative or quantitative, but the researcher adds the other component to gain additional insight
>
> **Transformative design:** In mixed-methods research, this design uses a theoretical perspective with a social justice focus to improve the well-being of vulnerable populations
>
> **Multiphase design:** In mixed-methods research, this design involves a series of quantitative and qualitative designs; each design and the findings inform the next phase

Case Study: Convergent Parallel Design: School Security and Discipline

Aaron Kupchik (2010) provides an excellent example of triangulation in practice in his book, *Homeroom Security*. His methodology would be classified as a convergent parallel design because both quantitative and qualitative methods were implemented at the same time and the findings were integrated. The research question was primarily interested in how school security measures, particularly the presence of police officers, affect students. In four high schools, two in a southwestern state and two in a mid-Atlantic state, Kupchik engaged in more than 100 hours of observation at each school, shadowing administrators and security guards, as well as surveying classrooms and common areas. He also conducted more than 100 semistructured interviews with administrators, security personnel, students, and parents. These interviews "sought to acquire an understanding of the respondents' views of the school rules and punishments, his or her experiences with school discipline, and his or her perceptions of school violence and appropriate responses to it" (Kupchik, 2010, p. 225). In addition to these two methods, student survey data were also collected at each school that, among other things, recorded students' experiences with punishment at school and their perceptions of the fairness of these incidents. Thus, to more fully understand the reality of school discipline, Kupchik used three very different research methods, each providing him with a somewhat different angle to examine the issue, and each method complemented the others' weaknesses.

The school observations allowed Kupchik to observe the interactions in the school in real time. He observed on numerous occasions how relatively minor problems escalated into larger problems as a result of police involvement, resulting in students unnecessarily being sent to the criminal justice system rather than having their issues dealt with at the school level only. With the in-depth interviews, Kupchik was able to identify how some of the school administrators perceived the behavior of the police officers in their schools. For example, one school administrator stated,

> The biggest problem that I see is that . . . police officers are trained to deal with adults . . . they are not trained to deal with children. . . . They deal with them terribly. In their day-to-day interactions . . . they deal with them like criminals, they do not trust anything they say, they assume they are lying before they even open their mouths. And it's not their fault. They've been trained to do that. (Kupchik, 2010, p. 108)

Finally, the survey data allowed him to make generalizations regarding perceptions and experiences of discipline to the larger student population. For example, the survey data indicated that boys were more likely to report getting in trouble for rule violations than girls, as were African American and Latino/Latina students compared with whites.

Of course, these are only a sampling of the many findings from this research. The central point we want to illustrate is how the use of all three methodologies provided a more complete picture of school discipline compared with the use of a single method. The research provided in-depth detailed descriptions of the reality of school discipline from both administrator and student perspectives. It also provided a quantitative assessment of students' experiences that could be generalized to a larger student population.

Case Study: Exploratory Sequential Design: American Indian Homicide

As noted previously, some mixed-methods designs begin with a qualitative method to explore a phenomenon and then proceed with a quantitative method for confirmatory purposes. This is referred to as an *exploratory sequential design*. This was the design used by one of the authors (Bachman, 1992) when studying the social causes of homicide within contemporary American Indian communities. This is a great example of this design because using this type of mixed-methods research was crucial for this research question. Although other researchers had noted high rates of American Indian homicide, virtually no attempts had been made to explore the factors that contributed to such high rates. Are the causal mechanisms that create these high rates the same as those that were documented in the population in general? Or are the social forces that were identified as increasing both African American and white homicide rates different from those forces that contribute to American Indian homicide? Because there was virtually no research examining the social factors related to American Indian homicide, Bachman first wanted to gain some insight and understanding of the structural and cultural conditions that may contribute to lethal violence at the individual level. Accordingly, she selected the qualitative method of intensive interviewing as her first method. Bachman conducted face-to-face interviews with homicide offenders at three Midwestern state prisons. Offenders responded to a lengthy set of open-ended questions and probes concerning the circumstances surrounding their crime, their life before the crime, and their attitudes about crime in general. Thus, she started with inductive research, beginning with qualitative interview data, which were then used to develop (induce) a general explanation (a theory) to account for the data.

The theoretical model that emerged from her interview data is displayed in Exhibit 11.2. The model demonstrates the causal forces of social disorganization, economic deprivation, a culture of honor or violence, and the psychological mechanisms of culture conflict and perceived powerlessness with the intervening variable of alcohol or drug abuse. Also included in the theoretical guide is the antecedent variable to each of these concepts: internal colonialism. Although this concept was not explicitly derived from the qualitative analysis, Bachman (1992) explained, "No model explaining any phenomenon with regard to American Indians would be complete without acknowledgment of the colonization process to which our government has subjected this population" (p. 36).

Using this theoretical model, Bachman next collected state- and county-level data on homicide rates from the Supplementary Homicide Reports (SHR) and combined these data with social indicators of poverty and social disorganization from the U.S. Census. Thus began the deductive phase of her research to test three hypotheses:

1. The higher the level of social disorganization within a reservation community, the higher the rate of homicide.

2. The higher the level of economic deprivation within a reservation community, the higher the rate of homicide.

3. The more traditional and integrated a reservation community, the lower the rate of homicide.

Exhibit 11.2   Theoretical Model for American Indian Homicide That Emerged From Bachman's Qualitative Interviews With American Indian Homicide Offenders

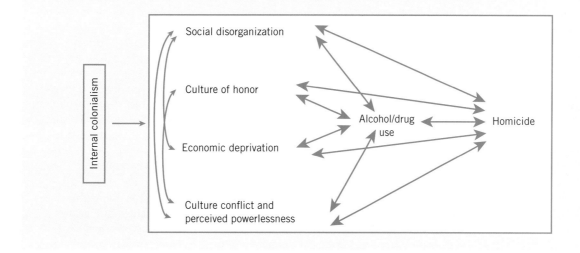

Results indicated that American Indian communities with higher levels of both social disorganization and economic deprivation also had higher rates of homicide. Bachman (1992) did not find support in her data for the third hypothesis. In addition to guiding her deductive research, the qualitative interview data also provided Bachman's research with a wealth of narratives that added meaning and depth to the statistical relationships that were found at the aggregate level. For example, many homicide offenders revealed what conditions of social disorganization and economic deprivation were like in their own lives. One offender talked about the reality of his disorganized childhood, being placed in multiple foster homes:

> I was pretty much living in foster homes since I was about two. I guess my parents weren't doing too good—you know, drinking and partying. My brother got put into a different foster home, but my sister and I got in the same one. After several moves, we all eventually got placed in the same home. We moved around quite a bit. (p. 38)

Finding support for relationships between the independent and dependent variables at two different levels—the individual level and the community level—provided validity to Bachman's (1992) conclusions that both social disorganization and economic deprivation are related to homicide in American Indian communities. T. T. Campbell and Fiske (1959) explain the validity-enhancing qualities of triangulation:

> If a hypothesis can survive the confrontation of a series of complementary methods of testing, it contains a degree of validity unattainable by one tested within the more constricted framework of a single method. . . . Findings from this latter approach must always be subject to the suspicion that they are method-bound: Will the comparison totter when exposed to an equally prudent but different testing method? (p. 82)

Case Study: Embedded Design: Investigating Rape

Testa and colleagues (Testa, Livingston, & VanZile-Tamsen, 2011) supplemented their quantitative study of violence against women with a qualitative component because violence against women is "a complex, multifaceted phenomenon, occurring within a social context that is influenced by gender norms, interpersonal relationships, and sexual scripts" and "understanding of these experiences of violence is dependent on the subjective meaning for the woman and cannot easily be reduced to a checklist" (p. 237). This was an embedded—QUAN(qual)—design.

Victims' responses to structured questions indicated an association between alcohol and rape, but when victims elaborated on their experiences in qualitative interviews, their comments led to a new way of understanding this quantitative association. Although this association has often been interpreted as suggesting "impaired judgment" about consent by intoxicated victims, the women interviewed by Testa et al. (2011) all revealed that they had had so much to drink that they were unconscious or at least unable to speak at the time of the rape. Testa and her colleagues (2011) concluded that the prevalence of this type of "incapacitated rape" required a new approach to the problem of violence against women:

> Qualitative analysis of our data has resulted in numerous "a-ha" types of insights that would not have been possible had we relied solely on quantitative data analysis (e.g., identification of incapacitated rape and sexual precedence, heterogeneity in the way that sexual assaults arise) and also helped us to understand puzzling quantitative

observations. . . . These insights, in turn, led to testable, quantitative hypotheses that supported our qualitative findings, lending rigor and convergence to the process. We never could have anticipated what these insights would be and that is what is both scary and exhilarating about qualitative data analysis, particularly for a scientist who has relied on quantitative data analysis and a priori hypothesis testing. The lengthy process of reading, coding, rereading, interpreting, discussing, and synthesizing among two or more coders is undeniably a major investment of time. (p. 242)

Testa and her colleagues concluded that insights yielded by the qualitative data analysis fully justified the time-consuming process of reading and rereading interviews, coding text, and discussing and reinterpreting the codes.

STRENGTHS AND LIMITATIONS OF MIXED METHODS

Combining qualitative and quantitative methods within one research project can strengthen the project's design by enhancing measurement validity, generalizability, causal validity, or authenticity. At the same time, combining methods creates challenges that may be difficult to overcome and ultimately limit the extent to which these goals are enhanced. This should be your golden rule: The choice of a data collection method should be guided in large part by the aspect of validity that is of most concern and the best method for answering your research question!

As you can see in Exhibit 11.3, none of these methods is superior to the others in all respects, and each varies in its suitability to different research questions and goals. Choosing among them for a particular investigation requires consideration of the research problem, opportunities and resources, prior research, philosophical commitments, and research goals.

True experimental designs are strongest for testing nomothetic causal hypotheses and are most appropriate for studies of treatment effects, as well as research questions that are believed to involve basic social/psychological processes. Random assignment reduces the possibility of preexisting differences between treatment and comparison groups to small, specifiable, chance levels, so many of the variables that might create a spurious association are controlled. But despite this clear advantage, an experimental design requires a degree of control that cannot always be achieved in other settings. Researchers may be unable to randomly assign participants to groups or have too few participants to assign to groups, and

Exhibit 11.3 Comparison of Three General Research Methods

Design	Measurement Validity	Generalizability	Type of Causal Assertions	Causal Validity
Experiments	+	−[a]	Nomothetic	+
Surveys	+	+/−	Nomothetic	+/−[b]
Participant Observation and Intensive Interviewing	−/+[c]	−	Idiographic	−

a. Experiments are designed to ensure causal validity, not generalizability.

b. Surveys are a weaker design for identifying causal effects than true experiments, but use of statistical controls can strengthen causal arguments. Also, only if a random sample is used to collect survey data and the response rate is high can results be generalized to the target population.

c. Reliability is low compared to surveys, and evaluation of measurement validity is often not possible. However, direct observations may lead to a greater understanding of the concepts being measured.

unfortunately, most field experiments also require more access arrangements and financial resources than can often be obtained. In lieu of these difficulties, quasi- and nonexperimental designs are used, but often at the cost of causal validity.

Surveys typically use standardized, quantitative measures of attitudes, behaviors, or social processes. Closed-ended questions are most common and are well suited for the reliable measurement of variables that have been studied in the past and whose meanings are well understood. Of course, surveys often include measures of many more variables than are included in an experiment, but this feature is not inherent in either design. Many surveys rely on random sampling for their selection of cases from some larger population, and this feature makes them preferable for research that seeks to develop generalizable findings. However, survey questionnaires can only measure what respondents are willing to report; they may not be adequate for studying behaviors or attitudes that are regarded as socially unacceptable. Also, surveys often are used to test hypothesized causal relationships. When variables that might create spurious relationships are included in the survey, they can be controlled statistically in the analysis and thus eliminated as rival causal influences.

In contrast, qualitative methods, such as participant observation and intensive interviewing, presume an exploratory measurement approach in which indicators of concepts are drawn from direct observation or in-depth commentary. This approach is most appropriate when it is not clear what meaning people attach to a concept or what sense they might make of particular questions about it. Qualitative methods also are suited to the exploration of new or poorly understood social settings when it is not even clear what concepts would help to understand the situation. Furthermore, these methods are useful in uncovering the process of a program or the implementation of an intervention. They also may be used instead of survey methods when the population of interest is not easily identifiable or seeks to remain hidden. For these reasons, qualitative methods tend to be preferred when exploratory research questions are posed or when new groups are investigated. But, of course, intensive measurement necessarily makes the study of large numbers of cases or situations difficult, resulting in the limitation of many field research efforts to small numbers of people or unique social settings. The individual

RESEARCH IN THE NEWS

Lacking Data on Gun Violence

In 1993, the Centers for Disease Control and Prevention (CDC) conducted a study that examined the effect of having a gun in the home and injurious outcomes, such as accidental shootings. The study found that residents who had guns in their homes were significantly more likely to be injured or die from a gun than residents in homes without guns. The *New York Times* reported in this article that after this finding, the National Rifle Association (NRA) lobbied to prevent taxpayer money from being spent on research that monitored the effects of guns, and Congress passed the Dickey Amendment in 1996 that essentially cut funding for the CDC's monitoring of gun violence. As a result, the agency that is tasked with monitoring threats to public health (including violence) cannot answer simple questions such as "Who is most likely to use a gun in a crime, and where does the gun come from?"

For Further Thought

1. If criminal justice agencies and hospitals are not collecting data on gun-related injuries and death, how can policies directed at preventing such injuries be evaluated?

2. What would you like to know about the original 1993 study conducted by the CDC?

Source: Kaplan, S. (2018, March 12). Congress quashed research into gun violence. Since then, 600,000 people have been shot. *New York Times.* Retrieved from https://www.nytimes.com/2018/03/12/health/gun-violence-research-cdc.html

field researcher may not require many financial resources, but the amount of time required for many field research projects serves as a barrier to many would-be field researchers.

A researcher should always consider whether data of another type should be collected in single-method studies and whether additional research using different methods is needed before the research question can be answered with sufficient confidence. But the potential for integrating methods and combining findings does not decrease the importance of single studies using just one method of data collection. The findings from well-designed studies in carefully researched settings are the necessary foundation for broader, more integrative methods. There is little point in combining methods that are poorly implemented or in merging studies that produced invalid results. Whatever the research question, we should consider the full range of methodological possibilities, make an informed and feasible choice, and then carefully carry out our strategy. As you saw in Chapter 2, research questions are never completely answered. Research findings regarding a particular question are added to the existing literature to inform future research, and the research circle continues.

COMPARING RESULTS ACROSS STUDIES

Meta-Analysis

Meta-analysis is a quantitative method for identifying patterns in findings across multiple studies of the same research question (Cooper & Hedges, 1994). Unlike a traditional literature review, which describes previous research studies verbally, meta-analyses treat previous studies as cases whose features are measured as variables and are then analyzed statistically. It is similar to conducting a survey in which the respondents are previous studies. Meta-analysis shows how evidence about interventions varies across research studies. If the methods used in these studies varied, then meta-analysis can be used to describe how this variation affected study findings. If social contexts or demographic characteristics varied across the studies, then a meta-analysis can indicate how social context or demographic characteristics affected study findings. Meta-analysis often accompanies systematic reviews that summarize what we know about the effectiveness of a particular intervention. By integrating different study samples and controlling for social context and demographic characteristics, meta-analysis enhances the generalizability of the findings. Meta-analysis is often used to provide systematic reviews to be used for evidence-based policies.

Meta-analysis can be used when a number of studies have attempted to answer the same research question with similar quantitative methods. It is not typically used for evaluating results from multiple studies that used different methods or measured different dependent variables. It is also not very sensible to use meta-analysis to combine study results when the original case data from these studies are available and can actually be combined and analyzed together (Lipsey & Wilson, 2001). Rather, meta-analysis is a technique to combine and statistically analyze the statistical findings in published research reports.

After a research problem is formulated about prior research, the literature must be searched systematically to identify the entire population of relevant studies. Typically, multiple bibliographic databases are used; some researchers also search for related dissertations and conference papers. Eligibility criteria must be specified carefully to determine which studies to include and which to omit as too different. Mark Lipsey and David Wilson (2001) suggest that eligibility criteria include the following:

- Distinguishing features. These include the specific intervention tested and perhaps the groups compared.

- Research respondents. These specify the population to which generalization is sought.

Meta-analysis: The quantitative analysis of findings from multiple studies

- Key variables. These must be sufficient to allow tests of the hypotheses of concern and controls for likely additional influences.

- Research methods. Apples and oranges cannot be directly compared, so some trade-off must be made between including the range of studies about a research question and excluding those that are so different in their methods as not to yield comparable data.

- Cultural and linguistic range. If the study population is going to be limited to English-language publications or in some other way, this must be acknowledged, and the size of the population of relevant studies in other languages should be estimated.

- Time frame. Social processes relevant to the research question may have changed for such reasons as historical events or new technologies, so temporal boundaries around the study population must be considered.

- Publication type. Will the analysis focus only on published reports in professional journals, or will it include dissertations and/or unpublished reports?

Once the studies are identified, their findings, methods, and other features are coded (e.g., sample size, location of sample, strength of the association between the independent and dependent variables). Statistics are then calculated to identify the average effect of the independent variable on the dependent variable, as well as the effect of methodological features and other characteristics of the studies (Cooper & Hedges, 1994). The **effect size** statistic is the key to capturing the association between the independent and dependent variables across multiple studies. The effect size statistic is a standardized measure of association—often the difference between the mean of the experimental group and the mean of the control group on the dependent variable, adjusted for the average variability in the two groups (Lipsey & Wilson, 2001).

The meta-analytic approach to synthesizing research results can produce more generalizable findings than those obtained with just one study. Methodological weaknesses in the studies included in the meta-analysis are still a problem; only when other studies without particular methodological weaknesses are included can we estimate effects with some confidence. In addition, before we can place any confidence in the results of a meta-analysis, we must be confident that all (or almost all) relevant studies were included and that the information we need to analyze was included in all (or most) of the studies (Matt & Cook, 1994).

One of the challenges of meta-analysis is that the authors of the articles to be reviewed may not always report sufficient information. For example, the study reports (whether a journal article or unpublished report) may not contain information about participant characteristics, an especially important variable if we are to consider the generalizability of the results to different population groups.

> **Effect size:**
> A standardized measure of association—often the difference between the mean of the experimental group and the mean of the control group on the dependent variable, adjusted for the average variability in the two groups

Case Study: Meta-Analysis: The Effectiveness of Antibullying Programs

The 2013 School Crime Supplement to the National Crime Victimization Survey reported that about 28% of teens between the ages of 12 and 18 had been bullied in the past six months. The effects of bullying are numerous and include perceived fear, behavior problems, negative consequences for school performance, depression, and other physical ailments. There have been many different programs designed to decrease bullying in schools, but the effectiveness of these programs remains largely unknown. To examine the effects of antibullying programs across studies, Ferguson, San Miguel, Kilburn, Sanchez, and Sanchez (2007) performed a meta-analysis of randomized experimental studies examining the efficacy of such programs.

Studies included in the Ferguson et al. (2007) meta-analysis had several selection criteria: (a) They had to be published between 1995 and 2006, (b) the outcome variables had to clearly measure some element of bullying behavior toward peers, (c) they had to involve some form of control group to test program effectiveness, (d) the intervention programs had to be school based, and (e) only manuscripts published in peer-reviewed journals were included. Results of the meta-analysis indicated that the impact of antibullying programs ranged from less than 1% for low-risk children to 3.6% for high-risk children. Ferguson and his colleagues (2007) stated, "Thus, it can be said that although anti-bullying programs produce a small amount of positive change, it is likely that this change is too small to be practically significant or noticeable" (p. 408).

Meta-analyses such as this make us aware of how hazardous it is to base understanding of social processes on single studies that are limited in time, location, and measurement. Of course, we need to have our wits about us when we read reports of meta-analytic studies. It is not a good idea to assume that a meta-analysis is the definitive word on a research question just because it cumulates the results of multiple studies.

Meta-analyses and meta-syntheses make us aware of how hazardous it is to base understandings of social processes on single studies that are limited in time, location, and measurement. Although one study may not support the hypothesis that we deduced from what seemed to be a compelling theory, this is not a sufficient basis for discarding the theory itself or even for assuming that the hypothesis is no longer worthy of consideration in future research. You can see that a meta-analysis combining the results of many studies may identify conditions for which the hypothesis is supported and others for which it is not.

Meta-Synthesis

Meta-synthesis is a related method used to analyze and integrate findings from qualitative studies (Thorne, Jensen, Kearney, Noblit, & Sandelowski, 2004). This type of analysis requires not just aggregating findings from different qualitative studies but also reinterpreting the data once in aggregate. As is the case for meta-analyses, attention to eligibility criteria for selection into a meta-synthesis is extremely important.

> Meta-synthesis: The qualitative analysis of findings from multiple qualitative studies

Case Study: Meta-Synthesis: Female Drug Dealers

Maher and Hudson (2007) performed a meta-synthesis examining the qualitative literature on women in the illicit-drug economy to identify and integrate key themes. The authors spelled out their methods meticulously, describing the characteristics they used to select studies that met their criteria. They first searched many databases (e.g., Criminal Justice Abstracts, Sociological Abstracts) for research using various key terms such as *drug market*, *drug economy*, and *women dealing*. Studies were selected only if they "generated findings in relation to female participation in the drug economy" and the "primary data collection used qualitative or ethnographic research" (Maher & Hudson, 2007, p. 809). Of the 36 studies located, only 15 met their criteria and provided thick descriptions of female experiences using field notes or narrative data from transcribed interviews. A sample of the selected studies included in the meta-synthesis is described in Exhibit 11.4.

> Thick description: A method used in case reports that clarifies the context and makes it possible for the reader vicariously to experience it

Exhibit 11.4   Selected Studies Included in a Meta-Synthesis

Author(s)	Study Location	Sample
Rosenbaum (1981)	San Francisco and New York	100 women
Adler (1985)	Southwest county close to Mexico border	65 dealers/smugglers, 6 women
E. M. Miller (1986)	Milwaukee	64 women "hustlers"
Waldorf et al. (1991)	San Francisco	80 sellers, 26 female
Taylor (1993)	Glasgow, Scotland	26 women
Maher (1997)	New York	211 women
Dunlap et al. (1997)	New York	111 dealers, 39 women
Sterk (1999)	Atlanta, Georgia	149 women
Denton (2001)	Melbourne, Australia	16 women recently released from prison

Source: Adapted from Maher and Hudson 2007.

After reading the qualitative material from the 15 studies examined, Maher and Hudson (2007) identified six themes that captured the nature and experience of women's participation in the illicit drug economy. One of the key findings was the gender-stratified nature of women's involvement; all studies, regardless of time or place, found that women tended to occupy subordinate roles to men, even those women identified as successful dealers. They also concluded that most women were introduced to dealing through relationships with sex partners. They concluded,

> Our results suggest that while women rely on a diverse range of income sources and juggle different roles both within the drug economy and in relation to dealing and domestic responsibilities, most women in most drug markets remain confined to low level and marginal roles. (Maher & Hudson, 2007, p. 821)

ETHICS AND MIXED METHODS

Researchers who combine methods must be aware of the ethical concerns involved in using each of the separate methods, but there are also some ethical challenges that are heightened in mixed-methods projects. One special challenge is defining the researcher's role in relation to the research participants. Every researcher creates an understanding about his or her role with research participants (Mertens, 2012). Researchers using quantitative methods often define themselves as outside experts who design a research project and collect research data using objective procedures that are best carried out without participant involvement. By contrast, qualitative researchers often define themselves as engaging in research in some type of collaboration with the community or group they are studying, with much input from their research participants into the research design and the collection and analysis of research data.

A researcher using mixed methods cannot simply adopt one of these roles: A researcher needs some degree of autonomy when designing quantitative research plans, but a researcher will not be able to collect intensive qualitative data if participants do not accord her or him some degree of trust as an insider. The challenge is compounded by the potential for different reactions of potential participants to the different roles. Authorities who control access to program clients or employees or to community members may be willing to agree to a structured survey but not to a long-term engagement with researchers as participant observers, so a mixed-methods project that spans programs, communities, or other settings may involve a biased sampling for the qualitative component. Natalia Luxardo, Graciela Colombo, and Gabriela Iglesias (2011) confronted this challenge in their study of Brazilian family violence services and, as a result, focused their qualitative research on one service that supported the value of giving voice to their service recipients.

Weighing both roles and the best combination of them is critical at the outset of a mixed-methods project, although the dilemma will be lessened if a project uses different researchers to lead the quantitative and qualitative components.

Complex mixed-methods projects in which quantitative surveying is interspersed with observational research or intensive interviews may also require the renegotiation of participant consent to the particular research procedures at each stage. As stated by Chih Hoong Sin (2005),

> Different stages and different components of research may require the negotiation of different types of consent, some of which may be more explicit than others. Sampling, contact, re-contact, and fieldwork can be underpinned by different conceptualization and operationalization of "informed consent." This behooves researchers to move away from the position of treating consent-seeking as an exercise that only occurs at certain points in the research process or only for certain types of research. Consent-seeking should not be thought of merely as an event. (p. 290)

Claire Wulf Winiarek, MA, Director of Collaborative Policy Engagement

Source: Claire Wulf Winiarek

Claire Wulf Winiarek didn't set her sights on research methods as an undergraduate in political science and international relations at Baldwin College, nor as a master's student at Old Dominion University; her goal was to make a difference in public affairs. It still is. She is currently director of collaborative policy engagement at WellPoint, a *Fortune* 50 health insurance company based in Indianapolis, Indiana. Her previous positions include working for a Virginia member of the U.S. House of Representatives, coordinating grassroots international human rights advocacy for Amnesty International's North Africa Regional Action Network, and working as director of Public Policy and Research at Amerigroup's Office of Health Reform Integration.

Early in her career, Winiarek was surprised by the frequency with which she found herself leveraging research methods. Whether she is analyzing draft legislation and proposed regulations, determining next year's department budget, or estimating potential growth while making the case for a new program, Winiarek has found that a strong foundation in research methods shapes her success. The increasing reliance of government and its private-sector partners on data and evidence-based decision making continues to increase the importance of methodological expertise.

Policy work informed by research has made for a very rewarding career:

> The potential for meaningful impact in the lives of everyday Americans is very real at the nexus of government and the private sector. Public policy—and how policy works in practice—has significant societal impact. I feel fortunate to help advance that nexus in a way that is informed not only by practice, evidence, and research but also by the voice of those impacted.

Winiarek's advice for students seeking a career like hers is clear:

> The information revolution is impacting all industries and sectors, as well as government and our communities. With this ever-growing and ever-richer set of information, today's professionals must have the know-how to understand and apply these data in a meaningful way. Research methods will create the critical and analytical foundation to meet the challenge, but internships or special research projects in your career field will inform that foundation with practical experience. Always look for that connection between research and reality.

CAREERS AND RESEARCH

CONCLUSION

We began this chapter by asking what mixed-methods research has to tell us about our social world. The mixed-methods examples from this chapter demonstrate that a research design is an integrated whole. Designing research means deciding how to measure empirical phenomena, how to identify causal connections, and how to generalize findings—not as separate decisions but in tandem, with each decision having implications for the others. The choice of a data collection method should be guided, in part, by the aspect of validity that is of most concern, but each aspect of validity must be considered in attempting to answer every research question. A basic question the researcher must ask is this: Will a mixed-methods approach give a better picture of the research target than a single-method approach? If the answer is yes, then the researcher must consider which combination of methods will offer the best mix of validity, generalizability, and rich, accurate data on the target research question.

The ability to apply diverse techniques to address different aspects of a complex research question is one mark of a sophisticated researcher. Awareness that one study's findings must be understood in the context of a larger body of research is another. And the ability to speculate on how the use of different methods might have altered a study's findings is a prerequisite for informed criticism of research.

Finally, realistic assessment of the weaknesses, as well as the strengths, of each method of data collection should help you to remember that humility is a virtue in research. Advancement of knowledge and clear answers to specific research questions are attainable with the tools you now have in your methodological toolbox. Perfection, however, is not a realistic goal. No matter what research method we use, our mental concepts cannot reflect exactly what we measured, our notions of causation cannot reveal a tangible causal force, and our generalizations always extend beyond the cases that were actually studied. This is not cause for disillusionment, but it should keep us from being excessively confident in our own interpretations or unreasonably resistant to change. Final answers to every research question we pose cannot be achieved; what we seek are new, ever more sophisticated questions for research.

KEY TERMS

Convergent parallel design   279
Effect size   288
Embedded design   281
Exploratory sequential design   279
Meta-analysis   287
Meta-synthesis   289
Mixed methods   278
Multiphase design   281
Thick description   289
Transformative design   281
Triangulation   278

HIGHLIGHTS

- The use of mixed methods is intentionally combining both quantitative and qualitative methods to study one research question.

- Mixed-methods research has been increasing for the past 25 years primarily because most researchers are convinced that research on most topics can be improved by using mixed methods.

- There are several designs available in mixed-methods research, including those that give equal weight to both quantitative and qualitative methodologies and those that give differential weight to one or the other method.

- Researchers can test statistically for patterns across multiple studies with meta-analysis. This technique can be used only in areas of research in which there have been many prior studies using comparable methods.

- Meta-synthesis is the analysis tool for assessing the results of multiple studies that have relied on qualitative methods.

Discussing Research

1. Some research projects use an "inverted pyramid" data collection strategy, with broad, quantitative measures gathered from a large population on top, narrowing to more intensive qualitative measures (focus groups, individual interviews) with a smaller subset of the population at the bottom. Design a research project that resembles such an inverted pyramid, showing what measures and what sample size and research subjects you would use at each level of the design.

2. Think of at least three areas of criminological research where you believe much research has been done—for example, understanding why some people engage in crime. Where are you likely to find such studies? You may wish to start by looking on ERIC, in JSTOR, and in Criminal Justice Abstracts, whichever database your library has. Do a literature search for this substantive area of inquiry with the words *and "mixed methods"* to find out about recent research on the topic that has utilized mixed methods. What do you find? Did mixing methods enhance the findings?

3. Testa (Testa et al., 2011) describes her own training as quantitative and then highlights some experiences that led her to integrate qualitative methods into her research. Would you describe your own training in research methods so far as primarily quantitative or qualitative? Have you had any experiences that lead you to consider the other methodology?

4. Which of the four types of mixed methods do you feel is likely to be useful for investigating the social world? Would you favor more single-method or more mixed-methods studies? Explain your reasoning.

5. Select a public setting in which there are many people on a regular basis, such as a sports game, a theater lobby, a coffee shop, or a popular public park. Observe as an ethnographer for 30 minutes on one day and then write up your notes. Before your next visit, a day later, develop a systematic observation schedule on which to record observations in the same setting in a structured manner. Record observations using the structured observation form on another day but in the same place and at about the same time of day. Compare the data you have collected with your ethnographic notes and with your systematic observation notes.

Finding Research on the Web

1. Go to the website for the online *Journal of Mixed-Methods Research* (mmr.sagepub.com). On the home page, click the button "Current Issue." When the table of contents for the current issue comes up, click on the abstracts for three of the articles, and for each article, write down two more methods that the authors used to conduct their research. Did any methods occur more than once? Were there any methods you had never heard of before?

2. Go to the home page of the *Journal of Mixed-Methods Research*, and click on the "most read." When the most-read article titles come up, read the abstracts for the top-five articles. What themes or main points do you see running through these articles? Based on the top-five abstracts, write a paragraph or two describing the most important issues currently being discussed or investigated by mixed-methods researchers.

3. Go to the National Criminal Justice Reference Service website (www.ncjrs.gov), and search for the term *mixed methods*. Find at least two studies that have used a mixed-methods approach. What strengths did this approach provide the study compared with using only one of the methods?

4. Find a research article that used both qualitative and quantitative research data (You can also find articles on the Student Study Site, **edge.sagepub.com/ bachmanfrccj5e.**). Make a list of the ways that you think the collection of qualitative data enhanced the findings and interpretations of quantitative data. Try to find some potential interpretations of the quantitative data that would have been incorrect if it were not for the additional insights garnered from the qualitative data.

Critiquing Research

1. Do you find the idea of a meta-analysis (or "study of studies") convincing? Find a review study on crime from the Campbell Collaboration (www .campbellcollaboration.org). Give at least two reasons why conclusions reached in this review may be more convincing than conclusions reached by the individual studies alone.

2. Using a case study provided in this chapter, list two ways the study may have been improved, such as the

sample, the measurement of concepts, and the selection of methods to study the research question(s). If you were going to design a study to investigate the same research question, provide an outline of the methodological and measurement strategy you would use.

Making Research Ethical

1. You learned in this book that Sampson and Raudenbush (1999) had observers drive down neighborhood streets in Chicago and record the level of disorder they observed. What should have been the observers' response if they observed a crime in progress? What if they just suspected that a crime was going to occur? What if the crime was a drug dealer interacting with a driver at a curb? What if it was a prostitute soliciting a customer? What, if any, ethical obligation does a researcher studying a neighborhood have to residents in that neighborhood? Should research results be shared at a neighborhood forum or community meeting?

2. Some research investigating the effects of alcohol have actually had research subjects drink to the point of intoxication (Exum, 2002). If you were a student member of your university's institutional review board, would you vote to approve a study such as this? Why, or why not? Would you ban an experiment that involves alcohol altogether or would you set certain criteria for the experimental conditions? What would such criteria be? What about female students who may be potentially pregnant? Can you think of any circumstances in which you would allow an experiment involving the administration of illegal drugs?

Developing a Research Proposal

Now is the time to mix your methods.

1. Add a component involving a second method to your research proposal. If you already developed alternative approaches in response to the exercises in earlier chapters, just write a justification for these additions that point out the potential benefits.

2. Consider the possible influences of social-context factors on the variables pertinent to your research question. Write a rationale for including a test for contextual influences in your proposed research.

3. Describe a method for studying the contextual influences in Question 2.

Performing Data Analysis in SPSS or Excel

Data for Exercise	
Dataset	**Description**
2013 YRBS.sav	The 2013 Youth Risk Behavior Survey (YRBS) is a national study of high school students. It focuses on gauging various behaviors and experiences of the adolescent population, including substance use and some victimization.
Monitoring the future 2013 grade 10.sav	This dataset contains variables from the 2013 Monitoring the Future (MTF) study. These data cover a national sample of 10th graders, with a focus on monitoring substance use and abuse.
Variables for Exercise	
Variable Name (dataset)	**Description**
Qn33 (YRBS)	Binary variable indicating if the respondent had drunk any alcohol in the past month, where 1 = *yes* and 2 = *no*
Qn43 (YRBS)	Binary variable indicating if the respondent had smoked cigarettes in the past month, where 1 = *yes* and 2 = *no*
Sex (YRBS)	Gender of the respondent, where 1 = *male* and 2 = *female*
Race4 (YRBS)	Four-category race measure, where 1 = *white*, 2 = *black*, 3 = *Hispanic*, and 4 = *other*
Past30cigs (MTF)	Binary variable indicating if the respondent had smoked cigarettes in the past month, where 1= *yes* and 0 = *no*

Variables for Exercise	
Variable Name (dataset)	**Description**
Past30drink (MTF)	Binary variable indicating if the respondent had drunk any alcohol in the past month, where 1 = *yes* and 0 = *no*
Gender (MTF)	Gender of the respondent, where 1 = *male* and 2 = *female*
V1070 (MTF)	Three-category race measure, where 1 = *black*, 2 = *white*, and 3 = *Hispanic*

1. We won't be able to do anything with mixed-methods data in the sense that we can't mix qualitative and quantitative data, as such an analysis is not well suited to SPSS and is *very* labor intensive. What we can do is look into triangulating and replicating findings across multiple datasets with similar measures. For this exercise, we'll look at whether there are any race and gender differences in smoking and drinking behaviors.

   a. Why would we want to compare results across multiple datasets?

   b. Does this allow us to establish (1) causal relationships, (2) that measures are reliable, (3) the validity of a measure? Why, or why not?

2. The MTF dataset is for 10th graders specifically, so you will need to make sure that the 2013 YRBS dataset has only 10th graders selected as well. To do this, go to "Data->select cases->if" and enter "grade=2" into the field. After this is done, we'll look into answering our questions:

   a. First, tabulate the YRBS variables "qn33" and "qn43" and the MTF variables "past30cigs" and "past30drink."

   b. Do these two datasets agree on the incidence rates of drinking and smoking? If not, can you think of any reasons for why they wouldn't agree?

3. Next, let's look at whether we can replicate any relationships across the two datasets, regardless of any differences in prevalence estimates. In particular, look at the relationship between race and gender and drinking and smoking in both datasets. The variables for race and gender are "race4" and "sex" in the YRBS and "gender" and "v1070" in MTF.

   a. Do you see any consistencies or similarities?

   b. What conclusions do you feel most comfortable making based on these comparisons? What do you think needs additional replication and testing?

12

SUMMARIZING AND REPORTING RESEARCH

Learning Objectives

1. Describe the three basic goals of research reports.

2. Identify unique problems that must be overcome in writing student papers, theses, applied research reports, and journal articles.

3. List the major sections of a research article.

4. Describe the elements that should be considered in writing research reports to ensure adherence to the ethical standard of honesty.

5. Discuss the motivations for plagiarism and the ways of avoiding suspicions of plagiarism.

6. Identify major steps in the review of research reports.

7. Understand the need to display results without redundant information using compressed displays.

⑤SAGE edge™

Master the content at edge
.sagepub.com/bachmanfrccj5e

WHAT DO WE HAVE IN MIND?

You learned in Chapter 2 that research is a circular process, so it is appropriate that we end this book where we began. The stage of reporting research results is also the point at which the need for new research is identified. It is the time when, so to speak, the rubber hits the road—when we have to make our research make sense to others. To whom will our research be addressed? How should we present our results to them? Should we seek to influence how our research report is used?

The primary goals of this chapter are to guide you in writing worthwhile reports of your own, displaying findings, and communicating with the public about research. This chapter gives particular attention to the writing process itself and points out how that process can differ when writing qualitative versus quantitative research reports. We highlight the goals of research reports, including expanding the discussion of participatory action research (PAR), which we introduced in Chapter 3. We will conclude by considering some of the ethical issues unique to the reporting process, with special attention to the problem of plagiarism.

RESEARCH REPORT GOALS

The research report will present research findings and interpretations in a way that reflects some combination of the researcher's goals, the research sponsor's goals, the concerns of the research subjects, and, perhaps, the concerns of a wider anticipated readership. Understanding the goals of these different groups will help the researcher begin to shape the final report even at the beginning of the research. In designing a proposal and in negotiating access to a setting for the research, commitments often must be made to produce a particular type of report or, at least, to cover certain issues in the final report. As the research progresses, feedback about the research from its participants, sponsoring agencies, collaborators, or other interested parties may suggest the importance of focusing on particular issues in the final report. Social researchers traditionally have tried to distance themselves from the concerns of such interested parties, paying attention only to what is needed to advance scientific knowledge. But in recent years, some social scientists have recommended bringing these interested parties into the research and reporting process itself.

Advance Scientific Knowledge

Most social science research reports are directed to other social scientists working in the area of study, so they reflect orientations and concerns that are shared within this community of interest. The traditional scientific approach encourages a research goal to advance scientific knowledge by providing reports to other scientists. This approach also treats value considerations as beyond the scope of science: "An empirical science cannot tell anyone what he should do but rather what he can do and under certain circumstances what he wishes to do" (M. Weber, 1949, p. 54).

The idea is that developing valid knowledge about how society is organized or how we live our lives does not tell us how society *should* be organized or how we *should* live our lives. There should, as a result, be a strict separation between the determination of empirical facts and the evaluation of these facts as satisfactory or unsatisfactory (M. Weber, 1949). Social scientists must not ignore value considerations, which are viewed as a legitimate basis for selecting a research problem to study. After the research is over and a report has been written, many scientists also consider it acceptable to encourage government officials or private organizations to implement the findings. During a research project, however, value considerations are to be held in abeyance.

Shape Social Policy

As we highlighted in our discussion of applied research in Chapter 10, many social scientists seek to influence social policy through their writing. By now, you have been exposed to several such examples in this text, including all the evaluation research. These particular studies, like much policy-oriented social science research, are similar to those that aim strictly to increase knowledge. In fact, these studies might even be considered contributions to knowledge first and to social policy debate second. What distinguishes the reports of these studies from strictly academic reports is their attention to policy implications.

Other social scientists who seek to influence social policy explicitly reject the traditional scientific, rigid distinction between facts and values (Sjoberg & Nett, 1968). Bellah and colleagues (Bellah, Madsen, Sullivan, Swidler, & Tipton, 1985) have instead proposed a model of "social science as public philosophy," in which social scientists focus explicit attention on achieving a more just society. Social science makes assumptions about the nature of persons, the nature of society, and the relation between persons and society. It also, whether it admits it or not, makes assumptions about good persons and a good society and considers how far these conceptions are embodied in our actual society:

> Social science as public philosophy, by breaking through the iron curtain between the social sciences and the humanities, becomes a form of social self-understanding or self-interpretation. . . . By probing the past as well as the present, by looking at "values" as much as at "facts," such a social science is able to make connections that are not obvious and to ask difficult questions. (p. 301)

This perspective suggests more explicit concern with public policy implications when reporting research results. But it is important to remember that we all are capable of distorting our research and our interpretations of research results to correspond to our own value preferences. The temptation to see what we want to see is enormous, and research reports cannot be deemed acceptable unless they avoid this temptation.

Organize Social Action—Participatory Action Research

For the same reasons that value questions are traditionally set apart from the research process, many social scientists consider the application of research a nonscientific concern. William

Foote Whyte has criticized this belief and proposed an alternative research and reporting strategy he calls **participatory action research (PAR)**. Whyte (1991) argues that social scientists must get "out of the academic rut" and engage in applied research to develop better understanding of social phenomena (p. 285).

In PAR, the researcher involves as active participants some members of the setting studied. Both the organizational members and the researcher are assumed to want to develop valid conclusions, to bring unique insights, and to desire change, but Whyte (1991) believed that these objectives were more likely to be obtained if the researcher collaborated actively with the persons he or she studied. PAR can bring researchers into closer contact with participants in the research setting through groups that discuss and plan research steps and then take steps to implement research findings. Stephen Kemmis and Robin McTaggart (2005) summarize the key features of PAR as "a spiral of self-reflecting cycles" involving

- planning a change,

- acting and observing the process and consequences of the change,

- reflecting on these processes and consequences,

- planning again, and

- acting and observing again.

In contrast with the formal reporting of results at the end of a research project, these cycles make research reporting an ongoing part of the research process.

Case Study: Seeking Higher Education for Inmates

While prison populations in the United States have been significantly increasing, access to college programs within prisons essentially has been eliminated. Primarily because of the "tough on crime" policies of the 1990s, by 1995, only eight of the existing 350 college programs in prisons remained open nationwide (Torre & Fine, 2005). To remedy this situation, Torre and Fine became involved in PAR to facilitate a college and college-bound program at the Bedford Hills Correctional Facility (BHCF), a maximum-security women's prison in New York. Michelle Fine was the principal investigator in the study determining the effects of the program, along with four prisoner researchers and four researchers from the Graduate Center of the City University of New York. This PAR team asked several questions: (a) Who are the women in the college program? (b) What is the impact of the college experience on inmate students and their children? (c) What is the impact of the college experience on the prison environment? (d) What is the impact of the college experience beyond college on recidivism? and (e) What is the cost of such a program to taxpayers? The researchers used a triangulated methodology employing quantitative analysis of recidivism rates and costs of the program, along with in-depth interviews with the participants; focus groups with inmates, faculty, children, and college presidents; and surveys of faculty who taught in the program. Although not using a randomized experimental design, Torre and Fine, along with their coinvestigators, tracked participants in the college program after release and found that women who had not participated in the program were 4 times more likely to be returned to custody than women who had participated.

The narratives from the interviews with college inmates also illuminated the positive benefits of the education. One inmate college student said,

Because when you take somebody that feels that they're not gonna amount to anything, and you put them in an environment, like, when you're in college it takes you away from the prison . . . it's like you're opening your mind to a whole different experience. (Torre & Fine, 2005, p. 582)

The positive impact of college on the inmates was also transferred to their children. The cost–benefit analysis of the program indicated that the savings based on decreased recidivism rates for those who attended the college far outweighed the initial cost of the program itself. In sum, with just a small grant from a private foundation, the PAR team brought together universities, prisoners, churches, community organizations, and prison administrators to resurrect a college at BHCF. The authors concluded, "Key elements of this program include broad-based community involvement, strong prisoner participation in design and governance, and the support of the prison administration" (p. 591). A full report of this research can be found at arj .sagepub.com/content/4/3/253.abstract. As you can see, PAR has the potential to be life changing for all those involved.

Dialogue With Research Subjects

Guba and Lincoln (1989) have carried the notion of involving research subjects and others in the design and reporting of research one step further. What they call the constructivist paradigm is a methodology that emphasizes the importance of exploring how different stakeholders in a social setting construct their beliefs. As we noted in Chapter 1, this approach rejects the assumption that there is a reality around us to be studied and reported on. Instead, social scientists operating in the constructivist paradigm try to develop a consensus among participants in some social process about how to understand the focus of inquiry, a program that is often evaluated. A research report will then highlight different views of the social program and explain how a consensus can be reached.

> Constructivist paradigm: Methodology based on the rejection of a belief in an external reality; it emphasizes the importance of exploring the way in which different stakeholders in a social setting construct their beliefs

The constructivist approach provides a useful way of thinking about how to best make sense of the complexity and subjectivity of the social world. Other researchers write reports intended to influence public policy, and often, their findings are ignored. Such neglect would be less common if social researchers gave more attention to the different meanings attached by participants to the same events, in the spirit of constructivist case reports. The philosophy of this approach is also similar to the utilization-based evaluation research approach advanced by Patton (1997; see Chapter 10) that involves all stakeholders in the research process.

TYPES OF RESEARCH REPORTS

Research projects designed to produce student papers and theses, applied research reports, and academic articles all have unique features that will influence the final research report. For example, student papers are written for a particular professor or for a thesis committee and often are undertaken with almost no financial resources and in the face of severe time constraints. Applied research reports are written for an organization or agency that usually also has funded the research and has expectations for a particular type of report. Journal articles are written for the larger academic community and will not be published until they are judged acceptable by some representatives of that community (e.g., after the article has gone through extensive peer review).

These unique features do not really match up so neatly with specific types of research products. For example, a student paper that is based on a research project conducted in collaboration with a work organization may face some constraints for a project designed to produce an applied research report. An academic article may stem from an applied research project conducted for a government agency. An applied research report often can be followed by an academic article on the same topic. In fact, one research study may lead to all three types of research reports as students write course papers or theses for professors who write both academic articles and applied research reports.

Student Papers and Theses

What is most distinctive about a student research paper or thesis is the audience for the final product: a professor or (for a thesis) a committee of professors. In light of this, it is important for you to seek feedback early and often about the progress of your research and about your professor's expectations for the final paper. Securing approval of a research proposal is usually the first step, but it should not be the last occasion for seeking advice prior to writing the final paper. Do not become too anxious for guidance, however. Professors require research projects, in part, so that their students can work through—at least somewhat independently—the many issues they confront. A great deal of insight into the research process can be gained in this way. So balance your requests for advice with some independent decision making.

Most student research projects can draw on few resources beyond the student's own time and effort, so it is important that the research plan not be overly ambitious. Keep the paper deadline in mind when planning the project, and remember that almost every researcher tends to underestimate the time required to carry out a project.

The Thesis Committee

Students who are preparing a paper for a committee, usually at the MA or PhD level, must be prepared to integrate the multiple perspectives and comments of committee members into a plan for a coherent final report. (The thesis committee chair should be the primary guide in this process; careful selection of faculty to serve on the committee also is important.) As much as possible, committee members should have complementary areas of expertise that are each important for the research project: perhaps one methodologist, one specialist in the primary substantive area of the thesis, and one specialist in a secondary area.

It is very important that you work with your committee members in an ongoing manner, both individually and collectively. In fact, it is vitally important to have a group meeting with all committee members at the beginning of the project to ensure that everyone on the committee supports the research plan. Doing this will avoid obstacles that arise due to miscommunication later in the research process.

Journal Articles

Peer review: A process in which a journal editor sends a submitted article to two or three experts who judge whether the paper should be accepted, revised and resubmitted, or rejected; the experts also provide comments to explain their decisions and guide any revisions

It is the **peer review** process that makes preparation of an academic journal article most unique. Similar to a grant review, the journal's editor sends submitted articles to two or three experts (peers), who are asked whether the paper should be accepted more or less as is, revised and then resubmitted, or rejected. Reviewers also provide comments—which are sometimes quite lengthy—to explain their decision and to guide any required revisions. The process is an anonymous one at most journals; reviewers are not told the author's name, and the author is not told the reviewers' names. Although the journal editor has the final say, editors' decisions are normally based on the reviewers' comments.

This peer review process must be anticipated in designing the final report. Peer reviewers are not pulled out of a hat. They are experts in the field or fields represented in the paper and usually have published articles themselves in that field. It is critical that the author be familiar with the research literature and be able to present the research findings as a unique contribution to that literature. In most cases, this hurdle is much harder to jump with journal articles than with student papers or applied research reports. In fact, most leading journals have a rejection rate of over 90%, so that hurdle is quite high indeed. Of course, there is also a certain luck of the draw involved in peer review. One set of two or three reviewers may be inclined to reject an article that another set of reviewers would accept. But in general, the anonymous peer review process results in higher quality research reports because articles are revised prior to publication in response to the suggestions and criticisms of the experts.

Criminological and criminal justice research is published in myriad journals within several disciplines, including criminology, law, sociology, psychology, and economics. As a result, there is no one formatting style by which all criminological literature abides. If, for example, you are submitting your paper to a psychology-related journal, you must abide by the formatting style dictated by the *Publication Manual of the American Psychological Association* (American Psychological Association, 2009). The easiest way to determine how to format a paper for a particular journal is to examine recent volumes of the journal and format your paper accordingly. Numerous articles are available on the Student Study Site. (The website is listed at the end of each chapter in this book.)

Despite the slight variations in style across journals, there are typically seven standard sections within a journal article, in addition to the title page (see Exhibit 12.1).

Exhibit 12.1 General Sections of a Journal Article

1. Abstract	This should be a concise and nonevaluative summary of your research paper (no more than 120 words) that describes the research problem, the sample, the method, and the findings.
2. Introduction	The body of a paper should open with an introduction that presents the specific problem under study and describes the research strategy. Before writing this section, you should consider the following questions: What is the point of the study? How do the hypotheses and the research design relate to the problem? What are the theoretical implications of the study, and how does the study relate to previous work in the area? What are the theoretical propositions tested, and how were they derived? A good introduction answers these questions in a few paragraphs by summarizing the relevant argument and the data, giving the reader a sense of what was done and why.
3. Literature Review	Discuss the relevant literature in a way that relates each previous study cited to your research but not in an exhaustive historical review. Citation of and specific credit to relevant earlier works is part of the researchers' scientific and scholarly responsibility. It is essential for the growth of cumulative science. This section should demonstrate the logical continuity between previous research and the research at hand. At the end of this section, you are ready to conceptually define your variables and formally state your hypotheses.
4. Method	Describe in detail how the study was conducted. Such a description enables the reader to evaluate the appropriateness of your methods and the reliability and validity of your results. It also permits experienced investigators to replicate the study if they so desire. In this section, you can include subsections that describe the sample, the independent and dependent variables, and the analytical or statistical procedure you will use to analyze the data.
5. Results	Summarize the results of the statistical or qualitative analyses performed on the data. This can include tables and figures that summarize findings. If statistical analyses are performed, tests of significance also should be highlighted.
6. Discussion	Take the opportunity to evaluate and interpret your results, particularly with respect to your original hypotheses and previous research. Here, you are free to examine and interpret your results, as well as draw inferences from them. In general, this section should answer the following questions: What have I contributed to the literature here? How has my study helped resolve the original problem? What conclusions and theoretical implications can I draw from my study? What are the limitations of my study? What are the implications for future research?
7. References	All citations in the manuscript must appear in the reference list, and all references must be cited in the text.

Applied Reports

Unlike journal articles, applied reports are usually commissioned by a particular government agency, corporation, or nonprofit organization. As such, the most important problem that applied researchers confront is the need to produce a final report that meets the funding organization's expectations. This is called the "hired gun" problem. Of course, the extent to which being a hired gun is a problem varies greatly with the research orientation of the funding organization and with the nature of the research problem posed. The ideal situation is to have few constraints on the nature of the final report, but sometimes research reports are suppressed or distorted because the researcher comes to conclusions that the funding organization does not like.

Applied reports that are written in a less highly charged environment can face another problem—even when they are favorably received by the funding organization, their conclusions are often ignored. This problem can be more a matter of the organization not really knowing how to use research findings than it not wanting to use them. This is not just a problem of the funding organization; many researchers are prepared only to present their findings, without giving any thought to how research findings can be translated into organizational policies or programs.

CURBING THE FRUSTRATIONS OF WRITING

> Perfectionism is the voice of the oppressor, the enemy of the people. It will keep you cramped and insane your whole life and it is the main obstacle between you and a shitty first draft. (Lamott, 1994, p. 28)

We often hear lamentations from students such as "It is impossible to know where to begin" or "I have a hard time getting started." To this we say only, "Begin wherever you are most comfortable, but begin early!" You do not have to start with the introduction; start in the method section if you prefer. The main point is to begin somewhere and then keep typing, keep typing, and keep typing! It is always easier to rewrite a paper than it is to write the first draft. The fine art of writing is really in the rewriting!

Those of you who began with a research proposal have a head start; you will find that the final report is much easier to write. It is very disappointing to discover that something important was left out when it is too late to do anything about it. We do not need to point out that students (and professional researchers) often leave final papers (and reports) until the last possible minute (often for understandable reasons, including other course work and job or family responsibilities). But be forewarned: The last-minute approach does not work for research reports.

A successful report must be well organized and clearly written. Getting to such a product is a difficult but not impossible goal. Consider the following principles formulated by experienced writers (Booth, Colomb, & Williams, 1995):

- Start with an outline.

- Respect the complexity of the task, and do not expect to write a polished draft in a linear fashion. Your thinking will develop as you write, causing you to reorganize and rewrite.

- Leave enough time for dead ends, restarts, revisions, and so on, and accept the fact that you will discard much of what you write.

- Write as fast as you comfortably can. Do not worry about spelling, grammar, and so on until you are polishing things up.

- Ask all the people whom you trust for their reactions to what you have written.

- Write as you go along, so you have notes and report segments drafted even before you focus on writing the report.

It is important to remember that no version of a manuscript is ever final. As you write, you will get new ideas about how to organize the report. Try them out. As you review the first draft, you will see many ways to improve your writing. Focus particularly on how to shorten and clarify your statements. Make sure each paragraph concerns only one topic. Remember the golden rule of good writing: Writing is revising!

Another useful tip is to use a method called **reverse outlining**. After you have written a first complete draft, outline it on a paragraph-by-paragraph basis, ignoring the actual section headings you used. See if the paper you wrote actually fits the outline you planned. How could the organization be improved?

> **Reverse outlining:** Outlining the sections in an already written draft of a paper or report to improve its organization in the next draft

Perhaps most importantly, leave yourself enough time so that you can revise—several times if possible—before turning in the final draft.

A well-written research report requires (to be just a bit melodramatic) blood, sweat, and tears and more time than you will at first anticipate. But the process of writing one will help you to write the next, and the issues you consider—if you approach your writing critically—will be sure to improve your subsequent research projects and sharpen your evaluations of others.

Those of you interested in a more focused discussion of writing in general (e.g., grammar, elements of style, emotional aspects of writing) should see Becker (1986), Booth et al. (1995), Mullins (1977), Strunk and White (1979), and Turabian (1967).

DISPLAYING DATA

If you have an interest in learning about quantitative statistics, you can see the chapter that is posted on the Student Study Site. Here, we want to focus on some additional methods of presenting statistical results that can improve research reports. Combined and compressed displays are used most often in applied research reports and government documents, but they can also help communicate findings more effectively in student papers and journal articles.

In a **combined frequency display**, the distributions for a set of conceptually similar variables with the same response categories are presented together, with common headings for the responses. For example, you could identify the variables in the leftmost column and the value labels along the top. Exhibit 12.2 is a combined display reporting the frequency distributions in percentage form for responses to the question, "How worried are you that you or someone in your family will become a victim of terrorism?" for the years 2002 through 2013. From this table, you can infer several pieces of information besides the basic distribution of attitudes. Except for the high blip in early October, when 24% of the population was very worried, for the most part, about 1 in 10 people have been very worried throughout the entire time period. However, there has been a noticeable increase in the percentage of the population who are not worried at all during this time.

> **Combined frequency display:** A table that presents together the distributions for a set of conceptually similar variables having the same response categories; common headings are used for the responses

> **Compressed frequency display:** A table that presents cross-classification data efficiently by eliminating unnecessary percentages, such as the percentage corresponding to the second value of a dichotomous variable

Compressed frequency displays can also be used to present cross-tabular data and summary statistics more efficiently, by eliminating unnecessary percentages (such as those corresponding to the second value of a dichotomous variable) and by reducing the need for repetitive labels. Exhibit 12.3 presents a compressed display used to highlight the percentages of students in Grades 9 through 12 who reported using marijuana at least once in the past 30 days by select student characteristics and year. It took many cross-tabulations to create

Respondents reporting fear that they or a family member will become a victim of terrorism United States, 2002–2013

Question: "How worried are you that you or someone in your family will become a victim of terrorism—very worried, somewhat worried, not too worried, or not worried at all?"

Date	Very Worried	Somewhat Worried	Not too Worried	Not Worried at All
Sept. 21–22, 2001	14	35	32	18
Oct. 5–6, 2001	24	35	27	14
Oct. 11–14, 2001	18	33	35	14
Oct. 19–21, 2001	13	30	33	23
Nov. 2–4, 2001	11	28	34	28
Nov. 26–27, 2001	8	27	34	30
March, 2002	12	33	32	23
April, 2002	8	27	39	25
May, 2002	9	31	37	22
September, 2002	8	30	37	25
January, 2003	8	31	36	25
February, 2003	8	28	33	31
March, 2003	8	30	38	24
August, 2003	11	30	33	26
December, 2003	9	28	38	25
January, 2004	5	23	42	30
February, 2004	10	30	36	24
October, 2004	13	34	33	20
December, 2004	13	28	34	25
January, 2005	10	28	37	24
June, 2005	8	30	36	26
July, 2005	14	33	30	23
December, 2005	11	30	37	22
August, 2006	11	34	34	21
June, 2007	12	32	33	22
July, 2007	13	34	31	21
September, 2008	9	29	38	24
December, 2009	12	27	34	28
January, 2010	9	33	35	22
August, 2011	9	27	32	31
April, 2013	11	29	33	27

0% 10% 20% 30% 40% 50% 60% 70% 80% 90% 100%

Legend:
☐ Very Worried   ☐ Somewhat Worried
☐ Not too Worried   ☐ Not Worried at All

Source: From Sourcebook of Criminal Justice Statistics Online. (2013). *Table 2.29.2013*. Data source: Gallup, Inc., The Gallup Poll [Online]. Available: http://www.gallup.com/poll/162074/post-boston-half-anticipate-terrorism-soon.aspx [May 6, 2013]. Table adapted by SOURCEBOOK staff.

Note: Most recent data available at publication

Exhibit 12.3 Compressed Display of the Percentage (Standard Errors in Parentheses) of Students in Grades 9–12 Who Reported Using Marijuana at Least One Time During the Previous 30 Days, by Selected Student Characteristics and Year

Location and student characteristic	1993	1995	1997	1999	2001	2003	2005	2007	2009	2011	2013	2015
1	2	3	4	5	6	7	8	9	10	11	12	13
Anywhere (including on school property) Total	17.7 (1.22)	25.3 (1.03)	26.2 (1.11)	26.7 (1.30)	235 (0.77)	22.4 (1.09)	205 (0.84)	19.7 (0.97)	20.8 (0.70)	23.1 (0.80)	23.4 (1.08)	21.7 (1.22)
Sex												
Male	20.6 (161)	28.4 (1.08)	30.2 (1.46)	30.8 (1.92)	27.9 (0.81)	25.1 (1.25)	22.1 (0.98)	22.4 (1.02)	23.4 (0.80)	25.9 (1.01)	25.4 (1.14)	23.2 (1.46)
Female	14.6 (1.02)	22.0 (1.44)	21.4 (1.04)	22.6 (0.96)	20.0 (0.87)	19.3 (0.96)	18.2 (0.99)	17.0 (1.13)	17.9 (0.87)	20.1 (0.95)	21.9 (1.28)	20.0 (1.33)
Race/ethnicity												
White	17.3 (1.41)	24.5 (1.49)	25.0 (1.56)	26.4 (1.59)	24.4 (1.04)	21.7 (1.2)	20.3 (1.11)	19.9 (1.28)	20.7 (0.93)	21.7 (1.09)	20.4 (1.36)	19.9 (1.67)
Black	18.6 (1.84)	28.6 (2.62)	28.2 (1.67)	26.4 (3.49)	21.8 (2.12)	23.9 (1.58)	20.4 (1.11)	21.5 (1.64)	22.2 (1.44)	25.1 (1.35)	28.9 (1.30)	27.1 (1.57)
Hispanic	19.4 (1.33)	27.8 (2.92)	28.6 (2.06)	28.2 (2.29)	24.6 (0.81)	23.8 (1.16)	23.0 (1.22)	18.5 (1.41)	21.6 (2.62)	24.4 (1.27)	27.6 (1.50)	24.5 (1.49)
Asian	—(†)	—(†)	—(†)	13.5 (2.04)	10.9 (2.12)	9.5 (2.21)	6.7 (1.64)	9.4 (1.63)	7.5 (1.40)	13.6 (3.75)	16.4 (2.99)	8.2 (1.58)
Pacific Islander	—(†)	—(†)	—(†)	33.8 (4.11)	21.9 (4.07)	28.1 (6.47)	12.4 (3.87)	28.7 (6.14)	24.8 (5.50)	31.1 (7.08)	23.4 (7.35)	17.4 (4.88)
American Indian/Alaska Native	17.4 (4.77)	28.0 (5.72)	44.2 (4.31)	36.2 (6.55)	36.4 (5.48)	32.8 (5.29)	30.3 (4.36)	27.4 (3.50)	31.6 (5.26)	47.4 (3.20)	35.5 (6.37)	26.9 (5.20)
Two or more races	—(†)	—(†)	—(†)	29.1 (4.00)	31.8 (3.22)	28.3 (5.57)	16.9 (2.43)	20.5 (2.73)	21.7 (2.33)	26.8 (2.10)	28.8 (2.55)	23.5 (2.18)
Grade												
9th	13.2 (1.10)	20.9 (1.83)	23.6 (1.95)	21.7 (1.84)	19.4 (1.25)	18.5 (1.52)	17.4 (1.16)	14.7 (1.02)	15.5 (0.97)	18.0 (1.11)	17.7 (1.13)	15.2 (0.98)
10th	16.5 (1.79)	25.5 (1.89)	25.0 (1.29)	27.8 (2.21)	24.8 (1.12)	22.0 (1.47)	20.2 (1.27)	19.3 (1.12)	21.1 (1.11)	21.6 (1.15)	23.5 (1.89)	20.0 (1.87)
11th	18.4 (1.77)	27.6 (1.35)	29.3 (1.81)	26.7 (2.47)	25.8 (1.33)	24.1 (1.56)	21.0 (1.24)	21.4 (1.49)	23.2 (1.52)	25.5 (1.44)	25.5 (1.37)	24.8 (4.77)
12th	22.0 (1.40)	26.2 (2.35)	26.6 (2.09)	31.5 (2.81)	26.9 (1.77)	25.8 (1.19)	22.8 (1.23)	25.1 (1.96)	24.6 (1.49)	28.0 (1.08)	27.7 (1.58)	27.6 (1.93)

Source: Musu-Gillette et al. 2018. Indicators of School Crime and Safety: 2017, Table 16.1.

Note: = unweighted sample size less than 15.

305

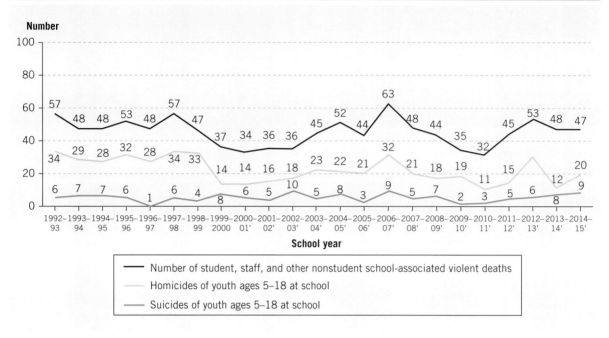

Source: Musu-Gillette, et al. 2018. Indicators of School Crime and Safety: 2017, Table 16.1.

this display, but not all of the percentages are presented—only those percentages necessary to convey the bivariate distribution are presented. With this display, readers can easily compare the likelihood of different students smoking marijuana over time. Interestingly, despite the fact that several states have now legalized recreational marijuana use (although it typically does not apply to those under the age of 21), the percentage of students using marijuana does not appear to have changed much over the past 20 years.

Combined and compressed statistical displays present a large amount of data in a relatively small space. To the experienced reader of statistical reports, such displays can convey much important information. They should be used with caution, however, because people who are not used to them may be baffled by the rows of numbers. Graphs can also provide an efficient tool for summarizing relationships among variables. A good example of the use of graphs is also reported in *Indicators of School Crime and Safety: 2017* (Musu-Gillette et al., 2018). Exhibit 12.4 presents the number of student, staff, and other nonstudent school-associated violent deaths and number of homicides and suicides of youth aged 5 to 19 at school from 1992 through 2015 (Musu-Gillette et al., 2018). As you can see, compressed displays in both table and graph form can be very illuminating!

SPECIAL CONSIDERATIONS FOR REPORTING QUANTITATIVE AND QUALITATIVE RESEARCH

The requirements for good research reports are similar, in many respects, for quantitative and qualitative research projects. Every research report should include good writing, a clear statement of the research question, an integrated literature, and a presentation of key findings with related discussion, conclusions, and limitations. The general sections of quantitative articles (Exhibit 12.1) also may be used by some authors of qualitative research reports. However, the differences between qualitative and quantitative research approaches mean that it is often desirable for research reports based on qualitative research to diverge in some respects from those reflecting quantitative research.

Reports based on qualitative research should be enriched in each section with elements that reflect the more holistic and reflexive approach of qualitative projects. The introduction should include background about the development of the researcher's interest in the topic, whereas the literature review should include some attention to the types of particular qualitative methods used in prior research. The methodology section should describe how the researcher gained access to the setting or individuals studied and the approach used to managing relations with research participants. The presentation of findings in qualitative studies may be organized into sections reflecting different themes identified in interviews or observational sessions. Quotes from participants or from observational notes should be selected to illustrate these themes, although qualitative research reports differ in the extent

Criminalizing Fraud Related to the OxyContin Crisis

You may have read about the way Purdue Pharma, the maker of OxyContin, falsely led medical doctors to believe that OxyContin was less habit forming than other opioid pain relievers, which has created a health care crisis in the United States. Since 1996, when OxyContin was introduced, there have been over 218,000 overdose deaths related to the drug. You may have also read about the doctors and pharmacists who essentially ran pill mills, dispensing OxyContin by the thousands. This article reports that the "financial muscle that has driven the spread of prescription opioids in the United States comes from distributors—companies that act as middlemen, trucking medications of all kinds from vast warehouses to hospitals, clinics, and drugstores." The article provides a trail of evidence that led to the attorneys general in three states—New York, Vermont, and Washington—to file civil suits against these distributors and the Southern District of New York to file the first criminal case against Rochester Drug Cooperative.

Several drug distributors have paid several hundred millions of dollars in fines for failing to monitor suspicious orders of opioids, but filling the orders did not stop. The article reports on the Congressional testimony by the chief executive of one distributor when he was asked about a rural West Virginia drugstore that was obtaining almost 10,000 pills a day. Representative Kathy Castor, a Florida Democrat, asked, "Don't you take responsibility? You saw that paying the penalties on your settlement agreements was a cost worth paying because you were making so much money?" The representative responded, "I wish we had moved earlier to stop shipping to that pharmacy."

For Further Thought

1. After reading this article, you may ask yourself, "How could the criminal justice system do a better job to deter executives like this from flouting the law?" What kind of research would you conduct to understand the thought processes of executives when making decisions regarding behavior they know to be illegal?

2. If you wanted to determine if shipments of a certain kind of drug decreased after companies paid fines for not monitoring the distribution of said drug appropriately, what kind of data would you need to have?

Source: Hakim, D., Rashbaum, W. K., & Rabin, R. C. (2019, April 22). The giants at the heart of the opioid crisis. *New York Times*. Retrieved from https://www.nytimes.com/2019/04/22/health/opioids-lawsuits-distributors.html?searchResultPosition=33

RESEARCH IN THE NEWS

to which the researcher presents findings in summary form or uses direct quotes to identify key issues. The findings sections in a qualitative report may alternate between presentations of quotes or observations about the research participants, the researcher's interpretations of this material, and some commentary on how the researcher reacted in the setting, although some qualitative researchers will limit their discussion of their reactions to the discussion section.

Reports on mixed-methods projects should include subsections in the methods section that introduce each method and then distinguish findings from qualitative and quantitative analyses in the findings section. Some mixed-methods research reports may present analyses that use both qualitative and quantitative data in yet another subsection, but others may just discuss implications of analyses of each type for the overall conclusions in the discussions and conclusions sections (Dahlberg, Wittink, & Gallo, 2010). When findings based on each method are presented, it is important to discuss explicitly both the ways in which the specific methods influenced findings obtained with those methods and the implications of findings obtained using both methods for the overall study conclusions.

ETHICS, POLITICS, AND REPORTING RESEARCH

It is at the time of reporting research results that the researcher's ethical duty to be honest becomes paramount. Here are some guidelines:

- Provide an honest accounting of how the research was carried out and where the initial research design had to be changed. Readers do not have to know about every change you made in your plans and each new idea you had, but they should be informed about major changes in hypotheses or research design.

- Maintain a full record of the research project so that questions can be answered if they arise. Many details will have to be omitted from all but the most comprehensive reports, but these omissions should not make it impossible to track down answers to specific questions about research procedures that may arise in the course of data analysis or presentation.

- Avoid "lying with statistics" or using graphs to mislead.

- Acknowledge the sponsors of the research. In part, this is so that others can consider whether this sponsorship may have tempted you to bias your results in some way. Make sure to also thank staff who made major contributions.

- Be sure that the order of authorship for coauthored reports is discussed in advance and reflects agreed-upon principles. Be sensitive to coauthors' needs and concerns.

Ethical research reporting should not mean ineffective reporting. You need to tell a coherent story in the report and to avoid losing track of the story in a thicket of minuscule details. You do not need to report every twist and turn in the conceptualization of the research problem or the conduct of the research, but be suspicious of reports that do not seem to admit to the possibility of any room for improvement. Social science is an ongoing enterprise in which one research report makes its most valuable contribution by laying the groundwork for another, more sophisticated research project. Highlight important findings in the research report, but use the report also to point out what are likely to be the most productive directions for future researchers.

COMMUNICATING WITH THE PUBLIC

Even following appropriate guidelines such as these, however, will not prevent controversy and conflict over research on sensitive issues. Does this mean that ethical researchers should avoid political controversy by sidestepping media outlets for their work? Many social scientists argue that the media offer one of the best ways to communicate the practical application of sociological knowledge and that when we avoid these opportunities, "some of the best sociological insights never reach policy makers because sociologists seldom take advantage of useful mechanisms to get their ideas out" (Wilson, 1998, p. 435).

The sociologist William Julius Wilson (1998) urges the following principles for engaging the public through the media:

1. Focus on issues of national concern, issues that are high on the public agenda.

2. Develop creative and thoughtful arguments that are clearly presented and devoid of technical language.

3. Present the big picture whereby the arguments are organized and presented so that the readers can see how the various parts are interrelated.

Ultimately, each researcher must make a decision about the most appropriate and important outlets for his or her work.

PLAGIARISM

It may seem depressing to end a book on research methods with a section on plagiarism, but it would be irresponsible to avoid the topic. Of course, you may have a course syllabus detailing instructor or university policies about plagiarism and specifying the penalties for violating that policy, so we're not simply going to repeat that kind of warning. You probably realize that the practice of selling term papers is revoltingly widespread (our search of *term papers* on Google returned over 2 million websites on June 3, 2019), so we're not going to just repeat that academic dishonesty is widespread. Instead, we will use this section to review the concept of plagiarism and to show how that problem connects to the larger issue of the integrity of social research. When you understand the dimensions of the problem and the way it affects research, you should be better able to detect plagiarism in other work and avoid it in your own.

> Plagiarism: Presenting as one's own the ideas or words of another person or persons for academic evaluation without proper acknowledgment

You learned in Chapter 3 that maintaining professional integrity—honesty and openness in research procedures and results—is the foundation for ethical research practice. When it comes to research publications and reports, being honest and open means avoiding plagiarism—that is, presenting as one's own the ideas or words of another person or persons for academic evaluation without proper acknowledgment (Hard, Conway, & Moran, 2006). In essence, plagiarism is a form of stealing.

An increasing body of research suggests that plagiarism is a growing problem on college campuses. For example, Hard et al. (2006) conducted an anonymous survey in one university and found very high plagiarism rates: 60.6% of students reported that they had copied "sentences, phrases, paragraphs, tables, figures or data directly or in slightly modified form from a book, article, or other academic source without using quotation marks or giving proper acknowledgment to the original author or source" (p. 1069), and 39.4% reported that they had "copied information from Internet [websites] and submitted it as [their] work" (p. 1069).

The plagiarism problem is not just about purchasing term papers—although that is really about as bad as it gets (Broskoske, 2005); plagiarism is also about what you do with the information you obtain from a literature review or an inspection of research reports. However, rest assured that this is not only about student papers; it also is about the work of established scholars and social researchers who publish reports that you want to rely on for accurate information. Several noted historians have been accused of plagiarizing passages that they used in popular books; some have admitted to not checking the work of their research assistants, to not keeping track of their sources, or to being unable to retrieve the data they claimed they had analyzed. Whether the cause is cutting corners to meet deadlines or consciously fudging facts, the effect is to undermine the trustworthiness of social research.

A primary way to avoid plagiarism is to maintain careful procedures for documenting the sources that you rely on for your own research and papers, but you should also think about how best to reduce temptations among others. After all, what people believe about what others do is a strong influence on their own behavior (Hard et al., 2006).

Reviewing the definition of plagiarism and how it is enforced by your discipline's professional association is an important first step. These definitions and procedures reflect a collective effort to help social scientists maintain standards throughout the discipline. Awareness is the first step (American Sociological Association [ASA], 1999). In addition, your college or university also has rules that delineate its definition of and consequences for plagiarism.

Researchers have an obligation to be familiar with their code of ethics (and other applicable ethics codes) and their application to sociologists' work. Lack of awareness or misunderstanding of an ethical standard is not, in itself, a defense to a charge of unethical conduct.

ASA's (1999) Code of Ethics, which is used by the American Society of Criminology and is similar to that of the Academy of Criminal Justice Sciences, includes an explicit prohibition of plagiarism:

14. Plagiarism

(a) In publications, presentations, teaching, practice, and service, sociologists explicitly identify, credit, and reference the author when they take data or material verbatim from another person's written work, whether it is published, unpublished, or electronically available.

(b) In their publications, presentations, teaching, practice, and service, sociologists provide acknowledgment of and reference to the use of others' work, even if the work is not quoted verbatim or paraphrased, and they do not present others' work as their own whether it is published, unpublished, or electronically available. (p. 16)

The next step toward combating the problem and temptation of plagiarism is to keep focused on the goal of social-research methods: investigating the social world. If researchers are motivated by a desire to learn about social relations, to study how people understand society, and to discover why conflicts arise and how they can be prevented, they will be as concerned with the integrity of their research methods as are those, like yourself, who read and use the results of their research. Throughout this text, you have been learning how to use research processes and practices that yield valid findings and trustworthy conclusions. Failing to report honestly and openly on the methods used or sources consulted derails progress toward that goal.

It works the same as cheating in school. When students are motivated only by the desire to ace their tests and receive better grades than others, they are more likely to plagiarize and use other illicit means to achieve that goal. Students who seek first to improve their understanding of the subject matter and to engage in the process of learning are less likely to plagiarize sources or cheat on exams (A. Kohn, 2008). They are also building the foundation for becoming successful social researchers who help others understand our world.

Mitchell Bezzina, BS, Cybersecurity Consultant

Source: Courtesy of Mitchell Bezzina

Mitchell has been a computer forensic examiner for over 15 years. He has conducted investigations centered on many areas of inquiry, including intellectual property theft, employee misconduct, fraud investigations, cross-border investigations, court orders, and regulatory inquiries. This work has spanned multiple jurisdictions and countries. With hands-on experience in security and digital investigations of every kind, he has designed, developed, and implemented operational and procedural policies for digital forensics, e-discovery, and engineering departments to gain production efficiencies and comply with business requirements.

While knowledge of computers is a must for the kind of work Mitchell does, the cyber world is constantly changing, so the main thing you need to have is curiosity and motivation to learn. Mitchell believes there are several career paths for someone interested in his line of work, including digital forensics, e-discovery, and incident response/threat intelligence. From there, your path is defined by your interests, as you will be investing more than 40 hours per week and doing what you love.

His advice to students is that they take as many computer and data analysis courses as possible and never stop learning. If you go into the consulting business, you also have to be able to communicate with several different stakeholders in both business and government. For this reason, it's also important to be able to communicate effectively, both verbally and in writing.

CONCLUSION

Much research lacks one or more of the three legs of validity—measurement validity, causal validity, or generalizability—and sometimes contributes more confusion than understanding about particular issues. Top journals generally maintain very high standards, partly because they have good critics in the review process and distinguished editors who make the final acceptance decisions. But some daily newspapers do a poor job of screening, and research reporting standards in many popular magazines, TV shows, and books are often abysmally poor. Keep your standards high and your view critical when reading research reports but not so high or so critical that you turn away from studies that make tangible contributions to the literature, even if they do not provide definitive answers. However, don't be so intimidated by the need to maintain high standards that you shrink from taking advantage of opportunities to conduct research yourself.

Of course, social-research methods are no more useful than the commitment of the researchers to their proper application. Research methods, like all knowledge, can be used poorly or well, for good purposes or bad, when appropriate or not. A claim that a belief is based on social science research in itself provides no extra credibility. As you have discovered throughout this book, we must first learn which methods were used, how they were applied, and whether the interpretations square with the evidence. To investigate the social world, we must keep in mind the lessons of research methods.

KEY TERMS

Combined frequency display   303
Compressed frequency
   display   303

Constructivist paradigm   299
Participatory action research
   (PAR)   298

Peer review   300
Plagiarism   309
Reverse outlining   303

- Proposal writing should be a time for clarifying the research problem, reviewing the literature, and thinking ahead about the report that will be required.

- Relations with research subjects and consumers should be developed in a manner that achieves key research goals and preparation of an effective research report. The traditional scientific approach of minimizing the involvement of research subjects and consumers in research decisions has been challenged by proponents of PAR and adherents of the constructivist paradigm.

- Research reports should include an introductory statement of the research problem, a literature review, a methodology section, a findings section with pertinent data displays, and a conclusions section that identifies any weaknesses in the research design and points out implications for future research and theorizing. This basic report format should be modified according to the needs of a particular audience.

- All reports should be revised several times and critiqued by others before they are presented in final form.

- Some of the data in many reports can be displayed more efficiently by using combined and compressed statistical displays.

- The central ethical concern in research reporting is to be honest. This honesty should include providing a truthful accounting of how the research was carried out, maintaining a full record about the project, using appropriate statistics and graphs, acknowledging the research sponsors, and being sensitive to the perspectives of coauthors.

- Plagiarism is a grievous violation of scholarly ethics. All direct quotes or paraphrased material from another author's work must be appropriately cited.

EXERCISES

Discussing Research

1. Select a recent article published in a peer-reviewed criminological or criminal justice–related journal and answer the following questions: How effective is the article in conveying the design and findings of the research? Could the article's organization be improved at all? Are there bases for disagreement about the interpretation of the findings?

2. Call a local criminal justice official and arrange for an interview. Ask the official about his or her experience with applied research reports and his or her conclusions about the value of social research and the best techniques for reporting to practitioners.

Finding Research on the Web

1. Go to the National Science Foundation's Law and Social Science Program website (nsf.gov/dir/index.jsp?org=sbe). What are the components that this program looks for in a proposed piece of research in the social sciences? Write a detailed outline for a research proposal to study a subject of your choice to be submitted to the National Science Foundation for funding.

2. Using the Internet, find five different examples of criminological research projects that have been completed. Briefly describe each. How does each differ in its approach to reporting the research results? To whom do you think the author(s) of each is reporting (i.e., who is the audience)? How do you think the predicted audience has helped to shape the author's approach to reporting the results? Be sure to note the websites at which you located each of your five examples.

3. Go to the Bureau of Justice's website (www.bjs.gov), and identify one research report based on data collected by BJS, such as the National Crime Victimization Survey. Now, find one article published in the scholarly literature that uses the same data. How does the government report differ from the scholarly article?

Critiquing Research

1. Rate four criminological journal articles for overall quality of the research and for effectiveness of the writing and data displays. Discuss how each could have been improved.

2. How firm a foundation do social-research methods provide for understanding the social world? Stage an in-class debate, with the pro and con arguments focusing on the variability of social-research findings across different social contexts and the difficulty of understanding human subjectivity.

Making Research Ethical

1. Some researchers do not make their data publicly available. As a result, other researchers are not able to replicate the original findings. Would you recommend legal regulations about the release of research data? What would those regulations be? Would they differ depending on the researcher's source of funding? Would you allow researchers exclusive access to their own data for some period of time after they have collected it?

2. Plagiarism is not a joke. What are the regulations on plagiarism of class papers at your school? What do you think the ideal policy would be? Should this policy take into account cultural differences in teaching practices and learning styles? Do you think this ideal policy is likely to be implemented? Why, or why not? Based on your experiences, do you believe that most student plagiarism is the result of misunderstanding about proper citation practices, or is it the result of

dishonesty? Do you think that students who plagiarize while in school are less likely to be honest as social researchers? Why, or why not?

3. Full disclosure of sources of research, as well as other medically related funding, has become a major concern for medical journals. Should researchers publishing in criminology and criminal justice journals also be required to fully disclose all sources of funding? Should full disclosure of all previous funds received by criminal justice agencies be required in each published article? What about disclosure of any previous jobs or paid consultations with criminal justice agencies? Write a short justification of the regulations you propose.

Developing a Research Proposal

Now it is time to bring all the elements of your proposal together.

1. Organize the proposal material you wrote for previous chapters in a logical order. Based on your research question, select the most appropriate research method as your primary method (see Chapters 5–8).

2. To add another component to your research design, select an additional research method that could contribute knowledge about your research question.

Performing Data Analysis in SPSS or Excel

Data for Exercise	
Dataset	**Description**
Youth.sav	This dataset is from a random sample of students from schools in a southern state. While not representative of the United States, it covers a variety of important delinquent behaviors and peer influences.

Variables for Exercise	
Variable Name	**Description**
D1	A binary variable based on the number of delinquent acts a respondent reported. A "0" indicates that the respondent reported one or fewer acts, while "1" indicates two or more
Lowcertain_bin	Binary indicator for if the respondent felt there was certainty that they'd be punished for delinquent behaviors, where 1 = *low certainty* and 0 = *high certainty*
Certain	A scale indicating how likely the individual feels it is that they will be punished for delinquent behavior. High values indicate high certainty.
Gender	A binary variable coded "0" for females and "1" for males
Delinquency	A scale indicating individual delinquency scores with "0" indicating the student engaged in no delinquency. The scale rages from 0 to a high of 120, with higher scores indicating higher engagement in delinquent behavior.

1. For this exercise, take a look at whether a person's expectation of punishment after delinquency is associated with the number of deviant behaviors a student engages in, as measured by the variable "delinquency."

   a. Run a frequency of the dependent variable "delinquency," and answer the following questions:

      i. What level of measurement is this item?

      ii. What form of descriptive analyses are appropriate?

      iii. How would you best represent these data in a graph?

   b. Based on your responses to Question 1a, conduct all appropriate descriptive analyses. Be sure to describe what you can about the data's distribution and what measures of central tendency are most appropriate. If one or another measure may produce misleading results, be sure to caution the reader as to why.

2. Repeat Question 1 for the independent variable, "lowcertain_bin." Again, describe the variable and how you would go about presenting it. Remember that you are only required to conduct the analyses that are appropriate.

3. On to the actual analysis! First, let's compare mean delinquency scores for "lowcertain_bin" and "delinquency." This can be done under "analyze-> means->compare means."

   a. What is the difference between the two group means?

   b. What do these results suggest substantively?

4. Now let's compare mean delinquency scores for males and females using the variable "gender." This can be done under "analyze->means->compare means."

   a. What is the difference between the two group means?

   b. What do these results suggest substantively?

GLOSSARY

Academy of Criminal Justice Science (ACJS) Code of Ethics: The Code of Ethics of ACJS sets forth (1) general principles and (2) ethical standards that underlie members of the academy's professional responsibilities and conduct, along with the (3) policies and procedures for enforcing those principles and standards; membership in the ACJS commits individual members to adhere to the ACJS Code of Ethics in determining ethical behavior in the context of their everyday professional activities

Adjacency matrix: A dataset containing information about the relations between the units of observation, sometimes called a *network matrix*

Alternate-forms reliability: A procedure for testing the reliability of responses to survey questions in which subjects' answers are compared after the subjects have been asked slightly different versions of the questions or when randomly selected halves of the sample have been administered to slightly different versions of the questions

Anchors: Key dates of important events, such as birthdays, that help trigger recall for respondents when using life calendars

Anonymity: Provided by research when no identifying information is recorded that could be used to link respondents to their responses

Applied research: Research that has an impact on policy and can be immediately utilized and applied

Arrestee Drug Abuse Monitoring (ADAM): A U.S. monitoring program that uses standardized drug-testing methodologies and predictive models to measure the consequences of drug abuse within each state and across state boundaries

Association: A criterion for establishing a causal relationship between two variables; variation in one variable is related to variation in another variable as a condition to determine causality

Authenticity: When the understanding of a social process or social setting is one that fairly reflects the various perspectives of participants in that setting

Availability sampling: Sampling in which elements are selected on the basis of convenience

Before-and-after design: A quasi-experimental design consisting of before–after comparisons involving the same variables and sometimes the same groups; these designs may include different groups in the pretests and posttests

Belmont Report: A 1979 National Commission for the Protection of Human Subjects of Biomedical and Behavioral Research report that established three basic ethical principles for the protection of human subjects, including respect for persons, beneficence, and justice

Beneficence: Minimizing possible harms and maximizing benefits in research

Betweenness centrality score: A statistic that measures the extent to which nodes connect to other nodes that are not directly linked to each other in SNA

Big Data: A very large dataset (e.g., containing thousands of cases) that is accessible in computer-readable form that is used to reveal patterns, trends, and associations between variables

Binary network: Distinguishes whether a relationship does or does not exist between nodes

Black-box evaluation: A type of evaluation that occurs when an evaluation of program outcomes ignores or does not identify the process by which the program produced the effect

Campbell Collaboration: An international research network that prepares and disseminates systematic reviews of social science evidence in crime and justice, education, and social welfare

Causal effect: When variation in one phenomenon (an **independent variable**) leads to or results in, on average, variation in another phenomenon (the **dependent variable**); also known as *idiographic perspective*

Causal validity: Exists when a conclusion that "*x* leads to or results in *y*" is correct; also known as *internal validity*

Census: Research in which information is obtained through the responses that all available members of an entire population give to questions

Certificate of confidentiality: Document that protects researchers from being legally required to disclose confidential information

Ceteris paribus: Latin phrase meaning "other things being equal"

Closed-ended question: A survey question that provides preformatted response choices for the respondent to circle or check; also called a *fixed-choice question*

Cluster: A naturally occurring, mixed aggregate of elements of the population

Cohort: Individuals or groups with a common starting point. Examples include "college class of 2010," "General Motors employees who started work between 2005 and 2006," and so on.

Combined frequency display: A table that presents together the distributions for a set of conceptually similar variables having the same response categories; common headings are used for the responses

Compensatory rivalry (John Henry effect): A type of contamination in experimental designs that occurs when control group members perceive that they are being denied some advantage that the experimental group members are getting and increase their efforts by way of compensation

Complete observation: A role in participant observation in which the researcher does not participate in group activities and is publicly defined as a researcher

Compressed frequency displays: A table that presents cross-classification data efficiently by eliminating unnecessary percentages, such as the percentage corresponding to the second value of a dichotomous variable

Computer-assisted personal interviewing (CAPI): An interview in which the interviewer carries a laptop computer programmed to display the interview questions and to process the responses that the interviewer types in, as well as to check that these responses fall within the allowed ranges

Computer-assisted qualitative data analysis: Uses special computer software to assist qualitative analyses through creation, application, and refinement of categories; tracing linkages between concepts; and making comparisons between cases and events

Computer-assisted self-interviewing (CASI): A system within which respondents interact with a computer-administered questionnaire by using a mouse and following audio instructions delivered via headphones

Computer-assisted telephone interview (CATI): An interview in which data collection and data entry can occur concurrently and data entry error is minimized. Most large surveys are performed in this way.

Computerized interactive voice response (IVR): Software that uses a touch-tone telephone to interact with people to acquire information from or enter data into the database

Concept: A mental image that summarizes a set of similar observations, feelings, or ideas

Conceptualization: The process of specifying what we mean by a term. In deductive research, conceptualization helps to translate portions of an abstract theory into testable hypotheses involving specific variables. In inductive research, conceptualization is an important part of the process used to make sense of related observations.

Constant: A characteristic or property that does not vary but takes on only one value

Construct validity: The type of validity that is established by showing that a measure is related to other measures as specified in a theory

Constructivist paradigm: Methodology based on rejection of belief in an external reality; it emphasizes the importance of exploring the way in which different stakeholders in a social setting construct their beliefs

Contamination: A source of causal invalidity that occurs when either the experimental or the comparison group is aware of the other group and is influenced in the posttest as a result

Content analysis: A research method for systematically analyzing and making inferences from text and other media

Content validity: The type of validity that exists when the full range of a concept's meaning is covered by the measure

Context: A focus on idiographic causal explanation. A particular outcome is understood as part of a larger set of interrelated circumstances.

Context effects: Occur in a survey when one or more questions influence how subsequent questions are interpreted

Contextual effects: Relationships among variables that vary among geographic units or other social settings

Contingent questions: Questions that are asked of only a subset of survey respondents

Continuous measure: A measure with numbers indicating the values of variables as points on a continuum

Control or comparison group: In an experiment or study, a group that receives no treatment

Convergent parallel design: In mixed-methods research, when quantitative and qualitative methods are implemented at the same time; the findings are integrated and interpreted together

Cost–benefit analysis: A type of evaluation research that compares program costs with the economic value of program benefits

Cost-effectiveness analysis: A type of evaluation research that compares program costs with actual program outcomes

Counterfactual: The outcome that would have occurred if the subjects who were exposed to the treatment actually were not exposed but otherwise had had identical experiences to those they underwent during the experiment

Cover letter: The letter sent with a mailed questionnaire. It explains the survey's purpose and auspices and encourages the respondent to participate.

Covert (complete) participation: A role in field research in which the researcher does not reveal his or her identity as a researcher to those who are observed. The covert participant has adopted the role of a complete participant.

Crime mapping: The process of using a geographic information system to conduct a special analysis of crime data and other police-related issues

Criterion validity: The type of validity that is established by comparing the scores obtained on the measure being validated with those obtained with a more direct or already validated measure of the same phenomenon

Critical theory: Focuses on examining structures, patterns, and meanings but rests on the premise that power differences have shaped these structures and patterns

Cronbach's alpha: A statistic that measures the reliability of items in an index or scale

Cross-population generalizability: Exists when findings about one group, population, or setting hold true for other groups, populations, or settings; also called *external validity*

Cross-sectional research design: A study in which data are collected at only one point in time

Debriefing: A researcher's informing of subjects after an experiment about the experiment's purposes and methods and evaluating subjects' personal reactions to the experiment

Deception: Used in social experiments to create more "realistic" treatments in which the true purpose of the research is not disclosed to participants, often within the confines of a laboratory

Deductive reasoning: The type of reasoning that moves from the general to the specific

Deductive research: The type of research in which a specific explanation is deduced from a general premise and is then tested; compare with *inductive research*

Dependent variable: A variable that is hypothesized to vary depending on or under the influence of the independent variable

Descriptive research: Research in which social phenomena are defined and described

Dichotomy: A variable having only two values

Differential attrition: A problem that occurs in experiments when comparison groups become different because subjects are more likely to drop out of one of the groups for various reasons

Discrete measure: A measure that classifies cases in distinct categories

Disproportionate stratified sampling: Sampling in which elements are selected from strata in different proportions from those that appear in the population

Double-barreled question: A single survey question that actually asks two questions but allows only one answer

Double-blind procedure: An experimental method in which neither the subjects nor the staff delivering experimental treatments know which subjects are getting the treatment and which are receiving the placebo

Double-negative question: A question or statement that contains two negatives, which can muddy the meaning

Ecological fallacy: An error in reasoning in which incorrect conclusions about individual-level processes are drawn from group-level data

Effect size: A standardized measure of association that is often the difference between the mean of the experimental group and the mean of the control group on the dependent variable

Efficiency analysis: A type of evaluation research that compares program costs with program effects. It can be either a cost–benefit analysis or a cost-effectiveness analysis.

Electronic survey: A survey that is sent and answered by computer, either through e-mail or on the Web

Elements: The individual entities of the population whose characteristics are to be measured

Embedded design: In mixed-methods research, when the primary method is qualitative or quantitative, but the researcher adds the other component to gain additional insight

Empirical generalizations: Statements that describe patterns found in data from a sample to the population

Endogenous change: A source of causal invalidity that occurs when natural developments or changes in the subjects, independent of the experimental treatment itself, account for some or all of the observed change from the pretest to the posttest

Enumeration units: Units that contain one or more elements and that are listed in a sampling frame

Epistemology: A branch of philosophy that studies how knowledge is gained or acquired

Ethnography: The study of a culture or cultures that some group of people share, using participant observation over an extended period of time

Evaluability assessment: A method to determine the possibility of a study being able to specifically identify the effects of a particular program within the available time and with the available resources

Evaluation research: Research about social programs or interventions

Event-based design: A type of longitudinal study in which data are collected at two or more points in time from individuals in a cohort; also known as a *cohort study*

Evidence-based policies: Programs and policies that are based on a systematic review of all available evidence that assesses what works and what doesn't

Ex post facto control group design: A nonexperimental design in which comparison groups are selected after the treatment or program has occurred

Exhaustive attributes: A variable's attributes or values are exhaustive when every case can be classified into one of the categories

Exhaustive response: A variable's attributes or values, in which every case can be classified as having one attribute

Expectancies of the experimental staff: A source of treatment misidentification in experiments that occurs when change among experimental subjects is due to the positive expectancies of the staff who are delivering the treatment rather than to the treatment itself; also called a *self-fulfilling prophecy*

Experimental approach: An approach in which the researcher randomly assigns individuals to two or more groups in a way that equates the characteristics of individuals in the groups, except for variation in the groups' exposure to the independent variable

Experimental group: In an experiment or study, the group of subjects that receives the treatment or experimental manipulation

Explanatory research: Research that seeks to identify causes or effects of social phenomena

Exploratory research: Research in which social phenomena are investigated without *a priori* expectations in order to develop an understanding of them

Exploratory sequential design: The qualitative method is implemented first, followed by the quantitative method

External event: A source of causal invalidity that occurs when events external to the study influence posttest scores; also called *history effects*

Face validity: The type of validity that exists when an inspection of items used to measure a concept suggests that they are appropriate at face value

Falsifiable: Being capable of being proven wrong; that is, having the capacity to be empirically tested and falsified

Federal Policy for the Protection of Human Subjects (Common Rule): Federal regulations established in 1991 that are based on the principles of the *Belmont Report* (see *Belmont Report*)

Feedback: Information about service delivery system outputs, outcomes, or operations that is available to any program inputs

Feminist research: Research with a focus on women's lives that often includes an orientation to personal experience, subjective orientations, the researcher's standpoint, and emotions

Fence-sitters: Survey respondents who see themselves as being neutral on an issue and choose a middle (neutral) response that is offered

Field experiment: An experiment that is conducted in a real-world setting

Field notes: Notes that describe what has been observed, heard, or otherwise experienced in a participant observation study; these notes usually are written after the observational session

Field research: Research in which natural social processes are studied as they happen and left relatively undisturbed

Filter question: A survey question used to identify a subset of respondents who then are asked other questions

Fixed-sample panel design (panel study): A type of longitudinal study in which data are collected from the same individuals—the panel—at two or more points in time

Floaters: Survey respondents who provide an opinion on a topic in response to a closed-ended question that does not include a "don't know" option even if they do not have an answer to the question but will choose "don't know" if it is available

Focus group: A qualitative method that involves unstructured group interviews in which the focus group leader actively encourages discussion among participants on the topics of interest

Freedom of Information Act (FOIA): This federal law stipulates that all persons have a right to access all federal agency records unless the records are specifically exempted

Geographic information system (GIS): The software tool that has made crime mapping increasingly available to researchers since the 1990s

Grounded theory: Systematic theory developed inductively, based on observations that are summarized into conceptual categories, reevaluated in the research setting, and gradually refined and linked to other conceptual categories

Group-administered survey: A survey that is completed by individual respondents who are assembled in a group

Hawthorne effect: A type of contamination in experimental designs that occurs when members of the treatment group change in terms of the dependent variable because their participation in the study makes them feel special

Hypothesis: A tentative statement about empirical reality involving a relationship between two or more variables

Idiographic causal explanation: An explanation that identifies the concrete, individual sequence of events, thoughts, or actions that resulted in a particular outcome for a particular individual or that led to a particular event; may be termed an *individualist* or *historicist explanation*

Idiosyncratic variation: Variation in responses to a question that is caused by individuals' reactions to particular words or ideas in the question instead of by variation in the concept that the question is intended to measure

Illogical reasoning: When someone prematurely jumps to conclusions or argues on the basis of invalid assumptions

Impact evaluation: Analysis of the extent to which a treatment or other service has an effect; also known as *impact analysis*

In-person interview: A survey in which an interviewer questions respondents and records their answers

Inaccurate observation: Observations based on faulty perceptions of empirical reality

Independent variable: A variable that is hypothesized to cause—or lead to—variation in the dependent variable

Index: A composite measure based on summing, averaging, or otherwise combining the responses to multiple questions that are intended to measure the same variable

Indicator: The question or other operation used to indicate the value of cases on a variable

Inductive reasoning: The type of reasoning that moves from the specific to the general

Inductive research: The type of research in which general conclusions are drawn from specific data; compare with *deductive research*

Informed consent: Human subjects in research must be able to voluntarily consent to participate

Inputs: Resources, raw materials, clients, and staff that go into a program

Institutional review board (IRB): A group of organizational and community representatives required by federal law to review the ethical issues in all proposed research that is federally funded, involves human subjects, or has any potential for harm to subjects

Integrated approaches: An orientation to evaluation research that expects researchers to respond to the concerns of people involved with the program, as well as to the standards and goals of the social scientific community

Intelligence-led policing: Using data, analysis, and criminal theory to guide police allocation and decision making

Intensive interviewing: A qualitative method that involves open-ended, relatively unstructured questioning in which the interviewer seeks in-depth information on the interviewee's feelings, experiences, and perceptions (Lofland & Lofland, 1984, p. 12); also called *in-depth interviewing*

Interitem reliability: An approach that calculates reliability based on the correlation among multiple items used to measure a single concept; also known as *internal consistency*

Interobserver reliability: When similar measurements are obtained by different observers rating the same persons, events, or places

Interpretive questions: Questions included in a questionnaire or interview schedule to help explain answers to other important questions

Interpretivism: The belief that reality is socially constructed and that the goal of social scientists is to understand what meanings people give to that reality. Max Weber termed the goal of interpretivist research *verstehen* (understanding).

Intersubjective agreement: Agreement between scientists about the nature of reality; often upheld as a more reasonable goal for science than certainty about an objective reality

Interval level of measurement: Represent fixed measurement units (e.g., the change in value from one unit to the next is equal and incremental) but have no absolute, or fixed, zero point

Interval-ratio level of measurement: A measurement of a variable in which the numbers indicating a variable's values represent fixed measurement units but may not have an absolute, or fixed, zero point, but it is assumed the values can be multiplied and divided

Interview schedule: The survey instrument containing the questions asked by the interviewer for an in-person interview or phone survey

Intraobserver reliability: Consistency of ratings by an observer of an unchanging phenomenon at two or more points in time; also known as *intrarater reliability*

Jottings: Brief notes that serve as memory joggers when writing actual field notes at a later time

Justice (in research): Distributing benefits and risks of research fairly

Level of measurement: The mathematical precision with which the values of a variable can be expressed. The nominal level of measurement, which is qualitative, has no mathematical interpretation; the quantitative levels of measurement (ordinal, interval, and ratio) are progressively more precise mathematically.

Life calendar: An instrument that helps respondents recall events in their past by displaying each month of a given year along with key dates noted within the calendar, such as birthdays, arrests, holidays, anniversaries, and so on

Likert-type responses: Survey responses in which respondents indicate the extent to which they agree or disagree with statements

Longitudinal research design: A study in which data are collected that can be ordered in time; also defined as research in which data are collected at two or more points in time

Mailed (self-administered) survey: A survey involving a mailed questionnaire to be completed by the respondent

Matching: A procedure for equating the characteristics of individuals in different comparison groups in an experiment or other longitudinal research

Measurement validity: Exists when a measurement actually measures what we think it does

Mechanism: A discernible process that creates a causal connection between two variables

Meta-analysis: The quantitative analysis of findings from multiple studies

Meta-synthesis: The qualitative analysis of findings from multiple qualitative studies

Mixed methods: Combining both qualitative and quantitative methods to study one research question

Mixed-mode surveys: Surveys that are conducted by more than one method, allowing the strengths of one survey design to compensate for the weaknesses of another and maximizing the likelihood of securing data from different types of respondents; for example, nonrespondents in a mailed survey may be interviewed in person or over the phone

Multiphase design: In mixed-methods research, this design involves a series of quantitative and qualitative designs; each design and the findings inform the next phase

Multistage cluster sampling: Sampling in which elements are selected in two or more stages, with the first stage being the random selection of naturally occurring clusters and the last stage being the random selection of multilevel elements within clusters

Mutually exclusive attributes: A variable's attributes or values are mutually exclusive when every case can be classified as having only one attribute

Mutually exclusive responses: Response choices on a survey that do not overlap

Needs assessment: A type of evaluation research that attempts to determine the needs of some population that might be met with a social program

Netnography: The use of ethnographic methods to study online communities; also termed *cyberethnography* and *virtual ethnography*

Ngrams: Frequency graphs produced by Google's database of all words printed in more than one third of the world's books over time (with coverage still expanding)

Nodelist: The dataset containing the nodes (units of observation) for a social-network analysis

Nodes: The basic units (e.g., people) in a network graph, sometimes called *actors* or *vertices*

Nominal level of measurement: Variables whose values have no mathematical interpretation; they vary in kind or quality but not in amount; also called *categorical level of measurement*, *qualitative level of measurement*, or *attribute*

Nomothetic causal explanation: A type of causal explanation involving the belief that variation in an independent variable will be followed by variation in the dependent variable, when all other things are equal

Nonequivalent control group design: A quasi-experimental design in which there are experimental and comparison groups that are designated before the treatment occurs but are not created by random assignment

Nonprobability sampling methods: Sampling methods in which the probability of selection of population elements is unknown

Nonresponse: People or other entities who do not participate in a study although they are selected for the sample

Nonspuriousness: A criterion for establishing a causal relationship between two variables; when a relationship between two variables is not due to variation in a third variable

Nuremberg war crimes trials: Court trials that exposed horrific medical experiments conducted by Nazi doctors and others in the name of science

Omnibus survey: A survey that covers a range of topics of interest to different social scientists

Open-ended question: A survey question to which the respondent replies in his or her own words, either by writing or by talking

Operation: A procedure for identifying or indicating the value of cases on a variable

Operationalization: The process of specifying the operations that will indicate the value of a variable for each case

Ordinal level of measurement: A measurement of a variable in which the numbers indicating the variable's value specify only the order of the cases, permitting *greater than* and *less than* distinctions

Outcomes: The impact of the program process on the cases processed

Outputs: The services delivered or new products produced by the program process

Overgeneralization: Occurs when we unjustifiably conclude that what is true for some cases is true for all cases

Participant observation: A qualitative method for gathering data that involves developing a sustained relationship with people while they go about their normal activities

Participatory action research (PAR): A type of research in which the researcher involves some organizational members as active participants throughout the process of studying an organization; the goal is to make changes in the organization or community

Peer review: A process in which a journal editor sends a submitted article to two or three experts who judge whether the paper should be accepted, revised and resubmitted, or rejected; the experts also provide comments to explain their decision and guide any revisions

Periodicity: A sequence of elements in a list to be sampled that varies in some regular, periodic pattern

Philip Zimbardo's Stanford Prison Experiment: A two-week experiment that simulated the prison life of both prisoners and guards that was ended in just six days because of what the simulation was doing to college students who participated

Phone survey: A survey in which interviewers question respondents over the phone and then record their answers

Phrenology: A now-defunct field of study, once considered a science in the 19th century, which held that bumps and fissures of the skull determined the character and personality of a person

Placebo effect: A source of treatment misidentification that can occur when subjects receive a treatment that they consider likely to be beneficial and improve because of the expectation rather than because of the treatment

Plagiarism: Presenting as one's own the ideas or words of another person or persons without proper acknowledgment

Policy research: A process in which research results are used to provide policy actors with recommendations for action that are based on empirical evidence and careful reasoning

Population: The entire set of elements (e.g., individuals, cities, states, countries, prisons, schools) in which we are interested

Positivism: The belief that there is a reality that exists quite apart from our own perception of it, although our knowledge of this reality may never be complete

Postpositivism: The belief that there is an empirical reality but that our understanding of it is limited by its complexity and by the biases and other limitations of researchers

Posttest: In experimental research, this is the measurement of an outcome (**dependent**) variable after an experimental intervention or treatment (**independent variable**)

Pretest: In experimental research, this is the measurement of an outcome (**dependent**) variable prior to an experimental intervention or treatment (**independent variable**)

Pretested: When a questionnaire is taken by a small subsample of respondents to uncover any problems with the questions or response categories

Privacy certificate: A document that protects researchers from being legally required to disclose confidential information

Probability of selection: The likelihood that an element will be selected from the population for inclusion in the sample. In a census, of all the elements of a population, the probability that any particular element will be selected is 1.0 because everyone will be selected. If half the elements in the population are sampled on the basis of chance (say, by tossing a coin), the probability of selection for each element is one half (0.5). When the size of the sample as a proportion of the population decreases, so does the probability of selection.

Probability sampling methods: Sampling methods that allow us to know in advance how likely it is that any element will be selected from the population for inclusion in the sample

Process evaluation: Evaluation research that investigates the process of service delivery; also known as *program monitoring*

Program process: The complete treatment or services delivered by the program

Program theory: A descriptive or prescriptive model of how a program operates and produces effects

Progressive focusing: The process by which a qualitative analyst interacts with the data and gradually refines his or her focus

Proportionate stratified sampling: A sampling method in which elements are selected from strata in exact proportion to their representation in the population

Pseudoscience: Dubious claims that are touted as "scientifically proven"; however, the evidence is not based on the principles of the scientific method

Purposive sampling: A nonprobability sampling method in which elements are selected for a purpose, usually because of their unique position

Qualitative data analysis: Techniques used to search and code textual, visual, or other content and to explore relationships among the resulting categories

Qualitative methods: Methods such as participant observation, intensive interviewing, and focus groups that are designed to capture social life as participants experience it rather than in categories predetermined by the researcher. Data that are treated as qualitative are mostly written or spoken words or observations that do not have a direct numerical interpretation.

Quantitative methods: Methods such as surveys and experiments that record variation in social life in terms of categories that vary in amount. Data that are treated as quantitative are either numbers or attributes that can be ordered in terms of magnitude.

Quasi-experimental design: A research design in which there is a comparison group that is comparable to the experimental group in critical ways, but subjects are not randomly assigned to the comparison and experimental groups

Questionnaire: The survey instrument containing the questions for a self-administered survey

Quota sampling: A nonprobability sampling method in which elements are selected to ensure that the sample represents certain characteristics in proportion to their prevalence in the population

Random assignment: A procedure by which each experimental subject is placed into the experimental and control groups randomly; also known as *randomization*

Random digit dialing (RDD): The random dialing by a machine of phone numbers within designated prefixes, which creates a random sample for phone surveys

Random number table: A table containing lists of numbers that are ordered solely on the basis of chance; it is used for drawing random samples

Random selection: The fundamental element of probability samples. The essential characteristic of random selection is that every element of the population has a known and independent chance of being selected into the sample.

Ratio level of measurement: A measurement of a variable in which the numbers indicating a variable's values represent fixed measuring units and an absolute zero point

Reactive effects: The changes in individual or group behavior that are due to being observed or otherwise studied

Reductionist fallacy: An error in reasoning that occurs when incorrect conclusions about group-level processes are based on individual-level data; also known as *reductionism*

Reference period: A time frame in which a survey question asks respondents to place a particular behavior (e.g., in the past six months)

Reflexivity: A narrative provided by the researcher that offers a reflection on the process of research, including any obstacles encountered

Regression effect: A source of causal invalidity that occurs when subjects who are chosen for a study because of their extreme scores on the dependent variable become less extreme on the posttest because of natural cyclical or episodic change

Relational data: Measures the contacts, connections, attachments, and ties that relate one unit to the next

Relations: The connections in a network graph, sometimes called *ties*, *links*, *arcs*, or *edges*

Reliability: A measure is reliable when it yields consistent scores or observations of a given phenomenon on different occasions; reliability is a prerequisite for measurement validity

Reliability measures: Special statistics that help researchers decide whether responses are consistent

Repeated cross-sectional design: A longitudinal study in which data are collected at two or more points in time from different samples of the same population; also known as a *trend study*

Replacement sampling: A method of sampling in which sample elements are returned to the sampling frame after being selected so they may be sampled again

Replication: Repetition of a study using the same research methods to answer the same research question

Representative sample: A sample that looks similar to the population from which it was selected in all respects that are potentially relevant to the study. The distribution of characteristics among the elements of a representative sample is the same as the distribution of those characteristics among the total population. In an unrepresentative sample, some characteristics are overrepresented or underrepresented.

Research circle: A diagram of the elements of the research process, including theories, hypotheses, data collection, and data analysis

Research question: A question that is answered through the collection and analysis of firsthand, verifiable, empirical data

Resistance to change: The reluctance to change our ideas in light of new information

Respect for persons: Treating persons as autonomous agents and protecting those with diminished autonomy

Reverse code: Recoding response choices that were originally coded to reflect both favorable and unfavorable attitudes toward a phenomenon as indicative of either all favorable or all unfavorable so the index is measuring the same thing

Reverse outlining: Outlining the sections in an already written draft of a paper or report to improve its organization in the next draft

Risk terrain modeling (RTM): Uses data from several sources to predict the probability of crime occurring in the future using the underlying factors of the environment that are associated with illegal behavior

Sample: A subset of elements from the larger population

Sample generalizability: Exists when a conclusion based on a sample, or subset, of a larger population holds true for that population

Sampling error: Any difference between the characteristics of a sample and the characteristics of the population from which it was drawn. The larger the sampling error, the less representative the sample is of the population.

Sampling frame: A list of all elements or other units containing the elements in a population

Sampling interval: The number of cases from one sampled case to another in a systematic random sample

Sampling units: Units listed at each stage of a multistage sampling design

Saturation point: The point at which subject selection is ended in intensive interviewing, when new interviews seem to yield little additional information

Science: A set of logical, systematic, documented methods for investigating nature and natural processes; the knowledge produced by these investigations

Secondary data analysis: Analysis of data collected by someone other than the researcher or the researcher's assistant

Selection bias: A source of internal (causal) invalidity that occurs when the characteristics of experimental and comparison groups are not equivalent

Selective distribution of benefits: An ethical issue about how much researchers can influence the benefits subjects receive as part of the treatment being studied in a field experiment

Selective observation: Choosing to look only at things that are in line with our preferences or beliefs

Serendipitous findings: Unexpected patterns in data that stimulate new ideas or theoretical approaches; also known as **anomalous findings**

Simple random sampling: A method of sampling in which every sample element is selected only on the basis of chance through a random process

Skip pattern: The unique combination of questions created in a survey by filter questions and contingent questions

Snowball sampling: A method of sampling in which sample elements are selected as they are identified by successive informants or interviewees

Social-network analysis (SNA): An approach to analysis and a set of methodological techniques that help researchers describe and explore relationships that both individuals and groups have with each other

Social networks: Types of relationships that can include many different forms, such as face to face, online and digital, economic transactions, interaction with a criminal justice agency, etc.

Social science: A set of logical, systematic, documented methods for investigating nature and natural processes; the knowledge produced by these investigations

Social science approaches: An orientation to evaluation research that expects researchers to emphasize the importance of researcher expertise and maintenance of autonomy from program stakeholders

Sociogram: A graph representing the social configurations, with individuals (or some other unit) represented by points and their social relationships to one another depicted by lines

Solomon four-group design: A type of experimental design that combines a randomized pretest/posttest control group design with a randomized posttest-only design, resulting in two experimental groups and two comparison groups

Split-ballot design: Unique questions or other modifications in a survey administered to randomly selected subsets of the total survey sample so that more questions can be included in the entire survey or so that responses to different question versions can be compared

Split-halves reliability: Reliability achieved when responses to the same questions by two randomly selected halves of a sample are about the same

Spurious: A relationship between two variables that is due to variation in a third variable

Stakeholder approaches: An orientation to evaluation research that expects researchers to be responsive primarily to the people involved with the program

Stakeholders: Individuals and groups who have some basis of concern with the program

Stanley Milgram's experiments on obedience to authority: Experiments by Stanley Milgram that sought to identify the conditions under which ordinary citizens would be obedient to authority figures' instructions to inflict pain on others

Statistical control: A technique used in nonexperimental research to reduce the risk of spuriousness. One variable is held constant so the relationship between two or more other variables can be assessed without the influence of variation in the control variable

Stratified random sampling: A method of sampling in which sample elements are selected separately from population strata that are identified in advance by the researcher

Subject fatigue: Problems caused by panel members growing weary of repeated interviews and dropping out of a study or becoming so used to answering the standard questions in the survey that they start giving stock or thoughtless answers

Survey research: Research in which information is obtained from a sample of individuals through their responses to questions about themselves or others

Survey: A popular and versatile research instrument using a question format; surveys can be self-administered or read by an interviewer

Systematic bias: Overrepresentation or underrepresentation of some population characteristics in a sample resulting from the method used to select the sample; a sample shaped by systematic sampling error is a biased sample

Systematic observation: A strategy that increases the reliability of observational data by using explicit rules that standardize coding practices across observers

Systematic random sampling: A method of sampling in which sample elements are selected from a list or from sequential files, with every *n*th element being selected after the first element is selected randomly within the first interval

Systematic review: A paper that attempts to gather relevant evaluative studies, critically appraise them, and come to judgments about what works using explicit, transparent, state-of-the-art methods

Systematic social observation (SSO): A strategy that increases the reliability of observational data by using explicit rules that standardize coding practices across observers

Tacit knowledge: In field research, a credible sense of understanding of social processes that reflects the researcher's awareness of participants' actions, as well as their words and of what they fail to state, feel deeply, and take for granted

Target population: A set of elements larger than or different from the population sampled, to which the researcher would like to generalize study findings

Test–retest reliability: A measurement showing that measures of a phenomenon at two points in time are highly correlated if the phenomenon has not changed or the measures have changed only as much as the phenomenon itself

Theoretical construct: A construct that describes what is important to look at to understand, explain, or predict a phenomenon

Theoretical sampling: A sampling method recommended for field researchers by Glaser and Strauss (1967). A theoretical sample is drawn in a sequential fashion, with settings or individuals selected for study as earlier observations or interviews indicate that these settings or individuals are influential.

Theory: A logically interrelated set of propositions about empirical reality. Examples of criminological theories are social learning, routine activities, labeling, general strain, and social disorganization theory.

Theory-driven evaluation: A program evaluation that is guided by a theory that specifies the process by which the program has an effect

Thick description: A method used in case reports that clarifies the context and makes it possible for the reader vicariously to experience it

Time order: A criterion for establishing a causal relationship between two variables. The variation in the independent variable must occur before the variation in the dependent variable

Time series design: A quasi-experimental design consisting of many pretest and posttest observations of the same group over an extended period; also known as *repeated-measures panel design*

Transformative design: In mixed-methods research, this design uses a theoretical perspective with a social justice focus to improve the well-being of vulnerable populations

Transparent: An important feature of the scientific method that requires procedures, methods, and data analyses of any study to be presented clearly for the purposes of replication

Treatment misidentification: A problem that occurs in an experiment when the treatment itself is not what causes the outcome but rather the outcome is caused by some intervening process that the research has not identified and is not aware of

Triangulation: The use of multiple methods to study one research question; also used to mean the use of two or more different measures of the same variable

True experiment: An experiment in which subjects are assigned randomly to an experimental group that receives the treatment or other manipulation of the independent variable and a comparison group that does not receive the treatment. Outcomes are measured in a posttest.

Tuskegee syphilis experiment: U.S. Public Health Service study of the "natural" course of syphilis that followed 399 low-income African American men from the 1930s to 1972, without providing them with penicillin after this was discovered as a treatment for the illness; the study was stopped after it was exposed in 1972

Units of analysis: The level of social life on which a research question is focused, such as individuals, groups, towns, or nations

Units of observation: The cases about which measures actually are obtained in a sample

Unobtrusive measure: A measurement based on physical traces or other data that are collected without the knowledge or participation of the individuals or groups that generated the data

Variable: A characteristic or property that can vary (take on different values or attributes)

REFERENCES

Abbott, A. (1992). From causes to events: Notes on narrative positivism. *Sociological Methods*, *20*(May), 428–455.

Academy of Criminal Justice Sciences (ACJS). (2000). *Code of ethics*. Retrieved September 26, 2009, from http://www.acjs.org.pubs./167_171_2922.cfm

Adair, G., Dushenko, T. W., & Lindsay, R. C. L. (1985). Ethical regulations and their impact on research practice. *American Psychologist*, *40*, 59–72.

Agnew, R. (2006). Storylines as a neglected cause of crime. *Journal of Research in Crime and Delinquency*, *43*(2), 119–147.

Aiden, E., & Michel, J.-B. (2013). *Uncharted: Big Data as a lens on human culture*. New York, NY: Riverhead Books.

Alfred, R. (1976). The church of Satan. In C. Glock & R. Bellah (Eds.), *The new religious consciousness* (pp. 180–202). Berkeley: University of California Press.

Allen, A. (2018, January 8). Common Rule delays irk research organizations. Politico. Retrieved from https://www.politico.com/newsletters/morning-ehealth/2018/01/08/common-rule-delays-irk-research-orgs-067230

Alper, M., Durose, M. R., & Markman, J. (2018). *2018 update on prisoner recidivism: A 9-year follow-up period (2005–2014)*. Washington, DC: Bureau of Justice Statistics, U.S. Department of Justice.

Altheide, D. L., & Johnson, J. M. (1994). Criteria for assessing interpretive validity in qualitative research. In N. K. Denzin & Y. S. Lincoln (Eds.), *The SAGE handbook of qualitative research* (pp. 485–499). Thousand Oaks, CA: Sage.

American Psychological Association. (2009). *Publication manual of the American Psychological Association* (6th ed.). Washington, DC: Author.

American Sociological Association. (1999). *Code of ethics and policies and procedures of the ASA Committee on professional ethics*. Washington, DC: Author.

Anderson, E. (1999). *Code of the street: Decency, violence, and the moral life of the inner city*. New York, NY: Norton.

Armstrong, K. (2008). *Ethnography and audience*. In P. Aasuutari, L. Bickman, & J. Brannen (Eds.), *The SAGE handbook of social research methods* (pp. 54–63). Thousand Oaks, CA: Sage.

Arwood, T., & Panicker, S. (2007). Assessing risk in social and behavioral sciences. *Collaborative institutional training initiative*. Retrieved June 5, 2008, from https://www.citiprogram.org/members/learners

Babor, T. F., Stephens, R. S., & Marlatt, G. A. (1987). Verbal report methods in clinical research on alcoholism: Response bias and its minimization. *Journal of Studies on Alcohol*, *48*(5), 410–424.

Bachman, R. (1992). *Death and violence on the reservation: Homicide, family violence, and suicide in American Indian populations*. Westport, CT: Auburn House.

Bachman, R. (2012). *Measuring rape and sexual assault: Comparing the National Crime Victimization Survey with other methodologies*. Paper presented at the National Academy of Sciences: Committee on National Statistics, June 2012.

Bachman, R., Kerrison, E., O'Connell, D., & Paternoster, R. (2013). *Roads diverge: Long-term patterns of relapse, recidivism, and desistance for a cohort of drug involved offenders*. Final Report. Grant Number 2008-IJ-CX-0017. Washington, DC: National Institute of Justice, U.S. Department of Justice.

Bachman, R., & Paternoster, R. (2017). *Statistics for Criminology and Criminal Justice*, 4th Edition, Thousand Oaks, CA: SAGE.

Ball, R. A., & Curry, G. D. (1995). The logic of definition in criminology: Purposes and methods for defining gangs. *Criminology*, *33*(2), 225–245.

Bandura, A., Ross, D., & Ross, S. A. (1963). Imitation of film-mediated aggressive models. *Journal of Abnormal and Social Psychology*, *66*, 3–11.

Barringer, F. (1993, June 4). Majority in poll back ban on handguns. *New York Times*, p. A14.

Baskin, D. R., & Sommers, I. B. (1998). *Casualties of community disorder: Women's careers in violent crime*. Boulder, CO: Westview.

Baumrind, Diana. (1964). "Some Thoughts on Ethics of Research: After Reading Milgram's `Behavioral Study of Obedience.'" *American Psychologist* 19 (6), 421–23.

Baumrind, D. (1985). Research using intentional deception: Ethical issues revisited. *American Psychologist*, *40*(2), 165–174.

Beals, J., Manson, S., Mitchell, C., Spicer, P., & AI-SUPERPFP Team. (2003). Cultural specificity and comparison in psychiatric epidemiology: Walking the tightrope in American Indian research. *Culture, Medicine and Psychiatry*, *27*(3), 259–289.

Becker, H. S. (1958). Problems of inference and proof in participant observation. *American Sociological Review*, *23*, 652–660.

Becker, H. S. (1986). *Writing for social scientists*. Chicago, IL: University of Chicago Press.

Bellah, R. N., Madsen, R., Sullivan, W. M., Swidler, A., & Tipton, S. M. (1985). *Habits of the heart: Individualism and commitment in American life*. New York, NY: Harper & Row.

Belli, Robert F., Frank P. Stafford, & Duane F. Alwin. (2009). *Calendar and Time Diary: Methods in Life Course Research*. Thousand Oaks, CA: SAGE.

Bench, L. L., & Allen, T. D. (2003). Investigating the stigma of prison classification: An experimental design. *Prison Journal*, *83*(4), 367–382.

Belousov, Konstantin, Tom Horlick-Jones, Michael Bloor, Jakov Gilinsky, Valentin Golbert, Jakov Kostikovsky, Michael Levi, & Dmitri Pentsov. (2007). Any Port in a Storm: Fieldwork Difficulties in Dangerous and Crisis-Ridden Settings. *Qualitative Research*, 7, 155–75.

Bergen, E., Antfolk, J., Jern, P., Alanko, K., & Santtila, P. (2013). Adults' sexual interest in children and adolescents online: A quasi-experimental study. *International Journal of Cyber Criminology*, *7*(2), 94–111.

Berk, R. A., Campbell, A., Klap, R., & Western, B. (1992). The deterrent effect of arrest: A Bayesian analysis of four field experiments. *American Sociological Review*, *57*, 698–708.

Bialik, C. (2015, April 6). The latest Kentucky riot is part of a long, destructive sports tradition. Retrieved August 24, 2015, from http://fivethirtyeight.com/datalab/the-latest-kentucky-riot-is-part-of-a-long-destructive-sports-tradition

Bichler, G., Lim, S., & Larin, E. (2017). Tactical social network analysis: Using affiliation networks to aid serial homicide investigation. *Homicide Studies, 21*(2), 133–158

Binder, A., & Meeker, J. W. (1993). Implications of the failure to replicate the Minneapolis Experimental findings. *American Sociological Review, 58*(December), 886–888.

Black, D. J. (Ed.). (1984). *Toward a general theory of social control*. Orlando, FL: Academic Press.

Black, M. C., Basile, K. C., Breiding, M. J., Smith, S. G., Walters, M. L., . . . Stevens, M. R. (2011). *The National Intimate Partner and Sexual Violence Survey (NISVS): 2010 summary report*. Atlanta, GA: National Center for Injury Prevention and Control, Centers for Disease Control and Prevention.

Boba, R. (2009). *Crime analysis with crime mapping*. Thousand Oaks, CA: Sage.

Booth, W. C., Colomb, G. G., & Williams, J. M. (1995). *The craft of research*. Chicago, IL: University of Chicago Press.

Boruch, R. F. (1997). *Randomized experiments for planning and evaluation: A practical guide*. Thousand Oaks, CA: Sage.

Braga, A.A., Weisburd, D., & Turchan, B. (2018) Focused deterrence strategies and crime control: An updated systematic review and meta-analysis of the empirical evidence. *Criminology & Public Policy, 17*, 205–250.

Braga, A. A., Weisburd, D. L., Waring, E. J., Mazerolle, L. G., Spelman, W., & Gajewski, F. (1999). Problem-oriented policing in violent crime places: A randomized controlled experiment. *Criminology, 37*(4), 541–580.

Brennan, T., & Austin, J. (1997). *Women in jail: Classification issues*. Washington, DC: Department of Justice, National Institute of Corrections.

Brewer, J., & Hunter, A. (1989). *Multimethod research: A synthesis of styles*. Newbury Park, CA: Sage.

Bridges, G. S., & Weis, J.G. (1989). Measuring violent behavior: Effects of study design on reported correlates of violence. In N. A. Weiner & M. E. Wolfgang (Eds.), *Violent crime, violent criminals* (pp. 14–34). Newbury Park, CA: Sage.

Broskoske, S. (2005). How to prevent paper recycling. *Teaching Professor, 19*, 1–4.

Burger, J. M. (2009). Replicating Milgram: Would people still obey today? *American Psychologist, 64*, 1–11.

Burt, M. R. (1996). Homelessness: Definitions and counts. In J. Baumohl (Ed.), *Homelessness in America* (pp. 15–23). Phoenix, AZ: Oryx.

Bushman, B. J. (1995). Moderating role of trait aggressiveness in the effects of violent media on aggression. *Journal of Personality and Social Psychology, 69*(5), 950–960.

Bushman, B. J., & Huesmann, R. L. (2012). Effects of media violence on aggression. In B. J. Bushman & R. L. Huesmann (Eds.), *Handbook of children and the media* (2nd ed., pp. 231–248). Thousand Oaks, CA: Sage.

Buzawa, E. S., & Buzawa, C. G. (1996). *Domestic violence: The criminal justice response* (2nd ed.). Thousand Oaks, CA: Sage.

Calvey, D. (2014). Covert ethnography in criminology: A submerged yet creative tradition. *Current Issues in Criminal Justice, 25*(1), 541–550.

Campbell, D. T., & Russo, M. J. (1999). *Social experimentation*. Thousand Oaks, CA: Sage.

Campbell, D. T., & Stanley, J. C. (1996). *Experimental and quasi-experimental designs for research*. Chicago, IL: Rand McNally.

Campbell, R. T. (1992). Longitudinal research. In E. F. Borgatta & M. L. Borgatta (Eds.), *Encyclopedia of sociology* (pp. 1146–1158). New York, NY: Macmillan.

Campbell, T. T., & Fiske, D. W. (1959). Convergent and discriminant validity by the multi-trait, multi-method matrix. *Psychological Bulletin, 56*, 126–139.

Cantor, D. (1984). *Comparing bounded and unbounded three- and six-month reference periods in rate estimation*. Washington, DC: Bureau of Social Science Research.

Cantor, D. (1985). Operational and substantive differences in changing the NCS reference period. In *Proceedings of the American Statistical Association, Social Statistics Section* (pp. 125–137). Washington, DC: American Statistical Association.

Caplan, J., & Kennedy, L. (2015). *Risk terrain modeling and the spatial dynamics of crime*. Los Angeles: University of California Press.

Carr, P. J., & Kefalas, M. J. (2009). *Hollowing out the middle: The rural brain drain and what it means for America*. Boston, MA: Beacon Press.

Carrington, P. J., & Schulenberg, J. L. (2008). Structuring police discretion: The effect on referrals to youth court. *Criminal Justice Policy Review, 19*, 349–367.

Carroll-Lind, J., Chapman, J., & Raskauskas, J. (2011). Children's perceptions of violence: The nature, extent, and impact of their experiences. *Social Policy Journal of New Zealand, 37*, 6–18.

Cava, A., Cushman, R., & Goodman, K. (2007). HIPAA and human subjects research. Collaborative Institutional Training Initiative. Retrieved June 5, 2008, from https://www.citiprogram.org/members/learners

Centers for Disease Control and Prevention (CDC). (2009). The Tuskegee timeline. Atlanta, GA: National Center for HIV/AIDS, Viral Hepatitis, STD, and TB Prevention. Retrieved from www.cdc.gov/tuskegee/timeline.htm

Chadwick, G. L. (2017). New final Common Rule published many changes are required. HRP Consulting Group. Retrieved from http://files.constantcontact.com/7ad07d0b001/7bd1f2ce-05e8-4d6a-bd2a-eaa-c1a6e9e25.pdf?ver=1485629966000

Chalk, R., & Garner, J. H. (2001). "Evaluating Arrest for Intimate Partner Violence: Two Decades of Research and Reform." *New Directions for Evaluation 90*: 9–23.

Chan, J., & Moses, L. B. (2017). Making sense of Big Data for security. *British Journal of Criminology, 57*, 299–319.

Chen, H. (1990). *Theory-driven evaluations*. Newbury Park, CA: Sage.

Chen, H.-T., & Rossi, P. H. (1987). The theory-driven approach to validity. *Evaluation and Program Planning, 10*, 95–103.

Christian, L., Keeter, S., Purcell, K., & Smith, A. (2010). *Assessing the cell phone challenge to survey research in 2010*. Washington, DC: Pew Research Center for the People & the Press and Pew Internet & American Life Project.

Coffey, A., & Atkinson, P. (1996). *Making sense of qualitative data: Complementary research strategies*. Thousand Oaks, CA: Sage.

Collins, P. H. (1991). Learning from the outsider within: The sociological significance of black feminist thought. In M. M. Fonow & J. A. Cook (Eds.), *Beyond methodology* (pp. 35–59). Bloomington: Indiana University Press.

Converse, J. M. (1984). Attitude measurement in psychology and sociology: The early years. In C. F. Turner & E. Martin (Eds.), *Surveying subjective phenomena* (Vol. 2, pp. 3–40). New York, NY: Russell Sage.

Cook, T. D., & Campbell, D. T. (1979). *Quasi-Experimentation: Design and analysis issues for field settings*. Chicago, IL: Rand McNally.

Cooper, H., & Hedges, L. V. (1994). Research synthesis as a scientific enterprise. In H. Cooper & L. V. Hedges (Eds.), *The handbook of research synthesis* (pp. 3–14). New York, NY: Russell Sage Foundation.

Core Institute. (2015). Core Alcohol and Drug Survey: Long form. Carbondale. IL: FIPSE Core Analysis Grantee Group, Core Institute, Student Health Programs, Southern Illinois University.

Corse, S. J., Hirschinger, N. B., & Zanis, D. (1995). The use of the Addiction Severity Index with people with severe mental illness. *Psychiatric Rehabilitation Journal*, *19*(1), 9–18.

Creswell, J. A., Klassen, A. C., Plano Clark, V. L., & Smith, K. (2011). *Best practices for mixed methods research in the health sciences*. Washington, DC: Office of Behavioral and Social Sciences Research.

Creswell, J. W., & Plano Clark, V. L. (2011). *Designing and conducting mixed methods research* (2nd ed.). Thousand Oaks, CA: Sage.

Crossland, C., Palmer, J., & Brooks, A. (2013). NIJ's program of research on violence against American Indian and Alaska Native Women. *Violence Against Women*, *19*(6), 771–790.

Dahlberg, B., Wittink, M. N., & Gallo, J. J. (2010). Funding and publishing integrated studies: Writing effective mixed methods manuscripts and grant proposals. In A. Tashakkori & C. Teddlie (Eds.), *The SAGE handbook of mixed methods in social & behavioral research* (2nd ed., pp. 775–802). Thousand Oaks, CA: Sage.

D'Amico, E. J., & Fromme, K. (2002). Brief prevention for adolescent risk-taking behavior. *Addiction*, *97*, 563–574.

Decker, S. H., & Van Winkle, B. (1996). *Life in the gang: Family, friends, and violence*. Cambridge, UK: Cambridge University Press.

Two Decades of Research and Reform." *New Directions for Evaluation* 90: 9–23.

Dentler, R. A. (2002). *Practicing sociology: Selected fields*. Westport, CT: Praeger.

Denzin, N. K., & Lincoln, Y. S. (1994). Introduction: Entering the field of qualitative research. In N. K. Denzin & Y. S. Lincoln (Eds.), *The SAGE handbook of qualitative research* (pp. 1–17). Thousand Oaks, CA: Sage.

Denzin, Norman, & Yvonna S. Lincoln. (2000). Introduction: The Discipline and Practice of Qualitative Research." In The *Handbook of Qualitative Research*, 2nd ed., edited by Norman Denzin and Yvonna S. Lincoln, pp. 1–28. Thousand Oaks, CA: SAGE.

Dillman, D. A. (2000). *Mail and Internet surveys: The tailored design method* (2nd ed.). New York, NY: John Wiley.

Dorsey, Tina L., & Marianne W. Zawitz. (2005). *Drugs and Crime Facts* (NCJ-165148). Washington, DC: Bureau of Justice Statistics, U.S. Department of Justice.

Duncombe, Jean, and Julie Jessop. (2002). 'Doing Rapport' and the Ethics of 'Faking Friendship.' In *Ethics in Qualitative Research*, edited by Melanie

Mauthner, Maxine Birch, Julie Jessop, and Tina Miller, 107–22. Thousand Oaks, CA: SAGE.

Eck, J. E., Chainey, S., Cameron, J. G., Leitner, M., & Wilson, R. E. (2005). *Crime mapping: Understanding hot spots*. Washington, DC: U.S. Department of Justice, National Institute of Justice.

Ellsberg, M., & Heise, L. (2005). *Researching violence against women: A practical guide for researchers and activists*. Washington, DC: World Health Organization, PATH.

Emerson, R. M. (Ed.). (1983). *Contemporary field research*. Prospect Heights, IL: Waveland.

Emerson, R. M., Fretz, R. I., & Shaw, L. L. (1995). *Writing ethnographic field notes*. Chicago, IL: University of Chicago Press.

Erikson, K. T. (1967). A comment on disguised observation in sociology. *Social Problems*, *12*, 366–373.

Esbensen, F.-A., Osgood, D. W., Peterson, D., Taylor, T. J., & Carson, D. C. (2013). Short- and long-term outcome results from a multisite evaluation of the GREAT Program. *Criminology & Public Policy*, *12*(3), 375–411.

Evans, R. (2007, September 1). Military scientists tested mustard gas on Indians. *The Guardian*. Retrieved from http://www.theguardian.com/uk/2007/sep/01/india.military

Exum, M. L. (2002). The application and robustness of the rational choice perspective in the study of intoxicated/angry intentions to aggress. *Criminology*, *40*, 933–966.

Farrington, D. P. (1977). The effects of public labeling. *British Journal of Criminology*, *17*(2), 112–125.

Fausset, R., & Kovaleski, S. (2018, February 15). Nikolas Cruz, Florida shooting suspect, showed 'early red flag.' *New York Times*. Retrieved from https://www.nytimes.com/2018/02/15/us/nikolas-cruz-florida-shooting.html

Federal Register. (2017). Federal Policy for the Protection of Human Subjects, 82(12, Part IX), 49 CFR Part *11*, 7149–7274. Retrieved from https://www.gpo.gov/fdsys/pkg/FR-2017-01-19/html/2017-01058.htm

Fenno, R. F., Jr. (1978). *Home style: House members in their districts*. Boston, MA: Little, Brown.

Ferguson, C. J., San Miguel, C., Kilburn, J. C., Sanchez, J. R., & Sanchez, P. (2007). The effectiveness of school-based anti-bullying programs: A meta-analytic review. *Criminal Justice Review*, *32*(4), 401–414.

Fink, A. (2020). *Conducting Research Literature Reviews* (5th Ed.). Thousand Oaks, CA: SAGE.

Fisher, B. (2009). The effects of survey question wording on rape estimates: Evidence from a quasi-experimental design. *Violence Against Women*, *15*, 133–147.

Fitterer, J., Nelson, T. A., & Nathoo, F. (2015). Predictive crime mapping. *Police, Practice, and Research*, *16*(2), 121–135.

Fontaine, N. M. G., Brendgen, M., Vitaro, F., & Tremblay, R. E. (2016). Compensatory and protective factors against violent delinquency in late adolescence: Results from the Montreal Longitudinal and Experimental Study. *Journal of Criminal Justice*, *45*, 54–62.

Fowler, F. J. (1988). *Survey research methods* (Rev. ed.). Newbury Park, CA: Sage.

Fowler, F. J. (1995). *Improving survey questions: Design and evaluation.* Thousand Oaks, CA: Sage.

Gill, H. E. (2004). Finding a middle ground between extremes: Notes on researching transnational crime and violence. *Anthropology Matters Journal, 6,* 1–9.

Giordano, P. C., Cernkovich, S. A., & Rudolph, J. L. (2002). Gender, crime, and desistance: Toward a theory of cognitive transformation. *American Journal of Sociology, 107,* 990–1064.

Glaser, B. G., & Strauss, A. L. (1967). *The discovery of grounded theory: Strategies for qualitative research.* London, UK: Weidenfeld and Nicholson.

Gobo, G. (2008). Re-conceptualizing generalization: Old issues in a new frame. In P. Alasuutari, L. Bickman, & J. Brannen (Eds.), *The SAGE handbook of social research methods* (pp. 193–213). Thousand Oaks, CA: Sage.

Goffman, E. (1961). *Asylums: Essays on the social situation of mental patients and other inmates.* Garden City, NY: Doubleday.

Goldfinger, S. M., Schutt, R. K., Seidman, L. J., Turner, W. M., Penk, W. E., & Tolomiczenko, G. S. (1996). Self-report and observer measures of substance abuse among homeless mentally ill persons in the cross-section and over time. *Journal of Nervous and Mental Disease, 184*(11), 667–672.

Goleman, D. (1993, September 7). Pollsters enlist psychologists in quest for unbiased results. *New York Times,* pp. C1, C11.

Gordon, R. (1992). *Basic interviewing skills.* Itasca, IL: Peacock.

Gottfredson, D. C., & Hirschi, T. (1990). *A general theory of crime.* Palo Alto, CA: Stanford University Press.

Grant, B. F., Dawson, D. A., Stinson, F. S., Chou, S. P., Dufour, M. C., & Pickering, R. P. (2004). The 12-month prevalence and trends in DSM-IV alcohol abuse and dependence: United States, 1991–1992 and 2001–2002. *Drug and Alcohol Dependence, 74,* 223–234.

Gray, K. M. (2011). Problem behaviors of students pursuing policing careers. *Policing, 34*(3), 541–552.

Groves, R. M., & Couper, M. P. (1998). *Nonresponse in household interview surveys.* New York, NY: John Wiley.

Gruenewald, P. J., Treno, A. J., Taff, G., & Klitzner, M. (1997). *Measuring community indicators: A systems approach to drug and alcohol problems.* Thousand Oaks, CA: Sage.

Guba, E. G., & Lincoln, Y. S. (1989). *Fourth generation evaluation.* Newbury Park, CA: Sage.

Guba, E. G., & Lincoln, Y. S. (1994). Competing paradigms in qualitative research. In N. K. Denzin & Y. S. Lincoln (Eds.), *The SAGE handbook of qualitative research* (pp. 110–117). Thousand Oaks, CA: Sage.

Gubrium, J. F., & Holstein, J. A. (1997). *The new language of qualitative method.* New York, NY: Oxford University Press.

Hafner, K. 2005. "In challenge to Google, Yahoo will scan books. *New York Times,* Oct 3.

Hagan, J. (1994). *Crime and disrepute.* Thousand Oaks, CA: Pine Forge Press.

Hage, J., & Meeker, B. F. (1988). *Social causality.* Boston, MA: Unwin Hyman.

Hagedorn, J. (1988). *People and folks.* Chicago, IL: Lake View Press.

Hakimzadeh, S., & Cohn, D. (2007). *English usage among Hispanics in the United States.* Washington, DC: Pew Hispanic Center. Retrieved August 21, 2015, from http://pewhispanic.org/files/reports/82.pdf

Haney, C., Banks, C., & Zimbardo, P. G. (1973). International dynamics in a simulated prison. *International Journal of Criminology and Penology, 1,* 69–97.

Hard, S. F., Conway, J. M., & Moran, A. C. (2006). Faculty and college student beliefs about the frequency of student academic misconduct. *Journal of Higher Education, 77,* 1058–1080.

Hasin, D. S., Stinson, F. S., Ogburn, E., & Grant, B. F. (2007). Prevalence, correlates, disability, and comorbidity of DSM-IV alcohol abuse and dependence in the United States: Results from the National Epidemiologic Survey on Alcohol and Related Conditions. *Archives of General Psychiatry, 64,* 830–842.

Heaton, J. (2008). Secondary analysis of qualitative data. In P. Alasuutari, L. Bickman, & J. Brannen (Eds.), *The SAGE handbook of social research methods* (pp. 506–535). Thousand Oaks, CA: Sage.

Heckathorn, D. D. (1997). Respondent-Driven sampling: A new approach to the study of hidden populations. *Social Problems, 44,* 174–199.

Hertenstein, M. (2013). *The tell: The little clues that reveal big truths about who we are.* New York, NY: Basic Books.

Hesse-Biber, S., & Leavy, P. L. (2007). *Feminist research: A primer.* Thousand Oaks, CA: Sage.

Hirschel, J. D., Hutchison III, I. W., & Dean, C. W. (1992). The failure of arrest to deter spouse abuse. *Journal of Research in Crime and Delinquency, 29*(1), 7–33.

Hirvonen, K. (2013). Sweden: When hate becomes the norm. *Race & Class, 55*(1), 78–86.

Hock, R. E. (2010). *The extreme searcher's internet handbook* (3rd Ed.). Medford, NJ: CyberAge Books.

Howell, J. C. (2003). *Preventing and reducing juvenile delinquency: A comprehensive framework.* Thousand Oaks, CA: Sage.

Hoyle, C., & Sanders, A. (2000). Police response to domestic violence. *The British Journal of Criminology, 40*(1), 14–36.

Huberman, A. M., & Miles, M. B. (1994). Data management and analysis methods. In N. K. Denzin, & Y. S. Lincoln (Eds.), *The SAGE handbook of qualitative research* (pp. 428–444). Thousand Oaks, CA: Sage.

Humphrey, N. (1992). *A history of the mind: Evolution and the birth of consciousness.* New York, NY: Simon & Schuster.

Humphreys, L. (1970). *Tearoom trade: Impersonal sex in public places.* Chicago, IL: Aldine.

Hunt, M. (1985). *Profiles of social research: The scientific study of human interactions.* New York, NY: Russell Sage Foundation.

Huston, P., & Naylor, C. D. (1996). Health services research: Reporting on studies using secondary data sources. *Canadian Medical Association Journal, 155,* 1697–1702.

Hyatt, J. M., & Ostermann, M. (2019). Better to stay home: Evaluating the impact of day reporting centers on offending. *Crime & Delinquency, 65*(1), 94–121.

Inciardi, J. A., & Harrison, L. D. (2000). Introduction: The concept of harm reduction. In J. A. Inciardi & L. D. Harrison (Eds.), *Harm reduction: National and international perspectives* (pp. 2–19). Thousand Oaks, CA: Sage.

James, N., & Busher, H. (2009). *Online interviewing.* Thousand Oaks, CA: Sage.

Johnson, D., & Bullock, M. (2009). The ethics of data archiving: Issues from four perspectives. In D. M. Mertens & P. E. Ginsberg (Eds.), *The handbook of social research ethics* (pp. 214–228). Thousand Oaks, CA: Sage.

Kaeble, D., & Cowhig, M. (2018). *Correctional populations in the United States, 2016*. Washington, DC: Bureau of Justice Statistics.

Karberg, J., & James, D. J. (2005). *Substance dependence, abuse, and treatment of jail inmates, 2002*. Washington, DC: Bureau of Justice Statistics, U.S. Department of Justice.

Kaufman, S. R. (1986). *The ageless self: Sources of meaning in late life*. Madison: University of Wisconsin Press.

Keenan, E. K. (2004). From sociocultural categories to socially located relations: Using critical theory in social work practice. *Families in Society: The Journal of Contemporary Social Services*, *85*(4), 539–548.

Keeter, S. (2008). *Survey research and cell phones: Is there a problem?* Presentation to the Harvard Program on Survey Research Spring Conference, New Technologies and Survey Research. Cambridge, MA: Institute of Quantitative Social Science, Harvard University, May 9.

Kemmis, S., & McTaggart, R. (2005). Participatory action research: Communicative action and the public sphere. In N. K. Denzin & Y. S. Lincoln (Eds.), *The SAGE handbook of qualitative research* (3rd ed., pp. 559–603). Thousand Oaks, CA: Sage.

Kennedy, D. M., Piehl, A. M., & Braga, A. A. (1996). Youth violence in Boston: Gun markets, serious youth offenders, and a use-reduction strategy. *Law and Contemporary Problems*, *59*, 147–196.

Kennedy, L. W., Caplan, J. M., & Piza, E. L. (2012). *A primer on the spatial dynamics of crime emergence and persistence*. Newark, NJ: Rutgers Center on Public Security.

Kiefer, S. (2015). *CITI Collaborative Institutional Training Initiative: Human subjects research: Special module for prisoners*. Retrieved August 8, 2015, from https://www.citiprogram.org/index.cfm?pageID=88

King, G., Keohane, R. O., & Verba, S. (1994). *Scientific inference in qualitative research*. Princeton, NJ: Princeton University Press.

Kitchener, K. S., & Kitchener, R. F. (2009). Social science research ethics: Historical and philosophical issues. In D. M. Mertens & P. E. Ginsberg (Eds.), *The handbook of social research ethics* (pp. 5–22). Thousand Oaks, CA: Sage.

Klein, M. W. (1971). *Street gangs and street workers*. Englewood Cliffs, NJ: Prentice Hall.

Knight, J. R., Wechsler, H., Kuo, M., Seibring, M., Weitzman, E. R., & Schuckit, M. A. (2002). Alcohol abuse and dependence among U.S. college students. *Journal of Studies on Alcohol*, *63*, 263–270.

Kobelarcik, E. L., Alexander, C. A., Singh, R. P., & Shapiro, G. M. (1983). Alternative reference periods for the national crime survey. In *Proceedings of the American Statistical Association: Section on Survey Methods*. Washington, DC.

Koegel, P. (1987). *Ethnographic perspectives on homeless and homeless mentally ill women*. Washington, DC: Alcohol, Drug Abuse, and Mental Health Administration, Public Health Service, U.S. Department of Health and Human Services.

Kohn, A. (2008). Who's cheating whom? *Education Digest*, *73*, 4–11.

Korn, J. H. (1997). *Illusions of reality: A history of deception in social psychology*. Albany: State University of New York Press.

Kozinets, R. V. (2010). *Netnography: Doing ethnographic research online*. Thousand Oaks, CA: Sage.

Kramer, A. D., Guillory, J. E., & Hancock, J. T. (2014). Experimental evidence of massive-scale emotional contagion through social networks. *Proceedings of the National Academy of Sciences*, *111*, 8788–8790.

Krebs, V. E. (2002). Mapping networks of terrorist cells. *Connections*, *24*(3), 43–52.

Kupchik, A. (2010). *Homeroom security: School discipline in an age of fear*. New York: New York University Press.

Kvale, S. (1996). *InterViews: An introduction to qualitative research interviewing*. Thousand Oaks, CA: Sage.

Kvale, S. (2002). The social construction of validity. In N. K. Denzin & Y. S. Lincoln (Eds.), *The qualitative inquiry reader* (pp. 229–325). Thousand Oaks, CA: Sage.

Labaw, P. (1980). *Advanced questionnaire design*. Cambridge, MA: ABT Books.

Lamott, A. (1994). *Bird by bird: Some instructions on writing and life*. New York, NY: Anchor.

LaRossa, R. (1995). Parenthood in Early Twentieth-Century America Project (PETCAP), 1900–1944 [Computer file]. Atlanta, GA: Georgia State University [producer], 1995.

Laub, J. H., & Sampson, R. J. (2003). *Shared beginnings, divergent lives: Delinquent boys to age 70*. Cambridge, MA: Harvard University Press.

Lavrakas, P. J. (1987). *Telephone survey methods: Sampling, selection, and supervision*. Newbury Park, CA: Sage.

Leakey, T., Lunde, K. B., Koga, K., & Glanz, K. (2004). Written parental consent and the use of incentives in a youth smoking prevention trial: A case study from Project SPLASH. *American Journal of Evaluation*, *25*, 509–523.

Lempert, R. (1989). Humility is a virtue: On the publicization of policy-relevant research. *Law & Society Review*, *23*, 146–161.

Lempert, R., & Sanders, J. (1986). *An invitation to law and social science: Desert, disputes, and distribution*. New York, NY: Longman.

Levine, J. P. (1976). The potential for crime overreporting in criminal victimization surveys. *Criminology*, *14*, 307–330.

Levitt, H. M., Todd-Swanger, R., & Butler, J. B. (2008). Male perpetrators' perspectives on intimate partner violence, religion, and masculinity. *Sex Roles: A Journal of Research*, *58*, 435–448.

Levy, P. S., & Lemeshow, S. (1999). *Sampling of populations: Methods and applications* (3rd ed.). New York, NY: Wiley.

Lewin, Tamar. (2001). Income Education Is Found to Lower Risk of New Arrest." *The New York Times*, November 16, p. A18.

Lieberson, S. (1985). *Making it count: The improvement of social research and theory*. Berkeley, CA: University of California Press.

Lipsey, M. W., & Wilson, D. B. (2001). *Practical meta-analysis*. Thousand Oaks, CA: Sage.

Litwin, M. S. (1995). *How to measure survey reliability and validity*. Thousand Oaks, CA: Sage.

Lo, C. C., Kim, Y. S., & Cheng, C. (2008). Offense specialization of arrestees: An event history analysis. *Crime and Delinquency*, *54*, 341–365.

Lockwood, D. (1996). Violent incidents among selected public school students in two large cities of the South and the southern Midwest, 1995:

[United States] [Computer file]. ICPSR version. Atlanta, GA: Clark Atlantic University [producer], 1996. Ann Arbor, MI: Inter-university Consortium for Political and Social Research [distributor], 1998.

Lovibond, S. H., Mithiran, X., & Adams, W. G. (1979). The effects of three experimental prison environments on the behaviour of non-convict volunteer subjects. *Australian Psychologist*, *14*, 273–287.

Luxardo, N., Colombo, G., & Iglesias, G. (2011). Methodological and ethical dilemmas encountered during field research of family violence experienced by adolescent women in Buenos Aires. *Qualitative Report*, *16*, 984–1000.

Madden, R. (2010). *Being ethnographic: A guide to the theory and practice of ethnography*. Thousand Oaks, CA: Sage.

Madfis, E. (2014). Averting school rampage: Student intervention amid a persistent code of silence. *Youth Violence & Juvenile Justice*, *12*(3), 229–241.

Maher, L., & Hudson, S. L. (2007). Women in the drug economy: A meta-synthesis of the qualitative literature. *Journal of Drug Issues*, *37*, 805–826.

Majchrzak, A., & Markus, M. L. (2014). *Methods for policy research: Taking socially responsible action* (2nd ed.). Thousand Oaks, CA: SAGE.

Mangione, T. W. (1995). *Mail surveys: Improving the quality*. Thousand Oaks, CA: Sage.

Marini, M. M., & Singer, B. (1988). Causality in the social sciences. In C. C. Clogg (Ed.), *Sociological methodology* (Vol. *18*, pp. 347–409). Washington, DC: American Sociological Association.

The Mark Twitchell case. (n.d.). *Edmonton Journal*. Retrieved August 5, 2019, from http://www.edmontonjournal.com/news/twitchell-case/index.html

Martin, L. L., & Kettner, P. M. (1996). *Measuring the performance of human service programs*. Thousand Oaks, CA: Sage.

Matt, G. E., & Cook, T. D. (1994). Threats to the validity of research syntheses. In H. M. Cooper & L. V. Hedge (Eds.), *The handbook of research synthesis* (pp. 503–520). New York, NY: Russell Sage Foundation.

Maxwell, J. A. (1996). *Qualitative research design: An interactive approach*. Thousand Oaks, CA: Sage.

Mayer-Schönberger, V., & Cukier, K. (2013). *Big Data: A revolution that will transform how we live, work, and think*. Boston, MA: Houghton Mifflin Harcourt.

McGarrell, E. F., Corsaro, N., Melde, C., Hipple, N. K., Bynum, T., & Cobbina, J. (2013). Attempting to reduce firearms violence through a Comprehensive Anti-Gang Initiative (CAGI): An evaluation of process and impact. *Journal of Criminal Justice*, *41*, 33–43.

McLellan, A. T., Luborsky, L., Cacciola, J., Griffith, J., Evans, F., Barr, H. L., & O'Brien, C. P. (1985). New data from the Addiction Severity Index: Reliability and validity in three centers. *Journal of Nervous and Mental Disease*, *173*(7), 412–423.

Mertens, D. M. (2012). Transformative mixed methods: Addressing inequities. *American Behavioral Scientist*, *56*, 802–813.

Milgram, S. (1963). Behavioral study of obedience. *Journal of Abnormal and Social Psychology*, *67*(3), 371–378.

Milgram, S. (1964). Issues in the "Study of Obedience": A reply to Baumrind. *American Psychologist*, *19*, 848–852.

Milgram, S. (1965). Some conditions of obedience and disobedience to authority. *Human Relations*, *18*, 57–75.

Milgram, S. (1974). *Obedience to authority: An experimental view*. New York, NY: Harper & Row.

Milgram, S. (1992). *The individual in a social world: Essays and experiments* (2nd ed.). New York, NY: McGraw-Hill.

Miller, A. G. (1986). *The Obedience Experiments: A case study of controversy in social science*. New York, NY: Praeger.

Miller, D. C. (1991). *Handbook of research design and social measurement* (5th ed.). Newbury Park, CA: Sage.

Miller, H. G., Gribble, J. N., Mazade, L. C., & Turner, C. F. (1998). Abortion and breast cancer: Fact or artifact? In A. Stone (Ed.), *The science of self-report* (pp. 123–141). Mahwah, NJ: Lawrence Erlbaum.

Miller, J. (2000). *One of the guys: Girls, gangs, and gender*. New York, NY: Oxford University Press.

Miller, J. (2003). An arresting experiment: Domestic violence victim experiences and perceptions. *Journal of Interpersonal Violence*, *18*, 695–716.

Miller, S. (1999). *Gender and community policing: Walking the talk*. Boston, MA: Northeastern University Press.

Miller, T. R., & Hendrie, D. (2008). *Substance abuse prevention dollars and cents: A cost-benefit analysis*. DHHS Pub. No. (SMA) 07-4298. Rockville, MD: Center for Substance Abuse Prevention, Substance Abuse and Mental Health Services Administration.

Miller, W. (1992). *Crime by youth gangs and groups in the United States*. Washington, DC: Office of Juvenile Justice and Delinquency Prevention.

Miller, W. L., & Crabtree, B. F. (1999). Clinical research: A multimethod typology and qualitative roadmap. In B. Crabtree & W. L. Miller (Eds.), *Doing qualitative research* (2nd ed., pp. 3–30). Thousand Oaks, CA: Sage.

Mills, C. W. (1959). *The sociological imagination*. New York, NY: Oxford University Press.

Moe, A. M. (2007). Silenced voices and structural survival—Battered women's help seeking. *Violence Against Women*, *13*(7), 676–699.

Mohr, L. B. (1992). *Impact analysis for program evaluation*. Newbury Park, CA: Sage.

Moore, J. W. (1978). *Homeboys: Gangs, drugs, and prison in the barrios of Los Angeles*. Philadelphia, PA: Temple University Press.

Moore, J. W. (1991). *Going down to the barrio: Homeboys and homegirls in change*. Philadelphia, PA: Temple University Press.

Moreno, J. L. (1953). *Who shall survive? Foundations of sociometry, group psychotherapy, and sociodrama*. Beacon, NY: Beacon House.

Morgan, D. L. (2014). *Integrating qualitative & quantitative methods: A pragmatic approach*. Thousand Oaks, CA: Sage.

Mosher, C. J., Miethe, T. D., & Phillips, D. M. (2002). *The mismeasure of crime*. Thousand Oaks, CA: Sage.

Mueller, B., Piccoli, S., & Southall, A. (2018, March 14). In Brooklyn apartment, four shot dead in apparent murder-suicide. *New York Times*. Retrieved from https://www.nytimes.com/2018/03/14/nyregion/brownsville-brooklyn-shooting.html?searchResultPosition=4

Mullins, C. J. (1977). *A guide to writing and publishing in the social and behavioral sciences*. New York, NY: John Wiley.

Musu-Gillette, L., Zhang, A., Wang, K., Zhang, J., Kemp, J., Diliberti, M., & Oudekerk, B. A. (2018). *Indicators of school crime and safety: 2017* (NCES 2018-036/NCJ 251413). Washington, DC: National Center for Education Statistics, U.S. Department of Education and Bureau of Justice Statistics, Office of Justice Programs, U.S. Department of Justice.

National Gang Center. (2014). *Gang-related definitions*. Retrieved September 18, 2015, from http://www.nationalgang center.gov/Legislation/Definitions

National Institute on Alcohol Abuse and Alcoholism (NIAAA). (1997). Alcohol metabolism. *Alcohol Alert, 35*(January), 1–4.

National Institute on Alcohol Abuse and Alcoholism (NIAAA). (2018). Alcohol facts and statistics. Retrieved from https://www.niaaa.nih.gov/alcohol-health/overview-alcohol-consumption/alcohol-facts-and-statistics

Nestor, P. G., & Schutt, R. K. (2012). *Research methods in psychology: Investigating human behavior*. Thousand Oaks, CA: Sage.

Neuendorf, K. A. (2002). *The content analysis guidebook*. Thousand Oaks, CA: Sage.

Nguyen, H., & Loughran, T. A. (2018). On the measurement and identification of turning points in criminology. *Annual Review of Criminology, 1*, 335–358.

O Dochartaigh, N. (2012). *Internet research skills*. Thousand Oaks, CA: SAGE.

O'Neal, E. N., & Spohn, C. (2017). When the perpetrator is a partner: Arrest and charging decisions in intimate partner sexual assault cases—A focal concerns analysis. *Violence Against Women, 23*(6), 707–729.

Orcutt, J. D., & Turner, J. B. (1993). "Shocking numbers and graphic accounts: Quantified images of drug problems in the print media." *Social Problems* 49 (May): 190–206.

Padilla, F. M. (1992). *The gang as an American enterprise*. New Brunswick, NJ: Rutgers University Press.

Pager, D. (2007). *Marked: Race, crime and finding work in an era of mass incarceration*. Chicago, IL: University of Chicago Press.

Papineau, D. (1978). *For science in the social sciences*. London, UK: Macmillan.

Parlett, M., & Hamilton, D. (1976). Evaluation as illumination: A new approach to the study of innovative programmes. In G. Glass (Ed.), *Evaluation studies review annual* (Vol. 1, pp. 140–157). Beverly Hills, CA: Sage.

Pasick, R. J., Stewart, S. L., Bird, J. A., & D'Onofrio, C. N. (2001). Quality of data in multiethnic health surveys. *Public Health Reports* (Washington, DC), *116*, 223–243.

Pate, A. M., & Hamilton, E. E. (1992). Formal and informal deterrents to domestic violence: The Dade County spouse assault experiment. *American Sociological Review, 57*, 691–697.

Paternoster, R. (1991). *Capital punishment in America*. New York, NY: Lexington.

Paternoster, R., Brame, R., Bachman, R., & Sherman, L. W. (1997). Do fair procedures matter? The effect of procedural justice on spouse assault. *Law & Society Review, 31*(1), 163–204.

Patton, M. Q. (1997). *Utilization-focused evaluation: The new century text* (3rd ed.). Thousand Oaks, CA: Sage.

Patton, M. Q. (2002). *Qualitative research & evaluation methods* (3rd ed.). Thousand Oaks, CA: Sage.

Pearson, G. (2009). The researcher as hooligan: Where "participant" observation means breaking the law. *International Journal of Social Research Methodology, 12*(3), 243–255.

Perry, G. (2013). *Behind the shock machine: The untold story of the notorious Milgram psychology experiments*. New York, NY: New Press.

Peterson, R. A. (2000). *Constructing effective questionnaires*. Thousand Oaks, CA: Sage.

Petrosino, A., & Lavenberg, J. (2007). Systematic reviews and meta-analyses: Best evidence on "what works" for criminal justice decision makers. *Western Criminology Review, 8*(1), 1–15.

Pew Research Center. (2019). Internet/broadband fact sheet. Retrieved from https://www.pewinternet.org/fact-sheet/internet-broadband

Piza, E. L., Gilchrist, A. M., Caplan, J. M., Kennedy, L. W., & O'Hara, B. A. (2016). The financial implications of merging proactive CCTV monitoring and directed police patrol: A cost–benefit analysis. *Journal of Experimental Criminology, 12*, 403–429.

Plano Clark, V. L., & Badiee, M. (2010). Research questions in mixed methods research. In A. Tashakkori & C. Teddlie (Eds.), *The SAGE handbook of mixed methods in social & behavioral research* (2nd ed., pp. 275–304). Thousand Oaks, CA: Sage.

Posavac, E. J., & Carey, R. G. (1997). *Program evaluation: Methods and case studies*. Upper Saddle River, NJ: Prentice Hall.

Presley, C. A., Meilman, P. W., & Lyerla, R. (1994). Development of the Core Alcohol and Drug Survey: Initial findings and future directions. *Journal of American College Health, 42*, 248–255.

Punch, M. (1994). Politics and ethics in qualitative research. In N. K. Denzin & Y. S. Lincoln (Eds.), *The SAGE handbook of qualitative research* (pp. 83–97). Thousand Oaks, CA: Sage.

QualiBank. (2014). UK data service. Retrieved from http://ukdata service.ac.uk/get-data/explore-online/qualibank/qualibank

Ragin, C. C. (1994). *Constructing social research*. Thousand Oaks, CA: Pine Forge Press.

Regoli, R. M., & Hewitt, J. D. (1994). *Delinquency in society: A child-centered approach*. New York, NY: McGraw-Hill.

Reicher, S., & Haslam, S. A. (2006). Rethinking the psychology of tyranny: The BBC prison study. *British Journal of Social Psychology, 45*, 1–40.

Reinharz, S. (1992). *Feminist methods in social research*. New York, NY: Oxford University Press.

Reiss, A. J., Jr. (1971). *The police and the public*. New Haven, CT: Yale University Press.

Reynolds, P. D. (1979). *Ethical dilemmas and social science research*. San Francisco, CA: Jossey-Bass.

Richards, T. J., & Richards, L. (1994). Using computers in qualitative research. In N. K. Denzin & Y. S. Lincoln, *The SAGE handbook of qualitative research* (pp. 445–462). Thousand Oaks, CA: Sage.

Richardson, L. (1995). Narrative and sociology. In J. Van Maanen (Ed.), *Representation in ethnography* (pp. 198–221). Thousand Oaks, CA: Sage.

Riedel, M. (2000). *Research strategies for secondary data: A perspective for criminology and criminal justice*. Thousand Oaks, CA: Sage.

Rios, V. (2011). *Punished: Policing the lives of Black and Latino boys*. New York: New York University Press.

Rodríguez, H., Trainor, J., & Quarantelli, E. L. (2006). Rising to the challenges of a catastrophe: The emergent and prosocial behavior following Hurricane Katrina. *Annals of the American Academy of Political and Social Science, 604*, 82–101.

Rosenberg, Morris. (1968). *The Logic of Survey Analysis*. New York, NY: Basic Books.

Rossi, P. H., & Freeman, H. E. (1989). *Evaluation: A systematic approach* (4th ed.). Newbury Park, CA: Sage.

Rubin, H. J., & Rubin, I. S. (1995). *Qualitative interviewing: The art of hearing data*. Thousand Oaks, CA: Sage.

Sampson, R. J., & Laub, J. H. (1990). Crime and deviance over the life course: The salience of adult social bonds. *American Sociological Review*, *55*(October), 609–627.

Sampson, R. J., & Laub, J. H. (1993). Structural variations in juvenile court processing: Inequality, the underclass, and social control. *Law & Society Review*, *22*(2), 285–311.

Sampson, R. J., & Raudenbush, S. W. (1999). Systematic social observation of public spaces: A new look at disorder in urban neighborhoods. *American Journal of Sociology*, *105*, 603–651.

Sampson, R. J., Raudenbush, S. W., & Earls, F. (1997). Neighborhoods and violent crime: A multilevel study of collective efficacy. *Science*, *277*, 918–924.

Sanchez-Jankowski, M. (1991). *Islands in the street*. Berkeley: University of California Press.

Savin, H. B. (1973). Professors and psychological researchers: Conflicting values in conflicting roles. *Cognition*, *2*, 147–149.

Schober, M. F. (1999). Making sense of survey questions. In M. G. Sirkin, D. J. Herrmann, S. Schechter, N. Schwartz, J. M. Tanur, & R. Tourangeau (Eds.), *Cognition and survey research* (pp. 77–97). New York, NY: Wiley.

Schofield, J. W. (2002). Increasing the generalizability of qualitative research. In A. M. Huberman & M. B. Miles (Eds.), *The qualitative researcher's companion* (pp. 171–203). Thousand Oaks, CA: Sage.

Schuman, H., & Presser, S. (1981). *Questions and answers in attitude surveys: Experiments on question form, wording, and context*. New York, NY: Academic Press.

Schwandt, T. A. (1994). Constructivist, interpretivist approaches to human inquiry. In N. K. Denzin & Y. S. Lincoln (Eds.), *Handbook of qualitative research* (pp. 118–137). Thousand Oaks, CA: Sage.

Scott, John. (2017). *Social Network Analysis*. 4th ed. Thousand Oaks, CA: SAGE.

Sechrest, L., & Sidani, S. (1995). Quantitative and qualitative methods: Is there an alternative? *Evaluation and Program Planning*, *18*, 77–87.

Seltzer, R. A. (1996). *Mistakes that social scientists make: Error and redemption in the research process*. New York, NY: St. Martin's.

Selwitz, A. S., Epley, N., & Erickson, J. (2013). Basic institutional review board (IRB): Regulations and review process. Miami, FL: Collaborative Institutional Training Initiative at the University of Miami. Retrieved from https://www.citiprogram.org

Shadish, W. R., Cook, T. D., & Leviton, L C. (Eds.). (1991). *Foundations of program evaluation: Theories of practice*. Thousand Oaks, CA: Sage.

Shepherd, J., Hill, D., Bristor, J., & Montalvan, P. (1996). Converting an ongoing health study to CAPI: Findings from the national health and nutrition study. In R. B. Warnecke (Ed.), *Health survey research methods conference proceedings* (pp. 159–164). Hyattsville, MD: U.S. Department of Health and Human Services.

Sherman, L. W. (1992). *Policing domestic violence: Experiments and dilemmas*. New York, NY: Free Press.

Sherman, L. W., & Berk, R. A. (1984). The specific deterrent effects of arrest for domestic assault. *American Sociological Review*, *49*, 261–272.

Sherman, L. W., Smith, D. A., Schmidt, J. D., & Rogan, D. P. (1992). Crime, punishment, and stake in conformity: Legal and informal control of domestic violence. *American Sociological Review*, *57*, 680–690.

Sieber, J. E. (1992). *Planning ethically responsible research: A guide for students and international review boards*. Thousand Oaks, CA: Sage.

Sin, C. H. (2005). Seeking informed consent: Reflections on research practice. *Sociology*, *39*, 277–294.

Sinozich, S., & Langton, L. (2014). *Rape and sexual assault victimization among college-aged females, 1995–2013*. Washington, DC: U.S. Department of Justice, Bureau of Justice Statistics.

Sjoberg, G., & Nett, R. (1968). *A methodology for social research*. New York, NY: Harper & Row.

Skinner, H. A., & Sheu, W.-J. (1982). Reliability of alcohol use indices: The lifetime drinking history and the MAST. *Journal of Studies on Alcohol*, *43*(11), 1157–1170.

Sloboda, Z., Stephens, R. C., Stephens, P. C., Grey, S. F., Teasdale, B., Hawthorne, R. D., . . . & Marquette, J. F. (2009). The Adolescent Substance Abuse Prevention Study: A randomized field trial of a universal substance abuse prevention program. *Drug and Alcohol Dependence*, *102*(1–3), 1–10.

Smith, E. L., & Cooper, A. D. (2013). *Homicide in the U.S. known to law enforcement, 2011*. Washington, DC: Bureau of Justice Statistics, U.S. Department of Justice.

Snelson, Chareen. (2016). Qualitative and Mixed Methods Social Media Research: A Review of the Literature. *International Journal of Qualitative Methods* 15 (1), 1–15.

Sobeck, J. L., Chapleski, E. E., & Fisher, C. (2003). Conducting research with American Indians. *Journal of Ethnic and Cultural Diversity*, *1*, 69–84.

Speiglman, R., & Spear, P. (2009). The role of institutional review boards: Ethics: Now you see them, now you don't. In D. M. Mertens, and P. E. Ginsberg (Eds.), *The handbook of social research ethics* (pp. 121–134). Thousand Oaks, CA: Sage.

St. Jean, P. K. B. (2007). *Pockets of crime: Broken windows, collective efficacy, and the criminal point of view*. Chicago, IL: University of Chicago Press.

Stake, R. E. (1995). *The art of case study research*. Thousand Oaks, CA: Sage.

Stansfield, R., & Williams, K. R. (2014). Predicting family violence recidivism using the DVSI-R. *Criminal Justice and Behavior*, *41*(2), 163–180.

Steiner, B., & Wooldredge, J. (2014). Comparing self-report to official measures of inmate misconduct. *Justice Quarterly*, *31*(6), 1074–1101.

Stewart, D. W. (1984). *Secondary research: Information sources and methods*. Beverly Hills, CA: Sage.

Stott, C., & Pearson, G. (2007). *Football hooliganism: Policing and the war on the English disease*. London, UK: Pennant Books.

Strunk, W., Jr., & White, E. B. (1979). *The elements of style* (3rd ed.). New York, NY: Macmillan.

Sudman, S. (1976). *Applied sampling*. New York, NY: Academic Press.

Sue, V. M., & Ritter, L. A. (2012). *Conducting online surveys* (2nd ed.). Thousand Oaks, CA: Sage.

Sulik, M. J., Huerta, S., Zerr, A. A., Eisenberg, N., Spinrad, T. L., Valiente, C., . . . Wilson, S. B. (2010). The factor structure of effortful control and measurement invariance across ethnicity and sex in a high-risk sample. *Journal of Psychopathology and Behavioral Assessment*, 32(1), 8–22.

Surrette, R. (1998). *Media, crime, and justice: Images and realities*. Belmont, CA: West/Wadsworth.

Tannenbaum, F. (1938). *Crime and the community*. New York, NY: Columbia University Press.

Taylor, B., & Woods, D. J. (2010). Injuries to officers and suspects in police use-of-force cases: A quasi-experimental evaluation. *Police Quarterly*, 13(3), 260–289.

Taylor, J., Boisvert, D., Sims, B., & Garver, C. (2013). An examination of gender and age in print media accounts of child abductions. *Criminal Justice Studies*, 26(2), 151–167.

Teddlie, C., & Tashakkori, A. (2010). Overview of contemporary issues in mixed methods research. In A. Tashakkori & C. Teddlie (Eds.), *The SAGE handbook of mixed methods in social and behavioral research* (2nd ed., pp. 1–41). Thousand Oaks, CA: Sage.

Testa, M., Livingston, J. A., & VanZile-Tamsen, C. (2011). Advancing the study of violence against women using mixed methods: Integrating qualitative methods into a quantitative research program. *Violence Against Women*, 17(2), 236–250.

Thornberry, T. P., Krohn, M., Lizotte, A., & Bushway, S. (2008). *The Rochester Youth Development Survey*. Albany, NY: Hindelang Criminal Justice Research Center, University of Albany.

Thorne, S., Jensen, L., Kearney, M. H., Noblit, G., & Sandelowski, M. (2004). Qualitative meta-synthesis: Reflections on methodological orientation and ideological agenda. *Qualitative Health Research*, 14, 1342–1365.

Thrasher, F. (1927). *The gang: A study of 1,313 gangs in Chicago*. Chicago, IL: University of Chicago Press.

Tinkler, P. (2013). *Using photographs in social and historical research*. Thousand Oaks, CA: Sage.

Tjaden, P., & Thoennes, N. (2000). Extent, nature, and consequences of intimate partner violence: Findings from the National Violence Against Women Survey. Washington, DC: National Institute of Justice, U.S. Department of Justice.

Tonry, M., & Moore, M. H. (1998). *Youth violence: Crime and justice* (Vol. 24). Chicago, IL: University of Chicago Press.

Torre, M. E., & Fine, M. (2005). Bar none: Extending affirmative action to higher education in prison. *Journal of Social Issues*, 61(3), 569–594.

Tourangeau, R. (2004). Survey research and societal change. *Annual Review of Psychology*, 55, 775–801.

Tourangeau, R., Conrad, F. G., & Couper, M. P. (2012). *The science of web surveys*. Oxford, England: Oxford University Press.

Tourangeau, R., & Smith, T. W. (1996). Asking sensitive questions: The impact of data collection mode, question format, and question context. *Public Opinion Quarterly*, 60, 275–301.

Tufte, E. R. (1983). *The visual display of quantitative information*. Cheshire, CT: Graphics.

Turabian, K. L. (1967). *A manual for writers of term papers, theses, and dissertations* (3rd rev. ed.). Chicago, IL: University of Chicago Press.

Turner, C. F., Ku, L., Rogers, S. M., Lindberg, L. D., Pleck, J. H., & Sonenstein, F. L. (1998). Adolescent sexual behavior, drug use, and violence: Increased reporting with computer survey technology. *Science*, 280, 867–873.

Turner, C. F., & Martin, E. (Eds.). (1984). *Surveying subjective phenomena* (2 vols.). New York, NY: Russell Sage Foundation.

Turner, S. P. (1980). *Sociological explanation as translation*. Cambridge, UK: Cambridge University Press.

Tyler, T. (1990). *Why people obey the law*. New Haven, CT: Yale University Press.

U.S. Census Bureau. (2010a). *$1.6 billion in 2010 census savings returned*. United States Department of Commerce News. Retrieved September 18, 2015, from https://www.census.gov/newsroom/releases/archives/2010_census/cb10-cn70.html

U.S. Census Bureau. (2010b). *Door-to-door visits begin for 2010 census*. United States Department of Commerce News. Retrieved September 18, 2015, from https://www.census.gov/newsroom/releases/archives/2010_census/cb10-cn59.html

U.S. Census Bureau. (2015). *Quick facts beta*. Retrieved September 18, 2015, from http://quickfacts.census.gov/qfd/states/00000.html

United States of America v. Zacarias Moussaoui. (2001, December). United States District Court for the Eastern District of Virginia, Alexandria Division. Indictment. Retrieved from https://fas.org/irp/world/para/docs/mous_indict.html

Vaillant, G. E. (1995). *The natural history of alcoholism revisited*. Cambridge, MA: Harvard University Press.

Van Maanen, J. (1995). An end to innocence: The ethnography of ethnography. In J. Van Maanen (Ed.), *Representation in ethnography* (pp. 1–35). Thousand Oaks, CA: Sage.

Vidich, A. J., & Lyman, S. M. (1994). Qualitative methods: Their history in sociology and anthropology. In N. K. Denzin & Y. S. Lincoln (Eds.), *The SAGE handbook of qualitative research* (pp. 23–59). Thousand Oaks, CA: Sage.

Vigil, J. D. (1988). *Barrio gangs*. Austin: University of Texas Press.

Viswanathan, M. (2005). *Measurement error and research design*. Thousand Oaks, CA: Sage.

Wallace, W. L. (1983). *Principles of scientific sociology*. New York, NY: Aldine.

Webb, E., Campbell, D. T., Schwartz, R. D., & Sechrest, L. (1966). *Unobtrusive measures: Nonreactive research in the social sciences*. Chicago, IL: Rand McNally. Revised in 2000.

Weber, M. (1949). *The methodology of the social sciences* (E. A. Shils & H. Finch, Trans. & Eds.). New York, NY: Free Press.

Weber, R. P. (1985). *Basic content analysis*. Beverly Hills, CA: Sage.

Weber, R. P. (1990). *Basic content analysis* (2nd ed.). Thousand Oaks, CA: Sage.

Wechsler, H., Davenport, A., Dowdall, G., Moeykens, B., & Castillo, S. (1994). Health and behavioral consequences of binge drinking in college: A national survey of students at 140 campuses. *Journal of the American Medical Association*, 272(21), 1672–1677.

Wechsler, H., Lee, J. E., Kuo, M., Seibring, M., Nelson, T. F., & Lee, H. (2002). Trends in college binge drinking during a period of increased prevention efforts. *Journal of American College Health*, 50, 203–217.

Weisburd, D., Wheeler, S., Waring, E., & Bode, N. (1991). *Crimes of the middle class: White-collar offenders in the federal courts.* New Haven, CT: Yale University Press.

Weiss, C. H. (1993). Where politics and evaluation research meet. *Evaluation Practice, 14,* 93–106.

Whyte, W. F. (1943). *Street corner society: The social structure of an Italian slum.* Chicago, IL: University of Chicago Press.

Whyte, W. F. (1955). *Street corner society* (2nd ed.). Chicago, IL: University of Chicago Press.

Whyte, W. F. (1991). *Social theory for social action: How individuals and organizations learn to change.* Newbury Park, CA: Sage.

Willer, D., & Walker, H. A. (2007). *Building experiments: Testing social theory.* Stanford, CA: Stanford University Press.

Williams, K.R. and Hawkins, R. (1986). Perceptual research on general deterrence: A critical overview. *Law & Society Review,* 20, 545–572.

Williams, B. N., & Stahl, M. (2008). An analysis of police traffic stops and searches in Kentucky: A mixed-methods approach offering heuristic and practical implications. *Policy Science, 41,* 221–243.

Williams, K. R. (2012). Family violence risk assessment: A predictive cross-validation study of the Domestic Violence Instrument-Revised (DVSI-R). *Law and Human Behavior, 36*(2), 120–129.

Williams, K. R., & Houghton, A. B. (2004). Assessing the risk of domestic violence reoffending: A validation study. *Law and Human Behavior, 28*(4), 437–455.

Wilson, W. J. (1998). Engaging publics in sociological dialogue through the media. *Contemporary Sociology, 27,* 435–438.

Wines, M. (2006, August 27). To fill notebooks, and then a few bellies. *New York Times.* Retrieved from http://www.nytimes.com/2006/08/27/weekinreview/27wines.html?_r=0

Witkin, S. L. (2001). The measure of things. *Social Work, 46,* 101–104.

Wolcott, H. F. (1995). *The art of fieldwork.* Walnut Creek, CA: AltaMira Press.

Wolf, N., Blitz, C. L., Shi, J., Bachman, R., & Siegel, J. (2006). Sexual violence inside prisons: Rates of victimization. *Journal of Urban Health, 83,* 835–846.

World Health Organization (WHO). (2005). *WHO multi-country study on women's health and domestic violence against women: Summary report of initial results on prevalence, health outcomes and women's responses.* Geneva, Switzerland: Author.

World Health Organization (WHO). (2013). *Management of substance abuse.* Retrieved September 18, 2015, from http://www.who.int/substance_abuse/facts/alcohol/en

Wyse, J. (2018). Older men's social integration after prison. *International Journal of Offender Therapy and Comparative Criminology, 62*(8), 2153–2173.

Xu, Y., Fiedler, M. L., & Flaming, K. H. (2005). Citizens' judgment discovering the impact of community policing: The broken windows thesis, collective efficacy, and citizens' judgment. *Journal of Research in Crime and Delinquency, 42,* 147–186.

Yang, S., Keller, F. B., & Zheng, L. (2017). *Social network analysis: Methods and examples.* Thousand Oaks, CA: Sage.

Zimbardo, P. G. (1973). On the ethics of intervention in human psychological research: With special reference to the Stanford Prison Experiment. *Cognition, 2,* 243–256.

Zimbardo, P. G. (2004). A situationist perspective on the psychology of evil: Understanding how good people are transformed into perpetrators. In A. G. Miller (Ed.), *The social psychology of good and evil: Understanding our capacity for kindness and cruelty* (pp. 21–50). New York, NY: Guilford.

Zimbardo, P. G. (2007). *The Lucifer effect: Understanding how good people turn evil.* New York, NY: Random House.

Zimbardo, P. G. (2008). *The Lucifer effect: Understanding how good people turn evil* (2nd ed.). New York, NY: Random House.

Zimbardo, P. G. (2009). *Revisiting the Stanford Prison Experiment: A lesson in the power of situation.* Retrieved July 2, 2009, from http://www.lucifereffect.com

INDEX

Prisoners, ethical issues related to, 63
Privacy certificates, 59
Probability of selection, 99
Probability sampling methods, 99, 100–106
Process evaluations, 258
Program monitoring, 258
Program processes, 256
Program theory, 263–264
Progressive focusing, 208
Proportionate stratified sampling, 103
Pseudoscience, vs. social science, 6–7
Publication of research, 51
Punished (Rios), 196
Purposive sampling, 108–109

QSR NVivo, 215–218, 219 (exhibit)
Qualitative data analysis, 208
   See also qualitative research methods
Qualitative levels of measurement, 76
Qualitative research methods
   overview, 186–191
   data analysis, 207–218
   ethical issues related to, 218–222
   focus groups, 206–207
   intensive interviewing, 202–206
   participant observation, 191–199
   vs. quantitative research methods, 14
   systematic observation, 199–202
Qualtrics, 175
Quantitative causal explanations, 120–123
Quantitative research methods, vs. qualitative research
   methods, 14
Quasi-experimental designs, 15, 132, 268–269
Questionnaires
   development of, 156–168
   organization of, 168–170
   See also surveys and survey research
Quota sampling, 107, 108 (exhibit)

Random assignment, 128, 266
Random digit dialing (RDD), 101–102
Randomization, 128
Random selection, 100
Ratio levels of measurement, 80
Raudenbush, Stephen W., 74, 200
Reactive effects, 193
Reasoning, errors in, 3–6
Recoding, 166
Reductionism, 113
Reductionist fallacy, 113
Reference periods, 161
Reflexivity, 212
Regression effects, 138
Relational data, 231
Relations, 231
Reliability, vs. measurement validity, 84–88
Reliability measures, 165
Repeated cross-sectional designs, 143
Repeated-measures panel designs, 134
Replacement sampling, 102
Replications, 32
Representative samples, 97

Research
   element of time in, 141–145
   institutional review boards (IRBs), 50, 61
   questions, 25–27
   standards, 36–39
   strategies for, 29–36
Research circles, 30–35
Researcher safety, 221
Research reports
   considerations for, 306–308
   data displays in, 303–306
   ethical issues related to, 308
   goals of, 296–299
   media and, 309
   plagiarism and, 309–310
   types of, 299–302
   writing, 302–303
Research spirals, 33, 34 (exhibit)
Resistance to change, 5–6
Respect for persons, 49
Respondent-driven sampling, 109
Reverse code, 166
Reverse outlining, 303
Revised Domestic Violence Screening Instrument
   (DVSI-R), 242
Ridgway, Gary Leon, 234–236
Rios, Victor, 186, 188–191, 193, 196, 212, 223
Risk, 221
Risk Skills Training Program (RSTP), 261
Risk terrain modeling (RTM), 241–242
Rochester Youth Development Study (RYDS), 8–9
Ross, Dorothea, 126
Ross, Sheila, 126

Safety, 221
Sample generalizability, 38, 96, 140–141
Samples and sampling
   overview, 93–98
   methods of, 98–111
   quality of, 110–111
   sampling error, 96
   sampling frames, 94
   sampling intervals, 102
   sampling units, 94
   theoretical sampling, 197–198
   units of analysis and, 111–114
   See also populations
Sampson, Robert J., 74, 200
Sandy Hook Elementary, 1
Saturation point, 203
Scales, 78
School shootings
   overview, 1
   beliefs about, 4 (exhibit)
   video games and, 142
Science, 6
Secondary data analysis
   overview, 15, 228–230
   Big Data, 238–243
   content analysis, 244–246
   crime mapping, 236–238
   ethical issues related to, 243, 247–249